PRENTICE HALL
LITERATURE

COPPER

BRONZE

SILVER

GOLD

PLATINUM

THE AMERICAN EXPERIENCE

THE BRITISH TRADITION

WORLD MASTERPIECES

PRENTICE HALL

LITERATURE
BRONZE

FOURTH EDITION

PRENTICE HALL
Upper Saddle River, New Jersey
Needham, Massachusetts

ISBN 0-13-838210-7

2 3 4 5 6 7 8 9 10 00   99 98 97 96

Art credits begin on page 809.

PRENTICE HALL
Simon & Schuster Education Group
A VIACOM COMPANY

STAFF CREDITS FOR PRENTICE HALL LITERATURE

Editorial: Ellen Bowler, Douglas McCollum, Philip Fried, Kelly Ackley, Eric Hausmann, Lauren Weidenman

Multicultural/ESL: Marina Liapunov, Barbara T. Stone

Marketing: Mollie Ledwith, Belinda Loh

National Language Arts Consultants: Ellen Lees Backstrom, Ed.D., Craig A. McGhee, Karen Massey, Vennisa Travers, Gail Witt

Permissions: Doris Robinson

Design: AnnMarie Roselli, Gerry Schrenk, Laura Bird

Media Research: Libby Forsyth, Suzi Myers, Martha Conway

Production: Suse Bell, Joan McCulley, Gertrude Szyferblatt

Computer Test Banks: Greg Myers, Cleasta Wilburn

Pre-Press Production: Kathryn Dix, Paula Massenaro, Carol Barbara

Print and Bind: Rhett Conklin, Matt McCabe

ACKNOWLEDGMENTS

Grateful acknowledgment is made to the following for permission to reprint copyrighted material:

Teresa Palomo Acosta
"My Mother Pieced Quilts" by Teresa Palomo Acosta. Reprinted by permission of the author.

T. D. Allen
"Grandfather" by Shirley Crawford. Copyright © 1970. Used by permission of T. D. Allen.

Américas Magazine
"Lather and Nothing Else" by Hernando Téllez. Reprinted from *Américas,* a bimonthly magazine published by the General Secretariat of the Organization of American States in English and Spanish. Reprinted by permission of *Américas* Magazine.

(Continued on page 805.)

CONTENTS

SHORT STORIES

DRAMA

POETRY

MYTHS AND FOLK TALES AROUND THE WORLD

PRENTICE HALL

LITERATURE
BRONZE

[Reading is] the key which admits us to the whole world of thought and fancy and imagination.
—*James Russell Lowell*

NOON WASH, 1991
Jonathan Green
The Collection of Mary and Michael James

SHORT STORIES

One of the best-loved forms of literature is the short story. It is a brief work of fiction containing made-up characters and events. Because short stories are brief, they do not take long to read. Usually you can start and finish one in a single sitting. Short stories are fun to read, presenting us with an endless variety of characters, places, and situations. In addition, they often reveal truths about life and so deepen our understanding of the human condition.

The basic meaning of the word *fiction* is "anything made up." Because short stories are made up from a writer's imagination, they are not just reports of events that actually happened. However, they are "made up" in another sense, too. They are put together from several basic elements: plot, characters, setting, and theme. The plot is the sequence of events in the story. The characters are, of course, the people, or sometimes the animals, that take part in the events. The setting is the time and place of the story. The theme is the central idea or insight into life that is revealed through the events of the story.

You will be learning more about these elements as you read the stories in this unit. As your understanding of these elements grows, so will the pleasure you gain from reading good fiction.

READING ACTIVELY

Short Stories

A short story is a work of fiction—literature in which characters and events are imagined by the author. Fiction allows you to explore new worlds, share joys and sorrows of characters, and learn from the invented experiences of others.

Reading short stories is an active process. It is a process in which you picture what is happening in the story and gather meaning from what you see in your mind. You do this by using the following active-reading strategies:

QUESTION You probably think of questions as you are reading. For example, have you wondered why characters act as they do, what causes events to happen, or why the writer includes certain information? Look for answers to these questions as you read.

VISUALIZE Use details in the story to make a picture in your mind. As you read along, change the picture as the story unfolds and your understanding increases. If you get confused, try to describe what confuses you. Use what you see in your mind to help clarify what you didn't understand at first.

PREDICT What do you think will happen? Look for hints in the story that seem to lead to a certain conclusion. As you keep reading, you can see if your predictions are right.

CONNECT Bring to the story what you know and what you have done. Make connections with your own knowledge and with situations or people you have known in your own life.

Also, make connections between different events in the story. Try to figure out how all the pieces of the story fit together.

RESPOND Think about what the story means. What does it say to you? What feelings do you have as you read? How has the story helped you to understand people and events?

Try to use these strategies as you read the stories in this unit. They will help you increase your enjoyment and understanding of literature.

On pages 3–9 you can see an example of active reading by Niki Grace of Franklin Heights School in Columbus, Ohio. The notes in the side column show Niki's thoughts and comments while reading "Lather and Nothing Else." Your own thoughts as you read may be different, because each reader brings something different to a story and takes away something different.

MODEL

Lather and Nothing Else

Hernando Téllez

He came in without a word. I was stropping[1] my best razor. And when I recognized him, I started to shake. But he did not notice. To cover my nervousness, I went on honing the razor. I tried the edge with the tip of my thumb and took another look at it against the light.

Meanwhile, he was taking off his cartridge-studded belt with the pistol holster suspended from it. He put it on a hook in the wardrobe and hung his cap above it. Then he turned full around toward me and, loosening his tie, remarked, "It's hot as the devil. I want a shave." With that he took his seat.

I estimated he had a four-days' growth of beard, the four days he had been gone on the last foray after our men. His face looked burnt, tanned by the sun.

I started to work carefully on the shaving soap. I scraped some slices from the cake, dropped them into the mug, then added a little lukewarm water, and stirred with the brush. The lather soon began to rise.

"The fellows in the troop must have just about as much beard as I." I went on stirring up lather.

"But we did very well, you know. We caught the leaders. Some of them we brought back dead; others are still alive. But they'll all be dead soon."

"How many did you take?" I asked.

"Fourteen. We had to go pretty far in to find them. But now they're paying for it. And not one will escape; not a single one."

He leaned back in the chair when he saw the brush in my hand, full of lather. I had not yet put the sheet on him. I was

Question: Who is "he"? Why does he make the other person so nervous?

Visualize: I can picture this man hanging up his pistol and showing off.

Respond: The barber is very quiet.

Question: Who is he killing and why?

---

1. stropping (sträp' iŋ) *v.*: The act of sharpening a blade to a fine edge on a thick band of leather called a strop.

certainly flustered. Taking a sheet from the drawer, I tied it around my customer's neck.

He went on talking. He evidently took it for granted that I was on the side of the existing regime.[2]

Connect: *He gets a thrill out of scaring people.*

"The people must have gotten a scare with what happened the other day," he said.

"Yes," I replied, as I finished tying the knot against his nape,[3] which smelt of sweat.

"Good show, wasn't it?"

"Very good," I answered, turning my attention now to the brush. The man closed his eyes wearily and awaited the cool caress of the lather.

I had never had him so close before. The day he ordered the people to file through the schoolyard to look upon the four rebels hanging there, my path had crossed his briefly. But the sight of those mutilated bodies kept me from paying attention to the face of the man who had been directing it all and whom I now had in my hands.

Question: *What type of captain is he?*

It was not a disagreeable face, certainly. And the beard, which aged him a bit, was not unbecoming. His name was Torres. Captain Torres.

I started to lay on the first coat of lather. He kept his eyes closed.

"I would love to catch a nap," he said, "but there's a lot to be done this evening."

I lifted the brush and asked, with pretended indifference: "A firing party?"

"Something of the sort," he replied, "but slower."

"All of them?"

"No, just a few."

I went on lathering his face. My hands began to tremble again. The man could not be aware of this, which was lucky for me. But I wished he had not come in. Probably many of our men had seen him enter the shop. And with the enemy in my house I felt a certain responsibility.

Predict: *The barber will have to make a decision about this "enemy."*

I would have to shave his beard just like any other, carefully, neatly, just as though he were a good customer, taking heed that not a single pore should emit a drop of blood. Seeing to it that the blade did not slip in the small whorls. Taking care

---

2. regime (rə zhēm') *n*.: A particular government or administration.
3. nape (nāp) *n*.: The back of the neck.

GENERAL WITH SWORD
Francisco Vidal
Courtesy of the Artist

that the skin was left clean, soft, shining, so that when I passed the back of my hand over it not a single hair should be felt. Yes. I was secretly a revolutionary, but at the same time I was a conscientious barber, proud of the way I did my job. And that four-day beard presented a challenge.

I took up the razor, opened the handle wide, releasing the blade, and started to work, downward from one sideburn. The blade responded to perfection. The hair was tough and hard; not very long, but thick. Little by little the skin began to show through. The razor gave out its usual sound as it gathered up layers of soap mixed with bits of hair. I paused to wipe it clean, and taking up the strop once more went about improving its edge, for I am a painstaking barber.

The man, who had kept his eyes closed, now opened them, put a hand out from under the sheet, felt of the part of his face that was emerging from the lather, and said to me, "Come at six o'clock this evening to the school."

Question: *What is he going to see at the school that scares him so much?*

"Will it be like the other day?" I asked, stiff with horror.

"It may be even better," he replied.

"What are you planning to do?"

"I'm not sure yet. But we'll have a good time."

Once more he leaned back and shut his eyes. I came closer, the razor on high.

"Are you going to punish all of them?" I timidly ventured.

"Yes, all of them."

The lather was drying on his face. I must hurry. Through the mirror, I took a look at the street. It appeared about as usual; there was the grocery shop with two or three customers. Then I glanced at the clock, two-thirty.

The razor kept descending. Now from the other sideburn downward. It was a blue beard, a thick one. He should let it grow like some poets, or some priests. It would suit him well. Many people would not recognize him. And that would be a good thing for him, I thought, as I went gently over all the throat line. At this point you really had to handle your blade skillfully, because the hair, while scantier, tended to fall into small whorls. It was a curly beard. The pores might open, minutely, in this area and let out a tiny drop of blood. A good barber like myself stakes his reputation on not permitting that to happen to any of his customers.

Connect: *He's not really concerned with the well-being of this particular customer.*

And this was indeed a special customer. How many of ours had he sent to their death? How many had he mutilated? It was best not to think about it. Torres did not know I was his enemy. Neither he nor the others knew it. It was a secret shared by very few, just because that made it possible for me to inform the revolutionaries about Torres's activities in the town and what he planned to do every time he went on one of his raids to hunt down rebels. So it was going to be very difficult to explain how it was that I had him in my hands and then let him go in peace, alive, cleanshaven.

Connect: *He is like a spy.*

Predict: *He will have to answer to his friends.*

His beard had now almost entirely disappeared. He looked younger, several years younger than when he had come in. I suppose that always happens to men who enter and leave barbershops. Under the strokes of my razor, Torres was rejuvenated; yes, because I am a good barber, the best in this town, and I say this in all modesty.

A little more lather here under the chin, on the Adam's apple, right near the great vein. How hot it is! Torres must be sweating just as I am. But he is not afraid. He is a tranquil man, who is not even giving thought to what he will do to his prisoners this evening. I, on the other hand, polishing his skin with this razor but avoiding the drawing of blood, careful with every stroke—I cannot keep my thoughts in order.

Visualize: *I can see his pulse.*

Confound the hour he entered my shop! I am a revolutionary but not a murderer. And it would be so easy to kill him. He deserves it. Or does he? No! No one deserves the sacrifice others make in becoming assassins. What is to be gained by it? Nothing. Others and still others keep coming, and the first kill the second, and then these kill the next, and so on until everything becomes a sea of blood. I could cut his throat, so, swish, swish! He would not even have time to moan, and with his eyes shut he would not even see the shine of the razor or the gleam in my eye.

Connect: *He believes in the saying, "Two wrongs don't make a right."*

But I'm shaking like a regular murderer. From his throat a stream of blood would flow on the sheet, over the chair, down on my hands, onto the floor. I would have to close the door. But the blood would go flowing, along the floor, warm, indelible, not to be stanched,[4] until it reached the street like a small scarlet river.

I'm sure that with a good strong blow, a deep cut, he would feel no pain. He would not suffer at all. And what would I do

---

4. stanched (stôncht) *v.*: Prevented from flowing.

GENERAL LOOKING AT THE ECLIPSE
Francisco Vidal
Courtesy of the Artist

then with the body? Where would I hide it? I would have to flee, leave all this behind, take shelter far away, very far away. But they would follow until they caught up with me. "The murderer of Captain Torres. He slit his throat while he was shaving him. What a cowardly thing to do." And others would say, "The avenger of our people. A name to remember"—my name here. "He was the town barber. No one knew he was fighting for our cause."

And so, which will it be? Murderer or hero? My fate hangs on the edge of this razor blade. I can turn my wrist slightly, put a bit more pressure on the blade, let it sink in. The skin will yield like silk, like rubber, like the strop. There is nothing more tender than a man's skin, and the blood is always there, ready to burst forth. A razor like this cannot fail. It is the best one I have.

But I don't want to be a murderer. No, sir. You came in to be shaved. And I do my work honorably. I don't want to stain my hands with blood. Just with lather, and nothing else. You are an executioner; I am only a barber. Each one to his job. That's it. Each one to his job.

The chin was now clean, polished, soft. The man got up and looked at himself in the glass. He ran his hand over the skin and felt its freshness, its newness.

"Thanks," he said. He walked to the wardrobe for his belt, his pistol, and his cap. I must have been very pale, and I felt my shirt soaked with sweat. Torres finished adjusting his belt buckle, straightened his gun in its holster, and, smoothing his hair mechanically, put on his cap. From his trousers pocket he took some coins to pay for the shave. And he started toward the door. On the threshold he stopped for a moment, and turning toward me he said,

"They told me you would kill me. I came to find out if it was true. But it's not easy to kill. I know what I'm talking about."

Hernando Téllez (1908–1966) served as a senator in his native Colombia, a consul to the city of Marseille, and a delegate to UNESCO. His written works include essays on political and social issues, translations of French drama, and a collection of stories, *Ashes for the Wind and Other Tales* (1950). "Lather and Nothing Else," perhaps the best known of these stories, has been translated into several languages.

Predict: He knows he will have to answer for his actions. He is too worried about how he will be remembered to act without thinking.

Question: What is the captain thinking at this point? Does he have any idea?

Respond: I think he will regret not killing the captain.

Connect: This shows that the captain is a brave man and does have feelings about killing people. The barber is probably in shock.

Respond: I wonder what will happen to the barber now. I admire him for not killing Torres, but I don't envy his having to look over his shoulder all the time from now on.

RESPONDING TO THE SELECTION

Your Response

1. Did you think that the barber would harm Captain Torres? Why or why not?

Recalling

2. How does the barber feel when Captain Torres enters the shop?
3. What has Captain Torres been doing for the past four days?
4. How does the barber help the rebels?

Interpreting

5. What is Captain Torres going to do in the evening?
6. Why does the barber decide not to harm Captain Torres?
7. Considering what Captain Torres says at the end of the story, what do you think he knows about the barber?

Applying

8. The barber's decision is a difficult one to make. What difficult decision have you made? Were you satisfied with the result?
9. After the barber has decided not to kill Captain Torres, he remarks to himself, "Each one to his job." Do you agree? Explain.

ANALYZING LITERATURE

Understanding Elements of Suspense

Authors often use seemingly unimportant details to create **suspense,** a feeling of excitement about what will happen. In "Lather and Nothing Else," the details in the description of Captain Torres's neck in the paragraph beginning, "A little more lather here under the chin" become important and create suspense when you realize that the barber must decide whether to shave his customer or kill him.

1. Identify two passages in which the barber describes his razor. How did these passages affect you as you read?

2. Reread the next-to-last paragraph of the story. What effect do the details in this passage have?

CRITICAL THINKING AND READING

Understanding Decisions

To understand the barber's decision, you must understand his reasons. Make a chart in which you list the Reasons for Killing Torres in one column and the Reasons for Not Killing Torres in a second column. Listing the reasons in the order they occur to the barber will help you understand how he made his decision.

1. Which column on your chart contains the greatest number of reasons?
2. Does your chart support the barber's decision? Why or why not?

THINKING AND WRITING

Writing an Interior Monologue

In the story, the barber has a "conversation" with himself in his own mind. This is called an **interior monologue.** Write your own interior monologue describing what Captain Torres might have been thinking as the barber went about shaving him. Read and compare your interior monologue with a classmate's.

LEARNING OPTION

Writing. Work with a classmate to write a short dramatic version of "Lather and Nothing Else." Start by writing down the dialogue as it appears in the story. Then write any additional pieces of dialogue based on what you think the two characters would be likely to say to each other in the barber's shop. Finally, you might use the script you have written to act out the story for the class.

Plot

THE CALLERS
Walter Ufer
National Museum of American Art
Smithsonian Institution

GUIDE FOR READING

Rikki-tikki-tavi

Plot

The **plot** is the sequence of events in a short story. In many stories the events follow a pattern you can recognize. First, the writer describes a **conflict**, which is a struggle between opposing sides or forces. As the story develops, this struggle becomes more and more intense. Then the story reaches a **climax,** the point at which the conflict is greatest. After the climax you learn the **resolution,** or outcome of the conflict, before the story ends. You will be able to see this sequence of events as you read "Rikki-tikki-tavi."

Focus

The main characters in "Rikki-tikki-tavi" are not people but animals native to Asia. The mongoose is a small, short-legged animal with a pointed nose, small ears, and a long, furry tail. The cobra is a very poisonous snake that expands the ribs near its head to form a hood shape just before striking. It was once believed that the mongoose is immune to the cobra's bite, but in truth, the mongoose is simply faster and more agile than the cobra. Write a few sentences about what you think a fight between these two animals would be like. Then, as you read, compare what you imagined with the battles between Rikki-tikki and the cobras.

Vocabulary

Knowing the following words will help you as you read "Rikki-tikki-tavi."

draggled (drag'ld) *adj.*: Wet and dirty (p. 13)
flinched (flinch't) *v.*: Moved back, as if away from a blow (p. 16)
mourning (morn' iŋ) *v.*: Feeling sorrow for the death of a loved one (p. 20)

consolation (kän' sə lā' shən) *n.*: Something that makes you feel better (p. 20)
cunningly (kun' iŋ lē) *adv.*: Cleverly (p. 20)

Rudyard Kipling

(1865–1936) was born in India, to British parents. While still a young man, he became famous for his stirring accounts of adventure and courage. In 1907 he received a major award, the Nobel Prize for Literature, for his novels, short stories, and poetry. "Rikki-tikki-tavi" comes from one of Kipling's most popular collections of short stories, *The Jungle Book.* Notice how Kipling makes "the great war" between the animal characters in this story seem just as important as a human conflict.

Rikki-tikki-tavi

Rudyard Kipling

This is the story of the great war that Rikki-tikki-tavi fought single-handed, through the bathrooms of the big bungalow in Segowlee cantonment.[1] Darzee, the tailor-bird, helped him, and Chuchundra,[2] the muskrat, who never comes out into the middle of the floor, but always creeps round by the wall, gave him advice; but Rikki-tikki did the real fighting.

He was a mongoose, rather like a little cat in his fur and his tail, but quite like a weasel in his head and his habits. His eyes and the end of his restless nose were pink; he could scratch himself anywhere he pleased, with any leg, front or back, that he chose to use; he could fluff up his tail till it looked like a bottle brush, and his war cry as he scuttled through the long grass, was: "*Rikk-tikk-tikki-tikki-tchk!*"

One day, a high summer flood washed him out of the burrow where he lived with his father and mother, and carried him, kicking and clucking, down a roadside ditch. He found a little wisp of grass floating there, and clung to it till he lost his senses. When he revived, he was lying in the hot sun on the middle of a garden path, very draggled indeed, and a small boy was saying: "Here's a dead mongoose. Let's have a funeral."

"No," said his mother; "let's take him in and dry him. Perhaps he isn't really dead."

---

1. **Segowlee cantonment** (sē gou′ lē kan tän′ mənt), *n.*: The living quarters for British troops in Segowlee, India.
2. **Chuchundra** (cho͞o chun′ drə)

They took him into the house, and a big man picked him up between his finger and thumb and said he was not dead but half choked; so they wrapped him in cotton wool, and warmed him, and he opened his eyes and sneezed.

"Now," said the big man (he was an Englishman who had just moved into the bungalow); "don't frighten him, and we'll see what he'll do."

It is the hardest thing in the world to frighten a mongoose, because he is eaten up from nose to tail with curiosity. The motto of all the mongoose family is, "Run and find out"; and Rikki-tikki was a true mongoose. He looked at the cotton wool, decided that it was not good to eat, ran all round the table, sat up and put his fur in order, scratched himself, and jumped on the small boy's shoulder.

"Don't be frightened, Teddy," said his father. "That's his way of making friends."

"Ouch! He's tickling under my chin," said Teddy.

Rikki-tikki looked down between the boy's collar and neck, snuffed at his ear, and climbed down to the floor, where he sat rubbing his nose.

"Good gracious," said Teddy's mother, "and that's a wild creature! I suppose he's so tame because we've been kind to him."

"All mongooses are like that," said her husband. "If Teddy doesn't pick him up by the tail, or try to put him in a cage, he'll run in and out of the house all day long. Let's give him something to eat."

They gave him a little piece of raw meat. Rikki-tikki liked it immensely, and when it was finished he went out into the veranda and sat in the sunshine and fluffed up his fur to make it dry to the roots. Then he felt better.

"There are more things to find out about in this house," he said to himself, "than all my family could find out in all their lives. I shall certainly stay and find out."

He spent all that day roaming over the house. He nearly drowned himself in the bathtubs, put his nose into the ink on a writing table, and burned it on the end of the big man's cigar, for he climbed up in the big man's lap to see how writing was done. At nightfall he ran into Teddy's nursery to watch how kerosene lamps were lighted, and when Teddy went to bed Rikki-tikki climbed up too; but he was a restless companion, because he had to get up and attend to every noise all through the night, and find out what made it. Teddy's mother and father came in, the last thing, to look at their boy, and Rikki-tikki was awake on the pillow. "I don't like that," said Teddy's mother; "he may bite the child." "He'll do no such thing," said the father. "Teddy's safer with that little beast than if he had a bloodhound to watch him. If a snake came into the nursery now—"

But Teddy's mother wouldn't think of anything so awful.

Early in the morning Rikki-tikki came to early breakfast in the veranda riding on Teddy's shoulder, and they gave him banana and some boiled egg; and he sat on all their laps one after the other, because every well-brought-up mongoose always hopes to be a house mongoose some day and have rooms to run about in, and Rikki-tikki's mother (she used to live in the General's house at Segowlee) had carefully told Rikki what to do if ever he came across Englishmen.

Then Rikki-tikki went out into the garden to see what was to be seen. It was a large garden, only half cultivated, with bushes as big as summer houses of Marshal Niel roses, lime and orange trees, clumps of bamboos, and thickets of high grass. Rikki-tikki licked his lips. "This is a splendid hunting ground," he said, and his tail grew bottle-brushy at the thought of it, and he scuttled up and down the garden, snuffing here and there till he heard very sorrowful voices in a thornbush.

It was Darzee, the tailorbird, and his wife. They had made a beautiful nest by pulling two big leaves together and stitching them up the edges with fibers, and had filled the hollow with cotton and downy fluff. The nest swayed to and fro, as they sat on the rim and cried.

"What is the matter?" asked Rikki-tikki.

"We are very miserable," said Darzee.

"One of our babies fell out of the nest yesterday and Nag[3] ate him."

"H'm!" said Rikki-tikki, "that is very sad—but I am a stranger here. Who is Nag?"

Darzee and his wife only cowered down in the nest without answering, for from the thick grass at the foot of the bush there came a low hiss—a horrid cold sound that made Rikki-tikki jump back two clear feet. Then inch by inch out of the grass rose up the head and spread hood of Nag, the big black cobra, and he was five feet long from tongue to tail. When he had lifted one third of himself clear of the ground, he stayed balancing to and fro exactly as a dandelion tuft balances in the wind, and he looked at Rikki-tikki with the wicked snake's eyes that never change their expression, whatever the snake may be thinking of.

"Who is Nag?" he said. "*I* am Nag. The great god Brahm[4] put his mark upon all our people when the first cobra spread his hood to keep the sun off Brahm as he slept. Look, and be afraid!"

He spread out his hood more than ever, and Rikki-tikki saw the spectacle mark on the back of it that looks exactly like the eye part of a hook-and-eye fastening. He was afraid for the minute; but it is impossible for a mongoose to stay frightened for any length of time, and though Rikki-tikki had never met a live cobra before, his mother had fed him on dead ones, and he knew that all a grown mongoose's business in life was to fight and eat snakes. Nag knew that too, and at the bottom of his cold heart he was afraid.

"Well," said Rikki-tikki, and his tail began to fluff up again, "marks or no marks, do you think it is right for you to eat fledglings out of a nest?"

Nag was thinking to himself, and watching the least little movement in the grass behind Rikki-tikki. He knew that mongooses in the garden meant death sooner or later for him and his family; but he wanted to get Rikki-tikki off his guard. So he dropped his head a little, and put it on one side.

"Let us talk," he said, "You eat eggs. Why should not I eat birds?"

"Behind you! Look behind you!" sang Darzee.

Rikki-tikki knew better than to waste time in staring. He jumped up in the air as high as he could go, and just under him whizzed by the head of Nagaina,[5] Nag's wicked wife. She had crept up behind him as he was talking, to make an end of him; and he heard her savage hiss as the stroke missed. He came down almost across her back, and if he had been an old mongoose he would have known that then was the time to break her back with one bite; but he was afraid of the terrible lashing return stroke of the cobra. He bit, indeed, but did not bite long enough, and he jumped clear of the whisking tail, leaving Nagaina torn and angry.

"Wicked, wicked Darzee!" said Nag, lashing up as high as he could reach toward the nest in the thornbush; but Darzee had built it out of reach of snakes; and it only swayed to and fro.

Rikki-tikki felt his eyes growing red and hot (when a mongoose's eyes grow red, he is angry), and he sat back on his tail and hind legs like a little kangaroo, and looked all around him, and chattered with rage. But Nag and Nagaina had disappeared into the grass. When a snake misses its stroke, it never says anything or gives any sign of what it means to do next. Rikki-tikki did not care to follow them, for he did not feel sure that he could manage two snakes at once. So he trotted off to the gravel path near the

---

3. Nag (Näg).

4. Brahm (bräm): An abbreviation of Brahma, the name of the chief god in the Hindu religion.

5. Nagaina (nə gī nə)

house, and sat down to think. It was a serious matter for him.

If you read the old books of natural history, you will find they say that when the mongoose fights the snake and happens to get bitten, he runs off and eats some herb that cures him. That is not true. The victory is only a matter of quickness of eye and quickness of foot—snake's blow against mongoose's jump—and as no eye can follow the motion of a snake's head when it strikes, that makes things much more wonderful than any magic herb. Rikki-tikki knew he was a young mongoose, and it made him all the more pleased to think that he had managed to escape a blow from behind. It gave him confidence in himself, and when Teddy came running down the path, Rikki-tikki was ready to be petted.

But just as Teddy was stooping, something flinched a little in the dust, and a tiny voice said: "Be careful. I am death!" It was Karait,[6] the dusty brown snakeling that lies for choice on the dusty earth; and his bite is as dangerous as the cobra's. But he is so small that nobody thinks of him, and so he does the more harm to people.

Rikki-tikki's eyes grew red again, and he danced up to Karait with the peculiar rocking, swaying motion that he had inherited from his family. It looks very funny, but it is so perfectly balanced a gait that you can fly off from it at any angle you please; and in dealing with snakes this is an advantage. If Rikki-tikki had only known, he was doing a much more dangerous thing than fighting Nag, for Karait is so small, and can turn so quickly, that unless Rikki bit him close to the back of the head, he would get the return stroke in his eye or lip. But Rikki did not know: his eyes were all red, and he rocked back and forth, looking for a good place to hold. Karait struck out. Rikki jumped sideways and tried to run in, but the wicked little dusty gray head lashed within a fraction of his shoulder, and he had to jump over the body, and the head followed his heels close.

Teddy shouted to the house: "Oh, look here! Our mongoose is killing a snake"; and Rikki-tikki heard a scream from Teddy's mother. His father ran out with a stick, but by the time he came up, Karait had lunged out once too far, and Rikki-tikki had sprung, jumped on the snake's back, dropped his head far between his fore legs, bitten as high up the back as he could get hold, and rolled away. That bite paralyzed Karait, and Rikki-tikki was just going to eat him up from the tail, after the custom of his family at dinner, when he remembered that a full meal makes a slow mongoose, and if he wanted all his strength and quickness ready, he must keep himself thin.

He went away for a dust bath under the castor-oil bushes, while Teddy's father beat the dead Karait. "What is the use of that?" thought Rikki-tikki. "I have settled it all"; and then Teddy's mother picked him up from the dust and hugged him, crying that he had saved Teddy from death, and Teddy's father said that he was a providence,[7] and Teddy looked on with big scared eyes. Rikki-tikki was rather amused at all the fuss, which, of course, he did not understand. Teddy's mother might just as well have petted Teddy for playing in the dust. Rikki was thoroughly enjoying himself.

That night, at dinner, walking to and fro among the wineglasses on the table, he could have stuffed himself three times over with nice things; but he remembered Nag and Nagaina, and though it was very pleasant to be patted and petted by Teddy's mother, and to sit on Teddy's shoulder, his eyes would get red from time to time, and he

---

6. Karait (kə rīt′)

7. a providence (präv′ ə dəns): A godsend; a valuable gift.

would go off into his long war cry of "*Rikk-tikk-tikki-tikki-tchk!*"

Teddy carried him off to bed, and insisted on Rikki-tikki sleeping under his chin. Rikki-tikki was too well bred to bite or scratch, but as soon as Teddy was asleep he went off for his nightly walk round the house, and in the dark he ran up against Chuchundra, the muskrat, creeping round by the wall. Chuchundra is a brokenhearted little beast. He whimpers and cheeps all the night, trying to make up his mind to run into the middle of the room, but he never gets there.

"Don't kill me," said Chuchundra, almost weeping. "Rikki-tikki don't kill me."

"Do you think a snake-killer kills muskrats?" said Rikki-tikki scornfully.

"Those who kill snakes get killed by snakes," said Chuchundra, more sorrowfully than ever. "And how am I to be sure that Nag won't mistake me for you some dark night?"

"There's not the least danger," said Rikki-tikki; "but Nag is in the garden, and I know you don't go there."

"My cousin Chua, the rat, told me—" said Chuchundra, and then he stopped.

"Told you what?"

"H'sh! Nag is everywhere, Rikki-tikki. You should have talked to Chua in the garden."

"I didn't—so you must tell me. Quick, Chuchundra, or I'll bite you!"

Chuchundra sat down and cried till the tears rolled off his whiskers. "I am a very poor man," he sobbed. "I never had spirit enough to run out into the middle of the room. H'sh! I mustn't tell you anything. Can't you *hear*, Rikki-tikki?"

Rikki-tikki listened. The house was as still as still, but he thought he could just catch the faintest *scratch-scratch* in the world—a noise as faint as that of a wasp walking on a windowpane—the dry scratch of a snake's scales on brickwork.

"That's Nag or Nagaina," he said to himself; "and he is crawling into the bathroom sluice. You're right, Chuchundra; I should have talked to Chua."

He stole off to Teddy's bathroom, but there was nothing there, and then to Teddy's mother's bathroom. At the bottom of the smooth plaster wall there was a brick pulled out to make a sluice for the bath water, and as Rikki-tikki stole in by the masonry curb where the bath is put, he heard Nag and Nagaina whispering together outside in the moonlight.

"When the house is emptied of people," said Nagaina to her husband, "*he* will have to go away, and then the garden will be our own again. Go in quietly, and remember that the big man who killed Karait is the first one to bite. Then come out and tell me, and we will hunt for Rikki-tikki together."

"But are you sure that there is anything to be gained by killing the people?" said Nag.

"Everything. When there were no people in the bungalow, did we have any mongoose in the garden? So long as the bungalow is empty, we are king and queen of the garden; and remember that as soon as our eggs in the melon bed hatch (as they may tomorrow), our children will need room and quiet."

"I had not thought of that," said Nag. "I will go, but there is no need that we should hunt for Rikki-tikki afterward. I will kill the big man and his wife, and the child if I can, and come away quietly. Then the bungalow will be empty, and Rikki-tikki will go."

Rikki-tikki tingled all over with rage and hatred at this, and then Nag's head came through the sluice, and his five feet of cold body followed it. Angry as he was, Rikki-tikki was very frightened as he saw the size of the big cobra. Nag coiled himself up, raised his head, and looked into the bathroom in the dark, and Rikki could see his eyes glitter.

"Now, if I kill him here, Nagaina will know;—and if I fight him on the open floor, the odds are in his favor. What am I to do?" said Rikki-tikki-tavi.

Nag waved to and fro, and then Rikki-tikki heard him drinking from the biggest water jar that was used to fill the bath. "That is good," said the snake. "Now, when Karait was killed, the big man had a stick. He may have that stick still, but when he comes in to bathe in the morning he will not have a stick. I shall wait here till he comes. Nagaina—do you hear me?—I shall wait here in the cool till daytime."

There was no answer from outside, so Rikki-tikki knew Nagaina had gone away. Nag coiled himself down, coil by coil, round the bulge at the bottom of the waterjar, and Rikki-tikki stayed still as death. After an hour he began to move, muscle by muscle, toward the jar. Nag was asleep, and Rikki-tikki looked at his big back, wondering which would be the best place for a good hold. "If I don't break his back at the first jump," said Rikki, "he can still fight; and if he fights—O Rikki!" He looked at the thickness of the neck below the hood, but that was too much for him; and a bite near the tail would only make Nag savage.

"It must be the head," he said at last; "the head above the hood; and, when I am once there, I must not let go."

Then he jumped. The head was lying a little clear of the water jar, under the curve of it; and, as his teeth met, Rikki braced his back against the bulge of the red earthenware to hold down the head. This gave him just one second's purchase,[8] and he made the most of it. Then he was battered to and fro as a rat is shaken by a dog—to and fro on the floor, up and down, and round in great

circles; but his eyes were red, and he held on as the body cartwhipped over the floor, upsetting the tin dipper and the soap dish and the fleshbrush, and banged against the tin side of the bath. As he held he closed his jaws tighter and tighter, for he made sure he would be banged to death, and, for the honor of his family, he preferred to be found with his teeth locked. He was dizzy, aching, and felt shaken to pieces when something went off like a thunderclap just behind him; a hot wind knocked him senseless and red fire singed his fur. The big man had been wakened by the noise, and had fired both barrels of a shotgun into Nag just behind the hood.

Rikki-tikki held on with his eyes shut, for now he was quite sure he was dead; but the head did not move, and the big man

---

8. purchase (pur′ chəs): In this case, a good hold on something.

picked him up and said: "It's the mongoose again, Alice; the little chap has saved *our* lives now." Then Teddy's mother came in with a very white face, and saw what was left of Nag, and Rikki-tikki dragged himself to Teddy's bedroom and spent half the rest of the night shaking himself tenderly to find out whether he really was broken into forty pieces, as he fancied.

When morning came he was very stiff, but well pleased with his doings. "Now I have Nagaina to settle with, and she will be worse than five Nags, and there's no knowing when the eggs she spoke of will hatch. Goodness! I must go and see Darzee," he said.

Without waiting for breakfast, Rikki-tikki ran to the thornbush where Darzee was singing a song of triumph at the top of his voice. The news of Nag's death was all over

the garden, for the sweeper had thrown the body on the rubbish heap.

"Oh, you stupid tuft of feathers!" said Rikki-tikki, angrily. "Is this the time to sing?"

"Nag is dead—is dead—is dead!" sang Darzee. "The valiant Rikki-tikki caught him by the head and held fast. The big man brought the bang-stick and Nag fell in two pieces! He will never eat my babies again."

"All that's true enough; but where's Nagaina?" said Rikki-tikki, looking carefully round him.

"Nagaina came to the bathroom sluice and called for Nag," Darzee went on; "and Nag came out on the end of a stick—the sweeper picked him up on the end of a stick and threw him upon the rubbish heap. Let us sing about the great, the red-eyed Rikki-tikki!" and Darzee filled his throat and sang.

"If I could get up to your nest, I'd roll all your babies out!" said Rikki-tikki. "You don't know when to do the right thing at the right time. You're safe enough in your nest there, but it's war for me down here. Stop singing a minute, Darzee."

"For the great, the beautiful Rikki-tikki's sake, I will stop," said Darzee. "What is it, O Killer of the terrible Nag!"

"Where is Nagaina, for the third time?"

"On the rubbish heap by the stables, mourning for Nag. Great is Rikki-tikki with the white teeth."

"Bother my white teeth! Have you ever heard where she keeps her eggs?"

"In the melon bed, on the end nearest the wall, where the sun strikes nearly all day. She had them there weeks ago."

"And you never thought it worthwhile to tell me? The end nearest the wall, you said?"

"Rikki-tikki, you are not going to eat her eggs?"

"Not eat exactly; no. Darzee, if you have a grain of sense you will fly off to the stables and pretend that your wing is broken, and let Nagaina chase you away to this bush! I must get to the melon bed, and if I went there now she'd see me."

Darzee was a featherbrained little fellow who could never hold more than one idea at a time in his head; and just because he knew that Nagaina's children were born in eggs like his own, he didn't think at first that it was fair to kill them. But his wife was a sensible bird, and she knew that cobra's eggs meant young cobras later on; so she flew off from the nest, and left Darzee to keep the babies warm, and continue his song about the death of Nag. Darzee was very like a man in some ways.

She fluttered in front of Nagaina by the rubbish heap, and cried out, "Oh, my wing is broken! The boy in the house threw a stone at me and broke it." Then she fluttered more desperately than ever.

Nagaina lifted up her head and hissed, "You warned Rikki-tikki when I would have killed him. Indeed and truly, you've chosen a bad place to be lame in." And she moved toward Darzee's wife, slipping along over the dust.

"The boy broke it with a stone!" shrieked Darzee's wife.

"Well! It may be some consolation to you when you're dead to know that I shall settle accounts with the boy. My husband lies on the rubbish heap this morning, but before night the boy in the house will lie very still. What is the use of running away? I am sure to catch you. Little fool, look at me!"

Darzee's wife knew better than to do *that*, for a bird who looks at a snake's eyes gets so frightened that she cannot move. Darzee's wife fluttered on, piping sorrowfully, and never leaving the ground, and Nagaina quickened her pace.

Rikki-tikki heard them going up the path from the stables, and he raced for the end of the melon patch near the wall. There, in the warm litter about the melons, very cunningly hidden, he found twenty-five eggs, about the size of a bantam's[9] eggs, but with whitish skin instead of shell.

"I was not a day too soon," he said; for he could see the baby cobras curled up inside the skin, and he knew that the minute they were hatched they could each kill a man or a mongoose. He bit off the tops of the eggs as fast as he could, taking care to crush the young cobras, and turned over the litter from time to time to see whether he had missed any. At last there were only three eggs left, and Rikki-tikki began to chuckle to himself, when he heard Darzee's wife screaming:

---

9. bantam's : A small chicken's.

"Rikki-tikki, I led Nagaina toward the house, and she has gone into the veranda, and—oh, come quickly—she means killing!"

Rikki-tikki smashed two eggs, and tumbled backward down the melon bed with the third egg in his mouth, and scuttled to the veranda as hard as he could put foot to the ground. Teddy and his mother and father were there at early breakfast; but Rikki-tikki saw that they were not eating anything. They sat stone-still, and their faces were white. Nagaina was coiled up on the matting by Teddy's chair, within easy striking distance of Teddy's bare leg, and she was swaying to and fro singing a song of triumph.

"Son of the big man that killed Nag," she hissed, "stay still. I am not ready yet. Wait a little. Keep very still, all you three. If you move I strike, and if you do not move I strike. Oh, foolish people, who killed my Nag!"

Teddy's eyes were fixed on his father, and all his father could do was to whisper, "Sit still, Teddy. You mustn't move. Teddy, keep still."

Then Rikki-tikki came up and cried: "Turn round, Nagaina; turn and fight!"

"All in good time," said she, without moving her eyes. "I will settle my account with *you* presently. Look at your friends, Rikki-tikki. They are still and white; they are afraid. They dare not move, and if you come a step nearer I strike."

"Look at your eggs," said Rikki-tikki, "in the melon bed near the wall. Go and look, Nagaina."

The big snake turned half round, and saw the egg on the veranda. "Ah-h! Give it to me," she said.

Rikki-tikki put his paws one on each side of the egg, and his eyes were blood-red. "What price for a snake's egg? For a young cobra? For a young king cobra? For the last—the very last of the brood? The ants are eating all the others down by the melon bed."

Nagaina spun clear round, forgetting everything for the sake of the one egg; and Rikki-tikki saw Teddy's father shoot out a big hand, catch Teddy by the shoulder, and drag him across the little table with the teacups, safe and out of reach of Nagaina.

"Tricked! Tricked! Tricked! *Rikk-tck-tck!*" chuckled Rikki-tikki. "The boy is safe, and it was I—I—I that caught Nag by the hood last night in the bathroom." Then he began to jump up and down, all four feet together, his head close to the floor. "He threw me to and fro, but he could not shake me off. He was dead before the big man blew him in two. I did it. *Rikki-tikki-tck-tck!* Come then, Nagaina. Come and fight with me. You shall not be a widow long."

Nagaina saw that she had lost her chance of killing Teddy, and the egg lay between Rikki-tikki's paws. "Give me the egg, Rikki-tikki. Give me the last of my eggs, and I will go away and never come back," she said, lowering her hood.

"Yes, you will go away, and you will never come back; for you will go to the rubbish heap with Nag. Fight, widow! The big man has gone for his gun! Fight!"

Rikki-tikki was bounding all round Nagaina, keeping just out of reach of her stroke, his little eyes like hot coals. Nagaina gathered herself together, and flung out at him. Rikki-tikki jumped up and backward. Again and again and again she struck, and each time her head came with a whack on the matting of the veranda and she gathered herself together like a watchspring. Then Rikki-tikki danced in a circle to get behind her, and Nagaina spun round to keep her head to his head, so that the rustle of her tail on the matting sounded like dry leaves blown along by the wind.

He had forgotten the egg. It still lay on the veranda, and Nagaina came nearer and nearer to it, till at last, while Rikki-tikki was drawing breath, she caught it in her mouth, turned to the veranda steps, and flew like an arrow down the path, with Rikki-tikki behind her. When the cobra runs for her life, she goes like a whiplash flicked across a horse's neck.

Rikki-tikki knew that he must catch her, or all the trouble would begin again. She headed straight for the long grass by the thornbush, and as he was running Rikki-tikki heard Darzee still singing his foolish little song of triumph. But Darzee's wife was wiser. She flew off her nest as Nagaina came along, and flapped her wings about Nagaina's head. If Darzee had helped they might have turned her; but Nagaina only lowered her hood and went on. Still, the instant's delay brought Rikki-tikki up to her, and as she plunged into the rat hole where she and Nag used to live, his little white teeth were clenched on her tail, and he went down with her—and very few mongooses, however wise and old they may be, care to follow a cobra into its hole. It was dark in the hole; and Rikki-tikki never knew when it might open out and give Nagaina room to turn and strike at him. He held on savagely, and struck out his feet to act as brakes on the dark slope of the hot, moist earth.

Then the grass by the mouth of the hole stopped waving, and Darzee said: "It is all over with Rikki-tikki! We must sing his death song. Valiant Rikki-tikki is dead! For Nagaina will surely kill him underground."

So he sang a very mournful song that he made up all on the spur of the minute, and just as he got to the most touching part the grass quivered again, and Rikki-tikki, covered with dirt, dragged himself out of the hole leg by leg, licking his whiskers. Darzee stopped with a little shout. Rikki-tikki shook some of the dust out of his fur and sneezed. "It is all over," he said. "The widow will never come out again." And the red ants that live between the grass stems heard him, and began to troop down one after another to see if he had spoken the truth.

Rikki-tikki curled himself up in the grass and slept where he was—slept and slept till it was late in the afternoon, for he had done a hard day's work.

"Now," he said, when he awoke, "I will go back to the house. Tell the Coppersmith, Darzee, and he will tell the garden that Nagaina is dead."

The Coppersmith is a bird who makes a noise exactly like the beating of a little hammer on a copper pot; and the reason he is always making it is because he is the town crier to every Indian garden, and tells all the news to everybody who cares to listen. As Rikki-tikki went up the path, he heard his "attention" notes like a tiny dinner gong; and then the steady "*Ding-dong-tock!* Nag is dead—*dong!* Nagaina is dead! *Ding-dong-tock!*" That set all the birds in the garden singing, and the frogs croaking; for Nag and Nagaina used to eat frogs as well as little birds.

When Rikki got to the house, Teddy and Teddy's mother and Teddy's father came out and almost cried over him; and that night he ate all that was given him till he could eat no more, and went to bed on Teddy's shoulder, where Teddy's mother saw him when she came to look late at night.

"He saved our lives and Teddy's life," she said to her husband. "Just think, he saved all our lives."

Rikki-tikki woke up with a jump, for all the mongooses are light sleepers.

"Oh, it's you," said he. "What are you bothering for? All the cobras are dead; and if they weren't, I'm here."

Rikki-tikki had a right to be proud of himself; but he did not grow too proud, and he kept that garden as a mongoose should keep it, with tooth and jump and spring and bite, till never a cobra dared show its head inside the walls.

Your Response

1. What would you enjoy or find interesting about the life Teddy and his family have in India? What about it would you dislike?

Recalling

2. When does Rikki first meet the cobras?
3. What is Nag and Nagaina's plan to get control of the bungalow?
4. How does Rikki protect Teddy's father and then Teddy from the cobras?
5. What happens to Nagaina at the end?

Interpreting

6. How do these animals resemble humans?
7. Compare and contrast the personalities of Rikki and the two cobras.
8. How is "the great war" in this story a battle between good and evil?

Applying

9. Why would Rikki's approach to problems in life work better than Darzee's?

ANALYZING LITERATURE

Understanding Plot

Plot is the sequence of events in a story. These events usually involve a **conflict,** or struggle between opposing sides. This struggle becomes the most intense at the **climax,** the point just before the conflict is resolved. The rest of the story is devoted to the **resolution,** or solving of the conflict.

The conflict in "Rikki-tikki-tavi" occurs between Rikki and the two cobras.

1. How does the first meeting between Rikki and the cobras make you want to read further?
2. Which battle occurs at the climax?
3. How is the conflict resolved?

CRITICAL THINKING AND READING

Putting Events in Chronological Order

In "Rikki-tikki-tavi" the events take place in **chronological order.** This means that they follow one another as time goes forward.

1. List the main events of the story in the order they occur.
2. About how much time passes between the first event in the story and the last?

THINKING AND WRITING

Writing a Story With a Strong Plot

In a story with a strong plot like "Rikki-tikki-tavi," the conflict rises to a climax and is then resolved. Imagine that a movie director has asked you to write such a story to serve as the basis for her next film. Brainstorm to think of a good idea for a conflict. Then use this idea to write a story with a strong plot. As you revise it, check to see that it has a climax and a resolution.

LEARNING OPTIONS

1. **Art.** By yourself or with a friend, develop a comic strip based on "Rikki-tikki-tavi." One of you might want to develop the stories and write the dialogue while the other draws the different frames of the cartoon. You could first illustrate the story itself and then develop your own episodes involving the main characters.
2. **Cross-curricular Connection.** Find out about some animals native to your region that do not get along. Learn as much about the animals' individual habits and their relationships as you can. You can find this information in nature books and periodicals such as *National Geographic.* Then prepare a brief presentation for the class, perhaps showing photographs or drawings.

GUIDE FOR READING

The Ransom of Red Chief

O. Henry

(1862–1910) was born William Sidney Porter in Greensboro, North Carolina. Under the pen name of O. Henry, he wrote about ordinary people with warmth, humor, and a touch of romance. After spending time in prison for embezzlement (a crime for which he may not have been guilty), O. Henry moved to New York City, where he gathered material for his stories. His understanding of human nature and of people on both sides of the law is evident in "The Ransom of Red Chief."

Conflict

A **conflict** is a struggle between opposing sides or forces. When conflict in a story occurs between one person and another or between a person and a force of nature, we say the conflict is **external.** When it occurs between opposing ideas or feelings within a character, we say the conflict is **internal.** "The Ransom of Red Chief" contains both external and internal conflicts.

Focus

The boy in this story is the kind of kid many people would call a "brat." He makes trouble for practically everyone he meets and seems, unfortunately, to have boundless energy. You have probably known someone you considered a brat. What qualities did this person have that made him or her bratty? What were your experiences with this person like? Write a brief character sketch of this or an imaginary brat. Include details about the person's behavior that make it clear why you would want to avoid him or her. As you read, compare your portrait with that of "Red Chief."

Vocabulary

Knowing the following words will help you as you read "The Ransom of Red Chief."

undeleterious (un del′ ə tir′ ē əs) *adj.*: Healthy; full of well-being (p. 25)

fraudulent (frô′ jə lənt) *adj.*: Acting with fraud or deceit (p. 25)

lackadaisical (lak′ ə dā′ zi kəl) *adj.*: Showing a lack of interest (p. 25)

elevation (el′ ə vā′ shən) *n.*: A high place (p. 25)

provisions (prō vizh′ ənz) *n.*: Food and supplies (p. 25)

stealthy (stel′ *th*ē) *adj.*: Secret; sly (p. 27)

sylvan (sil′ vən) *adj.*: Of or characteristic of woods and forests (p. 28)

somnolent (säm′ nə lent) *adj.*: Sleepy; drowsy (p. 28)

collaborated (kə lab′ ə rāt′ 'd) *v.*: Worked together (p. 29)

The Ransom of Red Chief

O. Henry

It looked like a good thing: but wait till I tell you. We were down South, in Alabama—Bill Driscoll and myself—when this kidnapping idea struck us. It was, as Bill afterward expressed it, "during a moment of temporary mental apparition"[1]; but we didn't find that out till later.

There was a town down there, as flat as a flannel-cake, and called Summit, of course. It contained inhabitants of as undeleterious and self-satisfied a class of peasantry as ever clustered around a Maypole.

Bill and me had a joint capital of about six hundred dollars, and we needed just two thousand dollars more to pull off a fraudulent town-lot scheme in Western Illinois with. We talked it over on the front steps of the hotel. Philoprogenitoveness,[2] says we, is strong in semi-rural communities; therefore, and for other reasons, a kidnapping project ought to do better there than in the radius of newspapers that send reporters out in plain clothes to stir up talk about such things. We knew that Summit couldn't get after us with anything stronger than constables and, maybe, some lackadaisical bloodhounds and

a diatribe[3] or two in the *Weekly Farmers' Budget*. So, it looked good.

We selected for our victim the only child of a prominent citizen named Ebenezer Dorset. The father was respectable and tight, a mortgage fancier and a stern, upright collection-plate passer and forecloser. The kid was a boy of ten, with bas-relief[4] freckles, and hair the color of the cover of the magazine you buy at the newsstand when you want to catch a train. Bill and me figured that Ebenezer would melt down for a ransom of two thousand dollars to a cent. But wait till I tell you.

About two miles from Summit was a little mountain, covered with a dense cedar brake.[5] On the rear elevation of this mountain was a cave. There we stored provisions.

One evening after sundown, we drove in a buggy past old Dorset's house. The kid was in the street, throwing rocks at a kitten on the opposite fence.

"Hey, little boy!" says Bill, "would you like to have a bag of candy and a nice ride?"

The boy catches Bill neatly in the eye with a piece of brick.

"That will cost the old man an extra five hundred dollars," says Bill, climbing over the wheel.

1. **apparition** (ap′ ə rish′ ən).: Bill is confusing words here. Instead of *apparition*, which is a strange ghostly figure, he means *aberration* (ab′ ər ā′ s̸hən), which is a departure from the normal, or a mental lapse.
2. **philoprogenitoveness** (fil′ ō prō jen′ ə tiv′ nəs) *n.*: Again the characters make an error with a word. The correct spelling of the word is philoprogenitiveness, not -toveness. The word means "the love of parents for their offspring."
3. **diatribe** (dī′ ə trīb′) *n.*: Attack; criticism.
4. **bas-relief** (bä′ ri lēf′) *adj.*: Standing out from the background; like a sculpture in which figures are carved on a flat surface so that they project.
5. **brake** (brāk) *n.*: A thicket, or area of thick underbrush and trees.

That boy put up a fight like a welter-weight cinnamon bear; but, at last, we got him down in the bottom of the buggy and drove away. We took him up to the cave, and I hitched the horse in the cedar brake. After dark I drove the buggy to the little village, three miles away, where we had hired it, and walked back to the mountain.

Bill was pasting court-plaster[6] over the scratches and bruises on his features. There was a fire burning behind the big rock at the entrance of the cave, and the boy was watching a pot of boiling coffee, with two buzzard tail-feathers stuck in his red hair. He points a stick at me when I come up, and says:

"Ha! cursed paleface, do you dare to enter the camp of Red Chief, the terror of the plains?"

"He's all right now," says Bill, rolling up his trousers and examining some bruises on his shins. "We're playing Indian. We're making Buffalo Bill's show[7] look like magic-lantern[8] views of Palestine in the town hall. I'm Old Hank, the Trapper, Red Chief's captive, and I'm to be scalped at daybreak. By Geronimo! that kid can kick hard."

Yes, sir, that boy seemed to be having the time of his life. The fun of camping out in a cave had made him forget that he was a captive himself. He immediately christened me Snake-eye, the Spy, and announced that, when his braves returned from the warpath, I was to be broiled at the stake at the rising of the sun.

Then we had supper; and he filled his mouth full of bacon and bread and gravy, and began to talk. He made a during-dinner speech something like this:

"I like this fine. I never camped out before; but I had a pet 'possum once, and I was nine last birthday. I hate to go to school. Rats ate up sixteen of Jimmy Talbot's aunt's speckled hen's eggs. Are there any real Indians in these woods? I want some more gravy. Does the trees moving make the wind blow? We had five puppies. What makes your nose so red, Hank? My father has lots of money. Are the stars hot? I whipped Ed Walker twice, Saturday. I don't like girls. You dassent catch toads unless with a string. Do oxen make any noise? Why are oranges round? Have you got beds to sleep on in this cave? Amos Murray has got six toes. A parrot can talk, but a money or a fish can't. How many does it take to make twelve?"

Every few minutes he would remember that he was a pesky redskin, and pick up his stick rifle and tiptoe to the mouth of the cave to rubber[9] for the scouts of the hated paleface. Now and then he would let out a war-whoop that made Old Hank the Trapper shiver. That boy had Bill terrorized from the start.

"Red Chief," says I to the kid, "would you like to go home?"

"Aw, what for?" says he. "I don't have any fun at home. I hate to go to school. I like to camp out. You won't take me back home again, Snake-eye, will you?"

"Not right away," says I. "We'll stay here in the cave awhile."

"All right!" says he. "That'll be fine. I never had such fun in all my life."

We went to bed about eleven o'clock. We spread down some wide blankets and quilts and put Red Chief between us. We weren't afraid he'd run away. He kept us awake for three hours, jumping up and reaching for his rifle and screeching: "Hist! pard," in

---

6. court-plaster: Sticky cloth used to cover minor wounds.

7. Buffalo Bill's show: William F. Cody (1846–1917), known as Buffalo Bill, was a frontier scout turned showman. His famous wild-West show featured extravagant displays of trick-shooting and horseback riding.

8. magic-lantern: Old-fashioned term for a projector showing still pictures from transparent slides.

9. rubber (rub′ ər) n.: Short for rubberneck, old slang term meaning "to stretch one's neck and gaze around with curiosity."

mine and Bill's ears, as the fancied crackle of a twig or the rustle of a leaf revealed to his young imagination the stealthy approach of the outlaw band. At last, I fell into a troubled sleep, and dreamed that I had been kidnapped and chained to a tree by a ferocious pirate with red hair.

Just at daybreak, I was awakened by a series of awful screams from Bill. They weren't yells, or howls, or shouts, or whoops, or yawps, such as you'd expect from a manly set of vocal organs—they were simply indecent, terrifying, humiliating screams, such as women emit when they see ghosts or caterpillars. It's an awful thing to hear a strong, desperate, fat man scream incontinently in a cave at daybreak.

I jumped up to see what the matter was. Red Chief was sitting on Bill's chest, with one hand twined in Bill's hair. In the other he had the sharp case-knife we used for slicing bacon; and he was industriously and re-

alistically trying to take Bill's scalp, according to the sentence that had been pronounced upon him the evening before.

I got the knife away from the kid and made him lie down again. But, from that moment, Bill's spirit was broken. He laid down on his side of the bed, but he never closed an eye again in sleep as long as that boy was with us. I dozed off for a while, but along toward sun-up I remembered that Red Chief had said I was to be burned at the stake at the rising of the sun. I wasn't nervous or afraid; but I sat up and lit my pipe and leaned against a rock.

"What you getting up so soon for, Sam?" asked Bill.

"Me?" says I. "Oh, I got a kind of pain in my shoulder. I thought sitting up would rest it."

"You're a liar!" says Bill. "You're afraid. You was to be burned at sunrise, and you was afraid he'd do it. And he would, too, if he could find a match. Ain't it awful, Sam? Do you think anybody will pay out money to get a little imp like that back home?"

"Sure," said I. "A rowdy kid like that is just the kind that parents dote on. Now, you and the Chief get up and cook breakfast, while I go up on the top of this mountain and reconnoiter."[10]

I went up on the peak of the little mountain and ran my eye over the contiguous[11] vicinity.[12] Over towards Summit I expected to see the sturdy yeomanry[13] of the village armed with scythes and pitchforks beating the countryside for the dastardly kidnappers. But what I saw was a peaceful landscape dotted with one man ploughing with a dun mule. Nobody was dragging the creek; no couriers dashed hither and yon, bringing tidings of no news to the distracted parents. There was a sylvan attitude of somnolent sleepiness pervading that section of the external outward surface of Alabama that lay exposed to my view. "Perhaps," says I to myself, "it has not yet been discovered that the wolves have borne away the tender lambkin from the fold. Heaven help the wolves!" says I, and I went down the mountain to breakfast.

When I got to the cave I found Bill backed up against the side of it, breathing hard, and the boy threatening to smash him with a rock half as big as a cocoanut.

"He put a red-hot boiled potato down my back," explained Bill, "and then mashed it with his foot; and I boxed his ears. Have you got a gun about you, Sam?"

I took the rock away from the boy and kind of patched up the argument. "I'll fix you," says the kid to Bill. "No man ever yet struck the Red Chief but he got paid for it. You better beware!"

After breakfast the kid takes a piece of leather with strings wrapped around it out of his pocket and goes outside the cave unwinding it.

"What's he up now?" says Bill, anxiously. "You don't think he'll run away, do you, Sam?"

"No fear of it," says I. "He don't seem to be much of a home body. But we've got to fix up some plan about the ransom. There don't seem to be much excitement around Summit on account of his disappearance; but maybe they haven't realized yet that he's gone. His folks may think he's spending the night with Aunt Jane or one of the neighbors. Anyhow, he'll be missed today. Tonight we must get a message to his father demanding the two thousand dollars for his return."

Just then we heard a kind of war-whoop,

---

10. reconnoiter (rek' ə noit' ər) v.: Examine an area to discover information.
11. contiguous (kən tig' yoo əs) adj.: Near; next; touching.
12. vicinity (və sin' ə tē) n.: Area; neighborhood.
13. yeomanry (yō' mən rē) n.: Landowners.

such as David might have emitted when he knocked out the champion Goliath. It was a sling that Red Chief had pulled out of his pocket, and he was whirling it around his head.

I dodged, and heard a heavy thud and a kind of a sigh from Bill, like a horse gives out when you take his saddle off. A rock the size of an egg had caught Bill just behind his left ear. He loosened himself all over and fell in the fire across the frying pan of hot water for washing the dishes. I dragged him out and poured cold water on his head for half an hour.

By and by, Bill sits up and feels behind his ear and says: "Sam, do you know who my favorite Biblical character is?"

"Take it easy," says I. "You'll come to your senses presently."

"King Herod,"[14] says he. "You won't go away and leave me here alone, will you, Sam?"

I went out and caught that boy and shook him until his freckles rattled.

"If you don't behave," says I, "I'll take you straight home. Now, are you going to be good, or not?"

"I was only funning," says he, sullenly. "I didn't mean to hurt Old Hank. But what did he hit me for? I'll behave, Snake-eye, if you won't send me home, and if you'll let me play the Black Scout today."

"I don't know the game," says I. "That's for you and Mr. Bill to decide. He's your playmate for the day. I'm going away for a while, on business. Now, you come in and make friends with him and say you are sorry for hurting him, or home you go, at once."

I made him and Bill shake hands, and then I took Bill aside and told him I was going to Poplar Grove, a little village three miles from the cave, and find out what I could about how the kidnapping had been regarded in Summit. Also, I thought it best to send a peremptory[15] letter to old man Dorset that day, demanding the ransom and dictating how it should be paid.

"You know, Sam," says Bill, "I've stood by you without batting an eye in earthquakes, fire and flood—in poker games, dynamite outrages, police raids, train robberies, and cyclones. I never lost my nerve yet till we kidnapped that two-legged skyrocket of a kid. He's got me going. You won't leave me long with him, will you, Sam?"

"I'll be back some time this afternoon," says I. "You must keep the boy amused and quiet till I return. And now we'll write the letter to old Dorset."

Bill and I got paper and pencil and worked on the letter while Red Chief, with a blanket wrapped around him, strutted up and down, guarding the mouth of the cave. Bill begged me tearfully to make the ransom fifteen hundred dollars instead of two thousand. "I ain't attempting," says he, "to decry[16] the celebrated moral aspect of parental affection, but we're dealing with humans, and it ain't human for anybody to give up two thousand dollars for that forty-pound chunk of freckled wildcat. I'm willing to take a chance at fifteen hundred dollars. You can charge the difference up to me."

So, to relieve Bill, I acceded, and we collaborated a letter that ran this way:

Ebenezer Dorset, Esq.:
   We have your boy concealed in a place far from Summit. It is useless for you or the most skilful detectives to attempt to find him. Absolutely, the only terms on which you can

---

14. King Herod (73–74 B.C.): King of Judea who ordered the killing of all male children under two years of age.

15. peremptory (pər emp′ tə rē) *adj.*: Decisive, commanding.
16. decry (dē krī′) *v.*: Speak out against strongly.

have him restored to you are these: We demand fifteen hundred dollars in large bills for his return; the money to be left at midnight tonight at the same spot and in the same box as your reply—as hereinafter described. If you agree to these terms, send your answer in writing by a solitary messenger tonight at half-past eight o'clock. After crossing Owl Creek on the road to Poplar Grove, there are three large trees about a hundred yards apart, close to the fence of the wheat field on the right-hand side. At the bottom of the fence-post, opposite the third tree, will be found a small pasteboard box.

The messenger will place the answer in this box and return immediately to Summit.

If you attempt any treachery or fail to comply with our demand as stated, you will never see your boy again.

If you pay the money as demanded, he will be returned to you safe and well within three hours. These terms are final, and if you do not accede to them no further communication will be attempted.

Two Desperate Men

I addressed this letter to Dorset, and put it in my pocket. As I was about to start, the kid comes up to me and says:

"Aw, Snake-eye, you said I could play the Black Scout while you was gone."

"Play it, of course," says I. "Mr. Bill will play with you. What kind of a game is it?"

"I'm the Black Scout," says Red Chief, "and I have to ride to the stockade to warn the settlers that the Indians are coming. I'm tired of playing Indian myself. I want to be the Black Scout."

"All right," says I. "It sounds harmless to

me. I guess Mr. Bill will help you foil the pesky savages."

"What am I to do?" asks Bill, looking at the kid suspiciously.

"You are the hoss," says Black Scout. "Get down on your hands and knees. How can I ride to the stockade without a hoss?"

"You'd better keep him interested," said I, "till we get the scheme going. Loosen up."

Bill gets down on his all fours, and a look comes in his eye like a rabbit's when you catch it in a trap.

"How far is it to the stockade, kid?" he asks, in a husky manner of voice.

"Ninety miles," says the Black Scout. "And you have to hump yourself to get there on time. Whoa, now!"

The Black Scout jumps on Bill's back and digs his heels in his side.

"For Heaven's sake," says Bill, "hurry back, Sam, as soon as you can. I wish we hadn't made the ransom more than a thousand. Say, you quit kicking me or I'll get up and warm you good."

I walked over to Poplar Grove and sat around the post-office and store, talking with the chaw-bacons[17] that came in to trade. One whiskerando says that he hears Summit is all upset on account of Elder Ebenezer Dorset's boy having been lost or stolen. That was all I wanted to know. I bought some smoking tobacco, referred casually to the price of black-eyed peas, posted my letter surreptitiously,[18] and came away. The postmaster said the mail-carrier would come by in an hour to take the mail to Summit.

When I got back to the cave Bill and the boy were not to be found. I explored the vicinity of the cave, and risked a yodel or two, but there was no response.

So I lighted my pipe and sat down on a

---

17. chaw-bacons: Old slang for yokels or hicks.
18. surreptitiously (sŭr′ əp tish′ əs lē) *adv.*: In a secret or sneaky way.

mossy bank to await developments.

In about half an hour I heard the bushes rustle, and Bill wabbled out into the little glade in front of the cave. Behind him was the kid, stepping softly like a scout, with a broad grin on his face. Bill stopped, took off his hat, and wiped his face with a red handkerchief. The kid stopped about eight feet behind him.

"Sam," says Bill, "I suppose you'll think

I'm a renegade,[19] but I couldn't help it. I'm a grown man with masculine proclivities[20] and habits of self-defense, but there is a time when all systems of egotism[21] and predominance[22] fail. The boy is gone. I sent him home. All is off. There was martyrs in old times," goes on Bill, "that suffered death rather than give up the particular graft they enjoyed. None of 'em ever was subjugated[23] to such supernatural tortures as I have been. I tried to be faithful to our articles of depredation;[24] but there came a limit."

"What's the trouble, Bill?" I asks him.

"I was rode," says Bill, "the ninety miles to the stockade, not barring an inch. Then, when the settlers was rescued, I was given oats. Sand ain't a palatable[25] substitute. And then, for an hour I had to try to explain to him why there was nothin' in holes, how a road can run both ways, and what makes the grass green. I tell you, Sam, a human can only stand so much. I takes him by the neck of his clothes and drags him down the mountain. On the way he kicks my legs black and blue from the knees down; and I've got to have two or three bites on my thumb and hand cauterized.[26]

"But he's gone"—continues Bill—"gone home. I showed him the road to Summit and kicked him about eight feet nearer there at one kick. I'm sorry we lose the ransom; but

it was either that or Bill Driscoll to the madhouse."

Bill is puffing and blowing, but there is a look of ineffable[27] peace and growing content on his rose-pink features.

"Bill," says I, "there isn't any heart disease in your family, is there?"

"No," says Bill, "nothing chronic except malaria and accidents. Why?"

"Then you might turn around," says I, "and have a look behind you."

Bill turns and sees the boy, and loses his complexion and sits down plump on the ground and begins to pluck aimlessly at grass and little sticks. For an hour I was afraid of his mind. And then I told him that my scheme was to put the whole job through immediately and that we would get the ransom and be off with it by midnight if old Dorset fell in with our proposition. So Bill braced up enough to give the kid a weak sort of smile and a promise to play the Russian in a Japanese war[28] with him as soon as he felt a little better.

I had a scheme for collecting that ransom without danger of being caught by counterplots that ought to commend itself to professional kidnappers. The tree under which the answer was to be left—and the money later on—was close to the road fence with big, bare fields on all sides. If a gang of constables should be watching for anyone to come for the note, they could see him a long way off crossing the fields or in the road. But no, sirree! At half-past eight I was up in that tree as well hidden as a tree toad, waiting for the messenger to arrive.

Exactly on time, a half-grown boy rides up the road on a bicycle, locates the pasteboard box at the foot of the fence-post, slips

---

19. renegade (ren′ ə gād) *n.*: Traitor; turncoat.
20. proclivities (prō kliv′ ə tēz) *n.*: Tendencies; habits.
21. egotism (ē′ gō tiz′ əm) *n.*: Selfishness; self-conceit.
22. predominance (prē däm′ ə nəns) *n.*: Authority; superiority.
23. subjugated (sub′ jə gāt′ əd) *v.*: Put under the control of.
24. depredation (dep′ rə dā′ shən) *n.*: Robbing; here Bill is referring to the rules they set up for the kidnapping.
25. palatable (pal′ ə tə bəl) *adj.*: Pleasant; acceptable.
26. cauterized (kôt′ ər īz′ d) *v.*: Burned so as to stop the spread of infection.

27. ineffable (in ef′ ə bəl) *adj.*: Too overwhelming to be described.
28. the Russian in a Japanese war: Reference to the Russo-Japanese War of 1905.

a folded piece of paper into it, and pedals away again back toward Summit.

I waited an hour and then concluded the thing was square. I slid down the tree, got the note, slipped along the fence till I struck the woods, and was back at the cave in another half an hour. I opened the note, got near the lantern, and read it to Bill. It was written with a pen in a crabbed hand,[29] and the sum and substance of it was this:

Two Desperate Men.

Gentlemen: I received your letter today by post, in regard to the ransom you ask for the return of my son.

---

29. crabbed hand: Handwriting that is hard to read because it is cramped and irregular.

I think you are a little high in your demands, and I hereby make you a counter-proposition, which I am inclined to believe you will accept. You bring Johnny home and pay me two hundred and fifty dollars in cash, and I agree to take him off your hands. You had better come at night, for the neighbors believe he is lost, and I couldn't be responsible for what they would do to anybody they saw bringing him back. Very respectfully,

Ebenezer Dorset

"Great pirates of Penzance," says I; "of all the impudent——"

But I glanced at Bill, and hesitated. He

had the most appealing look in his eyes I ever saw on the face of a dumb or a talking brute.

"Sam," says he, "what's two hundred and fifty dollars, after all? We've got the money. One more night of this kid will send me to a bed in Bedlam.[30] Besides being a thorough gentleman, I think Mr. Dorset is a spendthrift for making us such a liberal offer. You ain't going to let the chance go, are you?"

"Tell you the truth, Bill," says I, "this little he ewe lamb has somewhat got on my nerves too. We'll take him home, pay the ransom, and make our getaway."

We took him home that night. We got him to go by telling him that his father had bought a silver-mounted rifle and a pair of moccasins for him, and we were to hunt bears the next day.

It was just twelve o'clock when we knocked at Ebenezer's front door. Just at that moment when I should have been abstracting the fifteen hundred dollars from the box under the tree, according to the original proposition, Bill was counting out two hundred and fifty dollars into Dorset's hand.

When the kid found out we were going to leave him at home he started up a howl like a calliope[31] and fastened himself as tight as a leech to Bill's leg. His father peeled him away gradually, like a porous plaster.

"How long can you hold him?" asks Bill.

"I'm not as strong as I used to be," says old Dorset, "but I think I can promise you ten minutes."

"Enough," says Bill. "In ten minutes I shall cross the Central, Southern, and Middle Western States, and be legging it trippingly for the Canadian border."

And, as dark as it was, and as fat as Bill was, and as good a runner as I am, he was a good mile and a half out of Summit before I could catch up with him.

---

30. Bedlam: Short for St. Mary of Bethlehem, an old asylum for the insane in London.

31. calliope (kə līʹ ə pēʹ) *n.*: A keyboard instrument that has a series of steam whistles.

R ESPONDING TO THE SELECTION

Your Response

1. If you had been one of the kidnappers, would you have reacted the same way at the end?

Recalling

2. Why do Bill and Sam choose Ebenezer Dorset's son to kidnap?
3. Tell two things the boy does before he is kidnapped that should have warned Bill and Sam that he would be nothing but trouble.
4. What are the terms of the kidnappers' note?
5. What does Red Chief's father's note propose in response?

Interpreting

6. Outlaws are often described as "desperate criminals." Here the word *desperate* means "extremely dangerous." No doubt, this is the meaning Bill and Sam intend when they sign their ransom note "two desperate men." What meaning does O. Henry also want you to read into this word?
7. Why does Bill and Sam's plan backfire?
8. What clues at the beginning of the story hint at the humorous, unexpected events to come?

Applying

9. Have you or someone you know ever started a task that was thought to be very simple and

easy, only to have unforseen problems turn the simple project into a gigantic pain in the neck? Describe the experience.

ANALYZING LITERATURE

Understanding Conflict

A **conflict** is a struggle between opposing forces. Sometimes a conflict can get so out of hand, taking so many unexpected twists and turns, that the outcome is quite humorous.

1. How do the kidnappers come into conflict with Ebenezer Dorset?
2. Describe the conflict between the kidnappers and Red Chief.
3. Red Chief's antics force Bill to face an internal conflict: Should he betray the compact with his friend to preserve his sanity? While Sam is in Poplar Grove sending the ransom note, what does Bill decide to do? What surprise awaits Bill as he tells Sam of his treachery?
4. How are the conflicts resolved?

CRITICAL THINKING AND READING

Recognizing Stereotypes

In literature, **stereotypes** can be characters, expressions, or situations that conform to what is familiar and expected. In this story, O. Henry sets up a stereotypical situation, a kidnapping. He then turns it upside down to make what would normally be a tragic story quite funny.

1. What aspects of this situation fit the stereotype of a kidnapping story?
2. How are Bill and Sam not like typical kidnappers? Find evidence to support your answer.
3. How does Red Chief's behavior differ from that of a stereotypical kidnap victim?
4. How is Ebenezer Dorset's reply to the kidnap note different from what you would expect in a kidnap story?
5. Why is the story humorous?

6. What advice would you give to Bill and Sam before they set out to kidnap anyone else? (Keep your advice humorous.)

THINKING AND WRITING

Writing Diary Entries

Imagine that you are the boy, Red Chief. Step into his shoes and become a mischievous, obnoxious brat. Thinking as Red Chief thinks, write two diary entries for the two days of your adventure with Sam and Bill. Explain how you feel about camping out in the woods and playing with "Snake-eye" and "Old Hank." What are you thinking about? How are you feeling? As you look over your first draft, ask yourself, "Is this Red Chief speaking?" Revise any sentences that are not from his point of view.

LEARNING OPTIONS

1. **Language.** If you think some of the old-fashioned slang words used in "The Ransom of Red Chief" sound corny, take a look through the *New Dictionary of American Slang,* which your school or local librarian can help you find. In this dictionary you will discover that the word *rubberneck,* a form of which appears in this O. Henry story, was created in the 1880's by cowboys. Using this dictionary, *A Dictionary of Catch Phrases,* or the *Dictionary of American Idioms,* find five words or phrases that you think are particularly funny or interesting and share them with the class.
2. **Writing.** Write a sequel to "The Ransom of Red Chief." Imagine that the Dorset boy has run away from home and found Bill and Sam up north somewhere. How does the boy torture the kidnappers now? How will they get rid of him a second time? You might instead think up another caper for Bill and Sam to attempt in some other town. What scam will they try to pull off this time?

GUIDE FOR READING

James Ramsey Ullman

(1907–1971) was born in New York City, but his interest in mountain climbing made him "more familiar with Tibet than with Times Square." His work as a reporter, playwright, and play producer did not prevent him from traveling in pursuit of adventure. Though too ill to climb Mount Everest in Tibet himself, he assisted the American expedition that conquered this mountain in 1963. "A Boy and a Man" captures Ullman's love of climbing.

A Boy and a Man

Suspense

Suspense is the quality of a story that makes you want to keep reading until you learn how the events turn out. The word *suspense* comes from a Latin word meaning "suspended" or "uncertain," and uncertainty is an important part of suspense. You keep reading because the story is like a fascinating puzzle that fits together only at the end. Danger is another key ingredient in creating suspense. In many tales of suspense, the outcome is a matter of life or death. However, the danger in a suspenseful story does not have to be a physical threat. It can involve, for example, the possibility of losing a friend or failing a test.

The writer of "A Boy and a Man" wastes no time in creating suspense. As soon as the story opens, you are faced with a situation that is both uncertain and dangerous.

Focus

The Alps mountain range stretches across France, Italy, Switzerland, Germany, and Austria. As you climb up these towering mountains, the temperature drops two degrees (Fahrenheit) every 650 feet. Most of the peaks are covered with snow or ice all year round. In "A Boy and a Man," the man falls into a deep crack in an Alpine glacier. Imagine how you would feel if you were trapped in that icy hole, in danger of freezing to death. Write a brief inner monologue, conveying your thoughts about your predicament.

Vocabulary

Knowing the following words will help you as you read "A Boy and a Man."

crevasse (krə vas') *n.*: Deep crack (p. 37)

glacier (glā' shər) *n.*: Large mass of ice and snow (p. 37)

despair (di sper') *n.*: Loss of hope (p. 37)

prone (prōn) *adj.*: Lying face downward (p. 38)

taut (tôt) *adj.*: Tightly stretched (p. 39)

pummeled (pum' 'ld) *v.*: Beat (p. 39)

reconnoiter (rē kə noit' ər) *v.*: Look around (p. 41)

A Boy and a Man

from *Banner in the Sky*

James Ramsey Ullman

The crevasse was about six feet wide at the top and narrowed gradually as it went down. But how deep it was Rudi could not tell. After a few feet the blue walls of ice curved away at a sharp slant, and what was below the curve was hidden from sight.

"Hello!" Rudi called.

"Hello—" A voice answered from the depths.

"How far down are you?"

"I'm not sure. About twenty feet, I'd guess."

"On the bottom?"

"No. I can't even see the bottom. I was lucky and hit a ledge."

The voice spoke in German, but with a strange accent. Whoever was down there, Rudi knew, it was not one of the men of the valley.

"Are you hurt?" he called.

"Nothing broken—no," said the voice. "Just shaken up some. And cold."

"How long have you been there?"

"About three hours."

Rudi looked up and down the crevasse. He was thinking desperately of what he could do.

"Do you have a rope?" asked the voice.

"No."

"How many of you are there?"

"Only me."

There was a silence. When the voice spoke again, it was still quiet and under strict control. "Then you'll have to get help," it said.

Rudi didn't answer. To get down to Kurtal would take at least two hours, and for a party to climb back up would take three. By that time it would be night, and the man would have been in the crevasse for eight hours. He would be frozen to death.

"No," said Rudi, "it would take too long."

"What else is there to do?"

Rudi's eyes moved over the ice-walls: almost vertical, smooth as glass. "Have you an ax?" he asked.

"No. I lost it when I fell. It dropped to the bottom."

"Have you tried to climb?"

"Yes. But I can't get a hold."

There was another silence. Rudi's lips tightened, and when he spoke again his voice was strained. "I'll think of something," he cried. "I'll think of *something!*"

"Don't lose your head," the voice said. "The only way is to go down for help."

"But you'll—"

"Maybe. And maybe not. That's a chance we'll have to take."

The voice was as quiet as ever. And, hearing it, Rudi was suddenly ashamed. Here was he, safe on the glacier's surface, showing fear and despair, while the one below, facing almost certain death, remained calm and controlled. Whoever it was down there, it was a real man. A brave man.

Rudi drew in a long, slow breath. With his climbing-staff he felt down along the smooth surface of the ice walls.

"Are you still there?" said the voice.

"Yes," he said.

"You had better go."

"Wait—"

Lying flat on the glacier, he leaned over the rim of the crevasse and lowered the staff as far as it would go. Its end came almost to the curve in the walls.

"Can you see it?" he asked.

"See what?" said the man.

Obviously he couldn't. Standing up, Rudi removed his jacket and tied it by one sleeve to the curved end of the staff. Then, holding the other end, he again lay prone and lowered his staff and jacket.

"Can you see it now?" he asked.

"Yes," said the man.

"How far above you is it?"

"About ten feet."

Again the staff came up. Rudi took off his shirt and tied one of its sleeves to the dangling sleeve of the jacket. This time, as he lay down, the ice bit, cold and rough, into his bare chest; but he scarcely noticed it. With his arms extended, all the shirt and half the jacket were out of sight beneath the curve in the crevasse.

"How near are you now?" he called.

"Not far," said the voice.

"Can you reach it?"

"I'm trying."

There was the sound of scraping boot-nails; of labored breathing. But no pull on the shirtsleeve down below.

"I can't make it," said the voice. It was fainter than before.

"Wait," said Rudi.

For the third time he raised the staff. He took off his trousers. He tied a trouser-leg to the loose sleeve of the shirt. Then he pulled, one by one, at all the knots he had made: between staff and jacket, jacket and shirt, shirt and trousers. He pulled until the blood pounded in his head and the knots were as tight as his strength could make them. This done, he stepped back from the crevasse to the point where his toes had rested when he lay flat. With feet and hands he kicked and scraped the ice until he had made two holes. Then, lying down as before, he dug his toes deep into them. He was naked now, except for his shoes, stockings and underpants. The cold rose from the ice into his blood and bones. He lowered the staff and knotted clothes like a sort of crazy fishing line.

The trousers, the shirt and half of the jacket passed out of sight. He was leaning over as far as he could.

"Can you reach it now?" he called.

"Yes," the voice answered.

"All right. Come on."

"You won't be able to hold me. I'll pull you in."

"No you won't."

He braced himself. The pull came. His toes went taut in their ice-holds and his hands tightened on the staff until the knuckles showed white. Again he could hear a scraping sound below, and he knew that the man was clawing his boots against the ice-wall, trying both to lever himself up and to take as much weight as possible off the improvised lifeline. But the wall obviously offered little help. Almost all his weight was on the lifeline. Suddenly there was a jerk, as one of the knots in the clothing slipped, and the staff was almost wrenched from Rudi's hands. But the knot held. And his hands held. He tried to call down, "All right?" but he had no breath for words. From below, the only sound was the scraping of boots on ice.

How long it went on Rudi could never have said. Perhaps only for a minute or so. But it seemed like hours. And then at last— at last—it happened. A hand came into view around the curve of the crevasse wall: a hand gripping the twisted fabric of his jacket, and then a second hand rising slowly above it. A head appeared. A pair of shoulders. A face was raised for an instant and then lowered. Again one hand moved slowly up past the other.

But Rudi no longer saw it, for now his eyes were shut tight with the strain. His teeth were clamped, the cords of his neck bulged, the muscles of his arm felt as if he were being drawn one by one from the bones that held them. He began to lose his toe-holds. He was being dragged forward. Desperately, frantically, he dug in with his feet, pressed his whole body down, as if he could make it part of the glacier. Though all but naked on the ice, he was pouring with sweat. Somehow he stopped the slipping. Somehow he held on. But now suddenly the strain was even worse, for the man had reached the lower end of the staff. The slight "give" of the stretched clothing was gone, and in its place, was rigid deadweight on a length of wood. The climber was close now. But heavy. Indescribably heavy. Rudi's hands ached and burned, as if it were a rod of hot lead that they clung to. It was not a mere man he was holding, but a giant; or a block of granite. The pull was unendurable. The pain unendurable. He could hold on no longer. His hands were opening. It was all over.

And then it *was* over. The weight was gone. There was a scraping sound close beneath him; a hand on the rim of ice; a figure pulling itself up onto the lip of the crevasse. The man was beside Rudi, turning to him, staring at him.

"Why—you're just a boy!" he said in astonishment.

Rudi was too numb to move or speak. Taking the staff from him, the man pulled up the line of clothes, untied the knots and shook them out.

"Come on now. Quickly!" he said.

Pulling the boy to his feet, he helped him dress. Then he rubbed and pummeled him until at last Rudi felt the warmth of returning circulation.

"Better?" the man asked, smiling.

Rudi nodded. And finally he was able to speak again. "And you, sir," he said, "you are all right?"

The man nodded. He was warming himself now: flapping his arms and kicking his feet together. "A few minutes of sun and I'll be as good as new."

Nearby, a black boulder lay embedded in the glacial ice, and, going over to it, they sat down. The sunlight poured over them like a warm bath. Rudi slowly flexed his aching fingers and saw that the man was doing the same. And then the man had raised his eyes and was looking at him.

"It's a miracle how you did it," he said. "A boy of your size. All alone."

"It was nothing," Rudi murmured.

"Nothing?"

"I—I only—"

"Only saved my life," said the man.

For the first time, now, Rudi was really seeing him. He was a man of perhaps thirty, very tall and thin, and his face, too, was thin, with a big hawklike nose and a strong jutting chin. His weather-browned cheeks were clean-shaven, his hair black, his eyes deep-set and gray. And when he spoke, his voice was still almost as quiet as when it had been muffled by the ice-walls of the crevasse. He is—what?—Rudi thought. Not Swiss, he knew. Not French or German. English, perhaps? Yes, English. . . . And then suddenly a deep excitement filled him, for he knew who the man was.

"You are Captain Winter?" he murmured.

"That's right."

"And I—I have saved—I mean—"

Rudi stopped in confusion, and the Englishman grinned. "You've saved," he said, smiling, "one of the worst imbeciles that ever walked on a glacier. An imbecile who was so busy looking up at a mountain that he couldn't even see what was at his feet."

Rudi was wordless—almost stunned. He looked at the man, and then away in embarrassment, and he could scarcely believe what had happened. The name of Captain John Winter was known through the length and breadth of the Alps. He was the foremost mountaineer of his day, and during the past ten years had made more first ascents of great peaks than any other man alive. Rudi had heard that he had come to Kurtal a few days before. He had hoped that at least he would see him in the hotel or walking by in the street. But actually to meet him—and in this way! To pull him from a crevasse—save him. . . . It was incredible!

Captain Winter was watching him. "And you, son," he asked. "What is your name?"

Somehow the boy got his voice back. "Rudi," he said. "Rudi Matt."

"Matt?" Now it was the man's turn to be impressed. "Not of the family of the great Josef Matt?"

"He was my father," Rudi said.

Captain Winter studied him with his gray eyes. Then he smiled again. "I should have known," he said. "A boy who could do what you've done—"

"Did you know my father, sir?"

"No, unfortunately I didn't. He was before my day. But ever since I was a boy I have heard of him. In twenty years no one has come to the Alps and not heard of the great guide, Josef Matt."

Rudi's heart swelled. He looked away. His eyes fixed on the vast mountain that rose before them, and then he saw that Captain Winter was watching it too.

Unconsciously the Englishman spoke his thoughts. "Your father was—" He caught himself and stopped.

"Yes," said Rudi softly, "he was killed on the Citadel."

There was a silence. Captain Winter reached into a pocket and brought out an unbroken bar of chocolate. "Lucky I fell on the other side," he grinned.

He broke the bar in two and handed half to Rudi.

"Oh, no, sir, thank you. I couldn't."

"When I meet a boy your age who can't eat chocolate," said Winter, "I'll be glad to stay in a crevasse for good."

Rudi took it, and they sat munching. The sun was warm on their thawing bodies. Far above, it struck the cliffs and snowfields of the Citadel, so brightly that they had to squint against the glare.

Then there was Winter's quiet voice again. "What do you think, Rudi?"

"Think, sir?"

"Can it be climbed?"

"Climbed? The Citadel?"

"Your father thought so. Alone among all the guides of Switzerland, he thought so." There was another pause. "And I think so too," said Captain Winter.

The boy was peering again at the shining heights. And suddenly his heart was pounding so hard that he was sure the Englishman must be able to hear it. "Is—is that why you have come here, sir?" he asked. "To try to climb the Citadel?"

"Well, now—" Winter smiled. "It's not so simple, you know. For one thing, there's not a guide in the valley who would go with me."

"I have an uncle, sir. He is—"

"Yes, I know your uncle. Franz Lerner. He is the best in Kurtal, and I've spoken to him. But he would not go. Anything but that, he said. Any other peak, any route, any venture. But not *that*, he said. Not the Citadel."

"He remembers my father—"

"Yes, he remembers your father. They all remember him. And while they love and respect his memory, they all think he was crazy." Winter chuckled softly. "Now they think *I'm* crazy," he added. "And maybe they're right too," he said.

"What will you do, sir?" asked Rudi. "Not try it alone?"

"No, that crazy I'm not." Winter slowly stroked his long jaw. "I'm not certain what I'll do," he went on. "Perhaps I'll go over to the next valley. To Broli. I've been told there is a guide there—a man called Saxo. Do you know him?"

"Yes—Emil Saxo. I have never met him, but I have heard of him. They say he is a very great guide."

"Well, I thought perhaps I'd go and talk with him. After a while. But first I must rec-

onnoiter some more. Make my plans. Pick the route. If there *is* a route."

"Yes, there is! Of course there is!"

Rudi had not thought the words. They simply burst out from him. And now again he was embarrassed as the man looked at him curiously.

"So?" said Captain Winter. "That is interesting, Rudi. Tell me why you think so."

"I have studied the Citadel many times, sir."

"Why?"

"Because—because—" He stopped. He couldn't say it.

"Because you want to climb it yourself?"

"I am not yet a grown man, sir. I know I cannot expect—"

"I wasn't a grown man either," said the Captain, "when I first saw the Citadel. I was younger than you—only twelve—and my parents had brought me here for a summer holiday. But I can still remember how I felt when I looked up at it, and the promise I made myself that some day I was going to climb it." He paused. His eyes moved slowly upward. "Youth is the time for dreams, boy," he murmured. "The trick is, when you get older, not to forget them."

Rudi listened, spellbound. He had never heard anyone speak like that. He had not known a grown man could think and feel like that.

Then Winter asked:

"This east face, Rudi—what do you think of it?"

"Think of it, sir?"

"Could it be climbed?"

Rudi shook his head. "No, it is no good. The long chimney[1] there—you see. It looks all right; it could be done. And to the left, the

---

1. chimney (chim′ nē) *n.*: In mountain climbing, this word means a deep, narrow crack in a cliff face.

ledges"—he pointed—"they could be done too. But higher up, no. They stop. The chimney stops, and there is only smooth rock."

"What about the northeast ridge?"

"That is not good either."

"It's not so steep."

"No, it is not so steep," said Rudi. "But the rocks are bad. They slope out, with few places for holds."

"And the north face?"

Rudi talked on. About the north face, the west ridge, the southwest ridge. He talked quietly and thoughtfully, but with deep inner excitement, for this was the first time in his life that he had been able to speak to anyone of these things which he had thought and studied for so long. . . . And then suddenly he stopped, for he realized what he was doing. He, Rudi Matt, a boy of sixteen who worked in the kitchen of the Beau Site Hotel, was presuming to give his opinions to one of the greatest climbers in the world.

But Captain Winter had been listening intently. Sometimes he nodded. "Go on," he said now, as Rudi paused.

"But I am only—"

"Go on."

And Rudi went on . . .

"That doesn't leave much," said the captain a little later.

"No, sir," said the boy.

"Only the southeast ridge."

"Yes, sir."

"That was the way your father tried, wasn't it?"

"Yes, sir."

"And you believe it's the *only* way?"

"Yes, sir."

Captain Winter rubbed his jaw for a moment before speaking again. Then—"That also is very interesting to me, Rudi," he said quietly, "because it is what I believe too."

Later, they threaded their way down the Blue Glacier. For a while they moved in silence. Then Captain Winter asked:

"What do you do, Rudi?"

"Do, sir?"

"Are you an apprentice guide? A porter?"

Rudi swallowed. "No sir."

"What then?"

He could hardly say it. "A—dishwasher."

"A dishwasher?"

"In the Beau Site Hotel. It is my mother, sir. Since my father died, you see, she is afraid—she does not want—" Rudi swallowed again. "I am to go into the hotel business," he murmured.

"Oh."

Again they moved on without speaking. It was now late afternoon, and behind them the stillness was broken by a great roaring, as sun-loosened rock and ice broke off from the heights of the Citadel.

When they reached the path Rudi spoke again, hesitantly. "Will you please do me a favor, sir," he asked.

"Of course," said Winter.

"Before we come to the town we will separate. And you will please not tell anyone that I have been up here today?"

The Englishman looked at him in astonishment. "Not tell anyone? You save my life, boy, and you want me to keep it a secret?"

"It was nothing, sir. Truly. And if you say that I have been in the mountains, my mother and uncle will hear, and I will be in trouble." Rudi's voice took on a note of urgency. "You will not do it, sir? You will promise—please?"

Winter put a hand on his shoulder. "Don't worry," he said. "I won't get you in trouble." Then he smiled and added: "Master Rudi Matt—dishwasher."

They walked down the path. The sun sank. Behind them, the mountain roared.

RESPONDING TO THE SELECTION

Your Response

1. What about Rudi do you admire? Explain.

Recalling

2. How does Rudi make a lifeline?
3. Why is Rudi "almost stunned" when he learns the identity of the man he has saved?
4. How did Rudi's father die?

Interpreting

5. Captain Winter says, "Youth is the time for dreams." What is Rudi's secret dream?
6. Why has Rudi been unable to fulfill his dream?
7. Why do you think this story is called "A Boy and a Man"?

Applying

8. Why do people sometimes keep secret their dreams and plans?

ANALYZING LITERATURE

Understanding Suspense

Writers create **suspense** by describing situations that are both uncertain and dangerous. Such dangers can be either physical or emotional. Many readers enjoy suspenseful stories because they want to discover what happens in the end and whether the characters avoid the dangers that face them. "A Boy and a Man" is a story that is filled with suspense.

1. How is Captain Winter's situation at the start of the story uncertain and dangerous?
2. How do Rudi's repeated attempts to rescue Captain Winter increase the suspense?
3. What future dangers are hinted at in the conversation between Rudi and the Captain?

CRITICAL THINKING AND READING

Identifying Details That Create Suspense

A writer creates suspense through details that increase the uncertainty and danger. Notice the details in the following description of Rudi's attempt to make a lifeline for Captain Winter.

> "He tied a trouser-leg to the loose sleeve of the shirt. Then he pulled, one by one, at all the knots he had made: between staff and jacket, jacket and shirt, shirt and trousers."

As you read, you wonder whether these knots will hold.

1. Find the paragraph that begins "He braced himself . . ." (page 39). Point out the details in this and the next few paragraphs that help create suspense.
2. Which specific words and phrases make you feel this suspense?

THINKING AND WRITING

Writing About Suspense

Imagine that a magazine for teenagers is planning a special issue containing suspenseful stories. Think of stories you have read that would keep readers on the edge of their seats. Then choose the best one and write a letter to the editors of the magazine persuading them to use your story. (You may, of course, recommend "A Boy and a Man.") When revising your letter, make sure you have explained how your story contains the key ingredients of suspense: uncertainty and danger.

LEARNING OPTION

Cross-curricular Connection. On a globe or world map, find the Himalayas (southern Asia), the Andes (western South America), the Alps (Europe), and the Rocky Mountains (western North America). Then in an encyclopedia, find the highest peak in each mountain range as well as the average height of each range. Make a table listing the peaks from highest to lowest, including the mountain's name and its height. Also list the mountain ranges according to their average height. Share your table with the class.

A Boy and a Man 43

GUIDE FOR READING

The Mouth-Organ

Unexpected Endings

Unexpected Endings occur when an author concludes a story with an event that is very different from what you have been led to expect. Such endings can have various effects on readers, sometimes frightening them and sometimes, as in "The Mouth-Organ," charming them.

Focus

Locate Trinidad, the setting for "The Mouth-Organ," on the map on page 51. The island is in the Caribbean Sea, just off the coast of Venezuela. Trinidad is near the equator, so the climate is very humid. Temperatures, usually between 70° and 90° Fahrenheit, drop only a few degrees in January and February. Life in the countryside differs greatly from that in cities like the capital, Port-of-Spain. People living near sugar plantations in the rural Central Plain are usually poorer and less educated than those living in cities. People of Spanish, French, African, English, Asian Indian, and Chinese descent all contribute to Trinidad's culture.

To help you picture how life in rural Trinidad would differ from your life in the United States, make a chart like this one to contrast aspects of living on Trinidad with living in your hometown.

	Climate	People	Work	Play
Trinidad				
Your Town				

Sam Selvon

(1923–1994) was born on the Caribbean island of Trinidad. As a boy, he was exposed to both urban and rural life and to the different cultures of Trinidad's Asian Indian and African inhabitants. Over the years Selvon explored these cultures in his stories and novels. His passionate and sensitive portrayals of people and cultures earned him many awards, including The Humming Bird Medal (Gold), Trinidad's most prestigious literary honor.

Vocabulary

Knowing the following words will help you as you read "The Mouth-Organ."

knoll (nōl) *n.*: A small, rounded hill (p. 45)

lulling (lul' iŋ) *v.*: Calming by gentle sounds or motions (p. 45)

brooding (brōōd' iŋ) *n.*: Thinking in a worried way (p. 47)

elaboration (ē lab' ə ra' shən) *n.*: Gestures that make an action seem complicated (p. 47)

tangible (tan' jə b'l) *adj.*: Real or solid (p. 49)

The Mouth-Organ[1]

Sam Selvon

When the Christmas season was near Santo knew because the canefields[2] were in flower, and when the wind blew it was like a sea of rippling, feathery movement, and he used to stop on a little knoll in the evening to look at it on his way home from working in the fields with his father, and imagine it was a vast, soft bed and that the movement was lulling him to sleep. He used to spend a few minutes there thinking about what Christmas in the city was like; he could see the lights there coming to life miles away from the canefields.

Every year the carol singers came, and once one of them had told Santo about Father Christmas, and how the stores in the city were packed with toys, and how little children hung stockings on their beds, and in the morning when they woke the stockings were filled with toys left by a kind old man with a great, white beard who had come into the house when everyone was asleep.

When Santo heard the story he was amazed; he wanted to know if the children didn't have to pay for the toys. But the carol singer told him no, that the toys were gifts, that through a feeling of joy and thanksgiving for the birth of Jesus Christ, people gave gifts to each other. Santo looked into the

flames of the great fire, around which the villagers were gathered to sing carols, and marveled at this goodwill; in the village one thing was exchanged for another, but at no time of year did the people go mad and give things away for nothing.

"And who is the man who does come with all the toys?" he asked the girl from the city, rubbing his eyes as smoke came in his direction from the fire. "Where he come from?"

The girl told him and the other children who had gathered that the man was Father Christmas, and that he came from far away, in a country where white ice fell from the sky and it was so cold that if Santo went there he would surely die.

"But how this man come from quite there to Trinidad?" Santo persisted, and the other children raised their heads to listen to the answer, for it was a question they would have asked themselves. The girl told them that he came by any means of transportation, and that all the children in the world believed in him, and that they must believe too.

But when the carol singing was done, and the buns and sweets eaten, and the bottles of Coca-Cola empty and the balloons and toys and crackers were distributed, they were all a little doubtful of the girl's story. All except Santo, who thought it was a wonderful thing. He thought it was the most beautiful story he had ever heard, and, though he found it hard to believe, he found it harder still to put out of

---

1. Mouth-Organ: Another name for a harmonica.
2. canefields: Santo lives in Trinidad, where cane, a very tall tropical grass, is grown as a main source of sugar.

THINKING
Carlton Murrell
Courtesy of the Artist

his mind, for the very telling of it had been to him like a gift which he put away inside him, to think about when he was feeling lonely and poor. And so, this Christmas season, every evening he paused a little on the rising just at the edge of the village, and thought about how it had been at that time, and the story.

That night, in his hut with his father and mother and little sister, he asked his father if he had written the letter. Lalsingh, tired from the fields and with the thought of tomorrow's bread, snapped at his son from the corner of the hut where he sat consoling himself with a pipe.

"But *bap*[3] you did say you would write the letter to Father Christmas like how the carol girl did say," Santo said timidly, edging nearer to his mother for protection in case his father got angry.

"I don't believe that story the carol girl did say," his sister said. "If it really have a Father Christmas who does give away toys for nothing, why it is he never come in this village?"

"Well, none of we did know anything about him," said Santo quickly, for fear of losing his faith in the story. "And besides, the carol girl did say you have to believe." He turned again to his father. "*Bap*, you promising every night to write the letter for me."

"Keep quiet, boy, your father can't write, he don't know how to spell," his mother looked up from combing her daughter's hair.

Lalsingh might have remained wrapped in his brooding, but when he heard his wife decry his ignorance to the children he rose to his feet.

"Where the paper?" he demanded.

Santo ran to the corner where he had hidden the paper and pencil he had borrowed from a friend.

---

3. **bap:** Dialect term of endearment for a father, like "Dad" or "Pop."

"Where the thing to write with?" Lalsingh demanded as his son handed him the paper.

Pencil followed quickly. Lalsingh, with much elaboration squatted in the center of the hut and Santo put the oil-lamp next to him on the floor.

"What the carol girl say to write?" Lalsingh demanded.

"Well," Santo swallowed, "you just write to Father Christmas, and ask him to send a mouth-organ for me, please. Tell him I want it too bad, and that I believe he would give me. Tell him I is a good boy, that I does help you do the work . . ."

"Hold up, hold up," Lalsingh cried, and bent down to the paper on the floor, cupping his free hand and holding it over the paper so no one would see what he was doing. He got up after a few minutes and folded the piece of paper and put it in his pocket. "All right, I give it to somebody to post tomorrow," he told his son, and went back to his pipe in the corner.

The next day Lalsingh, driving a cartload of cane to the mill, remembered the letter and drew it from his pocket and looked at it. A circle there, a straight line and a crooked one there. Lalsingh had never written a word in his life. "I sorry for the boy," he said to himself, tearing the paper into scraps, "but still, is a bad thing for him to think his *bap* can't even write a letter." And he held out his hand while the cart rumbled on, and dropped the paper bit by bit among the cane.

That Christmas Eve, with old and young alike eagerly awaiting the carol singers, a villager who had a bicycle came riding in with the news that they couldn't pay their usual visit because something had gone wrong.

"What gone wrong?" they wanted to know.

The cyclist didn't know, all he knew was that something had gone wrong, and the leader of the carol singers sent a message to

say that if it were at all possible they would try and come for short while on Christmas morning.

Santo was so disappointed he could have cried. Somehow he had connected up the carol singers with his gift—if they didn't come, then how could Father Christmas send his mouth-organ? For Santo never expected that the man with the big beard would have time to visit his poor village when there were so many other children and places to visit. He had expected the carol girl to hand him the mouth-organ and say that Father Christmas had got his letter and had not forgotten him.

SUGAR CANE
Carlton Murrell
Courtesy of the Artist

the fire; it died into smoke, then ash, and after a while they drifted back to their huts.

Santo walked off by himself, clutching the story to his heart like a tangible thing. He went along the winding track to the main road where traffic passed to and from the city. For he still believed the carol singers would come. All he had now was the story of the man who brought toys from that far country for the little children, and, if he lost that, he would have nothing at all. He walked along the main road, a lonely, forlorn figure against the dark background of the fields.

In the car that was slowly approaching, a man who had just been Father Christmas at a children's party was sitting behind the wheel, playing a mouth-organ. The instrument was a little on his conscience, because he had taken it from the bag of toys which he had distributed, intending to amuse himself a little on the long drive back to the city. He was finding it difficult to steer properly and play the mouth-organ at the same time, as he had to keep pushing away the great, white beard which he still wore.

But it had been a good party at a wealthy home, and he had left the children happy. Suddenly his headlights picked up the slight figure of Santo some distance away, his head bowed as he walked slowly along the grass path at the side of the road. And on a sudden impulse, the man slowed down as he got near the boy, and leaning out of the window he shouted, "Happy Christmas!" and at the same time tossed the mouth-organ.

In the sudden rush of joy he felt as he acted on the impulse, the man pressed his foot to the accelerator and the car shot off. But not before he had seen the boy bend down and pick up the mouth-organ with a look of incredible wonder on his face, and something else which the man found hard to define as he drove to the city.

That was all he had wanted; it would have been enough to make him believe forever.

The villagers lit the fire and tried to make merry. They stood around talking and smoking, and some of the women made half-hearted attempts to sing the carols like the people from the city did. But no one tended

RESPONDING TO THE SELECTION

Your Response

1. Would you like to live in a place like Trinidad? Why or why not?
2. How do you feel about the way Santo's father treats him?

Recalling

3. How does Santo's response to the Father Christmas story differ from the responses of the other children?
4. What does Santo want his father to do?

Interpreting

5. Why does Santo's father cup his hand over the paper when he writes?
6. Why do you think the man in the car tosses the mouth-organ to Santo?
7. What is unexpected about the way Santo receives his Christmas wish?

Applying

8. What does this story suggest about believing in things that seem impossible?

ANALYZING LITERATURE

Understanding Unexpected Endings

An **unexpected ending** occurs when a story ends with an event that is different from the one you expect. In "The Mouth-Organ," certain details lead you to expect an unhappy ending. For example, Santo's father throws away the letter to Father Christmas.

1. Identify another detail that might lead you to expect an unhappy ending.
2. How was Santo's encounter with the man driving the car different from the Father Christmas story?

CRITICAL THINKING AND READING

Predicting an Ending

As you read "The Mouth-Organ," you probably had your own ideas about how it would end.

1. Explain how you thought the story would end. Identify details or events that led you to expect such an ending.
2. How was the ending you expected similar to what really happened? How was it different?

THINKING AND WRITING

Writing About a Surprise

Write about an event in your life that had a surprise ending. Was the ending better or worse than you had expected? Include details that made you expect a certain ending, and then describe how the unexpected ending came about. Revise your work to make sure the sequence of events is clear.

LEARNING OPTIONS

1. **Writing.** Imagine that you are Santo and that, a year after the story ends, you have learned to write. Compose a letter to a friend in a nearby village, telling him or her about the mouth-organ and the unusual way it came into your life. Try to write the letter in the way that Santo would.
2. **Cross-curricular Connection.** Find out all you can about the mouth-organ, or harmonica. Who invented it? What kind of music is played on it? If possible, borrow a mouth-organ and try it out. Libraries or music stores are good places to find information on how to play one. What does it sound like? Can you play a tune?

MULTICULTURAL CONNECTION

The Caribbean—A Mosaic of Cultures

If you look at the map on this page, you will see hundreds of islands below Florida that stretch out into the Atlantic Ocean. These are the Caribbean Islands, a colorful mosaic of many cultures.

Hispanics, a large part of the population of Cuba, Puerto Rico, and the Dominican Republic, are descendants of the first Spanish settlers. Also living on these islands are people of Portuguese, Italian, and French origin.

Descendants of enslaved Africans, who were brought to the islands hundreds of years ago to work on the sugar plantations, are the largest group of inhabitants of the is-

lands of Haiti, Barbados, and Jamaica. French culture also influences life in Haiti, a former French colony, and English culture plays a role in Jamaica and Barbados, former colonies of England. The tiny island of Curaçao, colonized by the Netherlands, shows Dutch influence.

Exploring on Your Own

Choose one of the islands in the Caribbean. Find out about its rich cultural heritage as reflected in its art, music, dance, ethnic foods, and the languages spoken there.

GUIDE FOR READING

Edward D. Hoch

(1930–   ), whose last name rhymes with "poke," was born in Rochester, New York. After graduating from the University of Rochester, he worked as a researcher for the Rochester Public Library and as a copy writer for an advertising company. Hoch has written many stories and novels in the mystery and science-fiction fields. In 1967 he won an award from the Mystery Writers of America for his short story "The Oblong Room." As you will see in "Zoo," Hoch has a lively imagination and a good sense of humor.

Zoo

Plot and Point of View

Point of view refers to the angle or position from which a writer tells a story. By choosing to look through the eyes of a particular character or group, a writer gives you a certain impression of the sequence of events. In "Zoo," the writer views the events from two different angles. He tells the first part of the story from the point of view of the Earth people. Then he lets you look through the eyes of the horse-spider people of Kaan. This change in point of view affects the way you understand the events of the story.

Focus

Zoos have been around for a long time. It is believed that people started making zoos as early as 4500 B.C.! Kings and other rulers have often had zoos built according to their own designs. In China about 1000 B.C., Wen Wang established a 1,500-acre zoological garden, which he named "The Garden of Intelligence." During his trek through Mexico in 1519, Hernando Cortes came upon a royal zoo so large that it needed a staff of 300 keepers.

Modern zoos are increasing efforts to house animals as naturally as possible, and some are investigating the use of televised images to avoid keeping animals in captivity at all. Write a few notes describing what you think zoos will be like in the future. How will they be different? What will be the same?

Vocabulary

Knowing the following words will help you as you read "Zoo."
interplanetary (in′ tər plan′ ə ter′ ē) *adj.*: Between planets (p. 53)

wonderment (wun′ dər mənt) *n.*: Astonishment (p. 53)

awe (ô) *n.*: A mixed feeling of fear and wonder (p. 53)

Zoo

Edward D. Hoch

The children were always good during the month of August, especially when it began to get near the twenty-third. It was on this day that the great silver spaceship carrying Professor Hugo's Interplanetary Zoo settled down for its annual six-hour visit to the Chicago area.

Before daybreak the crowds would form, long lines of children and adults both, each one clutching his or her dollar, and waiting with wonderment to see what race of strange creatures the Professor had brought this year.

In the past they had sometimes been treated to three-legged creatures from Venus, or tall, thin men from Mars, or even snakelike horrors from somewhere more distant. This year, as the great round ship settled slowly to earth in the huge tri-city parking area just outside of Chicago, they watched with awe as the sides slowly slid up to reveal the familiar barred cages. In them were some wild breed of nightmare—small, horse-like animals that moved with quick, jerking motions and constantly chattered in a high-pitched tongue. The citizens of Earth clustered around as Professor Hugo's crew quickly collected the waiting dollars, and soon the good Professor himself made an appearance, wearing his many-colored rainbow cape and top hat. "Peoples of Earth," he called into his microphone.

The crowd's noise died down and he continued. "Peoples of Earth, this year you see a real treat for your single dollar— the little-known horse-spider people of Kaan—brought to you across a million miles of

space at great expense. Gather around, see them, study them, listen to them, tell your friends about them. But hurry! My ship can remain here only six hours!"

And the crowds slowly filed by, at once horrified and fascinated by these strange creatures that looked like horses but ran up

Then, as the six-hour limit ran out, Professor Hugo once more took the microphone in hand. "We must go now, but we will return next year on this date. And if you enjoyed our zoo this year, telephone your friends in other cities about it. We will land in New York tomorrow, and next week on to London, Paris, Rome, Hong Kong, and Tokyo. Then on to other worlds!"

He waved farewell to them, and as the ship rose from the ground, the Earth peoples agreed that this had been the very best Zoo yet. . . .

Some two months and three planets later, the silver ship of Professor Hugo settled at last onto the familiar jagged rocks of Kaan, and the odd horse-spider creatures filed quickly out of their cages. Professor Hugo was there to say a few parting words, and then they scurried away in a hundred different directions, seeking their homes among the rocks.

In one house, the she-creature was happy to see the return of her mate and offspring. She babbled a greeting in the strange tongue and hurried to embrace them. "It was a long time you were gone. Was it good?"

And the he-creature nodded. "The little one enjoyed it especially. We visited eight worlds and saw many things."

The little one ran up the wall of the cave. "On the place called Earth it was the best. The creatures there wear garments over their skins, and they walk on two legs."

"But isn't it dangerous?" asked the she-creature.

"No," her mate answered. "There are bars to protect us from them. We remain right in the ship. Next time you must come with us. It is well worth the nineteen commocs it costs."

And the little one nodded. "It was the very best Zoo ever. . . ."

the walls of their cages like spiders. "This is certainly worth a dollar," one man remarked, hurrying away. "I'm going home to get the wife."

All day long it went like that, until ten thousand people had filed by the barred cages set into the side of the spaceship.

RESPONDING TO THE SELECTION

Your Response

1. Do you think something like Professor Hugo's zoo could someday actually exist? Why or why not?

Recalling

2. What impression do Earthlings have of the people from Kaan?
3. How do the Kaanians describe humans?

Interpreting

4. Compare and contrast the ways in which Earthlings and Kaanians view each other.
5. What does the way Professor Hugo runs his zoo suggest about him?

Applying

6. Why is it easier to understand a situation if you see it from more than one angle?

ANALYZING LITERATURE

Understanding Plot and Point of View

Point of view is the position from which a writer tells a story. Often a writer will describe the sequence of events as they are seen by a particular person or group. In "Zoo," however, the writer treats point of view in an unusual way. He allows you to see the events from two different angles.

1. Identify the place in the story where the point of view changes.
2. How would the story have been different if it were told only from the Earthlings' point of view?
3. How does the change in point of view make the story effective?

CRITICAL THINKING AND READING

Considering Other Points of View

In "Zoo," the Earthlings think of the Kaanians as "small, horse-like animals" that are best viewed in a zoo. The Kaanians think of themselves as normal but regard the Earthlings as possibly dangerous "creatures." Neither group considers the other group's point of view. When studying people whose ideas or customs appear strange, you can keep an open mind by imagining what they think of *your* customs and ideas.

1. Imagine that you are a visitor to Earth from a planet where people travel by rockets. Describe your first impression of cars.
2. Describe your reaction to humans if on your planet people had eyes in the front *and* back of their heads.

THINKING AND WRITING

Writing From Another Point of View

You have learned how the Earthlings and the Kaanians view the events of this story. However, Professor Hugo also must have a point of view. Imagine that the professor has kept a diary giving *his* impression of the story's events. List the type of entries the professor would make in his diary. Then use this list to write two diary pages indicating what the professor feels and thinks at each point in the story. When you revise these entries, make sure that the professor refers to himself as "I."

LEARNING OPTIONS

1. **Art.** Design the layout of a zoo. Decide how large it should be, what kind of animals will be kept there, and how each of the different habitats will look. You may want to draw your layout as a map, or you might construct a three-dimensional model of your zoo. Be prepared to discuss with your classmates the reasons for your design.
2. **Cross-curricular Connection.** Zoos do more than display animals. Contact a zoo in your area to find out what sort of scientific and educational programs are conducted there. Share your findings with your classmates.

Character

JOVENES, 1991
Tony Ortega
Courtesy of the Artist

GUIDE FOR READING

Paul Annixter

(1894–1985) was born Howard Allison Sturtzel in Minneapolis, Minnesota. While working a timber claim in northern Minnesota, Annixter began writing. He published more than five hundred stories and worked with his wife writing novels for young people. He said, "Our stories deal with some phase of human and animal interrelation, which offers to our minds a different and deeper sort of heart interest." "Last Cover" deals with this special relationship between a boy and a fox.

Last Cover

Character Traits

Character traits are the qualities that make a person an individual. For example, one person may appear to be calm, another excitable. One person may be musical, another athletic. Writers give their characters qualities that make them seem like real people. It is these character traits that determine how each character behaves and interacts with others.

Focus

As a class, make a list of the different kinds of animals that people have for pets. Then think about the reasons why they choose each kind. For example, why would someone want a pet boa constrictor or a pet tarantula? Discuss with your classmates what each of you enjoys about having a pet. Is it affection, companionship, or a connection to nature?

In the story "Last Cover," two boys develop a deep attachment to a pet fox. As you read, think about the boys' feelings for their pet and how they deal with their feelings when nature runs its course.

Vocabulary

Knowing the following words will help you as you read "Last Cover."

abetting (ə bet′ iŋ) *v.*: Helping or encouraging (p. 61)

passive (pas′ iv) *adj.*: Inactive (p. 61)

vixen (vik′ s'n) *n.*: A female fox (p. 61)

confound (kən found′) *v.*: Confuse (p. 64)

sanction (saŋk′ shən) *v.*: Support (p. 64)

crafty (kraf′ tē) *adj.*: Sly; cunning (p. 65)

wily (wī′ lē) *adj.*: Sly (p. 65)

sanctuary (saŋk′ chōō wer′ ē) *n.*: A place of protection (p. 65)

Last Cover

Paul Annixter

I'm not sure I can tell you what you want to know about my brother; but everything about the pet fox is important, so I'll tell all that from the beginning.

It goes back to a winter afternoon after I'd hunted the woods all day for a sign of our lost pet. I remember the way my mother looked up as I came into the kitchen. Without my speaking, she knew what had happened. For six hours I had walked, reading signs, looking for a delicate print in the damp soil or even a hair that might have told of a red fox passing that way—but I had found nothing.

"Did you go up in the foothills?" Mom asked.

I nodded. My face was stiff from held-back tears. My brother, Colin, who was going on twelve, got it all from one look at me and went into a heartbroken, almost silent, crying.

Three weeks before, Bandit, the pet fox Colin and I had raised from a tiny kit, had disappeared, and not even a rumor had been heard of him since.

"He'd have to go off soon anyway," Mom comforted. "A big, lolloping[1] fellow like him, he's got to live his life same as us. But he may come back. That fox set a lot of store by you boys in spite of his wild ways."

"He set a lot of store by our food, anyway," Father said. He sat in a chair by the kitchen window mending a piece of harness. "We'll be seeing a lot more of that fellow, never fear. That fox learned to pine for table scraps and young chickens. He was getting to be an egg thief, too, and he's not likely to forget that."

"That was only pranking when he was little," Colin said desperately.

From the first, the tame fox had made tension in the family. It was Father who said we'd better name him Bandit, after he'd made away with his first young chicken.

"Maybe you know," Father said shortly. "But when an animal turns to egg sucking he's usually incurable.. He'd better not come pranking around my chicken run again."

It was late February, and I remember the bleak, dead cold that had set in, cold that was a rare thing for our Carolina hills. Flocks of sparrows and snowbirds had appeared to peck hungrily at all that the pigs and chickens didn't eat.

"This one's a killer," Father would say of a morning, looking out at the whitened barn roof. "This one will make the shoats[2] squeal."

A fire snapped all day in our cookstove and another in the stone fireplace in the living room, but still the farmhouse was never warm. The leafless woods were bleak and empty, and I spoke of that to Father when I came back from my search.

---

1. lolloping (läl′ əp iŋ) *adj.*: Moving in a clumsy or relaxed way, bobbing up and down or from side to side.

2. shoats (shōts) *n.*: Young hogs.

"It's always a sad time in the woods when the seven sleepers are under cover," he said.

"What sleepers are they?" I asked. Father was full of woods lore.

"Why, all the animals that have got sense enough to hole up and stay hid in weather like this. Let's see, how was it the old rhyme named them?

> *Surly bear and sooty bat,*
> *Brown chuck and masked coon,*
> *Chippy-munk and sly skunk,*
> *And all the mouses*
> *'Cept in men's houses.*

"And man would have joined them and made it eight, Granther Yeary always said, if he'd had a little more sense."

"I was wondering if the red fox mightn't make it eight," Mom said.

Father shook his head. "Late winter's a high time for foxes. Time when they're out deviling, not sleeping."

My chest felt hollow. I wanted to cry like Colin over our lost fox, but at fourteen a boy doesn't cry. Colin had squatted down on the floor and got out his small hammer and nails to start another new frame for a new picture. Maybe then he'd make a drawing for the frame and be able to forget his misery. It had been that way with him since he was five.

I thought of the new dress Mom had brought home a few days before in a heavy cardboard box. That box cover would be fine for Colin to draw on. I spoke of it, and Mom's glance thanked me as she went to get it. She and I worried a lot about Colin. He was small for his age, delicate and blond, his hair much lighter and softer than mine, his eyes deep and wide and blue. He was often sick, and I knew the fear Mom had that he might be predestined.[3] I'm just ordinary, like Father. I'm the sort of stuff that can take it—tough and strong—but Colin was always sort of special.

---

3. predestined (prē des' tind) *adj.*: In this case, marked to die early.

Mom lighted the lamp. Colin began cutting his white cardboard carefully, fitting it into his frame. Father's sharp glance turned on him now and again.

"There goes the boy making another frame before there's a picture for it," he said. "It's too much like cutting out a man's suit for a fellow that's, say, twelve years old. Who knows whether he'll grow into it?"

Mom was into him then, quick. "Not a single frame of Colin's has ever gone to waste. The boy has real talent, Sumter, and it's time you realized it."

"Of course he has," Father said. "All kids have 'em. But they get over 'em."

"It isn't the pox[4] we're talking of," Mom sniffed.

"In a way it is. Ever since you started talking up Colin's art, I've had an invalid for help around the place."

Father wasn't as hard as he made out, I knew, but he had to hold a balance against all Mom's frothing.[5] For him the thing was the land and all that pertained to it. I was following in Father's footsteps, true to form, but Colin threatened to break the family tradition with his leaning toward art, with Mom "aiding and abetting him," as Father liked to put it. For the past two years she had had dreams of my brother becoming a real artist and going away to the city to study.

It wasn't that Father had no understanding of such things. I could remember, through the years, Colin lying on his stomach in the front room making pencil sketches, and how a good drawing would catch Father's eye halfway across the room, and how he would sometimes gather up two or three of them to study, frowning and muttering, one hand in his beard, while a great pride rose in Colin, and in me too. Most of Colin's drawings were of the woods and wild things, and there Father was a master critic. He made out to scorn what seemed to him a passive "white-livered" interpretation of nature through brush and pencil instead of rod and rifle.

At supper that night Colin could scarcely eat. Ever since he'd been able to walk, my brother had had a growing love of wild things, but Bandit had been like his very own, a gift of the woods. One afternoon a year and a half before, Father and Laban Small had been running a vixen through the hills with their dogs. With the last of her strength the she-fox had made for her den, not far from our house. The dogs had overtaken her and killed her just before she reached it. When father and Laban came up, they'd found Colin crouched nearby holding her cub in his arms.

Father had been for killing the cub, which was still too young to shift for itself, but Colin's grief had brought Mom into it. We'd taken the young fox into the kitchen, all of us, except Father, gone a bit silly over the little thing. Colin had held it in his arms and fed it warm milk from a spoon.

"Watch out with all your soft ways," Father had warned, standing in the doorway. "You'll make too much of him. Remember, you can't make a dog out of a fox. Half of that little critter has to love, but the other half is a wild hunter. You boys will mean a whole lot to him while he's kit, but there'll come a day when you won't mean a thing to him and he'll leave you shorn."

For two weeks after that Colin had nursed the cub, weaning it from milk to bits of meat. For a year they were always together. The cub grew fast. It was soon following Colin and me about the barnyard. It turned out to be a patch fox, with a saddle of darker fur across its shoulders.

---

4. the pox (päks): Any of a variety of diseases—like smallpox or chicken pox—that cause a rash on the skin.

5. frothing (frôth' iŋ) vb.: Here, speaking angrily.

I haven't the words to tell you what the fox meant to us. It was far more wonderful owning him than owning any dog. There was something rare and secret like the spirit of the woods about him, and back of his calm, straw-gold eyes was the sense of a brain the equal of a man's. The fox became Colin's whole life.

Each day, going and coming from school, Colin and I took long side trips through the woods, looking for Bandit. Wild things' memories were short, we knew; we'd have to find him soon or the old bond would be broken.

Ever since I was ten I'd been allowed to hunt with Father, so I was good at reading signs. But, in a way, Colin knew more about the woods and wild things than Father or me. What came to me from long observation, Colin seemed to know by instinct.

It was Colin who felt out, like an Indian, the stretch of woods where Bandit had his den, who found the first slim, small fox-print in the damp earth. And then, on an afternoon in March, we saw him. I remember the day well, the racing clouds, the wind rattling the tops of the pine trees and swaying the Spanish moss. Bandit had just come out of a clump of laurel; in the maze of leaves behind him we caught a glimpse of a slim red vixen, so we knew he had found a mate. She melted from sight like a shadow, but Bandit turned to watch us, his mouth open, his tongue lolling as he smiled his old foxy smile. On his thin chops, I saw a telltale chicken feather.

Colin moved silently forward, his movements so quiet and casual he seemed to be standing still. He called Bandit's name, and the fox held his ground, drawn to us with all his senses. For a few moments he let Colin actually put an arm about him. It was then I knew that he loved us still, for all of Father's warnings. He really loved us back, with a

fierce, secret love no tame thing ever gave. But the urge of his life just then was toward his new mate. Suddenly, he whirled about and disappeared in the laurels.

Colin looked at me with glowing eyes. "We haven't really lost him, Stan. When he gets through with his spring sparking[6] he may come back. But we've got to show ourselves to him a lot, so he won't forget."

"It's a go," I said.

"Promise not to say a word to Father," Colin said, and I agreed. For I knew by the chicken feather that Bandit had been up to no good.

A week later the woods were budding and the thickets were rustling with all manner of wild things scurrying on the love scent. Colin managed to get a glimpse of Bandit every few days. He couldn't get close though, for the spring running was a lot more important to a fox than any human beings were.

Every now and then Colin got out his framed box cover and looked at it, but he never drew anything on it; he never even picked up his pencil. I remember wondering if what Father had said about framing a picture before you had one had spoiled something for him.

I was helping Father with the planting now, but Colin managed to be in the woods every day. By degrees he learned Bandit's range, where he drank and rested and where he was likely to be according to the time of day. One day he told me how he had petted Bandit again, and how they had walked together a long way in the woods. All this time we had kept his secret from Father.

As summer came on, Bandit began to live up to the prediction Father had made. Accustomed to human beings he moved without fear about the scattered farms of the

---

6. sparking (spär′ kiŋ) n.: An old-fashioned term for courting.

COURTSHIP
Bonnie Marris
The Greenwich Workshop, Inc.

Last Cover 63

region, raiding barns and hen runs that other foxes wouldn't have dared go near. And he taught his wild mate to do the same. Almost every night they got into some poultry house, and by late June Bandit was not only killing chickens and ducks but feeding on eggs and young chicks whenever he got the chance.

Stories of his doings came to us from many sources, for he was still easily recognized by the dark patch on his shoulders. Many a farmer took a shot at him as he fled and some of them set out on his trail with dogs, but they always returned home without even sighting him. Bandit was familiar with all the dogs in the region, and he knew a hundred tricks to confound them. He got a reputation that year beyond that of any fox our hills had known. His confidence grew, and he gave up wild hunting altogether and lived entirely off the poultry farmers. By September the hill farmers banded together to hunt him down.

It was father who brought home that news one night. All time-honored rules of the fox chase were to be broken in this hunt; if the dogs couldn't bring Bandit down, he was to be shot on sight. I was stricken and furious. I remember the misery of Colin's face in the lamplight. Father, who took pride in all the ritual of the hunt, had refused to be a party to such an affair, though in justice he could do nothing but sanction any sort of hunt, for Bandit, as old Sam Wetherwax put it, had been "purely getting in the Lord's hair."

The hunt began next morning, and it was the biggest turnout our hills had known. There were at least twenty mounted men in the party and as many dogs. Father and I were working in the lower field as they passed along the river road. Most of the hunters carried rifles, and they looked ugly.

Twice during the morning I went up to the house to find Colin, but he was nowhere around. As we worked, Father and I could follow the progress of the hunt by the distant hound music on the breeze. We could tell just where the hunters first caught sight of the fox and where Bandit was leading the dogs during the first hour. We knew as well as if we'd seen it how Bandit roused another fox along Turkey Branch and forced it to run for him, and how the dogs swept after it for twenty minutes before they sensed their mistake.

Noon came, and Colin had not come in to eat. After dinner Father didn't go back to the field. He moped about, listening to the hound talk. He didn't like what was on any more than I did, and now and again I caught his smile of satisfaction when we heard the broken, angry notes of the hunting horn, telling that the dogs had lost the trail or had run another fox.

I was restless, and I went up into the hills in midafternoon. I ranged the woods for miles, thinking all the time of Colin. Time lost all meaning for me, and the short day was nearing an end, when I heard the horn talking again, telling that the fox had put over another trick. All day he had deviled the dogs and mocked the hunters. This new trick and the coming night would work to save him. I was wildly glad, as I moved down toward Turkey Branch and stood listening for a time by the deep, shaded pool where for years we boys had gone swimming, sailed boats, and dreamed summer dreams.

Suddenly, out of the corner of my eye, I saw the sharp ears and thin, pointed mask of a fox—in the water almost beneath me. It was Bandit, craftily submerged there, all but his head, resting in the cool water of the pool and the shadow of the two big beeches that spread above it. He must have run forty miles or more since morning. And he must have hidden in this place before. His knowing, crafty mask blended perfectly with the shadows and a mass of drift and branches that had collected by the bank of the pool. He was so still that a pair of thrushes flew up from the spot as I came up, not knowing he was there.

Bandit's bright, harried eyes were looking right at me. But I did not look at him direct. Some woods instinct, swifter than thought, kept me from it. So he and I met as in another world, indirectly, with feeling but without sign or greeting.

Suddenly I saw that Colin was standing almost beside me. Silently as a water snake, he had come out of the bushes and stood there. Our eyes met, and a quick and secret smile passed between us. It was a rare moment in which I really "met" my brother, when something of his essence flowed into me and I knew all of him. I've never lost it since.

My eyes still turned from the fox, my heart pounding. I moved quietly away, and Colin moved with me. We whistled softly as we went, pretending to busy ourselves along the bank of the stream. There was magic in it, as if by will we wove a web of protection about the fox, a ring-pass-not that none might penetrate. It was so, too, we felt, in the brain of Bandit, and that doubled the charm. To us he was still our little pet that we had carried about in our arms on countless summer afternoons.

Two hundred yards upstream, we stopped beside slim, fresh tracks in the mud where Bandit had entered the branch. The tracks angled upstream. But in the water the wily creature had turned down.

We climbed the far bank to wait, and Colin told me how Bandit's secret had been his secret ever since an afternoon three months before, when he'd watched the fox swim downstream to hide in the deep pool. Today he'd waited on the bank, feeling that Bandit, hard pressed by the dogs, might again seek the pool for sanctuary.

We looked back once as we turned homeward. He still had not moved. We didn't know until later that he was killed that same night by a chance hunter, as he crept out from his hiding place.

That evening Colin worked a long time on his framed box cover that had lain about the house untouched all summer. He kept at it all the next day too. I had never seen him work so hard. I seemed to sense in the air the feeling he was putting into it, how he was *believing* his picture into being. It was evening before he finished it. Without a word he handed it to Father. Mom and I went and looked over his shoulder.

It was a delicate and intricate pencil drawing of the deep branch pool, and there was Bandit's head and watching, fear-filled eyes hiding there amid the leaves and shadows, woven craftily into the maze of twigs and branches, as if by nature's art itself. Hardly a fox there at all, but the place where he was—or should have been. I recognized it instantly, but Mom gave a sort of incredulous sniff.

"I'll declare," she said, "It's mazy as a puzzle. It just looks like a lot of sticks and leaves to me."

Long minutes of study passed before Father's eye picked out the picture's secret, as few men's could have done. I laid that to Father's being a born hunter. That was a picture that might have been done especially for him. In fact, I guess it was.

Finally he turned to Colin with his deep, slow smile. "So that's how Bandit fooled them all," he said. He sat holding the picture with a sort of tenderness for a long time, while we glowed in the warmth of the shared secret. That was Colin's moment. Colin's art stopped being a pox to Father right there. And later, when the time came for Colin to go to art school, it was Father who was his solid backer.

Your Response

1. How did you feel during the hunt? Did you want Bandit to escape? Why or why not?

Recalling

2. Why does the father name the fox Bandit?
3. What do the farmers do when Bandit continues to attack their animals?
4. How does Bandit elude the farmers?
5. How does Colin use his art to explain this trick to his father?

Interpreting

6. The father has mixed feelings about Colin and his art. What are they?
7. How are the mother's and the father's attitudes about Colin's art changed at the end of the story when Colin shows them his picture?
8. In the next to the last paragraph, Stan says, "That was a picture that might have been done especially for him. In fact, I guess it was." Explain what Stan means.
9. What are two possible meanings of the title "Last Cover"?

Applying

10. Much of the communication in this story is done nonverbally—that is, without words. Give two examples of nonverbal communication in daily life.

ANALYZING LITERATURE

Understanding Character Traits

Character traits are the qualities that make a person an individual. There are many aspects of Colin's personality that make him special. As the story unfolds, Colin reveals these special traits in what he says and what he does.

1. Which of Colin's character traits make his mother and Stan worry about him?
2. Which of Colin's traits does his father at first not appreciate?

3. Which character traits allow Colin to find Bandit when no one else can?

CRITICAL THINKING AND READING

Comparing and Contrasting Characters

You can understand more about characters if you compare and contrast them. When you **compare** characters, you look at ways in which they are alike. When you **contrast** them, you look at ways in which they are different.

1. Name two character traits that Colin and Stan share.
2. Stan describes himself as "tough and strong." How does Colin differ?
3. Stan says, "Colin knew more about the woods and wild things than Father or me." While Stan learns of the woods through observation, how does Colin seem to know?

THINKING AND WRITING

Writing a Character Sketch

Think of a person you know well. Write a character sketch describing this person to someone who does not know him or her. First list all the traits that make this person special. Then write your first draft. As you revise your sketch, include enough details to make this person come alive for your reader. Replace any tired words with more vivid words. Finally, correct all spelling and punctuation mistakes and prepare a final draft.

LEARNING OPTIONS

1. **Language.** The distinctive appearance and behaviors of the fox have inspired numerous uses for the word *fox*. Look up *fox* in a dictionary. What were its original meanings? What plants, animals, and activities have *fox* in their names? Make a poster of five of these "*fox*-things."
2. **Art.** Draw Colin's picture, as you imagine it, of Bandit hiding in the stream. Review the description of the drawing in the story to help you.

MULTICULTURAL CONNECTION

The Artist in Different Cultures

You have probably observed the different attitudes toward art in this story. The artist—painter, sculptor, craftsperson—is viewed differently in different societies and occupies a special place in many cultures. In his or her art, an artist often reflects society while standing apart from it. An artist's role can be to celebrate what is good in a culture and criticize what he or she sees as wrong with it.

The artist in Spain. Such great artists as Spain's Francisco Goya and Pablo Picasso have condemned the senseless destruction of war in some of their finest paintings. Goya, who worked in the early nineteenth century, combined savage satire and harsh realism in his masterful series *Disasters of War.* Picasso's masterpiece *Guernica* depicts the annihilation of a Spanish village, bombed by the fascist rebels during the Spanish Civil War of the 1930's. The artist brilliantly distorts human and animal bodies to highlight the horrors of modern warfare.

In Africa. African artists have traditionally celebrated every aspect of life, from momentous occasions to everyday chores. Fine craftspeople add their unique touch to such mundane objects as baskets, bowls, and clothing. No artist more dramatically celebrates African life than the dancer. Special dances commemorate birth, adulthood, marriage, and even death. Each body movement has a meaning all its own and expresses the artist's feelings.

In Latin America. In Latin America, visual artists have used their creativity both to celebrate and to criticize society. Mexican muralists Diego Rivera and José Clemente Orozco created huge murals on public buildings to depict the history of their country from its Indian beginnings to contemporary times. Their epic art honors the glories of the past while criticizing the exploitation of the working class by the privileged few.

In Japan. In direct contrast, the self-effacing artists of Japan strive to create harmony with nature—not conflict with society. Artists and musicians evoke a tranquil mood in their art. The highly formalized nature of a landscape drawing or a Japanese garden presents a world that is orderly and at peace with itself. Traditional rites like the Japanese tea ceremony celebrate life's everyday moments. Like the African dance, the complicated rite of the tea ceremony calls on ordinary persons to become artists, celebrating the rich variety of life around them.

Discussing and Sharing

Talk with classmates about your favorite artists in the worlds of literature, music, and art. How do these artists celebrate or criticize our society?

GUIDE FOR READING

Broken Chain

Motivation

In stories as in life, people do things because they have reasons, or motives, for doing them. **Motivation** refers to the reasons behind actions. The word *motivation* contains the root *mot,* meaning "to move." Motivation moves a person forward, causing him or her to do something, to pursue a goal. Another word with the root *mot* is *emotion,* and people are certainly motivated to action by their emotions.

Focus

The story you are about to read concerns a boy living in southern California. Before it became the thirty-first state of the United States, the territory that is now California was ruled by the Mexican government. Many Hispanic families who lived there decided to stay after California became a state. As a result, Hispanic culture has remained a strong force in the area.

As you read "Broken Chain," you will come across several Spanish words and expressions. As a class, make a list of words that you use in everyday conversation that come from the Spanish language, such as *adios* and *rodeo.* What are the names of the Spanish or Mexican foods you have eaten? Spanish-speaking classmates can help identify other words that are used regularly in American speech.

Vocabulary

Knowing the following words will help you as you read "Broken Chain."

sullen (sul′ ən) *adj.*: Silent and keeping to oneself because angry or hurt (p. 69)

swaggered (swag′ ərd) *v.*: Walked in a showy, proud way (p. 69)

pampered (pam′ pərd) *v.*: Treated carefully; coaxed (p. 72)

retrieved (ri trēvd′) *v.*: Found and brought back (p. 73)

desperation (des pər ā shən) *n.*: Recklessness that comes from despair (p. 73)

Gary Soto

(1952–   ) was born and lives in California. He is the author of *Baseball in April and Other Stories,* a critically acclaimed collection of young adult short stories. He has also published several collections of poetry, including *The Elements of San Joaquin,* in which he explores the lives of migrant workers, and *Living Up the Street,* which won the American Book Award. Like other stories and poems by Soto, "Broken Chain" explores the lives of Mexican Americans living in California.

Broken Chain

Gary Soto

Alfonso sat on the porch trying to push his crooked teeth to where he thought they belonged. He hated the way he looked. Last week he did fifty sit-ups a day, thinking that he would burn those already apparent ripples on his stomach to even deeper ripples, dark ones, so when he went swimming at the canal next summer, girls in cut-offs would notice. And the guys would think he was tough, someone who could take a punch and give it back. He wanted "cuts" like those he had seen on a calendar of an Aztec warrior standing on a pyramid with a woman in his arms. (Even she had cuts he could see beneath her thin dress.) The calendar hung above the cash register at La Plaza.[1] Orsua, the owner, said Alfonso could have the calendar at the end of the year if the waitress, Yolanda, didn't take it first.

Alfonso studied the magazine pictures of rock stars for a hairstyle. He liked the way Prince looked—and the bass player from Los Lobos. Alfonso thought he would look cool with his hair razored into a V in the back and streaked purple. But he knew his mother wouldn't go for it. And his father, who was *puro Mexicano,*[2] would sit in his chair after work, sullen as a toad, and call him "sissy."

Alfonso didn't dare color his hair. But one day he had had it butched on the top, like in the magazines. His father had come home that evening from a softball game, happy that his team had drilled four homers in a thirteen-to-five bashing of Color Tile. He'd swaggered into the living room, but had stopped cold when he saw Alfonso and asked, not joking but with real concern, "Did you hurt your head at school? *¿Qué pasó?*"[3]

Alfonso had pretended not to hear his father and had gone to his room, where he studied his hair from all angles in the mirror. He liked what he saw until he smiled and realized for the first time that his teeth were crooked, like a pile of wrecked cars. He grew depressed and turned away from the mirror. He sat on his bed and leafed through the rock magazine until he came to the rock star with the butched top. His mouth was closed, but Alfonso was sure his teeth weren't crooked.

Alfonso didn't want to be the handsomest kid at school, but he was determined to be better-looking than average. The next day he spent his lawn-mowing money on a new shirt, and, with a pocketknife, scooped the moons of dirt from under his fingernails.

He spent hours in front of the mirror trying to herd his teeth into place with his thumb. He asked his mother if he could have

---

1. La Plaza (lä plä′ zä): Spanish for "town square"; in this case, a store in the town square.
2. *puro Mexicano* (p$\overline{oo}$′ r$\overline{o}$ me h$\overline{e}$ kä′ n$\overline{o}$): Spanish for "pure Mexican."

3. *¿Qué pasó?* (ke pä s$\overline{o}$′): Spanish for "What happened?"

braces, like Frankie Molina, her godson, but he asked at the wrong time. She was at the kitchen table licking the envelope to the house payment. She glared up at him. "Do you think money grows on trees?"

His mother clipped coupons from magazines and newspapers, kept a vegetable garden in the summer, and shopped at Penney's and K-Mart. Their family ate a lot of *frijoles*,[4] which was OK because nothing else tasted so good, though one time Alfonso had had Chinese pot stickers[5] and thought they were the next best food in the world.

He didn't ask his mother for braces again, even when she was in a better mood. He decided to fix his teeth by pushing on them with his thumbs. After breakfast that Saturday he went to his room, closed the door quietly, turned the radio on, and pushed for three hours straight.

He pushed for ten minutes, rested for five, and every half hour, during a radio commercial, checked to see if his smile had improved. It hadn't.

Eventually he grew bored and went outside with an old gym sock to wipe down his bike, a ten-speed from Montgomery Ward. His thumbs were tired and wrinkled and pink, the way they got when he stayed in the bathtub too long.

Alfonso's older brother, Ernie, rode up on *his* Montgomery Ward bicycle looking depressed. He parked his bike against the peach tree and sat on the back steps, keeping his head down and stepping on ants that came too close.

Alfonso knew better than to say anything when Ernie looked mad. He turned his bike over, balancing it on the handlebars and seat, and flossed the spokes with the sock. When he was finished, he pressed a knuckle to his teeth until they tingled.

Ernie groaned and said, "Ah, man."

Alfonso waited a few minutes before asking, "What's the matter?" He pretended not to be too interested. He picked up a wad of steel wool and continued cleaning the spokes.

Ernie hesitated, not sure if Alfonso would laugh. But it came out. "Those girls didn't show up. And you better not laugh."

"What girls?"

Then Alfonso remembered his brother bragging about how he and Frostie met two girls from Kings Canyon Junior High last week on Halloween night. They were dressed as gypsies, the costume for all poor Chicanas[6]—they just had to borrow scarves and gaudy red lipstick from their *abuelitas*.[7]

Alfonso walked over to his brother. He compared their two bikes: his gleamed like a handful of dimes, while Ernie's looked dirty.

"They said we were supposed to wait at the corner. But they didn't show up. Me and Frostie waited and waited like dummies. They were playing games with us."

Alfonso thought that was a pretty dirty trick but sort of funny too. He would have to try that some day.

"Were they cute?" Alfonso asked.

"I guess so."

"Do you think you could recognize them?"

"If they were wearing red lipstick, maybe."

Alfonso sat with his brother in silence, both of them smearing ants with their floppy

---

4. *frijoles* (frē hō′ les): Spanish for "beans."
5. Chinese pot stickers: Steamed or fried dumplings stuffed with meat or vegetables.

6. Chicanas (chē kä′ näs): Spanish for "girls of Mexican descent."
7. abuelitas (ä bwe lēē′ täs): Spanish for "grandmothers."

high tops. Girls could sure act weird, especially the ones you meet on Halloween.

Later that day, Alfonso sat on the porch pressing on his teeth. Press, relax; press, relax. His portable radio was on, but not loud enough to make Mr. Rojas come down the steps and wave his cane at him.

Alfonso's father drove up. Alfonso could tell by the way he sat in his truck, a Datsun with a different-colored front fender, that his team had lost their softball game. Alfonso got off the porch in a hurry because he knew his father would be in a bad mood. He went to the backyard, where he unlocked his bike, sat on it with the kickstand down, and pressed on his teeth. He punched himself in the stomach, and growled, "Cuts." Then he patted his butch and whispered, "Fresh."

After a while Alfonso pedaled up the street, hands in his pockets, toward Foster's Freeze, where he was chased by a ratlike Chihuahua. At his old school, John Burroughs Elementary, he found a kid hanging upside down on the top of a barbed-wire fence with a girl looking up at him. Alfonso skidded to a stop and helped the kid untangle his pants from the barbed wire. The kid was grateful. He had been afraid he would have to stay up there all night. His sister, who was Alfonso's age, was also grateful. If she had to go home and tell her mother that Frankie was stuck on a fence and couldn't get down, she would get scolded.

"Thanks," she said. "What's your name?"

Alfonso remembered her from his school and noticed that she was kind of cute, with ponytails and straight teeth. "Alfonso. You go to my school, huh?"

"Yeah. I've seen you around. You live nearby?"

"Over on Madison."

"My uncle used to live on that street, but he moved to Stockton."

"Stockton's near Sacramento, isn't it?"

"You been there?"

"No." Alfonso looked down at his shoes. He wanted to say something clever the way people do on TV. But the only thing he could think to say was that the governor lived in Sacramento. As soon as he shared this observation, he winced inside.

Alfonso walked with the girl and the boy as they started for home. They didn't talk much. Every few steps, the girl, whose name was Sandra, would look at him out of the corner of her eye, and Alfonso would look away. He learned that she was in seventh grade, just like him, and that she had a pet terrier named Queenie. Her father was a mechanic at Rudy's Speedy Repair, and her mother was a teacher's aide at Jefferson Elementary.

When they came to the street, Alfonso and Sandra stopped at her corner, but her brother ran home. Alfonso watched him stop in the front yard to talk to a lady he guessed was their mother. She was raking leaves into a pile.

ALONE
Diana Zelvin
Courtesy of the Artist

"I live over there," she said, pointing.

Alfonso looked over her shoulder for a long time, trying to muster enough nerve to ask her if she'd like to go bike riding tomorrow.

Shyly, he asked, "You wanna go bike riding?"

"Maybe." She played with a ponytail and crossed one leg in front of the other. "But my bike has a flat."

"I can get my brother's bike. He won't mind."

She thought a moment before she said, "OK. But not tomorrow. I have to go to my aunt's."

"How about after school on Monday?"

"I have to take care of my brother until my mom comes home from work. How 'bout four-thirty?"

"OK," he said. "Four-thirty." Instead of parting immediately, they talked for a while, asking questions like, "Who's your favorite group?" "Have you ever been on the Big Dipper at Santa Cruz?" and "Have you ever tasted pot stickers?" But the question-and-answer period ended when Sandra's mother called her home.

Alfonso took off as fast as he could on his bike, jumped the curb, and, cool as he could be, raced away with his hands stuffed in his pockets. But when he looked back over his shoulder, the wind raking through his butch, Sandra wasn't even looking. She was already on her lawn, heading for the porch.

That night he took a bath, pampered his hair into place, and did more than his usual set of exercises. In bed, in between the push-and-rest on his teeth, he pestered his brother to let him borrow his bike.

"Come on, Ernie," he whined. "Just for an hour."

"*Chale,*[8] I might want to use it."

"Come on, man, I'll let you have my trick-or-treat candy."

"What you got?"

"Three baby Milky Ways and some Skittles."

"Who's going to use it?"

Alfonso hesitated, then risked the truth. "I met this girl. She doesn't live too far."

Ernie rolled over on his stomach and stared at the outline of his brother, whose head was resting on his elbow. "*You* got a girlfriend?"

"She ain't my girlfriend, just a girl."

"What does she look like?"

"Like a girl."

"Come on, what does she look like?"

"She's got ponytails and a little brother."

"Ponytails! Those girls who messed with Frostie and me had ponytails. Is she cool?"

"I think so."

Ernie sat up in bed. "I bet you that's her."

Alfonso felt his stomach knot up. "She's going to be my girlfriend, not yours!"

"I'm going to get even with her!"

"You better not touch her," Alfonso snarled, throwing a wadded Kleenex at him. "I'll run you over with my bike."

For the next hour, until their mother threatened them from the living room to be quiet or else, they argued whether it was the same girl who had stood Ernie up. Alfonso said over and over that she was too nice to pull a stunt like that. But Ernie argued that she lived only two blocks from where those girls had told them to wait, that she was in the same grade, and, the clincher, that she had ponytails. Secretly, however, Ernie was jealous that his brother, two years younger than himself, might have found a girlfriend.

Sunday morning, Ernie and Alfonso stayed away from each other, though over breakfast they fought over the last tortilla. Their mother, sewing at the kitchen table, warned them to knock it off. At church they made faces at one another when the priest,

---

8. Chale (chä′ lē′): Spanish for "No way" or "Get lost."

Father Jerry, wasn't looking. Ernie punched Alfonso in the arm, and Alfonso, his eyes wide with anger, punched back.

Monday morning they hurried to school on their bikes, neither saying a word, though they rode side by side. In first period, Alfonso worried himself sick. How would he borrow a bike for her? He considered asking his best friend, Raul, for his bike. But Alfonso knew Raul, a paper boy with dollar signs in his eyes, would charge him, and he had less than sixty cents, counting the soda bottles he could cash.

Between history and math, Alfonso saw Sandra and her girlfriend huddling at their lockers. He hurried by without being seen.

During lunch Alfonso hid in metal shop so he wouldn't run into Sandra. What would he say to her? If he weren't mad at his brother, he could ask Ernie what girls and guys talk about. But he *was* mad, and anyway, Ernie was pitching nickels with his friends.

Alfonso hurried home after school. He did the morning dishes as his mother had asked and raked the leaves. After finishing his chores, he did a hundred sit-ups, pushed on his teeth until they hurt, showered, and combed his hair into a perfect butch. He then stepped out to the patio to clean his bike. On an impulse, he removed the chain to wipe off the gritty oil. But while he was unhooking it from the back sprocket, it snapped. The chain lay in his hand like a dead snake.

Alfonso couldn't believe his luck. Now, not only did he not have an extra bike for Sandra, he had no bike for himself. Frustrated, and on the verge of tears, he flung the chain as far as he could. It landed with a hard slap against the back fence and spooked his sleeping cat, Benny. Benny looked around, blinking his soft gray eyes, and went back to sleep.

Alfonso retrieved the chain, which was hopelessly broken. He cursed himself for

being stupid, yelled at his bike for being cheap, and slammed the chain onto the cement. The chain snapped in another place and hit him when it popped up, slicing his hand like a snake's fang.

"Ow!" he cried, his mouth immediately going to his hand to suck on the wound.

After a dab of iodine, which only made his cut hurt more, and a lot of thought, he went to the bedroom to plead with Ernie, who was changing to his after-school clothes.

"Come on, man, let me use it," Alfonso pleaded. "Please, Ernie, I'll do anything."

Although Ernie could see Alfonso's desperation, he had plans with his friend Raymundo. They were going to catch frogs at the Mayfair canal. He felt sorry for his brother, and gave him a stick of gum to make him feel better, but there was nothing he could do. The canal was three miles away, and the frogs were waiting.

Alfonso took the stick of gum, placed it in his shirt pocket, and left the bedroom with his head down. He went outside, slamming the screen door behind him, and sat in the alley behind his house. A sparrow landed in the weeds, and when it tried to come close, Alfonso screamed for it to scram. The sparrow responded with a squeaky chirp and flew away.

At four he decided to get it over with and started walking to Sandra's house, trudging slowly, as if he were waist-deep in water. Shame colored his face. How could he disappoint his first date? She would probably laugh. She might even call him *menso*.[9]

He stopped at the corner where they were supposed to meet and watched her house. But there was no one outside, only a rake leaning against the steps.

Why did he have to take the chain off? he scolded himself. He always messed things up

---

9. menso (men' sō): Spanish for "silly" or "stupid."

LA ESQUINA Y LA BICICLETA (detail)
Tony Ortega
Courtesy of the Artist

when he tried to take them apart, like the time he tried to repad his baseball mitt. He had unlaced the mitt and filled the pocket with cotton balls. But when he tried to put it back together, he had forgotten how it laced up. Everything became tangled like kite string. When he showed the mess to his mother, who was at the stove cooking dinner, she scolded him but put it back together and didn't tell his father what a dumb thing he had done.

Now he had to face Sandra and say, "I broke my bike, and my stingy brother took off on his."

He waited at the corner a few minutes, hiding behind a hedge for what seemed like forever. Just as he was starting to think about going home, he heard footsteps and knew it was too late. His hands, moist from worry, hung at his sides, and a thread of sweat raced down his armpit.

He peeked through the hedge. She was wearing a sweater with a checkerboard pattern. A red purse was slung over her shoulder. He could see her looking for him,

standing on tiptoe to see if he was coming around the corner.

What have I done? Alfonso thought. He bit his lip, called himself *menso*, and pounded his palm against his forehead. Someone slapped the back of his head. He turned around and saw Ernie.

"We got the frogs, Alfonso," he said, holding up a wiggling plastic bag. "I'll show you later."

Ernie looked through the hedge, with one eye closed, at the girl. "She's not the one who messed with Frostie and me," he said finally. "You still wanna borrow my bike?"

Alfonso couldn't believe his luck. What a brother! What a pal! He promised to take Ernie's turn next time it was his turn to do the dishes. Ernie hopped on Raymundo's handlebars and said he would remember that promise. Then he was gone as they took off without looking back.

Free of worry now that his brother had come through, Alfonso emerged from behind the hedge with Ernie's bike, which was mud-splashed but better than nothing. Sandra waved.

"Hi," she said.

"Hi," he said back.

She looked cheerful. Alfonso told her his bike was broken and asked if she wanted to ride with him.

"Sounds good," she said, and jumped on the crossbar.

It took all of Alfonso's strength to steady the bike. He started off slowly, gritting his teeth, because she was heavier than he thought. But once he got going, it got easier. He pedaled smoothly, sometimes with only one hand on the handlebars, as they sped up one street and down another. Whenever he ran over a pothole, which was often, she screamed with delight, and once, when it looked like they were going to crash, she placed her hand over his, and it felt like love.

RESPONDING TO THE SELECTION

Your Response

1. Have you ever found yourself in a predicament like Alfonso's with his broken bicycle? Explain.

Recalling

2. How does Alfonso meet Sandra?
3. What causes the argument between Alfonso and Ernie?
4. How does Alfonso finally get to ride with Sandra?

Interpreting

5. Which details indicate that Alfonso's family must be careful about money?
6. The broken chain is described as "a dead snake," and when Alfonso throws it, it jumps up, "slicing his hand like a snake's fang." Why are these images appropriate?
7. Do you think Alfonso needed to worry about impressing Sandra? Why or why not?

Applying

8. When Alfonso first talks to Sandra, he is shy and tongue-tied. Why do you think people are sometimes shy when they first meet someone new?

ANALYZING LITERATURE

Understanding Motivation

Motivation is the cause for characters' actions. Understanding a character's motives gives you a deeper insight into a story. For example, Alfonso wants to improve his outward appearance, so he exercises and tries to straighten his teeth.

1. After Sandra's mother calls her home, Alfonso rides away as confidently as he can. Identify two other things he does that are motivated by his desire to impress Sandra.
2. What things do Alfonso and Ernie do to show that, despite their fighting, they really do care about each other?

CRITICAL THINKING AND READING

Comparing and Contrasting Characters

When you **compare** characters, you show how they are alike. When you **contrast** them, you show their differences. Comparing and contrasting characters can help you better understand characters and stories.

1. List two ways in which Alfonso and Ernie are similar.
2. How is Ernie different from Alfonso?

THINKING AND WRITING

Solving a Problem

After realizing that he cannot use Ernie's bike, Alfonso becomes desperate and ends up peering through the hedge at Sandra, unable to talk to her until, unexpectedly, Ernie lends him the bike. Imagine that you are a friend of Alfonso's and that he has asked for your advice about his problem. Write him a letter in which you offer some ways that he could deal with the problem of the bicycle.

LEARNING OPTIONS

1. **Writing.** Imagine that you are Ernie or Sandra and that you want to tell a friend in another state about your first bicycle ride together. Write this friend a letter in which you convey what a good time you had. Include details about your riding partner and the excursion itself. Where did you go? How long did you ride?
2. **Speaking and Listening.** "Broken Chain" includes many Spanish words that help to bring to life the Mexican culture of the characters. Scan the story to find all the sentences that contain Spanish words or phrases. Use the pronunciation guides in the footnotes to practice saying the Spanish words, and take turns reading the sentences with a classmate. Then work together to write new sentences that use each of the Spanish words or phrases.

ONE WRITER'S PROCESS

Gary Soto and "Broken Chain"

PREWRITING

Finding an Idea Where do ideas for stories come from? They come from anywhere and everywhere: a distant memory or an event that happened yesterday, a newspaper article, a glimpse of an object from a car window, a daydream sprung from the imagination. All can be sources of ideas for writers.

Sometimes, though, a writer doesn't know what inspired an idea. Gary Soto can't say where he got the original idea for "Broken Chain." His aim, he says, was "simply to write a story about a boy who doubted his looks but who was still courageous about finding a girlfriend, even in the face of defeat."

The Doodle Method Once he had an idea, Soto, like all writers, still had to prepare for the actual writing. Soto didn't outline or plan "Broken Chain" before writing it. "I'm terrible at planning my writing," he admits. Instead, with the idea in the back of his mind, he relaxes and lets his thoughts simply flow. How does he do that? "Often, when I am ready to write, I will doodle on a yellow note pad and when something strikes me—a story line, an image, some word with a special ring—then *wham*, I am on my way."

Whatever Works Soto also has a set of work habits, what he calls his "superstitions," that help him write. For example, he always writes in the mornings, at exactly the same time, and he has to have three cups of coffee before he gets started. "It's always three cups," says Soto, "not two or four."

DRAFTING

One Sentence at a Time Soto writes quickly, getting the words on paper without worrying too much about them. "I will start with the first sentence," he says, "and then let that sentence go when it's reasonably polished and go to the next sentence." (Many writers, of course, don't bother to polish at all on the first draft.) By concentrating on one thing at a time—without stopping to go back and rewrite what he has already written—Soto keeps the drafting process moving along smoothly. "I look neither back nor forwards but usually at the paragraph in front of me."

Use What You Know For Soto an important aspect of writing "Broken Chain" was his focus on what he calls "local" experience. What does he mean by that? "As a writer," he says, "I'm chiefly interested in story telling, and the local color of characters facing up to a problem. . . ." For example, in "Broken Chain," Soto uses a broken bicycle chain to trigger Alfonso's anxiety about finding a girlfriend. For Soto such everyday details are a necessary part of local experience. "As one of my former teachers once said, 'Write about what you know best.' That's what I've been doing," he says.

Go With Your Strengths Even accomplished writers have trouble with certain things. Soto's stumbling block is dialogue. The hardest thing about writing "Broken Chain," he says, was making the characters sound real. "Sure, in book form, they may seem natural, but I nervously chewed my fingernails when I was writing a sentence like, 'Come on Ernie. Just an hour.'"

Soto is much more at ease writing description and dreaming up situations for his characters to face. He is the first to point out that there is not much dialogue in "Broken Chain." "What advances the story is description," he says, "not the chatter between characters."

REVISING

Soto calls himself an "impatient writer who likes to get the story done," and gives that as the reason why he seldom makes substantial revisions. "For other writers," he says, "revision may be more involved, where characters are added or deleted, verb tense is changed, the details are shrunk or inflated."

A Second Opinion Soto, however, does consult others about the finer details of his writing. He shares his stories first with his wife, who suggests changes. Then he prints out a second draft of the story for a friend who "will act as a serious copy editor."

The professional editor who worked on "Broken Chain" didn't change very much, but the small changes made a difference. The box below shows part of the third paragraph of "Broken Chain" as Soto originally wrote it, with the editor's handwritten changes. Study the changes for a minute. What effect do they have on the scene?

> Alfonso didn't dare color his hair.
> *one day had*
> But he had it butched on the top, like
> *s*
> in the magazine.

You can see that in addition to correcting a minor mistake, the editor changed the tense of the scene where Alfonso's father reacts to his haircut. By doing this, the editor turned the scene into a recollection of Alfonso's.

PUBLISHING

Pleasing Readers Gary Soto is lucky. He gets to see his words in print, between the covers of a real book. Even so, he struggles with self-doubt. "A lot of what I write never gets published," he says. "What keeps me going is that I know, through the practice of writing, something will eventually happen that pleases me and, perhaps, the reader."

Soto's readers have been pleased with "Broken Chain" and other stories in *Baseball in April,* and they have written letters telling him so. "I appreciate these letters," Soto says. "I'm glad for my readers. They tell me which stories they like best, but they never tell me why. I wish they would if they could."

As for Alfonso and Ernie, they may turn up again in future stories by Gary Soto. Although Soto sometimes forgets about the characters he has created for past stories, he says, "When I run across them again, I'm happy to see them. 'Hi, Alfonso! Hello, Ernie! It was really mean of me to break the bicycle chain.'"

THINKING ABOUT THE PROCESS

1. To what part of the writing process does Soto devote the most time and energy? Explain.
2. **Writing** Soto talks about the difficulty of making characters' dialogue sound real. Write a scene in which two characters have a conversation. First decide what kind of characters you'd like to write about. Think carefully about their ages, their backgrounds, and their likely interests. Write an exchange of dialogue that will convince your reader that these characters are "real."

GUIDE FOR READING

Lucille Clifton

(1936–   ) was born in Depew, New York. She has written about the strength of the courageous black women who raised their families with dignity during the harsh period of slavery and its aftermath. In addition to several books of poetry, she has written a book called *Generations,* which contains anecdotes that celebrate the lives of her father and mother. "The Luckiest Time of All" deals with a theme common in her work: the importance of a strong black woman in handing down a family's traditions to a new generation.

The Luckiest Time of All

Major and Minor Characters

A **major character** is the one on whom a story focuses. It is the character who plays the most important role. Because a major character shows several character traits, you learn the most about this character as you read a story. In contrast, a **minor character** plays only a small part in a story. Therefore, you learn only a little about each minor character.

Focus

People have carried or worn good-luck charms for hundreds of years. Long ago it was thought that such objects, also called *talismans,* possessed magic and protected the owner from evil. Some objects that are traditionally thought to bring good luck include a horseshoe, a rabbit's foot, and a four-leaf clover. Often a good-luck charm is just a common object that its owner thinks brings him or her luck. Do you have a good-luck charm? How did you come to think that it brought you luck? With several of your classmates, make a list of other good-luck charms that you have heard of. As you read, notice how a simple stone becomes a lucky stone for a character.

Vocabulary

In "The Luckiest Time of All," some words, particularly verbs, are spelled the way they are pronounced by the characters, such as *dancin* for *dancing* or *twirlin* for *twirling.* These spelling changes reflect spoken language. Since many people, particularly the characters in this story, drop the final *g* when they speak, these spellings reflect the way the words sound. You will be able to recognize these words from their context when you see them.

The Luckiest Time of All

from *The Lucky Stone*

Lucille Clifton

Mrs. Elzie F. Pickens was rocking slowly on the porch one afternoon when her Great-granddaughter, Tee, brought her a big bunch of dogwood blooms, and that was the beginning of a story.

"Ahhh, now that dogwood reminds me of the day I met your Great-granddaddy, Mr. Pickens, Sweet Tee.

"It was just this time, spring of the year, and me and my best friend Ovella Wilson, who is now gone, was goin to join the Silas Greene. Usta be a kinda show went all through the South, called it the Silas Greene show. Somethin like the circus. Me and Ovella wanted to join that thing and see the world. Nothin wrong at home or nothin, we just wanted to travel and see new things and have high times. Didn't say nothin to nobody but one another. Just up and decided to do it.

"Well, this day we plaited our hair and put a dress and some things in a crokasack[1] and started out to the show. Spring day like this.

"We got there after a good little walk and it was the world, Baby, such music and won-ders as we never had seen! They had everything there, or seemed like it.

"Me and Ovella thought we'd walk around for a while and see the show before goin to the office to sign up and join.

"While we was viewin it all we come up

MOM AND DAD
William H. Johnson
National Museum of American Art

---

1. crokasack, usually spelled *croker sack* (krō′ kər sak) *n.*: A bag made of burlap or similar material.

on this dancin dog. Cutest one thing in the world next to you, Sweet Tee, dippin and movin and head bowin to that music. Had a little ruffly skirt on itself and up on two back legs twistin and movin to the music. Dancin dancin dancin till people started throwin pennies out of they pockets.

"Me and Ovella was caught up too and laughin so. She took a penny out of her pocket and threw it to the ground where that dog was dancin, and I took two pennies and threw 'em both.

"The music was faster and faster and that dog was turnin and turnin. Ovella reached in her sack and threw out a little pin she had won from never being late at Sunday school. And me, laughin and all excited, reached in my bag and threw out my lucky stone!

"Well, I knew right off what I had done. Soon as it left my hand it seemed like I reached back out for it to take it back. But the stone was gone from my hand and Lord, it hit that dancin dog right on his nose!

"Well, he lit out after me, poor thing. He lit out after me and I flew! Round and round the Silas Greene we run, through every place me and Ovella had walked before, but now that dancin dog was a runnin dog and all the people was laughin at the new show, which was us!

"I felt myself slowin down after a while and I thought I would turn around a little bit to see how much gain that cute little dog was makin on me. When I did I got such a surprise! Right behind me was the dancin dog and right behind him was the finest fast runnin hero in the bottoms of Virginia.

"And that was Mr. Pickens when he was still a boy! He had a length of twine in his hand and he was twirlin it around in the air just like the cowboy at the Silas Greene and grinnin fit to bust.

"While I was watchin how the sun shined on him and made him look like an angel come to help a poor sinner girl, why, he twirled that twine one extra fancy twirl and looped it right around one hind leg of that dancin dog and brought him low.

"I stopped then and walked slow and shy to where he had picked up that poor dog to see if he was hurt, cradlin him and talkin to him soft and sweet. That showed me how kind and gentle he was, and when we walked back to the dancin dog's place in the show he let the dog loose and helped me to find my stone. I told him how shiny black it was and how it had the letter A scratched on one side. We searched and searched and at last he spied it!

"Ovella and me lost heart for shows then and we walked on home. And a good little way, the one who was gonna be your Great-granddaddy was walkin on behind. Seein us safe. Us walkin kind of slow. Him seein us safe. Yes." Mrs. Pickens' voice trailed off softly and Tee noticed she had a little smile on her face.

"Grandmama, that stone almost got you bit by a dog that time. It wasn't so lucky that time, was it?"

Tee's Great-grandmother shook her head and laughed out loud.

"That was the luckiest time of all, Tee Baby. It got me acquainted with Mr. Amos Pickens, and if that ain't luck, what could it be! Yes, it was luckier for me than for anybody, I think. Least mostly I think it."

Tee laughed with her Great-grandmother though she didn't exactly know why.

"I hope I have that kind of good stone luck one day," she said.

"Maybe you will someday," her Great-grandmother said.

And they rocked a little longer and smiled together.

RESPONDING TO THE SELECTION

Your Response

1. Have you ever met someone "by chance"? What were the circumstances?

Recalling

2. "The Luckiest Time of All" is a story within a story. Who tells the story about the lucky stone and the Silas Greene Show?
3. What is Great-grandmother's reason for believing that the stone was lucky for her?

Interpreting

4. What was Mr. Pickens's real intention in saving Great-grandmother from being bitten by the dog and in following her home?
5. What evidence in the story shows that Great-grandmother and Mr. Pickens had a happy life?

Applying

6. Which do you think brings success more, hard work or luck? Give reasons for your answer.

ANALYZING LITERATURE

Identifying Major and Minor Characters

The **major character** in a story is the one on whom the story focuses and thus the one you learn the most about. **Minor characters** play small roles in the development of a story.

1. Who is the major character in "The Luckiest Time of All"?
2. Point out three facts you learn about the major character.
3. Name one minor character.
4. What do you learn about this minor character?

CRITICAL THINKING AND READING

Making Inferences About Characters

An **inference** is a conclusion that you make based on the information given. An author does not always tell you everything there is to know about a character. Sometimes you must make inferences about the character's personality traits based on what the character says and does.

1. What inference can you make about Mr. Pickens based on the following facts?
   a. He cradles the dog and speaks softly to it.
   b. He sees the young women safely home.
2. Find two details in the story that support the inference that Great-grandmother is a happy, good-natured person.

THINKING AND WRITING

Writing About Luck

Think about a person you know who is successful. Make notes about how much of this person's success is due to luck and how much is due to hard work. Then prepare the first draft of a composition to present before your class telling whether you think luck or hard work is more important to success. Begin with a topic sentence that summarizes your opinion. Then give examples to support your opinion. When you revise, be sure you have given enough examples to convince your classmates of your opinion.

LEARNING OPTION

Speaking and Listening. Ask a parent, an older relative, or another adult you know to tell you stories from his or her past. You may either tape-record the stories or write them down in your own words. If you write them yourself, try to recall and use as many of the storyteller's actual words as you can. Include funny or individual ways of saying things, and try to reproduce slang words or phrases. Share the most interesting or entertaining stories with the class. You may even want to use a story as source material for your own creative writing.

GUIDE FOR READING

Piri Thomas

(1928–   ) grew up in the Spanish Harlem section of New York City. While serving time in jail as a young man, he began to write about his life. Later he published an autobiography called *Down These Mean Streets,* which describes his experiences in some of the city's toughest neighborhoods. Like Thomas himself, the two major characters in "Amigo Brothers" have a dream that helps them overcome the problems they encounter in their environment.

Amigo Brothers

More Than One Major Character

Many stories tell about the experiences of just one major character. Sometimes, however, a story contains two or more major characters. Each of them may have a variety of character traits, or ways of acting and looking at the world. The focus of this type of story is often on the relationship between the major characters.

"Amigo Brothers" has two major characters. During the story, the friendship between them is put to a difficult test.

Focus

Boxing as an organized sport with rules has existed at least since the second century B.C. If you've ever seen any amateur bouts nowadays, you know that they are three rounds long and that the winner is chosen by three judges.

The story you are about to read centers on a boxing match between two best friends. Does it seem odd that best friends could enjoy a sport that requires them to hit each other? Have you and a friend ever competed in a sport or a contest? Write about what it feels like to compete against a friend.

Vocabulary

Knowing the following words will help you as you read "Amigo Brothers."

barrage (bə räzh′) *n.*: A heavy attack (p. 84)

gnawing (nô′ iŋ) *adj.*: Tormenting; bothering (p. 86)

perpetual (pər pech′ oo wəl) *adj.*: Never stopping (p. 86)

dignitaries (dig′ nə ter′ ēz) *n.*: People holding high positions or offices (p. 87)

interwoven (in′ tər wōv′ ən) *v.*: Mixed together (p. 87)

nimble (nim′ b'l) *adj.*: Moving quickly and lightly (p. 88)

dispelled (dis peld′) *v.*: Driven away (p. 89)

feinted (fānt′ əd) *v.*: Pretended to make an attack (p. 89)

Amigo[1] Brothers

Piri Thomas

Antonio Cruz and Felix Varga were both seventeen years old. They were so together in friendship that they felt themselves to be brothers. They had known each other since childhood, growing up on the lower east side of Manhattan in the same tenement building on Fifth Street between Avenue A and Avenue B.

Antonio was fair, lean, and lanky, while Felix was dark, short, and husky. Antonio's hair was always falling over his eyes, while Felix wore his black hair in a natural Afro style.

Each youngster had a dream of someday becoming lightweight champion of the world. Every chance they had the boys worked out, sometimes at the Boys Club on 10th Street and Avenue A and sometimes at the pro's gym on 14th Street. Early morning sunrises would find them running along the East River Drive, wrapped in sweat shirts, short towels around their necks, and handkerchiefs Apache style around their foreheads.

While some youngsters were into street negatives, Antonio and Felix slept, ate, rapped,[2] and dreamt positive. Between them, they had a collection of *Fight* magazines second to none, plus a scrapbook filled with torn tickets to every boxing match they had ever attended, and some clippings of their own. If asked a question about any given fighter, they would immediately zip out from their memory banks divisions, weights, records of fights, knock-outs, technical knock-outs,[3] and draws or losses.

Each had fought many bouts representing their community and had won two gold-plated medals plus a silver and bronze medallion. The difference was in their style. Antonio's lean form and long reach made him the better boxer, while Felix's short and muscular frame made him the better slugger.[4] Whenever they had met in the ring for sparring sessions, it had always been hot and heavy.

Now, after a series of elimination bouts,[5] they had been informed that they were to meet each other in the division finals that were scheduled for the seventh of August, two weeks away—the winner to represent the Boys Club in the Golden Gloves Championship Tournament.

The two boys continued to run together along the East River Drive. But even when joking with each other, they both sensed a wall rising between them.

One morning less than a week before their bout, they met as usual for their daily work-out. They fooled around with a few jabs at the air, slapped skin, and then took off, running lightly along the dirty East River's edge.

---

1. amigo (ə mē′ gō) *adj.*: Spanish for "friend" (usually a noun).
2. rapped (rapt) *v.*: A slang term meaning "talked."

3. technical knock-outs: Occasions when a fight is stopped because one of the fighters is too hurt to continue, even though he is on his feet.
4. slugger (slug′ ər) *n.*: A boxer who relies more on the power of his punches than on his grace and form.
5. elimination bouts: A series of matches in which only the winners go on to fight in other matches.

Antonio glanced at Felix who kept his eyes purposely straight ahead, pausing from time to time to do some fancy leg work while throwing one-twos followed by upper cuts to an imaginary jaw. Antonio then beat the air with a barrage of body blows and short devastating lefts with an overhand jaw-breaking right. After a mile or so, Felix puffed and said, "Let's stop a while, bro. I think we both got something to say to each other." Antonio nodded. It was not natural to be acting as though nothing unusual was happening when two ace-boon buddies were going to be blasting each other within a few short days.

They rested their elbows on the railing separating them from the river. Antonio wiped his face with his short towel. The sunrise was now creating day.

Felix leaned heavily on the river's railing and stared across to the shores of Brooklyn. Finally, he broke the silence.

"Man, I don't know how to come out with it."

Antonio helped. "It's about our fight, right?"

"Yeah, right." Felix's eyes squinted at the rising orange sun.

"I've been thinking about it too, *panín*.[6] In fact, since we found out it was going to be me and you, I've been awake at night, pulling punches on you, trying not to hurt you."

"Same here. It ain't natural not to think about the fight. I mean, we both are *cheverote*[7] fighters and we both want to win. But only one of us can win. There ain't no draws in the eliminations."

Felix tapped Antonio gently on the shoulder. "I don't mean to sound like I'm bragging, bro. But I wanna win, fair and square."

Antonio nodded quietly. "Yeah. We both know that in the ring the better man wins. Friend or no friend, brother or no . . . "

Felix finished it for him. "Brother. Tony, let's promise something right here. Okay?"

"If it's fair, *hermano*,[8] I'm for it." Antonio admired the courage of a tugboat pulling a barge five times its welterweight size.

"It's fair, Tony. When we get into the ring, it's gotta be like we never met. We gotta be like two heavy strangers that want the same thing and only one can have it. You understand, don'tcha?"

"Sí, I know." Tony smiled. "No pulling punches. We go all the way."

"Yeah, that's right. Listen, Tony. Don't you think it's a good idea if we don't see each other until the day of the fight? I'm going to stay with my Aunt Lucy in the Bronx. I can use Gleason's Gym for working out. My manager says he got some sparring partners with more or less your style."

Tony scratched his nose pensively. "Yeah, it would be better for our heads." He held out his hand, palm upward. "Deal?"

"Deal." Felix lightly slapped open skin.

"Ready for some more running?" Tony asked lamely.

"Naw, bro. Let's cut it here. You go on. I kinda like to get things together in my head."

"You ain't worried, are you?" Tony asked.

"No way, man." Felix laughed out loud. "I got too much smarts for that. I just think it's cooler if we split right here. After the fight, we can get it together again like nothing ever happened."

The amigo brothers were not ashamed to hug each other tightly.

"Guess you're right. Watch yourself, Felix. I hear there's some pretty heavy dudes up in the Bronx. *Suavecito*,[9] okay?"

"Okay. You watch yourself too, *sabe*?"[10]

Tony jogged away. Felix watched his friend disappear from view, throwing rights and lefts. Both fighters had a lot of psyching up[11] to do before the big fight.

The days in training passed much too slowly. Although they kept out of each other's way, they were aware of each other's progress via the ghetto grapevine.

The evening before the big fight, Tony made his way to the roof of his tenement. In

---

6. panín (pä nēn'): Spanish for "pal."

7. cheverote (che ve rô' tä): Spanish for "great."

8. hermano (er mä' nô): Spanish for "brother."

9. suavecito (swä vä sē' tô): Spanish for "take it easy."

10. sabe (sä' bä): Spanish for "understand?"

11. psyching (sīk iŋ) **up:** A slang term meaning "getting themselves mentally ready."

the quiet early dark, he peered over the ledge. Six stories below the lights of the city blinked and the sounds of cars mingled with the curses and the laughter of children in the street. He tried not to think of Felix, feeling he had succeeded in psyching his mind. But only in the ring would he really know. To spare Felix hurt, he would have to knock him out, early and quick.

Up in the South Bronx, Felix decided to take in a movie in an effort to keep Antonio's face away from his fists. The flick was *The Champion* with Kirk Douglas, the third time Felix was seeing it.

The champion was getting hit hard. He was saved only by the sound of the bell.

Felix became the champ and Tony the challenger.

The movie audience was going out of its head. The challenger, confident that he had the championship in the bag, threw a left. The champ countered with a dynamite right.

Felix's right arm felt the shock. Antonio's face, superimposed on the screen, was hit by the awesome blow. Felix saw himself in the ring, blasting Antonio against the ropes. The challenger fell to the canvas.

When Felix finally left the theatre, he had figured out how to psyche himself for tomorrow's fight. It was Felix the Champion vs. Antonio the Challenger.

He walked up some dark streets, deserted except for small pockets of wary-looking kids wearing gang colors. Despite the fact that he was Puerto Rican like them, they eyed him as a stranger to their turf.[12] Felix did a fast shuffle, bobbing and weaving, while letting loose a torrent of blows that would demolish whatever got in its way. It seemed to impress the brothers, who went about their own business.

Finding no takers, Felix decided to split

to his aunt's. Walking the streets had not relaxed him, neither had the fight flick. All it had done was to stir him up. He let himself quietly into his Aunt Lucy's apartment and went straight to bed, falling into a fitful sleep with sounds of the gong for Round One.

Antonio was passing some heavy time on his rooftop. How would the fight tomorrow affect his relationship with Felix? After all, fighting was like any other profession. Friendship had nothing to do with it. A gnawing doubt crept in. He cut negative thinking real quick by doing some speedy fancy dance steps, bobbing and weaving like mercury.[13] The night air was blurred with perpetual motions of left hooks and right crosses. Felix, his *amigo* brother, was not going to be Felix at all in the ring. Just an opponent with another face. Antonio went to sleep, hearing the opening bell for the first round. Like his friend in the South Bronx, he prayed for victory, via a quick clean knock-out in the first round.

Large posters plastered all over the walls of local shops announced the fight between Antonio Cruz and Felix Vargas as the main bout.

The fight had created great interest in the neighborhood. Antonio and Felix were well liked and respected. Each had his own loyal following. Antonio's fans counted on his boxing skills. On the other side, Felix's admirers trusted in his dynamite-packed fists.

Felix had returned to his apartment early in the morning of August 7th and stayed there, hoping to avoid seeing Antonio. He turned the radio on to *salsa* music[14] sounds

---

12. turf (turf): A slang term meaning "a gang's territory."

13. mercury (mur′ kyoo rē): The element mercury, also known as quicksilver because it is so quick and fluid. This element was named after the Roman god Mercury, who because of his quick thinking and speed served as the messenger of the gods.

14. salsa (säl′ sə) **music:** Latin American dance music.

and then tried to read while waiting for word from his manager.

The fight was scheduled to take place in Tompkins Square Park. It had been decided that the gymnasium of the Boys Club was not large enough to hold all the people who were sure to attend. In Tompkins Square Park, everyone who wanted could view the fight, whether from ringside or window fire escapes or tenement rooftops.

The morning of the fight Tompkins Square was a beehive of activity with numerous workers setting up the ring, the seats, and the guest speakers' stand. The scheduled bouts began shortly after noon and the park had begun filling up even earlier.

The local junior high school across from Tompkins Square Park served as the dressing room for all the fighters. Each was given a separate classroom with desk tops, covered with mats, serving as resting tables. Antonio thought he caught a glimpse of Felix waving to him from a room at the far end of the corridor. He waved back just in case it had been him.

The fighters changed from their street clothes into fighting gear. Antonio wore white trunks, black socks, and black shoes. Felix wore sky blue trunks, red socks, and white boxing shoes. Each had dressing gowns to match their fighting trunks with their names neatly stitched on the back.

The loudspeakers blared into the open windows of the school. There were speeches by dignitaries, community leaders, and great boxers of yesteryear. Some were well prepared, some improvised on the spot. They all carried the same message of great pleasure and honor at being part of such a historic event. This great day was in the tradition of champions emerging from the streets of the lower east side.

Interwoven with the speeches were the sounds of the other boxing events. After the sixth bout, Felix was much relieved when his trainer Charlie said, "Time change. Quick knock-out. This is it. We're on."

Waiting time was over. Felix was escorted from the classroom by a dozen fans in white T-shirts with the word FELIX across their fronts.

Antonio was escorted down a different stairwell and guided through a roped-off path.

As the two climbed into the ring, the crowd exploded with a roar. Antonio and Felix both bowed gracefully and then raised their arms in acknowledgment.

Antonio tried to be cool, but even as the roar was in its first birth, he turned slowly to meet Felix's eyes looking directly into his. Felix nodded his head and Antonio responded. And both as one, just as quickly, turned away to face his own corner.

Bong—bong—bong. The roar turned to stillness.

"Ladies and Gentlemen, *Señores y Señoras*."[15]

The announcer spoke slowly, pleased at his bilingual efforts.

"Now the moment we have all been waiting for—the main event between two fine young Puerto Rican fighters, products of our lower east side. In this corner, weighing 134 pounds, Felix Vargas. And in this corner, weighing 133 pounds, Antonio Cruz. The winner will represent the Boys Club in the tournament of champions, the Golden Gloves. There will be no draw. May the best man win."

The cheering of the crowd shook the window panes of the old buildings surrounding Tompkins Square Park. At the center of the ring, the referee was giving instructions to the youngsters.

"Keep your punches up. No low blows. No punching on the back of the head. Keep

---

15. *Señores y Señoras* (se nyô räs ē se nyô räs): Spanish for "Gentlemen and Ladies."

your heads up. Understand. Let's have a clean fight. Now shake hands and come out fighting."

Both youngsters touched gloves and nodded. They turned and danced quickly to their corners. Their head towels and dressing gowns were lifted neatly from their shoulders by their trainers' nimble fingers. Antonio crossed himself. Felix did the same.

BONG! BONG! ROUND ONE. Felix and

Antonio turned and faced each other squarely in a fighting pose. Felix wasted no time. He came in fast, head low, half hunched toward his right shoulder, and lashed out with a straight left. He missed a right cross as Antonio slipped the punch and countered with one-two-three lefts that snapped Felix's head back, sending a mild shock coursing through him. If Felix had any small doubt about their friendship affecting their fight, it was being neatly dispelled.

Antonio danced, a joy to behold. His left hand was like a piston pumping jabs one right after another with seeming ease. Felix bobbed and weaved and never stopped boring in. He knew that at long range he was at a disadvantage. Antonio had too much reach on him. Only by coming in close could Felix hope to achieve the dreamed-of knockout.

Antonio knew the dynamite that was stored in his *amigo* brother's fist. He ducked a short right and missed a left hook. Felix trapped him against the ropes just long enough to pour some punishing rights and lefts to Antonio's hard midsection. Antonio slipped away from Felix, crashing two lefts to his head, which set Felix's right ear to ringing.

Bong! Both *amigos* froze a punch well on its way, sending up a roar of approval for good sportsmanship.

Felix walked briskly back to his corner. His right ear had not stopped ringing. Antonio gracefully danced his way toward his stool none the worse, except for glowing glove burns, showing angry red against the whiteness of his midribs.

"Watch that right, Tony." His trainer talked into his ear. "Remember Felix always goes to the body. He'll want you to drop your hands for his overhand left or right. Got it?"

Antonio nodded, spraying water out between his teeth. He felt better as his sore midsection was being firmly rubbed.

Felix's corner was also busy.

"You gotta get in there, fella." Felix's trainer poured water over his curly Afro locks. "Get in there or he's gonna chop you up from way back."

Bong! Bong! Round two. Felix was off his stool and rushed Antonio like a bull, sending a hard right to his head. Beads of water exploded from Antonio's long hair.

Antonio, hurt, sent back a blurring barrage of lefts and rights that only meant pain to Felix, who returned with a short left to the head followed by a looping right to the body. Antonio countered with his own flurry, forcing Felix to give ground. But not for long.

Felix bobbed and weaved, bobbed and weaved, occasionally punching his two gloves together.

Antonio waited for the rush that was sure to come. Felix closed in and feinted with his left shoulder and threw his right instead. Lights suddenly exploded inside Felix's head as Antonio slipped the blow and hit him with a pistonlike left catching him flush on the point of his chin.

Bedlam broke loose as Felix's legs momentarily buckled. He fought off a series of rights and lefts and came back with a strong right that taught Antonio respect.

Antonio danced in carefully. He knew Felix had the habit of playing possum when hurt, to sucker an opponent within reach of the powerful bombs he carried in each fist.

A right to the head slowed Antonio's pretty dancing. He answered with his own left at Felix's right eye that began puffing up within three seconds.

Antonio, a bit too eager, moved in too close and Felix had him entangled into a rip-roaring, punching toe-to-toe slugfest that brought the whole Tompkins Square Park screaming to its feet.

Rights to the body. Lefts to the head. Neither fighter was giving an inch. Suddenly a short right caught Antonio squarely on the chin. His long legs turned to jelly and his arms flailed out desperately. Felix, grunting like a bull, threw wild punches from every direction. Antonio, groggy, bobbed and weaved, evading most of the blows. Suddenly his head cleared. His left flashed out hard and straight catching Felix on the bridge of his nose.

Felix lashed back with a haymaker,[16] right off the ghetto streets. At the same instant, his eye caught another left hook from Antonio. Felix swung out trying to clear the pain. Only the frenzied screaming of those along ringside let him know that he had dropped Antonio. Fighting off the growing haze, Antonio struggled to his feet, got up, ducked, and threw a smashing right that dropped Felix flat on his back.

Felix got up as fast as he could in his own corner, groggy but still game. He didn't even hear the count. In a fog, he heard the roaring of the crowd, who seemed to have gone insane. His head cleared to hear the bell sound at the end of the round. He was very glad. His trainer sat him down on the stool.

In his corner, Antonio was doing what all fighters do when they are hurt. They sit and smile at everyone.

The referee signaled the ring doctor to check the fighters out. He did so and then gave his okay. The cold water sponges brought clarity to both *amigo* brothers. They were rubbed until their circulation ran free.

Bong! Round three—the final round. Up to now it had been tic-tac-toe, pretty much even. But everyone knew there could be no draw and that this round would decide the winner.

This time, to Felix's surprise, it was Antonio who came out fast, charging across the ring. Felix braced himself but couldn't ward off the barrage of punches. Antonio drove Felix hard against the ropes.

The crowd ate it up. Thus far the two had fought with *mucho corazón*.[17] Felix tapped his gloves and commenced his attack anew. Antonio, throwing boxer's caution to the winds, jumped in to meet him.

Both pounded away. Neither gave an inch and neither fell to the canvas. Felix's left eye was tightly closed. Claret red[18] blood poured from Antonio's nose. They fought toe-to-toe.

The sounds of their blows were loud in contrast to the silence of a crowd gone completely mute. The referee was stunned by their savagery.

Bong! Bong! Bong! The bell sounded over and over again. Felix and Antonio were past hearing. Their blows continued to pound on each other like hailstones.

Finally the referee and the two trainers pried Felix and Antonio apart. Cold water was poured over them to bring them back to their senses.

They looked around and then rushed toward each other. A cry of alarm surged through Tompkins Square Park. Was this a fight to the death instead of a boxing match?

The fear soon gave way to wave upon wave of cheering as the two *amigos* embraced.

No matter what the decision, they knew they would always be champions to each other.

BONG! BONG! BONG! "Ladies and Gentlemen. *Señores* and *Señoras*. The winner and representative to the Golden Gloves Tournament of Champions is . . ."

The announcer turned to point to the winner and found himself alone. Arm in arm the champions had already left the ring.

---

16. haymaker: A punch thrown with full force.

17. mucho corazón (moo′ chô kô rä sôn′): Spanish for "much courage."

18. claret (klar′ it) **red**: Purplish red.

Your Response

1. How do you feel when you have to be separated from a friend for a time? Explain.

Recalling

2. What dream do the boys share?
3. What event creates a wall between them?
4. What agreement do they make while jogging?
5. Describe the way the boys leave the ring at the end of the fight.

Interpreting

6. Why is boxing so important to Antonio and Felix?
7. Why do the boys decide not to see each other until the fight?
8. What do the boys discover they value as much as or more than winning?
9. *Amigo* means "friend." Why is "Amigo Brothers" an appropriate title for this story?

Applying

10. What advice would you give to friends who have to compete?

ANALYZING LITERATURE

Considering Two Major Characters

Some stories deal with more than one major character. In "Amigo Brothers," both Antonio and Felix are fully developed and have a variety of character traits. The writer gives them equal attention. You learn about these two characters as you watch the dream they share become the barrier that divides them.

1. Explain how the boys' relationship is tested in this story.
2. Show how the boys' friendship is stronger or weaker as a result of this test.

CRITICAL THINKING AND READING

Comparing and Contrasting Characters

When you **compare** two characters, you show how they are similar. When you **contrast** them, you show how they are different. Often, you can better understand stories with more than one major character by comparing and contrasting the characters. In "Amigo Brothers," for example, Antonio and Felix are different in height but similar in their love of boxing.

1. List three other ways in which the boys are similar.
2. Now list three ways in which they are different.
3. Which of these similarities and differences may have brought them together as friends?

THINKING AND WRITING

Writing a Comparison and Contrast

Compare and contrast Antonio and Felix. As you brainstorm for ideas, recall your lists of the ways that the boys are similar and different. Also, remember to use some of the key words that show similarities and differences. When you have finished, revise your work to make sure it is clear.

LEARNING OPTION

Community Connections. The two boys in "Amigo Brothers" are boxing for the chance to participate in the Golden Gloves tournament. This tournament actually exists in many cities throughout the United States. What competitive activities does your community have available for young people? In a group or on your own, contact your local Chamber of Commerce, YMCA or YWCA, and neighborhood recreational centers. Ask them to supply you with information about similar competitive activities as well as other programs available to people your age. Gather the information together into an information resource for your class.

GUIDE FOR READING

Two Kinds

Direct and Indirect Characterization

Characterization is the art of making people in a story real. Authors can present characters in a **direct** or an **indirect** way. They present characters directly by simply telling you what they want you to know about a character. They develop characters indirectly by letting the characters reveal their personalities through what they think, say, or do. The narrator in "Two Kinds" is a woman recounting a part of her childhood. Sometimes the narrator makes direct statements about the characters, including herself, while at other times she lets you learn about the characters indirectly through what they say and do.

Focus

One of the characters in "Two Kinds" came to the United States in 1949 in order to escape being killed in a war in her native China. What feelings might such a person have upon arriving in a much different culture? How might her attitudes toward living differ from those of her child, who has always lived in the United States? With a group of classmates, discuss some of the difficulties recent immigrants are likely to face in their new lives. Then discuss what misunderstandings might arise between a young American and his or her immigrant parents. As you read the story, compare your thoughts with those of the narrator.

Vocabulary

Knowing the following words will help you as you read "Two Kinds."

prodigy (präd′ ə jē) *n*.: A child of unusually high talent (p. 93)

reproach (ri prōch′) *n*.: Disgrace; blame (p. 94)

mesmerizing (mez′ mər īz′ iŋ) *adj*.: Hypnotizing (p. 95)

sauciness (sô′ sē nes) *n*.: Liveliness; spirit (p. 95)

reverie (rev′ ər ē) *n*.: Dreamy thinking or imagining (p. 97)

dawdled (dôd′ 'ld) *v*.: Wasted time by being slow (p. 98)

debut (dā byoo′) *n*.: First appearance in public (p. 98)

fiasco (fē as′ kō) *n*.: A complete failure (p. 99)

Amy Tan

(1952–) was born in Oakland, California, two and a half years after her parents moved to the United States from China. Her parents expected her to become a doctor full-time and a concert pianist in her spare time. Instead, Tan became a writer. "Two Kinds," an episode from the novel *The Joy Luck Club,* expresses a similar conflict between the hopes and expectations of Chinese-immigrant parents and the desire of their Americanized child to make her own choices.

Two Kinds
from *The Joy Luck Club*
Amy Tan

My mother believed you could be anything you wanted to be in America. You could open a restaurant. You could work for the government and get good retirement. You could buy a house with almost no money down. You could become rich. You could become instantly famous.

"Of course you can be prodigy, too," my mother told me when I was nine. "You can be best anything. What does Auntie Lindo know? Her daughter, she is only best tricky."

America was where all my mother's hopes lay. She had come here in 1949 after losing everything in China: her mother and father, her family home, her first husband, and two daughters, twin baby girls. But she never looked back with regret. There were so many ways for things to get better.

We didn't immediately pick the right kind of prodigy. At first my mother thought I could be a Chinese Shirley Temple.[1] We'd watch Shirley's old movies on TV as though they were training films. My mother would poke my arm and say, "*Ni kan*"[2]—You watch. And I would see Shirley tapping her feet, or singing a sailor song, or pursing her lips into a very round O while saying, "Oh my goodness."

"*Ni kan*," said my mother as Shirley's eyes flooded with tears. "You already know how. Don't need talent for crying!"

Soon after my mother got this idea about Shirley Temple, she took me to a beauty training school in the Mission district[3] and put me in the hands of a student who could barely hold the scissors without shaking. Instead of getting big fat curls, I emerged with an uneven mass of crinkly black fuzz. My mother dragged me off to the bathroom and tried to wet down my hair.

"You look like Negro Chinese," she lamented, as if I had done this on purpose.

The instructor of the beauty training school had to lop off these soggy clumps to make my hair even again. "Peter Pan[4] is very popular these days," the instructor assured my mother. I now had hair the length of a boy's, with straight-across bangs that hung at a slant two inches above my eyebrows. I liked the haircut and it made me actually look forward to my future fame.

In fact, in the beginning, I was just as excited as my mother, maybe even more so. I

---

1. Shirley Temple: Shirley Temple was the most popular child movie star of the 1930's. She starred in her first picture at the age of three and achieved stardom in *Stand Up and Cheer* in 1934.
2. Ni (nē) **kan** (kän)

3. Mission district: A residential district in San Francisco, a city on the coast of California.
4. Peter Pan: The main character of J. M. Barrie's play of the same name, Peter Pan is a young boy who runs away to Never-Never Land to escape growing up. The success of the play led to the popularity of a short, boyish hairstyle for young girls.

pictured this prodigy part of me as many different images, trying each one on for size. I was a dainty ballerina girl standing by the curtains, waiting to hear the right music that would send me floating on my tiptoes. I was like the Christ child lifted out of the straw manger, crying with holy indignity. I was Cinderella[5] stepping from her pumpkin carriage with sparkly cartoon music filling the air.

In all of my imaginings, I was filled with a sense that I would soon become *perfect*. My mother and father would adore me. I would be beyond reproach. I would never feel the need to sulk for anything.

But sometimes the prodigy in me became impatient. "If you don't hurry up and get me out of here, I'm disappearing for good," it warned. "And then you'll always be nothing."

Every night after dinner, my mother and I would sit at the Formica[6] kitchen table. She would present new tests, taking her examples from stories of amazing children she had read in *Ripley's Believe It or Not*, or *Good Housekeeping, Reader's Digest*, and a dozen other magazines she kept in a pile in our bathroom. My mother got these magazines from people whose houses she cleaned. And since she cleaned many houses each week, we had a great assortment. She would look through them all, searching for stories about remarkable children.

The first night she brought out a story about a three-year-old boy who knew the capitals of all the states and even most of the European countries. A teacher was quoted as saying the little boy could also pronounce the names of the foreign cities correctly.

"What's the capital of Finland?" my mother asked me, looking at the magazine story.

All I knew was the capital of California, because Sacramento was the name of the street we lived on in Chinatown. "Nairobi!"[7] I guessed, saying the most foreign word I could think of. She checked to see if that was possibly one way to pronounce "Helsinki"[8] before showing me the answer.

The tests got harder—multiplying numbers in my head, finding the queen of hearts in a deck of cards, trying to stand on my head without using my hands, predicting the daily temperatures in Los Angeles, New York, and London.

One night I had to look at a page from the Bible for three minutes and then report everything I could remember. "Now Jehoshaphat had riches and honor in abundance and . . . that's all I remember, Ma," I said.

And after seeing my mother's disappointed face once again, something inside of me began to die. I hated the tests, the raised hopes and failed expectations. Before going to bed that night, I looked in the mirror above the bathroom sink and when I saw only my face staring back—and that it would always be this ordinary face—I began to cry. Such a sad, ugly girl! I made high-pitched noises like a crazed animal, trying to scratch out the face in the mirror.

And then I saw what seemed to be the prodigy side of me—because I had never seen that face before. I looked at my reflection, blinking so I could see more clearly. The girl staring back at me was angry,

---

5. Cinderella: The main character in a fairy tale about a young girl who has been mistreated by her stepmother. Her fairy godmother appears and magically changes her dress into a beautiful gown. A pumpkin is changed into a carriage, allowing her to go to the prince's ball.

6. Formica (fôr mī′ kə): Tradename for heat-resistant plastic used for table and counter tops.

7. Nairobi (nī rō′ bē): The capital of Kenya, a country in eastern Africa.

8. Helsinki (hel′ siŋ kē)

powerful. This girl and I were the same. I had new thoughts, willful thoughts, or rather thoughts filled with lots of won'ts. I won't let her change me, I promised myself. I won't be what I'm not.

So now on nights when my mother presented her tests, I performed listlessly, my head propped on one arm. I pretended to be bored. And I was. I got so bored I started counting the bellows of the foghorns out on the bay while my mother drilled me in other areas. The sound was comforting and reminded me of the cow jumping over the moon. And the next day, I played a game with myself, seeing if my mother would give up on me before eight bellows. After a while I usually counted only one, maybe two bellows at most. At last she was beginning to give up hope.

Two or three months had gone by without any mention of my being a prodigy again. And then one day my mother was watching *The Ed Sullivan Show*[9] on TV. The TV was old and the sound kept shorting out. Every time my mother got halfway up from the sofa to adjust the set, the sound would go back on and Ed would be talking. As soon as she sat down, Ed would go silent again. She got up, the TV broke into loud piano music. She sat down. Silence. Up and down, back and forth, quiet and loud. It was like a stiff embraceless dance between her and the TV set. Finally she stood by the set with her hand on the sound dial.

She seemed entranced by the music, a little frenzied piano piece with this mesmerizing quality, sort of quick passages and then teasing lilting ones before it returned to the quick playful parts.

"*Ni kan*," my mother said, calling me

over with hurried hand gestures, "Look here."

I could see why my mother was fascinated by the music. It was being pounded out by a little Chinese girl, about nine years old, with a Peter Pan haircut. The girl had the sauciness of a Shirley Temple. She was proudly modest like a proper Chinese child. And she also did this fancy sweep of a curtsy, so that the fluffy skirt of her white dress cascaded slowly to the floor like the petals of a large carnation.

In spite of these warning signs, I wasn't worried. Our family had no piano and we couldn't afford to buy one, let alone reams of sheet music and piano lessons. So I could be generous in my comments when my mother bad-mouthed the little girl on TV.

"Play note right, but doesn't sound good! No singing sound," complained my mother.

"What are you picking on her for?" I said carelessly. "She's pretty good. Maybe she's not the best, but she's trying hard." I knew almost immediately I would be sorry I said that.

"Just like you," she said. "Not the best. Because you not trying." She gave a little huff as she let go of the sound dial and sat down on the sofa.

The little Chinese girl sat down also to play an encore of "Anitra's Dance" by Grieg.[10] I remember the song, because later on I had to learn how to play it.

Three days after watching *The Ed Sullivan Show*, my mother told me what my schedule would be for piano lessons and piano practice. She had talked to Mr. Chong, who lived on the first floor of our apartment

9. *The Ed Sullivan Show*: A popular variety show hosted by Ed Sullivan that ran from 1955 to 1971.

10. Grieg (grēg): Edvard Grieg (1843–1907) was a Norwegian composer. He became known as "the Voice of Norway" because he used material from his native country—folk tales and native poetry—for composing his music.

building. Mr. Chong was a retired piano teacher and my mother had traded house-cleaning services for weekly lessons and a piano for me to practice on every day, two hours a day, from four until six.

When my mother told me this, I felt as though I had been sent to hell. I whined and then kicked my foot a little when I couldn't stand it anymore.

"Why don't you like me the way I am? I'm *not* a genius! I can't play the piano. And even if I could, I wouldn't go on TV if you paid me a million dollars!" I cried.

ATELIER
Byron Birdsall
Artique, Ltd.

My mother slapped me. "Who ask you be genius?" she shouted. "Only ask you be your best. For you sake. You think I want you be genius? Hnnh! What for! Who ask you!"

"So ungrateful," I heard her mutter in Chinese. "If she had as much talent as she has temper, she would be famous now."

Mr. Chong, whom I secretly nicknamed Old Chong, was very strange, always tapping his fingers to the silent music of an invisible orchestra. He looked ancient in my eyes. He had lost most of the hair on top of his head and he wore thick glasses and had eyes that always looked tired and sleepy. But he must have been younger than I thought, since he lived with his mother and was not yet married.

I met Old Lady Chong once and that was enough. She had this peculiar smell like a baby that had done something in its pants. And her fingers felt like a dead person's, like an old peach I once found in the back of the refrigerator; the skin just slid off the meat when I picked it up.

I soon found out why Old Chong had retired from teaching piano. He was deaf. "Like Beethoven!"[11] he shouted to me. "We're both listening only in our head!" And he would start to conduct his frantic silent sonatas.[12]

Our lessons went like this. He would open the book and point to different things, explaining their purpose: "Key! Treble! Bass! No sharps or flats! So this is C major![13] Listen now and play after me!"

---

11. Beethoven (bā′ tō vən): Ludvig van Beethoven (1770–1827) is considered to be one of the greatest composers ever. Like Old Chong, Beethoven became deaf. His illness began in 1801 and became worse until he was completely deaf by 1817. Despite this handicap, Beethoven continued to compose and created some of his best pieces during this time.
12. sonatas (sə nät′ əz) n.: Musical compositions for one or two instruments.
13. Key! Treble! . . . C major!: Musical terms used in composing and reading music.

And then he would play the C scale a few times, a simple chord, and then, as if inspired by an old, unreachable itch, he gradually added more notes and running trills and a pounding bass until the music was really something quite grand.

I would play after him, the simple scale, the simple chord, and then I just played some nonsense that sounded like a cat running up and down on top of garbage cans. Old Chong smiled and applauded and then said, "Very good! But now you must learn to keep time!"

So that's how I discovered that Old Chong's eyes were too slow to keep up with the wrong notes I was playing. He went through the motions in half-time. To help me keep rhythm, he stood behind me, pushing down on my right shoulder for every beat. He balanced pennies on top of my wrists so I would keep them still as I slowly played scales and arpeggios.[14] He had me curve my hand around an apple and keep that shape when playing chords. He marched stiffly to show me how to make each finger dance up and down, staccato[15] like an obedient little soldier.

He taught me all these things, and that was how I also learned I could be lazy and get away with mistakes, lots of mistakes. If I hit the wrong notes because I hadn't practiced enough, I never corrected myself. I just kept playing in rhythm. And Old Chong kept conducting his own private reverie.

So maybe I never really gave myself a fair chance. I did pick up the basics pretty quickly, and I might have become a good pianist at that young age. But I was so determined not to try, not to be anybody different

that I learned to play only the most ear-splitting preludes, the most discordant hymns.

Over the next year, I practiced like this, dutifully in my own way. And then one day I heard my mother and her friend Lindo Jong both talking in a loud bragging tone of voice so others could hear. It was after church, and I was leaning against the brick wall wearing a dress with stiff white petticoats.[16] Auntie Lindo's daughter, Waverly, who was about my age, was standing farther down the wall about five feet away. We had grown up together and shared all the closeness of two sisters squabbling over crayons and dolls. In other words, for the most part, we hated each other. I thought she was snotty. Waverly Jong had gained a certain amount of fame as "Chinatown's Littlest Chinese Chess Champion."

"She bring home too many trophy," lamented Auntie Lindo that Sunday. "All day she play chess. All day I have no time do nothing but dust off her winnings." She threw a scolding look at Waverly, who pretended not to see her.

"You lucky you don't have this problem," said Auntie Lindo with a sigh to my mother.

And my mother squared her shoulders and bragged: "Our problem worser than yours. If we ask Jing-mei wash dish, she hear nothing but music. It's like you can't stop this natural talent."

And right then, I was determined to put a stop to her foolish pride.

A few weeks later, Old Chong and my mother conspired to have me play in a talent show which would be held in the church hall. By then, my parents had saved up enough to buy me a secondhand piano, a black Wurlitzer spinet[17] with a scarred

---

14. arpeggios (är pej′ ōz) *n.*: The notes in a chord played in quick succession instead of at the same time.

15. staccato (stə kät′ ō) *adj.*: Played with distinct breaks between notes.

16. petticoats (pet′ ē kōts′) *n.*: Lace′ or ruffles at the hemline of a skirt.

17. spinet (spin′ it) *n.*: A small, upright piano.

bench. It was the showpiece of our living room.

For the talent show, I was to play a piece called "Pleading Child" from Schumann's[18] *Scenes from Childhood*. It was a simple, moody piece that sounded more difficult than it was. I was supposed to memorize the whole thing, playing the repeat parts twice to make the piece sound longer. But I dawdled over it, playing a few bars and then cheating, looking up to see what notes followed. I never really listened to what I was playing. I daydreamed about being somewhere else, about being someone else.

The part I liked to practice best was the fancy curtsy: right foot out, touch the rose on the carpet with a pointed foot, sweep to the side, left leg bends, look up and smile.

My parents invited all the couples from the Joy Luck Club[19] to witness my debut. Auntie Lindo and Uncle Tin were there. Waverly and her two older brothers had also come. The first two rows were filled with children both younger and older than I was. The littlest ones got to go first. They recited simple nursery rhymes, squawked out tunes on miniature violins, twirled Hula Hoops,[20] pranced in pink ballet tutus,[21] and when they bowed or curtsied, the audience would sigh in unison, "Awww," and then clap enthusiastically.

When my turn came, I was very confident. I remember my childish excitement. It was as if I knew, without a doubt, that the prodigy side of me really did exist. I had no fear whatsoever, no nervousness. I remember thinking to myself, This is it! This is it! I looked out over the audience, at my mother's blank face, my father's yawn, Auntie Lindo's stiff-lipped smile, Waverly's sulky expression. I had on a white dress layered with sheets of lace, and a pink bow in my Peter Pan haircut. As I sat down I envisioned people jumping to their feet and Ed Sullivan rushing up to introduce me to everyone on TV.

And I started to play. It was so beautiful. I was so caught up in how lovely I looked that at first I didn't worry how I would sound. So it was a surprise to me when I hit the first wrong note and I realized something didn't sound quite right. And then I hit another and another followed that. A chill started at the top of my head and began to trickle down. Yet I couldn't stop playing, as though my hands were bewitched. I kept thinking my fingers would adjust themselves back, like a train switching to the right track. I played this strange jumble through two repeats, the sour notes staying with me all the way to the end.

When I stood up, I discovered my legs were shaking. Maybe I had just been nervous and the audience, like Old Chong, had seen me go through the right motions and had not heard anything wrong at all. I swept my right foot out, went down on my knee, looked up and smiled. The room was quiet, except for Old Chong, who was beaming and shouting, "Bravo! Bravo! Well done!" But then I saw my mother's face, her stricken face. The audience clapped weakly, and as I walked back to my chair, with my whole face quivering as I tried not to cry, I heard a little boy whisper loudly to his mother, "That was awful," and the mother whispered back, "Well, she certainly tried."

And now I realized how many people were in the audience, the whole world it

18. Schumann (shoo′ män): Robert Alexander Schumann (1810–1856) was a German composer and music critic and a leader of classical music's Romantic Movement.

19. Joy Luck Club: Four Chinese women who have been meeting for years to socialize, play games, and tell stories from the past.

20. Hula (hoo′ lə) **Hoops:** Light hoops twirled around the body by rotating the hips.

21. tutus (too′ tooz′) *n.*: Very short skirts worn by ballerinas.

seemed. I was aware of eyes burning into my back. I felt the shame of my mother and father as they sat stiffly throughout the rest of the show.

We could have escaped during intermission. Pride and some strange sense of honor must have anchored my parents to their chairs. And so we watched it all: the eighteen-year-old boy with a fake mustache who did a magic show and juggled flaming hoops while riding a unicycle. The breasted girl with white makeup who sang from *Madama Butterfly* and got honorable mention. And the eleven-year-old boy who won first prize playing a tricky violin song that sounded like a busy bee.

After the show, the Hsus, the Jongs, and the St. Clairs from the Joy Luck Club came up to my mother and father.

"Lots of talented kids," Auntie Lindo said vaguely, smiling broadly.

"That was somethin' else," said my father, and I wondered if he was referring to me in a humorous way, or whether he even remembered what I had done.

Waverly looked at me and shrugged her shoulders. "You aren't a genius like me," she said matter-of-factly. And if I hadn't felt so bad, I would have pulled her braids and punched her stomach.

But my mother's expression was what devastated me: a quiet, blank look that said she had lost everything. I felt the same way, and it seemed as if everybody were now coming up, like gawkers at the scene of an accident, to see what parts were actually missing. When we got on the bus to go home, my father was humming the busy-bee tune and my mother was silent. I kept thinking she wanted to wait until we got home before shouting at me. But when my father unlocked the door to our apartment, my mother walked in and then went to the back, into the bedroom. No accusations. No blame.

Amy Tan as a child playing the piano

And in a way, I felt disappointed. I had been waiting for her to start shouting, so I could shout back and cry and blame her for all my misery.

I assumed my talent-show fiasco meant I never had to play the piano again. But two days later, after school, my mother came out of the kitchen and saw me watching TV.

"Four clock," she reminded me as if it were any other day. I was stunned, as though she were asking me to go through the talent-show torture again. I wedged myself more tightly in front of the TV.

"Turn off TV," she called from the kitchen five minutes later.

I didn't budge. And then I decided. I didn't have to do what my mother said anymore. I wasn't her slave. This wasn't China. I had listened to her before and look what happened. She was the stupid one.

She came out from the kitchen and stood in the arched entryway of the living room. "Four clock," she said once again, louder.

"I'm not going to play anymore," I said nonchalantly. "Why should I? I'm not a genius."

She walked over and stood in front of the TV. I saw her chest was heaving up and down in an angry way.

"No!" I said, and I now felt stronger, as if my true self had finally emerged. So this was what had been inside me all along.

"No! I won't!" I screamed

She yanked me by the arm, pulled me off the floor, snapped off the TV. She was frighteningly strong, half pulling, half carrying me toward the piano as I kicked the throw rugs under my feet. She lifted me up and onto the hard bench. I was sobbing by now, looking at her bitterly. Her chest was heaving even more and her mouth was open, smiling crazily as if she were pleased I was crying.

"You want me to be someone that I'm not!" I sobbed. "I'll never be the kind of daughter you want me to be!"

"Only two kinds of daughters," she shouted in Chinese. "Those who are obedient and those who follow their own mind! Only one kind of daughter can live in this house. Obedient daughter!"

"Then I wish I wasn't your daughter. I wish you weren't my mother," I shouted. As I said these things I got scared. It felt like worms and toads and slimy things crawling out of my chest, but it also felt good, as if this awful side of me had surfaced, at last.

"Too late change this," said my mother shrilly.

And I could sense her anger rising to its breaking point. I wanted to see it spill over. And that's when I remembered the babies she had lost in China, the ones we never talked about. "Then I wish I'd never been born!" I shouted. "I wish I were dead! Like them."

It was as if I had said the magic words. Alakazam!—and her face went blank, her mouth closed, her arms went slack, and she backed out of the room, stunned, as if she were blowing away like a small brown leaf, thin, brittle, lifeless.

It was not the only disappointment my mother felt in me. In the years that followed, I failed her so many times, each time asserting my own will, my right to fall short of expectations. I didn't get straight A's. I didn't become class president. I didn't get into Stanford. I dropped out of college.

For unlike my mother, I did not believe I could be anything I wanted to be. I could only be me.

And for all those years, we never talked about the disaster at the recital or my terrible accusations afterward at the piano bench. All that remained unchecked, like a betrayal that was now unspeakable. So I never found a way to ask her why she had hoped for something so large that failure was inevitable.

And even worse, I never asked her what frightened me the most: Why had she given up hope?

For after our struggle at the piano, she never mentioned my playing again. The lessons stopped. The lid to the piano was closed, shutting out the dust, my misery, and her dreams.

So she surprised me. A few years ago, she offered to give me the piano, for my thirtieth birthday. I had not played in all those years. I saw the offer as a sign of forgiveness, a tremendous burden removed.

"Are you sure?" I asked shyly. "I mean, won't you and Dad miss it?"

"No, this your piano," she said firmly. "Always your piano. You only one can play."

"Well, I probably can't play anymore," I said. "It's been years."

"You pick up fast," said my mother, as if she knew this was certain. "You have natural talent. You could been genius if you want to."

"No I couldn't."

"You just not trying," said my mother. And she was neither angry nor sad. She said it as if to announce a fact that could never be disproved. "Take it," she said.

But I didn't at first. It was enough that she had offered it to me. And after that, every time I saw it in my parents' living room, standing in front of the bay windows, it made me feel proud, as if it were a shiny trophy I had won back.

Last week I sent a tuner over to my parents' apartment and had the piano reconditioned, for purely sentimental reasons. My mother had died a few months before and I had been getting things in order for my father, a little bit at a time. I put the jewelry in special silk pouches. The sweaters she had knitted in yellow, pink, bright orange—all the colors I hated—I put those in moth-proof boxes. I found some old Chinese silk dresses, the kind with little slits up the sides. I rubbed the old silk against my skin, then wrapped them in tissue and decided to take them home with me.

After I had the piano tuned, I opened the lid and touched the keys. It sounded even richer than I remembered. Really, it was a very good piano. Inside the bench were the same exercise notes with handwritten scales, the same secondhand music books with their covers held together with yellow tape.

I opened up the Schumann book to the dark little piece I had played at the recital. It was on the left-hand side of the page, "Pleading Child." It looked more difficult than I remembered. I played a few bars, surprised at how easily the notes came back to me.

And for the first time, or so it seemed, I noticed the piece on the right-hand side. It was called "Perfectly Contented." I tried to play this one as well. It had a lighter melody but the same flowing rhythm and turned out to be quite easy. "Pleading Child" was shorter but slower; "Perfectly Contented" was longer, but faster. And after I played them both a few times, I realized they were two halves of the same song.

RESPONDING TO THE SELECTION

Your Response

1. If you could have given the mother some advice, what would it have been?

Recalling

2. Name the ways the mother tries to make her daughter a prodigy.
3. Describe the narrator's experience at the talent show.
4. What happens when the mother tries to get the narrator to continue practicing the piano after the talent show?

Interpreting

5. The narrator's mother does not regret her losses in China because, in America, "There were so many ways for things to get better." How are her hopes for her daughter a reflection of this attitude?
6. Why does the narrator react as she does to her mother's efforts to change her?
7. The narrator recalls that what frightened her most about her mother was that she had "given up hope" after their last fight. Why does this frighten the narrator most?
8. Why does the narrator reclaim the piano years later?

9. Reread the last paragraph. How can "Perfectly Contented" and "Pleading Child" be two halves of the same song?

Applying

10. The narrator in the story says, "For unlike my mother, I did not believe I could be anything I wanted to be. I could only be me." Do you agree or disagree with her? Explain your answer. Is it possible to agree with both the mother and the daughter? Explain.

ANALYZING LITERATURE

Understanding Characterization

In "Two Kinds" Amy Tan uses both **direct** and **indirect characterization** to give flesh and blood to her characters—to bring them to life. For example, the narrator states directly, "My mother believed you could be anything you wanted to be in America." The author reveals this indirectly through her mother's actions and statements, such as when her mother says, "Of course you can be prodigy, too . . . You can be best anything."

Read the following direct statements made by the narrator. For each, find one example in the story that reveals the same trait indirectly.

1. "I had new thoughts, willful thoughts, or rather thoughts filled with lots of won'ts. I won't let her change me . . ."
2. "Mr. Chong, whom I secretly nicknamed Old Chong, was very strange . . ."

CRITICAL THINKING AND READING

Making Inferences About Character

An **inference** is a reasonable conclusion that you draw from information given. When an author uses indirect characterization, you must make inferences based on a character's thoughts, words, and actions.

What can you infer about the narrator's mother from the following lines from "Two Kinds"?

1. ". . . my mother had traded housecleaning services for weekly lessons and a piano for me to practice on every day . . ."
2. "'Only two kinds of daughters,' . . . 'Those who are obedient and those who follow their own mind! Only one kind of daughter can live in this house. Obedient daughter!'"

THINKING AND WRITING

Writing About Characters

Often, people view the same situation differently. In this story, the narrator and her mother view the narrator's abilities differently. Make two columns on a sheet of paper. In one column write the narrator's view of her abilities and hopes. In the other column, write the mother's view of her daughter's abilities and her hopes for her daughter. Write a description of these two views, and explain how the hopes and desires of the narrator and the mother determine how each views the narrator's abilities. When you revise, be sure you have clearly presented the reasons for the different views.

LEARNING OPTION

Cross-curricular Connection. Ask your music teacher or librarian for information about some famous child prodigies. They may be composers like Mozart, who lived in the eighteenth century, or instrumentalists like Midori and Joshua Bell, who perform today. Your local library may have recordings of music composed or performed by these talented people. Write a brief essay responding to what you learned about what it's like to be a prodigy and to the recordings you heard.

Setting

EARLY SUMMER ON THE FARM
Karl Rodko
Three Lions

All Summer in a Day

Setting

Setting is the time and place of a short story's action. In some stories, setting is little more than background, but in others it is of central importance. In "All Summer in a Day," for example, everything that happens depends on the setting: Venus, at a time when interplanetary travel is possible.

Focus

One of the "characters" in "All Summer in a Day" is a large, hot sphere. A straight line through its center would be almost 865,000 miles long, and its temperature averages about 15 million degrees Centigrade! The sphere, of course, is the sun.

The sun is more than a collection of scientific facts. Its influence often affects us personally. Have you ever noticed that your mood is better on sunny days or that the days in winter seem all too short? The characters in the story you are about to read live in a place where the sun hasn't shone for seven years! Write down some of your thoughts about what it would be like to go without seeing the sun for so long. How would you feel? What could be done to make up for the lack of sunshine?

Vocabulary

Knowing the following words will help you as you read "All Summer in a Day."

concussion (kən kush′ ən) *n.:* Violent shaking (p. 105)

slackening (slak′ 'n iŋ) *v.:* Becoming less active (p. 105)

surged (surj′d) *v.:* Moved in a violent swelling motion (p. 107)

immense (i mens′) *adj.:* Vast (p. 107)

tumultuously (too mul′ choo wəs lē) *adv.:* Noisily and violently (p. 108)

resilient (ri zil′ yənt) *adj.:* Springing back into shape (p. 108)

savored (sā′ vərd) *v.:* Enjoyed (p. 108)

Ray Bradbury

(1920–   ) was born in Waukegan, Illinois. As a boy, he was fascinated with magicians, circuses, and the stories of Edgar Allan Poe. These early interests influenced Bradbury's development as one of our best writers of fantasy and science fiction. His many honors and awards include membership in the National Institute of Arts and Letters. In "All Summer in a Day," you will enter Bradbury's world of gripping fantasy—a strange yet oddly believable world.

All Summer in a Day

Ray Bradbury

"Ready?"

"Ready."

"Now?"

"Soon."

"Do the scientists really know? Will it happen today, will it?"

"Look, look; see for yourself!"

The children pressed to each other like so many roses, so many weeds, intermixed, peering out for a look at the hidden sun.

It rained.

It had been raining for seven years; thousands upon thousands of days compounded and filled from one end to the other with rain, with the drum and gush of water, with the sweet crystal fall of showers and the concussion of storms so heavy they were tidal waves come over the islands. A thousand forests had been crushed under the rain and grown up a thousand times to be crushed again. And this was the way life was forever on the planet Venus and this was the schoolroom of the children of the rocket men and women who had come to a raining world to set up civilization and live out their lives.

"It's stopping, it's stopping!"

"Yes, yes!"

Margot stood apart from them, from these children who could never remember a time when there wasn't rain and rain and rain. They were all nine years old, and if there had been a day, seven years ago, when the sun came out for an hour and showed its face to the stunned world, they could not recall. Sometimes, at night, she heard them stir, in remembrance, and she knew they were dreaming and remembering gold or a yellow crayon or a coin large enough to buy the world with. She knew they thought they remembered a warmness, like a blushing in the face, in the body, in the arms and legs and trembling hands. But then they always awoke to the tatting drum, the endless shaking down of clear bead necklaces upon the roof, the walk, the gardens, the forests, and their dreams were gone.

All day yesterday they had read in class about the sun. About how like a lemon it was, and how hot. And they had written small stories or essays or poems about it:

> *I think the sun is a flower,*
> *That blooms for just one hour.*

That was Margot's poem, read in a quiet voice in the still classroom while the rain was falling outside.

"Aw, you didn't write that!" protested one of the boys.

"I did," said Margot. "I *did*."

"William!" said the teacher.

But that was yesterday. Now the rain was slackening, and the children were crushed in the great thick windows.

"Where's teacher?"

"She'll be back."

"She'd better hurry, we'll miss it!"

They turned on themselves, like a feverish wheel, all fumbling spokes.

Margot stood alone. She was a very frail girl who looked as if she had been lost in the rain for years and the rain had washed out

SUNRISE IV
Arthur Dove
Hirshhorn Museum and Sculpture Garden

the blue from her eyes and the red from her mouth and the yellow from her hair. She was an old photograph dusted from an album, whitened away, and if she spoke at all her voice would be a ghost. Now she stood, separate, staring at the rain and the loud wet world beyond the huge glass.

"What're *you* looking at?" said William.

Margot said nothing.

"Speak when you're spoken to." He gave her a shove. But she did not move; rather she let herself be moved only by him and nothing else.

They edged away from her, they would not look at her. She felt them go away. And this was because she would play no games with them in the echoing tunnels of the underground city. If they tagged her and ran, she stood blinking after them and did not follow. When the class sang songs about happiness and life and games

her lips barely moved. Only when they sang about the sun and the summer did her lips move as she watched the drenched windows.

And then, of course, the biggest crime of all was that she had come here only five years ago from Earth, and she remembered the sun and the way the sun was and the sky was when she was four in Ohio. And they, they had been on Venus all their lives, and they had been only two years old when last the sun came out and had long since forgotten the color and heat of it and the way it really was. But Margot remembered.

"It's like a penny," she said once, eyes closed.

"No, it's not!" the children cried.

"It's like a fire," she said, "in the stove."

"You're lying, you don't remember!" cried the children.

But she remembered and stood quietly

apart from all of them and watched the patterning windows. And once, a month ago, she had refused to shower in the school shower rooms, had clutched her hands to her ears and over her head, screaming the water mustn't touch her head. So after that, dimly, dimly, she sensed it, she was different and they knew her difference and kept away.

There was talk that her father and mother were taking her back to Earth next year; it seemed vital to her that they do so, though it would mean the loss of thousands of dollars to her family. And so, the children hated her for all these reasons of big and little consequence. They hated her pale snow face, her waiting silence, her thinness, and her possible future.

"Get away!" The boy gave her another push. "What're you waiting for?"

Then, for the first time, she turned and looked at him. And what she was waiting for was in her eyes.

"Well, don't wait around here!" cried the boy savagely. "You won't see nothing!"

Her lips moved.

"Nothing!" he cried. "It was all a joke, wasn't it?" He turned to the other children. "Nothing's happening today. *Is* it?"

They all blinked at him and then, understanding, laughed and shook their heads. "Nothing, nothing!"

"Oh, but," Margot whispered, her eyes helpless. "But this is the day, the scientists predict, they say, they *know*, the sun . . ."

"All a joke!" said the boy, and seized her roughly. "Hey, everyone, let's put her in a closet before teacher comes!"

"No," said Margot, falling back.

They surged about her, caught her up and bore her, protesting, and then pleading, and then crying, back into a tunnel, a room, a closet, where they slammed and locked the door. They stood looking at the door and saw it tremble from her beating and throwing herself against it. They heard her muffled cries. Then, smiling, they turned and went out and back down the tunnel, just as the teacher arrived.

"Ready, children?" She glanced at her watch.

"Yes!" said everyone.

"Are we all here?"

"Yes!"

The rain slackened still more.

They crowded to the huge door.

The rain stopped.

It was as if, in the midst of a film concerning an avalanche, a tornado, a hurricane, a volcanic eruption, something had, first, gone wrong with the sound apparatus, thus muffling and finally cutting off all noise, all of the blasts and repercussions and thunders, and then, second, ripped the film from the projector and inserted in its place a peaceful tropical slide which did not move or tremor. The world ground to a standstill. The silence was so immense and unbelievable that you felt your ears had been stuffed or you had lost your hearing altogether. The children put their hands to their ears. They stood apart. The door slid back and the smell of the silent, waiting world came in to them.

The sun came out.

It was the color of flaming bronze and it was very large. And the sky around it was a blazing blue tile color. And the jungle burned with sunlight as the children, released from their spell, rushed out, yelling, into the springtime.

"Now, don't go too far," called the teacher after them. "You've only two hours, you know. You wouldn't want to get caught out!"

But they were running and turning their faces up to the sky and feeling the sun on their cheeks like a warm iron; they were taking off their jackets and letting the sun burn their arms.

"Oh, it's better than the sun lamps, isn't it?"

"Much, much better!"

They stopped running and stood in the great jungle that covered Venus, that grew and never stopped growing, tumultuously, even as you watched it. It was a nest of octopi, clustering up great arms of fleshlike weed, wavering, flowering in this brief spring. It was the color of rubber and ash, this jungle, from the many years without sun. It was the color of stones and white cheeses and ink, and it was the color of the moon.

The children lay out, laughing, on the jungle mattress, and heard it sigh and squeak under them, resilient and alive. They ran among the trees, they slipped and fell, they pushed each other, they played hide-and-seek and tag, but most of all they squinted at the sun until tears ran down their faces, they put their hands up to that yellowness and that amazing blueness and they breathed of the fresh, fresh air and listened and listened to the silence which suspended them in a blessed sea of no sound and no motion. They looked at everything and savored everything. Then, wildly, like animals escaped from their caves, they ran and ran in shouting circles. They ran for an hour and did not stop running.

And then—

In the midst of their running one of the girls wailed.

Everyone stopped.

The girl, standing in the open, held out her hand.

"Oh, look, look," she said, trembling.

They came slowly to look at her opened palm.

In the center of it, cupped and huge, was a single raindrop.

She began to cry, looking at it.

They glanced quietly at the sky.

"Oh, Oh."

A few cold drops fell on their noses and their cheeks and their mouths. The sun faded behind a stir of mist. A wind blew cool around them. They turned and started to walk back toward the underground house, their hands at their sides, their smiles vanishing away.

A boom of thunder startled them and like leaves before a new hurricane, they tumbled upon each other and ran. Lightning struck ten miles away, five miles away, a mile, a half mile. The sky darkened into midnight in a flash.

They stood in the doorway of the underground for a moment until it was raining hard. Then they closed the door and heard the gigantic sound of the rain falling in tons and avalanches, everywhere and forever.

"Will it be seven more years?"

"Yes. Seven."

Then one of them gave a little cry.

"Margot!"

"What?"

"She's still in the closet where we locked her."

"Margot."

They stood as if someone had driven them, like so many stakes, into the floor. They looked at each other and then looked away. They glanced out at the world that was raining now and raining and raining steadily. They could not meet each other's glances. Their faces were solemn and pale. They looked at their hands and feet, their faces down.

"Margot."

One of the girls said, "Well . . .?"

No one moved.

"Go on," whispered the girl.

They walked slowly down the hall in the sound of cold rain. They turned through the doorway to the room in the sound of the storm and thunder, lightning on their faces, blue and terrible. They walked over to the closet door slowly and stood by it.

Behind the closet door was only silence.

They unlocked the door, even more slowly, and let Margot out.

RESPONDING TO THE SELECTION

Your Response

1. How do you think Margot's classmates will feel about her from now on?

Recalling

2. In what way is Margot's experience of the sun different from the experience of all the other children on Venus?
3. How does this difference affect the way Margot gets along with her classmates?
4. What do the children do to Margot just before the rain stops?
5. What happens to Margot at the very end?

Interpreting

6. What point is made about Margot when the story says that the rain had washed the blue from her eyes and the red from her mouth and the yellow from her hair?
7. How do the children feel when they remember what they have done to Margot?
8. Having read the story, what do you think the title, "All Summer in a Day," means?

Applying

9. What does this story suggest about the problems individuals face if their backgrounds or experiences make them different from others?

ANALYZING LITERATURE

Understanding Setting

The **setting** of a story is the time and place of the action. In "All Summer in a Day," Bradbury gives you many details that help you see what Venus is like. For example, in describing the constant rain he says that the children "always awoke to the tatting drum, the endless shaking down of clear bead necklaces upon the roof, the walk, the gardens, the forests. . . ."

1. Point out three other passages that give you a vivid impression of Venus.
2. What feature of the setting is most significant?

3. Find at least two details that suggest that the time of the action is the future.

CRITICAL THINKING AND READING

Understanding the Effect of Setting

"All Summer in a Day" is a story in which the setting greatly affects the plot. Since the events occur in a place where it nearly always rains, this setting affects the way the characters behave.

1. What details of the setting make the story possible?
2. How is Margot affected by life on Venus?
3. How do the other children feel about Venus?

THINKING AND WRITING

Writing About Setting

Imagine that you have just arrived on Ray Bradbury's imagined Venus. After spending a day or so looking around, you decide to write a letter to a friend on Earth telling what Venus is like. First list on paper those sights and other details you will focus on. Then write a letter that will give your friend a clear picture of where you are. When you revise your writing, ask, "Will my friend see what I am trying to convey? Is every sentence clear and specific?"

LEARNING OPTIONS

1. **Cross-curricular Connection.** Reread the descriptions of Venus in the story. Are they accurate and realistic? Use science textbooks, encyclopedias, and books on the planets to find out about Venus. What is it made of? What is the average temperature on the surface? Do any forms of life exist there?
2. **Writing.** In the story Margot writes a poem about the sun. What in nature do you feel strongly about: rainy days, the wind in the trees, clouds, or stars? Write a poem in which you express your feelings. It may be any length and may or may not rhyme.

GUIDE FOR READING

Song of the Trees

Setting and Conflict

Setting is the time and place of a story's action. A **conflict** is a struggle between opposing sides or forces. A story's setting can directly affect the conflict. As you read "Song of the Trees," think about how the setting, rural Mississippi during the 1930's, affects the conflict between the Logans and the lumbermen.

Focus

During the 1930's the United States and many nations around the world experienced a severe economic depression. During the Great Depression, banks failed, companies went out of business, and many people lost their jobs and their homes. You may have seen photographs taken during those years that show people waiting in long lines for food. "Song of the Trees" is set during that time.

Some people suffered doubly hard during the Depression, enduring acts of discrimination as well as economic hardship. The African American family in this story must take a stand in order to preserve both their property and their dignity. Have you ever had to stand up for yourself, in circumstances that seemed threatening? What did you do? Write a brief account of your experience, describing the feelings you had. As you read the story, notice how Cassie and her brothers take a stand in a difficult situation.

Vocabulary

Knowing the following words will help you as you read "Song of the Trees."

blissfully (blis′ fəl ē) *adv.*: Very happily (page 112)

finicky (fin′ i kē) *adj.*: Particular or fussy (page 112)

hovered (huv′ ərd) *v.*: Hung in the air (page 114)

menacing (men′ is iŋ) *adj.*: Threatening (page 117)

venomously (ve′ nəm əs lē) *adv.*: Full of ill will (page 117)

billowed (bil′ ōd) *v.*: Swelled like a wave (page 117)

elude (ē lood′) *v.*: To escape or keep away from (page 121)

cunningly (kun′ iŋ lē) *adv.*: In a tricky or sly way (page 123)

incredulously (in krej′ oo ləs lē) *adv.*: In a disbelieving way (page 124)

Mildred D. Taylor

(1943–   ) was born in Jackson, Mississippi, and grew up in Toledo, Ohio. In 1975 she published her first book, *Song of the Trees,* which won a Council on Interracial Books Award as well as a New York Times Outstanding Book of the Year award. The book is based on actual events that happened to her father when he was a young boy growing up in Mississippi. Taylor's 1977 book, *Roll of Thunder, Hear My Cry,* won the Newbery Award.

Song of the Trees

Mildred D. Taylor

"Cassie. Cassie, child, wake up now," Big Ma called gently as the new sun peeked over the horizon.

I looked sleepily at my grandmother and closed my eyes again.

"Cassie! Get up, girl!" This time the voice was not so gentle.

I jumped out of the deep feathery bed as Big Ma climbed from the other side. The room was still dark, and I stubbed my toe while stumbling sleepily about looking for my clothes.

"Shoot! Darn ole chair," I fussed, rubbing my injured foot.

"Hush, Cassie, and open them curtains if you can't see," Big Ma said. "Prop that window open, too, and let some of that fresh morning air in here."

I opened the window and looked outside. The earth was draped in a cloak of gray mist as the sun chased the night away. The cotton stalks, which in another hour would glisten greenly toward the sun, were gray. The ripening corn, wrapped in jackets of emerald and gold, was gray. Even the rich brown Mississippi earth was gray.

Only the trees of the forest were not gray. They stood dark, almost black, across the dusty road, still holding the night. A soft breeze stirred, and their voices whispered down to me in a song of morning greeting.

"Cassie, girl, I said open that window, not stand there gazing out all morning. Now, get moving before I take something to you," Big Ma threatened.

I dashed to my clothes. Before Big Ma had unwoven her long braid of gray hair, my pants and shirt were on and I was hurrying into the kitchen.

A small kerosene lamp was burning in a corner as I entered. Its light reflected on seven-year-old Christopher-John, short, pudgy, and a year younger than me, sitting sleepily upon a side bench drinking a large glass of clabber milk.[1] Mama's back was to me. She was dipping flour from a near-empty canister, while my older brother, Stacey, built a fire in the huge iron-bellied stove.

"I don't know what I'm going to do with you, Christopher-John," Mama scolded. "Getting up in the middle of the night and eating all that cornbread. Didn't you have enough to eat before you went to bed?"

"Yes'm," Christopher-John murmured.

"Lord knows I don't want any of my babies going hungry, but times are hard, honey. Don't you know folks all around here in Mississippi are struggling? Children crying 'cause they got no food to eat, and their daddies crying 'cause they can't get jobs so they can feed their babies? And you getting up in the middle of the night, stuffing yourself with cornbread!"

Her voice softened as she looked at the

---

1. clabber milk: Thickly curdled sour milk.

sleepy little boy. "Baby, we're in a depression.[2] Why do you think Papa's way down in Louisiana laying tracks on the railroad? So his children can eat—but only when they're hungry. You understand?"

"Yes'm," Christopher-John murmured again as his eyes slid blissfully shut.

"Morning, Mama," I chimed.

"Morning, baby," Mama said. "You wash up yet?"

"No'm."

"Then go wash up and call Little Man again. Tell him he's not dressing to meet President Roosevelt this morning. Hurry up now 'cause I want you to set the table."

Little Man, a very small six-year-old and a most finicky dresser, was brushing his hair when I entered the room he shared with Stacey and Christopher-John. His blue pants were faded, but except for a small grass stain on one knee, they were clean. Outside of his Sunday pants, these were the only pants he had, and he was always careful to keep them in the best condition possible. But one look at him and I knew that he was far from pleased with their condition this morning. He frowned down at the spot for a moment, then continued brushing.

"Man, hurry up and get dressed," I called. "Mama said you ain't dressing to meet the president."

"See there," he said, pointing at the stain. "You did that."

"I did no such thing. You fell all by yourself."

"You tripped me!"

"Didn't!"

"Did, too!"

"Hey, cut it out, you two!" ordered Stacey, entering the room. "You fought over that stupid stain yesterday. Now get moving, both of

you. We gotta go pick blackberries before the sun gets too high. Little Man, you go gather the eggs while Christopher-John and me milk the cows."

Little Man and I decided to settle our dispute later when Stacey wasn't around. With Papa away, eleven-year-old Stacey thought of himself as the man of the house, and Mama had instructed Little Man, Christopher-John, and me to mind him. So, like it or not, we humored him. Besides, he was bigger than we were.

I ran to the back porch to wash. When I returned to the kitchen, Mama was talking to Big Ma.

"We got about enough flour for two more meals," Mama said, cutting the biscuit dough. "Our salt and sugar are practically down to nothing and ———" She stopped when she saw me. "Cassie, baby, go gather the eggs for Mama."

"Little Man's gathering the eggs."

"Then go help him."

"But I ain't set the table yet."

"Set it when you come back."

I knew that I was not wanted in the kitchen. I looked suspiciously at my mother and grandmother, then went to the back porch to get a basket.

Big Ma's voice drifted through the open window. "Mary, you oughta write David and tell him somebody done opened his letter and stole that ten dollars he sent," she said.

"No, Mama. David's got enough on his mind. Besides, there's enough garden foods so we won't go hungry."

"But what 'bout your medicine? You're all out of it and the doctor told you good to ———"

"Shhhh!" Mama stared at the window. "Cassie, I thought I told you to go gather those eggs!"

"I had to get a basket, Mama!" I hurried off the porch and ran to the barn.

After breakfast when the sun was streak-

2. depression (dē presh′ ən) n.: A period of time in the 1930's when it was difficult for people to earn a living.

BEFORE DAWN, 1985
Romare Bearden
Public Library of Charlotte and Mecklenburg County

ing red across the sky, my brothers and I ambled into the coolness of the forest leading our three cows and their calves down the narrow cow path to the pond. The morning was already muggy, but the trees closed out the heat as their leaves waved restlessly, high above our heads.

"Good morning, Mr. Trees," I shouted. They answered me with a soft, swooshing sound. "Hear 'em, Stacey? Hear 'em singing?"

"Ah, cut that out, Cassie. Them trees ain't singing. How many times I gotta tell you that's just the wind?" He stopped at a sweet alligator gum, pulled out his knife and scraped off a glob of gum that had seeped through its cracked bark. He handed me half.

As I stuffed the gooey wad into my mouth, I patted the tree and whispered, "Thank you, Mr. Gum Tree."

Stacey frowned at me, then looked back at Christopher-John and Little Man walking far behind us, munching on their breakfast biscuits.

"Man! Christopher-John! Come on, now," he yelled. "If we finish the berry picking early, we can go wading before we go back."

Christopher-John and Little Man ran to catch up with us. Then, resuming their leisurely pace, they soon fell behind again.

A large gray squirrel scurried across our

path and up a walnut tree. I watched until it was settled amidst the tree's featherlike leaves; then, poking one of the calves, I said, "Stacey, is Mama sick?"

"Sick? Why you say that?"

" 'Cause I heard Big Ma asking her 'bout some medicine she's supposed to have."

Stacey stopped, a worried look on his face. "If she's sick, she ain't bad sick," he decided. "If she was bad sick, she'd been in bed."

We left the cows at the pond and, taking our berry baskets, delved deeper into the forest looking for the wild blackberry bushes.

"I see one!" I shouted.

"Where?" cried Christopher-John, eager for the sweet berries.

"Over there! Last one to it's a rotten egg!" I yelled, and off I ran.

Stacey and Little Man followed at my heels. But Christopher-John puffed far behind. "Hey, wait for me," he cried.

"Let's hide from Christopher-John," Stacey suggested.

The three of us ran in different directions. I plunged behind a giant old pine and hugged its warm trunk as I waited for Christopher-John.

Christopher-John puffed to a stop; then, looking all around, called, "Hey, Stacey! Cassie! Hey, Man! Y'all cut that out!"

I giggled and Christopher-John heard me.

"I see you Cassie!" he shouted, starting toward me as fast as his chubby legs would carry him. "You're it!"

"Not 'til you tag me," I laughed. As I waited for him to get closer, I glanced up into the boughs of my wintry-smelling hiding tree expecting a song of laughter. But the old pine only tapped me gently with one of its long, low branches. I turned from the tree and dashed away.

"You can't, you can't, you can't catch me,"

I taunted, dodging from one beloved tree to the next. Around shaggy-bark hickories and sharp-needled pines, past blue-gray beeches and sturdy black walnuts I sailed while my laughter resounded through the ancient forest, filling every chink. Overhead, the boughs of the giant trees hovered protectively, but they did not join in my laughter.

Deeper into the forest I plunged.

Christopher-John, unable to keep up, plopped on the ground in a pant. Little Man and Stacey, emerging from their hiding places, ran up to him.

"Ain't you caught her yet?" Little Man demanded, more than a little annoyed.

"He can't catch the champ," I boasted, stopping to rest against a hickory tree. I slid my back down the tree's shaggy trunk and looked up at its long branches, heavy with sweet nuts and slender green leaves, perfectly still. I looked around at the leaves of the other trees. They were still also. I stared at the trees, aware of an eerie silence descending over the forest.

Stacey walked toward me. "What's the matter with you, Cassie?" he asked.

"The trees, Stacey," I said softly, "they ain't singing no more."

"Is that all?" He looked up at the sky. "Come on, y'all. It's getting late. We'd better go pick them berries." He turned and walked on.

"But, Stacey, listen. Little Man, Christopher-John, listen."

The forest echoed an uneasy silence.

"The wind just stopped blowing, that's all," said Stacey. "Now stop fooling around and come on."

I jumped up to follow Stacey, then cried, "Stacey, look!" On a black oak a few yards away was a huge white X. "How did that get there?" I exclaimed, running to the tree.

"There's another one!" Little Man screamed.

"I see one too!" shouted Christopher-John.

Stacey said nothing as Christopher-John, Little Man and I ran wildly through the forest counting the ghostlike marks.

"Stacey, they're on practically all of them," I said when he called us back. "Why?"

Stacey studied the trees, then suddenly pushed us down.

"My clothes!" Little Man wailed indignantly.

"Hush, Man, and stay down," Stacey warned. "Somebody's coming."

Two white men emerged. We looked at each other. We knew to be silent.

"You mark them all down here?" one of the men asked.

"Not the younger ones, Mr. Andersen."

"We might need them, too," said Mr. Andersen, counting the X's. "But don't worry 'bout marking them now, Tom. We'll get them later. Also them trees up past the pond toward the house."

"The old woman agree to you cutting these trees?"

"I ain't been down there yet," Mr. Andersen said.

"Mr. Andersen . . ." Tom hesitated a moment, looked up at the silent trees, then back at Mr. Andersen. "Maybe you should go easy with them," he cautioned. "You know that David can be as mean as an ole jackass when he wanna be."

"He's talking about Papa," I whispered.

"Shhhh!" Stacey hissed.

Mr. Andersen looked uneasy. "What's that gotta do with anything?"

"Well, he just don't take much to any dealings with white folks." Again, Tom looked up at the trees. "He ain't afraid like some."

Mr. Andersen laughed weakly. "Don't worry 'bout that, Tom. The land belongs to his mama. He don't have no say in it. Besides, I guess I oughta know how to handle David Logan. After all, there are ways . . .

"Now, you get on back to my place and get some boys and start chopping down these trees," Mr. Andersen said. "I'll go talk to the old woman." He looked up at the sky. "We can almost get a full day's work in if we hurry."

Mr. Andersen turned to walk away, but Tom stopped him. "Mr. Andersen, you really gonna chop all the trees?"

"If I need to. These folks ain't got no call for them. I do. I got me a good contract for these trees and I aim to fulfill it."

Tom watched Mr. Andersen walk away; then, looking sorrowfully up at the trees, he shook his head and disappeared into the depths of the forest.

"What we gonna do, Stacey?" I asked anxiously. "They can't just cut down our trees, can they?"

"I don't know. Papa's gone . . ." Stacey muttered to himself, trying to decide what we should do next.

"Boy, if Papa was here, them ole white men wouldn't be messing with our trees," Little Man declared.

"Yeah!" Christopher-John agreed. "Just let Papa get hold of 'em and he gonna turn 'em every which way but loose."

"Christopher-John, Man," Stacey said finally, "go get the cows and take them home."

"But we just brought them down here," Little Man protested.

"And we gotta pick the berries for dinner," said Christopher-John mournfully.

"No time for that now. Hurry up. And stay clear of them white men. Cassie, you come with me."

We ran, brown legs and feet flying high through the still forest.

By the time Stacey and I arrived at the house, Mr. Andersen's car was already parked in the dusty drive. Mr. Andersen himself was seated comfortably in Papa's rocker

GEORGIA LANDSCAPE
Hale Aspacio Woodruff
National Museum of American Art

on the front porch. Big Ma was seated too, but Mama was standing.

Stacey and I eased quietly to the side of the porch, unnoticed.

"Sixty-five dollars. That's an awful lot of money in these hard times, Aunt Caroline," Mr. Andersen was saying to Big Ma.

I could see Mama's thin face harden.

"You know," Mr. Andersen said, rocking familiarly in Papa's chair, "that's more than David can send home in two months."

"We do quite well on what David sends home," Mama said coldly.

Mr. Andersen stopped rocking. "I suggest you encourage Aunt Caroline to sell them trees, Mary. You know, David might not always be able to work so good. He could possibly have . . . an accident."

Big Ma's soft brown eyes clouded over with fear as she looked first at Mr. Andersen, then at Mama. But Mama clenched her fists and said, "In Mississippi, black men do not have accidents."

"Hush, child, hush," Big Ma said hurriedly. "How many trees for the sixty-five dollars, Mr. Andersen?"

"Enough 'til I figure I got my sixty-five dollars' worth."

"And how many would that be?" Mama persisted.

Mr. Andersen looked haughtily at Mama. "I said I'd be the judge of that, Mary."

"I think not," Mama said.

Mr. Andersen stared at Mama. And Mama stared back at him. I knew Mr. Andersen didn't like that, but Mama did it anyway. Mr. Andersen soon grew uneasy under that piercing gaze, and when his eyes swiftly shifted from Mama to Big Ma, his face was beet-red.

"Caroline," he said, his voice low and menacing, "you're the head of this family and you've got a decision to make. Now, I need them trees and I mean to have them. I've offered you a good price for them and I ain't gonna haggle over it. I know y'all can use the money. Doc Thomas tells me that Mary's not well." He hesitated a moment, then hissed venomously, "And if something should happen to David . . ."

"All right," Big Ma said, her voice trembling. "All right, Mr. Andersen."

"No, Big Ma!" I cried, leaping onto the porch. "You can't let him cut our trees!"

Mr. Andersen grasped the arms of the rocker, his knuckles chalk white. "You certainly ain't taught none of your younguns how to behave, Caroline," he said curtly.

"You children go on to the back," Mama said, shooing us away.

"No, Mama," Stacey said. "He's gonna cut them all down. Me and Cassie heard him say so in the woods."

"I won't let him cut them," I threatened. "I won't let him! The trees are my friends and

ain't no mean ole white man gonna touch my trees————"

Mama's hands went roughly around my body as she carried me off to my room.

"Now, hush," she said, her dark eyes flashing wildly. "I've told you how dangerous it is . . ." She broke off in midsentence. She stared at me a moment, then hugged me tightly and went back to the porch.

Stacey joined me a few seconds later, and we sat there in the heat of the quiet room, listening miserably as the first whack of an ax echoed against the trees.

That night I was awakened by soft sounds outside my window. I reached for Big Ma, but she wasn't there. Hurrying to the window, I saw Mama and Big Ma standing in the yard in their night clothes and Stacey, fully dressed, sitting atop Lady, our golden mare. By the time I got outside, Stacey was gone.

"Mama, where's Stacey?" I cried.

"Be quiet, Cassie. You'll wake Christopher-John and Little Man."

"But where's he going?"

"He's going to get Papa," Mama said. "Now be quiet."

"Go on Stacey, boy," I whispered. "Ride for me, too."

As the dust billowed after him, Mama said, "I should've gone myself. He's so young."

Big Ma put her arm around Mama. "Now, Mary, you know you couldn't've gone. Mr. Andersen would miss you if he come by and see you ain't here. You done right, now. Don't worry, that boy'll be just fine."

Three days passed, hot and windless.

Mama forbade any of us to go into the forest, so Christopher-John, Little Man and I spent the slow, restless days hovering as close to the dusty road as we dared, listening to the foreign sounds of steel against the trees and the thunderous roar of those ancient loved ones as they crashed upon the earth. Sometimes Mama would scold us and tell us to come back to the house, but even she could not ignore the continuous pounding of the axes against the trees. Or the sight of the loaded lumber wagons rolling out of the forest. In the middle of washing or ironing or hoeing, she would look up sorrowfully and listen, then turn toward the road, searching for some sign of Papa and Stacey.

On the fourth day, before the sun had risen bringing its cloak of miserable heat, I saw her walking alone toward the woods. I ran after her.

She did not send me back.

"Mama," I said, "How sick are you?"

Mama took my hand. "Remember when you had the flu and felt so sick?"

"Yes'm."

"And when I gave you some medicine, you got well soon afterward?"

"Yes'm."

"Well, that's how sick I am. As soon as I get my medicine, I'll be all well again. And that'll be soon now that Papa's coming home," she said, giving my hand a gentle little squeeze.

The quiet surrounded us as we entered the forest. Mama clicked on the flashlight and we walked silently along the cow path to the pond. There, just beyond the pond, pockets of open space loomed before us.

"Mama!"

"I know, baby, I know."

On the ground lay countless trees. Trees that had once been such strong, tall things. So strong that I could fling my arms partially around one of them and feel safe and secure. So tall and leafy green that their boughs had formed a forest temple.

And old.

So old that Indians had once built fires at their feet and had sung happy songs of happy days. So old, they had hidden fleeing black

SPRING FEVER, 1978 (detail)
Romare Bearden
Courtesy of the Estate of Romare Bearden

men in the night and listened to their sad tales of a foreign land.

In the cold of winter when the ground lay frozen, they had sung their frosty ballads of years gone by. Or on a muggy, sweat-drenched day, their leaves had rippled softly, lazily, like restless green fingers strumming at a guitar, echoing their epic tales.

But now they would sing no more. They lay forever silent upon the ground.

Those trees that remained standing were like defeated warriors mourning their fallen dead. But soon they, too, would fall, for the white *X*'s had been placed on nearly every one.

"Oh, dear, dear trees," I cried as the gray light of the rising sun fell in ghostly shadows over the land. The tears rolled hot down my cheeks. Mama held me close, and when I felt her body tremble, I knew she was crying too.

When our tears eased, we turned sadly toward the house. As we emerged from the forest, we could see two small figures waiting impatiently on the other side of the road. As soon as they spied us, they hurried across to meet us.

"Mama! You and Cassie was in the forest," Little Man accused. "Big Ma told us!"

"How was it?" asked Christopher-John, rubbing the sleep from his eyes. "Was it spooky?"

"Spooky and empty," I said listlessly.

"Mama, me and Christopher-John wanna see too," Little Man declared.

"No, baby," Mama said softly as we crossed the road. "The men'll be down there soon, and I don't want y'all underfoot."

"But, Mama———" Little Man started to protest.

"When Papa comes home and the men are gone, then you can go. But until then, you stay out of there. You hear me, Little Man Logan?"

"Yes'm," Little Man reluctantly replied.

But the sun had been up only an hour when Little Man decided that he could not wait for Papa to return.

"Mama said we wasn't to go down there," Christopher-John warned.

"Cassie did," Little Man cried.

"But she was with Mama. Wasn't you, Cassie?"

"Well, I'm going too," said Little Man. "Everybody's always going someplace 'cepting me." And off he went.

Christopher-John and I ran after him. Down the narrow cow path and around the pond we chased. But neither of us was fast enough to overtake Little Man before he reached the lumbermen.

"Hey, you kids, get away from here," Mr. Andersen shouted when he saw us. "Now, y'all go on back home," he said, stopping in front of Little Man.

"We are home," I said. "You're the one who's on our land."

"Claude," Mr. Andersen said to one of the black lumbermen, "take these kids home." Then he pushed Little Man out of his way. Little Man pushed back. Mr. Andersen looked down, startled that a little black boy would do such a thing. He shoved Little Man a second time, and Little Man fell into the dirt.

Little Man looked down at his clothing covered with sawdust and dirt, and wailed, "You got my clothes dirty!"

I rushed toward Mr. Andersen, my fist in a mighty hammer, shouting, "You ain't got no right to push on Little Man. Why don't you push on somebody your own size—like me, you ole———"

The man called Claude put his hand over my mouth and carried me away. Christopher-John trailed behind us, tugging on the man's shirt.

"Put her down. Hey, mister, put Cassie down."

The man carried me all the way to the

pond. "Now," he said, "you and your brothers get on home before y'all get hurt. Go on, get!"

As the man walked away, I looked around. "Where's Little Man?"

Christopher-John looked around too.

"I don't know," he said. "I thought he was behind me."

Back we ran toward the lumbermen.

We found Little Man's clothing first, folded neatly by a tree. Then we saw Little Man, dragging a huge stick, and headed straight for Mr. Andersen.

"Little Man, come back here," I called.

But Little Man did not stop.

Mr. Andersen stood alone, barking orders, unaware of the oncoming Little Man.

"Little Man! Oh, Little Man, don't!"

It was too late.

Little Man swung the stick as hard as he could against Mr. Andersen's leg.

Mr. Andersen let out a howl and reached to where he thought Little Man's collar was. But, of course, Little Man had no collar.

"Run, Man!" Christopher-John and I shouted. "Run!"

"Why, you little . . ." Mr. Andersen cried, grabbing at Little Man. But Little Man was too quick for him. He slid right through Mr. Andersen's legs. Tom stood nearby, his face crinkling into an amused grin.

"Hey, y'all!" Mr. Andersen yelled to the lumbermen. "Claude! Get that kid!"

But sure-footed Little Man dodged the groping hands of the lumbermen as easily as if he were skirting mud puddles. Over tree stumps, around legs and through legs he dashed. But in the end, there were too many lumbermen for him, and he was handed over to Mr. Andersen.

For the second time, Christopher-John and I went to Little Man's rescue.

"Put him down!" we ordered, charging the lumbermen.

I was captured much too quickly, though not before I had landed several stinging blows. But Christopher-John, furious at seeing Little Man handled so roughly by Mr. Andersen, managed to elude the clutches of the lumbermen until he was fully upon Mr. Andersen. Then, with his mightiest thrust, he kicked Mr. Andersen solidly in the shins, not once, but twice, before the lumbermen pulled him away.

Mr. Andersen was fuming. He slowly took off his wide leather belt. Christopher-John, Little Man and I looked woefully at the belt, then at each other. Little Man and Christopher-John fought to escape, but I closed my eyes and awaited the whining of the heavy belt and its painful bite against my skin.

What was he waiting for? I started to open my eyes, but then the zinging whirl of the belt began and I tensed, awaiting its fearful sting. But just as the leather tip lashed into my leg, a deep familiar voice said, "Put the belt down, Andersen."

I opened my eyes.

"Papa!"

"Let the children go," Papa said. He was standing on a nearby ridge with a strange black box in his hands. Stacey was behind him holding the reins to Lady.

The chopping stopped as all eyes turned to Papa.

"They been right meddlesome," Mr. Andersen said. "They need teaching how to act."

"Any teaching, I'll do it. Now, let them go."

Mr. Andersen looked down at Little Man struggling to get away. Smiling broadly, he motioned our release. "Okay, David," he said.

As we ran up the ridge to Papa, Mr. Andersen said, "It's good to have you home, boy."

Papa said nothing until we were safely behind him. "Take them home, Stacey."

"But, Papa———"

"Do like I say, son."

BROTHERS, 1934
Malvin Gray Johnson
National Museum of American Art

Stacey herded us away from the men. When we were far enough away so Papa couldn't see us, Stacey stopped and handed me Lady's reins.

"Y'all go on home now," he said. "I gotta go help Papa."

"Papa don't need no help," I said. "He told you to come with us."

"But you don't know what he's gonna do."

"What?" I asked.

"He's gonna blow up the forest if they don't get out of here. So go on home where y'all be safe."

"How's he gonna do that?" asked Little Man.

"We been setting sticks of dynamite since the middle of the night. We ain't even been up to the house cause Papa wanted the sticks planted and covered over before the men came. Now, Cassie, take them on back to the house. Do like I tell you for once, will ya?" Then, without waiting for another word, he was gone.

"I wanna see," Little Man announced.

"I don't," protested Christopher-John.

"Come on," I said.

We tied the mare to a tree, then belly-crawled back to where we could see Papa and joined Stacey in the brush.

"Cassie, I told you . . ."

"What's Papa doing?"

The black box was now set upon a sawed-off tree stump, and Papa's hands were tightly grasping a T-shaped instrument which went into it.

"What's that thing?" asked Little Man.

"It's a plunger," Stacey whispered. "If Papa presses down on it, the whole forest will go pfffff!"

Our mouths went dry and our eyes went wide. Mr. Andersen's eyes were wide, too.

"You're bluffing, David," he said. "You ain't gonna push that plunger."

"One thing you can't seem to understand, Andersen," Papa said, "is that a black man's always gotta be ready to die. And it don't make me any difference if I die today or tomorrow. Just as long as I die right."

Mr. Andersen laughed uneasily. The lumbermen moved nervously away.

"I mean what I say," Papa said. "Ask anyone. I always mean what I say."

"He sure do, Mr. Andersen," Claude said, eyeing the black box. "He always do."

"Shut up!" Mr. Andersen snapped. "And the rest of y'all stay put." Then turning back to Papa, he smiled cunningly. "I'm sure you and me can work something out, David."

"Ain't nothing to be worked out," said Papa.

"Now, look here, David, your mama and me, we got us a contract . . ."

"There ain't no more contract," Papa replied coldly. "Now, either you get out or I blow it up. That's it."

"He means it, Mr. Andersen," another frightened lumberman ventured. "He's crazy and he sure 'nough means it."

"You know what could happen to you, boy?" Mr. Andersen exploded, his face beet-red again. "Threatening a white man like this?"

Papa said nothing. He just stood there, his hands firmly on the plunger, staring down at Mr. Andersen.

Mr. Andersen could not bear the stare. He turned away, cursing Papa. "You're a fool, David. A crazy fool." Then he looked around at the lumbermen. They shifted their eyes and would not look at him.

"Maybe we better leave, Mr. Andersen," Tom said quietly.

Mr. Andersen glanced at Tom, then turned back to Papa and said as lightly as he could, "All right, David, all right. It's your land. We'll just take the logs we got cut and get out." He motioned to the men. "Hey, let's get moving and get these logs out of here before this crazy fool gets us all killed."

"No," Papa said.

Mr. Andersen stopped, knowing that he could not have heard correctly. "What you say?"

"You ain't taking one more stick out of this forest."

"Now, look here———"

"You heard me."

"But you can't sell all these logs, David," Mr. Andersen exclaimed incredulously.

Papa said nothing. Just cast that piercing look on Mr. Andersen.

"Look, I'm a fair man. I tell you what I'll do. I'll give you another thirty-five dollars. An even hundred dollars. Now, that's fair, ain't it?"

"I'll see them rot first."

"But———"

"That's my last word," Papa said, tightening his grip on the plunger.

Mr. Andersen swallowed hard. "You won't always have that black box, David," he warned. "You know that, don't you?"

"That may be. But it won't matter none. 'Cause I'll always have my self-respect."

Mr. Andersen opened his mouth to speak, but no sound came. Tom and the lumbermen were quietly moving away, putting their gear in the empty lumber wagons. Mr. Andersen looked again at the black box. Finally, his face ashen, he too walked away.

Papa stood unmoving until the wagons and the men were gone. Then, when the sound of the last wagon rolling over the dry leaves could no longer be heard and a hollow silence filled the air, he slowly removed his hands from the plunger and looked up at the remaining trees standing like lonely sentries in the morning.

"Dear, dear old trees," I heard him call softly, "will you ever sing again?"

I waited. But the trees gave no answer.

RESPONDING TO THE SELECTION

Your Response

1. Do you think David Logan handles the situation well? Why or why not?
2. How would you feel at the story's end if you were Cassie or Stacey?

Recalling

3. Why is David Logan away from home in the beginning of the story?
4. Why does Anderson visit the Logans?
5. How does David Logan convince Anderson to stop cutting the trees?

Interpreting

6. Why doesn't Mama want Cassie and her brothers to know she is ill?

7. When Anderson visits the Logans, he says that David ". . . could possibly have . . . an accident." What does he really mean?
8. Why is David Logan ready to die to save the trees?

Applying

9. What is the value of having self-respect?

ANALYZING LITERATURE

Understanding Setting and Conflict

A story's **setting** is its time and place. A **conflict** is a struggle between opposing sides. Sometimes setting and conflict are related. For example, the conflict between the Logans and Anderson centers on the trees in the forest, where much of the story takes place.

1. Point out two things Cassie says that indicate her feelings about the trees.
2. What is Anderson's attitude toward the trees? How is it different from the Logans'?

CRITICAL THINKING AND READING

Recognizing a Historical Setting

Knowing that "Song of the Trees" takes place during the Great Depression of the 1930's can help you understand the seriousness of the Logans' situation.

1. How has the Logan family been affected by the Great Depression?
2. David Logan is no doubt aware of his family's needs when he refuses Anderson's offer of thirty-five more dollars. Knowing this, what is your impression of his actions?

THINKING AND WRITING

Extending a Story

Imagine that you are the author of "Song of the Trees" and that you want to write more about the Logans. Extend the story by writing what you think will happen over the next few months. What will happen to the Logan family? What will happen to the trees? What will Anderson do? Include dialogue in your story.

LEARNING OPTIONS

1. **Performance.** With other classmates act out the story's final scene, beginning with the appearance of David Logan. Cast each character that has dialogue, and choose someone to read the narration. Try to read the dialogue as the characters might really have spoken it.
2. **Community Connections.** Investigate the effects of the Great Depression on your community. Use your public library's archives to locate articles appearing in local newspapers about the economy in your area during the 1930's. Also, interview members of your community who remember life during the Depression. Ask them about their personal experiences and about the effects felt by the entire community. Use your findings to give a presentation to your classmates.
3. **Cross-curricular Connection.** Review the story for references to different kinds of trees. Make a list of these. Then investigate the ways in which these trees grow, look for pictures of full-grown examples of each, and identify the differences between them. For example, Cassie mentions a pine tree, which is a conifer, and a hickory tree, which is deciduous. Prepare a field guide to these trees for your classmates. In addition to pictures, your field guide should include tips on identifying the trees by their leaf types, bark texture, and so on.

GUIDE FOR READING

The Third Level

Time

Setting consists of both the place and the time of a story. Think of all the changes that occur over time. A person who lived in a city in the 1990's would probably know a very different place from someone who had lived in the same city in the 1890's. In "The Third Level," the main character lives in the present but longs to go back to the past.

Focus

You may have seen movies or television shows in which people are able to travel backward and forward in time. Have you ever wished you could be a time traveler? Have you read about a different time in your history books that was interesting to you? If you really could go back to an earlier time, where would you go? Maybe you would rather travel forward in time. Choose a time to which you would like to travel and write a brief set of reasons for your wanting to go there. What is most attractive about the time? What could you experience then that you cannot experience in the present?

In the story you are about to read, a man finds himself transported back to the year 1894, surprisingly and for a few brief moments. Because he really likes what he has seen, he tries again and again to re-create—and prolong—the experience.

Vocabulary

Knowing the following words will help you as you read "The Third Level."

refuge (ref′ yōōj) *n.*: A place of safety or shelter (p. 127)

arched (ärcht) *adj.*: Curved (p. 127)

currency (kʉr′ ən sē) *n.*: Money (p. 129)

premium (prē′ mē əm) *n.*: An additional charge (p. 129)

Jack Finney

(1911–1995) was best known for *Invasion of the Body Snatchers,* a novel about aliens who come to Earth and inhabit human bodies. Escape from the harsh present to a peaceful past is a common idea in Finney's writing. It appears in his novel *Time and Again* and runs through *I Love Galesburg in the Springtime,* a collection of short stories. It is also at the heart of the unusual story you are about to read.

The Third Level

Jack Finney

The presidents of the New York Central and the New York, New Haven and Hartford railroads will swear on a stack of timetables that there are only two. But I say there are three, because I've *been* on the third level at Grand Central Station.[1] Yes, I've taken the obvious step: I talked to a psychiatrist friend of mine, among others. I told him about the third level at Grand Central Station, and he said it was a waking-dream wish fulfillment. He said I was unhappy. That made my wife kind of mad, but he explained that he meant the modern world is full of insecurity, fear, war, worry and all the rest of it, and that I just want to escape. Well, who doesn't? Everybody I know wants to escape, but they don't wander down into any third level at Grand Central Station.

But that's the reason, he said, and my friends all agreed. Everything points to it, they claimed. My stamp collecting, for example; that's a "temporary refuge from reality." Well, maybe, but my grandfather didn't need any refuge from reality; things were pretty nice and peaceful in his day, from all I hear, and he started my collection. It's a nice collection, too, blocks of four of practically every U.S. issue, first-day covers, and so on. President Roosevelt collected stamps, too, you know.

Anyway, here's what happened at Grand Central. One night last summer I worked late at the office. I was in a hurry to get uptown to my apartment so I decided to take the subway from Grand Central because it's faster than the bus.

Now, I don't know why this should have happened to me. I'm just an ordinary guy named Charley, thirty-one years old, and I was wearing a tan gabardine[2] suit and a straw hat with a fancy band; I passed a dozen men who looked just like me. And I wasn't trying to escape from anything; I just wanted to get home to Louisa, my wife.

I turned into Grand Central from Vanderbilt Avenue, and went down the steps to the first level, where you take trains like the Twentieth Century. Then I walked down another flight to the second level, where the suburban trains leave from, ducked into an arched doorway heading for the subway— and got lost. That's easy to do. I've been in and out of Grand Central hundreds of times, but I'm always bumping into new doorways and stairs and corridors. Once I got into a tunnel about a mile long and came out in the lobby of the Roosevelt Hotel. Another time I came up in an office building on Forty-sixth Street, three blocks away.

Sometimes I think Grand Central is

---

1. Grand Central Station: A large train station in New York City.

2. gabardine (gab′ ər dēn′): A cloth of wool, cotton, rayon, or other material used for suits and dresses.

growing like a tree, pushing out new corridors and staircases like roots. There's probably a long tunnel that nobody knows about feeling its way under the city right now, on its way to Times Square, and maybe another to Central Park. And maybe—because for so many people through the years Grand Central *has* been an exit, a way of escape— maybe that's how the tunnel I got into . . . But I never told my psychiatrist friend about that idea.

The corridor I was in began angling left and slanting downward and I thought that was wrong, but I kept on walking. All I could hear was the empty sound of my own footsteps and I didn't pass a soul. Then I heard that sort of hollow roar ahead that means open space and people talking. The tunnel turned sharp left; I went down a short flight of stairs and came out on the third level at Grand Central Station. For just a moment I thought I was back on the second level, but I saw the room was smaller, there were fewer ticket windows and train gates, and the information booth in the center was wood and old-looking. And the man in the booth wore a green eyeshade and long black sleeve protectors. The lights were dim and sort of flickering. Then I saw why; they were open-flame gaslights.

There were brass spittoons[3] on the floor, and across the station a glint of light caught my eye; a man was pulling a gold watch from his vest pocket. He snapped open the cover, glanced at his watch, and frowned. He wore a derby hat,[4] a black four-button suit with tiny lapels, and he had a big, black, handle-bar mustache. Then I looked around and saw that everyone in the station was dressed like eighteen-ninety-something; I never saw so many beards, sideburns and fancy mustaches in my life. A woman walked in through the train gate; she wore a dress with leg-of-mutton sleeves[5] and skirts to the top of her high-buttoned shoes. Back of her, out on the tracks, I caught a glimpse of a locomotive, a very small Currier & Ives[6] locomotive with a funnel-shaped stack. And then I knew.

To make sure, I walked over to a newsboy and glanced at the stack of papers at his feet. It was the *World;* and the *World* hasn't been published for years. The lead story said something about President Cleveland. I've found that front page since, in the Public Library files, and it was printed June 11, 1894.

I turned toward the ticket windows knowing that here—on the third level at Grand Central—I could buy tickets that would take Louisa and me anywhere in the United States we wanted to go. In the year 1894. And I wanted two tickets to Galesburg, Illinois.

Have you ever been there? It's a wonderful town still, with big old frame houses, huge lawns and tremendous trees whose branches meet overhead and roof the streets. And in 1894, summer evenings were twice as long, and people sat out on their lawns, the men smoking cigars and talking quietly, the women waving palm-leaf fans, with the fireflies all around, in a peaceful world. To be back there with the First World War still twenty years off, and World War II over forty years in the future . . . I wanted two tickets for that.

The clerk figured the fare—he glanced at my fancy hatband, but he figured the fare—and I had enough for two coach tickets, one way. But when I counted out the money and looked up, the clerk was staring at me. He nodded at the bills. "That ain't money, mister," he said, "and if you're trying to skin me[7] you won't get very far," and he glanced at the cash drawer beside him. Of course the money in his drawer was old-style bills, half again as big as the money we use nowadays, and different-looking. I turned away and got out fast. There's nothing nice about jail, even in 1894.

And that was that. I left the same way I came, I suppose. Next day, during lunch hour, I drew three hundred dollars out of the bank, nearly all we had, and bought old-style currency (that *really* worried my psychiatrist friend). You can buy old money at almost any coin dealer's, but you have to pay a premium. My three hundred dollars bought less than two hundred in old-style bills, but I didn't care; eggs were thirteen cents a dozen in 1894.

But I've never again found the corridor that leads to the third level at Grand Central Station, although I've tried often enough.

Louisa was pretty worried when I told her all this, and didn't want me to look for the third level any more, and after a while I

---

3. spittoons (spi to͞onz′): Jarlike containers into which people spit. Spitting in public was a more accepted habit in the past.
4. derby hat: A stiff felt hat with a round crown and curved brim.
5. leg-of-mutton sleeves: Sleeves that puff out toward the shoulder and resemble a leg of mutton (lamb or sheep).
6. Currier & Ives: These 19th-century American print makers became famous for their pictures of trains, yachts, horses, and scenes of nature.

7. skin me: An old-fashioned way of saying "cheat me."

stopped; I went back to my stamps. But now we're *both* looking, every weekend, because now we have proof that the third level is still there. My friend Sam Weiner disappeared! Nobody knew where, but I sort of suspected because Sam's a city boy, and I used to tell him about Galesburg—I went to school there—and he always said he liked the sound of the place. And that's where he is, all right. In 1894.

Because one night, fussing with my stamp collection, I found—well, do you know what a first-day cover is? When a new stamp is issued, stamp collectors buy some and use them to mail envelopes to themselves on the very first day of sale; and the postmark proves the date. The envelope is called a first-day cover. They're never opened; you just put blank paper in the envelope.

That night, among my oldest first-day covers, I found one that shouldn't have been there. But there it was. It was there because someone had mailed it to my grandfather at his home in Galesburg; that's what the address on the envelope said. And it had been there since July 18, 1894—the postmark showed that—yet I didn't remember it at all. The stamp was a six-cent, dull brown, with a picture of President Garfield. Naturally, when the envelope came to Granddad in the mail, it went right into his collection and stayed there—till I took it out and opened it.

The paper inside wasn't blank. It read:

941 Willard Street
Galesburg, Illinois
July 18, 1894

Charley:

I got to wishing that you were right. Then I got to believing you were right. And, Charley, it's true; I found the third level! I've been here two weeks, and right now, down the street at the Daly's, someone is play-

ing a piano, and they're all out on the front porch singing, "Seeing Nellie home." And I'm invited over for lemonade. Come on back, Charley and Louisa. Keep looking till you find the third level! It's worth it, believe me!

The note was signed *Sam.*

At the stamp and coin store I go to, I found out that Sam bought eight hundred dollars' worth of old-style currency. That ought to set him up in a nice little hay, feed and grain business; he always said that's what he really wished he could do, and he certainly can't go back to his old business. Not in Galesburg, Illinois, in 1894. His old business? Why, Sam was my psychiatrist.

MULTICULTURAL CONNECTION

Time in Different Cultures

Charley, the hero in this story, wants to go back in time to a more peaceful, less rushed era. Today in most parts of the United States, time is carefully scheduled, filled with work and other activities. However, it was not always this way, and it is not necessarily so in all parts of the world.

Culture plays an important role in shaping people's attitudes toward time. In many other cultures, people have a very different notion of time. Punctuality is not valued in some countries. Time is not "of the essence" in Italy or Mexico where, for instance, theater performances and other events do not always begin on schedule, and late arrivals for meetings and other appointments are not out of the ordinary. In many parts of the world, the concept of "wasting time" is unknown.

For Discussion

What role does time play in your life?

RESPONDING TO THE SELECTION

Your Response

1. As it's described, is Galesburg in 1894 a place you would like to go? Why or why not?

Recalling

2. According to Charley's psychiatrist, why does Charley think he has been on the third level of Grand Central Station?
3. What is the first clue that he is in the Grand Central Station of the past?
4. Why is he unable to travel to Galesburg even after he gets currency that the ticket clerk will accept?
5. What proof does Charley get that the third level exists?

Interpreting

6. Describe the contrast the story presents between life in the modern world and life in Galesburg at the turn of the century.
7. What is the connection between this contrast and Charley's wanting to go to Galesburg?
8. As a psychiatrist, Sam must listen to the problems and fears of people living in the modern world. How might his work have led to his going to Galesburg?
9. What effect do you think Sam's letter has on Charley?

Applying

10. Many stories, novels, and films deal with escaping from the present into a more pleasant time, usually in the past. Do you think the idea of a past that is better than the present is, or is not, realistic? Explain why.

ANALYZING LITERATURE

Recognizing Time in a Setting

Time refers to the *when* of the action. Sometimes a story will shift from the present to the past. Then you have to determine from clues when the action is taking place.

1. What is the first detail that hints Charley has entered the Grand Central Station of 1894?
2. Identify at least three other details that show the third level is in the past.

CRITICAL THINKING AND READING

Understanding the Effects of Time

The time in which a story is set affects the characters. There is a close connection between how people live and when they live. As time changes, a society changes. For example, in "The Third Level" Charley's and Sam's unhappiness is linked to life in general in the modern world.

1. What view of modern life is given in the first paragraph of the story?
2. According to Sam, how has modern life affected Charley's mind?
3. What does Sam's letter to Charley say that suggests life in Galesburg in 1894 is better than life in modern-day New York?

THINKING AND WRITING

Writing a Time-Travel Story

Write a brief story in which a character—maybe yourself—steps into the past, experiences life as it was then lived, and suddenly returns to the present (perhaps changed by the strange experience). First select the time period for your story. List details about this period that you might use in your story; for example, for the 1890's you might list gaslights, long dresses, and streetcars. Figure out a way to get your character into the past and a way to return him or her to the present. You might also think about how the experience of the past will change the character's life in the future. Go over your writing to see whether you have managed to convey a vivid glimpse of the past time that you are presenting. Then share your story with your classmates.

GUIDE FOR READING

Rip Van Winkle

Passage of Time

As a story moves forward in time, not only do characters and events change, but the setting may change as well. How a place is described later in a story may be different from how it is described earlier. In "Rip Van Winkle," changes in the setting over time are especially important to the story as a whole.

Focus

The story you are about to read is set in the Catskill Mountains in New York State. These mountains are quite high, and their steep sides, dense forests, and rocky glens create some of the most beautiful scenery in the northeast United States.

Look at the painting on page 133. What kind of atmosphere does it create? What details in it let you know that the man and his dog are walking through a rugged mountain scene? Write down your impressions of the landscape depicted in the painting. What feelings does it evoke in you? Does it seem like a place you would like to visit? What kinds of things would you expect to happen there?

Vocabulary

Knowing the following words will help you as you read "Rip Van Winkle."

chivalrous (shiv'' l rəs) *adj.*: Courteous (p. 134)

martial (mär' shəl) *adj.*: Suitable for war (p. 134)

domestic (dō mes' tik) *adj.*: Of the home and family (p. 134)

obliging (ə blī' jiŋ) *adj.*: Ready to do favors (p. 135)

keener (kēn' ər) *adj.*: Sharper and quicker (p. 136)

wistfully (wist' fəl lē) *adj.*: Showing vague yearnings (p.137)

majestic (mə jes' tik) *adj.*: Grand; lofty (p. 137)

incomprehensible (in' käm pri hen' sə b'l) *adj.*: Not able to be understood (p. 138)

evidently (ev' ə dənt' lē) *adj.*: Obviously (p. 139)

melancholy (mel' ən käl' ē) *adj.*: Sad; gloomy (p. 139)

Washington Irving

(1783–1859) was the first American author to achieve fame in both Europe and America. While living in England as a young man, he read old German folk tales in search of subjects he could use for stories of his own. One tale strongly appealed to him. He changed its setting from Europe to America, made other changes, and thus created "Rip Van Winkle." The magical quality of this story comes in part from its source—a strange old folk tale passed down from generation to generation of fascinated listeners.

Rip Van Winkle

Washington Irving

RIP IN THE MOUNTAINS
Albertus Del Orient Browere
Shelburne Museum, Shelburne, Vermont

Whoever has made a voyage up the Hudson must remember the Catskill mountains. They are a branch of the great Appalachian family,[1] and are seen away to the west of the river, swelling up to a noble height, and lording it over the surrounding country. Every change of season, every change of weather, indeed every hour of the day, produces some change in the magical hues and shapes of these mountains, and they are regarded by all the good wives, far and near, as perfect barometers. When the weather is fair and settled, they are clothed in blue and purple, and print their bold outlines on the clear evening sky; but sometimes, when the rest of the landscape is cloudless, they will gather a hood of gray vapors about their summits,

---

1. Appalachian (ap′ə lā′ chən) **family:** A group of mountains extending from southern Quebec in Canada to northern Alabama.

which, in the last rays of the setting sun, will glow and light up like a crown of glory.

At the foot of these fairy mountains, the voyager may have seen the light smoke curling up from a village, whose shingle roofs gleam among the trees, just where the blue tints of the upland melt away into the fresh green of the nearer landscape. It is a little village, of great antiquity, having been founded by some of the Dutch colonists, in the early times of the province, just about the beginning of the government of the good Peter Stuyvesant,[2] (may he rest in peace!) and there were some of the houses of the original settlers standing within a few years,[3] built of small yellow bricks brought from Holland, having latticed windows and gable fronts,[4] surmounted with weathercocks.

In that same village, and in one of these very houses (which, to tell the precise truth, was sadly timeworn and weather-beaten), there lived many years since, while the country was yet a province of Great Britain, a simple good-natured fellow, of the name of Rip Van Winkle. He was a descendant of the Van Winkles who figured so gallantly in the chivalrous days of Peter Stuyvesant, and accompanied him to the siege of Fort Christina. He inherited, however, but little of the martial character of his ancestors. I have observed that he was a simple good-natured man; he was, moreover, a kind neighbor, and an obedient henpecked husband. Indeed, to the latter circumstance might be owing that meekness of spirit which gained him such universal popularity; for those men are most apt to be obsequious and conciliating abroad, who are under the discipline of shrews at home. Their tempers, doubtless, are rendered pliant and malleable in the fiery furnace of domestic tribulation which is worth all the sermons in the world for teaching the virtues of patience and long-suffering. A termagant[5] wife may, therefore, in some respects, be considered a tolerable blessing; and if so, Rip Van Winkle was thrice blessed.

Certain it is, that he was a great favorite among all the good wives of the village, who, as usual with the amiable sex, took his part in all family squabbles; and never failed, whenever they talked those matters over in their evening gossipings, to lay all the blame on Dame Van Winkle. The children of the village, too, would shout with joy whenever he approached. He assisted at their sports, made their playthings, taught them to fly kites and shoot marbles, and told them long stories of ghosts, witches, and Indians. Whenever he went dodging about the village, he was surrounded by a troop of them, hanging on his skirts, clambering on his back and playing a thousand tricks on him with impunity; and not a dog would bark at him throughout the neighborhood.

The great error in Rip's composition was an insuperable aversion to all kinds of profitable labor. It could not be from the want of perseverance; for he would sit on a wet rock, with a rod as long and heavy as a Tartar's lance,[6] and fish all day without a murmur, even though he should not be encouraged by a single nibble. He would carry a fowling piece[7] on his shoulder for hours together, trudging through woods and swamps, and up hill and down dale, to shoot

---

2. Peter Stuyvesant (stī′ və s′nt): The last governor of New Netherland, a Dutch colony, before it was taken over by the English in 1664 and renamed New York.

3. within a few years: Until recently. The story was written during the early part of the 19th century.

4. gable fronts: Triangular wall shapes where two roof slopes meet.

5. termagant (tər′ mə gənt) adj.: Scolding.

6. Tartar's (tär′ tərz) **lance:** The Tartars were a member of the Mongolian tribes that invaded Europe about 700 years ago; these warriors used lances, which are long and heavy spears.

7. fowling piece: A type of shotgun for hunting wild fowl or birds.

a few squirrels or wild pigeons. He would never refuse to assist a neighbor even in the roughest toil, and was a foremost man at all country frolics for husking Indian corn, or building stone fences; the women of the village, too, used to employ him to run their errands, and to do such little odd jobs as their less obliging husbands would not do for them. In a word, Rip was ready to attend to anybody's business but his own; but as to doing family duty, and keeping his farm in order, he found it impossible.

In fact, he declared it was of no use to work on his farm; it was the most pestilent[8] little piece of ground in the whole country; everything about it went wrong, and would go wrong, in spite of him. His fences were continually falling to pieces; his cow would either go astray, or get among the cabbages; weeds were sure to grow quicker in his fields than anywhere else; the rain always made a point of setting in just as he had some outdoor work to do; so that though his estate had dwindled away under his management, acre by acre, until there was little more left than a mere patch of Indian corn and potatoes, yet it was the worst conditioned farm in the neighborhood.

His children, too, were as ragged and wild as if they belonged to nobody. His son Rip, an urchin[9] begotten in his own likeness, promised to inherit the habits, with the old clothes of his father. He was generally seen trooping like a colt at his mother's heels, equipped in a pair of his father's cast-off galligaskins,[10] which he had much ado to hold up with one hand, as a fine lady does her train in bad weather.

Rip Van Winkle, however, was one of those happy mortals, of foolish, well-oiled dispositions, who take the world easy, eat white bread or brown, whichever can be got with least thought or trouble, and would rather starve on a penny than work for a pound.[11] If left to himself, he would have whistled life away in perfect contentment; but his wife kept continually dinning in his ears about his idleness, his carelessness, and the ruin he was bringing on his family. Morning, noon, and night, her tongue was incessantly going, and everything he said or did was sure to produce a torrent of household eloquence. Rip had but one way of replying to all lectures of the kind, and that, by frequent use, had grown into a habit. He shrugged his shoulders, shook his head, cast up his eyes, but said nothing. This, however, always provoked a fresh volley from his wife; so that he was fain[12] to draw off his forces, and take to the outside of the house—the only side which, in truth, belongs to a henpecked husband.

Rip's sole domestic adherent was his dog Wolf, who was as much henpecked as his master; for Dame Van Winkle regarded them as companions in idleness, and even looked upon Wolf with an evil eye, as the cause of his master's going so often astray. True it is, in all points of spirit befitting an honorable dog, he was as courageous an animal as ever scoured the woods—but what courage can withstand the ever-enduring and all-besetting terrors of a woman's tongue? The moment Wolf entered the house his crest fell, his tail drooped to the ground or curled between his legs, he sneaked about with a gallows air, casting many a sidelong glance at Dame Van Winkle, and at the least flourish of a broomstick or ladle, he would fly to the door with yelping precipitation.[13]

---

8. pestilent (pes′ t'l ənt) *adj.*: In this case, it means "annoying."

9. urchin (ər′ chin) *n.*: A mischievous boy.

10. galligaskins (gal′ i gas′ kinz) *n.*: Loosely fitting breeches worn in the 16th and 17th centuries.

11. pound (pound) *n.*: A British unit of money.

12. fain (fān) *adj.*: An old-fashioned word meaning "glad."

13. precipitation (pri sip′ ə tā′ shən) *n.*: Great speed.

Times grew worse and worse with Rip Van Winkle as years of matrimony rolled on; a tart temper never mellows with age, and a sharp tongue is the only edged tool that grows keener with constant use. For a long while he used to console himself, when driven from home, by frequenting a kind of perpetual club of the sages, philosophers, and other idle personages of the village; which held its sessions on a bench before a small inn, designated by a portrait of His Majesty George the Third. Here they used to sit in the shade through a long, lazy summer's day, talking listlessly over village gossip, or telling endless sleepy stories about nothing. But it would have been worth any statesman's money to have heard the profound discussions that sometimes took place when by chance an old newspaper fell into their hands from some passing traveler. How solemnly they would listen to the contents, as drawled out by Derrick Van Bummel, the schoolmaster, a dapper, learned little man, who was not to be daunted by the most gigantic word in the dictionary; and how sagely they would deliberate upon public events some months after they had taken place.

The opinions of this group were completely controlled by Nicholas Vedder, a patriarch of the village, and landlord of the inn, at the door of which he took his seat from morning till night, just moving sufficiently to avoid the sun and keep in the shade of a large tree; so that the neighbors could tell the hour by his movements as accurately as by a sundial. It is true, he was rarely heard to speak, but smoked his pipe incessantly. His adherents, however (for every great man has his adherents), perfectly understood

him, and knew how to gather his opinions. When anything that was read or related displeased him, he was observed to smoke his pipe vehemently, and to send forth short, frequent, and angry puffs; but when pleased, he would inhale the smoke slowly and tranquilly, and emit it in light and placid clouds; and sometimes, taking the pipe from his mouth, and letting the fragrant vapor curl about his nose, would gravely nod his head in token of perfect approbation.

From even this stronghold the unlucky Rip was at length routed by his termagant wife, who would suddenly break in upon the tranquillity of the assemblage and call the members all to naught; nor was that august personage, Nicholas Vedder himself, sacred from the daring tongue of this terrible virago,[14] who charged him outright with encouraging her husband in habits of idleness.

Poor Rip was at last reduced almost to despair; and his only alternative, to escape from the labor of the farm and clamor of his wife, was to take gun in hand and stroll away into the woods. Here he would sometimes seat himself at the foot of a tree, and share the contents of his wallet[15] with Wolf, with whom he sympathized as a fellow-sufferer in persecution. "Poor Wolf," he would say, "thy mistress leads thee a dog's life of it; but never mind, my lad, whilst I live thou shalt never want a friend to stand by thee!" Wolf would wag his tail, look wistfully in his master's face, and if dogs can feel pity I verily believe he reciprocated the sentiment with all his heart.

In a long ramble of the kind on a fine autumnal day, Rip had unconsciously scrambled to one of the highest parts of the Catskill mountains. He was after his favorite sport of squirrel shooting, and the still soli-

tudes had echoed and re-echoed with the reports of his gun. Panting and fatigued, he threw himself, late in the afternoon, on a green knoll, covered with mountain herbage, that crowned the brow of a precipice. From an opening between the trees he could overlook all the lower country for many a mile of rich woodland. He saw at a distance the lordly Hudson, far, far below him, moving on its silent but majestic course, with the reflection of a purple cloud, or the sail of a lagging bark,[16] here and there sleeping on its glassy bosom, and at last losing itself in the blue highlands.

On the other side he looked down into a deep mountain glen, wild, lonely, and shagged,[17] the bottom filled with fragments from the impending[18] cliffs, and scarcely lighted by the reflected rays of the setting sun. For some time Rip lay musing on this scene; evening was gradually advancing; the mountains began to throw their long blue shadows over the valleys; he saw that it would be dark long before he could reach the village, and he heaved a heavy sigh when he thought of encountering the terrors of Dame Van Winkle.

As he was about to descend, he heard a voice from a distance hallooing, "Rip Van Winkle! Rip Van Winkle!" He looked round, but could see nothing but a crow winging its solitary flight across the mountain. He thought his fancy[19] must have deceived him, and turned again to descend, when he heard the same cry ring through the still evening air: "Rip Van Winkle! Rip Van Winkle!"—at the same time Wolf bristled up his back, and giving a low growl, skulked to his master's

---

14. virago (vi rā′ gō) *n*.: A quarrelsome woman.
15. wallet (wôl′ it) *n*.: In this case, it means a bag for carrying provisions.

16. bark (bärk) *n*.: Any boat, especially a small sailing boat.
17. shagged (shagd) *adj*.: Shaggy or rough.
18. impending (im pend′ iŋ) *adj*.: An old-fashioned word for "overhanging."
19. fancy (fan′ sē) *n*.: An old-fashioned word for "imagination."

side, looking fearfully down into the glen. Rip now felt a vague apprehension stealing over him; he looked anxiously in the same direction, and perceived a strange figure slowly toiling up the rocks, and bending under the weight of something he carried on his back. He was surprised to see any human being in this lonely and unfrequented place, but supposing it to be some one of the neighborhood in need of his assistance, he hastened down to yield it.

On nearer approach he was still more surprised at the singularity of the stranger's appearance. He was a short, square-built old fellow, with thick bushy hair, and a grizzled[20] beard. His dress was of the antique Dutch fashion—a cloth jerkin[21] strapped round the waist—several pairs of breeches, the outer one of ample volume, decorated with rows of buttons down the sides and bunches at the knees. He bore on his shoulder a stout keg, that seemed full of liquor, and made signs for Rip to approach and assist him with the load. Though rather shy and distrustful of this new acquaintance, Rip complied with his usual alacrity; and mutually relieving one another, they clambered up a narrow gully, apparently the dry bed of a mountain torrent. As they ascended, Rip every now and then heard long rolling peals, like distant thunder, that seemed to issue out of a deep ravine, or rather cleft, between lofty rocks, toward which their rugged path conducted. He paused for an instant, but supposing it to be the muttering of one of these transient thundershowers which often take place in mountain heights, he proceeded. Passing through the ravine, they came to a hollow, like a small amphitheater, surrounded by perpendicular precipices,

over the brinks of which impending trees shot their branches, so that you only caught glimpses of the azure sky and the bright evening cloud. During the whole time, Rip and his companion had labored on in silence; for though the former marvelled greatly what could be the object of carrying a keg of liquor up this wild mountain, yet there was something strange and incomprehensible about the unknown that inspired awe and checked familiarity.

On entering the amphitheater, new objects of wonder presented themselves. On a level spot in the center was a company of odd-looking personages playing at ninepins. They were dressed in a quaint outlandish fashion; some wore short doublets,[22] others jerkins, with long knives in their belts, and most of them had enormous breeches, of similar style with that of the guide's. Their visages,[23] too, were peculiar; one had a large beard, broad face, and small piggish eyes; the face of another seemed to consist entirely of nose, and was surmounted by a white sugar-loaf hat,[24] set off with a little red cock's tail. They all had beards, of various shapes and colors. There was one who seemed to be the commander. He was a stout old gentleman, with a weather-beaten countenance,[25] he wore a laced doublet, broad belt and hanger,[26] high-crowned hat and feather, red stockings, and high-heeled shoes, with roses in them. The whole group reminded Rip of the figures in an old Flemish[27] painting, in the parlor of Dominie Van Shaick, the village parson, and which had been brought over from Holland at the time of the settlement.

22. doublets (dub′ lits) *n*.: Closefitting jackets.
23. visages (viz′ ij iz) *n*.: An old-fashioned word for "faces."
24. sugar-loaf hat: A hat shaped like a cone.
25. countenance (koun′ tə nəns) *n*.: An old-fashioned word for "face."
26. hanger (haŋ′ ər) *n*.: A short sword that hangs from the belt.
27. Flemish (flem′ ish) *adj*.: Referring to the former country of Flanders in northwest Europe.

20. grizzled (griz′ ′ld) *adj*.: An old-fashioned word for "gray."
21. jerkin (jər′ kin) *n*.: A short, closefitting jacket worn in the 16th and 17th centuries.

RIP VAN WINKLE ASLEEP
Albertus Del Orient Browere
Shelburne Museum, Shelburne, Vermont

What seemed particularly odd to Rip was, that though these folks were evidently amusing themselves, yet they maintained the gravest face, the most mysterious silence, and were, withal, the most melancholy party of pleasure he had ever witnessed. Nothing interrupted the stillness of the scene but the noise of the balls, which, whenever they were rolled, echoed along the mountains like rumbling peals of thunder.

As Rip and his companion approached them, they suddenly desisted from their play, and stared at him with such fixed, statuelike gaze, and such strange, lackluster[28]

countenances, that his heart turned within him, and his knees smote together. His companion, now emptied the contents of the keg into large flagons,[29] and made signs to him to wait upon the company. He obeyed with fear and trembling; they quaffed[30] the liquor in profound silence, and then returned to their game.

By degrees Rip's awe and apprehension subsided. He even ventured, when no eye was fixed upon him, to taste the beverage, which he found had much of the flavor of ex-

---

28. lackluster (lak′ lus′ tər) *adj.*: Lacking brightness, dull.

29. flagons (flag′ ənz) *n.*: A container for liquids with a handle, narrow neck, spout, and sometimes a lid.

30. quaffed (kwäft) *v.*: Drank in a thirsty way.

cellent Hollands.[31] He was naturally a thirsty soul, and was soon tempted to repeat the draft. One taste provoked another; and he reiterated his visits to the flagon so often that at length his senses were overpowered, his eyes swam in his head, his head gradually declined, and he fell into a deep sleep.

On waking, he found himself on the green knoll whence he had first seen the old man of the glen. He rubbed his eyes—it was a bright sunny morning. The birds were hopping and twittering among the bushes, and the eagle was wheeling aloft, and breasting the pure mountain breeze. "Surely," thought Rip, "I have not slept here all night." He recalled the occurrences before he fell asleep. The strange man with a keg of liquor—the mountain ravine—the wild retreat among the rocks—the woebegone party at ninepins—the flagon—"Oh! that flagon! that wicked flagon!" thought Rip—"what excuse shall I make to Dame Van Winkle?"

He looked round for his gun, but in place of the clean, well-oiled fowling piece, he found an old firelock lying by him, the barrel incrusted with rust, the lock falling of, and the stock worm-eaten. He now suspected that the grave roysters[32] of the mountain had put a trick upon him, and having dosed him with liquor, had robbed him of his gun. Wolf, too, had disappeared, but he might have strayed away after a squirrel or partridge. He whistled after him and shouted his name, but all in vain; the echoes repeated his whistle and shout, but no dog was to be seen.

He determined to revisit the scene of the last evening's gambol,[33] and if he met with any of the party, to demand his dog and gun. As he rose to walk, he found himself stiff in the joints, and wanting in his usual activity. "These mountain beds do not agree with me," thought Rip, "and if this frolic should lay me up with a fit of the rheumatism, I shall have a blessed time with Dame Van Winkle." With some difficulty he got down into the glen: he found the gully up which he and his companion had ascended the preceding evening; but to his astonishment a mountain stream was now foaming down it, leaping from rock to rock, and filling the glen with babbling murmurs. He, however, made shift to scramble up its sides, working his toilsome way through thickets of birch, sassafras, and witch hazel, and sometimes tripped up or entangled by the wild grapevines that twisted their coils or tendrils from tree to tree, and spread a kind of network in his path.

At length he reached to where the ravine had opened through the cliffs to the amphitheater; but no traces of such opening remained. The rocks presented a high impenetrable wall, over which the torrent came tumbling in a sheet of feathery foam, and fell into a broad deep basin, black from the shadows of the surrounding forest. Here, then, poor Rip was brought to a stand. He again called and whistled after his dog; he was only answered by the cawing of a flock of idle crows, sporting high in air about a dry tree that overhung a sunny precipice; and who, secure in their elevation, seemed to look down and scoff at the poor man's perplexities. What was to be done? The morning was passing away, and Rip felt famished for want of his breakfast. He grieved to give up his dog and gun; he dreaded to meet his wife; but it would not do to starve among the mountains. He shook his head, shouldered the rusty firelock, and with a heart full of trouble and anxiety, turned his steps homeward.

As he approached the village he met a number of people, but none whom he knew,

---

31. Hollands n.: Gin made in the Netherlands.
32. roysters (rois′ tərs) n.: An old-fashioned word for people who are having a good time at a party.
33. gambol (gam′ b'l) v.: Play, frolic.

which somewhat surprised him, for he had thought himself acquainted with everyone in the country round. Their dress, too, was of a different fashion from that to which he was accustomed. They all stared at him with equal marks of surprise, and whenever they cast their eyes upon him, invariably stroked their chins. The constant recurrence of this gesture induced Rip, involuntarily, to do the same, when, to his astonishment, he found his beard had grown a foot long!

He had now entered the outskirts of the village. A troop of strange children ran at his heels, hooting after him, and pointing at his gray beard. The dogs, too, not one of which he recognized for an old acquaintance, barked at him as he passed. The very village was altered; it was larger and more populous. There were rows of houses which he had never seen before, and those which had been his familiar haunts had disappeared. Strange names were over the doors—strange faces at the windows—every thing was strange. His mind now misgave him; he began to doubt whether both he and the world around him were not bewitched. Surely this was his native village, which he had left but the day before. There stood the Catskill mountains—there ran the silver Hudson at a distance—there was every hill and dale precisely as it had always been—Rip was sorely perplexed—"That flagon last night," thought he; "has addled[34] my poor head sadly!"

It was with some difficulty that he found the way to his own house, which he approached with silent awe, expecting every moment to hear the shrill voice of Dame Van Winkle. He found the house gone to decay—the roof fallen in, the windows shattered, and the doors off the hinges. A half-starved dog that looked like Wolf was skulking about it. Rip called him by name, but the cur snarled, showed his teeth, and passed on.

This was an unkind cut indeed—"My very dog," sighed poor Rip, "has forgotten me!"

He entered the house, which, to tell the truth, Dame Van Winkle had always kept in neat order. It was empty, forlorn, and apparently abandoned. This desolateness overcame all his fears—he called loudly for his wife and children—the lonely chambers rang for a moment with his voice, and then all again was silence.

He now hurried forth, and hastened to his old resort, the village inn—but it too was gone. A large rickety wooden building stood in its place, with great gaping windows, some of them broken and mended with old hats and petticoats, and over the door was painted, "The Union Hotel, by Jonathan Doolittle." Instead of the great tree that used to shelter the quiet little Dutch inn of yore, there now was reared a tall, naked pole, with something on the top that looked like a red nightcap,[35] and from it was fluttering a flag, on which was a singular assemblage of stars and stripes—all this was strange and incomprehensible. He recognized on the sign, however, the ruby face of King George, under which he had smoked so many a peaceful pipe; but even this was singularly metamorphosed.[36] The red coat was changed for one of blue and buff, a sword was held in the hand instead of a scepter, the head was decorated with a cocked hat, and underneath was painted in large characters, GENERAL WASHINGTON.

There was, as usual, a crowd of folk about the door, but none that Rip recollected. The very character of the people seemed changed. There was a busy, bustling, disputatious tone about it, instead of the accustomed drowsy tranquillity. He looked in vain for the sage Nicholas Vedder,

---

34. addled (ad''ld) v.: Muddled and confused.

35. red nightcap: A liberty cap, used by colonists to symbolize their freedom from Great Britain.
36. metamorphosed (met' ə môr' fōzd) v.: Changed.

with his broad face, double chin, and fair long pipe, uttering clouds of tobacco smoke instead of idle speeches; or Van Bummel, the school-master, doling forth the contents of an ancient newspaper. In places of these, a lean, bilious-looking[37] fellow, with his pockets full of handbills, was speaking vehemently about rights of citizens—elections—members of Congress—liberty—Bunker's Hill—heroes of seventy-six—and other words, which were a perfect Babylonish jargon[38] to the bewildered Van Winkle.

The appearance of Rip, with his long grizzled beard, his rusty fowling piece, his uncouth dress, and an army of women and children at his heels, soon attracted the attention of the tavern politicians. They crowded round him, eyeing him from head to foot with great curiosity. The orator bustled up to him, and, drawing him partly aside, inquired "on which side he voted?" Rip stared in vacant stupidity. Another short but busy little fellow pulled him by the arm, and, rising on tiptoe, inquired in his ear, "whether he was Federal or Democrat?"[39] Rip was equally at a loss to comprehend the question; when a knowing, self-important

37. bilious (bil′ yəs)-**looking** *adj.*: Looking cross or bad-tempered.
38. Babylonish (bab′ ə lō′ nish) **jargon:** A language he could not understand.

39. Federal or Democrat: Two political parties at that time.

RETURN OF RIP VAN WINKLE, 1829
John Quidor
National Gallery of Art, Washington

old gentleman in a sharp cocked hat made his way through the crowd, putting them to the right and left with his elbows as he passed, and planting himself before Van Winkle, with one arm akimbo,[40] the other resting on his cane, his keen eyes and sharp hat penetrating, as it were, into his very soul, demanded, in an austere tone, "what brought him to the election with a gun on his shoulder, and a mob at his heels, and whether he meant to breed a riot in the village?" "Alas! gentlemen," cried Rip, somewhat dismayed, "I am a poor, quiet man, a native of the place, and a loyal subject of the king, God bless him!"

Here a general shout burst from the bystanders—"A tory![41] a tory! a spy! a refugee! hustle him! away with him!" It was with great difficulty that the self-important man in the cocked hat restored order; and, having assumed a tenfold austerity of brow, demanded again of the unknown culprit, what he came there for, and whom he was seeking. The poor man humbly assured him that he meant no harm, but merely came there in search of some of his neighbors, who used to keep about the tavern.

"Well, who are they? Name them."

Rip bethought himself a moment, and inquired, "Where's Nicholas Vedder?"

There was a silence for a little while, when an old man replied, in a thin, piping voice, "Nicholas Vedder! why, he is dead and gone these eighteen years! There was a wooden tombstone in the churchyard that used to tell all about him, but that's rotten and gone too."

"Where's Brom Dutcher?"

"Oh, he went off to the army in the beginning of the war; some say he was killed at the storming of Stony Point[42]—others say he was drowned in a squall at the foot of Antony's Nose.[43] I don't know—he never came back again."

"Where's Van Bummel, the schoolmaster?"

"He went off to the wars, too, was a great militia general, and is now in Congress."

Rip's heart died away at hearing of these sad changes in his home and friends, and finding himself thus alone in the world. Every answer puzzled him too, by treating of such enormous lapses of time, and of matters which he could not understand; war—Congress—Stony Point—he had no courage to ask after any more friends, but cried out in despair, "Does nobody here know Rip Van Winkle?"

"Oh, Rip Van Winkle!" exclaimed two or three, "Oh, to be sure! that's Rip Van Winkle yonder, leaning against the tree."

Rip looked, and beheld a precise counterpart of himself, as he went up the mountain: apparently as lazy, and certainly as ragged. The poor fellow was now completely confounded. He doubted his own identity, and whether he was himself or another man. In the midst of his bewilderment, the man in the cocked hat demanded who he was, and what was his name.

"Goodness knows," exclaimed he, at his wit's end; "I'm not myself—I'm somebody else—that's me yonder—no—that's somebody else got into my shoes—I was myself last night, but I fell asleep on the mountain, and they've changed my gun, and everything's changed, and I'm changed, and I can't tell what's my name, or who I am!"

The bystanders began now to look at each other, nod, wink significantly, and tap

---

40. akimbo (ə kim′ bō) *adj.*: Hand on hip, with elbow pointing outward.
41. tory (tôr′ ē): A person who supported the British during the American Revolution.

42. Stony Point: A town on the Hudson River where a Revolutionary War battle was fought in 1779.
43. Antony's Nose: The name of a mountain on the Hudson River.

their fingers against their foreheads. There was a whisper, also, about securing the gun, and keeping the old fellow from doing mischief, at the very suggestion of which the self-important man in the cocked hat retired with some precipitation. At this critical moment a fresh, comely[44] women pressed through the throng to get a peep at the gray-bearded man. She had a chubby child in her arms, which, frightened at his looks, began to cry. "Hush, Rip," cried she, "hush, you little fool; the old man won't hurt you." The name of the child, the air of the mother, the tone of her voice, all awakened a train of recollections in his mind. "What is your name, my good woman?" asked he.

"Judith Gardenier."

"And your father's name?"

"Ah! poor man, Rip Van Winkle was his name, but it's twenty years since he went away from home with his gun and never has been heard of since—his dog came home without him; but whether he shot himself, or was carried away by the Indians, nobody can tell. I was then but a little girl."

Rip had but one question more to ask; but he put it with a faltering voice:

"Where's your mother?"

"Oh, she too had died but a short time since; she broke a blood vessel in a fit of passion at a New England peddler."

There was a drop of comfort, at least, in this intelligence.[45] The honest man could contain himself no longer. He caught his daughter and her child in his arms. "I am your father!" cried he—"Young Rip Van Winkle once—old Rip Van Winkle now! Does nobody know poor Rip Van Winkle?"

All stood amazed, until an old woman, tottering out from among the crowd, put her hand to her brow, and peering under it in his face for a moment, exclaimed, "Sure enough! it is Rip Van Winkle—it is himself! Welcome home again, old neighbor. Why, where have you been these twenty long years?"

Rip's story was soon told, for the whole twenty long years had been to him but as one night. The neighbors stared when they heard it; some were seen to wink at each other, and put their tongues in their cheeks: and the self-important man in the cocked hat, who, when the alarm was over, had returned to the field, screwed down the corners of his mouth, and shook his head—upon which there was a general shaking of the head throughout the assemblage.

It was determined, however, to take the opinion of old Peter Vanderdonk, who was seen slowly advancing up the road. He was a descendant of the historian of that name, who wrote one of the earliest accounts of the province. Peter was the most ancient inhabitant of the village, and well versed in all the wonderful events and traditions of the neighborhood. He recollected Rip at once, and corroborated his story in the most satisfactory manner. He assured the company that it was a fact, handed down from his ancestor the historian, that the Catskill mountains had always been haunted by strange beings. That it was affirmed that the great Henry Hudson, the first discoverer of the river and country,[46] kept a kind of vigil there every twenty years, with his crew of the *Half-Moon*; being permitted in this way to revisit the scenes of his enterprise, and keep a guardian eye upon the river, and the great city called by his name. That his father had once seen them in their old Dutch dresses playing at ninepins in a hollow of the mountain; and that he himself had heard, one

---

44. comely (kum' lē) *adj.*: Attractive, pretty.
45. intelligence (in tel' ə jəns) *n.*: In this case, it means "news."

---

46. country: The area around the Catskills.

summer afternoon, the sound of their balls, like distant peals of thunder.

To make a long story short, the company broke up, and returned to the more important concerns of the election. Rip's daughter took him home to live with her; she had a snug, well-furnished house, and a stout, cheery farmer for a husband, whom Rip recollected for one of the urchins that used to climb upon his back. As to Rip's son and heir, who was the ditto of himself, seen leaning against the tree, he was employed to work on the farm; but evinced an hereditary disposition to attend to anything else but his business.

Rip now resumed his old walks and habits; he soon found many of his former cronies, though all rather the worse for the wear and tear of time; and preferred making friends among the rising generation, with whom he soon grew into great favor.

Having nothing to do at home, and being arrived at that happy age when a man can be idle with impunity, he took his place once more on the bench at the inn door, and was reverenced as one of the patriarchs of the village, and a chronicle of the old times "before the war." It was some time before he could get into the regular track of gossip, or could be made to comprehend the strange events that had taken place during his torpor. How that there had been a revolutionary war—that the country had thrown off the yoke of old England—and that, instead of being a subject of his Majesty George the Third, he was now a free citizen of the United States.

Rip, in fact, was no politician; the changes of states and empires made but little impression on him; but there was one species of despotism under which he had long groaned, and that was—petticoat government. Happily that was at an end; he had got his neck out of the yoke of matrimony, and could go in and out whenever he pleased, without dreading the tyranny of Dame Van Winkle. Whenever her name was mentioned, however, he shook his head, shrugged his shoulders, and cast up his eyes; which might pass either for an expression of resignation to his fate, or joy at his deliverance.

He used to tell his story to every stranger that arrived at Mr. Doolittle's hotel. He was observed, at first, to vary on some points every time he told it, which was, doubtless, owing to his having so recently awaked. It at last settled down precisely to the tale I have related, and not a man, woman, or child in the neighborhood, but knew it by heart. Some always pretended to doubt the reality of it, and insisted that Rip had been out of his head, and that this was one point on which he always remained flighty. The old Dutch inhabitants, however, almost universally gave it full credit. Even to this day they never hear a thunderstorm of a summer afternoon about the Catskills, but they say Henry Hudson and his crew are at their game of ninepins; and it is a common wish of all henpecked husbands in the neighborhood, when life hangs heavy on their hands, that they might have a quieting draft out of Rip Van Winkle's flagon.

RESPONDING TO THE SELECTION

Your Response

1. Which part of the story did you find the most entertaining? Explain.

Recalling

2. How do the people in the village feel about Rip?
3. Describe "the great error" in Rip's character.
4. What does Rip see when he enters the amphitheater with the strange man carrying the keg?
5. When Rip awakes, what is the first sign that he has been asleep a very long time?
6. What changes does Rip discover in the village?

Interpreting

7. A sentence in the story says that a quarrelsome wife may be considered a blessing. What does this mean?
8. How do Dame Van Winkle's personality and Rip's personality differ?
9. Compare and contrast Rip's life after his long sleep with his earlier life.

Applying

10. Imagine that you have fallen into a long sleep like Rip's. What changes in your neighborhood and country do you think you would discover when you awoke?

ANALYZING LITERATURE

Recognizing the Passage of Time

Changes in appearance indicate that time has passed. When Rip awakes, such changes show vividly the advance of time. They are also linked with other kinds of change.

1. What historical and political changes have occurred during Rip's long sleep?
2. What change has occurred that will make Rip's life at home different from what it was before his long sleep?

CRITICAL THINKING AND READING

Comparing and Contrasting Settings

When you **compare** and **contrast** a setting at different times, you note similarities, or comparisons, and differences, or contrasts.

1. When Rip looks around after he awakes, what features of the natural world does he see that have not changed at all?
2. What is different about the mountain setting?
3. How has the village changed?
4. How is his home different from what it was?

THINKING AND WRITING

Describing a Place Then and Now

Think of a place that you know well and that you have seen change over time. What details about the place changed? Use these details to write a composition in which you contrast how a place looked before it changed and how it looked after. When you revise, make sure your description would be clear even to a reader who never saw the place you are writing about.

LEARNING OPTION

Cross-curricular Connection. The Hudson River Valley was once a favorite subject of American painters. Books about these painters are probably available in your local library. A few titles include *American Paradise, The Hudson River and Its Painters,* and *Charmed Places.* You may also find examples of these painters' works in general books on American art. Compare the paintings you find with Irving's description of the Catskills in the opening paragraphs of "Rip Van Winkle." Choose a favorite painter and prepare a brief presentation about his or her work to the class.

Theme

THE FOUR-LEAF CLOVER
Winslow Homer
The Detroit Institute of Arts

GUIDE FOR READING

Utzel and His Daughter, Poverty

Stated Theme

Theme is the general idea about life that is revealed through the story. In stories with a **stated theme**, the writer or one of the characters tells you this idea directly. "Utzel and His Daughter, Poverty" is a story with a stated theme.

Focus

The story you are going to read is about a lazy man named Utzel and his daughter, whose name is Poverty. How would you expect a character noted for his lazy behavior to look and act? What would you expect a character named Poverty to look like? Would she be tall, short, slight, or heavy? Jot down your ideas about what these two characters would look like. Compare your ideas with your classmates' to see if they are similar. When you finish reading, review your notes to see if you and the author Isaac Bashevis Singer think alike.

Vocabulary

Knowing the following words will help you as you read "Utzel and His Daughter, Poverty."

fitting (fit′ iŋ) *adj.*: Suitable; proper (p. 149)

reproached (ri prōcht′) *v.*: Blamed; scolded (p. 149)

consternation (kän′ stər nā′ shən) *n.*: Sudden confusion and frustration (p. 150)

diligently (dil′ ə jənt lē) *adv.*: With careful, steady effort (p. 152)

industrious (in dus′ trē əs) *adj.*: Hard-working (p. 152)

Isaac Bashevis Singer

(1904–1991), who was born in Poland, wrote primarily in Yiddish, a language spoken by East European Jews and some of their descendants. Singer came to the United States in 1935 and earned his living by writing for Yiddish newspapers. As his novels and short stories were translated into English, he became famous for his accounts of Jewish life in Eastern Europe. In 1978 he won the Nobel Prize for Literature. In "Utzel and His Daughter, Poverty," Singer entertains and teaches at the same time.

Utzel and His Daughter, Poverty

Isaac Bashevis Singer

Once there was a man named Utzel. He was very poor and even more lazy. Whenever anyone wanted to give him a job to do, his answer was always the same: "Not today."

"Why not today?" he was asked. And he always replied, "Why not tomorrow?"

Utzel lived in a cottage that had been built by his great-grandfather. The thatched roof needed mending, and although the holes let the rain in, they did not let the smoke from the stove out. Toadstools grew on the crooked walls and the floor had rotted away. There had been a time when mice lived there, but now there weren't any because there was nothing for them to eat. Utzel's wife had starved to death, but before she died she had given birth to a baby girl. The name Utzel gave his daughter was very fitting. He called her Poverty.

Utzel loved to sleep and each night he went to bed with the chickens. In the morning he would complain that he was tired from so much sleeping and so he went to sleep again. When he was not sleeping, he lay on his broken-down cot, yawning and complaining. He would say to his daughter, "Other people are lucky. They have money without working. I am cursed."

Utzel was a small man, but as his daughter, Poverty, grew, she spread out in all directions. She was tall, broad, and heavy. At fifteen she had to lower her head to get through the doorway. Her feet were the size of a man's and puffy with fat. The villagers maintained that the lazier Utzel got, the more Poverty grew.

Utzel loved nobody, was jealous of everybody. He even spoke with envy of cats, dogs, rabbits, and all creatures who didn't have to work for a living. Yes, Utzel hated everybody and everything, but he adored his daughter. He daydreamed that a rich young man would fall in love with her, marry her, and provide for his wife and his father-in-law. But not a young man in the village showed the slightest interest in Poverty. When her father reproached the girl for not making friends and not going out with young men, Poverty would say, "How can I go out in rags and bare feet?"

One day Utzel learned that a certain charitable society in the village loaned poor people money, which they could pay back in small sums over a long period. Lazy as he was, he made a great effort—got up, dressed, and went to the office of the society. "I would like to borrow five gulden,"[1] he said to the official in charge.

"What do you intend to do with the

---

1. gulden (gool'dən) *n*.: A coin that was once used in Germany, Austria, and other countries.

money?" he was asked. "We lend money only for useful purposes."

"I want to have a pair of shoes made for my daughter," Utzel explained. "If Poverty has shoes, she will go out with the young people of the village and some wealthy young man will surely fall in love with her. When they get married, I will be able to pay back the five gulden."

The official thought it over. The chances of anyone falling in love with Poverty were very small. Utzel, however, looked so miserable that the official decided to give him the loan. He asked Utzel to sign a promissory note and gave him five gulden.

Utzel had tried to order a pair of shoes for his daughter a few months before. Sandler the shoemaker had gone so far as to take Poverty's measurements, but the shoemaker had wanted his money in advance. From the charitable society Utzel went directly to the shoemaker and asked whether he still had Poverty's measurements.

"And supposing I do?" Sandler replied. "My price is five gulden and I still want my money in advance."

Utzel took out the five gulden and handed them to Sandler. The shoemaker opened a drawer and after some searching brought out the order for Poverty's shoes. He promised to deliver the new shoes in a week, on Friday.

Utzel, who wanted to surprise his daughter, did not tell her about the shoes. The following Friday, as he lay on his cot yawning and complaining, there was a knock on the door and Sandler came in carrying the new shoes. When Poverty saw the shoemaker with a pair of shiny new shoes in his hand, she cried out in joy. The shoemaker handed her the shoes and told her to try them on. But, alas, she could not get them on her puffy feet. In the months since the measurements had been taken, Poverty's feet had be-

come even larger than they were before. Now the girl cried out in grief.

Utzel looked on in consternation. "How is it possible?" he asked. "I thought her feet stopped growing long ago."

For a while Sandler, too, stood there puzzled. Then he inquired, "Tell me, Utzel, where did you get the five gulden?" Utzel explained that he had borrowed the money from the charitable loan society and had given them a promissory note in return.

"So now you have a debt," exclaimed Sandler. "That makes you even poorer than you were a few months ago. Then you had nothing, but today you have five gulden less than nothing. And since you have grown

poorer, Poverty has grown bigger, and naturally her feet have grown with her. That is why the shoes don't fit. It is all clear to me now."

"What are we going to do?" Utzel asked in despair.

"There is only one way out for you," Sandler said. "Go to work. From borrowing one gets poorer and from work one gets richer. When you and your daughter work, she will have shoes that fit."

The idea of working did not appeal to either of them, but it was even worse to have new shoes and go around barefoot. Utzel and Poverty both decided that immediately after the Sabbath they would look for work.

Utzel got a job as a water carrier. Poverty became a maid. For the first time in their lives, they worked diligently. They were kept so busy that they did not even think of the new shoes, until one Sabbath morning Poverty decided she'd try them on again. Lo and behold, her feet slipped easily into them. The new shoes fit.

At last Utzel and Poverty understood that all a man possesses he gains through work, and not by lying in bed and being idle. Even animals were industrious. Bees make honey, spiders spin webs, birds build nests, moles dig holes in the earth, squirrels store food for the winter. Before long Utzel got a better job. He rebuilt his house and bought some furniture. Poverty lost more weight. She had new clothes made and dressed prettily like the other girls of the village. Her looks improved, too, and a young man began to court her. His name was Mahir and he was the son of a wealthy merchant. Utzel's dream of a rich son-in-law came true, but by then he no longer needed to be taken care of.

Love for his daughter had saved Utzel. In his later years he became so respected he was elected a warden of that same charitable loan society from which he had borrowed five gulden.

On the wall of his office there hung the string with which Sandler had once measured Poverty's feet, and above it the framed motto: *Whatever you can do today, don't put off till tomorrow.*

RESPONDING TO THE SELECTION

Your Response

1. Have you ever put off doing something even though you knew you had to do it? What effects did your delaying have?

Recalling

2. Why does Utzel want to buy shoes for Poverty?
3. Why are the shoes Sandler makes for Poverty too small?
4. What advice does Sandler give Utzel?
5. What does Utzel realize after he starts to work?

Interpreting

6. Why is it "fitting" that Utzel called his daughter Poverty?
7. The writer says that "the lazier Utzel got, the more Poverty grew." What could this statement indicate besides the fact that the girl grew physically larger?
8. What does the writer mean by saying, "Love for his daughter had saved Utzel"?

Applying

9. Why does a person become stronger by loving someone else?

ANALYZING LITERATURE

Identifying the Stated Theme

The **theme,** or central idea, of a story may be **stated** directly by the writer or one of the characters. In "Utzel and His Daughter, Poverty," there are several statements of the theme.

1. Find the place in the story where the character Sandler states the theme.
2. Find the place where the author, Isaac Bashevis Singer, states it.
3. How does the framed motto Utzel hangs on the wall also indicate the theme?

CRITICAL THINKING AND READING

Paraphrasing the Stated Theme

Paraphrasing a statement means putting it into your own words. By paraphrasing the stated theme, you ensure that you understand the story's point. You gain more from your reading if you also think about this idea. It may be that you do not agree with what the writer is saying.

1. Paraphrase the stated theme of "Utzel and His Daughter, Poverty."
2. Do you agree or disagree with this idea? Why?

THINKING AND WRITING

Writing About a Motto

A **motto** is an expression that captures a person's goals or ideals. At the end of the story, Utzel chooses a motto for himself. Think about what his motto means and how it fits the way he has changed. Draft an essay explaining why you think it is or is not an appropriate motto for Utzel. Support your opinion with details from the story. Review your essay, adding details to make your opinion more persuasive. Prepare a final draft to share with your classmates.

LEARNING OPTIONS

1. **Speaking and Listening.** It's fun to imagine how a character in a story might actually sound. Clues the writer gives you and what you know about a character's personality can help you do this. For example, the narrator says that Utzel yawns and complains when speaking to his daughter. With a classmate read aloud the dialogue between Utzel and Sandler when Poverty tries on her new shoes (pages 150 and 152). What clues did you find about how the characters might sound?
2. **Writing.** Write a story of your own to illustrate the motto "Whatever you can do today, don't put off till tomorrow." Read your story in class.

GUIDE FOR READING

The Old Demon

Implied Theme

Stories often communicate important ideas about life, called **themes.** However, authors do not always state these ideas directly. Sometimes the theme of a story is **implied,** and you must figure it out for yourself. In "The Old Demon," for example, the theme is revealed through the actions of the major character, Mrs. Wang.

Focus

The demon referred to in the title of this story is a river that flows next to the village in which Mrs. Wang and her neighbors live. Use a dictionary to discover meanings of the word *demon.* Why might someone call a river a demon? To help you organize your thoughts, use a Venn diagram like the one below, exploring what you know about rivers on one side and about demons on the other. In the space where the two circles intersect, write any characteristics, such as a lack of respect for human life, that a river and a demon might have in common.

Vocabulary

Knowing the following words will help you as you read "The Old Demon."

coarse (kôrs) *adj.*: Inferior; crude; common (p. 158)

wheedle (hwēd' 'l) *v.*: Persuade a person by flattery or coaxing (p. 158)

inert (in urt') *adj.*: Without power to move (p. 159)

somberly (säm' bər lē) *adv.*: Gloomily; dully (p. 160)

tentatively (ten' tə tiv lē) *adv.*: Hesitantly; uncertainly (p. 163)

impetuous (im pech' ōō wəs) *adj.*: Moving with great force or violence (p. 164)

resolutely (rez' ə lōōt' lē) *adv.*: With a firm purpose (p. 164)

Pearl S. Buck

(1892–1973) was born in the United States, but her parents took her to China when she was still a baby. Altogether she lived in that country for nearly forty years and wrote about it in her stories, novels, plays, and essays. One of her novels about China, *The Good Earth,* was made into a successful motion picture. In 1938 Buck became the first American woman to win the Nobel Prize for Literature. "The Old Demon" gives a picture of Chinese life in the late 1930's, when China was invaded and occupied by Japan.

The Old Demon

Pearl S. Buck

Old Mrs. Wang knew, of course, that there was a war. Everybody had known for a long time that there was war going on and that Japanese were killing Chinese. But still it was not real and no more than hearsay since none of the Wangs had been killed. The Village of Three Mile Wangs on the flat banks of the Yellow River, which was old Mrs. Wang's clan village, had never seen a Japanese. This was how they came to be talking about Japanese at all.

It was evening and early summer, and after her supper Mrs. Wang had climbed the dike steps, as she did every day, to see how high the river had risen. She was much more afraid of the river than of the Japanese. She knew what the river would do. And one by one the villagers had followed her up the dike, and now they stood staring down at the malicious yellow water, curling along like a lot of snakes, and biting at the high dike banks.

"I never saw it as high as this so early," Mrs. Wang said. She sat down on a bamboo stool that her grandson, Little Pig, had brought for her, and spat into the water.

"It's worse than the Japanese, this old devil of a river," Little Pig said recklessly.

"Fool!" Mrs. Wang said quickly. "The river god will hear you. Talk about something else."

So they had gone on talking about the Japanese. . . . How, for instance, asked Wang, the baker, who was old Mrs. Wang's nephew twice removed, would they know the Japanese when they saw them?

Mrs. Wang at this point said positively, "You'll know them. I once saw a foreigner. He was taller than the eaves of my house and he had mud-colored hair and eyes the color of a fish's eyes. Anyone who does not look like us—that is a Japanese."

Then Little Pig spoke up in his disconcerting way. "You can't see them, Grandmother. They hide up in the sky in airplanes."

Mrs. Wang did not answer immediately. Once she would have said positively, "I shall not believe in an airplane until I see it." But so many things had been true which she had not believed—the Empress, for instance, whom she had not believed dead, was dead. The Republic,[1] again, she had not believed in because she did not know what it was. She still did not know, but they had said for a long time there had been one. So now she merely stared quietly about the dike where

---

1. The Republic: China became a republic, a state run by elected representatives, in 1912. Before that time, China had been ruled by emperors and empresses. When the Republic ended in 1949, China was taken over by communists.

they all sat around her. It was very pleasant and cool, and she felt nothing mattered if the river did not rise to flood.

"I don't believe in the Japanese," she said flatly.

They laughed at her a little, but no one spoke. Someone lit her pipe—it was Little Pig's wife, who was her favorite, and she smoked it.

"Sing, Little Pig!" someone called.

So Little Pig began to sing an old song in a high quavering voice, and old Mrs. Wang listened and forgot the Japanese. The evening was beautiful, the sky so clear and still that the willows overhanging the dike were reflected even in the muddy water. Everything was at peace. The thirty-odd houses which made up the village straggled along beneath them. Nothing could break this peace. After all, the Japanese were only human beings.

"I doubt those airplanes," she said mildly to Little Pig when he stopped singing.

But without answering her, he went on to another song.

Year in and year out she had spent the summer evenings like this on the dike. The first time she was seventeen and a bride, and her husband had shouted to her to come out of the house and up the dike, and she had come, blushing and twisting her hands together, to hide among the women while the men roared at her and made jokes about her. All the same, they had liked her. "A pretty piece of meat in your bowl," they had said to her husband. "Feet a trifle big," he had answered deprecatingly. But she could see he was pleased, and so gradually her shyness went away.

He, poor man, had been drowned in a flood when he was still young. And it had taken her years to get him prayed out of Buddhist purgatory.[2] Finally she had grown

tired of it, what with the child and the land all on her back, and so when the priest said coaxingly, "Another ten pieces of silver and he'll be out entirely," she asked, "What's he got in there yet?"

"Only his right hand," the priest said, encouraging her.

Well, then, her patience broke. Ten dollars! It would feed them for the winter. Besides, she had had to hire labor for her share of repairing the dike, too, so there would be no more floods.

"If it's only one hand, he can pull himself out," she said firmly.

She often wondered if he had, poor silly fellow. As like as not, she had often thought gloomily in the night, he was still lying there, waiting for her to do something about it. That was the sort of man he was. Well, some day, perhaps, when Little Pig's wife had had the first baby safely and she had a little extra, she might go back to finish him out of purgatory. There was no real hurry, though. . . .

"Grandmother, you must go in," Little Pig's wife's soft voice said. "There is a mist rising from the river now that the sun is gone."

"Yes, I suppose I must," old Mrs. Wang agreed. She gazed at the river a moment. The river—it was full of good and evil together. It would water the fields when it was curbed and checked, but then if an inch were allowed it, it crashed through like a soaring dragon. That was how her husband had been swept away—careless, he was, about his bit of the dike. He was always go-

---

2. Buddhist purgatory (bood′ist pur′ gə tôr′ē): Buddhism is a religion popular in China and other Asian countries. Some Buddhists believe in purgatory, a place where the souls of certain dead people must stay until they can be freed.

ing to mend it, always going to pile more earth on top of it, and then in a night the river rose and broke through. He had run out of the house, and she had climbed on the roof with the child and had saved herself and it while he was drowned. Well, they had pushed the river back again behind its dikes, and it had stayed there this time. Every day she herself walked up and down the length of the dike for which the village was responsible and examined it. The men laughed and said, "If anything is wrong with the dikes, Granny will tell us."

It had never occurred to any of them to move the village away from the river. The Wangs had lived there for generations, and some had always escaped the floods and had fought the river more fiercely than ever afterward.

Little Pig suddenly stopped singing.

"The moon is coming up!" he cried. "That's not good. Airplanes come out on moonlight nights."

"Where do you learn all this about airplanes?" old Mrs. Wang exclaimed. "It is tiresome to me," she said, so severely that no one spoke. In this silence, leaning upon the arm of Little Pig's wife she descended slowly the earthen steps which led down into the village, using her long pipe in the other hand as a walking stick. Behind her the villagers came down, one by one, to bed. No one moved before she did, but none stayed long after her.

And in her own bed at last, behind the blue cotton mosquito curtains which Little Pig's wife fastened securely, she fell peacefully asleep. She had lain awake a little while thinking about the Japanese and wondering why they wanted to fight. Only very coarse persons wanted wars. In her mind she saw large coarse persons. If they came one must wheedle them, she thought, invite them to drink tea, and explain to them, reasonably—

only why should they come to a peaceful farming village . . . ?

So she was not in the least prepared for Little Pig's wife screaming at her that the Japanese had come. She sat up in bed muttering, "The tea bowls—the tea—"

"Grandmother, there's no time!" Little Pig's wife screamed. "They're here—they're here!"

"Where?" old Mrs. Wang cried, now awake.

"In the sky!" Little Pig's wife wailed.

They had all run out at that, into the clear early dawn, and gazed up. There, like wild geese flying in autumn, were great bird-like shapes.

"But what are they?" old Mrs. Wang cried.

And then, like a silver egg dropping, something drifted straight down and fell at the far end of the village in a field. A fountain of earth flew up, and they all ran to see it. There was a hole thirty feet across, as big as a pond. They were so astonished they could not speak, and then, before anyone could say anything, another and another egg began to fall and everybody was running, running . . .

Everybody, that is, but Mrs. Wang. When Little Pig's wife seized her hand to drag her along, old Mrs. Wang pulled away and sat down against the bank of the dike.

"I can't run," she remarked. "I haven't run in seventy years, since before my feet were bound. You go on. Where's Little Pig?" She looked around. Little Pig was already gone. "Like his grandfather," she remarked, "always the first to run."

But Little Pig's wife would not leave her, not, that is, until old Mrs. Wang reminded her that it was her duty.

"If Little Pig is dead," she said, "then it is necessary that his son be born alive." And when the girl still hesitated, she struck at her gently with her pipe. "Go on—go on," she exclaimed.

So unwillingly, because now they could scarcely hear each other speak for the roar of the dipping planes, Little Pig's wife went on with the others.

By now, although only a few minutes had passed, the village was in ruins and the straw roofs and wooden beams were blazing. Everybody was gone. As they passed they had shrieked at old Mrs. Wang to come on, and she had called back pleasantly:

"I'm coming—I'm coming!"

But she did not go. She sat quite alone watching now what was an extraordinary spectacle. For soon other planes came, from where she did not know, but they attacked the first ones. The sun came up over the fields of ripening wheat, and in the clear summery air the planes wheeled and darted and spat at each other. When this was over, she thought, she would go back into the village and see if anything was left. Here and there a wall stood, supporting a roof. She could not see her own house from here. But she was not unused to war. Once bandits had looted their village, and houses had been burned then, too. Well, now it had happened again. Burning houses one could see often, but not this darting silvery shining battle in the air. She understood none of it— not what those things were, nor how they stayed up in the sky. She simply sat, growing hungry, and watching.

"I'd like to see one close," she said aloud. And at that moment, as though in answer, one of them pointed suddenly downward, and, wheeling and twisting as though it were wounded, it fell head down in a field which Little Pig had ploughed only yesterday for soybeans. And in an instant the sky was empty again, and there was only this wounded thing on the ground and herself.

She hoisted herself carefully from the earth. At her age she need be afraid of nothing. She could, she decided, go and see what it was. So, leaning on her bamboo pipe, she made her way slowly across the fields. Behind her in the sudden stillness two or three village dogs appeared and followed, creeping close to her in their terror. When they drew near to the fallen plane, they barked furiously. Then she hit them with her pipe.

"Be quiet," she scolded, "there's already been noise enough to split my ears!"

She tapped the airplane.

"Metal," she told the dogs. "Silver, doubtless," she added. Melted up, it would make them all rich.

She walked around it, examining it closely. What made it fly? It seemed dead. Nothing moved or made a sound within it. Then, coming to the side to which it tipped, she saw a young man in it, slumped into a heap in a little seat. The dogs growled, but she struck at them again and they fell back.

"Are you dead?" she inquired politely.

The young man moved a little at her voice, but did not speak. She drew nearer and peered into the hole in which he sat. His side was bleeding.

"Wounded!" she exclaimed. She took his wrist. It was warm, but inert, and when she let it go, it dropped against the side of the hole. She stared at him. He had black hair and a dark skin like a Chinese and still he did not look like a Chinese.

"He must be a Southerner," she thought. Well, the chief thing was, he was alive.

"You had better come out," she remarked. "I'll put some herb plaster on your side."

The young man muttered something dully.

"What did you say?" she asked. But he did not say it again.

"I am still quite strong," she decided after a moment. So she reached in and seized him about the waist and pulled him out slowly, panting a good deal. Fortunately he was rather a little fellow and very light. When she had him on the ground, he seemed to find his feet; and he stood shakily and clung to her, and she held him up.

"Now if you can walk to my house," she said, "I'll see if it is there."

Then he said something, quite clearly. She listened and could not understand a word of it. She pulled away from him and stared.

"What's that?" she asked.

He pointed at the dogs. They were standing growling, their ruffs[3] up. Then he spoke again, and as he spoke he crumpled to the ground. The dogs fell on him, so that she had to beat them off with her hands.

"Get away!" she shouted. "Who told *you* to kill him?"

And then, when they had slunk back, she heaved him somehow onto her back; and, trembling, half carrying, half pulling him, she dragged him to the ruined village and laid him in the street while she went to find her house, taking the dogs with her.

Her house was quite gone. She found the place easily enough. This was where it should be, opposite the water gate into the dike. She had always watched that gate herself. Miraculously it was not injured now, nor was the dike broken. It would be easy enough to rebuild the house. Only, for the present, it was gone.

So she went back to the young man. He was lying as she had left him, propped against the dike, panting and very pale. He had opened his coat and he had a little bag from which he was taking out strips of cloth

and a bottle of something. And again he spoke, and again she understood nothing. Then he made signs and she saw it was water he wanted, so she took up a broken pot from one of many blown about the street, and, going up the dike, she filled it with river water and brought it down again and washed his wound, and she tore off the strips he made from the rolls of bandaging. He knew how to put the cloth over the gaping wound and he made signs to her, and she followed these signs. All the time he was trying to tell her something, but she could understand nothing.

"You must be from the South, sir," she said. It was easy to see that he had education. He looked very clever. "I have heard your language is different from ours." She laughed a little to put him at his ease, but he only stared at her somberly with dull eyes. So she said brightly, "Now if I could find something for us to eat, it would be nice."

He did not answer. Indeed he lay back, panting still more heavily, and stared into space as though she had not spoken.

---

3. ruffs (rufs) *n.*: Bands of fur around their necks.

"You would be better with food," she went on. "And so would I," she added. She was beginning to feel unbearably hungry.

It occurred to her that in Wang, the baker's, shop there might be some bread. Even if it were dusty with fallen mortar, it

would still be bread. She would go and see. But before she went she moved the soldier a little so that he lay in the edge of shadow cast by a willow tree that grew in the bank of the dike. Then she went to the baker's shop. The dogs were gone.

The baker's shop was, like everything else, in ruins. No one was there. At first she saw nothing but the mass of crumpled earthen walls. But then she remembered that the oven was just inside the door, and the door frame still stood erect, supporting one end of the roof. She stood in this frame, and, running her hand in underneath the fallen roof inside, she felt the wooden cover of the iron caldron. Under this there might be steamed bread. She worked her arm delicately and carefully in. It took quite a long time, but, even so, clouds of lime and dust almost choked her. Nevertheless she was right. She squeezed her hand under the cover and felt the firm smooth skin of the big steamed bread rolls, and one by one she drew out four.

"It's hard to kill an old thing like me," she remarked cheerfully to no one, and she began to eat one of the rolls as she walked back. If she had a bit of garlic and a bowl of tea—but one couldn't have everything in these times.

It was at this moment that she heard voices. When she came in sight of the soldier, she saw surrounding him a crowd of other soldiers, who had apparently come from nowhere. They were staring down at the wounded soldier, whose eyes were now closed.

"Where did you get this Japanese, Old Mother?" they shouted at her.

"What Japanese?" she asked, coming to them.

"This one!" they shouted.

"Is he a Japanese?" she cried in the greatest astonishment. "But he looks like us—his eyes are black, his skin—"

"Japanese!" one of them shouted at her.

"Well," she said quietly, "he dropped out of the sky."

"Give me that bread!" another shouted.

"Take it," she said, "all except this one for him."

"A Japanese monkey eat good bread?" the soldier shouted.

"I suppose he is hungry also," old Mrs. Wang replied. She began to dislike these men. But then, she had always disliked soldiers.

"I wish you would go away," she said. "What are you doing here? Our village has always been peaceful."

"It certainly looks very peaceful now," one of the men said, grinning, "as peaceful as a grave. Do you know who did that, Old Mother? The Japanese!"

"I suppose so," she agreed. Then she asked, "Why? That's what I don't understand."

"Why? Because they want our land, that's why!"

"Our land!" she repeated. "Why, they can't have our land!"

"Never!" they shouted.

But all this time while they were talking and chewing the bread they had divided among themselves, they were watching the eastern horizon.

"Why do you keep looking east?" old Mrs. Wang now asked.

"The Japanese are coming from there," the man replied who had taken the bread.

"Are you running away from them?" she asked, surprised.

"There are only a handful of us," he said apologetically. "We were left to guard a village—Pao An, in the county of—"

"I know that village," old Mrs. Wang interrupted. "You needn't tell me. I was a girl there. How is the old Pao who keeps the tea-shop in the main street? He's my brother."

"Everybody is dead there," the man replied. "The Japanese have taken it—a great army of men came with their foreign guns and tanks, so what could we do?"

"Of course, only run," she agreed. Nevertheless she felt dazed and sick. So he was dead, that one brother she had left! She was now the last of her father's family.

But the soldiers were straggling away again leaving her alone.

"They'll be coming, those little black dwarfs," they were saying. "We'd best go on."

Nevertheless, one lingered a moment, the one who had taken the bread, to stare down at the young wounded man, who lay with his eyes shut, not having moved at all.

"Is he dead?" he inquired. Then, before Mrs. Wang could answer, he pulled a short knife out of his belt. "Dead or not, I'll give him a punch or two with this—"

But old Mrs Wang pushed his arm away.

"No, you won't," she said with authority. "If he is dead, then there is no use in sending him into purgatory all in pieces. I am a good Buddhist myself."

The man laughed. "Oh well, he is dead," he answered; and then, seeing his comrades already at a distance, he ran after them.

A Japanese, was he? Old Mrs. Wang, left alone with this inert figure, looked at him tentatively. He was very young, she could see, now that his eyes were closed. His hand, limp in unconsciousness, looked like a boy's hand, unformed and still growing. She felt his wrist but could discern no pulse. She leaned over him and held to his lips the half of her roll which she had not eaten.

"Eat," she said very loudly and distinctly. "Bread!"

But there was no answer. Evidently he was dead. He must have died while she was getting the bread out of the oven.

There was nothing to do then but to finish the bread herself. And when that was done, she wondered if she ought not to follow after Little Pig and his wife and all the villagers. The sun was mounting and it was growing hot. If she were going, she had better go. But first she would climb the dike and see what the direction was. They had gone straight west, and as far as eye could look westward was a great plain. She might even see a good-sized crowd miles away. Anyway, she could see the next village, and they might all be there.

So she climbed the dike slowly, getting very hot. There was a slight breeze on top of the dike and it felt good. She was shocked to see the river very near the top of the dike. Why, it had risen in the last hour!

"You old demon!" she said severely. Let the river god hear it if he liked. He was evil, that he was—so to threaten flood when there had been all this other trouble.

She stooped and bathed her cheeks and her wrists. The water was quite cold, as though with fresh rains somewhere. Then she stood up and gazed around her. To the west there was nothing except in the far distance the soldiers still half-running, and beyond them the blur of the next village, which stood on a long rise of ground. She had better set out for that village. Doubtless Little Pig and his wife were there waiting for her.

Just as she was about to climb down and start out, she saw something on the eastern horizon. It was at first only an immense cloud of dust. But, as she stared at it, very quickly it became a lot of black dots and shining spots. Then she saw what it was. It was a lot of men—an army. Instantly she knew what army.

"That's the Japanese," she thought. Yes,

above them were the buzzing silver planes. They circled about, seeming to search for someone.

"I don't know who you're looking for," she muttered, "unless it's me and Little Pig and his wife. We're the only ones left. You've already killed my brother Pao."

She had almost forgotten that Pao was dead. Now she remembered it acutely. He had such a nice shop—always clean, and the tea good and the best meat dumplings to be had and the price always the same. Pao was a good man. Besides, what about his wife and his seven children? Doubtless they were all killed, too. Now these Japanese were looking for her. It occurred to her that on the dike she could easily be seen. So she clambered hastily down.

It was when she was about halfway down that she thought of the water gate. This old river—it had been a curse to them since time began. Why should it not make up a little now for all the wickedness it had done? It was plotting wickedness again, trying to steal over its banks. Well, why not? She wavered a moment. It was a pity, of course, that the young dead Japanese would be swept into the flood. He was a nice-looking boy, and she had saved him from being stabbed. It was not quite the same as saving his life, of course, but still it was a little the same. If he had been alive, he would have been saved. She went over to him and tugged at him until he lay well under the top of the bank. Then she went down again.

She knew perfectly how to open the water gate. Any child knew how to open the sluice for crops. But she knew also how to swing open the whole gate. The question was, could she open it quickly enough to get out of the way?

"I'm only one old woman," she muttered. She hesitated a second more. Well, it would be a pity not to see what sort of a baby Little Pig's wife would have, but one could not see everything. She had seen a great deal in this life. There was an end to what one could see, anyway.

She glanced again to the east. There were the Japanese coming across the plain. They were a long clear line of black, dotted with thousands of glittering points. If she opened this gate, the impetuous water would roar toward them, rushing into the plains, rolling into a wide lake, drowning them, maybe. Certainly they could not keep on marching nearer and nearer to her, and to Little Pig and his wife who were waiting for her. Well, Little Pig and his wife—they would wonder about her—but they would never dream of this. It would make a good story— she would have enjoyed telling it.

She turned resolutely to the gate. Well, some people fought with airplanes and some with guns, but you could fight with a river, too, if it were a wicked one like this one. She wrenched out a huge wooden pin. It was slippery with silvery green moss. The rill of water burst into a strong jet. When she wrenched one more pin, the rest would give way themselves. She began pulling at it, and felt it slip a little from its hole.

"I might be able to get myself out of purgatory with this," she thought, "and maybe they'll let me have that old man of mine, too. What's a hand of his to all this? Then we'll—"

The pin slipped away suddenly, and the gate burst flat against her and knocked her breath away. She had only time to gasp, to the river:

"Come on, you old demon!"

Then she felt it seize her and lift her up to the sky. It was beneath her and around her. It rolled her joyfully hither and thither, and then, holding her close and enfolded, it went rushing against the enemy.

RESPONDING TO THE SELECTION

Your Response

1. What do you think you would have done if you had been living in Mrs. Wang's village when the Japanese attacked?

Recalling

2. How did Mrs. Wang save herself and her child when her husband died?
3. What did she do for her husband after his death?
4. Why do the other people of her village run away?
5. How does she try to protect her land from the enemy?

Interpreting

6. In what ways is Mrs. Wang a person who protects and supports life?
7. In what ways does Mrs. Wang share some of the river's strength?
8. Explain the meaning of the story's title.

Applying

9. Although the Japanese pilot is an enemy, Mrs. Wang tries to help him. Do you think it is easier to fight an enemy you cannot see than one you can see? Explain your answer.

ANALYZING LITERATURE

Recognizing an Implied Theme

An **implied theme** is an idea about life that is suggested through a story. In "The Old Demon," the theme is suggested by the character of Mrs. Wang.

1. How does Mrs. Wang show that she values her family and her village?
2. What does her attempt to rescue the pilot reveal about her?
3. Which of the following statements best seems to express the implied theme of the story? Explain your answer.

a. Do not become involved with matters outside your family or community.
b. War is evil.
c. People should protect and care for each other.

4. How would you express the theme?

CRITICAL THINKING AND READING

Summarizing a Story

A **summary** of a story is a brief form of it containing the most important events in the order they occurred. By summarizing a story with many events like "The Old Demon," you can remember it more easily. Follow these steps in preparing a summary:

1. Reread the story.
2. Decide which events are the most important.
3. List these events in the order they occurred.
4. Give a brief account of each one in your own words.

Practice your summarizing skills on "The Old Demon."

1. Write a summary of the story.
2. When revising your summary, make sure it is brief but includes the key events.

THINKING AND WRITING

Responding to the Implied Theme

In "The Old Demon," the writer suggests that a person who protects and cares for others should be admired. List the reasons why you agree or disagree with this idea. Include examples to support your reasons. Then use your list to write a composition explaining your position. As you revise your work, check to see whether you have backed up your argument with good examples. Finally, share your composition with your classmates.

GUIDE FOR READING

Leslie Marmon Silko

(1948–   ), who was born in Albuquerque, New Mexico, was raised as a Pueblo Indian. Though her background is not entirely Pueblo, she identifies strongly with this tradition. She has explored its meaning in her well-known novel *Ceremony* (1977). Silko once said about the Laguna Pueblo reservation: "This place I am from is everything I am as a writer and a human being." "Humaweepi, the Warrior Priest" communicates Silko's strong feeling for the Southwest and for American Indian ways.

from Humaweepi, the Warrior Priest

Key to Theme: Character

The way a character in a story grows or changes is often a key to the theme. Sometimes characters grow because they are helped by others. In "Humaweepi, the Warrior Priest," a Pueblo boy's uncle helps him to become a warrior priest by teaching him about nature and tribal traditions. By focusing on the boy's development, you can understand the implied theme of the story.

Focus

How would you describe a warrior priest? You probably have ideas about what a warrior does and what a priest does. How might they go together? Imagine that an older relative or friend has told you that you will be taught how to be a warrior priest. Make a list of things you think you should learn. How would these things be valuable to your family, your friends, and to your community? How would these skills and insights help you in your own life?

As you read the story, compare what Humaweepi learns to the things on your list. Are any of the things the same? How are they different?

Vocabulary

Knowing the following words will help you as you read "Humaweepi, the Warrior Priest."

clan (klan) *n.*: A group of people, usually relatives (p. 167)
crevasses (krə vas′ əz) *n.*: Deep cracks (p. 168)
lacy (lā′ sē) *adj.*: Having a delicate, open pattern, like lace (p. 168)
fragile (fraj′ 'l) *adj.*: Delicate; easily broken (p. 168)

derive (di rīv′) *v.*: To receive from someone or something (p. 169)
succulent (suk′ yо̄о lənt) *adj.*: Juicy (p. 169)
triumphantly (trī um′ fənt lē) *adv.*: Victoriously; successfully (p. 171)

from Humaweepi, the Warrior Priest

Leslie Marmon Silko

The old man didn't really teach him much; mostly they just lived. Occasionally Humaweepi would meet friends his own age who still lived with their families in the pueblo,[1] and they would ask him what he was doing; they seemed disappointed when he told them.

"That's nothing," they would say.

Once this had made Humaweepi sad and his uncle noticed. "Oh," he said when Humaweepi told him, "that shows you how little they know."

They returned to the pueblo for the ceremonials and special days. His uncle stayed in the kiva[2] with the other priests, and Humaweepi usually stayed with clan members because his mother and father had been very old when he was born and now they were gone. Sometimes during these stays, when the pueblo was full of the activity and excitement of the dances or the fiesta[3] when the Christians paraded out of the pueblo church carrying the saint, Humaweepi would wonder why he was living out in the hills with the old man. When he was twelve he thought he had it all figured out: the old man just wanted someone to live with him and help him with the goat and to chop wood and carry water. But it was peaceful in this place, and Humaweepi discovered that after all these years of sitting beside his uncle in the evenings, he knew the songs and chants for all the seasons, and he was beginning to learn the prayers for the trees and plants and animals. "Oh," Humaweepi said to himself, "I have been learning all this time and I didn't even know it."

Once the old man told Humaweepi to prepare for a long trip.

"Overnight?"

The old man nodded.

So Humaweepi got out a white cotton sack and started filling it with jerked venison,[4] piki bread,[5] and dried apples. But the old man shook his head sternly. It was late June then, so Humaweepi didn't bother to bring the blankets; he had learned to sleep on the ground like the old man did.

"Human beings are special," his uncle had told him once, "which means they can do anything. They can sleep on the ground like the doe and fawn."

And so Humaweepi had learned how to find the places in the scrub-oak thickets

---

1. pueblo (pweb′ lō) *n*.: A type of Native American village in the Southwest where families lived together in flat-roofed houses of stone or adobe.
2. kiva (kē′ və) *n*.: A large room in a pueblo dwelling used for religious or other purposes.
3. fiesta (fē eś′ tə) *n*.: A religious festival.

4. jerked venison: Deer meat that has been sliced into thin strips and dried in the sun to preserve it.
5. piki (pē′ kē) **bread:** Corn bread.

where the deer had slept, where the dry oak leaves were arranged into nests. This is where he and his uncle slept, even in the autumn when the nights were cold and Humaweepi could hear the leaves snap in the middle of the night and drift to the ground.

Sometimes they carried food from home, but often they went without food or blankets. When Humaweepi asked him what they would eat, the old man had waved his hand at the sky and earth around them. "I am a human being, Humaweepi," he said: "I eat anything." On these trips they had gathered grass roots and washed them in little sandstone basins made by the wind to catch rain water. The roots had a rich, mealy taste. Then they left the desert below and climbed into the mesa[6] country, and the old man had

led Humaweepi to green leafy vines hanging from crevasses in the face of the sandstone cliffs. "Wild grapes," he said as he dropped some tiny dark-purple berries into Humaweepi's open palms. And in the high mountains there were wild iris roots and the bulbs from wild tulips which grew among the lacy ferns and green grass beside the mountain streams. They had gone out like this in each season. Summer and fall, and finally, spring and winter. "Winter isn't easy," the old man had said. "All the animals are hungry—not just you."

So this time, when his uncle shook his head at the food, Humaweepi left it behind as he had many times before. His uncle took the special leather pouch off the nail on the wall, and Humaweepi pulled his own buckskin bundle out from under his mattress. Inside he had a few objects of his own. A dried blossom. Fragile and yellow. A smooth pink

---

6. mesa (mā′ sə) *adj.*: Flat tableland with steep sides (usually a noun).

quartz crystal in the shape of a star. Tiny turquoise beads the color of a summer sky. And a black obsidian[7] arrowhead, shiny and sharp. They each had special meaning to him, and the old man had instructed him to assemble these things with special meaning. "Someday maybe you will derive strength from these things." That's what the old man had said.

They walked west toward the distant blue images of the mountain peaks. The water in the Rio Grande was still cold. Humaweepi was aware of the dampness on his feet: when he got back from the journey he decided he would make sandals for himself because it took hours for his boots to dry out again. His uncle wore old sandals woven from twisted yucca[8] fiber and they dried out almost immediately. The old man didn't approve of boots and shoes—bad for you, he said. In the winter he wore buckskin moccasins and in the warm months, these yucca sandals.

They walked all day, steadily, stopping occasionally when the old man found a flower or herb or stone that he wanted Humaweepi to see. And it seemed to Humaweepi that he had learned the names of everything, and he said so to his uncle.

The old man frowned and poked at a small blue flower with his walking stick. "That's what a priest must know," he said and walked rapidly then, pointing at stones and shrubs. "How old are you?" he demanded.

"Nineteen," Humaweepi answered.

"All your life," he said, "every day, I have been teaching you."

After that they walked along in silence, and Humaweepi began to feel anxious; all of a sudden he knew that something was going to happen on this journey. That night they reached the white sandstone cliffs at the foot of the mountain foothills. At the base of these cliffs were shallow overhangs with sandy floors. They slept in the sand under the rock overhang; in the night Humaweepi woke up to the call of a young owl; the sky was bright with stars and a half-moon. The smell of the night air made him shiver and he buried himself more deeply in the cliff sand.

In the morning they gathered tumbleweed sprouts that were succulent and tender. As they climbed the cliffs there were wild grapevines, and under the fallen leaves around the vine roots, the old man uncovered dried grapes shrunken into tiny sweet raisins. By noon they had reached the first of the mountain streams. There they washed and drank water and rested.

The old man frowned and pointed at Humaweepi's boots. "Take them off," he told Humaweepi; "leave them here until we come back."

So Humaweepi pulled off his cowboy boots and put them under a lichen-covered[9] boulder near a big oak tree where he could find them. Then Humaweepi relaxed, feeling the coolness of air on his bare feet. He watched his uncle, dozing in the sun with his back against a big pine. The old man's hair had been white and long ever since Humaweepi could remember; but the old face was changing, and Humaweepi could see the weariness there—a weariness not from their little journey but from a much longer time in this world. Someday he will die, Humaweepi was thinking. He will be gone and I will be by myself. I will have to do the things he did. I will have to take care of things.

Humaweepi had never seen the lake be-

---

7. obsidian (əb sid′ ē ən) *adj.*: Made of hard, black glass that comes from volcanoes (usually a noun).
8. yucca (yuk′ ə) *adj.*: Plants with stiff sword-shaped leaves and white flowers (usually a noun).

9. lichen (lī′ kən)-**covered:** Covered with small plants forming a crustlike growth.

fore. It appeared suddenly as they reached the top of a hill covered with aspen trees. Humaweepi looked at his uncle and was going to ask him about the lake, but the old man was singing and feeding corn pollen from his leather pouch to the mountain winds. Humaweepi stared at the lake and listened to the songs. The songs were snowstorms with sounds as soft and cold as snowflakes; the songs were spring rain and wild ducks returning. Humaweepi could hear this; he could hear his uncle's voice become the night wind—high-pitched and whining in the trees. Time was lost and there was only the space, the depth, the distance of the lake surrounded by the mountain peaks.

When Humaweepi looked up from the lake he noticed that the sun had moved down into the western part of the sky. He looked around to find his uncle. The old man was below him, kneeling on the edge of the lake, touching a big gray boulder and singing softly. Humaweepi made his way down the narrow rocky trail to the edge of the lake. The water was crystal and clear like air; Humaweepi could see the golden rainbow colors of the trout that lived there. Finally the old man motioned for Humaweepi to come to him. He pointed at the gray boulder that lay half in the lake and half on the shore. It was then that Humaweepi saw what it was. The bear. Magic creature of the mountains, powerful ally to men. Humaweepi unrolled his buckskin bundle and picked up the tiny beads—sky-blue turquoise and coral that was dark red. He sang the bear song and stepped into the icy, clear water to lay the beads on bear's head, gray granite rock, resting above the lake, facing west.

> "Bear
> resting in the mountains
> sleeping by the lake

> Bear
> I come to you, a man,
> to ask you:
> Stand beside us in our battles
> walk with us in peace.
> Bear
> I ask you for your power
> I am the warrior priest
> I ask you for your power
> I am the warrior priest."

It wasn't until he had finished singing the song that Humaweepi realized what the words said. He turned his head toward the old man. He smiled at Humaweepi and nodded his head. Humaweepi nodded back.

Speaking to a friend, Humaweepi describes a trip he took with his uncle.

Humaweepi and his friend were silent for a long time. Finally Humaweepi said, "I'll tell you what my uncle told me, one winter, before he left. We took a trip to the mountain. It was early January, but the sun was warm and down here the snow was gone. We left early in the morning when the sky in the east was dark gray and the brightest star was still shining low in the western sky. I remember he didn't wear his ceremonial moccasins; he wore his old yucca sandals. I asked him about that.

"He said, 'Oh, you know the badger and the squirrel. Same shoes summer and winter,' but I think he was making that up, because when we got to the sandstone cliffs he buried the sandals in the sandy bottom of the cave where we slept and after that he walked on bare feet—up the cliff and along the mountain trail.

"There was snow on the shady side of the trees and big rocks, but the path we followed was in the sun and it was dry. I could hear

melting snow—the icy water trickling down into the little streams and the little streams flowing into the big stream in the canyon where yellow bee flowers grow all summer. The sun felt warm on my body, touching me, but my breath still made steam in the cold mountain air.

" 'Aren't your feet cold?' I asked him.

"He stopped and looked at me for a long time, then shook his head. 'Look at these old feet,' he said. 'Do you see any corns or bunions?'

"I shook my head.

" 'That's right,' he said, 'my feet are beautiful. No one has feet like these. Especially you people who wear shoes and boots.' He walked on ahead before he said anything else. 'You have seen babies, haven't you?' he asked.

"I nodded, but I was wondering what this had to do with the old man's feet.

" 'Well, then you've noticed their grandmothers and their mothers, always worried about keeping the feet warm. But have you watched the babies? Do they care? No!' the old man said triumphantly, 'they do not care. They play outside on a cold winter day, no shoes, no jacket, because they aren't cold.' He hiked on, moving rapidly, excited by his own words; then he stopped at the stream. 'But human beings are what they are. It's not long before they are taught to be cold and they cry for their shoes.'

"The old man started digging around the edge of a stream, using a crooked, dry branch to poke through the melting snow. 'Here,' he said as he gave me a fat, round root, 'try this.'

"I squatted at the edge of the rushing, swirling water, full of mountain dirt, churning, and rolling—rich and brown and muddy with ice pieces flashing in the sun. I held the root motionless under the force of the stream water; the ice coldness of the water felt pure and clear as the ice that clung to the rocks in midstream. When I pulled my hand back it was stiff. I shook it and the root and lifted them high toward the sky.

"The old man laughed, and his mouth was full of the milky fibers of the root. He walked up the hill, away from the sound of the muddy stream surging through the snowbanks. At the top of the hill there was a grove of big aspens; it was colder, and the snow hadn't melted much.

" 'Your feet,' I said to him. 'They'll freeze.

"The snow was up to my ankles now. He was sitting on a fallen aspen, with his feet stretched out in front of him and his eyes half closed, facing into the sun.

" 'Does the wolf freeze his feet?' the old man asked me.

"I shook my head.

" 'Well then,' he said.

" 'But you aren't a wolf,' I started to say.

"The old man's eyes opened wide and then looked at me narrowly, sharply, squinting and shining. He gave a long, wailing, wolf cry with his head raised toward the winter sky.

"It was all white—pale white—the sky, the aspens bare white, smooth and white as the snow frozen on the ground. The wolf cry echoed off the rocky mountain slopes around us; in the distance, I thought I heard a wailing answer."

Your Response

1. Would you like to learn the kinds of things that Humaweepi does? Why or why not?

Recalling

2. When Humaweepi was twelve, why did he think his uncle wanted them to live together?
3. What kinds of things has Humaweepi learned from his uncle through the years?
4. On one of their trips, how does his uncle respond when Humaweepi tells the barefoot old man that he isn't a wolf?

Interpreting

5. Why does Humaweepi's uncle take him on trips?
6. In his song Humaweepi asks the "Bear" for its "power." What kind of "power" do you think he wants?
7. Why do Humaweepi and his uncle nod at each other when the song is over?
8. Give three examples showing that Humaweepi's uncle feels close to nature.
9. At the beginning of the story, the author writes, "The old man didn't really teach him much, mostly they just lived." Do you think the author means you to take this statement at face value? Explain your answer.

Applying

10. Compare and contrast Humaweepi's education with the way most people learn in school.

ANALYZING LITERATURE

Understanding Theme

The way a character grows is often a good clue to the theme of a story. In "Humaweepi, the Warrior Priest," the boy realizes that "sitting beside his uncle," he had "been learning all this time and . . . didn't even know it."

1. Briefly describe what Humaweepi learns from his uncle.

2. What evidence is there that the old man wants Humaweepi to take his place after he dies?
3. Choose one of the following ideas and explain why it best expresses the story's theme:
   a. Tradition is less important than freedom of expression.
   b. Young people learn about traditions from their elders.
   c. It is harmful to live apart from other people.
4. How would you express the theme of this story?

CRITICAL THINKING AND READING

Recognizing the Writer's Purpose

In this story the writer teaches you about Native American traditions, while presenting insights into life. Just as Humaweepi learns from his uncle almost without knowing it, you also learn about the Pueblo heritage.

1. Find two examples that show that Native Americans have a deep understanding of plants or animals.
2. What evidence is there that Native Americans believe there is a living spirit in things that might not seem alive to others?
3. How is a "warrior priest" different from and similar to other teachers or religious leaders?

THINKING AND WRITING

Responding to Theme

Imagine that Humaweepi's uncle suddenly arrives at your door. He wants to take you and your best friend on one of his trips to the mountains. You want to go on the trip, but your friend is not as enthusiastic. List the reasons that would convince your friend to support the decision to go on the trip. Then use the list to write a persuasive note to your friend. When you are finished, revise the note to make sure it will work.

GUIDE FOR READING

Gwendolyn Brooks

(1917–   ) was born in Topeka, Kansas, and grew up in Chicago, Illinois. In 1950 she won the Pulitzer Prize for poetry, and she has received other honors for her writing. She once remarked on her work by saying, "I like to vivify [give life to] the universal fact . . . but the universal wears contemporary clothing very well." What Brooks meant by this is illustrated in "Home." The universal fact of people's attachment to their home is vividly depicted in this brief story of a black American family faced with the loss of theirs.

Home

Universal Theme

A **theme** is the central idea of a story, or the general idea about life that the story reveals. A **universal theme** is one that has meaning and importance for people all over the world. Usually such a theme will be implied rather than stated directly.

Focus

What comes to mind when you hear the word *home*? Do you see visual images in your mind? Do you recall special events? Do you feel certain emotions? Look at the definition of *home* below.

> **home** (hōm) *n.* **1** the place where one lives; one's house, apartment, etc. **2** the city, country, etc. where one was born or brought up **3** a unit of family life **4** the place where something began or where it developed

Do any or all these definitions say everything about your understanding of what a home is? Use a sunburst diagram like the one below to help you define what *home* means to you. On each of the rays, write one aspect or characteristic of a home.

As its title suggests, the story you are about to read is about what one family's home means to them. As you read, think about how closely your ideas of home resemble those of the characters in the story.

Vocabulary

Knowing the following words will help you as you read "Home."

obstinate (äb′ stə nət) *adj.*: Stubborn (p. 175)

emphatic (em fat′ ik) *adj.*: Felt with emphasis; forceful; definite (p. 175)

staccato (stə kät′ ō) *adj.*: Made up of sharp, separate little elements (p. 176)

emerged (ēmʉrjd′) *v.*: Became visible (p. 176)

Home

Gwendolyn Brooks

What had been wanted was this always, this always to last, the talking softly on this porch, with the snake plant in the jardiniere[1] in the southwest corner, and the obstinate slip from Aunt Eppie's magnificent Michigan fern at the left side of the friendly door. Mama, Maud Martha and Helen rocked slowly in their rocking chairs, and looked at the late afternoon light on the lawn, and at the emphatic iron of the fence and at the poplar tree.

These things might soon be theirs no longer. Those shafts and pools of light, the tree, the graceful iron, might soon be viewed possessively by different eyes.

Papa was to have gone that noon, during his lunch hour, to the office of the Home Owners' Loan. If he had not succeeded in getting another extension, they would be leaving this house in which they had lived for more than fourteen years. There was little hope. The Home Owners' Loan was hard. They sat, making their plans.

"We'll be moving into a nice flat[2] somewhere," said Mama. "Somewhere on South Park, or Michigan, or in Washington Park Court." Those flats, as the girls and Mama knew well, were burdens on wages twice the size of Papa's. This was not mentioned now.

"They're much prettier than this old house," said Helen. "I have friends I'd just as soon not bring here. And I have other friends that wouldn't come down this far for anything, unless they were in a taxi."

Yesterday, Maud Martha would have attacked her. Tomorrow she might. Today she said nothing. She merely gazed at a little hopping robin in the tree, her tree, and tried to keep the fronts of her eyes dry.

HER WORLD
Philip Evergood
The Metropolitan Museum of Art

---

1. jardiniere (jär′d'n ir′) *n.*: An ornamental bowl, pot, or stand for flowers or plants.
2. flat (flat) *n.*: An apartment.

"Well, I do know," said Mama, turning her hands over and over, "that I've been getting tireder and tireder of doing that firing.[3] From October to April, there's firing to be done."

"But lately we've been helping, Harry and I," said Maud Martha. "And sometimes in March and April and in October, and even in November, we could build a little fire in the fireplace. Sometimes the weather was just right for that."

She knew, from the way they looked at her, that this had been a mistake. They did not want to cry.

But she felt that the little line of white, somewhat ridged with smoked purple, and all that cream-shot saffron,[4] would never drift across any western sky except that in back of this house. The rain would drum with as sweet a dullness nowhere but here. The birds on South Park were mechanical birds, no better than the poor caught canaries in those "rich" women's sun parlors.

"It's just going to kill Papa!" burst out Maud Martha. "He loves this house! He *lives* for this house!"

"He lives for us," said Helen. "It's us he loves. He wouldn't want the house, except for us."

"And he'll have us," added Mama, "wherever."

"You know," Helen sighed, "if you want to know the truth, this is a relief. If this hadn't come up, we would have gone on, just dragged on, hanging out here forever."

"It might," allowed Mama, "be an act of God. God may just have reached down, and picked up the reins."

"Yes," Maud Martha cracked in, "that's what you always say—that God knows best."

Her mother looked at her quickly, decided the statement was not suspect, looked away.

Helen saw Papa coming. "There's Papa," said Helen.

They could not tell a thing from the way Papa was walking. It was that same dear little staccato walk, one shoulder down, then the other, then repeat, and repeat. They watched his progress. He passed the Kennedys', he passed the vacant lot, he passed Mrs. Blakemore's. They wanted to hurl themselves over the fence, into the street, and shake the truth out of his collar. He opened his gate—the gate—and still his stride and face told them nothing.

"Hello," he said.

Mama got up and followed him through the front door. The girls knew better than to go in too.

Presently Mama's head emerged. Her eyes were lamps turned on.

"It's all right," she exclaimed. "He got it. It's all over. Everything is all right."

The door slammed shut. Mama's footsteps hurried away.

"I think," said Helen, rocking rapidly, "I think I'll give a party. I haven't given a party since I was eleven. I'd like some of my friends to just casually see that we're homeowners."

---

3. firing (fīr′ iŋ) *n.*: Starting up and tending the fire in a stove or furnace.

4. saffron: (saf′ rən) An orange-yellow color.

Your Response

1. How would you feel about moving from where you live? Explain.

Recalling

2. What does Papa hope to do during his lunch hour to deal with this problem?
3. According to Helen, why does Papa want to keep the house?

Interpreting

4. How do Mama and the girls feel before Helen sees Papa returning?
5. How do Mama and the girls feel as they watch Papa approaching?
6. At the end Helen gets the idea of giving a party. What does this suggest about how she feels?

Applying

7. What are the conditions that would make moving to a new home a happy event?

ANALYZING LITERATURE

Understanding Universal Themes

A theme is **universal** when readers the world over can respond to it. "Home," for example, presents a black family living in Chicago sometime during this century. Yet the problem the family faces and the feelings these people have would be understood by people in China, South America, Italy, or anywhere else.

1. Find three passages in the story where love of home is revealed.
2. In your own words tell what idea the story suggests about love of home.
3. Why could people living anywhere respond to this idea?

CRITICAL THINKING AND READING

Reading Between the Lines

The expression *reading between the lines* means reading to grasp and understand what is not said directly. For example, consider this sentence from "Home": "The rain would drum with as sweet a dullness nowhere but here." In reality, the sound of rain is basically the same everywhere. What is said "between the lines" is that Maud Martha is so attached to her home that she cannot imagine how another house can be as pleasant when it is raining. What can you read between the lines of the following sentences from "Home"?

1. "What had been wanted was this always, this always to last, the talking softly on this porch . . ."
2. "The birds on South Park were mechanical birds, no better than the poor caught canaries in those 'rich' women's sun parlors."

THINKING AND WRITING

Writing About Theme

One critic has identified a theme in Gwendolyn Brooks's work as the need for stability, order, and beauty. Write a composition explaining how "Home" reveals that these three qualities are necessary for a good life. First, look for a passage in the story that suggests why each of these qualities is needed or wanted. (You may have to read between the lines to do this.) Then prepare your first draft. When you revise, check that your statements all support your main point. Share your composition with your classmates.

LEARNING OPTIONS

1. **Art.** Draw or paint a picture of the house in the story. Review the story to find details of the house's appearance.
2. **Writing.** Gwendolyn Brooks describes her characters precisely. For example, see the description of Papa's walk on page 176. Write a description of someone you know well. Include facial expressions and gestures. Show your writing to others who know the person and let them guess his or her identity.

GUIDE FOR READING

Isaac Asimov

(1920–1992) was born in Russia and raised in Brooklyn, New York. He has written hundreds of books, many of which are science fiction. Asimov's love of science fiction developed when he began reading the science-fiction magazines sold in his father's candy store. In a way this childhood reading can be considered the earliest inspiration for "Hallucination," a story in which Asimov probes the mysteries of communication between two worlds.

Hallucination

Theme in Science Fiction

The **theme** of a story is its central idea, or the general idea about life it reveals. In a science-fiction story, a science-fiction theme will often apply to life as we know it. Because the story is often set far away in space or time and the characters and events are strange and unusual, however, you are likely to see the theme in a new light— a way that makes it more vivid and memorable.

Focus

Have you ever discovered something remarkable but were then unable to convince anyone that it was true? To demonstrate how frustrating it can be, act out the following situation with a partner. One of you has spoken to an intelligent being from another planet. The other is a police officer who refuses to believe the story. What would the two say to each other? How could the police officer be convinced?

This role-playing will give you some idea of what the boy in "Hallucination" comes up against. He, too, has spoken to an intelligent life form on another planet and must convince some pretty stubborn adults that it is true.

Vocabulary

Knowing the following words will help you as you read "Hallucination."

technology (tek näl′ ə jē) *n.*: The ideas of science applied to practical problems (p. 179)

hexagonal (heks ag′ ə nəl) *adj.*: Six-sided (p. 183)

concave (kän kāv′) *adj.*: Empty and curved like the inside of a hollow ball (p. 183)

billowed (bil′ ōd) *v.*: Surged or swelled (p. 184)

tethered (teth′ ərd) *v.*: Fastened with a rope or chain (p. 185)

insolent (in′ sə lənt) *adj.*: Disrespectful (p. 188)

opaque (ō pāk′) *adj.*: Not letting light pass through (p. 190)

Hallucination

Isaac Asimov

Sam Chase arrived on Energy Planet on his 15th birthday.

It was a great achievement, he had been told, to have been assigned there, but he wasn't at all sure he felt that at the moment.

It meant a three-year separation from Earth and from his family, while he continued a specialized education in the field, and that was a sobering thought. It was not the field of education in which he was interested, and he could not understand why Central Computer had assigned him to this project, and that was downright depressing.

He looked at the transparent Dome overhead. It was quite high, perhaps a thousand meters high, and it stretched in all directions farther than he could clearly see. He asked, "Is it true that this is the only dome on the planet, sir?"

Donald Gentry, to whom the question had been addressed, smiled. He was a large man, a little chubby, with dark brown, good-natured eyes, not much hair, and a short, graying beard.

He said, "The only one, Sam. It's quite large, though, and most of the housing facilities are underground, where you'll find no lack of space. Besides, once your basic training is done, you'll be spending most of your time in space. This is just our planetary base."

"I see, sir," said Sam, a little troubled.

Gentry said, "I am in charge of our basic trainees, so I have to study their records carefully. It seems to me that this assignment was not your first choice. Am I right?"

Sam hesitated, and then decided he didn't have much choice but to be honest about it. He said, "I'm not sure that I'll do as well as I would like to in gravitational engineering."

"Why not? Surely the Central Computer, which evaluated your scholastic record and your social and personal background, can be trusted in its judgments. And if you do well, it will be a great achievement for you; for right here, we are at the cutting edge of a new technology."

"I know that, sir," said Sam. "Back on Earth, everyone is very excited about it. No one before has ever tried to get close to a neutron star[1] and make use of its energy."

"Yes?" Gentry asked. "I haven't been on Earth for two years. What else do they say about it? I understand there's considerable opposition."

His eyes probed the boy.

Sam shifted uneasily, aware he was being tested. He said, "There are people on Earth who say it's all too dangerous and might be a waste of money."

"Do you believe that?"

"It might be so, but most new technologies have their dangers, and many are worth

---

1. neutron star: A collapsed star made up of many densely packed neutrons, or uncharged atomic particles.

doing despite that. This one is, I think."

"Very good. What else do they say on Earth?"

"They say the Commander isn't well and that the project might fail without him." When Gentry didn't respond, Sam added, hastily, "That's what they say."

Gentry acted as though he didn't hear. He put his hand on Sam's shoulder and said, "Come, I've got to show you to your Corridor, introduce you to your roommate and explain what your initial duties will be." As they walked toward the elevator that would take them downward, he said, "What was your first choice of assignment, Chase?"

"Neurophysiology,[2] sir."

"Not a bad choice. Even today, the human brain continues to be a mystery. We know more about neutron stars than we do about the brain—as we found out when this project first began."

"Oh?"

"Indeed! At the start, various people at the base—it was much smaller and more primitive then—reported having experienced hallucinations. It never had any bad effect, and after a while, there were no further reports. We never found out the cause."

Sam stopped, and looked up and about again. "Was that why the Dome was built, Dr. Gentry?"

"No, not at all. We needed a place with a completely Earth-like environment, but we haven't isolated ourselves. People can go outside freely. There are no hallucinations being reported now."

Sam said, "The information I was given about Energy Planet is that there is no life on it except for plants and insects, and that they're harmless."

"That's right, but they're also inedible.

So we grow our own vegetables, and keep some small animals, right here under the Dome. Still, we've found nothing hallucinogenic about the planetary life."

"Anything unusual about the atmosphere, sir?"

Gentry looked down from his only slightly greater height and said, "Not at all. People have camped in the open overnight on occasion, and nothing has happened. It is a pleasant world. There are streams but

---

2. neurophysiology (noor′ ō fiz′ ē äl′ ə jē) *n.*: The study of the brain and nervous system.

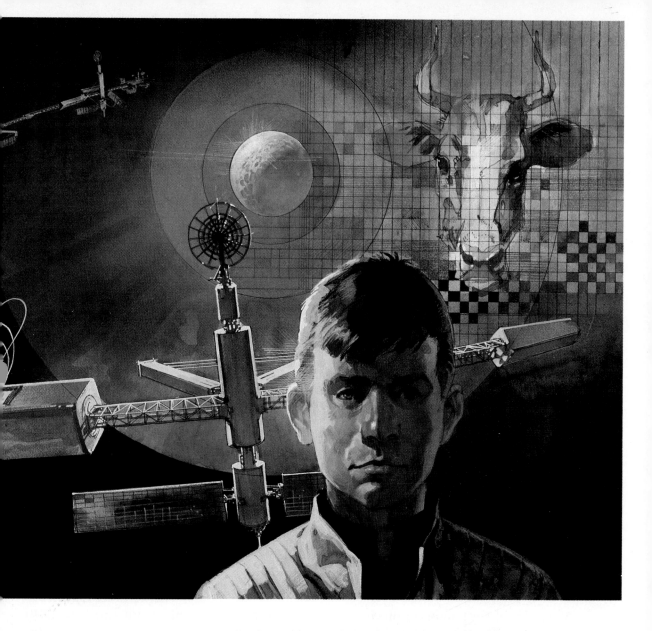

no fish, just algae[3] and water-insects. There is nothing to sting you or poison you. There are yellow berries that look delicious and taste terrible, but do no other harm. The weather's pretty nearly always good. There are frequent light rains, and it is sometimes windy, but there are no extremes of heat and cold."

---

3. algae (al′ jē) *n.*: Plants like seaweed that live in water or damp places.

"And no hallucinations anymore, Dr. Gentry?"

"You sound disappointed," said Gentry, smiling.

Sam took a chance. "Does the Commander's trouble have anything to do with the hallucinations, sir?"

The good nature vanished from Gentry's eyes. "What trouble do you refer to?"

Sam flushed, and they proceeded in silence.

Sam found few others in the Corridor he had been assigned to, but Gentry had explained it was a busy time at the forward station, where the power system was being built in a ring around the neutron star, the tiny object less than 10 miles across, that had all the mass of a normal star, and a magnetic field of incredible power.

It was a magnetic field that would be tapped. Energy would be led away in enormous amounts, and yet it would all be a pinprick, less than a pinprick to the star's rotational energy,[4] which was the ultimate source. It would take billions of years to bleed off all that energy, and in that time, dozens of populated planets, fed the energy through hyperspace, would have all they needed for an indefinite time.

Sharing Sam's room was Robert Gillette, a dark-haired, unhappy-looking young man. After cautious greetings had been exchanged, Robert revealed that he was 16 and had been "grounded" with a broken arm, though the break didn't show because it had been pinned internally.

Robert said, ruefully, "It takes a while before you learn to handle things in space. They may not have weight, but they have inertia,[5] and you have to allow for that."

Sam said, "They always teach you that . . ." He was going to say that it was taught in fourth-grade science, but realized that would be insulting, and stopped himself.

Robert caught the implication, however, and flushed. He said, "It's easy to know it in your head. It doesn't mean you get the proper reflexes till you've practiced quite a bit. You'll find out."

4. **rotational energy:** Energy that comes from the star's rotation, or turning.

5. **inertia** (in ur′ shə) n.: The tendency of an object to remain at rest if it is at rest, or to remain moving if it is moving—unless it is disturbed by an outside force.

Sam asked, "Is it very complicated to get to go outside?"

"No, but why do you want to go?"

"Have you ever been outside?"

"Sure."

Sam took a chance. He asked, very casually, "Did you ever see one of these hallucinations they talk about?"

Robert said, "*Who* talk about?"

Sam didn't answer directly. He said, "A lot of people used to see them—but they don't anymore. Or so they say."

"So *who* say?"

Sam took another chance. "Or if they see them, they keep quiet about them."

Robert said, gruffly, "Listen, don't get interested in these—whatever they are. If you start telling yourself you see—uh-something, you might be sent back. You'll lose your chance at a good education and an important career."

Sam shrugged and sat down on the unused bunk. "All right for this to be my bed?"

"It's the only other bed here," said Robert. He paused and then, as though to let bygones be bygones, said, "I'll show you around later."

"Thanks," said Sam. "What kind of a guy is the Commander?"

"He's aces. He knows more about hyperspatial technology than anyone, and he's got pull with the Space Agency, so we get the money and equipment we need."

Sam opened his trunk and, with his back to Robert, said, casually, "I hear he's not well."

"Things get him down. We're behind schedule, there are cost overruns, and like that."

"Depression, huh? Any connection, you suppose, with . . . ?"

Robert stirred impatiently in his seat. "Say, why are you so interested in all this?"

"Energy physics[6] isn't really my deal. Coming here. . . ."

"Well, here's where you are, mister, and you better make up your mind to it, or you'll get sent home, and then you won't be any-where—I'm going to the library."

Sam remained in the room alone—with his thoughts.

It was not at all difficult for Sam to get permission to leave the Dome.

The Corridor-Master nodded. "Fair enough, but you only get three hours, you know. And don't wander out of sight of the Dome. If we have to look for you, we'll find you, because you'll be wearing this," and he held out a transmitter, which Sam knew had been tuned to his own personal wavelength, one which had been assigned him at birth. "But if we have to go to that trouble, you won't be allowed out again for a pretty long time. And it won't look good on your record, either."

It won't look good on your record. Any reasonable career these days had to include experience and education in space, so it was an effective warning. No wonder people might have stopped reporting hallucina-tions, even if they saw them.

Even so, Sam was going to have to take his chance. After all, the Central Computer *couldn't* have sent him here just to do energy physics.

As far as looks were concerned, the planet might have been Earth—some part of Earth anyway, someplace where there were a few trees and low bushes and lots of tall grass.

There were no paths, and with his every

cautious step, the grass swayed, and flying creatures whirred upward with a soft, hiss-ing noise of wings.

One of them landed on his finger, and Sam looked at it curiously. It was very small and, therefore, hard to see in detail, but it seemed hexagonal, bulging above and con-cave below. There were many short, small legs so that when it moved it almost seemed to do so on tiny wheels. There were no signs of wings till it suddenly took off, and then four tiny, feathery objects unfurled.

What made the planet different from Earth, though, was the smell. It wasn't un-pleasant; it was just different. The plants must have an entirely different chemistry[7] from those on Earth.

The smell diminished with time, how-ever, as it saturated his nostrils. He found an exposed bit of rocky ledge he could sit on and considered the prospect. The sky was filled with lines of clouds, and the sun was periodically obscured, but the temperature was pleasant, and there was only a light wind. The air felt a bit damp.

Sam had brought a small hamper with two sandwiches, water and a canned drink.

He chewed away and thought: Why should there be hallucinations?

Surely, those accepted for a job as impor-tant as that of taming a neutron star would have been selected for mental stability. It would be surprising to have even one hallu-cinating, let alone a number of them. Was it a matter of chemical influences on the brain?

They would surely have checked that out.

Sam plucked a leaf, tore it in two and squeezed. He then put the torn edge to his

---

6. energy physics (fiz' iks): Physics is the science that deals with the properties of matter and energy; energy physics would be a branch of this science that studies energy especially.

7. chemistry (kem' is trē) *n.*: The chemical makeup and reaction of substances.

nose cautiously, and took it away again. A very acrid, unpleasant smell. He tried a blade of grass. Much the same.

Was the smell enough? It hadn't made him feel dizzy or in any way peculiar.

He used a bit of his water to rinse off the fingers that had held the plants, then finished his sandwiches slowly, trying to see if anything else might be considered unnatural.

All that greenery. There ought to be animals eating it, not just insects—or whatever those little things might be, with the gentle sighing of their tiny feathery wings and the very soft crackle of their munching of leaves and stalks.

What if there were a cow, a big, fat cow, doing the munching? And with the last mouthful of his second sandwich, Sam's munching stopped.

There was a kind of smoke in the air between himself and a line of hedges. It waved, billowed and altered, a very thin smoke. He blinked his eyes, then shook his head, but it was still there.

He swallowed hastily, closed his lunch box and slung it over his shoulder by its strap. He stood up.

MULTICULTURAL CONNECTION

Science Fiction Around the World

The world of science fiction. If you have ever dreamed about space voyages, time travel, and new worlds—or just plain down-to-earth but amazing scientific discoveries—you have been dreaming about the world of science fiction. Except for the basic requirement that it must be based on some scientific fact or speculation, science fiction has few limits and no standard definition. It is simply the fiction of daydreaming.

From ancient times to the twentieth century. Although this type of writing reached its peak in the twentieth century with the increase of scientific knowledge, writers had been spinning science-fiction tales for centuries, as far back as ancient Greece. Two modern science-fiction writers were France's Jules Verne, author of such classics as *From the Earth to the Moon* and *Twenty Thousand Leagues Under the Sea*, and Britain's H. G. Wells, author of such tales as *The Invisible Man* and *The Time Machine*.

Here at home. In the United States, a great deal of science fiction appeared in magazines. Two famous periodicals were *Amazing Stories*, the first total science-fiction magazine, edited by Hugo Gernsback, and *Astounding Science Fiction*, edited by the influential John W. Campbell, Jr. Many science-fiction giants, like Robert Heinlein and Isaac Asimov, began their careers with Campbell's magazine.

Around the world. Although America has been home to a large group of talented writers, other nations have also produced science-fiction greats. Among the notables: Arkady and Boris Strugatsky of the former Soviet Union, Stanislaw Lem of Poland, Sakyo Komatsu of Japan, and Jorge Luis Borges of Argentina.

Science fiction became popular around the world once the subject was transformed from written words to moving images. Perhaps two of the most memorable works are television's original *Star Trek* series and Stanley Kubrick's film *2001*, based on a story by British master Arthur C. Clarke.

Exploring on Your Own

Find out more about the science fiction of one of the countries mentioned here.

He felt no fear. He was only excited—and curious.

The smoke was growing thicker, and taking on a shape. Vaguely, it looked like a cow, a smoky, insubstantial shape that he could see through. Was it a hallucination? A creation of his mind? He had just been thinking of a cow.

Hallucination or not, he was going to investigate.

With determination, he stepped toward the cow outlined in smoke on the strange, far planet on which his education and career were to be advanced.

He was convinced there was nothing wrong with his mind. It was the "hallucination" that Dr. Gentry had mentioned, but it was no hallucination. Even as he pushed his way through the tall, rank, grass-like greenery, he noted the silence, and knew not only that it was no hallucination, but what it really *was*.

The smoke seemed to condense and grow darker, outlining the cow more sharply. It was as though the cow were being painted in the air.

Sam laughed, and shouted, "Stop! Stop! Don't use me; I don't know a cow well enough. I've only seen pictures. You're getting it all wrong."

It looked more like a caricature than a real animal, and, as he cried out, the outline wavered and thinned. The smoke remained, but it was as though an unseen hand had passed across the air to erase what had been written.

Then a new shape began to take form. At first, Sam couldn't quite make out what it was intended to represent, but it changed and sharpened quickly. He stared in surprise, his mouth hanging open and his hamper bumping emptily against his side.

The smoke was forming a human being. There was no mistake about it. It was forming accurately, as though it had a model it could imitate, and of course it did have one, for Sam was standing there.

It was becoming Sam, clothes and all, even the outline of the hamper and the strap over his shoulder. It was another Sam Chase.

It was still a little vague, wavering a bit, insubstantial, but it firmed as though it were correcting itself, and then, finally, it was steady.

It never became entirely solid. Sam could see the vegetation dimly through it, and when a gust of wind caught it, it moved a bit as though it were a tethered balloon.

But it was real. It was no creation of his mind. Sam was sure of that.

But he couldn't just stand there, simply facing it. Diffidently, he said, "Hello, there."

Somehow, he expected the Other Sam to speak too, and, indeed, its mouth opened and closed, but no sound came out. It might just have been imitating the motion of Sam's mouth.

Sam said, again, "Hello. Can you speak?"

There was no sound but his own voice, and yet there was a tickling in his mind, a conviction that they could communicate.

Sam frowned. What made him so sure of that? The thought seemed to pop into his mind.

He asked, "Is that what has appeared to other people—human people—my kind—on this world?"

No answering sound, but he was quite sure what the answer to this question was. This had appeared to other people, not necessarily in their own shape, but *something*. And it hadn't worked.

What made him so sure of *that*? Where did these convictions come from in answer to his questions?

Yes, of course, they *were* the answers to his questions. The Other Sam was putting thoughts into his mind. It was adjusting the tiny electric currents in his brain cells so that the proper thoughts would arise.

He nodded thoughtfully at *that* thought, and the Other Sam must have caught the significance of the gesture, for it nodded too.

It had to be so. First a cow had formed, when Sam had thought of a cow, and then it had shifted when Sam had said the cow was imperfect. The Other Sam could grasp his thoughts somehow, and if it could grasp them, then it could modify them, too, perhaps.

Was this what telepathy[8] was like, then?

---

8. telepathy (tə lep′ ə thē) *n.:* Communication between minds by exchanging thoughts.

It was not like talking. It was having thoughts, except that the thoughts originated elsewhere and were not created entirely of one's own mental operations. But how could you tell your own thoughts from thoughts imposed from outside?

Sam knew the answer to that at once. Right now, he was unused to the process. He had never had practice. With time, as he grew more skilled at it, he would be able to tell one kind of thought from another without trouble.

In fact, he could do it now, if he thought about it. Wasn't he carrying on a conversation, in a way? He was wondering, and then knowing. The wondering was his own ques-

Roy Andersen

tion, the knowing was the Other Sam's answer. Of course it was.

There! The "of course it was," just now, was an answer.

"Not so fast, Other Sam," said Sam aloud. "Don't go too quickly. Give me a chance to sort things out, or I'll just get confused."

He sat down suddenly on the grass, which bent away from him in all directions.

The Other Sam slowly tried to sit down as well.

Sam laughed, "Your legs are bending in the wrong place."

That was corrected at once. The Other Sam sat down, but remained very stiff from the waist up.

"Relax," said Sam.

Slowly, the Other Sam slumped, flopping a bit to one side, then correcting that.

Sam was relieved. With the Other Sam so willing to follow his lead, he was sure goodwill was involved. It was! Exactly!

"No," said Sam. "I said, not so fast. Don't go by my thoughts. Let me speak out loud, even if you can't hear me. *Then* adjust my thoughts, so I'll know it's an adjustment. Do you understand?"

He waited a moment and was then sure the Other Sam understood.

Ah, the answer had come, but not right away. Good!

"Why do you appear to people?" asked Sam.

He stared earnestly at the Other Sam, and knew that the Other Sam wanted to communicate with people, but had not succeeded.

But then, no answer to that question had really been required. The answer was obvious. But, then, *why* had they failed?

He put it in words. "Why did you fail? You are successfully communicating with me."

Sam was beginning to learn how to understand the alien manifestation. It was as though his mind were adapting itself to a new technique of communication, just as it would adapt itself to a new language. Or was the Other Sam influencing Sam's mind and teaching him the method without Sam even knowing it was being done?

What Sam found himself doing was letting his mind empty itself of immediate thoughts. After he asked this question, he let his eyes focus on nothing and his eyelids droop, as though he were about to drop off to sleep, and then he knew the answer. There was a little clicking—or something—in his mind, a signal that something had been put in from outside.

He now knew, for instance, that the Other Sam's previous attempts at communication had failed because the people to whom it had appeared had been frightened. They had doubted their own sanity. And because they feared, their minds—tightened. Their minds would not receive. The attempts at communication diminished, though they had never entirely stopped.

"But you're communicating with me," said Sam.

Sam was different from all the rest. He had not been afraid.

"Couldn't you have made them not afraid first? Then talked to them?"

It wouldn't work. The fear-filled mind resisted all. An attempt to change might damage. It would be wrong to damage a thinking mind. There had been one such attempt, but it had not worked.

"What is it you are trying to communicate, Other Sam?"

A wish to be left alone. *Despair!*

Despair was more than a thought; it was an emotion; it was a frightening sensation. Sam felt despair wash over him intensely, heavily, and yet, it was not part of himself.

He felt despair on the surface of his mind, keenly, but underneath it, where his own mind was, he was free of it.

Sam said, wonderingly, "It seems to me as though you're giving up. Why? Are we interfering with you?"

Human beings had built the Dome, cleared a large area of all planetary life and substituted their own. And once the neutron star had its power station; once floods of energy moved outward through hyperspace to power-thirsty worlds; more power stations would be built and still more. Then what would happen to *Home?* (There must be a name for the planet that the Other Sam used, but the only thought Sam found in his mind was *Home* and, underneath that, the thought *ours—ours—ours.*)

This planet was the nearest convenient base to the neutron star. It would be flooded with more and more people, more and more Domes, and their home would be destroyed.

"But you could change our minds if you had to, even if you damaged a few, couldn't you?"

If they tried, people would find them dangerous. People would work out what was happening. Ships would approach, and from a distance, use weapons to destroy the life on Home, and then bring in People-life instead. This could be seen in the people's minds. People had a violent history; they would stop at nothing.

"But what can I do?" Sam asked. "I'm just an apprentice. I've just been here a few days. What can I do?"

Fear. Despair.

There were no thoughts that Sam could work out, just the numbing layer of fear and despair.

He felt moved. It was such a peaceful world. They threatened nobody. They didn't even hurt minds, although they had the ability to do so.

It wasn't their fault they were near a neu-tron star. It wasn't their fault they were in the way of expanding humanity.

He said, "Let me think."

He thought, and there was the feeling of another mind watching. Sometimes his thoughts skipped forward, and he recognized a suggestion from outside.

There came the beginning of hope, Sam felt it, but wasn't certain.

He looked at the time-strip on his wrist and jumped a little. Far more time had passed than he had realized. His three hours were nearly up. "I must go back now," he said.

He opened his lunch hamper and removed the small thermos of water, drank from it thirstily, and emptied it. He placed the empty thermos under one arm. He removed the wrapping of the sandwich and stuffed it in his pocket.

The Other Sam wavered and turned smoky. The smoke thinned, dispersed and was gone.

Sam closed the hamper, swung it over his shoulder and turned toward the Dome.

His heart was hammering. Would he have the courage to go through with his plan? And if he did, would it work?

When Sam entered the Dome, the Corridor-Master was waiting for him, and said, as he looked ostentatiously at his own time-strip, "You shaved it rather fine, didn't you?"

Sam's lips tightened, and he tried not to sound insolent. "I had three hours, sir."

"And you took two hours and 58 minutes."

"That's less than three hours, sir."

"Hmm," the Corridor-Master was cold and unfriendly. "Dr. Gentry would like to see you."

"Yes, sir. What for?"

"He didn't tell me. But I don't like you cutting it that fine your first time out,

Chase. And I don't like your attitude, either, and I don't like an officer of the Dome wanting to see you. I'm just going to tell you once, Chase: If you're a trouble-maker, I won't want you in this Corridor. Do you understand?"

"Yes, Sir. But what trouble have I made?"

"We'll find that out soon enough."

Sam had not seen Donald Gentry since their one and only meeting when the young apprentice had reached the Dome. Gentry still seemed good-natured and kindly, and there was nothing in his voice to indicate anything else. He sat in a chair behind his desk, and Sam stood before it, his hamper still bumping his side.

Gentry said, "How are you getting along, Sam? Having an interesting time?"

"Yes, sir," said Sam.

"Still feeling you'd rather be doing something else, working somewhere else?"

Sam said, earnestly, "No, sir. This is a good place for me."

"Because you're interested in hallucinations?"

"Yes, sir."

"You've been asking others about it, haven't you?"

"It's an interesting subject to me, sir."

"Because you want to study the human brain?"

"Any brain, sir."

"And you've been wandering about outside the Dome, haven't you?"

"I was told it was permitted, sir."

"It is. But few apprentices take advantage of that so soon. Did you see anything interesting?"

Sam hesitated, then said, "Yes, sir."

"A hallucination?"

"No, sir." He said it quite positively.

Gentry stared at him for a few moments, and there was a kind of speculative hardening of his eyes. "Would you care to tell me what you did see? Honestly."

Sam hesitated again. Then he said, "I saw and spoke to an inhabitant of this planet, sir."

"An intelligent inhabitant, young man?"

"Yes, sir."

Gentry said, "Sam, we had reason to wonder about you when you came. The Central Computer's report on you did not match our needs, though it was favorable in many ways, so I took the opportunity to study you that first day. We kept our collective eye on you, and when you left to wander about the planet on your own, we kept you under observation."

"Sir," said Sam, indignantly, "that violates my right of privacy."

"Yes, it does, but this is a most vital project, and we are sometimes driven to bend the rules a little. We saw you talking with considerable animation for a substantial period of time."

"I just told you I was, sir."

"Yes, but you were talking to nothing; to empty air. You were experiencing a hallucination, Sam!"

Sam was speechless. A hallucination? It couldn't be a hallucination.

Less than half an hour ago, he had been speaking to the Other Sam; had been experiencing the thoughts of the Other Sam. He knew exactly what had happened then, and he was still the same Sam Chase he had been during that conversation and before. He put his elbow over his lunch hamper as though it were a connection with the sandwiches he had been eating when the Other Sam had appeared.

He said, with what was almost a stammer. "Sir—Dr. Gentry—it wasn't a hallucination. It was real."

Gentry shook his head. "My boy, I saw you talking with animation to nothing at all. I didn't hear what you said, but you were talking. Nothing else was there except plants. Nor was I the only one. There were two other witnesses, and we have it all on record."

"On record?"

"On a television cassette. Why should we lie to you, young man? This has happened before. At the start, it happened rather frequently. Now it happens only very rarely. For one thing, we tell the new apprentices of the hallucinations at the start, as I told you, and they generally avoid the planet until they are more acclimated, and then it doesn't happen to them."

"You mean you scare them," blurted out Sam, "so that it's not likely to happen. And they don't tell you if it does happen—but I wasn't scared."

Gentry shook his head. "I'm sorry you weren't, if that was what it would have taken to keep you from seeing things."

"I wasn't seeing things. At least, not things that weren't there."

"How do you intend to argue with a television cassette, which will show you staring at nothing?"

"Sir, what I saw was not opaque. It was smoky, actually; foggy, if you know what I mean."

"Yes, I do. It looked as a hallucination might look, not as reality. But the television set would have seen even smoke."

"Maybe not, sir. My mind must have been focused to see it more clearly. It was probably less clear to the camera than to me."

"It focused your mind, did it?" Gentry stood up, and he sounded rather sad. "That's an admission of hallucination. I'm really sorry, Sam, because you are clearly intelligent, and the Central Computer rated you highly—but we can't use you."

"Will you be sending me home, sir?"

"Yes, but why should that matter? You didn't particularly want to come here."

"I want to stay here *now*."

"But I'm afraid you cannot."

"You can't just send me home. Don't I get a hearing?"

"You certainly can, if you insist, but in that case, the proceedings will be official and will go on your record, so that you won't get another apprenticeship anywhere. As it is, if you are sent back unofficially, as better suited to an apprenticeship in neurophysiology, you might get that, and be better off, actually, than you are now."

"I don't want that. I want a hearing—before the Commander."

"Oh, no, not the Commander. He can't be bothered with that."

"It *must* be the Commander," said Sam, with desperate force, "or this project will fail."

"Unless the Commander gives you a hearing? Why do you say that? Come, you are forcing me to think that you are unstable in ways other than those involved with hallucinations."

"Sir," the words were tumbling out of Sam's mouth now. "The Commander is ill—they know that even on Earth—and if he gets too ill to work, this project will fail. I did not see a hallucination, and the proof is that I know why he is ill and how he can be cured."

"You're not helping yourself," said Gentry.

"If you send me away, I tell you the project will fail. Can it hurt to let me see the Commander? All I ask is five minutes."

"Five minutes? What if he refuses?"

"Ask him, sir. Tell him that I say the same thing that caused his depression can remove it."

"No, I don't think I'll tell him that. But I'll ask him if he'll see you."

The Commander was a thin man, not

very tall. His eyes were a deep blue, and they looked tired.

His voice was very soft, a little low-pitched and definitely weary.

"You're the one who saw the hallucination?"

"It was not a hallucination, Commander, it was real. So was the one you saw, Commander." (If that did not get him thrown out, Sam thought, he might have a chance. He felt his elbow tightening on his hamper again. He still had it with him.)

The Commander seemed to wince. "The one *I* saw?"

"Yes, Commander. It said it had hurt one person. They had to try with you because you were the Commander, and they—did damage."

The Commander ignored that and said, "Did you ever have any mental problems before you came here?"

"No, Commander. You can consult my Central Computer record."

Sam thought: *He* must have had problems, but they let it go because he's a genius and they had to have him.

Then he thought: Was that my own idea? Or had it been put there?

The Commander was speaking. Sam had almost missed it. He said, "What you saw can't be real. There is no intelligent life-form on this planet."

"Yes, sir. There is."

"Oh? And no one ever discovered it till you came here and did the job?" The Commander smiled very briefly. "I'm afraid I have no choice but to . . ."

"Wait, Commander," said Sam, in a strangled voice. "We know about the intelligent life-form. It's the insects, the little flying things."

"You say the insects are intelligent?"

"Not an individual insect by itself, but they fit together when they want to, like little jigsaws. They can do it in any way they want.

And when they do, their nervous systems fit together too, and build up. A lot of them *together* are intelligent."

The Commander's eyebrows lifted. "That's an interesting idea, anyway. Almost crazy enough to be true. How did you come to that conclusion, young man?"

"By observation, sir. Everywhere I walked, I disturbed the insects in the grass, and they flew about in all directions. But once the cow started to form, and I walked toward it, there was nothing to see or hear. The insects were gone. They had gathered together in front of me, and they weren't in the grass anymore. That's how I knew."

"You talked with a cow?"

"It was a cow at first, because that's what I thought of. But they had it wrong, so they switched and came together to form a human being—*me.*"

"You?" And then, in a lower voice, "Well, that fits anyway."

"Did you see it that same way too, Commander?"

The Commander ignored that. "And when it shaped itself like you, it could talk as you did? Is that what you're telling me?"

"No, Commander. The talking was in my mind."

"Telepathy?"

"Sort of."

"And what did it say to you—or think to you?"

"It wanted us to refrain from disturbing this planet. It wanted us not to take it over." Sam was all but holding his breath. The interview had lasted more than five minutes already, and the Commander was making no move to put an end to it, to send him home.

"Quite impossible."

"Why, Commander?"

"Any other base will double and triple the expense. We're having enough trouble getting grants as it is. Fortunately, it is all a hallucination, young man, and the problem

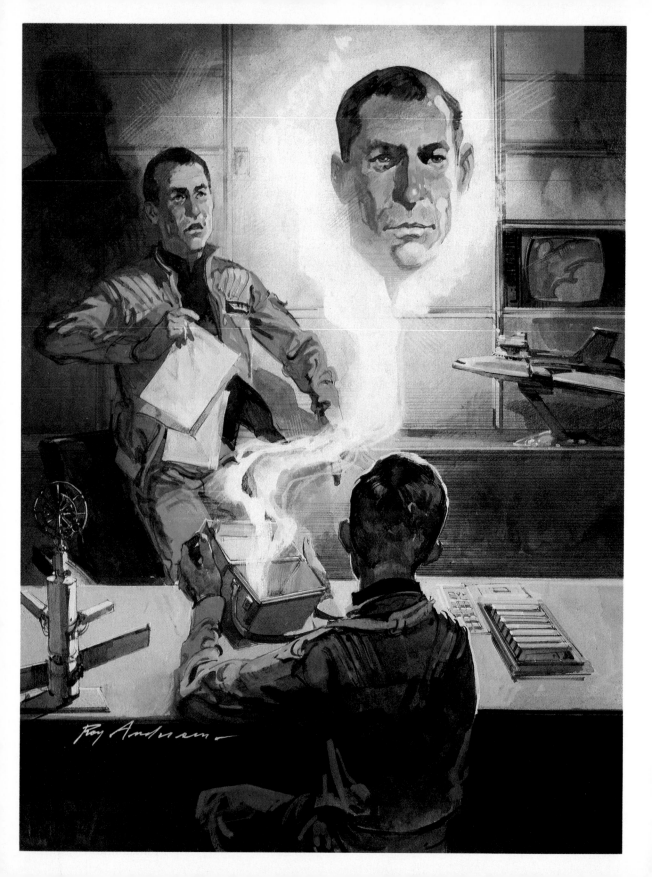

does not arise." He closed his eyes, then opened them and looked at Sam without really focusing on him. "I'm sorry, young man. You will be sent back—officially."

Sam gambled again. "We can't afford to ignore the insects, Commander. They have a lot to give us."

The Commander had raised his hand partway, as though about to give a signal. He paused long enough to say, "Really? What do they have that they can give us?"

"The one thing more important than energy, Commander. An understanding of the brain."

"How do you know that?"

"I can demonstrate it. I have them here." Sam seized his hamper and swung it forward onto the desk.

"What's that?"

Sam did not answer in words. He opened the hamper, and a softly whirring, smoky cloud appeared.

The Commander rose suddenly and cried out. He lifted his hand high, and an alarm bell sounded.

Through the door came Gentry, others behind him. Sam felt himself seized by the arms, and then a kind of stunned and motionless silence prevailed in the room.

The smoke was condensing, wavering, taking on the shape of a head; a thin head, with high cheekbones, a smooth forehead and receding hairline. It had the appearance of the Commander.

"I'm seeing things," croaked the Commander.

Sam said, "We're all seeing the same thing, aren't we?" He wriggled and was released.

Gentry said in a low voice, "Mass hysteria."[9]

"No," said Sam, "it's real." He reached toward the Head in midair and brought back his finger with a tiny insect on it. He flicked it, and it could just barely be seen making its way back to its companions.

No one moved.

Sam said, "Head, do you see the problem with the Commander's mind?"

Sam had the brief vision of a snarl in an otherwise smooth curve, but it vanished and left nothing behind. It was not something that could be easily put into human thought. He hoped the others experienced that quick snarl. Yes, they had. He knew it.

The Commander said, "There is no problem . . ." and stopped.

Sam said, "Can you adjust it. Head?"

Of course, they could not. It was not right to invade a mind.

Sam said, "Commander, give permission."

The Commander put his hands to his eyes and muttered something Sam did not make out. Then he said, clearly, "It's a nightmare, but I've been in one since . . . Whatever must be done, I give permission."

Nothing happened.

Or nothing seemed to happen.

And then slowly, little by little, the Commander's face lit in a smile.

He said, just above a whisper. "Astonishing. I'm watching a sun rise. It's been cold night for so long, and now I feel the warmth again." His voice rose high. "I feel wonderful."

The Head deformed at that point, turned into a vague, pulsing fog, then formed a curving, narrowing arrow that sped into the hamper. Sam snapped it shut.

He asked, "Commander, have I your permission to restore these little insect-things to their own world?"

"Yes, yes," said the Commander, dismissing that with a wave of his hand. "Gentry, call a meeting. We've got to change all our plans."

Sam had been escorted outside the Dome by a solid guard and had then been confined to his quarters in the Corridor for the rest of the day.

It was late when Gentry entered, stared at him thoughtfully, and said, "That was an amazing demonstration of yours. The entire incident has been fed into the Central Computer, and we now have a double project, neutron star energy and neurophysiology. I doubt that there will be any question about pouring money into this project now. And we'll have a group of neurophysiologists arriving eventually. Until then you're going to be working with those little things, those insects, and you'll probably end up the most important person here."

Sam said, "But will we leave their world to them?"

Gentry said, "We'll have to if we expect to get anything out of them, won't we? The Commander thinks we're going to build elaborate settlements in orbit about this world and shift all operations to them except for a skeleton crew in this Dome to maintain direct contact with the insects—or whatever we'll decide to call them. It will cost a great deal of money, and take time and labor, but it's going to be worth it. No one will question that."

Sam said, "Good!"

Gentry stared at him again, longer and more thoughtfully than before.

"My boy," he said, "it seems that what happened came about because you did not fear the supposed hallucination. Your mind remained open, and that was the whole difference. Why was that? Why weren't you afraid?"

Sam flushed. "I'm not sure, sir. As I look back on it, though, it seemed to me I was puzzled as to why I was sent here. I had been doing my best to study neurophysiology through my computerized courses and I knew very little about astrophysics.[10] The Central Computer had my record, all of it, the full details of everything I had ever studied, and I couldn't imagine why I had been sent here.

"Then, when you first mentioned the hallucinations, I thought, 'That must be it. I was sent here to look into it.' I just made up my mind that was the thing I had to do. I had no *time* to be afraid, Dr. Gentry. I had a problem to solve, and I—I had faith in the Central Computer. It wouldn't have sent me here, if I weren't up to it."

Gentry shook his head. "I'm afraid I wouldn't have had that much faith in that machine. But they say faith can move mountains, and I guess it certainly did in this case."

---

10. astrophysics (as' trō fiz' iks) *n*.: The science of the physical properties of the stars, planets, and other heavenly bodies.

RESPONDING TO THE SELECTION

Your Response

1. If, like Sam, you encountered a being from another planet, how would you react?

Recalling

2. Why are Sam, Dr. Gentry, and the Commander on Energy Planet?
3. What message does the "Other Sam" communicate to Sam?
4. Why does Sam succeed in communicating with the life form when others could not?
5. How does Sam convince the Commander not to send him back to Earth?
6. What changes will be made in the project as a result of all that Sam has done?

Interpreting

7. How is the intelligence of the life form different from human intelligence?
8. What conclusions does Sam come to about how the alien life form is communicating with him?

Applying

9. Gentry says to Sam, "My boy, it seems that what happened came about because you did not fear the supposed hallucination. Your mind remained open, and that was the whole difference." What real-life examples of open-mindedness and courage can you think of that have allowed people to gain knowledge that they otherwise could not have gained?

ANALYZING LITERATURE

Recognizing Theme in Science Fiction

The **theme** of a story is its central idea. In "Hallucination" the theme is revealed through what the main characters come to understand about the strange events taking place on an alien planet. The strangeness of the plot, of the aliens, and of the setting is what makes the theme stand out sharply.

1. Compare and contrast Sam's reaction to the alien life form he encounters with that of the Commander.
2. What does the story suggest about dealing with strange and unusual events?
3. What do you think is the theme of "Hallucination"?

CRITICAL THINKING AND READING

Looking at Reasoning

Reasoning is thinking logically. The part of the story in which Sam meets the alien life form reveals sound reasoning at work. Because of the way Sam reasons, events ultimately turn out favorably for him and the others assigned to Energy Planet.

1. Why does Sam reason that the reported hallucinations are highly unlikely?
2. When the cow appears before Sam, why does he reason that it is not a hallucination?
3. How does Sam figure out the way that the life form communicates?

THINKING AND WRITING

Writing Science Fiction

Imagine that you have been sent to Energy Planet shortly after the events presented in "Hallucination." Your duty is to send back to Earth reports on any strange or dangerous beings you meet outside the Dome. In your explorations you encounter one such being, and now you are writing a report about your adventure for an Information Committee on Earth made up of your classmates. Before you write the report, be sure you have assembled enough details to convey a full and clear picture of your experience. When you revise your work, keep in mind the question "Based on the information in my report, will people on Earth be able to visualize, or see, what I have seen?"

READING AND RESPONDING

The Short Story

As an active reader, you become involved with a story and gather meaning from it. You apply your active reading strategies to the plot, the characters, the setting, and the theme, which are the elements that work together to create an effective whole. Your response is your reaction to the story and its elements. It is what you think, what you feel, and what the story means to you.

RESPONDING TO PLOT The plot is what happens in a short story. The sequence of events in the plot center on a conflict, or struggle between opposing forces. Your understanding of the plot's structure will help you to make connections and predictions. Your involvement in the plot will affect your response to the way the conflict is resolved. For example, do you find the ending satisfying?

RESPONDING TO CHARACTERS Characters are the people—and sometimes the animals—in a story. Like real people, characters have traits and personalities that influence how they behave. They think and feel just as real people do. When you read, let yourself identify with the characters: Share their feelings and emotions, compare your own ideas with theirs, and think about what you would do in their place.

RESPONDING TO SETTING Setting is the time and the place in which the events in a story occur. The time might be in the past or in the future. It might cover just a minute or a span of years. The place might be a foreign country or someone's back yard. As you read actively, respond to the author's details about the setting. What kind of atmosphere or mood does the author create? How does the setting affect the plot and the characters? How does it affect you?

RESPONDING TO THEME Theme is the idea about life presented in a story. As you read, you will notice how the author has constructed the story to reveal the theme. Does the main character learn something about life? Is the theme stated or implied? What does this story say to you?

On pages 197–200 you can see an example of active reading and responding by Mario Sanchez of Flagstaff Junior High in Flagstaff, Arizona. The notes in the side column include Mario's thoughts and comments while reading "A Day's Wait." Your own thoughts as you read may be different, because each reader responds differently to a story.

MODEL

A Day's Wait

Ernest Hemingway

Title: *Who is waiting? What happens during this day?*

He came into the room to shut the windows while we were still in bed and I saw he looked ill. He was shivering, his face was white, and he walked slowly as though it ached to move.

"What's the matter, Schatz?"[1]

"I've got a headache."

"You better go back to bed."

"No. I'm all right."

"You go to bed. I'll see you when I'm dressed."

But when I came downstairs he was dressed, sitting by the fire, looking a very sick and miserable boy of nine years. When I put my hand on his forehead I knew he had a fever.

"You go up to bed," I said, "you're sick."

"I'm all right," he said.

When the doctor came he took the boy's temperature.

"What is it?" I asked him.

"One hundred and two."

Downstairs, the doctor left three different medicines in different colored capsules with instructions for giving them. One was to bring down the fever, another a purgative, the third to overcome an acid condition. The germs of influenza can only exist in an acid condition, he explained. He seemed to know all about influenza and said there was nothing to worry about if the fever did not go above one hundred and four degrees. This was a light epidemic[2] of flu and there was no danger if you avoided pneumonia.

Character: *Why is he arguing? Why not just go to bed?*

Setting: *Doctors hardly ever make house calls anymore. How long ago does this story take place?*

---

1. Schatz (shäts): A German term of affection, used here as a loving nickname.

2. epidemic (ep'ə dem' ik) *n.*: An outbreak of a contagious disease.

Plot and Character: *The boy should have fallen asleep. He shouldn't worry so much when there is obviously nothing he can do.*

Character: *What does he mean by "so far"?*

Plot: *He thinks something dreadful is going to happen.*

Plot and Character: *The father does not seem to be aware of the boy's fears.*

Setting: *It is wintertime, and these people live in the country.*

Back in the room I wrote the boy's temperature down and made a note of the time to give the various capsules.

"Do you want me to read to you?"

"All right. If you want to," said the boy. His face was very white and there were dark areas under his eyes. He lay still in the bed and seemed very detached from what was going on.

I read aloud from Howard Pyle's *Book of Pirates*; but I could see he was not following what I was reading.

"How do you feel, Schatz?" I asked him.

"Just the same, so far," he said.

I sat at the foot of the bed and read to myself while I waited for it to be time to give another capsule. It would have been natural for him to go to sleep, but when I looked up he was looking at the foot of the bed, looking very strangely.

"Why don't you try to go to sleep? I'll wake you up for the medicine."

"I'd rather stay awake."

After a while he said to me, "You don't have to stay in here with me, Papa, if it bothers you."

"It doesn't bother me."

"No, I mean you don't have to stay if it's going to bother you."

I thought perhaps he was a little lightheaded and after giving him the prescribed capsules at eleven o'clock I went out for a while. It was a bright, cold day, the ground covered with a sleet that had frozen so that it seemed as if all the bare trees, the bushes, the cut brush and all the grass and the bare ground had been varnished with ice. I took the young Irish setter for a little walk up the road and along a frozen creek, but it was difficult to stand or walk on the glassy surface and the red dog slipped and slithered and I fell twice, hard, once dropping my gun and having it slide away over the ice.

We flushed[3] a covey[4] of quail under a high clay bank with overhanging brush and I killed two as they went out of sight over the top of the bank. Some of the covey lit in trees but most of them scattered into brush piles and it was necessary to jump on the ice-coated mounds of brush several times be-

---

3. flushed (flusht) *v.*: Drove from hiding.
4. covey (kuv′ ē) *n.*: A small flock of birds.

fore they would flush. Coming out while you were poised unsteadily on the icy, springy brush they made difficult shooting, and I killed two, missed five, and started back pleased to have found a covey close to the house and happy there were so many left to find on another day.

At the house they said the boy had refused to let anyone come into the room.

"You can't come in," he said. "You mustn't get what I have."

I went up to him and found him in exactly the position I had left him, white-faced, but with the tops of his cheeks flushed by the fever, staring still, as he had stared at the foot of the bed.

I took his temperature.

"What is it?"

"Something like a hundred," I said. It was one hundred and two and four tenths.

"It was a hundred and two," he said.

"Who said so?"

"The doctor."

"Your temperature is all right," I said. "It's nothing to worry about."

"I don't worry," he said, "but I can't keep from thinking."

"Don't think," I said. "Just take it easy."

"I'm taking it easy," he said and looked straight ahead. He was evidently holding tight on to himself about something.

"Take this with water."

"Do you think it will do any good?"

"Of course it will."

I sat down and opened the *Pirate* book and commenced to read, but I could see he was not following, so I stopped.

"About what time do you think I'm going to die?" he asked.

"What?"

"About how long will it be before I die?"

"You aren't going to die. What's the matter with you?"

"Oh, yes, I am. I heard him say a hundred and two."

"People don't die with a fever of one hundred and two. That's a silly way to talk."

"I know they do. At school in France the boys told me you can't live with forty-four degrees. I've got a hundred and two."

He had been waiting to die all day, ever since nine o'clock in the morning.

"You poor Schatz," I said. "Poor old Schatz. It's like miles and kilometers.[5] You aren't going to die. That's a different thermometer. On that thermometer thirty-seven is normal. On this kind it's ninety-eight."

"Are you sure?"

"Absolutely," I said. "It's like miles and kilometers. You know, like how many kilometers we make when we do seventy miles in the car?"

"Oh," he said.

But his gaze at the foot of the bed relaxed slowly. The hold over himself relaxed too, finally, and the next day it was very slack and he cried very easily at little things that were of no importance.

---

5. kilometers (ki läm′ ə tərz) *n*.: A kilometer is 1,000 meters or about 5/8 of a mile.

Ernest Hemingway (1899–1961), who was born in Oak Park, Illinois, is one of America's most famous writers. He received the Nobel Prize for his novels and short stories. Hemingway lived an adventurous life, participating in both World War I and World War II and spending much time hunting and fishing. Many of his books, like *A Farewell to Arms* and *The Old Man and the Sea*, are based on such experiences. Many of these stories dramatize the importance of courage in the face of life's problems. "A Day's Wait" is not about adventures like these, but deals with a quieter kind of courage.

RESPONDING TO THE SELECTION

Your Response

1. How do you feel when you discover you have misunderstood something? Explain.

Recalling

2. Why does the boy think he will die?
3. How does the father explain the mistake to his son?

Interpreting

4. What is the meaning of the story's title?
5. What conflicting feelings does the boy have?
6. Describe two ways in which the boy shows courage or concern for others.
7. Why does the boy cry "very easily at little things" the next day?

Applying

8. In this story the boy shows a kind of quiet courage. What other characters in literature can you name who have shown quiet courage?

ANALYZING LITERATURE

Reviewing a Short Story

The elements of plot, character, setting, and theme work together to create a total effect. Apply all these elements to "A Day's Wait."

1. Give a brief summary of the story.
2. Describe the character of the boy.
3. What external conflict is present in the story? What internal conflict is present?
4. In what way does the setting—Europe—play an important role in this story?
5. What is the theme of the story?
6. What is the total effect of the story?

CRITICAL THINKING AND READING

Making Inferences About Conflict

The boy in "A Day's Wait" experiences a conflict, but the struggle is within his mind. Because the conflict occurs in the boy's mind, you do not learn about it directly. Instead, you learn about it by making inferences based on clues from what the boy says and does.

The trick of finding clues to the boy's conflict is to search for statements and actions that seem out of place. Such unusual behavior indicates that the boy is responding to an inner conflict rather than to the actual situation around him. For example, one clue to the conflict is that the boy seems "very detached."

1. Find two other examples of unusual actions (not words) that indicate the boy is experiencing a conflict.
2. Find two examples of unusual statements that point to the boy's internal conflict.

THINKING AND WRITING

Planning a Television Program

Imagine that your class is producing a program based on this story. As director, you have to write a memo telling the camera operator how to show the boy's internal conflict. Brainstorm to think of different camera shots that would reveal the boy's inner struggle. Then use these ideas to write a one-page memo. Explain why each shot you have chosen would be effective. As you revise your memo, make sure that the camera operator will be able to follow your directions.

LEARNING OPTION

Cross-curricular Connection. Had the boy in "A Day's Wait" known how to convert degrees Celsius to degrees Fahrenheit, he might have felt better sooner. You can make the conversion with a simple formula: $°F = \frac{9}{5} \times °C + 32$. To convert 30°C, for example, first multiply 30 by $\frac{9}{5}$ and then add 32. The answer is 86°F. Find the degrees Fahrenheit for 20°, 25°, 35°, and 40° Celsius. Then find out if the boy's friends were right about a temperature of 44 degrees Celsius.

YOUR WRITING PROCESS

WRITING AN EPILOGUE

Sometimes friends and neighbors move away and leave us wondering, "Whatever happened to ____?" Readers sometimes wonder about story characters in the same way. To satisfy this curiosity, authors sometimes write epilogues to their works. Epilogues are summaries of events that follow the end of a story. Imagine that you could write an epilogue to one of the stories in this unit. Which character would you focus on first? Which plot element would you explore further?

Focus

Assignment: Write an epilogue to a story.
Purpose: To answer questions that were raised in your mind by the story.
Audience: Fellow students who share your curiosity.

Prewriting

1. Pick the story. Chances are you will probably write the most interesting epilogue if you choose a story that intrigued you the first time around. Which of the stories left you wondering what was going to happen next?

2. Brainstorm with a partner or group. Find one or a group of classmates who chose the same story you did. Together, think of what might happen to each of the main characters if the story were to continue.

Student Model

Story: *A Boy and a Man*

characters	years later	20 years later
Rudi	Rudi becomes a famous guide.	Rudi buys a hotel of his own.
Captain Winter	Captain Winter retires and lives in England.	He is knighted by the Queen.

After you fill in your chart, choose the time frame you want to use in your epilogue.

3. Freewrite to create a clearer picture. Freewrite about the events of a particular time frame, filling in additional details. Before you know it, you will have the makings of an epilogue.

Drafting

1. Keep it brief. Remember that an epilogue is a summary of events rather than a full-fledged story. By answering a few essential questions—*who, what, when, where, why,* and *how*—you should be able to keep your narrative brief.

Student Model

"Song of the Trees"
Mr. Anderson, angry at David's interference in the woods, returns to David's home later that night with the other lumbermen. They break into the house while the family is asleep and carry David off. Mama and Big Ma arm themselves and, with the help of other families who have been threatened by Anderson, go after the lumbermen. They track the men to the lumbermill. Outnumbering them there, they manage to rescue David and chase Anderson and his men out of the area for good.

---

2. Tie up the loose ends. The purpose of your epilogue is to answer readers' questions. Don't include hints that will raise further questions in readers' minds.

Revising and Editing

1. Check your epilogue for "the facts." Did you include the *who, what, when, where, why,* and *how* as best as you could? If one of these elements is missing, now is the time to put it in.

2. Test your epilogue on peer editors. Exchange epilogues with another pair or group. Consider the following questions as you review your classmates' work:
- Does the epilogue answer questions that the story might raise in a reader's mind?
- Does it avoid raising further questions?
- Are the summarized events believable and consistent with those in the story?
- Is the summary clear and understandable?

3. Proofread your epilogue. You may have gotten so caught up in the events you were describing that you allowed sentence fragments and run-ons to sneak in. Check for these and correct them.

Grammar Tip
Run-ons and sentence fragments are closely related grammatical errors. A run-on sentence is two or more complete sentences that are not properly joined or separated. A fragment is a group of words that does not express a complete thought.

Options for Publishing
- Read your epilogue to the class and invite comments about it.
- Contribute your epilogue to a bulletin board display of stories and epilogues.
- Write a letter to the author or publisher of the short story and share your epilogue.

Reviewing Your Writing Process

1. How did you decide which short story to write an epilogue for? Explain.

2. Was it helpful to create a chart showing events set at different times? Explain.

YOUR WRITING PROCESS

WRITING A PROBLEM-SOLVING NOTE

Characters in well-written stories have a way of bringing us into their world. We can come to feel like their friends or even members of their family. Think about the short stories you have read. At any point did you wish that you could have stepped into the story and helped a character out of a sticky situation? Imagine that you are a friend or relative of one of the fictional characters in this unit. You are aware of the character's latest dilemma and are prepared to offer your valuable advice.

> **Focus**
>
> **Assignment:** Write a note of advice to a character in a story.
> **Purpose:** To help the character solve a problem.
> **Audience:** A fictional character.

Prewriting

1. Whose problem is *really* interesting? All good stories have at least one problem that brings the characters into conflict within themselves or with one another. Which character's problem interests you the most? With a partner or a small group, look through the stories in this unit. Take turns discussing them, focusing on each character's main problem.

2. Brainstorm to find solutions. At this stage don't limit yourself to logical solutions to a character's problem. Sometimes what at first seems to be an illogical idea can lead to a reasonable suggestion. Try mapping your ideas with a diagram like the one that follows.

Character: _____

Character's main problem: _____

_____

Solution 1:	Solution 2:	Solution 3:
_____	_____	_____
_____	_____	_____

3. Evaluate each solution. From your chart you can see many potential solutions for each problem. With your partner or peer group, evaluate each solution. List the advantages and disadvantages of each, then decide on the best one.

4. Break down the solution into smaller steps. After you have chosen a solution, figure out how your character will arrive at it. What should the character do first, next, last?

Student Model

Story: "Two Kinds"   Character: Narrator
<u>Main problem</u>: She doesn't have enough belief in herself to want to succeed at anything.
<u>Best solution</u>: She can build self-confidence by succeeding at something she feels comfortable doing.
<u>Outline of steps</u>:
1. She should confide in her mother and ask her mother to help her meet her goal.
2. She should choose an activity she enjoys.
3. She should set a specific goal for the activity, such as doing it longer, faster, or better than before.

---

6. Decide "when" to write the note. At what moment in the story will your character "receive" your note? (Remember that the character doesn't know what will happen next.)

Drafting

1. As you write, refer to your outline of steps. In this way your advice will be logical and clear to your character. Discuss each step by pointing out its advantages to the character and to others in the story.

2. Keep the tone optimistic. Remember that you are writing a note to someone you care about. You will want to encourage that character to remain hopeful as he or she works toward solving the problem at hand.

Revising

1. Role-play with a classmate. Ask a partner to read and respond to your note as your character might. Have him or her answer questions like the following:
• Is my advice clear and understandable?
• Do I convince you to follow my advice? Why or why not?
2. Proofread your note. Check to see that your finished note is free of errors in grammar and punctuation.

PARADE CURTAIN AFTER PICASSO
© *David Hockney, 1980*

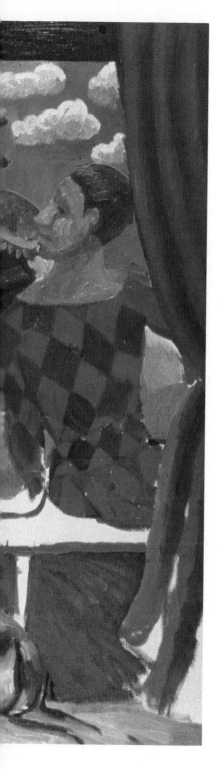

DRAMA

The word *drama* leaves a thrill in the air. Hear the word and you immediately think of the excitement of the theater with live actors on the stage and a live audience offering its applause. Or you recall the pleasure of drama brought into your home through television or radio or into the cinema through movies.

Since drama is meant to be performed, when you read it, you must imagine how it would appear on the stage or screen, or, if it is a radio play, how it would sound over the radio or on a tape cassette. The story of the drama is told mainly through dialogue, or conversation between characters. From what the characters say, you discover what they are feeling and what they are like. In addition, stage directions describe how the characters would move or act before an audience. The sets are the re-creation of settings on the stage; the props, the physical objects the characters use; the costumes, the clothes the characters wear; and the sound effects, the planned noise that accompanies the play. Each of these devices helps create the world of the play on the stage.

Just as a short story may be divided into episodes, a short play may be divided into scenes. Just as a novel is divided into chapters, a full-length play is divided into acts.

In this unit you will encounter plays on a variety of topics and for a variety of media. You will read a stage play, a television play, and a full-length play based on a famous book.

READING ACTIVELY

Drama

Drama is a story told in dialogue by performers before an audience. When we think of drama, we think of stage plays and the exciting world of the theater—actors, costumes, stage sets, and lights. Drama, however, includes more than the theater; television plays and radio plays are drama too. Even movies are a form of drama. In all these kinds of drama, actors make a world come alive before an audience.

Plays are meant to be performed, but it is possible just to read a play. When you read a play, you can make it come alive by staging it in your imagination. The play you are reading is a script. It contains not only the words that the actors speak but also the stage directions the playwright provides to indicate how to put on the play. Stage directions tell what the stage should look like, what the characters wear, how they speak their lines, and where they move.

Stage directions use a particular vocabulary. *Right, left, up, down,* and *center* refer to areas of the stage as the actors see it. To help you visualize what is meant when a stage direction tells an actor to move down left, for example, picture the stage like this:

THE STAGE

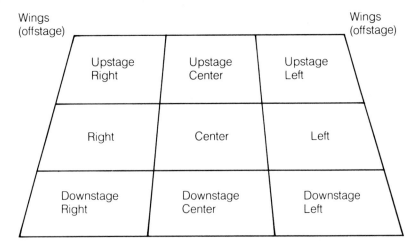

Wings (offstage) ... Wings (offstage)

Upstage Right	Upstage Center	Upstage Left
Right	Center	Left
Downstage Right	Downstage Center	Downstage Left

Curtain

Television plays and film scripts have their own kinds of directions; these are camera directions. *Fade in, fade out, long shot, close up* should make sense to you. *Pan* means "to move the camera to follow a moving object or to create a panoramic scene." These directions emphasize character or actions.

Just as you read short stories actively, you should also read drama actively. Reading actively includes trying to see the play in your mind while you continually question the meaning of what the actors are saying and doing.

Use the following strategies to help you read drama actively. They will help you to enjoy and appreciate the plays in this unit.

VISUALIZE Use the directions and information supplied by the playwright to picture the stage and the characters in action. Hear their voices. Go beyond the stated words and actions to create the scene in your mind.

QUESTION As you meet the characters, ask yourself what each character is like. What situation does each character face? What motives and traits does each character reveal by his or her words and actions?

PREDICT Building on the play's conflict and the characters' words and actions, predict what you think will happen. How will the conflict be resolved? What will become of each character?

CLARIFY If a character's words or actions are not clear to you, stop and try to make sense of them. Look for answers to your questions and check your predictions.

SUMMARIZE Pause occasionally to review what has happened. Put the characters' actions and words together. What is the story being told?

RESPOND Think about all the elements of the play. What does the play mean? Is it purely entertainment, or is there a message? What does it say to you?

Using these strategies when you read drama will help you to be a more effective reader. You will be better able to understand the conflict of the play and its resolution and to apply your understanding to your own life.

GUIDE FOR READING

The Flying Tortilla Man
Scenes 1 and 2

Dialogue

What the characters in a play say to one another is called **dialogue.** Not only can dialogue tell you what the characters are like, it can also give you information about the setting and plot of the play. By paying close attention to the dialogue in *The Flying Tortilla Man,* you will learn a lot about the different characters, their relationships, and their world.

Denise Chávez

(1948–   ), while still a young girl, began writing about life in a small border town in New Mexico. Since then, she has continued to express her feelings about her Southwest origins through writing and through acting in her own one-woman shows. Her story collection, *The Last of the Menu Girls,* and her many plays, including *The Flying Tortilla Man,* reflect her dedication to the people of the Southwest. As she herself has said, "These are people who endure."

Focus

Who might the flying tortilla man be? Well, a tortilla is a thin, round cake made of cornmeal used in several Mexican dishes. So a "tortilla man" might be someone who makes or eats tortillas. That doesn't seem odd, but why would a tortilla man fly? Take a few minutes to brainstorm about the image of a flying tortilla man. Then write a brief character sketch of the kind of person you think would fit this unusual description. What does he have to do with tortillas? Why does he fly? How is he able to fly? Where would you probably meet such a person? What would the experience of meeting him be like?

Vocabulary

Knowing the following words will help you as you read Scenes 1 and 2 of *The Flying Tortilla Man.*

forbidding (fər bid′ iŋ) *adj.*: Looking harmful or unpleasant (p. 212)

morose (mə rōs′) *adj.*: Bad-tempered (p. 212)

sarcastically (sär kas′ tik lē) *adv.*: In a mocking or sneering manner (p. 215)

wary (wer′ ē) *adj.*: Cautious (p. 217)

impudence (im′ pyo͞o dəns) *n.*: Lack of respect (p. 217)

disarray (dis ə rā′) *n.*: Untidiness (p. 219)

conniving (kə nīv′ iŋ) *adj.*: Scheming in an underhanded way (p. 221)

malice (mal′ is) *n.*: Ill will or spite (p. 221)

The Flying Tortilla¹ Man

Denise Chávez

"Beautiful or not, it is my native land. A relative or not, he is a fellow countryman."

Chinese Proverb

CHARACTERS

Carlos age twelve	**Nora** early thirties	**Cotil** age fifteen
Bennie age fourteen	**Neno** age twelve	**Fatty Campbell** age fifty-five
Elias age thirteen	**Hermano Gil** age forty-five	**The Birds/Old Women**
Oscar age eighteen	**Bertina** early fifties	**The Tortilla Man** ageless
Tudi age twenty		

Scene 1

[It is late evening on a hot summer night in Cuchillo,² New Mexico. The heat permeates the walls of an aluminum building that houses a small but prosperous tortilla factory. The odor of cooked maize³ hangs heavy in the air. The building seems collapsible, barely grounded to the earth. The factory is in full swing preparing for the day's orders. A screen door is held in place by two long wooden planks.

The radio jumps to a lively Mexican station, XELO, and casts a lyrical spell over the grinding, pulsating machines. Several teenage boys are at their posts, silhouetted against machines in an eerie, yellow-maize darkness that creeps inside the factory and finds relief in the midst of activity.

CARLOS *carries a pan of maize from a large metal trough to a machine that rinses the corn. He is a thin yet muscular boy of unspoiled character, gentle and filled with a natural goodness, a dreamer.* CARLOS *stands not far from* ELIAS, *who supervises the maize in the grinding machine and changes the pans of crushed corn that go to the cutter as a finished masa.⁴* ELIAS *is a mischievous adolescent with thick burnt red hair and fair skin, appropriately named "El Güero."⁵ Next to* ELIAS *stands* NENO, *guarding the cutting machines. He is about the same age as*

---

1. tortilla (tôr tē′ yə): A thin, flat, round cake of cornmeal baked on a griddle.
2. Cuchillo (kōō chē′ yō)
3. maize (māz): Corn.

4. masa (mä′ sä): Spanish for "dough."
5. "El Güero" (el gwe′ rō): Spanish for "a man with light skin and hair."

CARLOS, *somewhat tired and sickly-looking, with a dark chinless face. Not far from* NENO *stands* BENNIE, *who pushes the dough through the cutting machine roller. He is silent and shy, lean and greyhound-like. At the end of the cooking conveyor belt sit* OSCAR *and* NORA, *taking turns counting out a dozen tortillas and spreading them, fanlike, on the metal shelf where they are packaged by the roving* BENNIE. OSCAR *is fat, jolly, and toothy.* NORA *is a cheerful woman, who is somewhat simple-minded, yet she works with amazing speed and agility.*

At the far end of the factory stands the office, a tucked-away bastion of power amid the heat and sweat. Inside is a large metal desk covered with orders and business papers. Beside the desk stands a counter full of frozen products from the factory: flour and corn tortillas, taco shells, tamales.[6] At the desk, behind the closed and forbidding door, sits TUDI, *who oversees the factory with a hard, anxious eye. He is a good-looking, somewhat morose young man. He is not the actual boss but simply manages the factory in the owner's stead. The radio plays . . . all are intense and involved in the swinging, swaying creation of the tortillas.*]

NENO. It's hot!

OSCAR. So, why don't you work in an ice plant?

ELIAS. Quiet, you guys, this is my favorite song!

OSCAR. [*Laughing to himself*] This one, ese,[7] are you kidding me?

---

6. taco (tä′ kō) **shells, tamales** (tä mä′ les): Tacos are folded and dried tortillas filled with shredded meat and vegetables. Tamales are minced meat, tomato sauce, and red peppers rolled in a soft tortilla and baked or steamed.

7. ese (e′ se): Spanish for "man," as in "hey, man."

[*All are momentarily caught up in the dramatically sad tune coming from the radio: another song about lost love.*]

NENO. What am I doing here? I can't think . . . I can't breathe . . . it's so hot!

OSCAR. You're not paid to think, man; you're paid to sweat!

NENO. I gotta get out of here . . . my head is on fire. Trade with me, Elias . . .

ELIAS. Heck no, Neno. I got my own work to do. You start doing it once, and you'll want to do it all the time.

CARLOS. I'll trade, Neno.

ELIAS. They play this song to me this one night and you guys won't shut up.

OSCAR. What's so special about tonight? It don't feel so special to me.

ELIAS. It's a special request from my girl!

OSCAR. You have a girl, Güero? Who would want a pale worm like you?

ELIAS. None of your business, horsemouth!

OSCAR. You called in the song yourself tonight, corn face, before you came in to work. Isn't that right, Nora? Doesn't have a girl at all, unless it's Nora here. Are you sweethearts with La Nica,[8] Elias? NicaNora, NicaNora, NicaNora, old metate[9] face. [OSCAR *sings to* NORA, *who is first oblivious to him and then joins in, clapping her hands and humming, in a strange and haunting way.* NENO *is beginning to look progressively worse, and* ELIAS *makes ugly scowling faces at* OSCAR, *who encourages* BENNIE *to join him in his crazed chanting.*] NicaNora, NicaNora,

---

8. La Nica (lä nē′ kä): Oscar's nonsense name for Nora.

9. metate (me tä′ te): Spanish for "grinding stone."

NicaNora, old metate face! Laugh, Nica, laugh!

ELIAS. You're jealous!

OSCAR. Of La Nica? Heck, man, I see her every day—that's enough for me.

NORA. Funny, Oscar, funny! [NORA *continues to clap her hands.*]

OSCAR. Be quiet, Nora, and get back to work! The Boss gonna get on our case. We got lots of work to do . . .

[NORA *hums.*]

CARLOS. Nora hasn't done anything to you, Oscar; leave her alone!

OSCAR. *You* leave *me* alone, Mr. Corn Lifter. I was only making fun.

ELIAS. You tell him, Carlos . . . trying to make believe that La Nica is my girlfriend. That old hag, I'd rather drown in the irrigation ditch!

CARLOS. Leave her alone, Elias!

OSCAR. But she's his ruca,[10] ese . . .

ELIAS. If you're such a good boy, Carlos, be quiet . . . shut your mouth, okay?

CARLOS. Where's Tudi? He's been gone a long time. I'm worried about Neno.

NORA. Tudi? Tudi?

OSCAR. Shut up and get to work!

CARLOS. Don't talk to her that way, Oscar. Show some respect!

OSCAR. To a crazy woman?

ELIAS. You think you're so good, Carlos . . . well, you're the one that's crazy!

---

10. ruca (ro͞o′ kä): Spanish slang for "girlfriend."

That's what happens when you don't have real parents. When you're an orphan! And when you live with people that ain't your kin, in a house full of strangers!

CARLOS. I have parents!

ELIAS. You call those two—the stringbean and the squash—your parents? Heck, man, they have a houseful of kids, like rabbits, over there at that place.

CARLOS. They're good to me.

ELIAS. It's because they feel sorry.

NORA. Carlitos, good boy!

ELIAS. See, even La Nica feels sorry.

OSCAR. Go on Elias; you're finally showing a little nerve. Nica might fall in love with your strength!

BENNIE. You guys better be still. Tudi might come back!

OSCAR. Let him come back. I'll show him who OSCAR SALCEDO is!

LOS CHOLOS, 1985
Tony Ortega
Courtesy of the Artist

ELIAS. Híjole,[11] Oscar, you couldn't whip a mouse!

OSCAR. Be careful, you bleached earthworm!

ELIAS. You're going to get it one of these days, you fat hyena!

BENNIE. Be quiet! Be quiet, or we'll get in trouble! Tudi's in his office!

OSCAR. So El Tudi is in the office, huh? I don't trust that guy. He always looks like a dog who wants to bark. Too much power. Wooo! What do you say, Nica?

NORA. Where's Tudi? Tudi is a nice man.

CARLOS. Her name is Nora.

OSCAR. [*Referring to* NORA *as he counts tortillas*] So what does she know anyway? All she can do is count to twelve. Ay, this heat! It gets into your blood and drives you crazy. After so many years, you start counting all the time. Stupid things you start counting for nothing. All this heat . . . it affects your brain. It starts suddenly, like with Neno, until one day you're as dry in the head as Nica, right, Nenito? Where'd he go?

CARLOS. He's at the washer.

BENNIE. Don't let Tudi see you, Neno; it'll go rough for us!

ELIAS. So who cares! You've all got baked corn for brains, anyway!

NENO. I don't feel good. I'm going outside. [NENO *starts for the door and suddenly faints.* CARLOS, ELIAS, *and* BENNIE *run to him, followed by* NORA. OSCAR *remains behind.*]

OSCAR. [*Paying no attention to the others, he continues talking.*] You just keep counting, that's all . . .

---

11. Híjole (ē' hō le): Spanish exclamation, meaning "Oh yeah!"

CARLOS. What's wrong, Neno?

BENNIE. He's sick!

ELIAS. You're really a smart one, Bennie. Is that why you work here?

BENNIE. What about you, Güero? The light too bright for you out there in the world? You need to be in this cave, eh?

OSCAR. [*Still oblivious to the others,* OSCAR *continues to count tortillas.*] Ten . . . eleven . . . twelve . . .

CARLOS. Help me take him outside. He needs some fresh air.

OSCAR. He's got the rot. It just happens.

ELIAS. You must be an advanced case.

OSCAR. Sooner or later . . .

ELIAS. Would you shut up?

OSCAR. It gets you.

ELIAS. Is that why you're still here after all these years?

[*The boys carry* NENO *outside and lean him up against the steps.* NORA *has gone to the water trough near the maize bags and dips her apron in and returns to the steps. She uses her apron as a towel on* NENO's *forehead.* NENO *is in a daze.*]

CARLOS. Thank you, Nora.

NORA. [*In a soothing voice*] Neno, Nenito. Good boy, Nenito.

[NENO *unsteadily gets to his feet with the help of* NORA *and* CARLOS.]

ELIAS. Oh, he's okay.

[BENNIE, ELIAS, CARLOS, NORA *and* NENO *file back inside the building.*]

BENNIE. We'd better get back to work!

OSCAR. Since when have you worked around here, Bennie? And you, Nica. Where have you been, you lazy good-for-nothing? Who do you think you are, wiping people's foreheads? And who does Neno think he is? Hey, I already did more than my share of work, so where is everybody?

[NORA *runs back, confused. Her movements are pointed and jittery.*]

NORA. Sorry, Nora so sorry. Oscar not mad with Nora. She's sorry.

OSCAR. Back to work, back to work! They can hear you in the other room, the bosses, the big shots. They can hear you out here like rats in the night. Isn't that right, Nica, like rats?

NORA. [*Making a ratlike face*] Like rats, like rats.

CARLOS. Leave her alone, Oscar . . . she hasn't done anything to you. She was only trying to help Neno out.

OSCAR. It'll go bad for us all, Carlos. You get back to work.

CARLOS. He's sick!

OSCAR. He's got the corn rot and the fever that comes nights working at a place like this. It starts flowing in your blood.

ELIAS. [*Sarcastically*] What are you anyway, a doctor?

OSCAR. And you're the nurse!

CARLOS. I can't leave him alone. He's sick!

OSCAR. Oh, that's right . . . you're the one who doesn't have anyone to take care of you, so you take care of the world.

TUDI. [*Coming in and looking around suspiciously*] What's going on? Why aren't you working?

NENO. I'll be okay in a few minutes.

BENNIE. Didn't I tell you guys?

TUDI. Get to work! All of you!

CARLOS. Neno isn't feeling well, Tudi, I . . .

TUDI. Get to work, Carlos. We have orders to fill. It's late. The night's almost over and we're behind. Go on, all of you!

CARLOS. Neno is sick. He needs to rest. Maybe he should go home.

TUDI. We can't have this, Carlos. We have orders to fill. This isn't the first time someone has played a trick, pretending to be sick . . .

CARLOS. Feel his head . . .

TUDI. Huerfanito,[12] you, Carlos . . . help Neno get back to his job. He'll make it, all right. Now, boys, I've been in the office, thinking. [OSCAR *snickers.*] And I've come up with a new set of rules.

OSCAR. Not again!

TUDI. Quiet! Number one: one break every three hours, depending how far behind we are. Number two: no eating or drinking on the job. Number three: no visiting of an extended nature.

OSCAR. Number four: No breathing! Visiting, man, are you joking me? Who's there to visit en esta maldita cueva?[13]

TUDI. Number four: more than one absence, constitutes dismissal. Number five: we will all work together as a happy, united working force, producing as best as we can, without strife and dissension.

BENNIE. Dissension, what's dissension?

---

12. **Huerfanito** (wer fän ē′ tō): Spanish for "little orphan."
13. **en esta maldita cueva** (en es′ tä mäl dē′ tä kwe′ vä): Spanish for "in this cursed cave."

TUDI. Quiet! Now then, I'll be available to talk to you guys any time. Remember that I'm the boss in place of our BOSS, who is gone. I am the absolute head in his place, and I demand respect and will treat you accordingly. Come on, boys, let's be friends!

OSCAR. After all that . . . man, are you pulling my leg? It's a joke, Tudi.

CARLOS. I'm taking Neno home, Tudi.

ELIAS. Let them go, let them go . . . they're nothing but trouble.

OSCAR. Those two didn't do a thing all night.

NORA. Nice boys, Tudi, they're my friends.

TUDI. La Nica's very talkative tonight. She seems to be on your side, Carlos. Why are you helping Neno anyway? You know none of them would ever lift a finger for you. You could die right here on the job.

OSCAR. Carlos was just standing around doing nothing, Tudi.

CARLOS. I was helping my friend. I'm taking him home.

TUDI. If you do that, you might not have a job when you get back.

CARLOS. You just can't *not* help someone. Especially a friend, someone you work with. Look at him, Tudi . . . he looks bad. Friendship is more than just standing by while someone is sick. Neno and I are friends.

TUDI. Go on, Carlos. Get outta here. Just try and come back. You're always getting in my way. Take your friend home. Just take him home. He's worthless!

NENO. I'm feeling better; really, I am. I can go to work, Carlos. I can go . . . [*He appears ready to faint and then recovers a bit.*] I can go home alone, Carlos; you stay here. Let me go alone.

CARLOS. I'm taking you home! I care more about you than all the tortillas in the world!

ELIAS. Ah, they'll be back, begging for a job!

TUDI. Just you wait and see what happens, Carlos. Go on with you! Don't come back!

NORA. Goodbye. Goodbye, my friends. See you soon.

OSCAR. You make me laugh, Nica. You really make me laugh! [*He starts laughing. They all join in.* CARLOS *and* NENO *exit.*]

[*It is a rainy, windy night. The lightning crackles the breeze, and the boys look small and helpless against the sky. They don't have too far to go to* NENO'S *but they make their way slowly and cautiously, pausing under the archways and porches, huddling together against the fury of the oncoming storm.* CARLOS *knocks at* NENO'S *door. A woman answers and takes* NENO *in, then closes the door.* CARLOS *stands there long after they have gone in, unsure of what to do. He then dashes out of the doorway and runs madly to the next shelter. A delicate-looking man of above-average height with a fine, smooth face and warm, small eyes is standing there, also seeking shelter. They look at one another for a few seconds, the boy and the man, both dreamers.*]

TORTILLA MAN. Where are you, boy?

[CARLOS *is not sure he heard the old gentleman correctly. He is taken aback by the seemingly strange question. Often* THE TORTILLA MAN *will ask questions that seem to make no sense whatsoever, and yet they really do.*]

CARLOS. [*In an uncertain voice*] Where am I going, sir?

TORTILLA MAN. Where are you?

CARLOS. I don't understand.

TORTILLA MAN. That's what's wrong with everyone. They're out of touch; they don't know where they are, especially in the middle of a storm. They're lost, going from one place to another, from one thing to another.

CARLOS. WHO are you?

TORTILLA MAN. You don't know me?

CARLOS. [*Suddenly wary*] What do you want?

TORTILLA MAN. What makes you think I want anything?

CARLOS. If you'll excuse me, sir, I'll have to leave you and get back to work.

TORTILLA MAN. If I were you, I'd stay around and talk awhile. It's too early to be running off, and besides, your Boss hasn't decided to take you back yet. Wait up, boy; talk to an old man . . . tell him where you are.

CARLOS. Who are you? You seem to know a lot. You're not from here, are you?

TORTILLA MAN. I remember Cuchillo when there was nothing out here but rocks and weeds and the bare sky to wear as a hat . . . when you blessed yourself for another day in this wilderness and prayed for rain . . .

CARLOS. You don't look *that* old . . .

TORTILLA MAN. No impudence, boy, just listen to me. For he who teaches you for one day is your father for life. I read that in a book.

CARLOS. I can barely read, and I don't have a father.

TORTILLA MAN. You do now, boy. We're in the same line of work.

CARLOS. Tortillas?

TORTILLA MAN. Well, yes and no. Mostly yes.

CARLOS. I don't have a job now. I've been fired. I don't know whether I should go back and beg—they said I would—or whether I should go home . . . I mean, where I live. My parents,

Hermano Gil[14] and Bertina, they'll be mad at me. I finally got this job and now it's gone!

TORTILLA MAN. You'll go back to the factory, of course. No one should ever avoid what needs to be done.

CARLOS. Yes, I thought so, too. How did you know?

TORTILLA MAN. We do the same work.

CARLOS. You make tortillas, too?

TORTILLA MAN. In a way, yes, but we'll come to that later. We both make things grow, come alive.

CARLOS. We do?

TORTILLA MAN. We do, Carlos!

CARLOS. You know my name!

TORTILLA MAN. Boy, you look like a Carlos— long, gangly, a real weed, a Carlos who is growing.

CARLOS. You talk funny!

TORTILLA MAN. Boy, you look funny, all wet and long!

[*They both laugh.*]

CARLOS. Who are you?

TORTILLA MAN. I'm The Flying Tortilla Man.

CARLOS. The Tortilla Man? You run a factory, like our boss? He's never there, so Tudi takes his place. I never have seen the boss; I don't even know who he is . . .

CARLOS. [*Realizing* THE TORTILLA MAN *might be his boss*] You aren't . . .

TORTILLA MAN. I make things grow.

CARLOS. But tortillas don't grow! They're a dead thing . . . they're just corn that becomes bread and that's eaten and is gone . . .

---

14. Hermano Gil (er män′ ō hēl): Spanish for "Brother Gil (Gilberto)."

TORTILLA MAN. But, Carlos, tortillas are more than that . . . they're life to so many people. They're magic offerings; they're alive as the land, and as flat!

CARLOS. They are, huh? What's your real name?

TORTILLA MAN. Juan.

CARLOS. You're Mr. Juan, The Tortilla Man; pleased to meet you.

TORTILLA MAN. Enchanted. We are enchanted to meet you.

CARLOS. Who's we?

TORTILLA MAN. Why, the Magic Tortilla, of course.

CARLOS. [*Looking around*] Where is it?

TORTILLA MAN. [*Putting his arm around* CAR-LOS's *shoulder and speaking confidentially*] I couldn't bring it out in this rain, could I?

I AM YOUR MEXICAN COWBOY, 1989
Jose Esteban Martinez
Vorpal Gallery, New York

CARLOS. [*Disappointed*] I guess not.

TORTILLA MAN. Now . . . back to work . . . they're waiting for you.

CARLOS. They are?

TORTILLA MAN. Don't be impudent, boy . . . don't you trust me?

CARLOS. Yes . . . yes, I do! But I know I don't have a job anymore.

TORTILLA MAN. Who says? You just wait and see. Carlos, you just wait and see. You just can't stop something from growing.

CARLOS. I'll try . . . I'll try . . .

TORTILLA MAN. Grow, boy. Let them see you grow, in front of their eyes! [*He laughs an infectious, clear laugh that is warm and comforting.*] You'll see. It's waiting there to grow . . . they can't stop you. They can't stop you . . . they'll try . . . Now, goodbye, think of me, and run, run . . .

[CARLOS *runs into the darkness of a now-clear night. He is full of energy. He suddenly stops to say something to* THE TORTILLA MAN, *who has vanished.*]

CARLOS. THANK YOU! Sir . . . Mr. Juan . . . goodbye . . . he says he makes things grow, but how? Magic tortillas? And he says the sky is a hat . . .

[CARLOS *runs back to the factory and walks in. Everyone is working noisily. The radio competes with the tortilla machine for dominance.*]

TUDI. [*Seeing* CARLOS, *he signals for him to come closer.*] It's about time . . . what took you so long?

CARLOS. I was getting some fresh air; it's too hot in here . . .

OSCAR. There, what'd I tell you . . . the rot . . . it starts nights . . .

ELIAS. Shut up!!

TUDI. Well, get back to work! We have orders to fill and the night is half over, and we've just begun!

OSCAR. You're lucky, man . . . you're just lucky. Isn't that right, Nica?

NORA. Hello, Carlitos. Hello. How's your Mama?

OSCAR. What a memory!

NORA. Lucky boy, lucky boy.

CARLOS. [*Back at his post, he rinses out the maize.*] I'm fine, Nora . . . I'm just fine! How are you?

[*Blackout. End of scene one.*]

Scene 2

[*The orphanage where* CARLOS *lives with his foster parents,* HERMANO GIL *and* BERTINA. *It is a large, rambling house with about twenty-five children and teen-agers and two frazzled adults. The orphans are not juvenile delinquents, merely displaced and disoriented people.* CARLOS's *room is set off from the main house. It is a small junk-filled closet/shed that serves as a storage area and utility room, as well as* CARLOS's *room. Spread about the room are boxes full of cloth remnants, paper, old toys, and empty luggage; up against the wall, near* CARLOS's *bed, are some old picture frames, an old hoe, and some posters, as well as a beat-up, much-used vacuum cleaner. Nonetheless, despite its disarray, the room has a certain personal coziness, as if someone has tried his best to make a living space of his own and half succeeded. There is a small night table next to the bed and a chest of drawers nearby. On the table is an old decorated cigar box, with* CARLOS *written on the outside. It is* CARLOS's *private property and per-sonal joy. Inside the box are an old dried feather, a small fossil, a large rubber band tied into a series of amazing knots, a soft red handkerchief, two glass marbles, and a picture of a sickly old woman in black. It is a picture of Isa,* CARLOS's *guardian after the death of his mother, whom he hardly knew.* CARLOS *is sleeping. It is about six A.M. He has not been in bed very long. A man is singing. It is* HERMANO GIL. *He is a short, smallish man who works in the kitchen of a Mexican restaurant. He is energetic and sprightly despite the hour. He has a dark complexion that seems even darker in the half-light.*

The house is asleep for the most part, and the lights have a dim, early-morning quality. CARLOS *sleeps in a twisted position. Suddenly, the door opens to his room, and his foster father,* HERMANO GIL, *wanders in, looking for something in the dark room. He accidentally falls against the sleeping* CAR-LOS. HERMANO GIL *gets up and continues his search for a suitcase of his that is somewhere in the room.*]

HERMANO GIL. This is the last time I'll bother you, any one of you . . . this time I'm leaving for good! I'll take a job as a singer. [*He sings a few bars from a Mexican love ballad in Spanish.*] I'll come up in the world at last. Half my life spent in someone else's kitchen, cleaning up. That's no kind of life. Then I have to come home to a house full of strangers. I told Bertina, "Don't do it, Bert." I said, "I can't take it." She didn't listen. "I can't be a father to the entire world; we have a daughter of our own. Isn't that enough, woman? I'm leaving . . . I'm leaving . . ."

CARLOS. [*He has awakened and is sitting up on the bed, listening.*] Papa, wait, don't leave!

HERMANO GIL. I'm not your Papa . . . let me pack.

CARLOS. [*In a tired and sleepy voice*] We'll miss you, Papa!

HERMANO GIL. I have to leave. I can't go on living in a hallway in a house full of lost children. What am I talking about? I just work in a kitchen. [*Looking at* CARLOS] You're nothing to me!

CARLOS. Don't say that, Papa. We love you!

HERMANO GIL. All my life in a kitchen . . . for what? To run a house for stray dogs and cats . . . all my money going to feed twenty-five hungry mouths . . . as if Bertina and Cotil and I didn't have our own problems.

[HERMANO GIL *sits down on the edge of the bed. He puts his hand on the side of his head and sighs. He is holding a ragged suitcase. As* HERMANO GIL *is bemoaning his fate, he accidentally knocks over* CARLOS's *cigar box, and the contents fall to the floor.* CARLOS *scrambles to retrieve the objects, but* HERMANO GIL *has swooped them up and holds them in his dark and unsteady hands.*]

CARLOS. Papa!

HERMANO GIL. So why do you keep this junk? Isn't there enough here already to crowd into your life?

CARLOS. These are *my* things—they mean something to *me*! They remind me of people and places and times I've loved. They're alive to me.

HERMANO GIL. This seashell is dead, son. There was a life here once, but where is it now? Show me, if you can. Can it talk to you? Can it tell you how it feels to be buried in the sand and come up to the sky as a rock, a hardened thing, an outline of something that was once alive? No, son, these are dead things—they have no use. You keep them because you are a silly dreamer like I used to be and because you make up stories to pass away your silly time. Like how you are going to be a singer and come up in the world . . . [*Referring to his own broken life,* HERMANO GIL

breaks down and cries. CARLOS *comforts him.* HERMANO GIL *wipes his eyes and looks at the knots in the rubber band.*] This game of knots, this game of glass. Of what use is it? [*He cries a bit more and then looks at the picture.*] Who is this old pan face? She has the skin of an old wrinkled prune . . . This is what I mean, Carlitos! Your name is Carlos; I forget with all the names. I forget, son, so many people pass through here and go away with not so much as a thank you for the food. They leave their mugres[15]—stuff, son, stuff—behind for us to collect and store in this room. [*He looks at the feather and the rock.*] What is this? What does this mean? This dirty old bird feather and this rock?

CARLOS. It's not a rock, Papa; it's a fossil.

HERMANO GIL. It's a dirty old rock and this is a chicken feather! Like the ones whose necks I used to wring when I was a boy . . . [*He imitates the wringing of a chicken's neck.*] Squawk!

CARLOS. It's a seashell.

HERMANO GIL. So it is, Juanito.

CARLOS. Carlos, Papa . . . Let me have my things, please, Papa . . . please.

HERMANO GIL. [*Referring to the photograph*] This is the deadest thing of all, in black, like a spider.

CARLOS. That's Isa, my mother's aunt. She took care of me when Mama died.

HERMANO GIL. [*Touched*] Here, son . . . [*He puts the objects on the bed.*] Keep your treasures. You may be a fool, but you have a heart, and no man—not even the worst of us—can go against that. Keep your treasures. You'll need them out there in the world. Keep your feathers, your rocks, and your old lady's knot-

---

15. mugres (mōō′ gres)

ted life. [*He gets up.*] I don't want anything to do with strangers anymore. You've worn me out. I'm tired of trying to feed and clothe the world.

[CARLOS *takes his things and puts them back in the box. Then he goes to the chest of drawers and puts the box on top of it, under some clothing, just as* COTIL *comes in.* COTIL *is a conniving young lady of fifteen, who besides being prone to fits of unthinking and unsolicited malice, is a chubby romantic.*]

COTIL. Hiding things again, lazy boy?

CARLOS. Good morning, Cotil.

COTIL. Papa, Mama wants you to get ready for work.

HERMANO GIL. I told you, I'm leaving. This is it, Cotil. You're the only flesh and blood of mine in this infernal household. Why should I remain the father of this faceless screaming brood? Tell me!

COTIL. Mama wants you to come and eat, or the atole[16] will get cold.

HERMANO GIL. EAT? Child, how can I eat the fruit of my labor with a mouth full of sand? Let the maggots take it!

COTIL. Papa, you better go before Mama comes to get you. And you, lazy boy, get up. You've already slept long enough.

HERMANO GIL. Leave him alone.

COTIL. If I do, Papa, he'll sleep all day.

HERMANO GIL. He's one of the few people that works around here. Let him rest! Go away!

COTIL. I'll tell Mama!

HERMANO GIL. Tell her . . . tell her!

COTIL. You'd better get up, Carlos. I'll tell

Mama you steal and hide things. I'll show her where you put them.

HERMANO GIL. Out, out!

COTIL. He's got you believing him, Papa!

HERMANO GIL. Flesh of my flesh, blood of my blood . . . [COTIL *exits with a wicked smile.* HERMANO GIL *rises and gets ready to go to breakfast.*] Can you put away the suitcase, Carlitos? I am a bit hungry, now that I think about it. Carlos, you and me, we'll go away someday, just the two of us, just the two of us old fossils and we'll never come back . . .

BERTINA. [*Yelling from the kitchen*] Gil, honey, come on. Come and have breakfast, or you'll be late for work.

HERMANO GIL. [*Speaking to* CARLOS] We'll have to make a few plans before we can leave . . . I'm coming . . . I'm coming, Bert!

CARLOS. I'm sorry, Papa; I'll help you. I'll go away and become rich, and I'll send you lots of money. I'll make you happy.

HERMANO GIL. Ha! Go back to bed and dream some more, son. Rub your magic things together and pray for someone to show you the way. Ask for money first, then loaves of bread and fish. Pray for rain, boy. This is New Mexico and our souls are dry! No, boy, go back to bed, but first put up the suitcase, so I'll know where to find it the next time . . . Thanks, son . . . [HERMANO GIL *pauses in the doorway.*] It's so nice, so nice to believe in miracles . . . so keep your dried-out turkey feathers, who knows . . . who really knows . . .

[BERTINA *is at the door, with* COTIL *beside her.* BERTINA *is in her early fifties, a plump, kindly woman who is gracious and tactful.*]

COTIL. I told you, Mama. I told you they were talking and plotting, making all kinds of plans. Carlos is a troublemaker, Mama. I've always told you that.

_____
16. atole (ä tō′ le): Spanish for a hot corn cereal.

HERMANO GIL. Hello, Bert. Good morning to my dear and beloved wife and darling daughter.

COTIL. Carlos is a snake, Mama!

HERMANO GIL. Shut up, my darling girl. Now go run and sharpen your tongue while your Mama and I eat breakfast.

BERTINA. Go on, Cotil; your father is hungry.

COTIL. But MAMA!

BERTINA. I only say things once. You know that. What would you like for breakfast, Gilito?

HERMANO GIL. I thought you decided already. You take care of things like that, Bert. You always do.

BERTINA. We'll start with a little atole . . . chile . . . [*They exit.*]

COTIL. What about Carlos? He's still in bed, Mama!

HERMANO GIL. Let the world sleep! I'm going to have my atolito. You have all day to run your mother ragged, Cotil. I don't know how she does it. I don't know how you do it, Bert. A house full of children, both young and old.

BERTINA. I love them as I love you, Gilito . . . that's all. We're all God's children . . .

HERMANO GIL. But twenty-five!

COTIL. [*Standing at the door to* CARLOS's *room*] I saw you hide that box, Carlitos Warlitos. Such a good boy wouldn't have secrets.

CARLOS. I don't.

COTIL. Then show me what's in the box!

CARLOS. They're personal things.

COTIL. Nothing is personal in this house.

CARLOS. Let me sleep!

COTIL. You're a lazy orphan, and my Mama and Papa don't really love you. They only put up with you because you don't have parents or a house.

CARLOS. Leave me alone . . . please, Cotil.

COTIL. I'll never leave you alone—never!

CARLOS. You hate me, don't you?

COTIL. Yes! You orphan!

CARLOS. [*Sitting on the bed*] Why? Why? I haven't done anything to you!

COTIL. You think you're better than us.

CARLOS. No, I don't!

COTIL. You have secrets!

CARLOS. Why do you hate me so much, Cotil? [*It is a tense, electric moment.*]

COTIL. I don't know . . . but I do! [*She slams the door and leaves. She thinks twice about it and returns.*] Get up, you lazy, yawning nobody, or I'll tell Mama about your secrets!

[COTIL *exits and leaves* CARLOS *very hurt and stunned.*]

CARLOS. What have I done that everyone hates me? I'm quiet and I work hard and all they do is yell at me. Get to work! Get to work! You better straighten up and show respect! I don't understand. Who can tell me what's going wrong? [CARLOS *goes to the chest of drawers and removes the box from underneath the clothing. He looks at the photograph and then at the fossil.*] Hello, Isa. What can you tell me today? Gone to see some friends? And you, Carlos, do you have any friends? [*Thinking aloud,* CARLOS *remembers* MR. JUAN.] Where are you now, Mr. Juan? [*Remembering* THE TORTILLA MAN'S *words*] He said they'll try and stop you. They'll try but they can't . . . because for some reason, a person wants to keep growing . . . [CARLOS *goes back to sleep.*]

RESPONDING TO THE SELECTION

Your Response

1. Would you like someone like Carlos for a friend? Explain.
2. What advice would you give Carlos about how to deal with the people around him?

Recalling

3. What are the working conditions like at the tortilla factory?
4. Where does Carlos live? What is unusual about his home life?

Interpreting

5. What are some reasons the characters in the factory do not get along very well?
6. The Tortilla Man says to Carlos, "You just can't stop something from growing." What do you think he means?
7. Why does Cotil dislike Carlos so much?

Applying

8. Sometimes a person who is the most caring toward others is treated with little care in return. Why do you think this is so?

ANALZING LITERATURE

Understanding Dialogue

What characters say, the **dialogue,** tells you a lot about the characters and gives you information about what is going on in the play. For example, at the end of Scene 2, the dialogue between Carlos and Cotil tells us much about their relationship.

1. What does the dialogue tell you about how Cotil feels about Carlos? Explain.
2. Do you think their relationship has always been this way? Why or why not?
3. How important do you think Carlos's cigarbox will be later in the play? Why?

CRITICAL THINKING AND READING

Making Inferences About Characters

What characters say and how you imagine them saying it can help you make inferences about them. For example, you can tell from Oscar's responses to Neno in Scene 1 that he is sarcastic and insensitive. Review the portion of Scene 1 before Carlos exits with Neno.

1. Jot down several words you would use to describe each character.
2. Do you think any of these characters will change by the end of the play? Explain.

THINKING AND WRITING

Writing About a Dialogue

Look back over the first part of the play and choose a segment of dialogue, maybe ten or twenty lines, that you really liked. Why did you like it? What did it tell you about the characters? Did you learn anything about the plot or the theme of the play? Write an explanation of why you think this dialogue is particularly effective.

LEARNING OPTION

Performance. With several classmates choose a scene or part of a scene from the play and perform it for the class. To prepare, assign roles and practice reading the dialogue as you imagine each character would actually speak. You might discuss among yourselves what you think each character is really like before beginning. Also check the stage directions for clues about how the characters speak. Afterward, encourage the rest of the class to respond to your interpretations of the characters.

GUIDE FOR READING

The Flying Tortilla Man
Scenes 3 through 9

Staging

When you see a play in a theater, the scenery and lighting help you understand where and when a scene is taking place. You can also see what the characters are doing as they talk. When you read a play, however, you need to imagine the setting and the characters' actions. Stage directions, which are usually set off by brackets, provide a lot of this information. Stage directions tell you about the setting, that is, where and when a scene is taking place. They also tell you what the characters are doing on stage. As you read the rest of *The Flying Tortilla Man,* read the stage directions carefully. They will help you to imagine the setting and the characters' actions as they might occur if you were seeing the play performed.

Focus

The scenery and props (the physical objects that the actors use, such as furniture and personal items) of a scene in a play together make up what is called a "set." In the first part of *The Flying Tortilla Man,* there were three different sets: the tortilla factory, the street where Carlos meets Mr. Juan, and the orphanage. Find the stage directions (in italics) that describe each of the three sets. Then, in your own words, summarize the appearance of each. What does the scenery look like? What props do the actors playing the characters use?

Vocabulary

Knowing the following words will help as you read Scenes 3 through 9 of *The Flying Tortilla Man.*

furtively (fur′ tiv lē) *adv.*: In a sly or sneaky way (p. 228)

solitary (säl′ ə ter ē) *adj.*: Single; lone (p. 229)

melodious (mə lō′ dē əs) *adj.*: Pleasing to hear (p. 229)

distinguished (di stiŋ′ gwisht) *adj.*: Famous or outstanding (p. 230)

rudders (rud′ ərz) *n.*: Flat pieces of wood or metal attached to the rear of a boat or aircraft and used for steering (p. 230)

vandal (van′ d'l) *n.*: A person who damages or destroys things on purpose (p. 235)

curfew (kur′ fyoo) *n.*: A time at night past which people must not be outside (p. 238)

Scene 3

[*Early the next evening, outside the factory. The workers have not yet arrived. We can hear whispers in the distance.*]

ELIAS. I'm here behind the building. To the right. Did you have any trouble?

COTIL. I had to sneak out of the house.

ELIAS. Will you get into trouble?

COTIL. Oh, no! I can do just about anything and my Mama won't care. She likes me. I'm the favorite.

ELIAS. What about your Papa?

COTIL. What about him? He does what my Mama says.

ELIAS. [*Coming closer to* COTIL, *he puts his arms around her.*] Cotil, how are you?

COTIL. [*Moving away*] We don't have much time. Is everything ready?

ELIAS. Yes, Cotil. Oscar and I have gone over the plans many times. There's no doubt that we'll get Carlos—and good this time. Who does he think he is, walking all over Oscar and me like we were rocks under his feet?

COTIL. He's that way. He needs to be taught a lesson. He strolls through our house like he owns it, like he was my own true brother.

ELIAS. I'm glad I'm not your brother! Why don't you stay awhile?

COTIL. I have to go or Mama will get suspicious. You see, lucky for us, Carlos left the house to do an errand for Papa, and I snuck into his room and got this . . . [*She brings* CARLOS'S *cigar box from behind her back and shows it to* ELIAS.] See, it says CARLOS on it. That way, when the robbery is reported, everyone will figure he stole the stuff.

ELIAS. I'm glad you came, my dove, my little sunshine.

COTIL. Let's get on with it, okay?

ELIAS. Okay, okay. This is the plan: after work we stick around, Oscar and I. He opens the locks—he's real good at that—then we go into the office and fool around the safe. We mess up the room and leave. When Tudi comes in tomorrow morning, he sees Carlos's box and he figures out who broke in.

COTIL. Are you sure it'll work?

ELIAS. Aren't I Elias Macias? Hey, babe, by tomorrow Carlos will be fired. We'll have put him in his place. It's taken time to settle accounts with that goody-goody. Say, babe, can't you stay awhile?

COTIL. I have to get home. I just wanted to make sure everything is going okay.

ELIAS. Will you think of me?

COTIL. I do every night, Elias, just before I go to sleep.

ELIAS. Really?

COTIL. Yeah, now go on . . . listen to the radio . . . for a sign from me . . .

ELIAS. Cotil, the guys don't believe I have a girlfriend. How come you don't want to go out with me in public? [COTIL *looks away from him with an annoyed expression.*] Well, okay . . . until tomorrow. We'll celebrate the downfall of that plaster saint. There's no one worse than someone who smiles a lot with phony goodness . . . Goodnight, Cotil.

COTIL. Goodbye. Make sure that all goes well. [*She exits.*]

ELIAS. My Cotil . . . will you dedicate a song for me tonight? Ay! [*He sighs and exits with* CARLOS'S *box.*]

[*It is now about eight P.M. Everyone starts to arrive. By the side of the road stand four old women in black, who later become* THE BIRDS, TIN TAN, TON, *and* MABEL.]

WOMAN ONE. [*Referring to the boys coming in for work at the tortilla factory*] Those boys, it's disgraceful . . .

WOMAN TWO. Where is he?

WOMAN THREE. Who?

WOMAN FOUR. The boy.

WOMAN TWO. I don't see him.

WOMAN ONE. The rascally thin one, over there, over there.

WOMAN FOUR. His parents were killed when he was nothing . . .

WOMAN ONE. He was very small, wrinkled from his mother . . .

LA MESERA (THE WAITRESS), 1923
Abraham Angel
Museo de Arte Moderno—INBA, Mexico

WOMAN THREE. Full of his father's sweat . . .

WOMAN TWO. They were killed?

WOMAN FOUR. He's always been alone, like the sore on the side of the mouth, turned inside with a life of its own . . .

WOMAN ONE. There he goes . . .

WOMAN TWO. Who?

WOMAN FOUR. He's all alone . . .

WOMAN THREE. The boy . . .

[*The boys come up.* TUDI *is the first to arrive. He opens up the tortilla factory, turns on the lights and the machines.* BENNIE *and* OSCAR *are behind him, followed by* CARLOS *and* ELIAS. NORA *wanders in last.* ELIAS *is carrying a paper bag with the cigar box inside. He and* OSCAR *wink to each other.*]

TUDI. Hello, boys!

ALL. Hello, Tudi!

CARLOS. How are you, Tudi?

TUDI. I just said hello.

NORA. Hello, hello. I'm fine.

TUDI. I'm ready for work. How about everyone else?

[*Various grumbles, moans, sighs, and a belch can be heard.*]

OSCAR. I'm ready to go out on the town, to do anything but slave in this furnace.

ELIAS. (*Looking at* OSCAR] We'll have to set off some fireworks later on, eh, Oscar? Won't we?

TUDI. What's this? All of a sudden two fighting dogs become friends. It must be the end of the world.

ELIAS. We've come to an understanding.

OSCAR. Some common ground.

TUDI. Probably some common hate. Don't forget about rule number three: socializing too much.

OSCAR. Oh, yes, sir, Mr. Tudi.

NORA. Hello, hello, hello. I'm fine.

TUDI. Okay, okay, let's get to work. [*Talking to* OSCAR] Are you setting up, Oscar?

ELIAS. Yes, we've got it all worked out . . . right, Oscar?

TUDI. Ready, Carlos . . . Nora?

NORA. Ready, Tudi, ready.

CARLOS. I'm glad to see you and Oscar have become friends, Elias.

TUDI. Something must be wrong.

ELIAS. Finally something is right. We discovered a way to settle old debts.

TUDI. Get to work, you bums. We've been here ten minutes and you haven't done a bit of work. Hurry up there, Nora!

NORA. Okay, Tudi, I hurry.

OSCAR. Here it comes, folks . . . THE TORTILLA EXPRESS!!

[*The action is speeded up. The machines roar, night goes by. Suddenly, it is early morning and the work is done.* TUDI *is beginning to turn off the lights and lock up.*]

ELIAS. Hey, Oscar, did you hear about Neno?

OSCAR. What happened, man?

ELIAS. You were right.

TUDI. You guys must really be sick. Are you actually agreeing with him, Elias?

ELIAS. Neno's got the corn rot.

OSCAR. He does?

CARLOS. What's this, Elias? What's wrong?

ELIAS. Neno's got the rot. He's in bed. He's really sick. They don't know if he's going to make it.

TUDI. He was always sickly. The first time I saw him he looked like a stale sausage, very dark with bloody eyes. He was never healthy.

OSCAR. I've said it again and again . . . it'll get you sooner or later. It gets into your blood after awhile and then there's no going back. You're lost.

CARLOS. Neno is really sick? We should go see him.

ELIAS. Not me! I might get the rot from being near him.

OSCAR. He was never a friend of mine. Too puny and dark.

ELIAS. I never knew him that well.

NORA. Nora all finished with work. She go home.

CARLOS. I'll walk you, Nora.

OSCAR. Uuucheee, it's too funny!

ELIAS. They're sweethearts, Oscar!

TUDI. Get out of here, you worms! I haven't got all day to put up with a bunch of lazy, rascally caterpillars. I have to lock up.

CARLOS. [*Speaking gently to* NORA] Neno's sick.

NORA. Where's Nenito?

OSCAR. Why do you bother with her? She can't understand you. One . . . two . . . three . . . four . . . five . . . six . . . seven . . . eight . . . nine . . . ten . . . eleven . . . twelve—

that's all she understands. The two of you keep trying to make sense, and no one can understand.

CARLOS. Let's go, Nora.

NORA. Goodbye, my friends.

TUDI. Go on, I have my work to do.

CARLOS. Have a nice day, Tudi!

TUDI. Haven't you left yet?

ELIAS. I'm going.

TUDI. Well, hurry up!

ELIAS. Bye, you guys.

CARLOS. Bye, Elias.

ELIAS. [*To* OSCAR] Hey, man, I'll walk with you.

TUDI. So goodbye already . . . this must be the end of the world.

OSCAR. Let's go.

[*They exit and disappear around the building. They wait until* TUDI *has locked up and has gone.* CARLOS *and* NORA *have left.* OSCAR *and* ELIAS *emerge from the shadows and furtively slip into the doorway.* OSCAR *begins fiddling with the door lock.*]

ELIAS. Where'd you learn that?

OSCAR. You think I've been making tortillas all my life? I'm a T.V.I.[1] graduate.

ELIAS. I never knew you were so smart, Oscar.

OSCAR. Haven't I told you all this time?

ELIAS. But who listens?

OSCAR. Did Cotil come?

---

1. T.V.I.: Technical and Vocational Institute.

ELIAS. She gave me something that will put our Carlos in real trouble. See, it's a box with his name on it. When we get inside the office, we'll drop it on the floor for Tudi to find. It's all settled. We'll get him yet!

[*They go inside quietly. Once they open the office door, they rummage around the room, dropping the box, and then leave as quietly and as quickly as possible. While they have been doing this,* NORA *has returned, looking for* NENO. *She sees what is going on but does not fully comprehend its significance. She slips away. Meanwhile,* CARLOS *has returned to wait for* THE TORTILLA MAN *under the same stoop. He is tired and sleepy. He sits back, leaning up against the door, and falls into a heavy sleep. He hears the sounds of voices, then a solitary voice—first far away, then near. It is a soothing, melodious voice, the type one hears in dreams. It has a sweet clarity and richness that comes from a height and flows past the dreamer until it is there beside him.* CARLOS *feels a coolness and a movement but is unsure of where he is. Suddenly he feels a warm tingling sensation on his face.* CARLOS *is startled and jumps up. This sudden movement jars him out of the dream. He is now awake.*]

FLYING TILES, 1965
Francisco Toledo
Mary-Anne Martin/Fine Art, New York

CARLOS. Where am I? [*Although he finds himself in mid-air, on a smooth disc, he is reassured to see* THE TORTILLA MAN.]

TORTILLA MAN. Don't be impudent, boy. Where do you think you are?

CARLOS. Where am I?

TORTILLA MAN. Why do you ask so many questions? Just look around. Open your eyes and really see. We're flying over the Rio Grande now.

CARLOS. We are??? [*He jumps around and makes the Flying Tortilla take a nose dive.*]

TORTILLA MAN. I wouldn't do that if I were you, Carlosssssss . . . [THE TORTILLA MAN *looks nervous, but quickly regains control of the ship.* CARLOS *holds on for dear life. He is glued to the firm spongy mass under him and stares, wide-eyed. The Flying Tortilla is a flat spongy disc about six feet across and four feet wide. It is a blue color, with multicolored spots. Tough and durable, it has been made by a Master Tortilla Maker,* MR. JUAN *himself. It has no seats to speak of, just two slightly raised air pockets that serve as seats.* THE TORTILLA MAN *is wearing a historical costume of the fifteenth century, complete with armor. He looks proud and distinguished and a bit older than before. On the side of the Flying Tortilla is a flag of an unknown country with a feather on top. At the sides are rudders of dough. In the middle are several large sacks of baking powder, used to raise and lower the ship, much like the sand bags used in balloons. Once airborne, the Magic Blue Corn Tortilla floats on air currents and the occasional boost from various birds who happen to be flying by.*] You should never do that, Carlos!

CARLOS. Are we on an airplane or a ship?

TORTILLA MAN. I must have asked questions, too, when I was a boy, so I'll have to be patient. Yes, we are on a ship. The Magic Flying Blue Corn Tortilla. There seems to be no satisfying you with answers . . . that's good. Yes, Carlos, right now we are . . . let me see . . . [THE TORTILLA MAN *looks at a compass, checks the feather, and moistens his finger with saliva, then holds it up a foot or so from his face.*] We are about two miles due west of Cuchillo as the birds fly.

CARLOS. [*Embracing* THE TORTILLA MAN *with a mixture of fear and glee*] We are?

TORTILLA MAN. Boy, once you get over your wonder, you can start dealing with life. Sit up there . . . you're slouched over like you're afraid.

CARLOS. [*Peering over the edge of the Flying Tortilla*] I am!

TORTILLA MAN. You, my young explorer, afraid of this . . . [THE TORTILLA MAN *begins to jump up and down on the tortilla.*]

CARLOS. [*Begging* THE TORTILLA MAN *to stop*] Oh please, Mr. Juan, won't you stop doing that? I think I'll just sit here, if you don't mind.

TORTILLA MAN. This isn't like you, Carlos. We're on an adventure. You just can't sit there and watch the birds fly by. You have to jump in or, in this case, fly on . . .

CARLOS. How far up are we?

TORTILLA MAN. About three cloud lengths and a half . . . I can check . . . [*He makes a motion to go to the back of the ship.*]

CARLOS. No, that isn't necessary. Is this . . . a . . . tortilla?

TORTILLA MAN. Nothing but the best for me . . . blue corn.

CARLOS. How does it fly?

TORTILLA MAN. Up, Carlos, up! Now then, here we have the front and lateral rudders. I had a lot of trouble perfecting them. It seems the birds would fly by and nibble on them between meals. Lost a lot of rudders that way. I used to carry a parachute for safety. But since I've put those letters on the side, it's been better.

CARLOS. M.F.T.V.F. What does it mean, Mr. Juan?

TORTILLA MAN. Glad to see you relaxing, Carlos. I hate to see tense young people. Why, those letters mean MAGIC FLYING TORTILLA VERY FATTENING. Birds are very conscious of their figures. To an extreme you might say. They never stop talking about it, but oh, how they love to eat! You don't do that, do you, Carlos?

CARLOS. Do you really talk to the birds?

TORTILLA MAN. Yes, and usually in a loud voice. They're hard of hearing. I talk to them when I have time. We're always so busy. Now for the rest of the tour. How you do ask questions! The best thing is not to ask but to listen. You'll find out things much faster that way. Not enough listening these days. Here is my flag, Carlos. My compass and baking powder bags. [*He pauses and looks at* CARLOS.] I'm waiting for questions.

CARLOS. What flag is that?

TORTILLA MAN. Why it's my own, of course. It's the flag of growth. [*The flag is in burnt desert colors. It shows the mountains, the rivers, and the plants of the desert. In the forefront is a plant with its root system exposed.*] This is the land, dry and burnt. To someone who doesn't know its ways, it is like thirst—there is no in-between. Our land is a land of mountains and rivers, dry things and growing things. Our roots are in the earth and we feel

the nourishment of the sky. This is *my* flag . . . what's yours?

CARLOS. I don't have a flag of my own.

TORTILLA MAN. You don't? Well, then you shall have to make one.

CARLOS. [*Discovering his box on the Flying Tortilla*] My cigar box! What is it doing here?

TORTILLA MAN. You were thinking about it, perhaps?

CARLOS. Why, that's my feather up there with your flag!

TORTILLA MAN. I needed a compass. You see, birds tell the direction by the way their feathers blow, and besides, it's a nice feather.

CARLOS. My father calls it an old ugly chicken feather.

TORTILLA MAN. Has he ever had his own feather? [CARLOS *shakes his head no.*] Well, then, how would he know?

CARLOS. It *is* an old feather!

TORTILLA MAN. Don't let the birds hear you say that. They may never forgive us! They don't exactly hold grudges, but it'll go better for us if we keep on their good side; the other side can be most uncomfortable. They give us a push now and then when the air current is low, so we can really use their help. You see, we fly by current. I ignite special minerals and then sprinkle that mixture over baking powder and whoosh! We are off! The staying up part is the only thing I've never really quite figured out yet.

CARLOS. Ohhhh! [*He looks down fearfully.*] How do you land?

TORTILLA MAN. By dropping bags of powder much the way a balloon drops sand.

I AM SINGING AT YOUR WINDOW, 1988
Jose Esteban Martinez
Vorpal Gallery, New York

CARLOS. But, Mr. Juan, that's not the way it works!

TORTILLA MAN. It isn't? Oh, what does it matter? Why must everything work the same way for everybody?

CARLOS. All of this is hard to believe.

TORTILLA MAN. Just look down there . . . isn't it breathtaking? That's my trail down there. The Juan de Oñate Trail.[2] That's the way I came up through Mexico and all the way north to Santa Fe. When I came through here, there was nothing . . . Imagine that!

CARLOS. Oñate, the explorer? We learned about him in school. He was from Spain, but he came up from Mexico to explore. He was a conquistador. I did a report on him.

TORTILLA MAN. Him? You mean me!

CARLOS. You? But you're The Tortilla Man, Mr. Juan.

TORTILLA MAN. So I am.

CARLOS. How can you be two people at once? Mexican and Spanish? Modern and old?

---

2. The Juan de Oñate (hwän de ō nyä′ te) **Trail:** The route taken by the Spanish explorer Juan de Oñate.

TORTILLA MAN. Carlos, my boy, when are you going to stop asking questions? Too many questions! [*He pushes out two bags of baking powder.*] We're going to land and walk around. [*He adjusts the compass.*] Now then, take a seat, Carlos. The landing may be a bit rough. I think a bird heard you earlier.

CARLOS. You mean about the feather?

TORTILLA MAN. Ssshhh! Birds are terrible spellers, so kindly spell out that word henceforth. Very good diction but lousy spellers. [*The Magic Tortilla floats down and lands on a rocky hill.*] I thought you'd like this place. I understand you collect fossils.

CARLOS. Yes, I do!

TORTILLA MAN. Well, look around you, Carlos. We have some good ones here. This used to be under water many, many years ago. All of this was once part of a great vast ocean.

CARLOS. Where are we now?

TORTILLA MAN. It's hard to believe, I know, but we are at the bottom of the sea! Find your fossil. We have all the time in the world. Find your fossil!

[*They stand together a moment.* CARLOS *picks up a fossil and puts it in his cigar box. They wander about collecting fossils for a while and then reboard the ship and head due north to an area of white sand.* THE TORTILLA MAN *has brought a lunch, and they take a break. They collect some sand, which* CARLOS *puts in his box, then head back to Cuchillo.*]

TORTILLA MAN. It's getting late, Carlos. Are you tired? We must go on . . .

CARLOS. I could never be tired with you, Mr. Juan. I'm too happy.

TORTILLA MAN. You're a good boy, Carlos.

CARLOS. That's the problem! I don't want to be a good boy! I want to be a person. Nobody really likes good boys.

TORTILLA MAN. That *is* a problem. I see what you mean. It seems you can't be too good or too bad. It's hard. The solution is just to be yourself. Be truthful, and you won't have to worry about being at any far end. You'll be in the middle with yourself.

CARLOS. But it's so hard!

TORTILLA MAN. When will you learn not to be impudent, boy! Trust me, and trust yourself above all. Here we are!

[*They drag the Flying Tortilla with a rope that is attached. They then sit by the side of the river, happy but exhausted.*]

CARLOS. I want this time to last forever!

TORTILLA MAN. It will, my friend, but shhh! Let's listen to the birds. They're talking . . . see, there they are on the Magic Flying Tortilla . . .

[*The* FOUR OLD WOMEN, *now* BIRDS, *peck at the Flying Tortilla.*]

TON. I'm hungry, Tin . . .

TIN. Me too, Ton.

TAN. I haven't eaten in days.

MABEL. Weeks . . .

TON. Months . . .

TIN. Years . . .

TAN. When was it, anyway?

MABEL. When The Flying Tortilla Man was on his way south . . .

TON. I don't know if I would have lasted if he hadn't come by . . .

TIN. I was dying for even a moldy, dried-out crust, a few crumbs . . . anything!

TAN. How about a nice big juicy earthworm?

MABEL. I'm a vegetarian.

TON. Against your religion, eh?

MABEL. No, against my waistline.

TIN. Always prancing about with her airs she is!

TON. Look who's talking!

TIN. What about you, Ton-Tona?

TON. Don't call me that, please.

TIN. Against your religion?

TAN. Oh, yes, a nice big juicy baked earthworm would be nice, with lots of gravy and a bird's nest salad . . . [*She cries out.*] Bird does not live by bread alone!

MABEL. Stop it! I feel faint!

TAN. Can it be? Can it be? Oh, dear, The Tortilla Man is coming back this way. He's spotted us. See him, Mabel? Girls, take courage. Here he comes. [*They all bow.*] Oh, great Tortilla Man!

TON. Image of hope, blessed Tortilla!

TIN. Blessed be the Holy Name of Tortilla,

MABEL. Thank you, Mr. Juan. [*She stuffs her face with some tortilla.*] Food!

TIN. Now who's watching her figure?

TAN. Not me, I don't have problems!

TON. Nor me!

MABEL. You're all as crazy as magpies!

TIN. That's a terrible insult, Mabel!

TAN. Will you be quiet! They're just about ready to take off, and I'm still hungry! I'm still so hungry I can't think or move!

TON. [*Speaking to the others*] She never could!

MABEL. Girls, please, we have to be off. Mr. Juan is nearly ready to leave. Settle down and get in formation. That's right!

[*They dress right and do a drill. Then, they fly off.*]

BIRDS. Thank you, Mr. Juan!

TORTILLA MAN. [*As he inspects the ship*] Rudders don't look too damaged. Really, those birds are all right, Carlos. They do give me a push now and then. Now hop aboard . . . we have to go home.

CARLOS. Do we have to, Mr. Juan?

TORTILLA MAN. We have things to do. We have our work, our families. And there's the fiesta[3] coming up. I have to get ready for that.

CARLOS. I don't have a real family, and I'm so tired of making tortillas!

TORTILLA MAN. There you go again. It's not what you do but how you do it. And as for having a family, you have people who love you . . . and you have yourself. So many people don't have themselves, Carlos. So what does it matter how many brothers and sisters you have? Why all of us are brothers and sisters!

CARLOS. I've heard all those things before!

TORTILLA MAN. Yes, but did you listen to them? Or ask yourself *why* people were saying such things? Now be still with yourself and don't talk about you know what—

————————
3. fiesta (fē es' tä): Spanish for "festival" or "celebration."

because our friends might be listening. They might think we're saying one thing when we really mean another. Carlos, are you tired? Rest there on the Magic Tortilla. Before you know it, we'll be in Cuchillo. Close your eyes, sleep, sleep!

[CARLOS *is getting sleepy, almost against his will.*]

CARLOS. I'm not really sleepy. It's been the happiest day of my life!

TORTILLA MAN. Stretch out there and rest!

CARLOS. Just for a moment, Mr. Juan. A little nap, that's all I need. You won't leave me, will you?

TORTILLA MAN. No, I won't leave you, ever . . . remember these things, Carlitos, and sleep, sleep . . .

CARLOS. [*In a far away voice*] Mr. Juan, where's my box? I had it right here . . .

TORTILLA MAN. Sleep . . . you need it, boy, to be strong . . .

Scene 4

[*Outside the factory the next morning.* CARLOS *wakes to find himself in the same position he was in on the Flying Tortilla. His body is cold and cramped. He is surprised to find himself on the steps of the tortilla factory.* TUDI *shakes him as* OSCAR *and* ELIAS *stand nearby.*]

TUDI. Wake up! Wake up, you rascal!

CARLOS. Mr. Juan, where is my box? I had it right here.

ELIAS. There you are, Tudi. He admits his guilt.

OSCAR. It was Carlos who broke into your office, Tudi, and tried to get in the safe.

ELIAS. Oscar and I were walking by and noticed the lights were still on. Then we saw Carlos sleeping here. That's when we called you, Tudi.

TUDI. Thank you, boys! I'll make it up to you. Fortunately, the snake wasn't able to get into the safe, but he sure made a mess of things. How did you get in, Carlos? Oh, you're going to be sorry that you ever saw this place. You'll never forget this day!

CARLOS. I don't understand. I was with Mr. Juan!

ELIAS. Don't lie to us, you thief!

OSCAR. He's a sneaky one. Don't believe him, Tudi.

ELIAS. I'm very surprised, Tudi. He always seemed so good.

CARLOS. I don't understand all this . . . what's happening?

TUDI. Don't lie to me, Carlos. And here I was thinking of promoting you. Vandal, you broke into my office and tried to rob my safe; and when you couldn't break in, you made a mess of things!

ELIAS. And you dropped this . . . [*He shows off* CARLOS's *cigar box.*]

CARLOS. My box, where did you find it?

OSCAR. He admits it! Remember this, Elias. We're witnesses!

ELIAS. We'll sue! Won't we, Tudi?

TUDI. We'll sue! You'll be sorry you were ever born. They'll probably send you to the boys' home in Springer.

OSCAR. Not that!

ELIAS. That's where all the hardened criminals go. A cousin of mine is there, so I know.

CARLOS. You're all wrong! I wasn't here at all. I was flying with Mr. Juan.

ELIAS. Who is this Mr. Juan, anyway?

CARLOS. He's a friend of mine.

OSCAR. Listen to that story, would you, Tudi!

TUDI. Stop lying to us, Carlos. You're making up these crazy stories to lead us off the track.

CARLOS. You've got it all wrong. I can show you. Give me the box, please.

ELIAS. Oh no, that's important evidence.

OSCAR. If you were flying around, show us your wings. Show us your wings! That's a funny one!

TUDI. Let's go!

CARLOS. Where? I'm not guilty. I tell you, I'm not guilty!

TUDI. This is a matter for the Sheriff's Office.

OSCAR. [*He turns to* CARLOS, *almost impressed.*] You little thief, you've hit the big time!

ELIAS. Is Fatty in today? I thought he went fishing on Wednesdays.

TUDI. The law is always at hand.

OSCAR. What does that mean?

TUDI. Sounds good, doesn't it?

CARLOS. But you have it all wrong!

OSCAR. Man, if I were you, I'd start praying. No one can face Fatty Campbell and not feel helpless fear.

TUDI. Go on, march. March, there. Go on, march! Oscar, you run ahead and tell Bertina and Hermano Gil. They'll want to hear about this. Tell them to meet us at the Sheriff's Office. Forward now, to justice!

Scene 5

[*The Sheriff's Office. It is near the Plaza on Calle del Sol street. It consists of several rooms. The lobby has a desk and chairs and a long, orange plastic couch for visitors. A magazine rack is near the couch and has old copies of* Ford Times, The Ranch News, *and last Thursday's paper. On the wall is a calendar from Corney Hawkins Olds. Next to that is a Navy picture of Company 1435, U.S. Naval Training Center, Great Lakes, Illinois, and beside that is a horseshoe and a picture of President John F. Kennedy.*]

FATTY. Where were you the night of the 10th?

CARLOS. With Mr. Juan.

ELIAS. There he goes again with that fabulous story.

FATTY. [*He admonishes* ELIAS.] Whoa there, boy. Order in the court. What do you mean speaking out of turn!

ELIAS. Tell us the truth now, Carlos!

CARLOS. I *have* been telling the truth.

BERTINA. No child of mine was ever a disgrace to our home, son.

HERMANO GIL. Please, Carlos, tell Mr. Fatty the truth.

FATTY. Order, order in the court! [ELIAS, BERTINA, HERMANO GIL *and the others settle down and look at* FATTY.] Ahem. It's about time. [*To* CARLOS] Were you not found near the scene of the crime by these two young fellows? [*He peers at* ELIAS *and* OSCAR *very closely.*] I think I know you two from somewhere.

CARLOS. Yes, I was, Mr. Fatty. I fell asleep with Mr. Juan, and he must have carried me back to the factory.

FATTY. *Who* is this mysterious Mr. Juan?

HERMANO GIL. Pay no attention to him, Sheriff.

ELIAS. He keeps talking about a Mr. Juan who flies.

TUDI. He's unstable. That's all there is to it. He needs help.

BERTINA. Oh, shut your mouth, Tudi.

HERMANO GIL. Bertina, my love . . . Bert, settle down.

CARLOS. Mr. Juan is a friend of mine.

TUDI. It's all your fault, Bertina! I shouldn't have listened to you and given the boy a chance at the factory. Now look what he's done! He's ruined my business.

BERTINA. It's not *your* business, you little toad. Nothing was stolen, your honor.

HERMANO GIL. My love, please.

FATTY. Settle down, folks. I know emotions run high, but this is a court of law . . . and I am the law. Settle down there, folks!

HERMANO GIL. Can we settle this out of court, Mr. Fatty?

COTIL. Of course not, Papa! This is a matter of public concern.

NOUVEAUX RICHES, 1941
Antonio Ruiz
The Museum of Modern Art, New York

HERMANO GIL. Nothing was stolen except a bag of frozen tamales . . . that's all . . .

[ELIAS *looks at* OSCAR, *who shrugs his shoulders as if to say, "I was hungry."*]

TUDI. That's all! I'll sue, Gil. My reputation is ruined. Have you seen that mess in the office? I'll sue! I'll sue!

FATTY. Whoa there. As judge and jury, I take the reins of the law in my hands. Having viewed the evidence and spoken to the accused and the witnesses, I now proclaim the verdict of this court, Filmore P. Campbell presiding, this eleventh day of June, in the year of, etcetera. Isn't it about time for lunch, Gil? What time do you have?

BERTINA. He's just a boy! He never meant to hurt anyone. He's a good boy, your honor.

ELIAS. So what's the verdict?

FATTY. Don't I know you from somewhere, sonny?

COTIL. Mama, we have to abide by the verdict.

HERMANO GIL. I can't believe a boy of mine could do this. How could you, son?

CARLOS. Papa . . . you must believe me . . . I'm innocent!

ELIAS. As innocent as a snake!

COTIL. He's a liar, Papa. Don't you know that already?

ELIAS. Sentence him!

OSCAR. Show no mercy!

FATTY. I hereby sentence you, Carlos Campo, to a week's labor on the Plaza, early curfew, and a fine of twenty dollars for court costs. Case closed. We have the fiesta coming up, and we'll need all the help we can get. Report

at five A.M. to Fernando at the water tower. Court dismissed. [*He speaks to* ELIAS.] I know you from somewhere. Don't you have a cousin . . . ?

ELIAS. You must be thinking of someone else, Mr. Fatty.

TUDI. I demand a retrial! Who's going to clean up my office? What about the tamales? My mother made them for me, and I was taking them home. I demand a retrial!

FATTY. Go back and sell a few tortillas!

TUDI. I'll sue!

BERTINA. He's just a child! Can't you understand that?

FATTY. Clear the court . . . clear the court. It's my lunchtime. Someone mention tamales?

TUDI. *This* is justice?

FATTY. Insulting the court—five dollars!

TUDI. I'll write my congressman.

FATTY. Threatening the law—ten dollars.

TUDI. Now wait a minute!

FATTY. Harassing the court—fifteen dollars.

ELIAS. Man, Tudi, you better leave while you can. It doesn't look good for you.

HERMANO GIL. After all these years, son, how could you break your father's heart? You were my only hope, Carlos. I felt as if you were my true son, my flesh and blood. Now you're a stranger!

[*He walks away with* BERTINA *and* COTIL, *who is gloating.*]

COTIL. Papa, I told you he was a sneak!

CARLOS. Papa! I'm innocent!

HERMANO GIL. Don't talk to me. Let's go, Bert.

BERTINA. That's all right, son. Dinner's at six. We're having papitas con chorizo.[4]

HERMANO GIL. How can anyone eat with a mouthful of sand?

COTIL. Hey, Carlos, bad luck!

ELIAS. Where are you going now, Cotil?

COTIL. I'm busy. I'm going home with Mama. So don't you bother me.

ELIAS. How can you say that to me after all I've done for you?

COTIL. You were always too young for me.

OSCAR. Hey, Elias, I know something we can do.

ELIAS. Leave me alone, man.

OSCAR. So what happened to our friendship?

ELIAS. I have better things to do. Out of my way.

[*They all exit.* CARLOS *and* FATTY *are left in the courtroom.*]

FATTY. Come on, sonny, cheer up. It's not the end of the world. When I was a kid, I got into a few scrapes. What's it matter, huh? You want part of a tuna fish sandwich? Some chips? Now, cheer up. Here's the evidence. Don't tell anyone I gave it back to you. Run along now. I haven't got all day. I haven't eaten my lunch yet. Now, sonny, you watch those stories . . . they'll get you in a mess of trouble.

CARLOS. They aren't stories . . . it's the truth! It's really the truth!

---

4. **papitas con chorizo** (pä pē′ täs kōn chō rē′ sō): Spanish for "potatoes with sausage."

Scene 6

[CARLOS's *room late that night. He is sitting on the bed, when he decides to get up and get his box from the chest of drawers.*]

CARLOS. [*Looking up at the ceiling*] Where were you, Mr. Juan, when I needed you? Where are you now? Why do you always leave me? [*Dejectedly*] I am as lonely and sad as the day the men from the church carry the body of God around the Plaza in that wooden box on Good Friday.[5] The people are all in black, singing with dried voices and moaning to themselves. They stop in front of doors that are closed. He said many things but not where he was from or where he went. He comes and goes, and I want to be angry with him, but I can't. I can feel him close sometimes, when it matters. He knows, he really knows me . . . and he cares. Mr. Tortilla Man, come back. Stay awhile with your Carlos. He needs friends. Because people hate him when he is good and love him when he is bad. [*He looks down at the cigar box.*] Should I open it? What of our fossils and sand? Will they be there? [*He opens the box.*] Where are they? What's this? It's a little note. "Remember, Carlos. Your friend, Mr. Juan, The Flying Tortilla Man." That's all, just a note and this—a small hard edge of tortilla. Of what use is it? [*He throws the tortilla away and then retrieves it.*] Oh, well. It's something! He said many things, but not where he came from and where he went. He said many things . . . "Remember," he said, "remember." But what? What?

[CARLOS *goes to sleep and has fitful dreams. The* OLD WOMEN/BIRDS *call out his name in a dream sequence. "There he is . . .*

---

5. **the men from the church . . . Good Friday:** On the Friday before Easter in some places, the Catholic Church holds a reenactment of the death of Christ.

who . . . ," and he sees all the people from the court scene. He wakes up in a sweat, clutching the cigar box; then he drifts off to sleep again.]

Scene 7

[*The next morning in the Plaza.* CARLOS *is sweeping the bandstand. He looks forlorn and miserable.* NORA *comes up to him.*]

NORA. What's wrong with boy?

CARLOS. Hello, Nora.

NORA. What's wrong with Carlitos?

CARLOS. I lost my job.

NORA. So sad. I miss Carlos at job. Oscar and Elias no like Nora—make fun all time. Neno? Neno?

CARLOS. He's still very sick.

NORA. Neno! I look for him last night. Saw Oscar and Elias at the job.

CARLOS. What was that, Nora?

NORA. Neno good boy—lose job? I look for him last night after Carlos walk Nora home. See Oscar and Elias make mess.

CARLOS. They said I tried to break into Tudi's office last night.

NORA. Oh no, no. Oh no, that Elias and Oscar do.

CARLOS. No, Nora. They said that about *me.*

NORA. Oscar and Elias go in and throw things around.

CARLOS. What are you saying?

NORA. Nora see them.

CARLOS. Have you told anyone?

NORA. I tell you. Nora see Elias and Oscar make mess.

CARLOS. [*Grabbing her hand*] Let's go, Nora. Let's go see Fatty!

NORA. I don't know Fatty.

Scene 8

[*The Sheriff's Office.*]

FATTY. This is a highly unusual case. I've taken the liberty to call in two witnesses.

CARLOS. Nora told us how she saw Elias and Oscar break into Tudi's office and throw things around.

FATTY. That's fine, son; but what proof do we have?

CARLOS. Nora told us! She's a witness!

FATTY. [*Taking* CARLOS *aside*] Son, she's not well. Loca en la cabeza.[6] You know what I mean? I think she made it up to help you. [*He speaks to* OSCAR *and* ELIAS.] What do you boys say?

ELIAS. Carlos is trying to defend himself. It was a good try, but it won't work.

NORA. Oscar with Elias.

OSCAR. Go away, Nora.

NORA. She see. She see. Elias call Oscar stupid fat boy behind his back.

ELIAS. Don't listen to her, Oscar. She's not all there.

NORA. Elias hate Oscar. He told me. [*She looks at* OSCAR.] Say that night that you a stupid boy and he smart one.

ELIAS. Don't believe her, Oscar!

─────────────

6. Loca en la cabeza (lō′ kä en lä kä be′ sä): Spanish for "crazy in the head."

OSCAR. Well, how do you like that! After all we've been through! You never did like me, man. He was there, Fatty. He made me do it!

ELIAS. You stupid fool! Why'd you take those tamales? I told you not to!

OSCAR. I was hungry! Fatty, it was Elias's idea. He told me about it and asked me to help. We were trying to get back at Carlos for being such a baby. I thought Elias was my friend, but he's the type that talks about you behind your back. He's just a lousy tortilla bum with the rot!

ELIAS. Will you shut up!! He's the sick one, Sheriff. He's got the rot. He's making things up!

OSCAR. I'm smarter than you, Elias, you little punk. I can pick any lock I want to. What can you do besides give directions and tell people what to do? What do you know, anyway?

NORA. Carlos come back to work now?

CARLOS. I was innocent all the time, Mr. Fatty.

FATTY. So it seems. The law is never tricked. Justice rules. Call Bertina, Gil, and Tudi. Court's in session. The retrial is about to begin.

CARLOS. Why did you do this, Elias?

ELIAS. It was Cotil's idea. She made me do it. She wanted to get back at you for everything.

OSCAR. [*Looking at* CARLOS] You were always a better friend to me than Elias, Carlos.

CARLOS. It's all right, Oscar. I forgive you.

OSCAR. It was Elias's fault. He's full of poison blood.

ELIAS. It's the rot, man. I got the rot! It was Cotil made me do it . . .

CARLOS. I forgive you too, Elias.

ELIAS. You always talked too much, Nora.

NORA. Thank you, all my friends! Go to work now?

Scene 9

[*The fossil beds.* CARLOS *and* THE TORTILLA MAN *are sitting on a rock shelf reviewing the past few days' events. It is a peaceful twilight in New Mexico.*]

CARLOS. And so, Mr. Juan, everything finally worked out. Where were you all that time? You could have told the Sheriff that I wasn't guilty.

TORTILLA MAN. When will you learn not to be impudent, boy? The truth of the matter is that I was getting ready for the fiesta, and anyway, you handled things pretty nicely.

CARLOS. I don't know what I would have done without Nora.

TORTILLA MAN. I told her to take care of you.

CARLOS. Do you know her?

TORTILLA MAN. Oh, blessed tortillas, yes! We're dear old friends. And besides, I was with you all the time. Remember that night you looked inside your cigar box? You were thinking of me, and I heard you. I said hello. I'm sorry I had to take the sand and the fossil. You see, I thought it was the best way. Things can't be too easy for us, or we don't appreciate them. We don't grow that way! Here's your fossil and the sand. [THE TORTILLA MAN *hands them to* CARLOS.] Remember me when you see them.

CARLOS. Will you go away before the fiesta, Mr. Juan? Neno was to play the part of the Indian scout, Jusephe,[7] but he's still a little

---

7. Jusephe (h$\overline{oo}$ se′ fe): A Native Mexican scout who guided Juan de Oñate on one of his expeditions.

weak, so they asked me to take the role. This is my first time in the fiesta play. When I grow up, I want to play the part of Oñate. But how can anyone play that part, if you're the real Oñate? Why don't *you* play the part?

TORTILLA MAN. We'll have to work out something by that time, Carlos.

CARLOS. Elias and Oscar have to work in the Plaza now, in my place, but the Sheriff is letting them take part in the parade. All of us have roles in the pageant play! Will you be in the parade? You said something about getting ready for the fiesta.

TORTILLA MAN. Oh, I have a very small part. Nothing that anyone couldn't play if they really wanted to.

CARLOS. Will I see you?

TORTILLA MAN. If you don't, I shall be very sorry. Now, remember to see, not to look. I might seem a bit different from myself, but it's me. You can never really change a person inside, no matter what you do.

CARLOS. Mama is making the costumes. Cotil is playing the part of a Señorita,[8] but she still won't talk to me.

TORTILLA MAN. She'll get over it.

CARLOS. Even if you're not good, some people still don't like you.

TORTILLA MAN. Remember what I said, we're all from the same country. We have the sky which covers our heads and the earth which warms our feet. We don't have time to be anywhere in between where we can't feel that power. Some people call it love. I call it I.W.A.

CARLOS. I.W.A.? What does that mean?

TORTILLA MAN. Inside We're Alike. Now I must leave you.

CARLOS. Can we go for a ride on the Flying Tortilla some time?

TORTILLA MAN. Anytime you like, Carlos.

[*The Magic Tortilla takes off with a huge blast, and soon* CARLOS *and* THE TORTILLA MAN *are floating in space. Flash to the Plaza, the town fiesta, in honor of the founding of Cuchillo by Don Juan de Oñate. The Plaza is decorated with bright streamers and flowers, and booths completely circle it. There are food booths as well as game booths. The parade begins at North Cotton Street. First come the Spanish soldiers in costume, with* TUDI *leading.* ELIAS *and* OSCAR *wear a cow costume and are led by a radiantly beautiful* NORA. HERMANO GIL *plays the part of one of Oñate's generals, and* BERTINA *is a noblewoman. She is followed by* COTIL, *and behind* COTIL *is* FATTY, *in a tight-fitting suit of armor and a helmet with the insignia of the Spanish army.[9] He is the Master of Ceremonies. The parade marches forward. Jusephe, played by* CARLOS, *leads the Royal Entourage.[10]* CARLOS *is followed by Don Juan de Oñate (*THE FLYING TORTILLA MAN*), a small old man with twinkling eyes.*]

ELIAS. Hey, Oscar, who's that old man next to Carlos?

OSCAR. Let me see. [OSCAR *sticks his head out of the cow's rear end.*] That's El Boss, Señor

---

8. Señorita (se nyỏ rē′ tä): Spanish word for an unmarried woman.

9. insignia (in sig′ nē ə) **of the Spanish army:** The badges or emblems that identify members of the army.

10. Royal Entourage (än′ too räzh): The group of attendants with the representative of the King, Juan de Oñate.

THREE DAYS AND THREE NIGHTS, 1985
Paul Sierra
Gwenda Jay Gallery, Chicago

López[11]—he owns the factory. He lives at one of those rest homes, but every year he comes out and plays Oñate. He's been doing it as long as I can remember.

ELIAS. So that's the original Tortilla Man, eh? He looks as old as the hills and as dusty.

OSCAR. I can't go on much longer . . . it's hot!

ELIAS. So go work in an ice plant. Get it? Man, you have no sense of humor.

***

11. **El Boss, Señor López** (el bôs se nyôr′ lō′ pes): The boss, Mister Lopez.

OSCAR. You wouldn't have a sense of humor if you were back here!

[*They march forward, and when* FATTY *gets to the bandstand, he makes an announcement.* CARLOS *sees* NENO *and yells to him.* NENO *is sitting on the side, resting in the sun, and looks much better.*]

CARLOS. Hey, Neno! Neno, how are you?

NENO. I'm getting better, Carlos . . . I'm going to make it!

ELIAS. Move over, Oscar. There's Neno. I don't want germs to float over this way.

NORA. Come on, little cow; go see Neno.

OSCAR. Can't you do anything, Elias? She's going near you-know-who-with-you-know-what. The Rot!

NORA. Neno, Neno!

FATTY. As Master of Ceremonies and Sheriff of the Cuchillo Municipality, I, Filmore P. Campbell, welcome you inhabitants to our annual fiesta in honor of the founding of Cuchillo by Don Juan de Oñate.

[*The crowd cheers, and there is a great noise of firecrackers and shouts.* THE BIRDS *are seen from a distance, viewing all the festivities.*]

MABEL. There he is . . .

TIN. Who?

TAN. The boy.

TON. Are you going to start that again?

MABEL. I don't know what you're talking about.

TAN. What are they doing down there?

TIN. Who?

MABEL. The people in the Plaza.

TAN. They're laughing and having a good time.

TIN. You mean the ones out there? [*She peers into the audience.*]

MABEL. [*Looking out as well*] Oh, yes, they've been here awhile, haven't they?

TAN. I think they've had a good time, too. Don't you, Ton?

TON. They look a little happier than when they came in.

TIN. Do you think so?

TAN. But what about the people in the Plaza? What's all that about down there? That parade and all the noise?

MABEL. Horses make me nervous.

TON. Everything makes you nervous or unhappy or fat.

MABEL. I like a good story now and then, something to pass the time.

TON. Oh, you and your time!

TAN. It's so nice to just sit here and smell the sky and the sunshine, and feel the sounds of life . . .

MABEL. How can you smell the sky, you crazy bird? You have it all mixed up!

TON. Leave Tan alone, Mabel. She's all right. She's just being Tan.

MABEL. I guess you're right. She just can't help being Tan. Poor dear!

TIN. Are they getting nervous out there? [*Referring to the audience*]

TON. No, but I think it's time to go home now.

TIN. Why? I was having so much fun!

TON. It's just time.

TAN. Will we come back here again?

TIN. We'd better. I'm getting hungry just thinking about it.

MABEL. What are you silly birds talking about?

TAN. What's all the noise about anyway?

[*They fly off.*]

TON. When will you listen, silly bird?

TAN. What was that? I couldn't hear you! "Listen." Did you say, "listen"? [*In a faraway voice*] Can't you just smell the sky?

Your Response

1. The Tortilla Man says, "Things can't be too easy for us, or we don't appreciate them." Do you agree or disagree with this statement? Why?

Recalling

2. How does Cotil plan to teach Carlos a lesson?
3. Who finally helps Carlos prove his innocence?

Interpreting

4. What reason do Elias and Oscar have for suddenly becoming friends?
5. Why do you think everyone believed that Carlos was guilty?
6. Why does Oscar confess to the break-in?
7. What does Carlos learn about life from the Tortilla Man?

Applying

8. The Tortilla Man tells Carlos to "remember to see, not to look." How might this advice help people in everyday life?

ANALYZING LITERATURE

Understanding Staging

Staging a play means making it come to life on a stage. Staging includes actors' movements, scenery, lighting, and special effects. In *The Flying Tortilla Man,* the staging includes a number of unusual features, such as the huge blue tortilla.

1. Which details in the stage directions in Scene 3 help create a dreamlike atmosphere?
2. How is Carlos's ride on the Magic Blue Corn Tortilla staged differently than the more "realistic" scenes in the play?
3. What challenges would someone staging the scenes with Tin, Tan, and Ton face?

CRITICAL THINKING AND READING

Relating Staging to Dramatic Purpose

The staging in *The Flying Tortilla Man* often gives you important information that the dialogue alone does not. For instance, when Oscar and Elias break into the office, the stage directions say that Nora sees them.

1. What do you learn about the relationship between Carlos and the Tortilla Man through their movements rather than their dialogue?
2. In Scene 6 how do the stage directions add to what Carlos is saying?

THINKING AND WRITING

Writing About Staging

Imagine that you are directing a production of *The Flying Tortilla Man* for your school and that you must tell the stagehands how to stage the scene on the Magic Flying Blue Tortilla. What should the set look like and which props are needed? Write a memo with your instructions. Also explain how you are going to give the impression of the tortilla flying. Check to be sure your descriptions and the steps involved are clearly written.

LEARNING OPTIONS

1. **Writing.** Imagine that you can look five years into the future and see what will happen to the characters in *The Flying Tortilla Man.* Choose two characters from the play and write a paragraph on each describing what the person will be like and what they will be doing. Compare your predictions with some of your classmates'.
2. **Art.** Design costumes for some of the characters in the play. You may simply draw how the costumes should look, or you may want to use colored paper and fabric to make a collage. Refer to the stage directions for details about the characters' appearances.

GUIDE FOR READING

The Monsters Are Due on Maple Street

Conflict in Drama

Conflict, a struggle between opposing forces, is basic to drama. A play is usually based on one of the fundamental kinds of conflict. These include conflict between individuals, between an individual and society, between an individual and nature, and between an individual and himself or herself. Although one type of conflict will be central to a play, other types will often be present, too.

Focus

The Monsters Are Due on Maple Street is a *teleplay,* a play written for television. As such, it has an important feature that stage plays do not—camera directions. These directions tell you how the play would look on television; however, you need to know a few technical terms to understand them. *Pan* means to move the camera to scan a scene or to follow a moving object. *Cut* means to switch suddenly from one scene or setting to another. What do you think *fade in, fade out, close-up,* and *long shot* mean?

Now imagine this scene: You and some friends are in a room in one of your homes. Strange things start to happen: Lights go on and off by themselves, chairs and tables move, weird noises are heard. In a small group, brainstorm and write down the possible effects of these strange goings-on. Use your experience watching television to visualize them on screen.

Vocabulary

Knowing the following words will help you as you read *The Monsters Are Due on Maple Street.*

flustered (flus′ tərd) *v.:* Made nervous (p. 249)

sluggishly (slug′ ish lē) *adv.:* As if lacking energy (p. 250)

assent (ə sent′) *n.:* Agreement (p. 250)

persistently (pər sist′ ənt lē) *adv.:* Firmly and steadily (p. 250)

defiant (di fī′ ənt) *adj.:* Boldly resisting (p. 251)

metamorphosis (met′ ə môr′ fə sis) *n.:* A change of form (p. 252)

scapegoat (skāp′ gōt′) *n.:* A person or group blamed for the mistakes or crimes of others (p. 256)

Rod Serling

(1924–1975) was born and raised in New York State. He is best known as the creator of the television series *The Twilight Zone.* In this series, Serling presented a number of science-fiction plays that highlighted his views of life and society on this planet. *The Monsters Are Due on Maple Street* raises the question of whether the real monsters are up there or down here.

The Monsters Are Due on Maple Street

Rod Serling

CHARACTERS

Narrator
Figure One
Figure Two

Residents of Maple Street

Steve Brand	Charlie's Wife	Mrs. Goodman
Mrs. Brand	Tommy	Woman
Don Martin	Sally, Tommy's	Man One
Pete Van Horn	Mother	Man Two
Charlie	Les Goodman	

ACT I

[*Fade in on a shot of the night sky. The various nebulae and planet bodies stand out in sharp, sparkling relief, and the camera begins a slow pan across the Heavens.*]

NARRATOR'S VOICE. There is a fifth dimension beyond that which is known to man. It is a dimension as vast as space, and as timeless as infinity. It is the middle ground between light and shadow—between science and superstition. And it lies between the pit of man's fears and the summit of his knowledge. This is the dimension of imagination. It is an area which we call The Twilight Zone.

[*The camera has begun to pan down until it passes the horizon and is on a sign which reads "Maple Street." Pan down until we are shooting down at an angle toward the street below. It's a tree-lined, quiet residential American street, very typical of the small town. The houses have front porches on which people sit and swing on gliders, conversing across from house to house. Steve Brand polishes his car parked in front of his house. His neighbor, Don Martin, leans against the fender watching him. A Good Humor man rides a bicycle and is just in the process of stopping to sell some ice cream to a couple of kids. Two women gossip on the front lawn. Another man waters his lawn.*]

NARRATOR'S VOICE: Maple Street, U.S.A., late summer. A tree-lined little world of front

porch gliders, hop scotch, the laughter of children, and the bell of an ice cream vendor.

[*There is a pause and the camera moves over to a shot of the Good Humor man and two small boys who are standing alongside, just buying ice cream.*]

NARRATOR'S VOICE. At the sound of the roar and the flash of light it will be precisely 6:43 P.M. on Maple Street.

[*At this moment one of the little boys, Tommy, looks up to listen to a sound of a tremendous screeching roar from overhead. A flash of light plays on both their faces and then it moves down the street past lawns and porches and rooftops and then disappears.*

Various people leave their porches and stop what they're doing to stare up at the sky. Steve Brand, the man who's been pol-

ishing his car, now stands there transfixed, staring upwards. He looks at Don Martin, his neighbor from across the street.]

STEVE. What was that? A meteor?

DON. [*Nods*] That's what it looked like. I didn't hear any crash though, did you?

STEVE. [*Shakes his head*] Nope. I didn't hear anything except a roar.

MRS. BRAND. [*From her porch*] Steve? What was that?

STEVE. [*Raising his voice and looking toward porch*] Guess it was a meteor, honey. Came awful close, didn't it?

MRS. BRAND. Too close for my money! Much too close.

[*The camera pans across the various por-*

ches to people who stand there watching and talking in low tones.]

NARRATOR'S VOICE. Maple Street. Six-forty-four P.M. on a late September evening. [*A pause*] Maple Street in the last calm and reflective moment . . . before the monsters came!

[*The camera slowly pans across the porches again. We see a man screwing a light bulb on a front porch, then getting down off the stool to flick the switch and finding that nothing happens.*

Another man is working on an electric power mower. He plugs in the plug, flicks on the switch of the power mower, off and on, with nothing happening.

Through the window of a front porch, we see a woman pushing her finger back and forth on the dial hook. Her voice is indistinct and distant, but intelligible and repetitive.]

WOMAN. Operator, operator, something's wrong on the phone, operator!

[*Mrs. Brand comes out on the porch and calls to Steve.*]

MRS. BRAND. [*Calling*] Steve, the power's off. I had the soup on the stove and the stove just stopped working.

WOMAN. Same thing over here. I can't get anybody on the phone either. The phone seems to be dead.

[*We look down on the street as we hear the voices creep up from below, small, mildly disturbed voices highlighting these kinds of phrases:*]

VOICES.
Electricity's off.
Phone won't work.
Can't get a thing on the radio.
My power mower won't move, won't work at all.

Radio's gone dead!

[*Pete Van Horn, a tall, thin man, is seen standing in front of his house.*]

VAN HORN. I'll cut through the back yard . . . See if the power's still on on Floral Street. I'll be right back!

[*He walks past the side of his house and disappears into the back yard.*

The camera pans down slowly until we're looking at ten or eleven people standing around the street and overflowing to the curb and sidewalk. In the background is Steve Brand's car.]

STEVE. Doesn't make sense. Why should the power go off all of a sudden, and the phone line?

DON. Maybe some sort of an electrical storm or something.

CHARLIE. That don't seem likely. Sky's just as blue as anything. Not a cloud. No lightning. No thunder. No nothing. How could it be a storm?

WOMAN. I can't get a thing on the radio. Not even the portable.

[*The people again murmur softly in wonderment and question.*]

CHARLIE. Well, why don't you go downtown and check with the police, though they'll probably think we're crazy or something. A little power failure and right away we get all flustered and everything.

STEVE. It isn't just the power failure, Charlie. If it was, we'd still be able to get a broadcast on the portable.

[*There's a murmur of reaction to this. Steve looks from face to face and then over to his car.*]

STEVE. I'll run downtown. We'll get this all straightened out.

[*He walks over to the car, gets in it, turns the key. Looking through the open car door, we see the crowd watching him from the other side. Steve starts the engine. It turns over sluggishly and then just stops dead. He tries it again and this time he can't get it to turn over. Then, very slowly and reflectively, he turns the key back to "off" and slowly gets out of the car.*

The people stare at Steve. He stands for a moment by the car, then walks toward the group.]

STEVE. I don't understand it. It was working fine before . . .

DON. Out of gas?

STEVE. [*Shakes his head*] I just had it filled up.

WOMAN. What's it mean?

CHARLIE. It's just as if . . . as if everything had stopped. [*Then he turns toward* STEVE.] We'd better walk downtown. [*Another murmur of assent at this.*]

STEVE. The two of us can go, Charlie. [*He turns to look back at the car.*] It couldn't be the meteor. A meteor couldn't do *this*.

[*He and Charlie exchange a look, then they start to walk away from the group.*

We see Tommy, a serious-faced fourteen-year-old in spectacles who stands a few feet away from the group. He is halfway between them and the two men, who start to walk down the sidewalk.]

TOMMY. Mr. Brand . . . you better not!

STEVE. Why not?

TOMMY. They don't want you to.

[*Steve and Charlie exchange a grin, and Steve looks back toward the boy.*]

STEVE. *Who* doesn't want us to?

TOMMY. [*Jerks his head in the general direction of the distant horizon*] Them!

STEVE. Them?

CHARLIE. Who are them?

TOMMY. [*Very intently*] Whoever was in that thing that came by overhead.

[*Steve knits his brows for a moment, cocking his head questioningly. His voice is intense.*]

STEVE. What?

TOMMY. Whoever was in that thing that came over. I don't think they want us to leave here.

[*Steve leaves Charlie and walks over to the boy. He kneels down in front of him. He forces his voice to remain gentle. He reaches out and holds the boy.*]

STEVE. What do you mean? What are you talking about?

TOMMY. They don't want us to leave. That's why they shut everything off.

STEVE. What makes you say that? Whatever gave you that idea?

WOMAN. [*From the crowd*] Now isn't that the craziest thing you ever heard?

TOMMY. [*Persistently but a little intimidated by the crowd*] It's always that way, in every story I ever read about a ship landing from outer space.

WOMAN. [*To the boy's mother, Sally, who stands on the fringe of the crowd*] From outer space, yet! Sally, you better get that boy of yours up to bed. He's been reading too many comic books or seeing too many movies or something.

SALLY. Tommy, come over here and stop that kind of talk.

STEVE. Go ahead, Tommy. We'll be right

back. And you'll see. That wasn't any ship or anything like it. That was just a . . . a meteor or something. Likely as not—[*He turns to the group, now trying to weight his words with an optimism he obviously doesn't feel but is desperately trying to instill in himself as well as the others.*] No doubt it did have something to do with all this power failure and the rest of it. Meteors can do some crazy things. Like sunspots.

DON. [*Picking up the cue*] Sure. That's the kind of thing—like sunspots. They raise Cain with[1] radio reception all over the world. And this thing being so close—why, there's no telling the sort of stuff it can do. [*He wets his lips, smiles nervously.*] Go ahead, Charlie. You and Steve go into town and see if that isn't what's causing it all.

[*Steve and Charlie again walk away from the group down the sidewalk. The people watch silently.*

Tommy stares at them, biting his lips, and finally calling out again.]

TOMMY. *Mr. Brand!*

[*The two men stop again. Tommy takes a step toward them.*]

TOMMY. Mr. Brand . . . please don't leave here.

[*Steve and Charlie stop once again and turn toward the boy. There's a murmur in the crowd, a murmur of irritation and concern as if the boy were bringing up fears that shouldn't be brought up; words which carried with them a strange kind of validity that came without logic but nonetheless registered and had meaning and effect. Again we hear a murmur of reaction from the crowd.*

Tommy is partly frightened and partly defiant as well.]

---

1. **raise Cain with:** Badly disturb.

TOMMY. You might not even be able to get to town. It was that way in the story. Nobody could leave. Nobody except—

STEVE. Except who?

TOMMY. Except the people they'd sent down ahead of them. They looked just like humans. And it wasn't until the ship landed that—

[*The boy suddenly stops again, conscious of the parents staring at them and of the sudden hush of the crowd.*]

SALLY. [*In a whisper, sensing the antagonism of the crowd*] Tommy, please son . . . honey, don't talk that way—

MAN ONE. That kid shouldn't talk that way . . . and we shouldn't stand here listening to him. Why this is the craziest thing I ever heard of. The kid tells us a comic book plot and here we stand listening—

[*Steve walks toward the camera, stops by the boy.*]

STEVE. Go ahead, Tommy. What kind of story was this? What about the people that they sent out ahead?

TOMMY. That was the way they prepared things for the landing. They sent four people. A mother and a father and two kids who looked just like humans . . . but they weren't.

[*There's another silence as Steve looks toward the crowd and then toward Tommy. He wears a tight grin.*]

STEVE. Well, I guess what we'd better do then is to run a check on the neighborhood and see which ones of us are really human.

[*There's laughter at this, but it's a laughter that comes from a desperate attempt to lighten the atmosphere. It's a release kind* of laugh. The people look at one another in the middle of their laughter.]

CHARLIE. There must be somethin' better to do than stand around makin' bum jokes about it. [*Rubs his jaw nervously*] I wonder if Floral Street's got the same deal we got. [*He looks past the houses.*] Where is Pete Van Horn anyway? Didn't he get back yet?

[*Suddenly there's the sound of a car's engine starting to turn over.*

We look across the street toward the driveway of Les Goodman's house. He's at the wheel trying to start the car.]

SALLY. Can you get it started, Les? [*He gets out of the car, shaking his head.*]

GOODMAN. No dice.

[*He walks toward the group. He stops suddenly as behind him, inexplicably and with a noise that inserts itself into the silence, the car engine starts up all by itself. Goodman whirls around to stare toward it.*

The car idles roughly, smoke coming from the exhaust, the frame shaking gently.

Goodman's eyes go wide, and he runs over to his car.

The people stare toward the car.]

MAN ONE. He got the car started somehow. He got his car started!

[*The camera pans along the faces of the people as they stare, somehow caught up by this revelation and somehow, illogically, wildly, frightened.*]

WOMAN. How come his car just up and started like that?

SALLY. All by itself. He wasn't anywheres near it. It started all by itself.

[*Don approaches the group, stops a few feet away to look toward Goodman's car and then back toward the group.*]

DON. And he never did come out to look at that thing that flew overhead. He wasn't even interested. [*He turns to the faces in the group, his face taut and serious.*] Why? Why didn't he come out with the rest of us to look?

CHARLIE. He always was an oddball. Him and his whole family. Real oddball.

DON. What do you say we ask him?

[*The group suddenly starts toward the house. In this brief fraction of a moment they take the first step toward performing a metamorphosis that changes people from a group into a mob. They begin to head purposefully across the street toward the house at the end. Steve stands in front of them. For a moment their fear almost turns their walk into a wild stampede, but Steve's voice, loud, incisive, and commanding, makes them stop.*]

STEVE. Wait a minute . . . wait a minute! Let's not be a mob!

[*The people stop as a group, seem to pause for a moment, and then much more quietly and slowly start to walk across the street. Goodman stands alone facing the people.*]

GOODMAN. I just don't understand it. I tried to start it and it wouldn't start. You saw me. All of you saw me.

[*And now, just as suddenly as the engine started, it stops and there's a long silence that is gradually intruded upon by the frightened murmuring of the people.*]

GOODMAN. I don't understand. I swear . . . I don't understand. What's happening?

DON. Maybe you better tell us. Nothing's working on this street. Nothing. No lights, no power, no radio. [*And then meaningfully*] Nothing except one car—yours!

[*The people pick this up and now their murmuring becomes a loud chant filling the air with accusations and demands for action. Two of the men pass Don and head toward Goodman, who backs away, backing into his car and now at bay.*]

GOODMAN. Wait a minute now. You keep your distance—all of you. So I've got a car that starts by itself—well, that's a freak thing, I admit it. But does that make me some kind of a criminal or something? I don't know why the car works—it just does!

[*This stops the crowd momentarily and now Goodman, still backing away, goes toward his front porch. He goes up the steps and then stops to stand facing the mob.*

We see a long shot of Steve as he comes through the crowd.]

STEVE. [*Quietly*] We're all on a monster kick, Les. Seems that the general impression holds that maybe one family isn't what we think they are. Monsters from outer space or something. Different than us. Fifth columnists[2] from the vast beyond. [*He chuckles.*] You know anybody that might fit that description around here on Maple Street?

GOODMAN. What is this, a gag or something? This a practical joke or something?

[*We see a close-up of the porch light as it suddenly goes out. There's a murmur from the group.*]

GOODMAN. Now I suppose that's supposed to incriminate me! The light goes on and off. That really does it, doesn't it?

[*He looks around the faces of the people.*] I just don't understand this—[*He wets his lips, looking from face to face.*] Look, you all know me. We've lived here five years. Right

_____

2. **Fifth columnists:** People who help an invading enemy from within their own country.

in this house. We're no different from any of the rest of you! We're no different at all. Really . . . this whole thing is just . . . just weird—

WOMAN. Well, if that's the case, Les Goodman, explain why—[*She stops suddenly, clamping her mouth shut.*]

GOODMAN. [*Softly*] Explain what?

STEVE. [*Interjecting*] Look, let's forget this—

CHARLIE. [*Overlapping him*] Go ahead, let her talk. What about it? Explain what?

WOMAN. [*A little reluctantly*] Well . . . sometimes I go to bed late at night. A couple of times . . . a couple of times I'd come out on the porch and I'd see Mr. Goodman here in the wee hours of the morning standing out in front of his house . . . looking up at the sky. [*She looks around the circle of faces.*] That's right, looking up at the sky as if . . . as if he were waiting for something. [*A pause*] As if he were looking for something.

[*There's a murmur of reaction from the crowd again.*

We cut suddenly to a group shot. As Goodman starts toward them, they back away frightened.]

GOODMAN. You know really . . . this is for laughs. You know what I'm guilty of? [*He laughs.*] I'm guilty of insomnia. Now what's the penalty for insomnia? [*At this point the laugh, the humor, leaves his voice.*] Did you hear what I said? I said it was insomnia. [*A pause as he looks around, then shouts.*] I said it was insomnia! You fools. You scared, frightened rabbits, you. You're sick people, do you know that? You're sick people—all of you! And you don't even know what you're starting because let me tell you . . . let me tell you—this thing you're starting—that should frighten you. As God is my witness . . . you're letting something begin here that's a nightmare!

ACT II

[*We see a medium shot of the Goodman entry hall at night. On the side table rests an unlit candle. Mrs. Goodman walks into the scene, a glass of milk in hand. She sets the milk down on the table, lights the candle with a match from a box on the table, picks up the glass of milk, and starts out of scene.*

Mrs. Goodman comes through her porch door, glass of milk in hand. The entry hall, with table and lit candle, can be seen behind her.

Outside, the camera slowly pans down the sidewalk, taking in little knots of people who stand around talking in low voices. At the end of each conversation they look toward Les Goodman's house. From the various houses we can see candlelight but no electricity, and there's an all-pervading quiet that blankets the whole area, disturbed only by the almost whispered voices of the people as they stand around. The camera pans over to one group where Charlie stands. He stares across at Goodman's house.

We see a long shot of the house. Two men stand across the street in almost sentry-like poses. Then we see a medium shot of a group of people.]

SALLY. [*A little timorously*] It just doesn't seem right, though, keeping watch on them. Why . . . he was right when he said he was one of our neighbors. Why, I've known Ethel Goodman ever since they moved in. We've been good friends—

CHARLIE. That don't prove a thing. Any guy who'd spend his time lookin' up at the sky early in the morning—well, there's something wrong with that kind of person. There's something that ain't legitimate. Maybe under normal circumstances we could let it go by, but these aren't normal circumstances. Why, look at this street! Nothin' but candles. Why, it's like goin' back into the dark ages or somethin'!

[*Steve walks down the steps of his porch, walks down the street over to Les Goodman's house, and then stops at the foot of the steps. Goodman stands there, his wife behind him, very frightened.*]

GOODMAN. Just stay right where you are, Steve. We don't want any trouble, but this time if anybody sets foot on my porch, that's what they're going to get—trouble!

STEVE. Look, Les—

GOODMAN. I've already explained to you people. I don't sleep very well at night sometimes. I get up and I take a walk and I look up at the sky. I look at the stars!

MRS. GOODMAN. That's exactly what he does. Why this whole thing, it's . . . it's some kind of madness or something.

STEVE. [*Nods grimly*] That's exactly what it is—some kind of madness.

CHARLIE'S VOICE. [*Shrill, from across the street*] You best watch who you're seen with, Steve! Until we get this all straightened out, you ain't exactly above suspicion yourself.

STEVE. [*Whirling around toward him*] Or you, Charlie. Or any of us, it seems. From age eight on up!

WOMAN. What I'd like to know is—what are we gonna do? Just stand around here all night?

CHARLIE. There's nothin' else we can do! [*He turns back looking toward Steve and Good-*

man again.] One of 'em'll tip their hand. They got to.

STEVE. [*Raising his voice*] There's something you can do, Charlie. You could go home and keep your mouth shut. You could quit strutting around like a self-appointed hanging judge and just climb into bed and forget it.

CHARLIE. You sound real anxious to have that happen, Steve. I think we better keep our eye on you too!

DON. [*As if he were taking the bit in his teeth, takes a hesitant step to the front*] I think everything might as well come out now. [*He turns toward Steve.*] Your wife's

done plenty of talking, Steve, about how odd you are!

CHARLIE. [*Picking this up, his eyes widening*] Go ahead, tell us what she's said.

[*We see a long shot of Steve as he walks toward them from across the street.*]

STEVE. Go ahead, what's my wife said? Let's get it all out. Let's pick out every idiosyncrasy of every single man, woman, and child on the street. And then we might as well set up some kind of kangaroo court.[1] How about a firing squad at dawn, Charlie, so we can

---

1. kangaroo court: An unofficial court that does not follow normal rules.

get rid of all the suspects? Narrow them down. Make it easier for you.

DON. There's no need gettin' so upset, Steve. It's just that . . . well . . . Myra's talked about how there's been plenty of nights you spent hours down in your basement workin' on some kind of radio or something. Well, none of us have ever seen that radio—

[*By this time Steve has reached the group. He stands there defiantly close to them.*]

CHARLIE. Go ahead, Steve. What kind of "radio set" you workin' on? I never seen it. Neither has anyone else. Who you talk to on that radio set? And who talks to you?

STEVE. I'm surprised at you, Charlie. How come you're so dense all of a sudden? [*A pause*] Who do I talk to? I talk to monsters from outer space. I talk to three-headed green men who fly over here in what look like meteors.

[*Steve's wife steps down from the porch, bites her lip, calls out.*]

MRS. BRAND. Steve! Steve, please. [*Then looking around, frightened, she walks toward the group.*] It's just a ham radio set, that's all. I bought him a book on it myself. It's just a ham radio set. A lot of people have them. I can show it to you. It's right down in the basement.

STEVE. [*Whirls around toward her*] Show them nothing! If they want to look inside our house—let them get a search warrant.

CHARLIE. Look, buddy, you can't afford to—

STEVE. [*Interrupting*] Charlie, don't tell me what I can afford! And stop telling me who's dangerous and who isn't and who's safe and who's a menace. [*He turns to the group and shouts.*] And you're with him, too—all of you! You're standing here all set to crucify—all set to find a scapegoat—all desperate to point

some kind of a finger at a neighbor! Well now look, friends, the only thing that's gonna happen is that we'll eat each other up alive—

[*He stops abruptly as Charlie suddenly grabs his arm.*]

CHARLIE. [*In a hushed voice*] That's not the only thing that can happen to us.

[*Cut to a long shot looking down the street. A figure has suddenly materialized in the gloom and in the silence we can hear the clickety-clack of slow, measured footsteps on concrete as the figure walks slowly toward them. One of the women lets out a stifled cry. The young mother grabs her boy as do a couple of others.*]

TOMMY. [*Shouting, frightened*] It's the monster! It's the monster!

[*Another woman lets out a wail and the people fall back in a group, staring toward the darkness and the approaching figure.*

We see a medium group shot of the people as they stand in the shadows watching. Don Martin joins them, carrying a shotgun. He holds it up.]

DON. We may need this.

STEVE. A shotgun? [*He pulls it out of Don's hand.*] Good Lord—will anybody think a thought around here? Will you people wise up? What good would a shotgun do against—

[*Now Charlie pulls the gun from Steve's hand.*]

CHARLIE. No more talk, Steve. You're going to talk us into a grave! You'd let whatever's out there walk right over us, wouldn't yuh? Well, some of us won't!

[*He swings the gun around to point it toward the sidewalk.*

The dark figure continues to walk toward them.]

The group stands there, fearful, apprehensive, mothers clutching children, men standing in front of wives. Charlie slowly raises the gun. As the figure gets closer and closer he suddenly pulls the trigger. The sound of it explodes in the stillness. There is a long angle shot looking down at the figure, who suddenly lets out a small cry, stumbles forward onto his knees and then falls forward on his face. Don, Charlie, and Steve race forward over to him. Steve is there first and turns the man over. Now the crowd gathers around them.]

STEVE. [Slowly looks up] It's Pete Van Horn.

DON. [In a hushed voice] Pete Van Horn! He was just gonna go over to the next block to see if the power was on—

WOMAN. You killed him, Charlie. You shot him dead!

CHARLIE. [Looks around at the circle of faces, his eyes frightened, his face contorted] But . . . but I didn't know who he was. I certainly didn't know who he was. He comes walkin' out of the darkness—how am I supposed to know who he was? [He grabs Steve.] Steve—you know why I shot! How was I supposed to know he wasn't a monster or something? [He grabs Don now.] We're all scared of the same thing. I was just tryin' to . . . tryin' to protect my home, that's all! Look, all of you, that's all I was tryin' to do. [He looks down wildly at the body.] I didn't know it was somebody we knew! I didn't know—

[There's a sudden hush and then an intake of breath. We see a medium shot of the living room window of Charlie's house. The window is not lit, but suddenly the house lights come on behind it.]

WOMAN. [In a very hushed voice] Charlie . . . Charlie . . . the lights just went on in your house. Why did the lights just go on?

DON. What about it, Charlie? How come you're the only one with lights now?

GOODMAN. That's what I'd like to know.

[A pause as they all stare toward Charlie.]

GOODMAN. You were so quick to kill, Charlie, and you were so quick to tell us who we had to be careful of. Well, maybe you had to kill. Maybe Peter there was trying to tell us something. Maybe he'd found out something and came back to tell us who there was amongst us we should watch out for—

[Charlie backs away from the group, his eyes wide with fright.]

CHARLIE. No . . . no . . . it's nothing of the sort! I don't know why the lights are on. I swear I don't. Somebody's pulling a gag or something.

[He bumps against Steve, who grabs him and whirls him around.]

STEVE. A gag? A gag? Charlie, there's a dead man on the sidewalk and you killed him! Does this thing look like a gag to you?

[Charlie breaks away and screams as he runs toward his house.]

CHARLIE. No! No! Please!

[A man breaks away from the crowd to chase Charlie.

We see a long angle shot looking down as the man tackles Charlie and lands on top of him. The other people start to run toward them. Charlie is up on his feet, breaks away from the other man's grasp, lands a couple of desperate punches that push the man aside. Then he forces his way, fighting, through the crowd to once again break free, jumps up on his front porch. A rock thrown from the group smashes a window alongside of him, the broken glass flying past him. A couple of pieces cut him. He stands there perspiring, rumpled, blood *running down from a cut on the cheek. His wife breaks away from the group to throw herself into his arms. He buries his face against her. We can see the crowd converging on the porch now.*]

VOICES.
It must have been him.
He's the one.
We got to get Charlie.

[*Another rock lands on the porch. Now Charlie pushes his wife behind him, facing the group.*]

CHARLIE. Look, look I swear to you . . . it isn't me . . . but I do know who it is . . . I swear to you, I do know who it is. I know who the monster is here. I know who it is that doesn't belong. I swear to you I know.

GOODMAN. [*Shouting*] What are you waiting for?

WOMAN. [*Shouting*] Come on, Charlie, come on.

MAN ONE. [*Shouting*] Who is it, Charlie, tell us!

DON. [*Pushing his way to the front of the crowd*] All right, Charlie, let's hear it!

[*Charlie's eyes dart around wildly.*]

CHARLIE. It's . . . it's . . .

MAN TWO. [*Screaming*] Go ahead, Charlie, tell us.

CHARLIE. It's . . . it's the kid. It's Tommy. He's the one!

[*There's a gasp from the crowd as we cut to a shot of Sally holding her son Tommy. The boy at first doesn't understand and then, realizing the eyes are all on him, buries his face against his mother.*]

SALLY. [*Backs away*] That's crazy! That's crazy! He's a little boy.

WOMAN. But he knew! He was the only one who knew! He told us all about it. Well, how did he know? How *could* he have known?

[*The various people take this up and repeat the question aloud.*]

VOICES.
How could he know?
Who told him?
Make the kid answer.

DON. It was Charlie who killed old man Van Horn.

WOMAN. But it was the kid here who knew what was going to happen all the time. He was the one who knew!

[*We see a close-up of Steve.*]

STEVE. Are you all gone crazy? [*Pause as he looks about*] Stop.

[*A fist crashes at Steve's face, staggering him back out of the frame of the picture.*

There are several close camera shots suggesting the coming of violence. A hand fires a rifle. A fist clenches. A hand grabs the hammer from Van Horn's body, etc. Meanwhile, we hear the following lines.]

DON. Charlie has to be the one—Where's my rifle—

WOMAN. Les Goodman's the one. His car started! Let's wreck it.

MRS. GOODMAN. What about Steve's radio—He's the one that called them—

MR. GOODMAN. Smash the radio. Get me a hammer. Get me something.
STEVE. Stop—Stop—

CHARLIE. Where's that kid—Let's get him.

MAN ONE. Get Steve—Get Charlie—They're working together.

[*The crowd starts to converge around the mother, who grabs the child and starts to run with him. The crowd starts to follow, at first walking fast, and then running after him.*

We see a full shot of the street as suddenly Charlie's lights go off and the lights in another house go on. They stay on for a moment, then from across the street other lights go on and then off again.]

MAN ONE. [*Shouting*] It isn't the kid . . . it's Bob Weaver's house.

WOMAN. It isn't Bob Weaver's house, it's Don Martin's place.

CHARLIE. I tell you it's the kid.

DON. It's Charlie. He's the one.

[*We move into a series of close-ups of various people as they shout, accuse, scream, interspersing these shots with shots of houses as the lights go on and off, and then slowly in the middle of this nightmarish morass of sight and sound the camera starts to pull away, until once again we've reached the opening shot looking at the Maple Street sign from high above.*

The camera continues to move away until we dissolve to a shot looking toward the metal side of a space craft, which sits shrouded in darkness. An open door throws out a beam of light from the illuminated interior. Two figures silhouetted against the bright lights appear. We get only a vague feeling of form, but nothing more explicit than that.]

FIGURE ONE. Understand the procedure now? Just stop a few of their machines and radios and telephones and lawn mowers . . . throw them into darkness for a few hours, and then you just sit back and watch the pattern.

FIGURE TWO. And this pattern is always the same?

FIGURE ONE. With few variations. They pick the most dangerous enemy they can find . . . and it's themselves. And all we need do is sit back . . . and watch.

FIGURE TWO. Then I take it this place . . . this Maple Street . . . is not unique.

FIGURE ONE. [*Shaking his head*] By no means. Their world is full of Maple Streets. And we'll go from one to the other and let them destroy themselves. One to the other . . . one to the other . . . one to the other—

[*Now the camera pans up for a shot of the starry sky and over this we hear the Narrator's voice.*]

NARRATOR'S VOICE. The tools of conquest do not necessarily come with bombs and explosions and fallout. There are weapons that are simply thoughts, attitudes, prejudices— to be found only in the minds of men. For the record, prejudices can kill and suspicion can destroy and a thoughtless frightened search for a scapegoat has a fallout all its own for the children . . . and the children yet unborn. [*A pause*] And the pity of it is . . . that these things cannot be confined to . . . The Twilight Zone!

RESPONDING TO THE SELECTION

Your Response

1. If you were living on Maple Street, what would you do to stop the people from turning into a dangerous mob?

Recalling

2. What are the first signs that something strange is happening on Maple Street?
3. What does Tommy think has happened?
4. Why do the people become suspicious of Les Goodman?
5. Why do they turn against Steve Brand?
6. Why does Charlie shoot Pete Van Horn?
7. What happens after the shooting?
8. What is the real cause of the strange occurrences on Maple Street?

Interpreting

9. Why does the group of friendly neighbors turn into a dangerous mob?
10. How does the appearance of the aliens at the end affect your view of the preceding action?
11. How do the events of the play prove the narrator's statement: "The tools of conquest do not necessarily come with bombs and explosions and fallout"?
12. Who are the real "monsters"?

Applying

13. Why do you think people's behaviors change when they're in a group?

Recognizing Conflict in Drama

Conflict is a struggle between opposing forces. Understanding the different conflicts present will help you better understand the play.

1. How does Serling's play show conflict between individuals?
2. How does the play show conflict between individuals and society?
3. What other conflict occurs in the play?
4. What is the central conflict of the play?

CRITICAL THINKING AND READING

Identifying Invalid Conclusions

A **valid conclusion** is based on strong evidence or sound reasoning. For example, when Don Martin says that an electrical storm may have caused the loss of power on Maple Street, Charlie forms a valid conclusion. He says, "That don't seem likely. Sky's just as blue as anything. Not a cloud. No lightning. No thunder. . . ." His conclusion is valid because it is based on evidence.

An **invalid conclusion** is not well founded. It is based on little or no evidence, on faulty evidence, or on poor thinking. For example, when phones, portable radios, and lawn mowers stop working, Charlie concludes that an electrical-power failure has occurred. But if that were so, portable radios operating on batteries or transistors would be working—and they are not. Charlie's thinking is not sound and his conclusion is invalid.

1. Analyze the crowd's conclusion that Les Goodman is guilty of something. Why is their conclusion invalid? (What is wrong with their evidence and thinking?)

2. Point out two other similar invalid conclusions made about characters in the play. Explain why each is invalid.

THINKING AND WRITING

Extending the Play

Imagine that the producers of *The Monsters Are Due on Maple Street* have asked you to write an additional scene for the play. It will fit in right after the dialogue between the two figures near the end and before the narrator's concluding words. The setting is Maple Street on the following morning. Write a scene that shows the new situation there. When you revise your scene, make sure it follows naturally from all that happens before. Finally proofread your scene and prepare a final draft.

LEARNING OPTIONS

1. **Writing.** Look over the creative writing in your writing portfolio, especially any short stories, dialogues, or plays. Choose one piece and adapt it for television. Add appropriate camera directions to your piece of writing.

2. **Performance.** If you or your school or library has access to a video camera, try filming a scene from *The Monsters Are Due on Maple Street,* using the different camera techniques you have learned about. You might show your film to your family or class.

3. **Cross-curricular Connection.** Find out as much as you can about a radio broadcast that was made on Halloween night in 1938 by Orson Welles and the Mercury players. The radio script was written by Howard Koch and based on the famous novel *The War of the Worlds.* What "event" in Grovers Mill, New Jersey, did it "report"? How did people react to it? How was this reaction like the one in *The Monsters Are Due on Maple Street?*

GUIDE FOR READING

Charles Dickens

(1812–1870) was born in Portsmouth, England. He took upon himself the support of his family when he was twelve years old. For the rest of his life, he remembered what it was like to be poor. His sympathy for his fellow human beings is powerfully expressed in his story "A Christmas Carol."

Israel Horovitz (1939–   ) has great respect for Dickens and this story. He has written, "I come to this work humbly, under the pressures of great respect for the Master: Charles Dickens."

A Christmas Carol: Scrooge and Marley, Act I

Plot and Exposition

The **plot** of a play usually begins by introducing a conflict. The conflict rises to a climax, or high point of excitement or emotion. Then, as the play comes to a close, the excitement dies down, any unanswered questions about the story are answered, and the curtain falls.

Exposition is the revealing (exposing) of information needed to understand the action shown on stage. It often explains events that occurred before the start of the onstage events.

Focus

Charles Dickens created many memorable characters, one of whom is Mr. Scrooge. In fact the name *Scrooge* has become part of our everyday vocabulary. Make a web diagram or a sunburst diagram similar to the one below, and write on it all the ideas that come to mind when you hear the word *Scrooge*. As you read this play, notice the characteristics of the character Scrooge that match your ideas.

Vocabulary

Knowing the following words will help you as you read *A Christmas Carol: Scrooge and Marley*.

implored (im plôrd') *v.*: Asked or begged earnestly (p. 265)
morose (mə rōs') *adj.*: Gloomy; ill-tempered (p. 266)
destitute (des' tə tōōt') *adj.*: Living in complete poverty (p. 268)

misanthrope (mis' ən throp') *n.*: A person who hates or distrusts everyone (p. 270)
void (void) *n.*: Total emptiness (p. 270)
ponderous (pän' dər əs) *adj.*: Very heavy; bulky (p. 272)

A Christmas Carol: Scrooge and Marley

from *A Christmas Carol* by Charles Dickens

Israel Horovitz

THE PEOPLE OF THE PLAY

Jacob Marley, a specter

Ebenezer Scrooge, not yet dead, which is to say still alive

Bob Cratchit, Scrooge's clerk

Fred, Scrooge's nephew

Thin Do-Gooder

Portly Do-Gooder

Specters (Various), carrying money-boxes

The Ghost of Christmas Past

Four Jocund Travelers

A Band of Singers

A Band of Dancers

Little Boy Scrooge

Young Man Scrooge

Fan, Scrooge's little sister

The Schoolmaster

Schoolmates

Fezziwig, a fine and fair employer

Dick, young Scrooge's co-worker

Young Scrooge

A Fiddler

More Dancers

Scrooge's Lost Love

Scrooge's Lost Love's Daughter

Scrooge's Lost Love's Husband

The Ghost of Christmas Present

Some Bakers

Mrs. Cratchit, Bob Cratchit's wife

Belinda Cratchit, a daughter

Martha Cratchit, another daughter

Peter Cratchit, a son

Tiny Tim Cratchit, another son

Scrooge's Niece, Fred's wife

The Ghost of Christmas Future, a mute Phantom

Three Men of Business

Drunks, Scoundrels, Women of the Streets

A Charwoman

Mrs. Dilber

Joe, an old second-hand goods dealer

A Corpse, very like Scrooge

An Indebted Family

Adam, a young boy

A Poulterer

A Gentlewoman

Some More Men of Business

ACT I

Scene 1

[*Ghostly music in auditorium. A single spotlight on* JACOB MARLEY, D.C. *He is ancient; awful, dead-eyed. He speaks straight out to auditorium.*]

MARLEY. [*Cackle-voiced*] My name is Jacob Marley and I am dead. [*He laughs.*] Oh, no, there's no doubt that I am dead. The register of my burial was signed by the clergyman, the clerk, the undertaker . . . and by my chief mourner . . . Ebenezer Scrooge . . . [*Pause; remembers*] I am dead as a door-nail.

[*A spotlight fades up, Stage Right, on* SCROOGE, *in his counting-house,[1] counting. Lettering on the window behind* SCROOGE *reads: "SCROOGE AND MARLEY, LTD." The spotlight is tight on* SCROOGE's *head and shoulders. We shall not yet see into the offices and setting. Ghostly music continues, under.* MARLEY *looks across at* SCROOGE; *pitifully. After a moment's pause*]

I present him to you: Ebenezer Scrooge . . . England's most tightfisted hand at the grindstone, Scrooge! a squeezing, wrenching, grasping, scraping, clutching, covetous, old sinner! secret, and self-contained, and solitary as an oyster. The cold within him freezes his old features, nips his pointed nose, shrivels his cheek, stiffens his gait; makes his eyes red, his thin lips blue; and speaks out shrewdly in his grating voice. Look at him. Look at him . . .

[SCROOGE *counts and mumbles.*]

SCROOGE. They owe me money and I will collect. I will have them jailed, if I have to. They owe me money and I will collect what is due me.

[MARLEY *moves towards* SCROOGE; *two steps. The spotlight stays with him.*]

MARLEY. [*Disgusted*] He and I were partners for I don't know how many years. Scrooge was my sole executor, my sole administrator, my sole assign, my sole residuary legatee,[2] my sole friend and my sole mourner. But Scrooge was not so cut up by the sad event of my death, but that he was an excellent man of business on the very day of my funeral, and solemnized[3] it with an undoubted

---

1. counting house: An office for keeping financial records and writing business letters.

2. my sole executor (ig zek′yə tər), **my sole administrator, my sole assign** (ə sīn′), **my sole residuary legatee** (ri zij′ oo wer′ ē leg′ ə tē′): All legal terms.

3. solemnized (säl′ əm nīzd′) v. : Honored or remembered; Marley is being ironic.

bargain. [*Pauses again in disgust*] He never painted out my name from the window. There it stands, on the window and above the warehouse door: Scrooge and Marley. Sometimes people new to our business call him Scrooge and sometimes they call him Marley. He answers to both names. It's all the same to him. And it's cheaper than painting in a new sign, isn't it? [*Pauses; moves closer to* SCROOGE] Nobody has ever stopped him in the street to say, with gladsome looks, "My dear Scrooge, how are you? When will you come to see me?" No beggars implored him to bestow a trifle, no children ever ask him what it is o'clock, no man or woman now, or ever in his life, not once, inquire the way to such and such a place. [MARLEY *stands next to* SCROOGE *now. They share, so it seems, a spotlight.*] But what

does Scrooge care of any of this? It is the very thing he likes! To edge his way along the crowded paths of life, warning all human sympathy to keep its distance.

[*A ghostly bell rings in the distance.* MARLEY *moves away from* SCROOGE, *now, heading* D. *again. As he does, he "takes" the light:* SCROOGE *has disappeared into the black void beyond.* MARLEY *walks* D.C., *talking directly to the audience. Pauses*]

The bell tolls and I must take my leave. You must stay a while with Scrooge and watch him play out his scroogey life. It is now the story: the once-upon-a-time. Scrooge is busy in his counting-house. Where else? Christmas eve and Scrooge is busy in his counting-house. It is cold, bleak, biting weather outside: foggy withal: and, if you listen closely, you can hear the people in the court go wheezing up and down, beating their hands upon their breasts, and stamping their feet upon the pavement stones to warm them . . .

[*The clocks outside strike three.*]

Only three! and quite dark outside already: it has not been light all day this day.

[*This ghostly bell rings in the distance again.* MARLEY *looks about him. Music in.* MARLEY *flies away.*] (N.B. *Marley's comings and goings should, from time to time, induce the explosion of the odd flash-pot.* I.H.)

Scene 2

[*Christmas music in, sung by a live chorus, full. At conclusion of song, sound fades under and into the distance. Lights up in set: offices of Scrooge and Marley, Ltd.* SCROOGE *sits at his desk, at work. Near him is a tiny fire. His door is open and in his line of vision, we see* SCROOGE'S *clerk,* BOB CRATCHIT, *who sits in a dismal tank of a cubicle, copying letters. Near* CRATCHIT *is a fire so tiny as to barely cast a light: perhaps it is one pitifully glowing coal?* CRATCHIT *rubs his hands together, puts on a white comforter[4] and tries to heat his hands around his candle.* SCROOGE'S NEPHEW *enters, unseen.*]

SCROOGE. What are you doing, Cratchit? Acting cold, are you? Next, you'll be asking to replenish your coal from my coal-box, won't you? Well, save your breath, Cratchit! Unless you're prepared to find employ elsewhere!

NEPHEW. [*Cheerfully; surprising* SCROOGE] A merry Christmas to you, Uncle! God save you!

SCROOGE. Bah! Humbug![5]

---

4. comforter (kum′ fər tər) *n.*: A long, woolen scarf.
5. Humbug (hum′ bug′) *interj.*: Nonsense! (can also be used as a noun to mean nonsense or something done to cheat or deceive).

NEPHEW. Christmas a "humbug," Uncle? I'm sure you don't mean that.

SCROOGE. I do! Merry Christmas? What right do you have to be merry? What reason have you to be merry? You're poor enough!

NEPHEW. Come, then. What right have you to be dismal? What reason have you to be morose? You're rich enough.

SCROOGE. Bah! Humbug!

NEPHEW. Don't be cross, Uncle.

SCROOGE. What else can I be? Eh? When I live in a world of fools such as this? Merry Christmas? What's Christmastime to you but a time of paying bills without any money; a time for finding yourself a year older, but not an hour richer. If I could work my will, every idiot who goes about with "Merry Christmas" on his lips, should be boiled with his own pudding, and buried with a stake of holly through his heart. He should!

NEPHEW. Uncle!

SCROOGE. Nephew! You keep Christmas in your own way and let me keep it in mine.

NEPHEW. Keep it! But you don't keep it, Uncle.

SCROOGE. Let me leave it alone, then. Much good it has ever done you!

NEPHEW. There are many things from which I have derived good, by which I have not profited, I daresay. Christmas among the rest. But I am sure that I always thought of Christmas time, when it has come round— as a good time: the only time I know of, when men and women seem to open their shut-up hearts freely, and to think of people below them as if they really were fellow-passengers to the grave, and not another race of creatures bound on other journeys. And therefore, Uncle, though it has never put a scrap of gold or silver in my pocket, I believe that it *has* done me good, and that it *will* do me good; and I say, God bless it!

[*The* CLERK *in the tank applauds, looks at the furious* SCROOGE *and pokes out his tiny fire, as if in exchange for the moment of impropriety.* SCROOGE *yells at him.*]

SCROOGE. [*To the* CLERK] Let me hear another sound from *you* and you'll keep your Christmas by losing your situation. [*To the* NEPHEW] You're quite a powerful speaker, sir. I wonder you don't go into Parliament.[6]

NEPHEW. Don't be angry, Uncle. Come! Dine with us tomorrow.

SCROOGE. I'd rather see myself dead than see myself with your family!

NEPHEW. But, why? Why?

SCROOGE. Why did you get married?

NEPHEW. Because I fell in love.

SCROOGE. That, sir, is the only thing that you have said to me in your entire lifetime which is even more ridiculous than "Merry Christmas"! [*Turns from* NEPHEW] Good afternoon.

NEPHEW. Nay, Uncle, you never came to see me before I married either. Why give it as a reason for not coming now?

SCROOGE. Good afternoon, Nephew!

NEPHEW. I want nothing from you; I ask nothing of you; why cannot we be friends?

SCROOGE. Good afternoon!

NEPHEW. I am sorry with all my heart, to find you so resolute. But I have made the trial in homage to Christmas, and I'll keep my Christmas humor to the last. So A Merry Christmas, Uncle!

SCROOGE. Good afternoon!

NEPHEW. And A Happy New Year!

SCROOGE. Good afternoon!

NEPHEW. [*He stands facing* SCROOGE.] Uncle, you are the most . . . [*Pauses*] No, I shan't. My Christmas humor is intact . . . [*Pause*] God bless you, Uncle . . . [NEPHEW *turns and starts for the door; he stops at* CRATCHIT's *cage.*] Merry Christmas, Bob Cratchit . . .

CRATCHIT. Merry Christmas to you sir, and a very, very happy New Year . . .

SCROOGE. [*Calling across to them*] Oh, fine, a perfection, just fine . . . to see the perfect pair of you: husbands, with wives and children to support . . . my clerk there earning fifteen shillings a week . . . and the perfect pair of you, talking about a Merry Christmas! [*Pauses*] I'll retire to Bedlam![7]

NEPHEW. [*To* CRATCHIT] He's impossible!

CRATCHIT. Oh, mind him not, sir. He's getting on in years, and he's alone. He's noticed your visit. I'll wager your visit has warmed him.

NEPHEW. Him? Uncle Ebenezer Scrooge? *Warmed?* You are a better Christian than I am, sir.

CRATCHIT. [*Opening the door for* NEPHEW; *two* DO-GOODERS *will enter, as* NEPHEW *exits*] Good day to you, sir, and God bless.

NEPHEW. God bless . . . [*One man who enters is portly, the other is thin. Both are pleasant.*]

CRATCHIT. Can I help you, gentlemen?

---

6. Parliament (pär′ lə mənt): The national legislative body of Great Britain, in some ways like the American Congress.

7. Bedlam (bed′ ləm): A hospital in London for the mentally ill.

THIN MAN. [*Carrying papers and books; looks around* CRATCHIT *to* SCROOGE] Scrooge and Marley's, I believe. Have I the pleasure of addressing Mr. Scrooge, or Mr. Marley?

SCROOGE. Mr. Marley has been dead these seven years. He died seven years ago this very night.

PORTLY MAN. We have no doubt his liberality is well represented by his surviving partner . . . [*Offers his calling card*]

SCROOGE. [*Handing back the card; un-looked at*] . . . Good afternoon.

THIN MAN. This will take but a moment, sir . . .

PORTLY MAN. At this festive season of the year, Mr. Scrooge, it is more than usually desirable that we should make some slight provision for the poor and destitute, who suffer greatly at the present time. Many thousands are in want of common necessities; hundreds of thousands are in want of common comforts, sir.

SCROOGE. Are there no prisons?

PORTLY MAN. Plenty of prisons.

SCROOGE. And aren't the Union workhouses still in operation?

THIN MAN. They are. Still. I wish that I could say that they are not.

SCROOGE. The Treadmill[8] and the Poor Law[9] are in full vigor, then?

THIN MAN. Both very busy, sir.

---

8. the Treadmill (tred′ mil′): A kind of mill wheel turned by the weight of persons treading steps arranged around it; this device was used to punish prisoners in jails.

9. the Poor Law: A series of laws were passed in England from the 17th century on to help the poor; changes to the law in 1834 gave responsibility for this relief to the national government but did not provide much aid for the poor.

SCROOGE. Ohhh, I see. I was afraid, from what you said at first, that something had occurred to stop them from their useful course. [*Pauses*] I'm glad to hear it.

PORTLY MAN. Under the impression that they scarcely furnish Christian cheer of mind or body to the multitude, a few of us are endeavoring to raise a fund to buy the Poor some meat and drink, and means of warmth. We choose this time, because it is a time, of all others, when Want is keenly felt, and Abundance rejoices. [*Pen in hand; as well as notepad*] What shall I put you down for, sir?

SCROOGE. Nothing!

PORTLY MAN. You wish to be left anonymous?

SCROOGE. I wish to be left alone! [*Pauses; turns away; turns back to them*] Since you ask me what I wish, gentlemen, that is my answer. I help to support the establishments that I have mentioned: they cost enough: and those who are badly off must go there.

THIN MAN. Many can't go there; and many would rather die.

SCROOGE. If they would rather die, they had better do it, and decrease the surplus population. Besides—excuse me—I don't know that.

THIN MAN. But you might know it!

SCROOGE. It's not my business. It's enough for a man to understand his own business, and not to interfere with other people's. Mine occupies me constantly. Good afternoon, gentlemen! [*Scrooge turns his back on the gentlemen and returns to his desk.*]

PORTLY MAN. But, sir, Mr. Scrooge . . . think of the poor.

SCROOGE. [*Turns suddenly to them. Pauses*] Take your leave of my offices, sirs, while I am still smiling.

[*The* THIN MAN *looks at the* PORTLY MAN. *They are undone. They shrug. They move to door. Cratchit hops up to open it for them.*]

THIN MAN. Good day, sir . . . [*To* CRATCHIT] A merry Christmas to you, sir . . .

CRATCHIT. Yes. A Merry Christmas to both of you . . .

PORTLY MAN. Merry Christmas . . .

[CRATCHIT *silently squeezes something into the hand of the* THIN MAN.]

THIN MAN. What's this?

CRATCHIT. Shhhh . . .

[CRATCHIT *opens the door; wind and snow whistle into the room.*]

THIN MAN. Thank you, sir, thank you.

[CRATCHIT *closes the door and returns to his workplace.* SCROOGE *is at his own counting table. He talks to* CRATCHIT *without looking up.*]

SCROOGE. It's less of a time of year for being merry, and more a time of year for being loony . . . if you ask me.

CRATCHIT. Well, I don't know, sir . . .

[*The clock's bell strikes six o'clock.*]

Well, there it is, eh, six?

SCROOGE. Saved by six bells, are you?

CRATCHIT. I must be going home . . . [*He snuffs out his candle and puts on his hat.*] I hope you have a . . . very very lovely day tomorrow, sir . . .

SCROOGE. Hmmm. Oh, you'll be wanting the whole day tomorrow, I suppose?

CRATCHIT. If quite convenient, sir.

SCROOGE. It's not convenient, and it's not fair. If I was to stop half-a-crown for it, you'd think yourself ill-used, I'll be bound?

[CRATCHIT *smiles faintly.*]

CRATCHIT. I don't know, sir . . .

SCROOGE. And yet, you don't think me ill-used, when I pay a day's wages for no work . . .

CRATCHIT. It's only but once a year . . .

SCROOGE. A poor excuse for picking a man's pocket every 25th of December! But I suppose you must have the whole day. Be here all the earlier the next morning!

CRATCHIT. Oh, I will, sir. I will. I promise you. And, sir . . .

SCROOGE. Don't say it, Cratchit.

CRATCHIT. But let me wish you a . . .

SCROOGE. Don't say it, Cratchit. I warn you . . .

CRATCHIT. Sir!

SCROOGE. Cratchit!

[CRATCHIT *opens the door.*]

CRATCHIT. All right, then, sir . . . well . . . [*Suddenly*] Merry Christmas, Mr. Scrooge!

[*And he runs out the door, shutting same behind him.* SCROOGE *moves to his desk; gathering his coat, hat, etc. A* BOY *appears at his window. . . . .*]

BOY. [*Singing*] "Away in a manger . . ."

[SCROOGE *seizes his ruler and whacks at the image of the* BOY *outside. The* BOY *leaves.*]

SCROOGE. Bah! Humbug! Christmas! Bah! Humbug! [*He shuts out the light.*]

A note on the crossover, following Scene 2:

[SCROOGE *will walk alone to his rooms from his offices. As he makes a long slow cross of the stage, the scenery should change. Christmas music will be heard, various people will cross by* SCROOGE, *often smiling happily.*

There will be occasional pleasant greetings tossed at him.

SCROOGE, *in contrast to all, will grump and mumble. He will snap at passing boys, as might a horrid old hound.*

In short, SCROOGE's *sounds and movements will define him in contrast from all other people who cross the stage: he is the misanthrope, the malcontent, the miser. He is* SCROOGE.

This statement of SCROOGE's *character, by contrast to all other characters, should seem comical to the audience.*

During SCROOGE's *crossover to his rooms, snow should begin to fall. All passers-by will hold their faces to the sky, smiling, allowing snow to shower them lightly.* SCROOGE, *by contrast, will bat at the flakes with his walking-stick, as might an insomniac swat at a sleep-stopping, middle-of-the-night swarm of mosquitoes. He will comment on the blackness of the night, and, finally, reach his rooms and his encounter with the magical specter:* MARLEY, *his eternal mate.*]

Scene 3

SCROOGE. No light at all . . . no moon . . . *that* is what is at the center of a Christmas Eve: dead black: void . . .

[SCROOGE *puts his key in the door's keyhole. He has reached his rooms now. The door knocker changes and is now* MARLEY'S *face. A musical sound; quickly: ghostly.* MARLEY's *image is not at all angry, but looks at* SCROOGE *as did the old* MARLEY *look at* SCROOGE. *The hair is curiously stirred; eyes* wide open, dead: absent of focus. SCROOGE *stares wordlessly here. The face, before his very eyes, does deliquesce.*[10] *It is a knocker again.* SCROOGE *opens the door and checks the back of same, probably for* MARLEY'S *pigtail. Seeing nothing but screws and nuts,* SCROOGE *refuses the memory.*]

Pooh, pooh!

[*The sound of the door closing resounds throughout the house as thunder. Every room echoes the sound.* SCROOGE *fastens the door and walks across the hall to the stairs, trimming his candle as he goes; and then he goes slowly up the staircase. He checks each room: sitting room, bedroom, lumber-room. He looks under the sofa, under the table: nobody there. He fixes his evening gruel on the hob,*[11] *changes his jacket.* SCROOGE *sits near the tiny low-flamed fire, sipping his gruel. There are various pictures on the walls: all of them now show likenesses of* MARLEY. SCROOGE *blinks his eyes.*]

Bah! Humbug!

[SCROOGE *walks in a circle about the room. The pictures change back into their natural images. He sits down at the table in front of the fire. A bell hangs overhead. It begins to ring, of its own accord. Slowly, surely, begins the ringing of every bell in the house. They continue ringing for nearly half a minute.* SCROOGE *is stunned by the phenomenon. The bells cease their ringing all at once. Deep below* SCROOGE, *in the basement of the house, there is the sound of clanking, of some enormous chain being dragged across the floors; and now up the stairs. We hear doors flying open.*]

---

10. deliquesce (del' ə kwes') *v.*: Melt away.
11. gruel (grōō' əl) **on the hob** (häb): A thin broth warming on a ledge at the back or side of the fireplace.

Bah still! Humbug still! This is not happening! I won't believe it!

[MARLEY'S GHOST *enters the room. He is horrible to look at: pigtail, vest, suit as usual, but he drags an enormous chain now, to which is fastened cash-boxes, keys, padlocks, ledgers, deeds, and heavy purses fashioned of steel. He is transparent.* MARLEY *stands opposite the stricken* SCROOGE.]

How now! What do you want of me?

MARLEY. Much!

SCROOGE. Who are you?

MARLEY. Ask me who I *was*.

SCROOGE. Who *were* you then?

MARLEY. In life, I was your business partner: Jacob Marley.

SCROOGE. I see . . . can you sit down?

MARLEY. I can.

SCROOGE. Do it then.

MARLEY. I shall. [MARLEY *sits opposite* SCROOGE, *in the chair across the table, at the front of the fireplace.*] You don't believe in me.

SCROOGE. I don't.

MARLEY. Why do you doubt your senses?

SCROOGE. Because every little thing affects them. A slight disorder of the stomach makes them cheat. You may be an undigested bit of beef, a blot of mustard, a crumb of cheese, a fragment of an underdone potato. There's more of gravy than of grave about you, whatever you are!

[*There is a silence between them.* SCROOGE *is made nervous by it. He picks up a toothpick.*]

Humbug! I tell you: humbug!

[MARLEY *opens his mouth and screams a ghosty, fearful scream. The scream echoes about each room of the house. Bats fly, cats screech, lightning flashes.* SCROOGE *stands and walks backwards against the wall.* MARLEY *stands and screams again. This time, he takes his head and lifts it from his shoulders. His head continues to scream.* MARLEY'S *face again appears on every picture in the room: all screaming.* SCROOGE, *on his knees before* MARLEY.]

Mercy! Dreadful apparition,[12] mercy! Why, O! why do you trouble me so?

MARLEY. Man of the worldly mind, do you believe in me, or not?

SCROOGE. I do. I must. But why do spirits such as you walk the earth? And why do they come to me?

MARLEY. It is required of every man that the spirit within him should walk abroad among his fellow-men, and travel far and wide; and if that spirit goes not forth in life, it is condemned to do so after death. [MARLEY *screams again; a tragic scream; from his ghosty bones.*] I wear the chain I forged in life. I made it link by link, and yard by yard. Is its pattern strange to *you*? Or would you know, you, Scrooge, the weight and length of the strong coil you bear yourself? It was full as heavy and long as this, seven Christmas Eves ago. You have labored on it, since. It is a ponderous chain.

[*Terrified that a chain will appear about his body,* SCROOGE *spins and waves the unwanted chain away. None, of course, appears. Sees* MARLEY *watching him dance about the room.* MARLEY *watches* SCROOGE; *silently.*]

SCROOGE. Jacob. Old Jacob Marley, tell me more. Speak comfort to me, Jacob . . .

---

12. apparition (ap´ ə rish´ ən) *n.*: Ghost.

MARLEY. I have none to give. Comfort comes from other regions, Ebenezer Scrooge, and is conveyed by other ministers, to other kinds of men. A very little more, is all that is permitted to me. I cannot rest, I cannot stay, I cannot linger anywhere . . . [*He moans again.*] my spirit never walked beyond our counting-house—mark me!—in life my spirit never roved beyond the narrow limits of our money-changing hole; and weary journeys lie before me!

SCROOGE. But you were always a good man of business, Jacob.

MARLEY. [*Screams word "business"; a flashpot explodes with him.*] BUSINESS!!! Mankind was my business. The common welfare was my business; charity, mercy, forbearance, benevolence, were, all, my business. [SCROOGE *is quaking.*] Hear me, Ebenezer Scrooge! My time is nearly gone.

SCROOGE. I will, but don't be hard upon me. And don't be flowery, Jacob! Pray!

MARLEY. How is it that I appear before you in a shape that you can see, I may not tell. I have sat invisible beside you many and many a day. That is no light part of my penance. I am here tonight to warn you that you have yet a chance and hope of escaping my fate. A chance and hope of my procuring, Ebenezer.

SCROOGE. You were always a good friend to me. Thank'ee!

MARLEY. You will be haunted by Three Spirits.

SCROOGE. Would that be the chance and hope you mentioned, Jacob?

MARLEY. It is.

SCROOGE. I think I'd rather not.

MARLEY. Without their visits, you cannot hope to shun the path I tread. Expect the first one tomorrow, when the bell tolls one.

SCROOGE. Couldn't I take 'em all at once, and get it over, Jacob?

MARLEY. Expect the second on the next night at the same hour. The third upon the next night when the last stroke of twelve has ceased to vibrate. Look to see me no more. Others may, but you may not. And look that, for your own sake, you remember what has passed between us!

[MARLEY *places his head back upon his shoulders. He approaches the window and beckons to* SCROOGE *to watch. Outside the window, specters[13] fly by, carrying money-boxes and chains. They make a confused sound of lamentation.* MARLEY, *after listening a moment, joins into their mournful dirge. He leans to the window and floats out into the bleak, dark night. He is gone.*]

SCROOGE. [*Rushing to the window*] Jacob! No, Jacob! Don't leave me! I'm frightened!

[*He sees that* MARLEY *has gone. He looks outside. He pulls the shutter closed, so that the scene is blocked from his view. All sound stops. After a pause, he re-opens the shutter and all is quiet, as it should be on Christmas Eve. Carolers carol out of doors, in the distance.* SCROOGE *closes the shutter and walks down the stairs. He examines the door by which* MARLEY *first entered.*]

No one here at all! Did I imagine all that? Humbug! [*He looks about the room.*] I did imagine it. It only happened in my foulest dream-mind, didn't it? An undigested bit of . . .

[*Thunder and lightning in the room; suddenly*]

Sorry! Sorry!

[*There is silence again. The lights fade out.*]

---

13. specters (spek′ tərz) *n.:* Ghosts.

Scene 4

[*Christmas music, choral, "Hark the Herald Angels Sing," sung by an onstage choir of children, spotlighted,* D.C. *Above,* SCROOGE *in his bed, dead to the world, asleep, in his darkened room. It should appear that the choir is singing somewhere outside of the house, of course, and a use of scrim[14] is thus suggested. When the singing is ended, the choir should fade out of view and* MAR-LEY *should fade into view, in their place.*]

MARLEY. [*Directly to audience*] From this point forth . . . I shall be quite visible to you, but invisible to him. [*Smiles*] He will feel my presence, nevertheless, for, unless my senses fail me completely, we are—you and I—witness to the changing of a miser: that one, my partner in life, in business, and in eternity: that one: Scrooge. [*Moves to staircase, below* SCROOGE] See him now. He endeavors to pierce the darkness with his ferret eyes.[15] [*To audience*] See him, now. He listens for the hour.

[*The bells toll.* SCROOGE *is awakened and quakes as the hour approaches one o'clock, but the bells stop their sound at the hour of twelve.*]

SCROOGE. [*Astonished*] Midnight! Why this isn't possible. It was past two when I went to bed. An icicle must have gotten into the clock's works! I couldn't have slept through the whole day and far into another night. It isn't possible that anything has happened to the sun, and this is twelve at noon! [*He runs to window; unshutters same; it is night.*] Night, still. Quiet, normal for the season, cold. It is certainly not noon. I cannot in any way afford to lose my days. Securities come

---

14. scrim (skrim) *n.:* A light, semi-transparent curtain.

15. ferret eyes: A ferret is a small, weasellike animal used for hunting rabbits; this expression means to look persistently, the way a ferret hunts.

due, promissory notes,[16] interest on investments: these are things that happen in the daylight! [*He returns to his bed.*] Was this a dream?

[MARLEY *appears in his room. He speaks to the audience.*]

MARLEY. You see? He does not, with faith, believe in me fully, even still! Whatever will it take to turn the faith of a miser from money to men?

SCROOGE. Another quarter and it'll be one and Marley's ghosty friends will come. [*Pauses; listens*] Where's the chime for one? [*Ding, dong*] A quarter *past* [*Repeats*] Half-past! [*Repeats*] A quarter to it! But where's the heavy bell of the hour one? This is a game in which I lose my senses! Perhaps, if I allowed myself another short doze . . .

MARLEY. . . . Doze, Ebenezer, doze.

[*A heavy bell thuds its one ring; dull and definitely one o'clock. There is a flash of light.* SCROOGE *sits up, in a sudden. A hand draws back the curtains by his bed. He sees it.*]

SCROOGE. A hand! Who owns it! Hello!

[*Ghosty music again, but of a new nature to the play. A strange figure stands before* SCROOGE—*like a child, yet at the same time like an old man: white hair, but unwrinkled skin, long, muscular arms, but delicate legs and feet. Wears white tunic; lustrous belt cinches waist. Branch of fresh green holly in its hand, but has its dress trimmed with fresh summer flowers. Clear jets of light spring from the crown of its head. Holds cap in hand. The Spirit is called* PAST.]

Are you the Spirit, sir, whose coming was foretold to me?

---

16. promissory (präm′ i sôr′ ē) **notes:** Written promises to pay someone a certain sum of money.

PAST. I am.

MARLEY. Does he take this to be a vision of his green grocer?

SCROOGE. Who, and what are you?

PAST. I am the Ghost of Christmas Past.

SCROOGE. Long past?

PAST. Your past.

SCROOGE. May I ask, please, sir, what business you have here with me?

PAST. Your welfare.

SCROOGE. Not to sound ungrateful, sir, and really, please do understand that I am plenty obliged for your concern, but, really, kind spirit, it would have done all the better for my welfare to have been left alone altogether, to have slept peacefully through this night.

PAST. Your reclamation, then. Take heed!

SCROOGE. My what?

PAST. [*Motioning to* SCROOGE *and taking his arm*] Rise! Fly with me! [*He leads* SCROOGE *to the window.*]

SCROOGE. [*Panicked*] Fly, but I am a mortal and cannot fly!

PAST. [*Pointing to his heart*] Bear but a touch of my hand *here* and you shall be upheld in more than this!

[SCROOGE *touches the* SPIRIT's *heart and the lights dissolve into sparkly flickers. Lovely crystals of music are heard. The scene dissolves into another. Christmas music again*]

Scene 5

[SCROOGE *and the* GHOST OF CHRISTMAS PAST *walk together across an open stage. In the background, we see a field that is open; covered by a soft, downy snow: a country road.*]

SCROOGE. Good Heaven! I was bred in this place. I was a boy here!

[SCROOGE *freezes, staring at the field beyond.* MARLEY's *ghost appears beside him; takes* SCROOGE's *face in his hands, and turns his face to the audience.*]

MARLEY. You see this Scrooge: stricken by feeling. Conscious of a thousand odors floating in the air, each one connected with a thousand thoughts, and hopes, and joys, and care long, long forgotten. [*Pause*] This one—this Scrooge—before your very eyes, returns to life, among the living. [*To audience, sternly*] You'd best pay your most careful attention. I would suggest rapt.[17]

[*There is a small flash and puff of smoke and* MARLEY *is gone again.*]

---

17. rapt (rapt) *adj.*: Giving complete attention, totally carried away by something.

PAST. Your lip is trembling, Mr. Scrooge. And what is that upon your cheek?

SCROOGE. Upon my cheek? Nothing . . . a blemish on the skin from the eating of over-much grease . . . nothing . . . [*Suddenly*] Kind Spirit of Christmas Past, lead me where you will, but *quickly!* To be stagnant in this place is, for me, *unbearable!*

PAST. You recollect the way?

SCROOGE. Remember it! I would know it blindfolded! My bridge, my church, my winding river! [*Staggers about, trying to see it all at once. He weeps again.*]

PAST. These are but shadows of things that have been. They have no consciousness of us.

[*Four jocund travelers enter, singing a Christmas song in four-part harmony—* "God Rest Ye Merry Gentlemen."]

SCROOGE. Listen! I know these men! I know them! I remember the beauty of their song!

PAST. But, why do you remember it so happily? It is Merry Christmas that they say to one another! What is Merry Christmas to you, Mr. Scrooge? Out upon Merry Christmas, right? What good has Merry Christmas ever done you, Mr. Scrooge? . . .

SCROOGE. [*After a long pause*] None. No good. None . . . [*He bows his head.*]

PAST. Look, you, sir, a school ahead. The schoolroom is not quite deserted. A solitary child, neglected by his friends, is left there still.

[SCROOGE *falls to the ground; sobbing as he sees, and we see, a small boy, the young* SCROOGE, *sitting and weeping, bravely, alone at his desk: alone in a vast space, a void.*]

SCROOGE. I cannot look on him!

PAST. You must, Mr. Scrooge, you must.

SCROOGE. It's me. [*Pauses; weeps*] Poor boy. He lived inside his head . . . alone . . . [*Pauses; weeps*] poor boy. [*Pauses; stops his weeping*] I wish . . . [*Dries his eyes on his cuff*] ah! it's too late!

PAST. What is the matter?

SCROOGE. There was a boy singing a Christmas Carol outside my door last night. I should like to have given him something: that's all.

PAST. [*Smiles; waves his hand to* SCROOGE] Come. Let us see another Christmas.

[*Lights out on little boy. A flash of light. A puff of smoke. Lights up on older boy*]

SCROOGE. Look! Me, again! Older now! [*Realizes*] Oh, yes . . . still alone.

[*The boy—a slightly older* SCROOGE—*sits alone in a chair, reading. The door to the room opens and a young girl enters. She is much, much younger than this slightly older* SCROOGE. *She is, say, six, and he is, say, twelve. Elder* SCROOGE *and the* GHOST OF CHRISTMAS PAST *stand watching the scene, unseen.*]

FAN. Dear, dear brother, I have come to bring you home.

BOY. Home, little Fan?

FAN. Yes! Home, for good and all! Father is so much kinder than he ever used to be, and home's like heaven! He spoke so gently to me one dear night when I was going to bed that I was not afraid to ask him once more if you might come home; and he said "yes" . . . you should; and sent me in a coach to bring you. And you're to be a man and are never to come back here, but first, we're to be together all the Christmas long, and have the merriest time in the world.

BOY. You are quite a woman, little Fan!

[*Laughing; she drags at* BOY, *causing him to stumble to the door with her. Suddenly we hear a mean and terrible voice in the hallway, Off. It is the* SCHOOLMASTER.]

SCHOOLMASTER. Bring down Master Scrooge's travel box at once! He is to travel!

FAN. Who is that, Ebenezer?

BOY. O! Quiet, Fan. It is the Schoolmaster, himself!

[*The door bursts open and into the room bursts with it the* SCHOOLMASTER.]

SCHOOLMASTER. Master Scrooge?

BOY. Oh, Schoolmaster. I'd like you to meet my little sister, Fan, sir . . .

[*Two boys struggle on with* SCROOGE'S *trunk.*]

FAN. Pleased, sir . . . [*She curtsies.*]

SCHOOLMASTER. You are to travel, Master Scrooge.

SCROOGE. Yes, sir. I know sir . . .

[*All start to exit, but* FAN *grabs the coattail of the mean old* SCHOOLMASTER.]

BOY. Fan!

SCHOOLMASTER. What's this?

FAN. Pardon, sir, but I believe that you've forgotten to say your goodbye to my brother, Ebenezer, who stands still now awaiting it . . . [*She smiles, curtsies, lowers her eyes.*] pardon, sir.

SCHOOLMASTER. [*Amazed*] I . . . uh . . . harumph . . . uhh . . . well, then . . . [*Outstretches hand*] Goodbye, Scrooge.

BOY. Uh, well, goodbye, Schoolmaster . . .

[*Lights fade out on all but* BOY *looking at* FAN; *and* SCROOGE *and* PAST *looking at them.*]

SCROOGE. Oh, my dear, dear little sister, Fan . . . how I loved her.

PAST. Always a delicate creature, whom a breath might have withered, but she had a large heart . . .

SCROOGE. So she had.

PAST. She died a woman, and had, as I think, children.

SCROOGE. One child.

PAST. True. Your nephew.

SCROOGE. Yes.

PAST. Fine, then. We move on, Mr. Scrooge. That warehouse, there? Do you know it?

SCROOGE. Know it? Wasn't I apprenticed[18] there?

---

18. apprenticed (ə pren′ tist) *v.*: Receiving financial support and instruction in a trade in return for work.

PAST. We'll have a look.

[*They enter the warehouse. The lights crossfade with them, coming up on an old man in Welsh wig:* FEZZIWIG.]

SCROOGE. Why, it's old Fezziwig! Bless his heart; it's Fezziwig, alive again!

[FEZZIWIG *sits behind a large, high desk, counting. He lays down his pen; looks at the clock: seven bells sound.*]

Quittin' time . . .

FEZZIWIG. Quittin' time . . . [*He takes off his waistcoat and laughs; calls off*] Yo ho, Ebenezer! Dick!

[DICK WILKINS *and* EBENEZER SCROOGE—*a young man version—enter the room.* DICK *and* EBENEZER *are* FEZZIWIG's *apprentices.*]

SCROOGE. Dick Wilkins, to be sure! My fellow-'prentice! Bless my soul, yes. There he is. He was very much attached to me, was Dick. Poor Dick! Dear, dear!

FEZZIWIG. Yo ho, my boys. No more work tonight. Christmas Eve, Dick. Christmas, Ebenezer!

[*They stand at attention in front of* FEZZIWIG; *laughing*]

Hilli-ho! Clear away, and let's have lots of room here! Hilli-ho, Dick! Chirrup, Ebenezer!

[*The young men clear the room, sweep the floor, straighten the pictures, trim the lamps, etc. The space is clear now. A fiddler enters, fiddling.*]

Hi-ho, Matthew! Fiddle away . . . where are my daughters?

[*The* FIDDLER *plays. Three young daughters of* FEZZIWIG *enter followed by six young male suitors. They are dancing to the music. All employees come in: workers, clerks, housemaids, cousins, the baker, etc.*

All dance. Full number wanted here. Throughout the dance, food is brought into the feast. It is "eaten" in dance, by the dancers. EBENEZER danced with all three of the daughters, as does DICK. They compete for the daughters, happily, in the dance. FEZZIWIG dances with his daughters. FEZ-ZIWIG dances with DICK and EBENEZER. The music changes: MRS. FEZZIWIG enters. She lovingly scolds her husband. They dance. She dances with EBENEZER, lifting him and throwing him about. She is enormously fat. When the dance is ended, they all dance off, floating away, as does the music. SCROOGE and the GHOST OF CHRISTMAS PAST stand alone now. The music is gone.]

PAST. It was a small matter, that Fezziwig made those silly folks so full of gratitude.

SCROOGE. Small!

PAST. Shhh!

[Lights up on DICK and EBENEZER]

DICK. We are blessed, Ebenezer, truly, to have such a master as Mr. Fezziwig!

YOUNG SCROOGE. He is the best, best, the very and absolute best! If ever I own a firm of my own, I shall treat my apprentices with the same dignity and the same grace. We have learned a wonderful lesson from the master, Dick!

DICK. Ah, that's a fact, Ebenezer. That's a fact!

PAST. Was it not a small matter, really? He spent but a few pounds[19] of his mortal money on your small party. Three or four

---

19. pounds (pŏundz) *n.*: A common type of money used in Great Britain.

pounds, perhaps. Is that so much that he deserves such praise as you and Dick so lavish now?

SCROOGE. It isn't that! It isn't that, Spirit. Fezziwig had the power to make us happy or unhappy; to make our service light or burdensome; a pleasure or a toil. The happiness he gave is quite as great as if it cost him a fortune.

PAST. What is the matter?

SCROOGE. Nothing particular.

PAST. Something, I think.

SCROOGE. No, no. I should like to be able to say a word or two to my clerk just now! That's all!

[EBENEZER *enters the room and shuts down all the lamps. He stretches and yawns. The* GHOST OF CHRISTMAS PAST *turns to* SCROOGE; *all of a sudden.*]

PAST. My time grows short! Quick!

[*In a flash of light,* EBENEZER *is gone, and in his place stands an* OLDER SCROOGE, *this one a man in the prime of his life. Beside him stands a young woman in a mourning dress. She is crying. She speaks to the man, with hostility.*]

WOMAN. It matters little . . . to you, very little. Another idol has displaced me.

MAN. What idol has displaced you?

WOMAN. A golden one.

MAN. This is an even-handed dealing of the world. There is nothing on which it is so hard as poverty; and there is nothing it professes to condemn with such severity as the pursuit of wealth!

WOMAN. You fear the world too much. Have I not seen your nobler aspirations fall off one by one, until the master-passion, Gain, engrosses you? Have I not?

SCROOGE. No!

MAN. What then? Even if I have grown so much wiser, what then? Have I changed towards you?

WOMAN. No . . .

MAN. Am I?

WOMAN. Our contract is an old one. It was made when we were both poor and content to be so. You *are* changed. When it was made, you were another man.

MAN. I was not another man: I was a boy.

WOMAN. Your own feeling tells you that you were not what you are. I am. That which promised happiness when we were one in heart is fraught with misery now that we are two . . .

SCROOGE. No!

WOMAN. How often and how keenly I have thought of this, I will not say. It is enough that I *have* thought of it, and can release you . . .

SCROOGE. [*Quietly*] Don't release me, madame . . .

MAN. Have I ever sought release?

WOMAN. In words. No. Never.

MAN. In what then?

WOMAN. In a changed nature; in an altered spirit. In everything that made my love of any worth or value in your sight. If this has never been between us, tell me, would you seek me out and try to win me now? Ah, no!

SCROOGE. Ah, yes!

MAN. You think not?

WOMAN. I would gladly think otherwise if I could, heaven knows! But if you were free today, tomorrow, yesterday, can even I believe that you would choose a dowerless girl[20]—you who in your very confidence with her weigh everything by Gain; or, choosing her, do I not know that your repentance and regret would surely follow? I do; and I release you. With a full heart, for the love of him you once were.

SCROOGE. Please, I . . . I . . .

MAN. Please, I . . . I . . .

WOMAN. Please. You may—the memory of what is past half makes me hope you will—have pain in this. A very, very brief time, and you will dismiss the memory of it, as an unprofitable dream, from which it happened well that you awoke. May you be happy in the life that you have chosen for yourself . . .

SCROOGE. No!

WOMAN. Yourself . . . alone . . .

SCROOGE. No!

WOMAN. Goodbye, Ebenezer . . .

SCROOGE. Don't let her go!

MAN. Goodbye.

SCROOGE. No!

[*She exits.* SCROOGE *goes to younger man: himself.*]

You fool! Mindless loon! You fool!

MAN. [*To exited woman*] Fool. Mindless loon. Fool . . .

SCROOGE. Don't say that! Spirit, remove me from this place.

PAST. I have told you these were shadows of the things that have been. They are what they are. Do not blame me, Mr. Scrooge.

SCROOGE. Remove me! I cannot bear it!

[*The faces of all who appeared in this scene are now projected for a moment around the stage: enormous, flimsy, silent.*]

Leave me! Take me back! Haunt me no longer!

[*There is a sudden flash of light: a flare. The* GHOST OF CHRISTMAS PAST *is gone.* SCROOGE *is, for the moment, alone onstage. His bed is turned down, across the stage. A small candle burns now in* SCROOGE'S *hand. There is a child's cap in his other hand. He slowly crosses the stage to his bed, to sleep.* MARLEY *appears behind* SCROOGE, *who continues his long, elderly cross to bed.* MARLEY *speaks directly to the audience.*]

MARLEY. Scrooge must sleep now. He must surrender to the irresistible drowsiness caused by the recognition of what was. [*Pauses*] The cap he carries is from ten lives past: his boyhood cap . . . donned atop a hopeful hairy head . . . askew, perhaps, or at a rakish angle. Doffed now in honor of regret.[21] Perhaps even too heavy to carry in his present state of weak remorse . . .

[SCROOGE *drops the cap. He lies atop his bed. He sleeps. To audience*]

He sleeps. For him, there's even more trouble ahead. [*Smiles*] For you? The play house tells me there's hot cider, as should be your anticipation for the specter Christmas Present and Future, for I promise you both. [*Smiles again*] So, I pray you hurry back to your seats refreshed and ready for a miser—to turn his coat of gray into a blazen Christmas holly-red.

[*A flash of lightning. A clap of thunder. Bats fly. Ghosty music.* MARLEY *is gone.*]

---

20. a dowerless (dou′ ər les) **girl:** A girl without a dowery, the property or wealth a woman brought to her husband at marriage.

21. donned . . . regret: To *don* and *doff* a hat means to put it on and take it off; *askew* means "crooked," and *at a rakish angle* means "having a dashing or jaunty look."

RESPONDING TO THE SELECTION

Your Response

1. What do you think is the meanest thing that Scrooge does in Act I? Why?
2. Has Scrooge hurt himself as well as others? Explain.

Recalling

3. What relationship did Scrooge and Marley have in the past?
4. For what purpose does Scrooge's nephew come to see Scrooge?
5. How does Scrooge respond to Cratchit's request for Christmas Day off?

Interpreting

6. How do the scenes of Scrooge's past reveal a change in him?
7. How does Scrooge react to each of these scenes?

Applying

8. Do you think people who are like Scrooge are ever really happy? Why or why not?

ANALYZING LITERATURE

Understanding Plot and Exposition

The **plot** of a play is the sequence of its incidents and events. The first part of the plot is called the **exposition.** Here the opening situation is established, major characters are introduced, and the central problem of the play is made clear. Also, here earlier events are revealed.

Once the opening situation is established, the plot of the play develops until the climax is reached. The part of the play that builds up to the climax is called the rising action.

1. Describe the situation established in Scene 1 of *A Christmas Carol: Scrooge and Marley.*
2. What earlier events are disclosed here?
3. What problem does Scrooge have?
4. As you were reading Act I, what thoughts or questions did you have about how the story would turn out?

CRITICAL THINKING AND READING

Recognizing Foreshadowing

Foreshadowing is the use of hints or clues to suggest future events. For example, in his speech at the end of Act I, Marley says of Scrooge: "For him, there's even more trouble ahead." When reading or viewing a play, you should be alert to such hints or clues.

1. Early in Scene 5, Scrooge says to the Ghost of Christmas Past, "There was a boy singing a Christmas Carol outside my door last night. I should like to have given him something . . ." How might this statement be a hint of a future development?
2. Find one other example of foreshadowing present in Act I.

THINKING AND WRITING

Retelling *A Christmas Carol*

Imagine that you are going to entertain a group of young children by telling them the story of *A Christmas Carol,* Act I. Write a summary of the five scenes that you have just read so that if it were read aloud it would be a lively, easy-to-follow story that your young readers would understand and enjoy. Revise your summary to make sure it contains the important events.

LEARNING OPTIONS

1. **Performance.** With your classmates choose a scene from Act I to present as a dramatic reading or to act out. If you read the scene, be sure to include the stage directions so the class can imagine the action. If you act it, think of ways to make up for not being able to do everything the stage directions call for.
2. **Cross-curricular Connection.** Find and display pictures—paintings or prints like those of Currier and Ives—that show Christmas scenes from the nineteenth century. Discuss how fashions and traditions have changed.

GUIDE FOR READING

A Christmas Carol: Scrooge and Marley, Act II

Character and Theme

A **character** in a play is portrayed, in part, by what he or she says in the dialogue. If the play is performed onstage, then the acting will greatly affect the portrayal. The actor's facial expressions, gestures, movements, speaking style, and so on, will make the character come alive. To understand a character when you are reading a play, therefore, imagine an actor performing the lines.

The **theme** of a play is its central idea, or insight into life. One way to arrive at the theme of a play is to notice how the main character changes. If you can explain why the main character changes for the better, or for the worse, you probably are very close to understanding the theme.

Focus

In Act II Scrooge is visited by the Ghosts of Christmas Present and Christmas Future. Both ghosts show him things that cause great changes in his character. What if you could see twenty years into your own future? What would you want to find out about yourself and others? Make a list of two or three important things you would want to find out. As you read, compare your list with what Scrooge sees and discovers about himself.

Vocabulary

Knowing the following words will help you as you read Act II of *A Christmas Carol: Scrooge and Marley.*

astonish (ə stän′ ish) *v.*: Amaze (p. 283)

compulsion (kəm pul′ shən) *n.*: A driving, irresistible force (p. 285)

severe (sə vir′) *adj.*: Harsh (p. 285)

meager (mē′ gər) *adj.*: Of poor quality; small in amount (p. 286)

threadbare (thred′ ber) *adj.*: Worn; shabby (p. 287)

audible (ô′ də b'l) *adj.*: Loud enough to be heard (p. 291)

gnarled (närld) *adj.*: Knotty and twisted (p. 291)

dispelled (dis peld′) *v.*: Scattered and driven away; made to vanish (p. 297)

ACT II

Scene 1

[*Lights. Choral music is sung. Curtain.* SCROOGE, *in bed, sleeping, in spotlight. We cannot yet see the interior of his room.* MARLEY, *opposite, in spotlight equal to* SCROOGE'S. MARLEY *laughs. He tosses his hand in the air and a flame shoots from it, magically, into the air. There is a thunder clap, and then another; a lightning flash, and then another. Ghostly music plays under. Colors change.* MARLEY's *spotlight has gone out and now reappears, with* MARLEY *in it, standing next to the bed and the sleeping* SCROOGE. MARLEY *addresses the audience directly.*]

MARLEY. Hear this snoring Scrooge! Sleeping to escape the nightmare that is his waking day. What shall I bring to him now? I'm afraid nothing would astonish old Scrooge now. Not after what he's seen. Not a baby boy, not a rhinoceros, nor anything in between would astonish Ebenezer Scrooge just now. I can think of nothing . . . [*Suddenly*] that's it! Nothing! [*He speaks confidentially.*] I'll have the clock strike one and, when he awakes expecting my second messenger, there will be no one . . . nothing. Then I'll have the bell strike twelve. And then one again . . . and then nothing. Nothing . . . [*Laughs*] nothing will . . . astonish him. I think it will work.

[*The bell tolls one.* SCROOGE *leaps awake.*]

SCROOGE. One! One! This is it: time! [*Looks about the room*] Nothing!

[*The bell tolls midnight.*]

Midnight! How can this be? I'm sleeping backwards.

[*One again*]

Good heavens! One again! I'm sleeping back and forth! [*A pause.* SCROOGE *looks about.*] Nothing! Absolutely nothing!

[*Suddenly, thunder and lightning.* MARLEY *laughs and disappears. The room shakes and glows. There is suddenly springlike music.* SCROOGE *makes a run for the door.*]

MARLEY. Scrooge!

SCROOGE. What?

MARLEY. Stay you put!

SCROOGE. Just checking to see if anyone is in here.

[*Lights and thunder again: more music.* MARLEY *is of a sudden gone. In his place sits the* GHOST OF CHRISTMAS PRESENT—*to be called in the stage directions of the play,* PRESENT—*center of room. Heaped up on the floor, to form a kind of throne, are turkeys, geese, game, poultry, brawn, great joints of meat, suckling pigs, long wreaths of sausages, mince-pies, plum puddings, barrels of oysters, red hot chestnuts, cherry-cheeked apples, juicy oranges, luscious pears, immense twelfth cakes, and seething bowls of punch, that make the chamber dim with their delicious steam. Upon this throne sits* PRESENT, *glorious to see. He bears a torch, shaped as a Horn of Plenty.[1]* SCROOGE *hops out of the door, and then peeks back again into his bedroom.* PRESENT *calls to* SCROOGE.]

PRESENT. Ebenezer Scrooge. Come in, come in! Come in and know me better!

SCROOGE. Hello. How should I call you?

PRESENT. I am the Ghost of Christmas Present. Look upon me.

---

1. Horn of Plenty: A horn overflowing with fruits, flowers, and grain, standing for wealth and abundance.

[PRESENT *is wearing a simple green robe. The walls around the room are now covered in greenery, as well. The room seems to be a perfect grove now: leaves of holly, mistletoe and ivy reflect the stage lights. Suddenly, there is a mighty roar of flame in the fireplace and now the hearth burns with a lavish, warming fire. There is an ancient scabbard girdling the* GHOST'*s middle, but without sword. The sheath is gone to rust.*]

You have never seen the like of me before?

SCROOGE. Never.

PRESENT. You have never walked forth with younger members of my family; my elder brothers born on Christmases past.

SCROOGE. I don't think I have. I'm afraid I've not. Have you had many brothers, Spirit?

PRESENT. More than eighteen hundred.

SCROOGE. A tremendous family to provide for! [PRESENT *stands*] Spirit, conduct me where you will. I went forth last night on compulsion, and learnt a lesson which is working now. Tonight, if you have aught to teach me, let me profit by it.

PRESENT. Touch my robe.

[SCROOGE *walks cautiously to* PRESENT *and touches his robe. When he does, lightning flashes, thunder claps, music plays. Blackout*]

Scene 2

[*PROLOGUE:* MARLEY *stands spotlit, L. He speaks directly to the audience.*]

MARLEY. My ghostly friend now leads my living partner through the city's streets.

[*Lights up on* SCROOGE *and* PRESENT]

See them there and hear the music people make when the weather is severe, as it is now.

[*Winter music. Choral group behind scrim, sings. When the song is done and the stage is re-set, the lights will fade up on a row of shops, behind the singers. The choral group will hum the song they have just completed now and mill about the streets,[2] carrying their dinners to the bakers' shops and restaurants. They will, perhaps, sing about being poor at Christmastime, whatever.*]

PRESENT. These revelers, Mr. Scrooge, carry their own dinners to their jobs, where they will work to bake the meals the rich men and women of this city will eat as their Christ-mas dinners. Generous people these . . . to care for the others, so . . .

[PRESENT *walks among the choral group and a sparkling incense[3] falls from his torch on to their baskets, as he pulls the covers off of the baskets. Some of the choral group become angry with each other.*]

MAN #1. Hey, you, watch where you're going.

MAN #2. Watch it yourself, mate!

[PRESENT *sprinkles them directly, they change.*]

MAN #1. I pray go in ahead of me. It's Christmas. You be first!

MAN #2. No, no, I must insist that YOU be first!

MAN #1. All right, I shall be, and gratefully so.

MAN #2. The pleasure is equally mine, for being able to watch you pass, smiling.

MAN #1. I would find it a shame to quarrel on Christmas Day . . .

MAN #2. As would I.

MAN #1. Merry Christmas then, friend!

MAN #2. And a Merry Christmas straight back to you!

[*Church bells toll. The choral group enter the buildings; the shops and restaurants; they exit the stage, shutting their doors closed behind them. All sound stops.* SCROOGE *and* PRESENT *are alone again.*]

SCROOGE. What is it you sprinkle from your torch?

PRESENT. Kindness.

----

2. mill about the streets: Walk around aimlessly.

3. incense (in′ sens) *n.*: Any of various substances that produce a pleasant odor when burned.

SCROOGE. Do you sprinkle your kindness on any particular people or on all people?

PRESENT. To any person kindly given. And to the very poor most of all.

SCROOGE. Why to the very poor most?

PRESENT. Because the very poor need it most. Touch my heart . . . here, Mr. Scrooge. We have another journey.

[SCROOGE *touches the* GHOST's *heart and music plays, lights change color, lightning flashes, thunder claps. A choral group appears on the street, singing Christmas carols.*]

Scene 3

[MARLEY *stands spotlit in front of a scrim on which is painted the exterior of* CRATCHIT's *four-roomed house. There is a flash and a clap and* MARLEY *is gone. The lights shift color again, the scrim flies away, and we are in the interior of the* CRATCHIT *family home.* SCROOGE *is there, with the* SPIRIT (PRESENT), *watching* MRS. CRATCHIT *set the table, with the help of* BELINDA CRATCHIT *and* PETER CRATCHIT, *a baby, pokes a fork into the mashed potatoes on his highchair's tray. He also chews on his shirt collar.*]

SCROOGE. What is this place, Spirit?

PRESENT. This is the home of your employee, Mr. Scrooge. Don't you know it?

SCROOGE. Do you mean Cratchit, Spirit? Do you mean this is Cratchit's home?

PRESENT. None other.

SCROOGE. These children are his?

PRESENT. There are more to come presently.

SCROOGE. On his meager earnings! What foolishness!

PRESENT. Foolishness, is it?

SCROOGE. Wouldn't you say so? Fifteen shilings[4] a week's what he gets!

PRESENT. I would say that he gets the pleasure of his family, fifteen times a week times the number of hours a day! Wait, Mr. Scrooge. Wait, listen and watch. You might actually learn something . . .

MRS. CRATCHIT. What has ever got your precious father then? And your brother, Tiny Tim? And Martha warn't as late last Christmas by half an hour!

[MARTHA *opens the door, speaking to her mother as she does.*]

MARTHA. Here's Martha, now, Mother! [*She laughs. The* CRATCHIT CHILDREN *squeal with delight.*]

BELINDA. It's Martha, Mother! Here's Martha!

PETER. Marthmama, Marthmama! Hullo!

BELINDA. Hurrah! Martha! Martha! There's such an enormous goose for us, Martha!

MRS. CRATCHIT. Why, bless your heart alive, my dear, how late you are!

MARTHA. We'd a great deal of work to finish up last night, and had to clear away this morning, Mother.

MRS. CRATCHIT. Well, never mind so long as you are come. Sit ye down before the fire, my dear, and have a warm, Lord bless ye!

BELINDA. No, no! There's Father coming. Hide, Martha, hide!

[MARTHA *giggles and hides herself.*]

MARTHA. Where? Here?

PETER. *Hide, hide!*

BELINDA. Not there! *THERE!*

---

4. **fifteen shillings:** A small amount of money for a week's work.

[MARTHA *is hidden.* BOB CRATCHIT *enters, carrying* TINY TIM *atop his shoulder. He wears a threadbare and fringeless comforter hanging down in front of him.* TINY TIM *carries small crutches and his small legs are bound in an iron frame brace.*]

BOB and **TINY TIM.** Merry Christmas.

BOB. Merry Christmas my love, Merry Christmas Peter, Merry Christmas Belinda. Why, where is Martha?

MRS. CRATCHIT. Not coming.

BOB. Not coming? Not coming upon Christmas Day?

MARTHA. [*Pokes head out*] Ohhh, poor Father. Don't be disappointed.

BOB. What's this?

MARTHA. 'Tis I!

BOB. Martha! [*They embrace.*]

TINY TIM. Martha! Martha!

MARTHA. Tiny Tim!

[TINY TIM *is placed in* MARTHA's *arms.* BELINDA *and* PETER *rush him offstage.*]

BELINDA. Come, brother! You must come hear the pudding singing in the copper.

TINY TIM. The pudding? What flavor have we?

PETER. Plum! Plum!

TINY TIM! Oh, Mother! I love plum!

[*The children exit the stage, giggling.*]

MRS. CRATCHIT. And how did little Tim behave?

BOB. As good as gold, and even better. Somehow he gets thoughtful sitting by himself so much, and thinks the strangest things you ever heard. He told me, coming home, that he hoped people saw him in the church, be-cause he was a cripple, and it might be pleasant to them to remember upon Christmas Day, who made lame beggars walk and blind men see. [*Pauses*] He has the oddest ideas sometimes, but he seems all the while to be growing stronger and more hearty . . . one would never know. [*Hears* TIM's *crutch on floor outside door*]

PETER. The goose has arrived to be eaten!

BELINDA. Oh, mama, mama, it's beautiful.

MARTHA. It's a perfect goose, Mother!

TINY TIM. To this Christmas goose, Mother and Father I say . . . [*Yells*] Hurrah! Hurrah!

OTHER CHILDREN. [*Copying* TIM] Hurrah! Hurrah!

[*The family sits round the table.* BOB *and* MRS. CRATCHIT *serve the trimmings, quickly. All sit; all bow heads; all pray.*]

BOB. Thank you, dear Lord, for your many gifts . . . our dear children; our wonderful meal; our love for one another; and the warmth of our small fire— [*Looks up at all*] A merry Christmas to us, my dear. God bless us!

ALL. [*Except* TIM] Merry Christmas! God bless us!

TINY TIM. [*In a short silence*] God bless us every one.

[*All freeze. Spotlight on* PRESENT *and* SCROOGE]

SCROOGE. Spirit, tell me if Tiny Tim will live.

PRESENT. I see a vacant seat . . . in the poor chimney corner, and a crutch without an owner, carefully preserved. If these shadows remain unaltered by the future, the child will die.

SCROOGE. No, no, kind Spirit! Say he will be spared!

PRESENT. If these shadows remain unaltered by the future, none other of my race will find him here. What then? If he be like to die, he had better do it, and decrease the surplus population.

[SCROOGE *bows his head. We hear* BOB's *voice speak* SCROOGE's *name.*]

BOB. Mr. Scrooge . . .

SCROOGE. Huh? What's that? Who calls?

BOB. [*His glass raised in a toast*] I'll give you Mr. Scrooge, the Founder of the Feast!

SCROOGE. Me, Bob? You toast *me*?

PRESENT. Save your breath, Mr. Scrooge. You can't be seen or heard.

MRS. CRATCHIT. The Founder of the Feast, indeed! I wish I had him here, that miser Scrooge. I'd give him a piece of my mind to feast upon, and I hope he'd have a good appetite for it!

BOB. My dear! Christmas Day!

MRS. CRATCHIT. It should be Christmas Day, I am sure, on which one drinks the health of such an odious, stingy, unfeeling man as Mr. Scrooge . . .

SCROOGE. Oh, Spirit, must I? . . .

MRS. CRATCHIT. You know he is, Robert! Nobody knows it better than you do, poor fellow!

BOB. This is Christmas Day, and I should like to drink to the health of the man who employs me and allows me to earn my living and our support and that man is Ebenezer Scrooge . . .

MRS. CRATCHIT. I'll drink to his health for your sake and the day's, but not for his sake . . . a Merry Christmas and a Happy New Year to you, Mr. Scrooge, wherever you may be this day!

SCROOGE. Just here, kind madam . . . out of sight, out of sight . . .

BOB. Thank you, my dear. Thank you.

SCROOGE. Thank *you*, Bob . . . and Mrs. Cratchit, too. No one else is toasting me, . . . not now . . . not ever. Of that I am sure . . .

BOB. Children . . .

ALL. Merry Christmas to Mr. Scrooge.

BOB. I'll pay you sixpence, Tim, for my favorite song.

TINY TIM. Oh, Father, I'd so love to sing it, but not for pay. This Christmas goose—this feast—you and Mother, my brother and sisters close with me: that's my pay—

BOB. Martha, will you play the notes on the lute,[5] for Tiny Tim's song.

BELINDA. May I sing, too, Father?

BOB. We'll all sing.

[*They sing a song about a tiny child lost in the snow—probably from Wordsworth's poem.* TIM *sings the lead vocal; all chime in for the chorus. Their song fades under, as* THE GHOST OF CHRISTMAS PRESENT *speaks.*]

---

5. lute (lo͞ot) *n.*: An old-fashioned stringed instrument like a guitar.

PRESENT. Mark my words, Ebenezer Scrooge. I do not present the Cratchits to you because they are a handsome, or brilliant family. They are not handsome. They are not brilliant. They are not well-dressed, or tasteful to the times. Their shoes are not even waterproofed by virtue of money or cleverness spent. So when the pavement is wet, so are the insides of their shoes and the tops of their toes. These are the Cratchits, Mr. Scrooge. They are not highly special. They are happy, grateful, pleased with one another, contented with the time and how it passes. They don't sing very well, do they? But, nonetheless, they do sing . . . [*Pauses*] think of that, Scrooge. Fifteen shillings a week and they do sing . . . hear their song until its end.

SCROOGE. I am listening.

[*The chorus sings full volume now, until . . . the song ends here.*]

Spirit, it must be time for us to take our leave. I feel in my heart that it is . . . that I must think on that which I have seen here . . .

PRESENT. Touch my robe again . . .

[SCROOGE *touches* PRESENT's *robe. The lights fade out on the* CRATCHITS, *who sit, frozen, at the table.* SCROOGE *and* PRESENT *in a spotlight now. Thunder, lightning, smoke. They are gone.*]

Scene 4

[MARLEY *appears D.L. in single spotlight. A storm brews. Thunder and lightning.* SCROOGE *and* PRESENT *"fly" past, U. The storm continues, furiously, and, now and again,* SCROOGE *and* PRESENT *will zip past in their travels.* MARLEY *will speak straight out to the audience.*]

MARLEY. The Ghost of Christmas Present, my co-worker in this attempt to turn a miser, flies about now with that very miser, Scrooge, from street to street, and he points out partygoers on their way to Christmas parties. If one were to judge from the numbers of people on their way to friendly gatherings, one might think that no one was left at home to give anyone welcome . . . but that's not the case, is it? Every home is expecting company and . . . [*He laughs.*] Scrooge is amazed.

[SCROOGE *and* PRESENT *zip past again. The lights fade up around them. We are in the* NEPHEW's *home, in the living room,* PRESENT *and* SCROOGE *stand watching the* NEPHEW: FRED *and his wife, fixing the fire.*]

SCROOGE. What is this place? We've moved from the mines!

PRESENT. You do not recognize them?

SCROOGE. It is my nephew! . . . and the one he married . . .

[MARLEY *waves his hand and there is a lightning flash. He disappears.*]

FRED. It strikes me as sooooo funny, to think of what he said . . . that Christmas was a humbug, as I live! He believed it!

WIFE. More shame for him, Fred!

FRED. Well, he's a comical old fellow, that's the truth.

WIFE. I have no patience with him.

FRED. Oh, I have! I am sorry for him; I couldn't be angry with him if I tried. Who suffers by his ill whims? Himself, always . . .

SCROOGE. It's me they talk of, isn't it, Spirit?

FRED. Here, wife, consider this. Uncle Scrooge takes it into his head to dislike us, and he won't come and dine with us. What's the consequence?

WIFE. Oh . . . you're sweet to say what I think you're about to say, too, Fred . . .

FRED. What's the consequence? He don't lose much of a dinner by it, I can tell you that!

WIFE. Ooooooo, Fred! Indeed, I think he loses a very good dinner . . . ask my sisters, or your bachelor friend. Topper . . . ask any of them. They'll tell you what old Scrooge, your uncle, missed: a dandy meal!

FRED. Well, that's something of a relief, wife. Glad to hear it! [*He hugs his wife. They laugh. They kiss.*] The truth is, he misses much yet. I mean to give him the same chance every year, whether he likes it or not, for I pity him. Nay, he is my only uncle and I feel for the old miser . . . but, I tell you, wife: I see my dear and perfect mother's face on his own wizened cheeks and brow: brother and sister they were, and I cannot erase that from each view of him I take . . .

WIFE. I understand what you say, Fred, and I am with you in your yearly asking. But he never will accept, you know. He never will.

FRED. Well, true, wife. Uncle may rail at Christmas till he dies. I think I shook him some with my visit yesterday . . . [*Laughing*] I refused to grow angry . . . no matter how nasty he became . . . [*Whoops*] It was HE who grew angry, wife! [*They both laugh now.*]

SCROOGE. What he says is true, Spirit . . .

FRED and **WIFE.** Bah, humbug!

FRED. [*Embracing his wife*] There is much laughter in our marriage, wife. It pleases me. You please me . . .

WIFE. And you please me, Fred. You are a good man . . . [*They embrace.*] Come now. We must have a look at the meal . . . our guests will soon arrive . . . my sisters, Topper . . .

FRED. A toast first . . . [*He hands her a glass.*] A toast to Uncle Scrooge . . . [*Fills their glasses*]

WIFE. A toast to him?

FRED. Uncle Scrooge has given us plenty of merriment. I am sure, and it would be ungrateful not to drink to his health. And I say . . . *Uncle Scrooge!*

WIFE. [*Laughing*] You're a proper loon,[6] Fred . . . and I'm a proper wife to you . . . [*She raises her glass.*] *Uncle Scrooge!* [*They drink. They embrace. They kiss.*]

SCROOGE. Spirit, please, make me visible! Make me audible! I want to talk with my nephew and my niece!

[*Calls out to them. The lights that light the room and* FRED *and wife fade out.* SCROOGE *and* PRESENT *are alone, spotlit.*]

PRESENT. These shadows are gone to you now, Mr. Scrooge. You may return to them later tonight in your dreams. [*Pauses*] My time grows short, Ebenezer Scrooge. Look you on me! Do you see how I've aged?

SCROOGE. Your hair has gone gray! Your skin, wrinkled! Are spirits' lives so short?

PRESENT. My stay upon this globe is very brief. It ends tonight.

SCROOGE. Tonight?

PRESENT. At midnight. The time is drawing near!

---

6. a proper loon: A silly person.

[*Clock strikes 11:45.*]

Hear those chimes? In a quarter hour, my life will have been spent! Look, Scrooge, man. Look you here.

[*Two gnarled baby dolls are taken from* PRESENT'S *skirts.*]

SCROOGE. Who are they?

PRESENT. They are Man's children, and they cling to me, appealing from their fathers. The boy is Ignorance; the girl is Want. Beware them both, and all of their degree, but most of all beware this boy, for I see that written on his brow which is doom, unless the writing be erased. [*He stretches out his arm. His voice is now amplified: loudly and oddly.*]

SCROOGE. Have they no refuge or resource?

PRESENT. Are there no prisons? Are there no workhouses? [*Twelve chimes*] Are there no prisons? Are there no workhouses?

[*A* PHANTOM, *hooded, appears in dim light, D., opposite.*]

Are there no prisons? Are there no workhouses?

[PRESENT *begins to deliquesce.* SCROOGE *calls after him.*]

SCROOGE. Spirit, I'm frightened! Don't leave me! Spirit!

PRESENT. Prisons? Workhouses? Prisons? Workhouses . . .

[*He is gone.* SCROOGE *is alone now with the* PHANTOM, *who is, of course, the* GHOST OF CHRISTMAS FUTURE. *The* PHANTOM *is shrouded in black. Only its outstretched hand is visible from under his ghostly garment.*]

SCROOGE. Who are you, Phantom? Oh, yes, I think I know you! You are, are you not, the Spirit of Christmas Yet to Come? [*No reply*] And you are about to show me the shadows of the things that have not yet happened, but will happen in time before us. Is that not so, Spirit?

[*The* PHANTOM *allows* SCROOGE *a look at his face. No other reply wanted here. A nervous giggle here*]

Oh, Ghost of the Future, I fear you more than any Specter I have seen! But, as I know that your purpose is to do me good and as I hope to live to be another man from what I was, I am prepared to bear you company.

[FUTURE *does not reply, but for a stiff arm, hand and finger set, pointing forward.*]

Lead on, then, lead on. The night is waning fast, and it is precious time to me. Lead on, Spirit!

[FUTURE *moves away from* SCROOGE *in the same rhythm and motion employed at its arrival.* SCROOGE *falls into the same pattern, a considerable space apart from the* SPIRIT. *In the space between them,* MARLEY *appears. He looks to* FUTURE *and then to* SCROOGE. *He claps his hands. Thunder and lightning. Three* BUSINESSMEN *appear, spotlighted singularly: One is D.L.; One is D.R.; One is U.C. Thus, six points of the stage should now be spotted in light.* MARLEY *will watch this scene from his position,* C. SCROOGE *and* FUTURE *are R. and L. of C.*]

FIRST BUSINESSMAN. Oh, no, I don't know much about it either way, I only know he's dead.

SECOND BUSINESSMAN. When did he die?

FIRST BUSINESSMAN. Last night, I believe.

SECOND BUSINESSMAN. Why, what was the matter with him? I thought he'd never die, really . . .

FIRST BUSINESSMAN. [*Yawning*] Goodness knows, goodness knows . . .

THIRD BUSINESSMAN. What has he done with his money?

SECOND BUSINESSMAN. I haven't heard. Have you?

FIRST BUSINESSMAN. Left it to his Company, perhaps. Money to money; you know the expression . . .

THIRD BUSINESSMAN. He hasn't left it to *me*. That's all I know . . .

FIRST BUSINESSMAN. [*Laughing*] Nor to me . . . [*Looks at* SECOND BUSINESSMAN] You, then? You got his money???

SECOND BUSINESSMAN. [*Laughing*] Me, me, his money? Nooooo! [*They all laugh.*]

THIRD BUSINESSMAN. It's likely to be a cheap funeral, for upon my life, I don't know of a living soul who'd care to venture to it. Suppose we make up a party and volunteer?

SECOND BUSINESSMAN. I don't mind going if a lunch is provided, but I must be fed, if I make one.

FIRST BUSINESSMAN. Well, I am the most disinterested among you, for I never wear black gloves, and I never eat lunch. But I'll offer to go, if anybody else will. When I come to think of it, I'm not all sure that I wasn't his most particular friend; for we used to stop and speak whenever we met. Well, then . . . bye, bye!

SECOND BUSINESSMAN. Bye, bye . . .

THIRD BUSINESSMAN. Bye, bye . . .

[*They glide offstage in three separate directions. Their lights follow them.*]

SCROOGE. Spirit, why did you show me this? Why do you show me businessmen from my streets as they take the death of Jacob Marley. That is a thing past. You are *future*!

[JACOB MARLEY *laughs a long, deep laugh. There is a thunder clap and lightning flash, and he is gone.* SCROOGE *faces* FUTURE, *alone on stage now.* FUTURE *wordlessly stretches out his arm-hand-and-finger-set, pointing into the distance, U. There, above them, Scoundrels "fly" by, half-dressed and slovenly. When this scene has passed, a woman enters the playing area. She is almost at once followed by a second woman: and then a man in faded black: and then, suddenly, an old man, who smokes a pipe. The old man scares the other three. They laugh, anxious.*]

FIRST WOMAN. Look here, old Joe, here's a chance! If we haven't all three met here without meaning it!

OLD JOE. You couldn't have met in a better place. Come into the parlor. You were made free of it long ago, you know; and the other two an't strangers [*He stands: shuts a door. Shrieking*] We're all suitable to our calling. We're well matched. Come into the parlor. Come into the parlor . . .

[*They follow him D.* SCROOGE *and* FUTURE *are now in their midst, watching: silent. A truck comes in on which is set a small wall with fireplace and a screen of rags, etc. All props for the scene.*]

Let me just rake this fire over a bit . . .

[*He does. He trims his lamp with the stem of his pipe. The* FIRST WOMAN *throws a large bundle on to the floor. She sits beside it, crosslegged: defiantly.*]

FIRST WOMAN. What odds then? What odds, Mrs. Dilber? Every person has a right to take care of themselves. HE always did!

MRS. DILBER. That's true indeed! No man more so!

FIRST WOMAN. Why, then, don't stand staring as if you was afraid, woman! Who's the wiser? We're not going to pick holes in each other's coats, I suppose?

MRS. DILBER. No, indeed! We should hope not!

FIRST WOMAN. Very well, then! That's enough. Who's the worse for the loss of a few things like these? Not a dead man, I suppose?

MRS. DILBER. [*Laughing*] No, indeed!

FIRST WOMAN. If he wanted to keep 'em after he was dead, the wicked old screw, why wasn't he natural in his lifetime? If he had been, he'd have had somebody to look after him when he was struck with Death, instead of lying gasping out his last there, alone by himself.

MRS. DILBER. It's the truest word that was ever spoke. It's a judgment on him.

FIRST WOMAN. I wish it were a heavier one, and it should have been, you may depend on it, if I could have laid my hands on anything else. Open that bundle, old Joe, and let me know the value of it. Speak out plain. I'm not afraid to be the first, nor afraid for them to see it. We knew pretty well that we were helping ourselves, before we met here. I believe. It's no sin. Open the bundle, Joe.

FIRST MAN. No, no, my dear! I won't think of letting you being the first to show what you've . . . earned . . . earned from this. I throw in mine. [*He takes a bundle from his shoulder, turns it upside down, and emp-*

ties its contents out on to the floor.] It's not very extensive, see . . . seals . . . a pencil case . . . sleeve buttons . . .

MRS. DILBER. Nice sleeve buttons, though . . .

FIRST MAN. Not bad, not bad . . . a brooch there . . .

OLD JOE. Not really valuable, I'm afraid . . .

FIRST MAN. How much, old Joe?

OLD JOE. [*Writing on the wall with chalk*] A pitiful lot, really. Ten and six and not a sixpence more!

FIRST MAN. You're not serious!

OLD JOE. That's your account and I wouldn't give another sixpence if I was to be boiled for not doing it. Who's next?

MRS. DILBER. Me! [*Dumps out contents of her bundle*] Sheets, towels, silver spoons, silver sugar-tongs . . . some boots . . .

OLD JOE. [*Writing on wall*] I always give too much to the ladies. It's a weakness of mine and that's the way I ruin myself. Here's your total comin' up . . . two pounds-ten . . . if you asked me for another penny, and made it an open question, I'd repent of being so liberal and knock off half-a-crown.

FIRST WOMAN. And now do MY bundle, Joe.

OLD JOE. [*Kneeling to open knots on her bundle*] So many knots, madam . . . [*He drags out large curtains; dark*] What do you call this? Bed curtains!

FIRST WOMAN. [*Laughing*] Ah, yes, bed curtains!

OLD JOE. You don't mean to say you took 'em down, rings and all, with him lying there?

FIRST WOMAN. Yes, I did, why not?

OLD JOE. You were born to make your fortune and you'll certainly do it.

FIRST WOMAN. I certainly shan't hold my hand, when I can get anything in it by reaching it out, for the sake of such a man as he was, I promise you, Joe. Don't drop that lamp oil on those blankets, now!

OLD JOE. His blankets?

FIRST WOMAN. Whose else's do you think? He isn't likely to catch cold without 'em, I daresay.

OLD JOE. I hope that he didn't die of anything catching? Eh?

FIRST WOMAN. Don't you be afraid of that. I ain't so fond of his company that I'd loiter about him for such things if he did. Ah! You may look through that shirt till your eyes ache, but you won't find a hole in it, nor a threadbare place. It's the best he had, and a fine one, too. They'd have wasted it, if it hadn't been for me.

OLD JOE. What do you mean "They'd have wasted it?"

FIRST WOMAN. Putting it on him to be buried in, to be sure. Somebody was fool enough to do it, but I took it off again . . . [*She laughs, as do they all, nervously.*] If calico[7] ain't good enough for such a purpose, it isn't good enough then for anything. It's quite as becoming to the body. He can't look uglier than he did in that one!

SCROOGE. [*A low-pitched moan emits from his mouth; from the bones.*] OOOOOOOoo oooOOOOOoooooOOOOOOOooooooOOOOO OoooooOO!

OLD JOE. One pound six for the lot. [*He produces a small flannel bag filled with*

---

7. **calico** (kal′ ə kō) *n.*: A coarse and cheap cloth.

money. *He divvies it out. He continues to pass around the money as he speaks. All are laughing.*] That's the end of it, you see! He frightened every one away from him while he was alive, to profit us when he was dead! Hah ha ha!

ALL. HAHAHAHAhahahahahahah!

SCROOGE. *OOOoooOOOoooOOOoooOOOooo OOoooOOoooOOOooo!* [*He screams at them.*] Obscene demons! Why not market the corpse itself, as sell its trimming??? [*Suddenly*] Oh, Spirit, I see it, I see it! This unhappy man—this stripped-bare corpse . . . could very well be my own. My life holds parallel! My life ends that way now!

[SCROOGE *backs into something in the dark behind his spotlight.* SCROOGE *looks at* FUTURE, *who points to the corpse.* SCROOGE *pulls back the blanket. The corpse is, of course,* SCROOGE, *who screams. He falls aside the bed; weeping.*]

Spirit, this is a fearful place. In leaving it, I shall not leave its lesson, trust me. Let us go!

[FUTURE *points to the corpse.*]

Spirit, let me see some tenderness connected with a death, or that dark chamber, which we just left now, Spirit, will be forever present to me.

[FUTURE *spreads his robes again. Thunder and lightning. Lights up, U., in the Cratchit home setting.* MRS. CRATCHIT *and her daughters, sewing*]

TINY TIM'S VOICE. [*Off*] And He took a child and set him in the midst of them.

SCROOGE. [*Looking about the room; to* FUTURE] Huh? Who spoke? Who said that?

MRS. CRATCHIT. [*Puts down her sewing*] The color hurts my eyes. [*Rubs her eyes*] That's

better. My eyes grow weak sewing by candlelight. I shouldn't want to show your father weak eyes when he comes home . . . not for the world! It must be near his time . . .

PETER. [*In corner, reading. Looks up from book*] Past it, rather. But I think he's been walking a bit slower than usual these last few evenings, Mother.

MRS. CRATCHIT. I have known him walk with . . . [*Pauses*] I have know him walk with Tiny Tim upon his shoulder and very fast indeed.

PETER. So have I, Mother! Often!

DAUGHTER. So have I.

MRS. CRATCHIT. But he was very light to carry and his father loved him so, that it was not trouble—no trouble.

[BOB, *at door*]

And there is your father at the door.

[BOB CRATCHIT *enters. He wears a comforter. He is cold, forlorn.*]

PETER. Father!

BOB. Hello, wife, children . . .

[*The daughter weeps; turns away from* CRATCHIT.]

Children! How good to see you all! And you, wife. And look at this sewing! I've no doubt, with all your industry, we'll have a quilt to set down upon our knees in church on Sunday!

MRS. CRATCHIT. You made the arrangements today, then, Robert, for the . . . service . . . to be on Sunday.

BOB. The funeral. Oh, well, yes, yes, I did. I wish you could have gone. It would have done you good to see how green a place it is. But you'll see it often, I promised him that I would walk there on Sunday, after the service. [*Suddenly*] My little, little child! My little child!

ALL CHILDREN. [*Hugging him*] Oh, Father . . .

BOB. [*He stands*] Forgive me. I saw Mr. Scrooge's nephew, who you know I'd just met once before, and he was so wonderful to me, wife . . . he is the most pleasant-spoken gentleman I've ever met . . . he said "I am heartily sorry for it and heartily sorry for your good wife. If I can be of service to you in any way, here's where I live." And he gave me this card.

PETER. Let me see it!

BOB. And he looked me straight in the eye, wife, and said, meaningfully, "I pray you'll come to me, Mr. Cratchit, if you need some help. I pray you do." Now it wasn't for the sake of anything that he might be able to do for us, so much as for his kind way. It seemed as if he had known our Tiny Tim and felt with us.

MRS. CRATCHIT. I'm sure that he's a good soul.

BOB. You would be surer of it, my dear, if you saw and spoke to him. I shouldn't be at all surprised, if he got Peter a situation.

MRS. CRATCHIT. Only hear that, Peter!

MARTHA. And then, Peter will be keeping company with someone and setting up for himself!

PETER. Get along with you!

BOB. It's just as likely as not, one of these days, though there's plenty of time for that, my dear. But however and whenever we part from one another, I am sure we shall none of us forget poor Tiny Tim—shall we?—or this first parting that was among us?

ALL CHILDREN. Never, Father, never!

BOB. And when we recollect how patient and mild he was, we shall not quarrel easily among ourselves, and forget poor Tiny Tim in doing it.

ALL CHILDREN. No, Father, never!

LITTLE BOB. I am very happy, I am, I am, I am very happy.

[BOB *kisses his little son, as does* MRS. CRATCHIT, *as do the other children. The family is set now in one sculptural embrace. The lighting fades to a gentle pool of light, tight on them.*]

SCROOGE. Specter, something informs me that our parting moment is at hand. I know it, but I know not how I know it.

[FUTURE *points to the other side of the stage. Lights out on Cratchits.* FUTURE *moves slowing, gliding.* SCROOGE *follows.* FUTURE *points opposite.* FUTURE *leads* SCROOGE *to a wall and a tombstone. He points to the stone.*]

Am *I* that man those ghoulish parasites[8] so gloated over? [*Pauses*] Before I draw nearer to that stone to which you point, answer me one question. Are these the shadows of things that will be, or the shadows of things that MAY be, only?

[FUTURE *points to the gravestone.* MARLEY *appears in light well U. He points to grave as well. Gravestone turns front and grows to ten feet high. Words upon it: EBENEZER SCROOGE. Much smoke billows now from the grave. Choral music here.* SCROOGE *stands looking up at gravestone.* FUTURE *does not at all reply in mortals' words, but*

---

8. ghoulish parasites (gool' ish par' ə sïts): The man and women who stole and divided Scrooge's goods after he died.

points once more to the gravestone. The stone undulates and glows. Music plays, beckoning SCROOGE. SCROOGE reeling in terror]

Oh, no. Spirit! Oh, no, no!

[FUTURE's *finger still pointing*]

Spirit! Hear me! I am not the man I was. I will not be the man I would have been but for this intercourse. Why show me this, if I am past all hope?

[FUTURE *considers* SCROOGE's *logic. His hand wavers.*]

Oh, Good Spirit, I see by your wavering hand that your good nature intercedes for me and pities me. Assure me that I yet may change these shadows that you have shown me by an altered life!

[FUTURE's *hand trembles; pointing has stopped.*]

I will honor Christmas in my heart and try to keep it all the year. I will live in the Past, the Present, and the Future. The Spirits of all Three shall strive within me. I will not shut out the lessons that they teach. Oh, tell me that I may sponge away the writing that is upon this stone!

[SCROOGE *makes a desperate stab at grabbing* FUTURE's *hand. He holds it firm for a moment, but* FUTURE, *stronger than* SCROOGE, *pulls away.* SCROOGE *is on his knees, praying.*]

Spirit, dear Spirit, I am praying before you. Give me a sign that all is possible. Give me a sign that all hope for me is not lost. Oh, Spirit, kind Spirit, I beseech thee: give me a sign . . .

[FUTURE *deliquesces, slowly, gently. The* PHANTOM's *hood and robe drop gracefully to* the ground in a small heap. Music in. There is nothing in them. They are mortal cloth. The Spirit is elsewhere. SCROOGE *has his sign.* SCROOGE *is alone. Tableau. The lights fade to black.*]

Scene 5

[*The end of it.* MARLEY, *spotlighted, opposite* SCROOGE, *in his bed, spotlighted.* MARLEY *speaks to audience, directly.*]

MARLEY. [*He smiles at* SCROOGE.] The firm of Scrooge and Marley is doubly blessed; two misers turned; one, alas, in Death, too late; but the other miser turned in Time's penultimate nick.[9] Look you on my friend, Ebenezer Scrooge . . .

SCROOGE. [*Scrambling out of bed; reeling in delight*] I will live in the Past, in the Present, and in the Future! The Spirits of all Three shall strive within me!

MARLEY. [*He points and moves closer to* SCROOGE's *bed.*] Yes, Ebenezer, the bedpost is your own. Believe it! Yes, Ebenezer, the room is your own. Believe it!

SCROOGE. Oh, Jacob Marley! Wherever you are, Jacob, know ye that I praise you for this! I praise you . . . and heaven . . . and Christmastime! [*Kneels facing away from* MARLEY] I say it to ye on my knees, old Jacob, on my knees! [*He touches his bed curtains.*] Not torn down. My bed curtains are not at all torn down! Rings and all, here they are! They are here: I am here: the shadows of things that would have been, may now be dispelled. They will be, Jacob! I know they will be! [*He chooses clothing for the day. He tries different pieces of clothing and settles,*

---

9. in Time's penultimate nick: Just at the last moment.

perhaps, on a dress suit, plus a cape of the bed clothing: something of color.] I am light as a feather, I am happy as an angel, I am as merry as a schoolboy. [*Yells out window and then out to audience*] Merry Christmas to everybody! Merry Christmas to everybody! A Happy New Year to all the world! Hallo here! Whoop! Whoop! Hallo! Hallo! I don't know what day of the month it is! I don't care! I don't know anything! I'm quite a baby! I don't care! I don't care a fig! I'd much rather be a baby than be an old wreck like me or Marley! (Sorry, Jacob, wherever ye be!) Hallo! Hallo there!

[*Church bells chime in Christmas Day. A small boy, named* ADAM, *is seen now D.R., as a light fades up on him.*]

Hey, you boy! What's today? What day of the year is it?

ADAM. Today, sir? Why, it's Christmas Day!

SCROOGE. It's Christmas Day, is it? Whoop! Well, I haven't missed it after all, have I? The Spirits did all they did in one night. They can do anything they like, right? Of course they can! Of course they can!

ADAM. Excuse me, sir?

SCROOGE. Huh? Oh, yes, of course, what's your name, lad?

[SCROOGE *and* ADAM *will play their scene from their own spotlights.*]

ADAM. Adam, sir.

SCROOGE. Adam! What a fine, strong name! Do you know the poulterer's[10] in the next street but one, at the corner?

ADAM. I certainly should hope I know him, sir!

SCROOGE. A remarkable boy! An intelligent boy! Do you know whether the poulterer's have sold the prize turkey that was hanging up there? I don't mean the little prize turkey, Adam, I mean the big one!

ADAM. What, do you mean the one they've got that's as big as me?

SCROOGE. I mean, the turkey the size of Adam: that's the bird!

ADAM. It's hanging there now, sir.

SCROOGE. It is? Go and buy it! No, no, I am absolutely in earnest. Go and buy it and tell 'em to bring it here, so that I may give them

---

10. poulterer's (pōl′ tər ərz) *n.*: A British word for a store that sells chickens, turkeys, and geese.

the directions to where I want it delivered, as a gift. Come back here with the man, Adam, and I'll give you a shilling. Come back here with him in less than five minutes, and I'll give you half-a-crown!

ADAM. Oh, my sir! Don't let my brother in on this.

[ADAM *runs offstage.* MARLEY *smiles.*]

MARLEY. An act of kindness is like the first green grape of summer: one leads to another and another and another. It would take a queer man indeed to not follow an act of kindness with an act of kindness. One simply whets the tongue for more . . . the taste of kindness is too too sweet. Gifts—goods—are lifeless. But the gift of goodness one feels in the giving is full of life. It . . . is . . . a . . . wonder.

[*Pauses; moves closer to* SCROOGE, *who is totally occupied with his dressing and arranging of his room and his day. He is making lists, etc.* MARLEY *reaches out to* SCROOGE.]

ADAM. [*Calling, off*] I'm here! I'm here!

[ADAM *runs on with a man, who carries an enormous turkey.*]

Here I am, sir. Three minutes flat! A world record! I've got the poultryman and he's got the poultry! [*He pants, out of breath.*] I have earned my prize, sir, if I live . . .

[*He holds his heart, playacting.* SCROOGE *goes to him and embraces him.*]

SCROOGE. You are truly a champion, Adam . . .

MAN. Here's the bird you ordered, sir . . .

SCROOGE. Oh, my, MY!!! Look at the size of that turkey, will you! He never could have stood upon his legs, that bird! He would have snapped them off in a minute, like sticks of sealingwax! Why you'll never be able to carry that bird to Camden-Town. I'll give you money for a cab . . .

MAN. Camden-Town's where it's goin', sir?

SCROOGE. Oh, I didn't tell you? Yes, I've written the precise address down just here on this . . . [*Hands paper to him*] Bob Cratchit's house. Now he's not to know who sends him this. Do you understand me? Not a word . . . [*Handing out money and chuckling*]

MAN. I understand, sir, not a word.

SCROOGE. Good. There you go then . . . this is for the turkey . . . [*Chuckle*] and this is for the taxi. [*Chuckle*] . . . and this is for your world-record run, Adam . . .

ADAM. But I don't have change for that, sir.

SCROOGE. Then keep it, my lad. It's Christmas!

ADAM. [*He kisses* SCROOGE's *cheek, quickly.*] Thank you, sir. Merry, Merry Christmas! [*He runs off.*]

MAN. And you've given me a bit overmuch here, too, sir . . .

SCROOGE. Of course I have, sir. It's Christmas!

MAN. Oh, well, thanking you, sir. I'll have this bird to Mr. Cratchit and his family in no time, sir. Don't you worry none about that. Merry Christmas to you, sir, and a very happy New Year, too . . .

[*The man exits.* SCROOGE *walks in a large circle about the stage, which is now gently lit. A chorus sings Christmas music far in the distance. Bells chime as well, far in the distance. A gentlewoman enters and passes.* SCROOGE *is on the streets now.*]

SCROOGE. Merry Christmas, madam . . .

WOMAN. Merry Christmas, sir . . .

[*The portly businessman from the first act enters.*]

SCROOGE. Merry Christmas, sir.

PORTLY MAN. Merry Christmas, sir.

SCROOGE. Oh, you! My dear sir! How do you do? I do hope that you succeeded yesterday! It was very kind of you. A Merry Christmas.

PORTLY MAN. Mr. Scrooge?

SCROOGE. Yes, Scrooge is my name though I'm afraid you may not find it very pleasant. Allow me to ask your pardon. And will you have the goodness to— [*He whispers into the man's ear.*]

PORTLY MAN. Lord bless me! My dear Mr. Scrooge, are you *serious!?!*

SCROOGE. If you please. Not a farthing[11] less. A great many back payments are included in it, I assure you. Will you do me that favor?

PORTLY MAN. My dear sir, I don't know what to say to such munifi—

SCROOGE. [*Cutting him off*] Don't say anything, please. Come and see me. Will you?

PORTLY MAN. I will! I will! Oh I will, Mr. Scrooge! It will be my pleasure!

SCROOGE. Thank'ee, I am much obliged to you. I thank you fifty times. Bless you!

[*Portly man passes offstage, perhaps by moving backwards.* SCROOGE *now comes to the room of his* NEPHEW *and* NIECE. *He stops at the door, begins to knock on it, loses his courage, tries again, loses his courage again, tries again, fails again, and then backs off and runs at the door, causing a tremendous bump against it. The* NEPHEW

---

11. farthing (fär′ thiŋ) *n.:* A small British coin.

and NIECE *are startled.* SCROOGE, *poking head into room*]

Fred!

NEPHEW. Why, bless my soul! Who's that?

NEPHEW and **NIECE.** [*Together*] How now? Who goes?

SCROOGE. It's I. Your Uncle Scrooge.

NIECE. Dear heart alive!

SCROOGE. I have come to dinner. May I come in, Fred?

NEPHEW. *May you come in???!!!* With such pleasure for me you may, Uncle!!! What a treat!

NIECE. What a treat, Uncle Scrooge! Come in, come in!

[*They embrace a shocked and delighted* SCROOGE. FRED *calls into the other room.*]

NEPHEW. Come in here, everybody, and meet my Uncle Scrooge! He's come for our Christmas party!

[*Music in. Lighting here indicates that day has gone to night and gone to day again. It is early, early morning.* SCROOGE *walks alone from the party, exhausted, to his offices, opposite side of the stage. He opens his offices. The offices are as they were at the start of the play.* SCROOGE *seats himself with his door wide open so that he can see into the tank, as he awaits.* CRATCHIT, *who enters, head down, full of guilt.* CRATCHIT *starts writing almost before he sits.*]

SCROOGE. What do you mean by coming in here at this time of day, a full eighteen minutes late, Mr. Cratchit? Hallo, sir? Do you hear me?

BOB. I am very sorry, sir. I *am* behind my time.

SCROOGE. You are? Yes, I certainly think you are. Step this way, sir, if you please . . .

BOB. It's only but once a year, sir . . . it shall not be repeated. I was making rather merry yesterday and into the night . . .

SCROOGE. Now, I'll tell you what, Cratchit. I am not going to stand this sort of thing any longer. And therefore . . .

[*He stands and pokes his finger into* BOB's *chest.*]

I am . . . about . . . to . . . raise . . . your salary.

BOB. Oh, no, sir, I . . . [*Realizes*] what did you say, sir?

SCROOGE. A Merry Christmas, Bob . . . [*He claps* BOB's *back.*] A merrier Christmas, Bob, my good fellow! than I have given you for many a year. I'll raise your salary and endeavor to assist your struggling family and we will discuss your affairs this very afternoon over a bowl of smoking bishop.[12] Bob! Make up the fires and buy another coal scuttle before you dot another i, Bob. It's too cold in this place! We need warmth and cheer, Bob Cratchit! Do you hear me? DO . . . YOU . . . HEAR . . . ME?

[BOB CRATCHIT *stands, smiles at* SCROOGE. BOB CRATCHIT *faints. Blackout. As the main lights black out, a spotlight appears on* SCROOGE. C. *Another on* MARLEY. *He talks directly to the audience.*]

MARLEY. Scrooge was better than his word. He did it all and infinitely more; and to Tiny Tim, who did NOT die, he was a second father. He became as good a friend, as good a master, as good a man, as the good old city

---

12. smoking bishop: A hot, sweet, orange-flavored drink.

knew, or any other good old city, town, or borough in the good old world. And it was always said of him that he knew how to keep Christmas well, if any man alive possessed the knowledge. [*Pauses*] May that be truly said of us, and all of us. And so, as Tiny Tim observed . . .

TINY TIM. [*Atop* SCROOGE'S *shoulder*] God Bless Us, Every One . . .

[*Lights up on chorus, singing final Christmas Song.* SCROOGE *and* MARLEY *and all spirits and other characters of the play join in. When the song is over, the lights fade to black.*]

RESPONDING TO THE SELECTION

Your Response

1. Do you believe in Scrooge's change of heart? Why or why not?

Recalling

2. What fate does the Ghost of Christmas Present foretell for Tiny Tim?
3. What four sights does the Ghost of Christmas Future show Scrooge?
4. How does Scrooge live up to his promise in the final scene?

Interpreting

5. Contrast the attitudes of Cratchit and his wife toward Scrooge when they toast him.
6. What does this difference in attitudes indicate about each of these characters?
7. What does Scrooge mean when he says, "I will live in the Past, the Present, and the Future"?
8. The name Scrooge has come to stand for anyone who is miserly and heartless. Explain why the name as it is usually used would not fit Scrooge as he is at the end of the play.

Applying

9. Charles Dickens lived in the nineteenth century. Do you think the message of his play applies to our world today?

ANALYZING LITERATURE

Connecting Character and Theme

Theme is the central idea or insight about life revealed in a work of literature. Because Scrooge is of central importance to the play, understanding why he changes will help reveal the theme.

1. (a) Find three places in Act II where Scrooge's reactions show him changing for the better. (b) What causes him to change?
2. Using your answers to the preceding question, write a brief statement of the theme.

CRITICAL THINKING AND READING

Supporting an Opinion of a Character

Although an opinion cannot be proven false, a sound opinion is one that is supported by facts. For instance, to support an opinion that Scrooge is willing to change, you could mention his statement to the Ghost of Christmas Present: "Tonight, if you have aught to teach me, let me profit by it."

1. In Act II, Scene 3, Scrooge observes the Cratchits at home. What does Scrooge say that could support the opinion that he is developing feelings of kindness or compassion?
2. Write a one-sentence description of Scrooge as he is at the end of the play. Support your statement with two details from the final scene.

THINKING AND WRITING

Writing a Review of a Play

A review of a play does two things: It gives the reader a clear idea of what the play is about, and it gives the reviewer's opinion of the play. Write a review of *A Christmas Carol: Scrooge and Marley.* First list details of the story to give students who read the play next an idea of what it is about. Then jot down your thoughts on why you liked or did not like it. When you revise, make sure your review is fair and useful to someone thinking about reading the play.

ONE WRITER'S PROCESS

Israel Horovitz and A Christmas Carol: Scrooge and Marley

PREWRITING

Facing a Challenge When a Baltimore theater asked Israel Horovitz to adapt *A Christmas Carol* for the stage, he was faced with a particular challenge. From the seventh grade on, Horovitz had found reading Dickens something of a chore. "I hated reading Charles Dickens so completely," he says, "so absolutely, it took an enormous amount of courage to take on the adaptation."

Today, however, Horovitz is convinced that the English writer was a "masterful storyteller." If Dickens were alive today, Horovitz declares, "he would be our greatest television writer, or perhaps screenwriter."

DRAFTING

Staying Faithful to Dickens Horovitz had seen other Dickens adaptations, both on film and stage, but believed that "no one else had done an adaptation that was faithful to Dickens's own writing."

One Important Change Horovitz departed from Dickens's story in one respect. He gave the character Jacob Marley increased importance and frequently had him appear on stage while remaining invisible to Scrooge. In this way Marley can comment to the audience on what is occurring. Horovitz made sure, however, that "everything Marley says is taken directly from Dickens's own narrative." The playwright even memorized whole passages from the story "so that whenever I had to add a few lines of language to 'bridge' speeches and ideas, I was able to imitate Dickens's own language."

REVISING

First Alone, and Then With Others Horovitz wrote his draft of *Scrooge and Marley* "entirely on my own." Then, however, an old theater friend, the play's director, and even the actors "pitched in and helped me 'finish' the play . . . cut and change specific speeches, tighten and focus the play."

According to Horovitz, "This is business as usual for a playwright. The writing is an initially singular, lonely sport. But, in the end, it's very collaborative." Horovitz likes working with others; he calls the experience of collaborating "my kind of party."

PUBLISHING

A Global Stage Horovitz's plays have been produced all over the world and translated into thirty languages. He has even directed some of his plays in French, "a language I learned not in school, but in the rehearsal hall, speaking only lines memorized from my own plays!"

THINKING ABOUT THE PROCESS

1. Horovitz considers the help he gets finishing his plays a kind of "party." How do you think this attitude about revising could help you with your own writing?
2. **Write Your Own Adaptation** With some classmates, select a passage from a favorite story or novel that is especially dramatic. Then transform this passage into a scene from a play.

YOUR WRITING PROCESS

CREATIVE WRITING: WRITING A SPEECH

"Everything written is as good as it is dramatic."

Robert Frost

Imagine that you are a television scriptwriter. Your network has purchased the rights to produce one of the plays in this unit, but the script falls short of the allotted time slot by about three minutes. The director wants to lengthen the play by including a long speech by one speaker, and you have been asked to write it. The speech can occur at any point in the play, but it should include one character's thoughts, feelings, and observations.

Focus

Assignment: Write a speech that will become part of one of the plays in this unit.

Purpose: To extend the play by three minutes.

Audience: The television audience.

Prewriting

1. Study a dramatic speech or two. Read some long speeches in plays from this unit. For example, Marley has a long speech at the opening of *A Christmas Carol: Scrooge and Marley.* What makes his speech different from the rest of the play? Jot down a list of qualities that you think a long speech should have.

2. Consider possibilities. Think about each of the plays in this unit, and make some notes in a chart like the one that follows. Identify some places in the play where a speech could be inserted. Then decide what the speech might reveal about the character.

Student Model

Play	Where Speech Could Be Inserted	What It Reveals
"Monsters"	Before Figure One's voice at end	Don's thoughts and fears about Charlie and what is happening
"A Christmas Carol"	End of Act I, Scene iii	More of Scrooge's fear turning to disbelief then back to fear

3. Time is of the essence. Read a portion of a play aloud so that you can see how much dialogue and action take up three minutes of time.

4. Try on the voice. Imagine that you are the character who will be giving the speech. Freewrite, using the character's voice. What are you afraid of? What do you want to happen? What do you care about most?

Drafting

1. Dialogue *and* action. Remember that the three minutes can include both talk and action. Ask yourself what would be the best balance of these two elements for the speech you are writing.

2. Use smooth-and-easy transitions. Your speech should not seem different from the rest of the play. Don't change the setting, add a new plot twist, or do anything else that could jar or upset the flow of the action. Make sure that the end of your speech leads smoothly and logically to what follows.

Revising and Editing

1. Eliminate unnecessary words. Make your speech brief and concise. Don't waste words. If a word or phrase does not contribute to the speech, eliminate it!

> ### Student Model
>
> **Scrooge:** And now let us go ~~to your~~ home and enjoy the ~~finest, the best, the~~ most wonderful Christmas ever, with ~~your family~~, your wife, and your children, and with the wisdom of the past, present, and future!

2. Listen to your speech. Direct a reading that includes your speech and the surrounding dialogue. Assign your speech to a speaker, but assign the dialogue around your speech to several other students. Then listen carefully to the performance. Does your speech work as a bridge between what comes before and what follows? Does the speech make sense in itself? Take notes as you listen and ask for opinions from your "cast."

3. Use informal language. Remember that your words should sound like those your character would actually use. Include partial sentences, contractions, exclamations, and slang where appropriate. Make the style consistent with that in the existing script.

Grammar Tip

In all the plays in this unit, the writers use **ellipses** (. . .) to capture the flavor of speech. Sometimes ellipses indicate an unfinished thought, as in the following bit of dialogue from *A Christmas Carol: Scrooge and Marley:* "Please, I . . ." Other times, they indicate hesitation, as in this passage from *The Monsters Are Due on Maple Street:* "Then I take it this place . . . this Maple Street . . . is not unique."

Options for Publishing

- Tape-record students reading the portion of the play that includes your speech. Then play the recording for the class.
- Take the part of the speaker and present your speech to the class. You might even want to wear an appropriate costume or use props as you deliver your speech.
- After you have shared your speech, keep it in your portfolio.

Reviewing Your Writing Process

1. What was the most difficult part of writing your speech? Why?

2. Did you find it easier to write the speech itself or the stage directions? Explain.

YOUR WRITING PROCESS

EXPOSITION/PERSUASION: WRITING A CASTING MEMO

"The horror of that moment," the King went on, "I shall never forget!"

"You will," the Queen said, "if you don't make a memorandum of it."

Lewis Carroll

The job of a casting director is to match each role in a play or film with the perfect actor to play that role. Imagine that a casting director has asked you to write a memo describing a character in a play and recommending an actor to play that character. You can choose from among a broad range of well-known actors, or you may want to select a talented friend.

> **Focus**
>
> **Assignment:** Write a casting memo.
> **Purpose:** To describe a character in a play and recommend an actor to play that character.
> **Audience:** Your boss, the casting director.

Prewriting

1. Review the characters. Look back through the plays in this unit and list the characters that you imagined most clearly. Beside each name jot down a few descriptive phrases about that character. Also write a note or two to remind yourself why this character captured your interest. You might start with the phrase: "This character interested me because _____."

2. Who is available? With a partner make a list of your favorite actors or of your friends who enjoy acting. You might even flip through an entertainment magazine or two for ideas. Keeping in mind the roles you are offering, discuss with your partner whether certain actors are suitable for a role.

3. What is a memo? Memo is short for *memorandum*, a brief written communication used in business. (The term comes from a Latin word meaning "to be remembered.") If possible, look at some models of memos and note their style. For example, memos often begin with headings like the one in the model that follows. It is easy to see at a glance what the memo is about. ("Re" is short for "regarding.")

4. Scan the stage directions for details. Playwrights often include details, as part of the stage directions, about a character's appearance. Once you have decided which play you would like to cast, look through the script for such clues.

Drafting

1. Remember what the assignment asks for. The assignment asks for two things: a description of the character and a recommendation. Devote the first part of your memo to the description of the character and the second to your recommendation of an actor.

2. Keep the words flowing. Don't try to perfect your words and ideas at this stage. Just get them down on paper. You may want to write yourself a note in brackets if something puzzles you.

Revising and Editing

1. Is your memo businesslike? In revising your memo, eliminate passages where you have wandered off the track or have gotten caught up in your own opinions. You do not need to retell the story or to state obvious facts.

Student Model

Jacob Marley is "ancient, awful, dead-eyed" according to Israel Horovitz. He is a ghost, in fact, ~~and I have always been afraid of ghosts since I was a child. Jacob Marley was Scrooge's business partner.~~ He should be frightening to look at.

2. Read your draft aloud. Ask a classmate to listen to your draft and offer suggestions. Read it slowly and make notes to yourself as you go. Often you can hear an awkward or wordy phrase that your eyes may have missed. Then listen to your classmate's draft and offer suggestions.

RECLINING WOMAN, 1952
John Robinson

NONFICTION

Many people who love reading believe that the most interesting literature being written today is nonfiction. Nonfiction does not deal with imaginary people or events but with real life. The characters are real people and the events are actual happenings. If a work of nonfiction is concerned mainly with ideas or opinions, they are ideas or opinions taken from real life.

The world of nonfiction is a wide one. It includes true stories of people's lives and experiences. It includes thoughtful writings that instruct, persuade, or inform you. It includes diaries, speeches, letters, and magazine articles. Nonfiction is created by men and women who use words well. What they write has clarity, liveliness, interest, and style. When you read the nonfiction in this unit, try to notice these qualities. They contribute much to your reading enjoyment.

READING ACTIVELY

Nonfiction

Nonfiction is a type of literature that deals with real people, events, and ideas. Nonfiction may instruct you, entertain you, keep you informed about the world, or satisfy your curiosity about real people and things.

Reading nonfiction actively means interacting with and responding to the information the author presents. You can do this through the following strategies:

QUESTION Preview the material before you read it. Certain questions may come to mind: What is the author's purpose for writing? How does the author support the points presented? Why does the author include certain information? Look for answers to your questions as you read.

PREDICT Predict what the author will say about the topic. How will the author support his or her points? Make new predictions as you go along.

CONNECT Think of what you already know about the topic, and make connections to what the author is saying. Take in new facts and ideas as you read, and connect these to what you know. This will help you to understand the information presented.

EVALUATE What do you think of the author's conclusions? What have you learned?

RESPOND Think about what the author has said. Allow yourself to respond personally. How do you feel about the topic? What will you do with this information?

Try to use these strategies as you read the selections in this unit. They will help you increase your enjoyment and understanding of nonfiction.

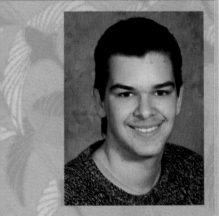

On pages 311–315 you can see an example of active reading by Craig Browning of Cass Technical School in Detroit, Michigan. The notes in the side column include Craig's thoughts and comments while reading "In Search of Our Mothers' Gardens." Your own thoughts as you read may be different, because each reader responds differently to an essay.

MODEL

from In Search of Our Mothers' Gardens

Alice Walker

Question: *Is the writer in search of actual gardens? Or will they represent something else?*

My mother made all the clothes we wore, even my brothers' overalls. She made all the towels and sheets we used. She spent the summers canning vegetables and fruits. She spent the winter evenings making quilts enough to cover all our beds.

Connect: *My mother doesn't make our clothes, can vegetables, or make quilts, but she has always worked hard to make sure we have what we need.*

During the "working" day, she labored beside—not behind—my father in the fields. Her day began before sunup, and did not end until late at night. There was never a moment for her to sit down, undisturbed, to unravel her own private thoughts; never a time free from interruption—by work or the noisy inquiries of her many children. And yet, it is to my mother—and all our mothers who were not famous—that I went in search of the secret of what has fed that muzzled[1] and often mutilated,[2] but vibrant,[3] creative spirit that the black woman has inherited, and that pops out in wild and unlikely places to this day.

Predict: *The fact that her mother worked beside her father indicates to me that she will be shown to be a woman with a lot of pride.*

But when, you will ask, did my overworked mother have time to know or care about feeding the creative spirit?

The answer is so simple that many of us have spent years discovering it. We have constantly looked high, when we should have looked high—and low.

For example: in the Smithsonian Institution[4] in Washington, D.C., there hangs a quilt unlike any other in the world. In fanciful,[5] inspired, and yet simple and identifiable figures,

Evaluate: *The author identifies with how this woman can create such beauty from limited resources like rags. She sees the artwork as a triumph over oppression.*

---

1. muzzled (muz′ 'ld) *adj.*: Prevented from expressing itself.
2. mutilated (myo͞ot′ 'l at′ id) *adj.*: Damaged or injured.
3. vibrant (vī′ brənt) *adj.*: Lively and energetic.
4. Smithsonian Institution: A group of museums with exhibits in the fields of science, art, and history.
5. fanciful (fan′ si fəl) *adj.*: Playfully imaginative.

it portrays the story of the Crucifixion.[6] It is considered rare, beyond price. Though it follows no known pattern of quilt-making, and though it is made of bits and pieces of worthless rags, it is obviously the work of a person of powerful imagination and deep spiritual feeling. Below this quilt I saw a note that says it was made by "an anonymous[7] Black woman in Alabama, a hundred years ago."

If we could locate this "anonymous" black woman from Alabama, she would turn out to be one of our grandmothers—an artist who left her mark in the only materials she could afford, and in the only medium her position in society allowed her to use.

Question: How does the parents' artwork flow through the children? How are the parents' ideas carried on by the child?

And so our mothers and grandmothers have, more often than not anonymously, handed on the creative spark, the seed of the flower they themselves never hoped to see: or like a sealed letter they could not plainly read.

And so it is, certainly, with my own mother. Unlike "Ma" Rainey's songs,[8] which retained their creator's name even while blasting forth from Bessie Smith's mouth,[9] no song or poem will bear my mother's name. Yet so many of the stories that I write, that we all write, are my mother's stories. Only recently did I fully realize this: that through years of listening to my mother's stories of her life, I have absorbed not only the stories themselves, but something of the manner in which she spoke, something of the urgency that involves the knowledge that her stories—like her life—must be recorded. It is probably for this reason that so much of what I have written is about characters whose counterparts in real life are so much older than I am.

Connect: Many people look to their elders for wisdom.

Evaluate: It has taken the author many years to realize that it was through her art that her mother lived.

But the telling of these stories, which came from my mother's lips as naturally as breathing, was not the only way my mother showed herself as an artist. For stories, too, were subject to being distracted, to dying without conclusion. Dinners must be started, and cotton must be gathered before the big rains. The artist that was and is my mother showed itself to me only after many years. This is what I finally noticed:

---

6. the Crucifixion (kro͞o′ sə fik′ shən): Jesus Christ's suffering and death on the cross.

7. anonymous (ə nän′ ə məs) *adj.*: With no name known.

8. "Ma" Rainey's songs: Gertrude ("Ma") Rainey, one of America's first blues singers, lived during the early years of this century.

9. Bessie Smith's mouth: Bessie Smith was a well-known blues singer (1898?–1937) who knew and learned from "Ma" Rainey.

Like Mem, a character in *The Third Life of Grange Copeland*,[10] my mother adorned with flowers whatever shabby house we were forced to live in. And not just your typical straggly[11] country stand of zinnias, either. She planted ambitious gardens—and still does—with over fifty different varieties of plants that bloom profusely from early March until late November. Before she left home for the fields, she watered her flowers, chopped up the grass, and laid out new beds. When she returned from the fields she might divide clumps of bulbs, dig a cold pit,[12] uproot and replant roses, or prune branches from her taller bushes or trees—until night came and it was too dark to see.

Whatever she planted grew as if by magic, and her fame as a grower of flowers spread over three counties. Because of her creativity with her flowers, even my memories of poverty are seen through a screen of blooms—sunflowers, petunias, roses, dahlias, forsythia, spirea, delphiniums, verbena . . . and on and on.

And I remember people coming to my mother's yard to be given cuttings from her flowers; I hear again the praise showered on her because whatever rocky soil she landed on, she

Predict: *The essay will show how the author's mother made sure she could always appreciate the beauty around her.*

Evaluate: *What seems to be only a screen actually turns the ugliness into beauty.*

---

10. *The Third Life of Grange Copeland:* The title of a novel by Alice Walker.
11. straggly (strag' lē) *adj.*: Spread out in an irregular way.
12. cold pit: A hole in which seedlings are planted at the beginning of the spring.

Connect: *People love to see beauty.*

Evaluate: *In the process of creating art, the mother becomes a living, breathing work of art herself.*

Question: *Is she saying that the women held their families together with a hard hand as well as a soft touch? Does a mother take on the hardness of the world to protect her children?*

turned into a garden. A garden so brilliant with colors, so original in its design, so magnificent with life and creativity, that to this day people drive by our house in Georgia—perfect strangers and imperfect strangers—and ask to stand or walk among my mother's art.

I notice that it is only when my mother is working in her flowers that she is radiant, almost to the point of being invisible—except as Creator: hand and eye. She is involved in work her soul must have. Ordering the universe in the image of her personal conception of Beauty.

Her face, as she prepares the Art that is her gift, is a legacy[13] of respect she leaves to me, for all that illuminates and cherishes life. She has handed down respect for the possibilities—and the will to grasp them.

For her, so hindered and intruded upon in so many ways, being an artist has still been a daily part of her life. This ability to hold on, even in very simple ways, is work black women have done for a very long time.

This poem is not enough, but it is something, for the woman who literally covered the holes in our walls with sunflowers:

> They were women then
> My mama's generation
> Husky of voice—Stout of
> Step
> With fists as well as
> Hands
> How they battered down
> Doors
> And ironed
> Starched white
> Shirts
> How they led
> Armies
> Headragged[14] Generals
> Across mined[15]
> Fields

---

13. legacy (leg′ ə sē) *n.*: Something handed down by a parent or an ancestor.

14. headragged (hed′ rag′d) *adj.*: With head wrapped around by a rag or kerchief.

15. mined (mīnd) *adj.*: Filled with buried explosives that are set to go off when stepped on.

> *Booby-trapped*[16]
> *Kitchens*
> *To discover books*
> *Desks*
> *A place for us*
> *How they knew what we*
> *Must know*
> *Without knowing a page*
> *Of it*
> *Themselves.*

Predict: *We will see how, through her mother's self-sacrifice, the child has become educated.*

Guided by my heritage of a love of beauty and a respect for strength—in search of my mother's garden, I found my own.

And perhaps in Africa over two hundred years ago, there was just such a mother; perhaps she painted vivid and daring decorations in oranges and yellows and greens on the walls of her hut; perhaps she sang—in a voice like Roberta Flack's[17]—*sweetly* over the compounds of her village; perhaps she wove the most stunning mats or told the most ingenious[18] stories of all the village storytellers. Perhaps she was herself a poet—though only her daughter's name is signed to the poems that we know.

Respond: *Our lives are reflections of the legacy left by our ancestors.*

Perhaps Phillis Wheatley's[19] mother was also an artist.

Perhaps in more than Phillis Wheatley's biological life is her mother's signature made clear.

---

16. booby-trapped (bo͞o′ bē trapt) *adj.*: With bombs or mines hidden and set to go off when someone touches or lifts an object.
17. Roberta Flack's: Roberta Flack is a contemporary black singer.
18. ingenious (in jēn′ yəs) *adj.*: Clever and inventive.
19. Phillis Wheatley's: Phillis Wheatley (1753?–1784) was a poet, considered the first important black writer in America.

Alice Walker (1944–   ), who was born in Eatonton, Georgia, is a black writer concerned with social injustice. A poet, novelist, biographer, and essayist, Walker has written widely about the experiences of women and black individuals and families. Her novel *The Color Purple*, which was made into a movie, was awarded a Pulitzer Prize in 1983. A major influence on Walker's life and writing has been her mother. She dedicated her novel *The Third Life of Grange Copeland* "for my mother, who made a way out of no way."

RESPONDING TO THE SELECTION

Your Response

1. Whom do you consider creative? How does that person express his or her creativity?

Recalling

2. In what two ways did Walker's mother reveal herself as an artist?
3. What legacies, or gifts, has Walker's mother given her daughter?

Interpreting

4. What does Walker mean when she writes, "We have constantly looked high, when we should have looked high—and low"?
5. Do you think Walker's poem is a fitting tribute to her mother? Explain your answer.
6. Explain the following statement: "In search of my mother's garden, I found my own."
7. Why does Walker call this selection "In Search of *Our* Mothers' Gardens" instead of "In Search of *My* Mother's Garden"?

Applying

8. In what way are the signatures of our parents and grandparents made clear through us?

ANALYZING LITERATURE

Understanding Essays About People

An essay is a work of nonfiction. One common topic for an essay is a remembered person. Often an essay about a remembered person contains anecdotes, or little stories, that reveal what the person is like. However, such an essay presents not only a vivid portrait of the subject but also explains the subject's importance to the writer. In this way the essay reveals both the subject and the writer.

1. In what way does Walker present her mother as a unique individual? In what way does she present her as representative of black women in general?
2. How would you describe Walker's attitude toward her mother?

CRITICAL THINKING AND READING

Understanding the Main Idea

The **main idea** is the most important idea the writer presents. In an essay the main idea is often expressed in a thesis statement near the beginning. The rest of the essay contains information that supports or clarifies the main idea.

1. Look again at the first two paragraphs. Which sentence expresses the main idea? Restate the main idea in your own words.
2. How does the anecdote of the quilt hanging in the Smithsonian Institution clarify the main idea?
3. Find one other detail that supports the main idea.
4. Find the sentence near the end of the selection that again expresses the main idea. Restate this sentence in your own words.

THINKING AND WRITING

Writing About a Remembered Person

List people who have been important in your life. Choose the person you think you can describe most fully. Next, list everything you can remember about this person, such as appearance, traits, quirks. Select details you would include in an essay. Write a first draft telling your best friend why this person is significant to you. When you review your essay, make sure you have included enough details to support your main idea. Prepare a final draft and share it with your classmates.

LEARNING OPTION

Cross-curricular Connection. Explore the music of famous African American singers. In her essay Alice Walker mentions Bessie Smith and Roberta Flack. Records and tapes by both singers are probably available in a nearby library, or your family members or friends might own some. Explore other African American singers of the past, such as Billie Holliday. Then listen to African American singers of today. How has the music changed over time?

Biographies and
Personal Accounts

SELF PORTRAIT, 1934
Malvin Johnson
National Museum of American Art

Eugenie Clark and the Sleeping Sharks

Biography

A **biography** is an account of a person's life written by someone else. Biographies often focus on the accomplishments of the people they describe. They also tell you about the difficulties these people had to overcome in order to reach their goals. An author usually chooses as the subject of the biography someone who has achieved something significant. Subjects of biographies may include baseball stars, political leaders, poets, kings and queens, generals, and scientists. "Eugenie Clark and the Sleeping Sharks," for example, is about a scientist with an unusual interest.

Focus

Have you ever seen a real shark in an aquarium, or have you seen sharks only on television and in the movies? Write down a brief account of what you know about sharks and how you feel about them. Do they frighten you? Do you find them fascinating? After reading this biography of Eugenie Clark, look at your writing to see if you have changed your mind at all about this mysterious animal.

Vocabulary

Knowing the following words will help you as you read "Eugenie Clark and the Sleeping Sharks."

assortment (ə sôrt′ mənt) *n.*: A group or collection of different kinds of things (p. 319)

repellent (ri pel′ ənt) *n.*: Something that pushes away (p. 319)

oozed (o͞ozd) *v.*: Flowed or leaked slowly (p. 319)

commotion (kə mō′ shən) *n.*: Noisy reaction; confusion (p. 322)

elusive (i lo͞o′ siv) *adj.*: Hard to find (p. 322)

diligently (dil′ ə jənt lē) *adv.*: With hard work; carefully (p. 324)

maneuver (mə no͞o′ vər) *n.*: A planned movement or procedure (p. 326)

Margery Facklam

(1927–   ) has been fascinated by the animal kingdom since she was a child. She pursued this interest by working as a volunteer at the Buffalo Zoo, in Buffalo, New York, and later she became the zoo's Educational Coordinator. She has also written a number of books about people involved with nature. In this biographical sketch, she tells about a scientist whose life-long study of sharks has earned her the nickname of the "shark lady."

Eugenie Clark
and the Sleeping Sharks

Margery Facklam

Sunlight sparkled on bright blue-green water as a small boat dropped anchor. Three divers wearing black wet suits adjusted their scuba gear. One diver leaned over the side of the boat and peered into the water. It was so clear he could see the rainbow assortment of fishes swimming around the coral reef.[1]

"Sharks below," he called.

"No problem," a second diver answered calmly. "Use this," she said, handing cans of shark repellent to the others.

When they had sprayed themselves all over with the repellent, the divers put on their masks and flipped backward out of the boat into the warm water. Two tiger sharks began to circle the divers. Silently they picked up speed to attack, but as they closed in on the swimmers, they slammed on invisible brakes. Suddenly their mouths seemed to be frozen open. They shook their heads as though trying to get rid of something. And the divers went about exploring the coral reef, unconcerned about the sharks.

So far, that scene is only make-believe. There is no shark repellent that really keeps sharks away, but there may be soon because Dr. Eugenie Clark was curious about a little fish called the Moses sole.

In 1960, Eugenie was netting fish in the Red Sea when she came across the fish known scientifically as *Pardachirus*; local fishermen called it the Moses sole. When she touched the fish, a milky substance oozed from the pores along its fins. It was slippery, and her fingers felt tingly and tight, the way they might feel if they fell asleep.

The Moses sole is a flatfish, like the flounder you buy at the market, and it got its name from a traditional story told in Israel. According to the legend, when Moses parted the Red Sea, this little fish was caught in the middle and split in half. Each half became a sole.

Eugenie is an ichthyologist,[2] a scientist who studies fish. She was working at the Marine Laboratory at the Hebrew University in Elat, Israel, when she decided to find out more about the sole's poison. A scientist had reported the poisonous substance in 1871, but no one had studied it further. When Eugenie tested it on sea urchins, starfish, and reef fishes, she found that small doses killed these creatures quickly. She began to wonder how it would work on larger fishes, especially sharks.

Three reef whitetip sharks lived in a tank at the laboratory, and they ate anything

---

1. coral reef: A ridge near the surface of the water made of countless skeletons of tiny ocean animals.

2. ichthyologist (ik′ thē äl′ ə jist)

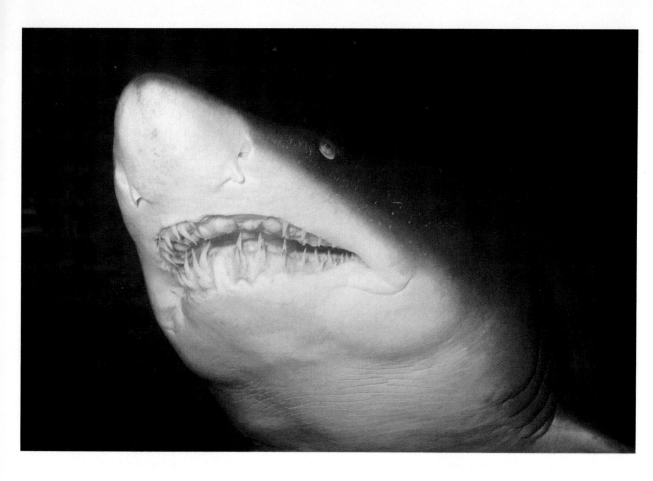

dropped into the water. One day as Eugenie was experimenting with the fish, she found one small Moses sole that had not been completely "milked" of its poison. She put a string through its gills, which did not hurt it, and lowered the fish into the shark's tank. The moment the sole touched the water, the sharks swept toward it with mouths open wide. But when they got within a few feet of the fish on the string, the sharks' jaws seemed to be frozen open. They dashed away, shaking their heads as though trying to get rid of something awful. For six hours Eugenie watched the sharks approach the sole, and the reactions were the same each time the sharks swam near the poisonous fish.

The use of this poison as a shark repellent was an exciting idea. So far everything invented to keep sharks away has not worked on all sharks all the time. Streams of air bubbles used as a barrier along beaches eventually attracted sharks, who seemed to enjoy the feeling of the bubbles as they swam through them. Different dyes that swimmers can release in the water only hide the swimmer from the shark temporarily but cannot keep a really hungry shark away. Lifeboats on ships and Navy planes are sometimes equipped with plastic bags large enough to hold a person. Stranded in the water, the person inflates the top ring and crawls into the tubelike bag. A shark cannot follow the scent of a human inside this bag, nor can it see kicking legs or blood from a wound. But such bags are not carried as regular equipment by swimmers at an ocean beach. A substance that can be sprayed on, the way mosquito repellent is, would be perfect.

But before Eugenie could experiment further on the Moses sole, she had to leave the Elat laboratory, and other work claimed her attention for many years. It wasn't until 1974 that she was able to collect some of the fish and test the shark-stopping poison. After dozens of experiments in tanks and in the sea, a final test was arranged to find out how free-swimming sharks reacted to the live Moses sole.

An eighty-foot shark line, with ten shorter lines dropping from it, was stretched close to the rocky Israeli coastline three feet underwater at a point where a ledge dropped off to a depth of one thousand feet. Each of the ten dropper lines was baited with parrot fish, groupers, nonpoisonous flatfish, and the Moses sole. As Eugenie, her fourteen-year-old son, and other assistants snorkeled[3] quietly along the underwater ledge and watched the sharks approach the bait at dawn or sunset, they saw the poison at work.

One by one the fish were gulped down by hungry sharks, but the Moses sole remained untouched. When Eugenie wiped the skin of a Moses sole with alcohol to remove the poison and tossed the fish into the water, a shark would instantly eat it. It was an excit-

ing discovery—a substance that could really stop a shark. Further work is being done now to make a chemical compound like the poison of the Moses sole that can be used as a reliable commercial shark repellent.

Eugenie knew she wanted to be an ichthyologist long before she knew the word meant "someone who studies fish." Her father died when she was very small, and she lived in New York City with her mother. When her mother had to work on Saturdays, Eugenie went to the old aquarium in Battery Park at the tip of Manhattan. The hours went quickly for her as she watched the colorful reef fishes and the graceful sea turtles. It wasn't long before she had her own collection of guppies and swordtail platys, and she became the youngest member of the Queens County Aquarium Society. She learned to keep careful records of her fish and their scientific names.

All during elementary school and high school, her mother encouraged her in her new interest. When she went to Hunter College in New York for a degree in biology, Mrs. Clark, aware of the limited job possibilities for women, suggested that Eugenie add typing and shorthand to her studies. But Eugenie never had the time or interest to do it. When she graduated from Hunter College during World War II, there were not many jobs for biologists, so she worked for a while at the Celanese Corporation as a chemist and attended graduate school at night.

She wrote later on, "In the field of science, a Ph.D. degree is handy to have although not absolutely necessary. One of the most brilliant and accomplished ichthyologists in the country never went to college, although later he became a university professor. But a person without a formal education has a more difficult time proving his worth, especially when applying for a position. A Ph.D. among your qualifications helps start

---

3. snorkeled (snôr′ k'ld) v.: Swam underwater using a snorkel, or breathing tube, that extends above the surface of the water.

things out on the right foot. I hoped to get this degree . . . my career had enough other disadvantages for a woman."

In 1947, the U.S. Fish and Wildlife Service was planning a survey of the Philippine Island area for possible fisheries. They needed a person who knew fish and chemistry. Eugenie was qualified. She applied for the job and got it.

"Several people were surprised that a girl had been hired for the job. Then it was called to someone's attention in Washington that I was the only female scientist on the program. Some commotion followed. I got as far as Hawaii, but my passport was mysteriously delayed because, they told me, the FBI had to check my Oriental [Eugenie's mother is Japanese] origin and connections. As far as I know they are still checking. They never did tell me I was cleared. After weeks of waiting, I accepted my fate and handed in my resignation to waiting hands. They hired a man in my place."

Being stranded in Hawaii was no hardship for Eugenie. For an ichthyologist, the freedom to dive among the fascinating fishes around the Hawaiian volcanic reefs[4] was as satisfying as being a cat free to roll in a meadow of catnip. But even that ended. She said later, "The longer you put off graduate studies, the harder it is to find the time and enthusiasm to go back to school." So she went back.

It takes years of study and research to complete a Ph.D. Very often the original research requires going into the field to learn about the subject firsthand.

"Women scientists have to buck some difficulties when it comes to field work," said Eugenie, "but I had one decided advantage. A man in my position often has a family to support and is not free to travel. I was independent and free to go anywhere and do anything I liked, and there was only my own neck to risk."

Eugenie went many places. She learned to dive while studying at Scripps Institute of Oceanography in California. She used her diving skills constantly in Micronesia in the Pacific Ocean, where she collected the *plectognaths* she was studying. These are small fish that live mostly in tropical waters near coral reefs. They include the triggerfish, porcupine fish, puffer, filefish, and boxfish.

One of her research fellowships took her to the Red Sea, where she found the Moses sole and collected the elusive garden eels that burrow in the ocean bottom. They are long, smooth fish that sway gently with the water currents as they feed upon small ocean creatures.

In Cairo, Egypt, Eugenie married a doctor she had met during her studies in the United States. When they returned to the States, Eugenie began the less glamorous part of being a scientist—sorting through notes and writing the scientific results of things she had found. And she began to raise a family.

In 1955, she was delighted to be asked to start a marine laboratory in Florida. Her husband was ready to open a medical office, and he agreed that Florida would be a good place to live. With their first two children, they moved to Florida's west coast, and Eugenie became the director of the Cape Haze Marine Laboratory. At first the laboratory was only a small wooden building, twelve by twenty feet, built on skids[5] so it could be moved if the first site did not work out. There was a dock and a boat for collecting.

---

4. volcanic reefs: Reefs built up on sunken volcanoes.

5. skids (skidz) *n.*: Planks or logs on which a heavy object can be slid.

Eugenie decided her first job should be to collect and identify all the local fishes.

The day after she arrived, she received a phone call from a doctor who needed shark livers for cancer research. She checked with the man who was going to handle the boat, and even before supplies were unpacked, they were in the shark-hunting business.

There are about 250 different sharks in the world, ranging in size from the 24-inch dogfish studied in biology classes to the 60-foot giant whale shark that eats plankton[6] and is so gentle that divers have hung onto its fins for a short ride. In between are the man-eaters we hear horror stories about. All the sharks belong to a group of fishes called cartilaginous. They have skeletons made not of bone but of cartilage, that bendable tissue our ears and noses are made of. And all the sharks are torpedo-shaped predators. They have many sets of razor-sharp teeth that they can fold back into a nonbiting position or thrust forward, ready to slice easily into prey. When a tooth is lost, another moves into place quite quickly.

The shark's always-staring eyes give it an evil appearance. It cannot blink or close its eyes for sleep, but it has a membrane that can cover the eye for protection.

Eugenie and her assistant began collecting some of the eighteen species of sharks found off the west coast of Florida. As she dissected hammerhead, nurse, lemon, and sand sharks on the dock, her children, neighbors, and children of visiting scientists watched. Sometimes she gave them jobs to do—measuring parts of the intestines, washing out a shark stomach, or hosing the dock after the dissection. Some of the sharks brought in on lines survived, and Eugenie wanted to know as much about the live animals as she knew about the organs she was weighing and measuring.

A stockaded pen, forty by seventy feet, was built next to the dock to hold the live sharks. A tiger shark, named Hazel, and a reddish color nurse shark, named Rosy, were two of the first guests in the pen, and a new problem arose. Nosy visitors, ignoring signs and fences, poked around and teased the animals. Eugenie was worried that both people and sharks would be hurt. When several of the sharks were killed by trespassers, Eugenie began to talk to groups in the community, especially at schools. She explained what sharks eat and how they live. Whenever people know about an animal, they fear it less. Soon the newspapers labeled her the "shark lady." It is a name that has stayed with her in spite of all her research with other sea creatures.

It wasn't long before Eugenie was involved in finding out how sharks learn. She enjoyed working with the live sharks day after day and getting to know the individual personalities of the animals.

When she set up experiments in which sharks would have to hit a target to receive the reward of food, one scientist warned her, "Don't be discouraged. It may take months." But he was wrong. The sharks learned quickly. When two lemon sharks learned that they could press an empty target and get food for it, Eugenie thought up harder problems for them to solve.

She trained them to swim to the end of the seventy-foot pen to pick up food after they pressed the target; and the female shark, who usually hung back and waited for the male to go first, quickly learned that if she circled the food drop area, she could pick up the male's reward while he was still at the target.

Eugenie stopped the tests during the winter months when the sharks lost interest

---

6. plankton (plaŋk′ tən) *n.*: Very small animal and plant life that floats or drifts in the water.

in food, but she found that the sharks remembered everything they had learned when spring training began. She moved on to more complicated learning. She used targets of different sizes, shapes, and designs, and she found that sharks of the same species, like other animals, have great individual differences. Some are smarter than others.

Scientists from all over the world visited the Cape Haze laboratory, studying everything from parasites[7] on sharks to microscopic life on algae. By the time Eugenie had been the laboratory's director for ten years, she had four children who enjoyed diving and helping her underwater explorations.

When Eugenie heard that there were "sleeping" sharks a diver could swim right up to, she was determined to find out more about them. With her daughter, Aya, and some research assistants, she went to Mexico's beautiful Isla Mujeres[8] off the tip of the Yucatán Peninsula.[9] There, in the warm, clear underwater caves, she found the great, sleek sharks of the requiem[10] family—the notorious man-eaters. They were lying on the floor of the caves, looking half-asleep even though their open, staring eyes watched the divers swim toward them.

Ordinarily, these sharks must keep moving. They swim constantly in order to keep the oxygen-rich water flowing through their mouths and out over the gills. When they rest on the bottom, they must pump water over the gills, and that takes more energy than leisurely swimming. But in the caves the sharks were motionless. Even with di-

vers churning up water and sand, and even with the glare of photographers' lights, the sharks acted as though they were tranquilized.

Eugenie and her team measured the depth and temperature of the water in the cave. They mapped the water currents by dropping dyes in the water and following their paths. They took water and rock samples for chemical analysis. And they noticed how clean the sharks looked compared to those caught by local fishermen. These cave sharks were not infested with the parasites found on most sharks.

They watched the "shark's faithful housekeeper," the small remora fish, as it worked around the eyes and mouths and into the gill slits of the resting sharks. The remora is a fish whose dorsal fin has evolved into a kind of suction disk on the top of its head. It can hitch a ride on a shark, sea turtle, whale, or even a ship by means of this suction disk. The remora picks up pieces of food dropped by its host. In the caves, however, these remoras worked diligently. Could it be that these "sleeping" sharks gathered in the caves for a health treatment? Were the caves cleaning stations?

Eugenie discovered fresh water seeping into the caves, diluting the sea water. There was less salt in the caves than in the open ocean. She remembered that when she was a kid she would put her saltwater fish into fresh water for a little while so that the parasites would drop off. Perhaps the same thing was happening with the sharks. Maybe these eighteen-foot tiger and reef sharks were intelligent enough to seek comfort in the caves.

Eugenie had taught sharks to ring a bell and push targets for meals and to distinguish right from wrong targets at the Florida laboratory. "Surely," she said, "they are capable of learning that in water of below-

---

7. parasites (par′ ə sīts) *n.*: Animals that live on other organisms in order to get food, protection, or both. Often, parasites harm the organisms on which they live.

8. Isla Mujeres (ēs′ lä moō her′ is)

9. Yucatán (yoō′ kä tän′) **Peninsula:** A projection of land, located mostly in southeast Mexico, that separates the Caribbean Sea from the Gulf of Mexico.

10. requiem (rek′ wē əm)

normal salinity, a condition they apparently must sense, annoying parasites loosen their grip."

The sharks may not know the water is less salty, but they know it feels good, so they go there. There are three such caves known around Mexico. Recently, some underwater caves full of sharks were reported around Japan. So many divers swarmed into the caves, catching sharks by the hundreds for food, that by the time Eugenie got to Japan to see them, the sharks had learned it was not safe to go to that cleaning station. Another cave was discovered near Japan, but Eugenie and other scientists are keeping its location secret to protect the sharks.

When asked about her life as a scientist, Eugenie said, "Being a scientist and a woman has some advantages, some disad-

vantages. It balances out. It takes some time to prove yourself initially, but then you get more credit than a man when you do accomplish something. For example, I am a diver, and when I dive into a cave with sharks it seems to be much more amazing than when a man does it."

The "shark lady" publicity has followed Eugenie, and no matter what she does, people think of her as the spear-carrying shark hunter. But she said, "I get just as excited about the garden eels in the Red Sea. Perhaps the discovery that thrilled me the most was the first hermaphroditic vertebrate,[11] a fish that changes sex."

---

11. **vertebrate** (vər′ tə brāt′): An animal with a backbone.

Looking for an excuse to go swimming one hot July day, Eugenie decided to take a census of the fish around a certain coral reef near the Cape Haze laboratory. She watched a tiny grouper fish, called *Serranus*. There were dozens of females swollen with eggs that would have to be laid and fertilized. But she could not find any males. No matter how long she followed some of these fish or what time of day she watched, no males appeared.

For a year she found no answers. But after many dives and long hours in the lab looking at fish under the microscope and watching live fish in lab tanks, she finally solved the mystery. *Serranus* is an hermaphrodite—an animal with both male and female parts. There are a few vertebrates that start life as one sex and turn into another, functioning as both in a lifetime, but never at the same time. *Serranus* turned out to be the first vertebrate found in which every individual could function at the same time as a male and female, able to fertilize itself. It seems, however, that this self-fertilization is used only in an emergency when a mate is not available. It was an exciting discovery that will probably lead to other investigations.

Eugenie Clark obviously loves what she does. "If from my research mankind gains some practical application or benefit, this is added delight and satisfaction to my work," she said. "But this is not what drives me to study late into the night or to watch a fish on the bottom making some strange maneuver until all the air in my scuba tank is gone and I hold my breath for those last few seconds."

MULTICULTURAL CONNECTION

Shark Folklore

Just as the author of this selection is fascinated by sharks, people throughout the world have been fascinated and often frightened by these large fish.

You don't have to see the movie *Jaws* to be afraid of sharks. In fact, in the twentieth century, these huge fish with terrifying jaws have come to be viewed as terrifying monsters. You may be surprised to learn, therefore, that not all cultures share this negative view of the shark and that in many cultures, the shark is revered and worshiped.

Legends about sharks. The folklore of the Solomon Islands in the South Pacific depicts sharks as almost human because they are believed to shelter the souls of people's ancestors. According to an ancient legend, a woman on one of the islands gave birth to a sharklike child, and through this child, sharks inherited human souls. Since then, there has been a bond between sharks and the inhabitants of the islands, who trust sharks and believe that they cannot be harmed by them.

Myths about sharks. In the myths of other Pacific islands, like Hawaii and Samoa, sharks are also portrayed favorably. They are thought of as just and compassionate, helping to guide lost fishermen safely back to shore.

Curiously, sharks were not mentioned in ancient European mythology or in animal legends like *Aesop's Fables*. More recently, however, they have been frequently described in the journals of sailors and explorers, and in novels about the sea.

Exploring on Your Own

You can learn more about how sharks are perceived in different cultures by further researching the mythology of people who live close to the sea.

RESPONDING TO THE SELECTION

Your Response

1. Would you like to observe sharks up close? Why or why not?

Recalling

2. Describe the experiment Clark set up in 1974 to test the effectiveness of the poison from the Moses sole.
3. How did Clark's being a woman work against her goal to become a scientist? In what ways did it serve as an advantage?
4. What did Clark discover about the "sleeping" sharks?

Interpreting

5. What qualities of a good scientist does Clark display?
6. What does Clark's response to the killing of her sharks by trespassers reveal about her?

Applying

7. Clark said, "But a person without a formal education has a more difficult time proving his worth, especially when applying for a position." Why do you think this is so?

ANALYZING LITERATURE

Understanding Biography

A **biography** is an account of a person's life written by someone else.

1. Is Eugenie Clark a good subject for a biography? Why or why not?
2. How do you think the author wants you to feel about her subject, Dr. Clark?

CRITICAL THINKING AND READING

Learning About the Scientific Method

The term **scientific method** refers to the systematic way in which scientists try to solve a prob-

lem. The basic steps in this method are the following:

    a. Stating the problem to be solved
    b. Gathering information about the problem
    c. Making a hypothesis, which is a possible explanation that can be tested
    d. Performing experiments to test the hypothesis
    e. Reaching a conclusion

With these steps in mind, look again at the passage on the "sleeping" sharks.

1. What problem was Dr. Clark trying to solve?
2. Show how she followed the second and third steps of the scientific method.
3. Think of an experiment that would test her hypothesis.

THINKING AND WRITING

Writing a Biography

Imagine that you want to make a television documentary about a person's life. You must convince the producers that your choice is a good one. Brainstorm to decide on a subject, and list some of the unusual or exciting events in this person's life. Then write a short biography of this person that will persuade the producers to use your idea. When you revise your biography, make sure you have included information about the difficulties that this person overcame.

LEARNING OPTION

Community Connections. Have you ever wondered what job or profession you might like as an adult? Think about two or three jobs that interest you and find out more about them. Discover what qualifications you need for each job, what subjects you should take in high school, and how much, if any, college education or other special training you might need. With your classmates use your findings to set up a vocational information center, making available the information all of you have found on different career possibilities.

GUIDE FOR READING

No Gumption

Autobiography

An **autobiography** is a person's own account of his or her life. Like biographies, autobiographies often focus on conflicts and struggles. However, an autobiography can reveal more about its subject's thoughts and feelings because the writer and the subject are the same person.

Focus

Role-play with a partner the following situation. One of you is trying to sell T-shirts to raise money for a local youth center. The other partner is an adult walking by. What would you say to the adult to get his or her attention? Give a good sales pitch for buying a T-shirt. Pay attention to your body language as well as to what you say. The partner portraying the customer should resist buying a shirt. After a few attempts at a sale, describe what you found easy about it and what you found difficult. Remember your responses as you read "No Gumption," which is about a boy who is not very good at selling things.

Vocabulary

Knowing the following words will help you as you read "No Gumption."

gumption (gump′ shən) *n.*: Courage and enterprise (p. 329)

appraisal (ə prā′ z′l) *n.*: Judgment of something's or someone's quality (p. 329)

paupers (pô′ pərz) *n.*: People who are very poor (p. 329)

interrogations (in ter′ ə gā′ shənz) *n.*: Situations where a person is formally questioned (p. 330)

crucial (kro͞o′ shəl) *adj.*: Of great importance (p. 331)

accessible (ak ses′ ə b′l) *adj.*: Easy to get (p. 331)

aptitude (ap′ tə to͞od′) *n.*: Talent; ability (p. 332)

maxims (mak′ simz) *n.*: Wise sayings (p. 334)

Russell Baker

(1925–   ) grew up in Virginia and New Jersey. When he was in the seventh grade, he decided to become a writer since "making up stories must surely be almost as much fun as reading them." As it turned out, he became a reporter rather than a fiction writer. He has won awards both for his newspaper column and for *Growing Up,* a book about his life. In this selection from his autobiography, you will learn about his failure in the business world—at a very young age!

No Gumption

Russell Baker

I began working in journalism when I was eight years old. It was my mother's idea. She wanted me to "make something" of myself and, after a level-headed appraisal of my strengths, decided I had better start young if I was to have any chance of keeping up with the competition.

The flaw in my character which she had already spotted was lack of "gumption." My idea of a perfect afternoon was lying in front of the radio rereading my favorite Big Little Book,[1] *Dick Tracy Meets Stooge Viller.* My mother despised inactivity. Seeing me having a good time in repose, she was powerless to hide her disgust. "You've got no more gumption than a bump on a log," she said. "Get out in the kitchen and help Doris do those dirty dishes."

My sister Doris, though two years younger than I, had enough gumption for a dozen people. She positively enjoyed washing dishes, making beds, and cleaning the house. When she was only seven she could carry a piece of short-weighted cheese back to the A&P, threaten the manager with legal action, and come back triumphantly with the full quarter-pound we'd paid for and a few ounces extra thrown in for forgiveness. Doris could have made something of herself if she hadn't been a girl. Because of this defect, however, the best she could hope for was a career as a nurse or schoolteacher, the only work that capable females were considered up to in those days.

This must have saddened my mother, this twist of fate that had allocated all the gumption to the daughter and left her with a son who was content with Dick Tracy and Stooge Viller. If disappointed, though, she wasted no energy on self-pity. She would make me make something of myself whether I wanted to or not. "The Lord helps those who help themselves," she said. That was the way her mind worked.

She was realistic about the difficulty. Having sized up the material the Lord had given her to mold, she didn't overestimate what she could do with it. She didn't insist that I grow up to be President of the United States.

Fifty years ago parents still asked boys if they wanted to grow up to be President, and asked it not jokingly but seriously. Many parents who were hardly more than paupers still believed their sons could do it. Abraham Lincoln had done it. We were only sixty-five years from Lincoln. Many a grandfather who walked among us could remember Lincoln's

---

1. Big Little Book: A small, inexpensive, illustrated book that often portrayed the adventures of comic strip heroes like Dick Tracy.

time. Men of grandfatherly age were the worst for asking if you wanted to grow up to be President. A surprising number of little boys said yes and meant it.

I was asked many times myself. No, I would say, I didn't want to grow up to be President. My mother was present during one of these interrogations. An elderly uncle, having posed the usual question and exposed my lack of interest in the Presidency, asked, "Well, what *do* you want to be when you grow up?"

I loved to pick through trash piles and collect empty bottles, tin cans with pretty labels, and discarded magazines. The most de-sirable job on earth sprang instantly to mind. "I want to be a garbage man," I said.

My uncle smiled, but my mother had seen the first distressing evidence of a bump budding on a log. "Have a little gumption, Russell," she said. Her calling me Russell was a signal of unhappiness. When she approved of me I was always "Buddy."

When I turned eight years old she decided that the job of starting me on the road toward making something of myself could no longer be safely delayed. "Buddy," she said one day, "I want you to come home right after school this afternoon. Somebody's coming and I want you to meet him."

When I burst in that afternoon she was in conference in the parlor with an executive of the Curtis Publishing Company. She introduced me. He bent low from the waist and shook my hand. Was it true as my mother had told him, he asked, that I longed for the opportunity to conquer the world of business?

My mother replied that I was blessed with a rare determination to make something of myself.

"That's right," I whispered.

"But have you got the grit, the character, the never-say-quit spirit it takes to succeed in business?"

My mother said I certainly did.

"That's right," I said.

He eyed me silently for a long pause, as though weighing whether I could be trusted to keep his confidence, then spoke man-to-man. Before taking a crucial step, he said, he wanted to advise me that working for the Curtis Publishing Company placed enormous responsibility on a young man. It was one of the great companies of America. Perhaps the greatest publishing house in the world. I had heard, no doubt, of the *Saturday Evening Post*?

Heard of it? My mother said that everyone in our house had heard of the *Saturday Post* and that I, in fact, read it with religious devotion.

Then doubtless, he said, we were also familiar with those two monthly pillars of the magazine world, the *Ladies Home Journal* and the *Country Gentleman*.

Indeed we were familiar with them, said my mother.

Representing the *Saturday Evening Post* was one of the weightiest honors that could be bestowed in the world of business, he said. He was personally proud of being a part of that great corporation.

My mother said he had every right to be.

Again he studied me as though debating whether I was worthy of a knighthood. Finally: "Are you trustworthy?"

My mother said I was the soul of honesty.

"That's right," I said.

The caller smiled for the first time. He told me I was a lucky young man. He admired my spunk. Too many young men thought life was all play. Those young men would not go far in this world. Only a young man willing to work and save and keep his face washed and his hair neatly combed could hope to come out on top in a world such as ours. Did I truly and sincerely believe that I was such a young man?

"He certainly does," said my mother.

"That's right," I said.

He said he had been so impressed by what he had seen of me that he was going to make me a representative of the Curtis Publishing Company. On the following Tuesday, he said, thirty freshly printed copies of the *Saturday Evening Post* would be delivered at our door. I would place these magazines, still damp with the ink of the presses, in a handsome canvas bag, sling it over my shoulder, and set forth through the streets to bring the best in journalism, fiction, and cartoons to the American public.

He had brought the canvas bag with him. He presented it with reverence fit for a chasuble.[2] He showed me how to drape the sling over my left shoulder and across the chest so that the pouch lay easily accessible to my right hand, allowing the best in journalism, fiction, and cartoons to be swiftly extracted and sold to a citizenry whose happiness and security depended upon us soldiers of the free press.

The following Tuesday I raced home from school, put the canvas bag over my

---

2. chasuble (chaz' yoob'l) *n.*: A sleeveless outer garment worn by priests.

shoulder, dumped the magazines in, and, tilting to the left to balance their weight on my right hip, embarked on the highway of journalism.

We lived in Belleville, New Jersey, a commuter town at the northern fringe of Newark. It was 1932, the bleakest year of the Depression. My father had died two years before, leaving us with a few pieces of Sears, Roebuck furniture and not much else, and my mother had taken Doris and me to live with one of her younger brothers. This was my Uncle Allen. Uncle Allen had made something of himself by 1932. As salesman for a soft-drink bottler in Newark, he had an income of $30 a week; wore pearl-gray spats,[3] detachable collars, and a three-piece suit; was happily married; and took in threadbare relatives.

With my load of magazines I headed toward Belleville Avenue. That's where the people were. There were two filling stations at the intersection with Union Avenue, as well as an A&P, a fruit stand, a bakery, a barber shop, Zuccarelli's drugstore, and a diner shaped like a railroad car. For several hours I made myself highly visible, shifting position now and then from corner to corner, from shop window to shop window, to make sure everyone could see the heavy black lettering on the canvas bag that said *The Saturday Evening Post*. When the angle of the light indicated it was suppertime, I walked back to the house.

"How many did you sell, Buddy?" my mother asked.

"None,"

"Where did you go?"

"The corner of Belleville and Union Avenues."

"What did you do?"

"Stood on the corner waiting for somebody to buy a *Saturday Evening Post*."

"You just stood there?"

"Didn't sell a single one."

"For God's sake, Russell!"

Uncle Allen intervened. "I've been thinking about it for some time," he said, "and I've about decided to take the *Post* regularly. Put me down as a regular customer." I handed him a magazine and he paid me a nickel. It was the first nickel I earned.

Afterwards my mother instructed me in salesmanship. I would have to ring doorbells, address adults with charming self-confidence, and break down resistance with a sales talk pointing out that no one, no matter how poor, could afford to be without the *Saturday Evening Post* in the home.

I told my mother I'd changed my mind about wanting to succeed in the magazine business.

"If you think I'm going to raise a good-for-nothing," she replied, "you've got another think coming." She told me to hit the streets with the canvas bag and start ringing doorbells the instant school was out next day. When I objected that I didn't feel any aptitude for salesmanship, she asked how I'd like to lend her my leather belt so she could whack some sense into me. I bowed to superior will and entered journalism with a heavy heart.

My mother and I had fought this battle almost as long as I could remember. It probably started even before memory began, when I was a country child in northern Virginia and my mother, dissatisfied with my father's plain workman's life, determined that I would not grow up like him and his people, with calluses on their hands, overalls on their backs, and fourth-grade educations in their heads. She had fancier ideas of life's

---

3. spats (spats) *n.*: Pieces of cloth or leather that cover the upper part of the shoe or ankle.

possibilities. Introducing me to the *Saturday Evening Post*, she was trying to wean me as early as possible from my father's world where men left with lunch pails at sunup, worked with their hands until the grime ate into the pores, and died with a few sticks of mail-order furniture as their legacy. In my mother's vision of the better life there were desks and white collars, well-pressed suits, evenings of reading and lively talk, and perhaps—if a man were very, very lucky and hit the jackpot, really made something important of himself—perhaps there might be a fantastic salary of $5,000 a year to support a big house and a Buick with a rumble seat[4] and a vacation in Atlantic City.

And so I set forth with my sack of magazines. I was afraid of the dogs that snarled behind the doors of potential buyers. I was timid about ringing the doorbells of strangers, relieved when no one came to the door, and scared when someone did. Despite my mother's instructions, I could not deliver an engaging sales pitch. When a door opened I simply asked, "Want to buy a *Saturday Evening Post*?" In Belleville few persons did. It was a town of 30,000 people, and most weeks I rang a fair majority of its doorbells. But I rarely sold my thirty copies. Some weeks I canvassed the entire town for six days and still had four or five unsold magazines on Monday evening; then I dreaded the coming of Tuesday morning, when a batch of thirty fresh *Saturday Evening Posts* was due at the front door.

"Better get out there and sell the rest of those magazines tonight," my mother would say.

I usually posted myself then at a busy intersection where a traffic light controlled

commuter flow from Newark. When the light turned red I stood on the curb and shouted my sales pitch at the motorists.

"Want to buy a *Saturday Evening Post*?"

One rainy night when car windows were sealed against me I came back soaked and with not a single sale to report. My mother beckoned to Doris.

"Go back down there with Buddy and show him how to sell these magazines," she said.

Brimming with zest, Doris, who was then seven years old, returned with me to the corner. She took a magazine from the bag, and when the light turned red she

---

4. rumble seat: In early automobiles, an open seat in the rear of the car that could be folded shut.

strode to the nearest car and banged her small fist against the closed window. The driver, probably startled at what he took to be a midget assaulting his car, lowered the window to stare, and Doris thrust a *Saturday Evening Post* at him.

"You need this magazine," she piped, "and it only costs a nickel."

Her salesmanship was irresistible. Before the light changed half a dozen times she disposed of the entire batch. I didn't feel humiliated. To the contrary. I was so happy I decided to give her a treat. Leading her to the vegetable store on Belleville Avenue, I bought three apples, which cost a nickel, and gave her one.

"You shouldn't waste money," she said.

"Eat your apple." I bit into mine.

"You shouldn't eat before supper," she said. "It'll spoil your appetite."

Back at the house that evening, she dutifully reported me for wasting a nickel. Instead of a scolding, I was rewarded with a pat on the back for having the good sense to buy fruit instead of candy. My mother reached into her bottomless supply of maxims and told Doris, "An apple a day keeps the doctor away."

By the time I was ten I had learned all my mother's maxims by heart. Asking to stay up past normal bedtime, I knew that a refusal would be explained with, "Early to bed and early to rise, makes a man healthy, wealthy, and wise." If I whimpered about having to get up early in the morning, I could depend on her to say, "The early bird gets the worm."

The one I most despised was, "If at first you don't succeed, try, try again." This was the battle cry with which she constantly sent me back into the hopeless struggle whenever I moaned that I had rung every doorbell in town and knew there wasn't a single potential buyer left in Belleville that week. After listening to my explanation, she handed me the canvas bag and said, "If at first you don't succeed . . ."

Three years in that job, which I would gladly have quit after the first day except for her insistence, produced at least one valuable result. My mother finally concluded that I would never make something of myself by pursuing a life in business and started considering careers that demanded less competitive zeal.

One evening when I was eleven I brought home a short "composition" on my summer vacation which the teacher had graded with an A. Reading it with her own schoolteacher's eye, my mother agreed that it was top-drawer seventh grade prose and complimented me. Nothing more was said about it immediately, but a new idea had taken life in her mind. Halfway through supper she suddenly interrupted the conversation.

"Buddy," she said, "maybe you could be a writer."

I clasped the idea to my heart. I had never met a writer, had shown no previous urge to write, and hadn't a notion how to become a writer, but I loved stories and thought that making up stories must surely be almost as much fun as reading them. Best of all, though, and what really gladdened my heart, was the ease of the writer's life. Writers did not have to trudge through the town peddling from canvas bags, defending themselves against angry dogs, being rejected by surly strangers. Writers did not have to ring doorbells. So far as I could make out, what writers did couldn't even be classified as work.

I was enchanted. Writers didn't have to have any gumption at all. I did not dare tell anybody for fear of being laughed at in the schoolyard, but secretly I decided that what I'd like to be when I grew up was a writer.

RESPONDING TO THE SELECTION

Your Response

1. Do you agree with Russell's mother that he has no "gumption"? Why or why not?

Recalling

2. How does Russell's mother try to repair his flaw when he is eight?
3. How does Russell feel about selling magazines?
4. What does his mother conclude after he has worked at his job for three years?
5. What is his mother's new plan for his career?

Interpreting

6. What qualities prevent him from being a good salesman? How might these same qualities help him in his chosen career?
7. How does Baker show a sense of humor in the way that he writes about this part of his life? Do you think he thought the situation humorous at the time the events were happening to him? Find evidence to support your answer.
8. How does Baker's sense of humor affect your reaction to the essay?

Applying

9. How does the description of Doris in the third paragraph show the different expectations people had for boys and for girls? Have these expectations changed since the time that this selection takes place? Support your answer.

ANALYZING LITERATURE

Understanding Autobiography

A person's account of his or her own life is called an **autobiography.** Such accounts include not only the facts of the writers' lives but their thoughts and feelings as well. In "No Gumption," Russell Baker gives you first-hand information about what happened when his mother tried to make him into a successful salesman at the age of eight.

1. What is the main problem that Baker faces during this part of his life?
2. Find a passage where he reveals his thoughts or feelings about this problem.
3. Would his account have been as humorous if he had written it as a boy? Why or why not?
4. Why is it that the passage of time can make events that seemed terrible when they happened now seem humorous?
5. How might the account of these events be different if Doris had written it?

CRITICAL THINKING AND READING

Comparing and Contrasting Characters

Comparing characters means seeing how they are similar. **Contrasting** them means finding how they are different. Although the main character of an autobiography is the writer, other characters will appear also. By comparing and contrasting these characters with the writer, you can gain a better idea of his or her personality.

1. How do Russell's and Doris's attitudes toward household chores differ?
2. Why was Doris better at selling magazines?
3. How does the incident where Russell buys an apple reveal a difference between them?
4. In what ways are both Doris and Russell admirable?

THINKING AND WRITING

Writing an Autobiographical Sketch

You have just started writing to a student your age in another country. Now that you have agreed to exchange letters, you want to tell this student something about your life. Think of a problem you faced when you were in kindergarten or first grade that now seems humorous to you. Before writing about this incident in a letter, list the most interesting and amusing parts of the story. Then turn this list into a humorous autobiographical sketch. When you revise your letter, make sure your description is clear and humorous. Then proofread your letter and prepare a final draft.

GUIDE FOR READING

Ernesto Galarza

(1905–1984) was born in the Mexican town of Jalcocotán. When his family resettled in California, they struggled to make ends meet. Ernesto was a good student. He eventually became a gifted teacher and writer. *Barrio Boy,* his most successful book, tells the story of his childhood in California. In this section from *Barrio Boy,* he tells of the frightening experience of attending school for the first time in a new country.

from Barrio Boy

The Narrator in Autobiography

The **narrator** of a work is the person who tells the story. In an autobiography the narrator is the writer telling you about his or her life. Ernesto Galarza, for example, is the narrator of *Barrio Boy.* Like most writers of autobiography, he refers to himself as "I" and tells you his thoughts and feelings about people and events.

Focus

Sometimes making a big change in your life can be difficult. For instance, have you always gone to the same school? Maybe you have moved to a new school once in your life, or possibly more than once. If you have changed schools, write about the way you felt when starting at the new school. If you've always attended the same school, describe how you would feel if you found out you had to move to a new school. Your writing will help you understand the boy's feelings in the essay you are about to read.

Vocabulary

Knowing the following words will help you as you read this excerpt from *Barrio Boy.*

barrio (bär′ ē ō) *n.*: Part of a town or city where most of the people are Hispanic (p. 337)

menace (men′ is) *n.*: Danger; threat (p. 337)

formidable (fôr′ mə də bəl) *adj.*: Impressive (p. 338)

mobilized (mō′ bə līzd′) *v.*: Put into motion (p. 338)

interpreter (in tʉr′ prə tər) *n.*: Someone who translates from one language into another (p. 338)

radiant (rā′ dē ənt) *adj.*: Shining brightly (p. 338)

consultations (kän′ səl tā′ sʰənz) *n.*: Discussions (p. 338)

persistently (pər sis′ tənt lē) *adv.*: Constantly (p. 338)

grieving (grēv′ iŋ) *v.*: Feeling sorrow for a loss (p. 339)

from **Barrio Boy**

Ernesto Galarza

My mother and I walked south on Fifth Street one morning to the corner of Q Street and turned right. Half of the block was occupied by the Lincoln School. It was a three-story wooden building, with two wings that gave it the shape of a double-T connected by a central hall. It was a new building, painted yellow, with a shingled roof that was not like the red tile of the school in Mazatlán. I noticed other differences, none of them very reassuring.

We walked up the wide staircase hand in hand and through the door, which closed by itself. A mechanical contraption screwed to the top shut it behind us quietly.

Up to this point the adventure of enrolling me in the school had been carefully rehearsed. Mrs. Dodson had told us how to find it and we had circled it several times on our walks. Friends in the *barrio* explained that the director was called a principal, and that it was a lady and not a man. They assured us that there was always a person at the school who could speak Spanish.

Exactly as we had been told, there was a sign on the door in both Spanish and English: "Principal." We crossed the hall and entered the office of Miss Nettie Hopley.

Miss Hopley was at a roll-top desk to one side, sitting in a swivel chair that moved on wheels. There was a sofa against the opposite wall, flanked by two windows and a door that opened on a small balcony. Chairs were set around a table and framed pictures hung on the walls of a man with long white hair and another with a sad face and a black beard.

The principal half turned in the swivel chair to look at us over the pinch glasses crossed on the ridge of her nose. To do this she had to duck her head slightly as if she were about to step through a low doorway.

What Miss Hopley said to us we did not know but we saw in her eyes a warm welcome and when she took off her glasses and straightened up she smiled wholeheartedly, like Mrs. Dodson. We were, of course, saying nothing, only catching the friendliness of her voice and the sparkle in her eyes while she said words we did not understand. She signaled us to the table. Almost tiptoeing across the office, I maneuvered myself to keep my mother between me and the gringo lady. In a matter of seconds I had to decide whether she was a possible friend or a menace. We sat down.

Then Miss Hopley did a formidable thing. She stood up. Had she been standing when we entered she would have seemed tall. But rising from her chair she soared. And what she carried up and up with her was a buxom superstructure,[1] firm shoulders, a straight sharp nose, full cheeks slightly molded by a curved line along the nostrils, thin lips that moved like steel springs, and a high forehead topped by hair gathered in a bun. Miss Hopley was not a giant in body but when she mobilized it to a standing position she seemed a match for giants. I decided I liked her.

She strode to a door in the far corner of the office, opened it and called a name. A boy of about ten years appeared in the doorway. He sat down at one end of the table. He was brown like us, a plump kid with shiny black hair combed straight back, neat, cool, and faintly obnoxious.

Miss Hopley joined us with a large book and some papers in her hand. She, too, sat down and the questions and answers began by way of our interpreter. My name was Ernesto. My mother's name was Henriqueta. My birth certificate was in San Blas. Here was my last report card from the Escuela Municipal Numero 3 para Varones of Mazatlán,[2] and so forth. Miss Hopley put things down in the book and my mother signed a card.

As long as the questions continued, Doña[3] Henriqueta could stay and I was secure. Now that they were over, Miss Hopley saw her to the door, dismissed our interpreter and without further ado took me by the hand and strode down the hall to Miss Ryan's first grade.

Miss Ryan took me to a seat at the front of the room, into which I shrank—the better to survey her. She was, to skinny, somewhat runty me, of a withering height when she patrolled the class. And when I least expected it, there she was, crouching by my desk, her blond radiant face level with mine, her voice patiently maneuvering me over the awful idiocies of the English language.

During the next few weeks Miss Ryan overcame my fears of tall, energetic teachers as she bent over my desk to help me with a word in the pre-primer. Step by step, she loosened me and my classmates from the safe anchorage of the desks for recitations at the blackboard and consultations at her desk. Frequently she burst into happy announcements to the whole class. "Ito can read a sentence," and small Japanese Ito, squint-eyed and shy, slowly read aloud while the class listened in wonder: "Come, Skipper, come. Come and run." The Korean, Portuguese, Italian, and Polish first graders had similar moments of glory, no less shining than mine the day I conquered "butterfly," which I had been persistently pronouncing in standard Spanish as boo-ter-flee. "Children," Miss Ryan called for attention. "Ernesto has learned how to pronounce *butterfly!*" And I proved it with a perfect imitation of Miss Ryan. From that celebrated success, I was soon able to match Ito's progress as a sentence reader with "Come, butterfly, come fly with me."

Like Ito and several other first graders who did not know English, I received private lessons from Miss Ryan in the closet, a narrow hall off the classroom with a door at each end. Next to one of these doors Miss Ryan placed a large chair for herself and a small one for me. Keeping an eye on the class

---

1. buxom superstructure: Full figure.
2. Escuela Municipal Numero 3 para Varones of Mazatlán (es kwä lə mōō nē sē päl nōō′me rô träs pärä vä rō′nas mä sät län′): Municipal School Number 3 for Boys of Mazatlán.
3. doña (dô′ nyä): A Spanish title of respect meaning "lady" or "madam".

through the open door she read with me about sheep in the meadow and a frightened chicken going to see the king, coaching me out of my phonetic ruts in words like *pasture*, *bow-wow-wow*, *hay*, and *pretty*, which to my Mexican ear and eye had so many unnecessary sounds and letters. She made me watch her lips and then close my eyes as she repeated words I found hard to read. When we came to know each other better, I tried interrupting to tell Miss Ryan how we said it in Spanish. It didn't work. She only said "oh" and went on with *pasture*, *bow-wow-wow*, and *pretty*. It was as if in that closet we were both discovering together the secrets of the English language and grieving together over the tragedies of Bo-Peep. The main reason I was graduated with honors from the first grade was that I had fallen in love with Miss Ryan. Her radiant, nononsense character made us either afraid not to love her or love her so we would not be afraid, I am not sure which. It was not only that we sensed she was with it, but also that she was with us.

Like the first grade, the rest of the Lincoln School was a sampling of the lower part of town where many races made their home.

from *Barrio Boy*   339

My pals in the second grade were Kazushi, whose parents spoke only Japanese; Matti, a skinny Italian boy; and Manuel, a fat Portuguese who would never get into a fight but wrestled you to the ground and just sat on you. Our assortment of nationalities included Koreans, Yugoslavs, Poles, Irish, and home-grown Americans.

At Lincoln, making us into Americans did not mean scrubbing away what made us originally foreign. The teachers called us as our parents did, or as close as they could pronounce our names in Spanish or Japanese. No one was ever scolded or punished for speaking in his native tongue on the playground. Matti told the class about his mother's down quilt, which she had made in Italy with the fine feathers of a thousand geese. Encarnación acted out how boys learned to fish in the Philippines. I astounded the third grade with the story of my travels on a stagecoach, which nobody else in the class had seen except in the museum at Sutter's Fort. After a visit to the Crocker Art Gallery and its collection of heroic paintings of the golden age of California, someone showed a silk scroll with a Chinese painting. Miss Hopley herself had a way of expressing wonder over these matters before a class, her eyes wide open until they popped slightly. It was easy for me to feel that becoming a proud American, as she said we should, did not mean feeling ashamed of being a Mexican.

RESPONDING TO THE SELECTION

Your Response

1. Have you ever felt the way young Ernesto felt in his new school? Explain.

Recalling

2. Why is Ernesto nervous at the start of this selection?
3. How does Miss Hopley reassure him?
4. Why is he afraid of Miss Ryan at first?
5. How does Miss Ryan make Ernesto and his classmates feel successful?

Interpreting

6. Explain the writer's statement that Miss Ryan was both "with it" and "with us."
7. What is the main problem that Ernesto faces during this part of his life?

8. What is the meaning of the title?

Applying

9. What qualities does a person need in order to make someone feel at home in a strange situation?
10. How would you make foreign students feel more at home in a school?

ANALYZING LITERATURE

Thinking About the Narrator

The **narrator** of a work is the person who tells the story. The narrator of an autobiography is the author. However, the narrator often tells about a different time in life. In this selection, the older, maturer Ernesto Galarza tells about the young boy Ernesto.

Narrators of autobiographies, like Ernesto Galarza, refer to themselves as "I" and tell you their thoughts and feelings about the events of their lives. In this selection from *Barrio Boy,* Galarza focuses on the problems he faced and overcame as a new, Spanish-speaking student in an American school.

1. Find three places where Galarza refers to himself as "I."
2. Identify two passages where Galarza reports his thoughts or feelings.
3. Most readers probably feel glad when Galarza overcomes his problems. Why might readers be less involved if Galarza himself were not the narrator?
4. In what ways do you think the narrator Ernesto Galarza is different from the young boy Ernesto? Find evidence to support your answer.

CRITICAL THINKING AND READING

Understanding Stereotypes

A **stereotype** is a negative idea about the traits or behavior of a group of people. This idea does not let you see the individuals of that group for who they are. For example, Ernesto feels threatened by "tall, energetic teachers." Since Miss Ryan is a member of this group, he is afraid of her. However, as he begins to know her, he realizes that his stereotype was wrong.

1. Judging by Galarza's experience, what is the best way to overcome stereotypes?
2. Galarza comments, "At Lincoln, making us into

Americans did not mean scrubbing away what made us originally foreign." What does he mean by this statement?

THINKING AND WRITING

Writing About a School Experience

Imagine that a young friend of yours is about to go to a new school. You want to encourage that person. To do so, write an account of your own first time in a strange situation. Write an autobiographical sketch that your young friend will enjoy. When you revise the sketch, make sure you have used the word "I" when talking about yourself, just as Galarza does. Proofread your account and share it with your classmates.

LEARNING OPTIONS

1. **Multicultural Activity.** What would you do if a new student who did not speak English joined your class? What would you do to make the person comfortable? How would you communicate? Role-play with a friend such a scene. You or some of your classmates may be able to role-play some of your actual experiences when a new student has come into the class.
2. **Writing.** Have you ever known a teacher or other adult of whom you were afraid, but only at first? What about him or her frightened you? How did your feelings toward this person change? Write an autobiographical sketch about your experiences with an impressive person whom you came to admire.

GUIDE FOR READING

A Time of Beginnings

Third-Person Narrative in Autobiography

While in most autobiographies the writers refer to themselves as "I," Jade Snow Wong refers to herself by name or as "she." This method of writing is called **third-person narrative.** Wong explains this unusual practice in the introduction to her autobiography, telling readers about the importance of modesty in the Chinese tradition. According to this tradition, it is "unnecessary to sign works of art and unbecoming to talk at length using 'I' or 'me.'"

Jade Snow Wong

(1922–   ) grew up in San Francisco's Chinatown. As a girl, she tried to learn American customs while her parents followed a traditional Chinese way of life. Wong tells about this period of her life in her popular autobiography *Fifth Chinese Daughter* (1950). In 1975, she published the story of her adult life in *No Chinese Stranger.* "A Time of Beginnings," which comes from that later book, describes how she fought against odds to become an artist and a businesswoman.

Focus

Do you ever make things with your hands? Maybe you enjoy sewing clothes or building unusual things like birdhouses. Maybe you build models, make collages, or cook. You might even make ceramics as does Jade Snow Wong, the subject of the autobiography you are about to read. With a group of three or four classmates, discuss what kind of work you do with your hands. Each of you should share why you enjoy the activity. Does making things always come easy for you, or do you sometimes feel frustrated? As you read, compare your experiences with Jade Snow Wong's.

Vocabulary

Knowing the following words will help you as you read "A Time of Beginnings."

ironically (ī rän′ ik lē) *adv.*: In a way different from what is expected (p. 343)

prevalent (prev′ ə lənt) *adj.*: Widely accepted (p. 343)

utilizing (yōōt′ 'l īz′ iŋ) *v.*: Using (p. 343)

catastrophe (kə tas′ trə fē) *n.*: Sudden disaster or misfortune (p. 345)

immeasurably (i mezh′ ər əb′ lē) *adv.*: Extremely; very (p. 345)

comparable (käm′ pər ə b'l) *adj.*: Similar (p. 345)

liability (lī′ ə bil′ ə tē) *n.*: Disadvantage (p. 345)

aesthetically (es thet′ ik lē) *adv.*: From an artistic point of view (p. 347)

A Time of Beginnings

Jade Snow Wong

After Jade Snow began working in Mr. Fong's window, which confined her clay spatters, her activity revealed for the first time to Chinatown residents an art which had distinguished Chinese culture. Ironically, it was not until she was at college that she became fascinated with Tang and Sung Dynasty[1] achievements in clay, a thousand years ago.

Her ability to master pottery made her father happy, for Grandfather Wong believed that a person who could work with his hands would never starve. When Father Wong was young, Grandfather made him learn how to hand-pierce and stitch slipper soles, and how to knot Chinese button heads, both indispensable in clothing. But to Mother Wong, the merits of making pottery escaped her—to see her college-educated daughter up to her elbows in clay, and more clay flying around as she worked in public view, was strangely unladylike. As for Chinatown merchants, they laughed openly at her, "Here comes the girl who plays with mud. How many bowls could you sell today?" Probably they thought: Here is a college graduate foolish enough to dirty her hands.

It has been the traditional belief from Asia to the Middle East, with Japan the exception, that scholars do not soil their hands and that a person studied literature in order to escape hard work. (This attitude is still prevalent in most Asian countries outside of the People's Republic of China and Japan.)

From the first, the local Chinese were not Jade Snow's patrons. The thinness and whiteness of porcelains imported from China and ornate decorations which came into vogue during the late Ching Dynasty[2] satisfied their tastes. They could not understand why "silly Americans" paid dollars for a hand-thrown bowl[3] utilizing crude California colored clays, not much different from the inexpensive peasant ware of China. That the Jade Snow Wong bowl went back to an older tradition of understated beauty was not apparent. They could see only that she wouldn't apply a dragon or a hundred flowers.

Many years later when Jade Snow met another atypical artist, a scholar and calligrapher[4] born and educated in China, he was to say to her, "I shudder if the majority of people look at my brush work and say it is pretty, for then I know it is ordinary and I have failed. If they say they do not understand it, or even that it is ugly, I am happy, for I have succeeded."

---

1. Tang and Sung (soong) **Dynasty:** A dynasty is a succession of rulers who belong to the same family. The period of the Tang Dynasty was 618–906 and that of the Sung Dynasty 960–1279.

2. Ching Dynasty: This dynasty lasted from 1644 to 1912.

3. hand-thrown bowl: A bowl shaped by hand on a potter's wheel, which spins the clay around.

4. calligrapher (kə lig′ rə fər) n.: Someone skilled in the art of beautiful handwriting.

However, there were enough numbers of the American public who bought Jade Snow's pottery to support her modestly. The store window was a temporary experiment which proved what she needed to know. In the meantime, her aging father, who was fearful that their home and factory might be in a redevelopment area, made a down payment with lifetime savings to purchase a small white wooden building with six rentable apartments at the perimeter of Chinatown. Jade Snow agreed to rent the two tiny empty ground-floor storefronts which he did not yet need, one for a display room, with supplies and packing center at its rear, the other for the potter's wheel, kiln,[5] glazing booth,[6] compressor,[7] and other equipment. Now, instead of paying Mr. Fong a commission on gross sales, she had bills to pay. Instead of sitting in a window, she worked with doors thrown open to the street.

Creativeness was 90 percent hard work and 10 percent inspiration. It was learning from errors, either from her lack of foresight or because of the errors of others. The first firing[8] in an unfamiliar new gas kiln brought crushing disappointment when the wares blew up into tiny pieces. In another firing,

5. kiln (kiln) n.: An oven to bake pottery.

6. glazing booth: A place to apply glaze, a glassy finish, to pottery.
7. compressor: (kəm pres' ər): A machine for compressing air or gas.
8. firing (fīr' iŋ) n.: The application of heat to harden or glaze pottery.

glaze results were uneven black and dark green, for the chemical supply house had mistakenly labeled five pounds of black copper oxide as black iron oxide. One morning there was a personal catastrophe. Unaware of a slow leak all night from the partially opened gas cock, she lit a match at the kiln. An explosion injured both hands, which took weeks to heal.

The day-to-day work of potterymaking tested her deepest discipline. A "wedged" ball of clay (prepared by kneading) would be "thrown" (shaped) on the potter's wheel, then dried overnight and trimmed, sometimes decorated with Chinese brush or bamboo tools. It took about a hundred thoroughly dried pieces to fill a kiln for the first firing that transformed fragile mud walls into hard bisque ware.[9] Glazes, like clays the results of countless experiments, were then applied to each piece. A second twelve-hour firing followed, with the temperatures raised hour by hour up to the final maturing point of somewhere around 2,000 degrees Fahrenheit. Then the kiln was turned off for twenty-four hours of cooling. Breakage was a potential hazard at every stage; each step might measure short in technical and artistic accomplishment. A piece she worked on diligently could disappoint. Another made casually had been enhanced successively until it delighted. One piece in ten might be of exhibition quality, half might be salable, and the others would be flawed "seconds" she would discard.

Yet Jade Snow never wavered from her belief that if moments in time could result in a thing of beauty that others could share, those moments were immeasurably satisfying. She owned two perfect Sung tea bowls. Without copying, she tried to make her pottery "stand up" in strength and grace to that standard.

It became routine to work past midnight without days off. Hand work could not be rushed; failures had to be replaced, and a host of other unanticipated business chores suddenly manifested themselves. She had kept comparable hours when she worked all through college to meet her expenses. Again, the hope of reaching valued goals was her spur. If she should fail, then she could accept what tradition dictated for most Chinese daughters—to be a wife, daughter-in-law, and mother. But unlike her college, the American business world was not dedicated to helping her. Because she was pioneering in a new venture, her identity was a liability. Her brains and hands were her only assets. How could she convert that liability? How could she differ from other struggling potters?

To enlarge her production base, she experimented with enamels[10] on copper forms conceived in the fluid shapes of her pottery, layering jewel tones for brilliant effects. They differed from the earth tints of clay and attracted a new clientele. With another kiln and new equipment, she made functional forms, believing that fine things should become part of the user's everyday life. The best results were submitted to exhibitions. Some juries rejected them, some accepted, and others awarded prizes.

To reach a market larger than San Francisco, she wrote to store buyers around the country, and, encouraged, she called on them. Traveling to strange cities far across the United States, as a rare Oriental woman alone in hotel dining rooms, she developed strong nerves against curious stares. That trip produced orders. Stipulated delivery and

---

9. bisque (bisk) **ware:** Unglazed pottery.

10. enamels (i nam′′ls) *n.*: Glassy colored substances used as coatings on metal, glass, and pottery.

cancellation dates made it necessary to hire first one and then more helpers who had to be trained, checked, kept busy and happy.

The strains increased. So did the bills, and she borrowed in small amounts from her sympathetic father, who said, "A hundred dollars is easy to come by, but the first thousand is very, very tricky. Look at the ideograph[11] for hundred—solidly square. Look at it for thousand—pointed, slippery. The ancients knew this long ago." When hundreds were not enough, tactful Western friends offered help. Oldest Brother, noticing her worries and struggles, sniffed scornfully. "You'll be out of business in a year."

She had learned to accept family criticism in silence, but she was too deeply involved to give up. Money was a worry, but creating was exciting and satisfying. These were lonely years. Jade Snow's single-minded pursuit did not allow her pleasant interludes with friends. To start a kiln at dawn, then watch till its critical maturing moment, which could happen any time between early evening and midnight or later (when gas pressure was low, it took until the next dawn), kept her from social engagements.

Then, gradually, signs indicated that she was working in the right direction. The first was a letter from the Metropolitan Museum of Art in New York, where the Eleventh Ceramic National Syracuse Show had been sent. The curator wrote, "We think the green, gold and ivory enamel bowl a skillful piece of workmanship and are anxious to add it to our collections." They referred to a ten-inch shallow bowl which Jade Snow had made.

A reviewer in *Art Digest* wrote, "In plain enamels without applied design, Jade Snow

Wong of San Francisco seemed to this critic to top the list."

Recognition brought further recognition. National decorating magazines featured her enamels, and in the same year, 1947, the Museum of Modern Art installed an exhibit by Mies Van der Rohe[12] which displayed 100 objects of fine design costing less than $100. A note introducing this exhibit read, "Every so often the Museum of Modern Art selects and exhibits soundly designed objects available to American purchasers in the belief that this will encourage more people to use beautiful things in their everyday life. . . ."

---

11. ideograph (id′ē ə graf′) n.: A symbol that stands for a thing or idea without expressing the sounds that make up its name.

12. Mies Van der Rohe (mēz′ van dər rō′ə): Ludwig Mies Van der Rohe (1886–1969) was a German-born American architect.

Two of Jade Snow's enamels, a dinner plate in Chinese red and a dessert plate in grayish gold, were included in the exhibition, which subsequently went to Europe.

So it did not seem unusual to receive an interviewer from *Mademoiselle*, but it was indeed unexpected to receive one of the magazine's ten awards for 1948 to women outstanding in ten different fields. They invited Jade Snow to fly to New York to claim her silver medal.

The more deeply one delves into a field, the more one realizes limitations. When Bernard Leach, the famous English potter, accepted an invitation from Mills College to teach a special course, Jade Snow attended. Another summer, Charles Merritt came from Alfred University's staff to give a course in precise glaze chemistry. Again, she commuted to Oakland. She became friends with these two unusual teachers. Both agreed that in pottery making, one never found a final answer. A mass-produced bathtub may be a technical triumph; yet a chemically balanced glaze on a pot can be aesthetically dull. Some of the most pleasing glaze effects could never be duplicated, for they were the combination of scrapings from the glaze booth. Like the waves of the sea, no two pieces of pottery art can be identical.

After three years of downs, then ups, the business promised to survive. Debts had been cleared. A small staff could handle routine duties. A steady clientele of San Franciscans came to her out-of-the-way shop. A beginning had been made.

RESPONDING TO THE SELECTION

Your Response

1. Do you admire Jade Snow Wong? Why or why not?

Recalling

2. How did Wong defy traditional Chinese ways? How did she defy the traditional expectations of the time for women?
3. The ideograph for hundred is 百 and for thousand is 千. According to Wong's father, what is the significance of these ideographs?

Interpreting

4. What do you infer about Wong from her success in reaching a market beyond San Francisco? What other incidents support this inference?
5. In what way was Wong's identity a liability? In what way were her brains and hands her only assets?
6. Explain the significance of the last line.

Applying

7. Jade Snow Wong says that her work did not allow her to spend much time with friends. Do you think it is worth making such a sacrifice to reach a goal? Why or why not?
8. Another artist says to Wong, "I shudder if the majority of people look at my brush work and say it is pretty, for then I know it is ordinary and I have failed." What is the difference between an artistic success and a popular success? Can a person be both? Support your answer.

ANALYZING LITERATURE

Understanding Third-Person Narrative

This autobiography is unusual because Jade Snow Wong uses **third-person narrative,** referring to herself as "she" rather than "I." In keeping with the Chinese tradition of modesty, she records her struggles and successes as a potter as if she were talking about someone else.

1. Look at the paragraph beginning, "It became routine . . . ," on page 345. Reread it, changing every *she* to *I* and every *her* to *my*.
2. Compare and contrast your version of the paragraph with the original.
3. Wong uses third-person narrative so it will not seem that she is boasting. What else in her account shows her modesty?

CRITICAL THINKING AND READING

Distinguishing Details

Autobiographies contain both objective and subjective details. An **objective detail** is a description of an event or object in the world outside the writer's mind. For example, when Jade Snow Wong says that she received an award from *Mademoiselle* in 1948, this is an objective detail. A **subjective detail** is a description of the writer's thoughts or feelings or opinions and judgments. Wong's statement that "creating was exciting and satisfying" is a subjective detail.

Find three objective details Wong gives about herself. Find three subjective details.

THINKING AND WRITING

Writing a Third-Person Sketch

Imagine that you are doing the task you wrote about before reading this selection. Suddenly you actually have the power to leave your body and watch yourself at work. Write a description of the way you look from your new perspective. Include in this description not only what your hands and body are doing but also your ideas and feelings. To help you with your writing, use the list you made for the earlier writing assignment. When you revise what you have written, make sure you have referred to yourself by name or as "he" or "she," just as Jade Snow Wong does.

Essays for Enjoyment

ICED COFFEE
Fairfield Porter
Private Collection

GUIDE FOR READING

Cat on the Go

Narrative Essay

An **essay** is a kind of musing, or thinking, upon a subject. It takes the form of a brief and personal discussion of any topic that a writer wants to consider. A **narrative essay** explores the subject by telling a true story. This type of essay may remind you of an autobiographical sketch. In an autobiography, however, the writer is always the central character, while a narrative essay may focus on a character other than the writer. The narrative essay "Cat on the Go," for instance, centers on the actions of Oscar, a friendly and restless cat.

Focus

Some people say they don't like cats because cats lack the personalities that dogs have. Lovers of cats disagree, stating that cats have personalities just as winning as dogs'. What do you think? Write down your opinion, and then see if it is supported by the behavior of the cat in the essay.

Vocabulary

Knowing the following words will help you as you read "Cat on the Go."

grotesquely (grō tesk′ lē) *adv.*: In a strange or distorted way (p. 351)

emaciated (i mā′ shē āt′ əd) *adj.*: Extremely thin; starving (p. 351)

sieve (siv) *n.*: Utensil with many tiny openings; strainer (p. 353)

inevitable (in ev′ ə tə b'l) *adj.*: Certain to happen (p. 353)

sauntered (sôn′ tərd) *v.*: Strolled (p. 354)

distraught (dis trôt′) *adj.*: Extremely upset (p. 355)

despondent (di spän′ dənt) *adj.*: Lacking hope; depressed (p. 355)

intrigued (in trēgd′) *v.*: Fascinated (p. 356)

consolation (kän′ sə lā′ shən) *n.*: Comfort (p. 359)

surreptitiously (sʉr′ əp tish′ əs lē) *adv.*: Secretly (p. 360)

James Herriot

(1916–1995) was born James Alfred Wight in Scotland. However, he used the name Herriot when writing about his experiences as a veterinarian in Yorkshire, an English county. Herriot's books are famous for their lively descriptions of the characters he met, both animal and human. "Cat on the Go," which comes from his book *All Things Wise and Wonderful,* describes a cat that loves to go visiting.

Cat on the Go

James Herriot

One winter evening Tristan shouted up the stairs from the passage far below.

"Jim! Jim!"

I went out and stuck my head over the bannisters. "What is it, Triss?"

"Sorry to bother you, Jim, but could you come down for a minute?" The upturned face had an anxious look.

I went down the long flights of steps two at a time and when I arrived slightly breathless on the ground floor Tristan beckoned me through to the consulting room at the back of the house. A teenage girl was standing by the table, her hand resting on a stained roll of blanket.

"It's a cat," Tristan said. He pulled back a fold of the blanket and I looked down at a large, deeply striped tabby. At least he would have been large if he had had any flesh on his bones, but ribs and pelvis stood out painfully through the fur and as I passed my hand over the motionless body I could feel only a thin covering of skin.

Tristan cleared his throat. "There's something else, Jim."

I looked at him curiously. For once he didn't seem to have a joke in him. I watched as he gently lifted one of the cat's hind legs and rolled the abdomen into view. There was a gash on the ventral surface[1] through which a coiled cluster of intestines spilled grotesquely onto the cloth. I was still shocked and staring when the girl spoke.

"I saw this cat sittin' in the dark, down Brown's yard. I thought 'e looked skinny, like, and a bit quiet and I bent down to give 'im a pat. Then I saw 'e was badly hurt and I went home for a blanket and brought 'im round to you."

"That was kind of you," I said. "Have you any idea who he belongs to?"

The girl shook her head. "No, he looks like a stray to me."

"He does indeed." I dragged my eyes away from the terrible wound. "You're Marjorie Simpson, aren't you?"

"Yes."

"I know your Dad well. He's our postman."

"That's right." She gave a half smile then her lips trembled.

"Well, I reckon I'd better leave 'im with you. You'll be going to put him out of his misery. There's nothing anybody can do about . . . about that?"

I shrugged and shook my head. The girl's eyes filled with tears, she stretched out a hand and touched the emaciated animal then turned and walked quickly to the door.

"Thanks again, Marjorie," I called after the retreating back. "And don't worry—we'll look after him."

In the silence that followed, Tristan and I looked down at the shattered animal. Under the surgery lamp it was all too easy to

---

1. **ventral** (ven' trəl) **surface:** The surface near or on the belly.

see. He had almost been disemboweled[2] and the pile of intestines was covered in dirt and mud.

"What d'you think did this?" Tristan said at length. "Has he been run over?"

"Maybe," I replied. "Could be anything. An attack by a big dog or somebody could have kicked him or struck him." All things were possible with cats because some people seemed to regard them as fair game for any cruelty.

Tristan nodded. "Anyway, whatever happened, he must have been on the verge of starvation. He's a skeleton. I bet he's wandered miles from home."

"Ah well," I sighed. "There's only one thing to do. Those guts are perforated in several places. It's hopeless."

Tristan didn't say anything but he whistled under his breath and drew the tip of his forefinger again and again across the furry cheek. And, unbelievably, from somewhere in the scraggy chest a gentle purring arose.

The young man looked at me, round eyed. "My God, do you hear that?"

"Yes . . . amazing in that condition. He's a good-natured cat."

Tristan, head bowed, continued his stroking. I knew how he felt because, although he preserved a cheerfully hard-boiled attitude to our patients he couldn't kid me about one thing; he had a soft spot for cats. Even now, when we are both around the sixty mark, he often talks to me about the cat he has had for many years. It is a typical relationship—they tease each other unmercifully—but it is based on real affection.

"It's no good, Triss," I said gently. "It's got to be done." I reached for the syringe but

---

2. disemboweled (dis′ im bou′ əld) v.: Lost its intestines.

something in me rebelled against plunging a needle into that mutilated body. Instead I pulled a fold of the blanket over the cat's head.

"Pour a little ether onto the cloth," I said. "He'll just sleep away."

Wordlessly, Tristan unscrewed the cap of the ether bottle and poised it above the head. Then from under the shapeless heap of blanket we heard it again; the deep purring which increased in volume till it boomed in our ears like a distant motorcycle.

Tristan was like a man turned to stone, hand gripping the bottle rigidly, eyes staring down at the mound of cloth from which the purring rose in waves of warm friendly sound.

At last he looked up at me and gulped. "I don't fancy this much, Jim. Can't we do something?"

"You mean, put that lot back?"

"Yes."

"But the bowels are damaged—they're like a sieve in parts."

"We could stitch them, couldn't we?"

I lifted the blanket and looked again. "Honestly, Triss, I wouldn't know where to start. And the whole thing is filthy."

He didn't say anything, but continued to look at me steadily. And I didn't need much persuading. I had no more desire to pour ether onto that comradely purring than he had.

"Come on, then," I said. "We'll have a go."

With the oxygen bubbling and the cat's head in the anesthetic mask we washed the whole prolapse[3] with warm saline.[4] We did it again and again but it was impossible to remove every fragment of caked dirt. Then we started the painfully slow business of stitching the many holes in the tiny intestines,

and here I was glad of Tristan's nimble fingers which seemed better able to manipulate the small round-bodied needles than mine.

Two hours and yards of catgut[5] later, we dusted the patched up peritoneal[6] surface with sulfanilamide[7] and pushed the entire mass back into the abdomen. When I had sutured muscle layers and skin everything looked tidy but I had a nasty feeling of sweeping undesirable things under the carpet. The extensive damage, all that contamination—peritonitis[8] was inevitable.

"He's alive, anyway, Triss," I said as we began to wash the instruments. "We'll put him onto sulfapyridine and keep our fingers crossed." There were still no antibiotics at that time but the new drug was a big advance.

The door opened and Helen came in. "You've been a long time, Jim." She walked over to the table and looked down at the sleeping cat. "What a poor skinny little thing. He's all bones."

"You should have seen him when he came in." Tristan switched off the sterilizer and screwed shut the valve on the anesthetic machine. "He looks a lot better now."

She stroked the little animal for a moment. "Is he badly injured?"

"I'm afraid so, Helen," I said. "We've done our best for him but I honestly don't think he has much chance."

"What a shame. And he's pretty, too. Four white feet and all those unusual colors." With her finger she traced the faint bands of auburn and copper-gold among the gray and black.

---

3. prolapse (prō′ laps) n.: An internal organ—here, the intestines—that has fallen out of place.

4. saline (sā′ līn) n.: A salt solution.

5. catgut (kat′ gut′) n.: A tough string or thread used in surgery.

6. peritoneal (per′ it ′n ē′ əl) adj.: Having to do with the membrane that lines the abdomen.

7. sulfanilamide (sul′ fə nil′ ə mīd) n.: Sulfa drugs were used to treat infections before penicillin was discovered and other antibiotics were created.

8. peritonitis (per′ it ′n īt′ əs) n.: Inflammation of the abdominal lining.

Tristan laughed. "Yes, I think that chap has a ginger Tom somewhere in his ancestry."

Helen smiled, too, but absently, and I noticed a broody look about her. She hurried out to the stock room and returned with an empty box.

"Yes . . . yes . . ." she said thoughtfully. "I can make a bed in this box for him and he'll sleep in our room, Jim."

"He will?"

"Yes, he must be warm, mustn't he?"

"Of course."

Later, in the darkness of our bed-sitter,[9] I looked from my pillow at a cozy scene. Sam in his basket on one side of the flickering fire and the cat cushioned and blanketed in his box on the other.

As I floated off into sleep it was good to know that my patient was so comfortable, but I wondered if he would be alive in the morning. . . .

I knew he was alive at 7:30 a.m. because my wife was already up and talking to him. I trailed across the room in my pajamas and the cat and I looked at each other. I rubbed him under the chin and he opened his mouth in a rusty miaow. But he didn't try to move.

"Helen," I said. "This little thing is tied together inside with catgut. He'll have to live on fluids for a week and even then he probably won't make it. If he stays up here you'll be spooning milk into him umpteen times a day."

"Okay, okay." She had that broody look again.

It wasn't only milk she spooned into him over the next few days. Beef essence, strained broth and a succession of sophisticated baby foods found their way down his

---

9. bed-sitter: A British term for a one-room apartment.

throat at regular intervals. One lunch time I found Helen kneeling by the box.

"We shall call him Oscar," she said.

"You mean we're keeping him?"

"Yes."

I am fond of cats but we already had a dog in our cramped quarters and I could see difficulties. Still I decided to let it go.

"Why Oscar?"

"I don't know." Helen tipped a few drops of chop gravy onto the little red tongue and watched intently as he swallowed.

One of the things I like about women is their mystery, the unfathomable part of them, and I didn't press the matter further. But I was pleased at the way things were going. I had been giving the sulfapyridine every six hours and taking the temperature night and morning, expecting all the time to encounter the roaring fever, the vomiting and the tense abdomen of peritonitis. But it never happened.

It was as though Oscar's animal instinct told him he had to move as little as possible because he lay absolutely still day after day and looked up at us—and purred.

His purr became part of our lives and when he eventually left his bed, sauntered through to our kitchen and began to sample Sam's dinner of meat and biscuit it was a moment of triumph. And I didn't spoil it by wondering if he was ready for solid food; I felt he knew.

From then on it was sheer joy to watch the furry scarecrow fill out and grow strong, and as he ate and ate and the flesh spread over his bones the true beauty of his coat showed in the glossy medley of auburn, black and gold. We had a handsome cat on our hands.

Once Oscar had fully recovered, Tristan was a regular visitor.

He probably felt, and rightly, that he, more than I, had saved Oscar's life in the first place and he used to play with him for long periods. His favorite ploy was to push his leg round the corner of the table and withdraw it repeatedly just as the cat pawed at it.

Oscar was justifiably irritated by this teasing but showed his character by lying in wait for Tristan one night and biting him smartly[10] in the ankle before he could start his tricks.

From my own point of view Oscar added many things to our menage.[11] Sam was delighted with him and the two soon became firm friends, Helen adored him and each evening I thought afresh that a nice cat washing his face by the hearth gave extra comfort to a room.

Oscar had been established as one of the family for several weeks when I came in from a late call to find Helen waiting for me with a stricken face.

"What's happened?" I asked.

"It's Oscar—he's gone!"

"Gone? What do you mean?"

"Oh, Jim, I think he's run away."

I stared at her. "He wouldn't do that. He often goes down to the garden at night. Are you sure he isn't there?"

"Absolutely. I've searched right into the yard. I've even had a walk round the town. And remember." Her chin quivered. "He . . . he ran away from somewhere before."

I looked at my watch. "Ten o'clock. Yes, that is strange. He shouldn't be out at this time."

As I spoke the front door bell jangled. I galloped down the stairs and as I rounded the corner in the passage I could see Mrs. Heslington, the vicar's[12] wife, through the glass. I threw open the door. She was holding Oscar in her arms.

"I believe this is your cat, Mr. Herriot," she said.

"It is indeed, Mrs. Heslington. Where did you find him?"

She smiled. "Well it was rather odd. We were having a meeting of the Mothers' Union at the church house and we noticed the cat sitting there in the room."

"Just sitting . . .?"

"Yes, as though he were listening to what we were saying and enjoying it all. It was unusual. When the meeting ended I thought I'd better bring him along to you."

"I'm most grateful, Mrs. Heslington." I snatched Oscar and tucked him under my arm. "My wife is distraught—she thought he was lost."

It was a little mystery. Why should he suddenly take off like that? But since he showed no change in his manner over the ensuing week we put it out of our minds.

Then one evening a man brought in a dog for a distemper[13] inoculation and left the front door open. When I went up to our flat I found that Oscar had disappeared again. This time Helen and I scoured the marketplace and side alleys in vain and when we returned at half past nine we were both despondent. It was nearly eleven and we were thinking of bed when the doorbell rang.

It was Oscar again, this time resting on the ample stomach of Jack Newbould. Jack was a gardener at one of the big houses. He hiccuped gently and gave me a huge benevolent smile. "Brought your cat, Mr. Herriot."

"Gosh, thanks, Jack!" I said, scooping up Oscar gratefully. "Where the devil did you find him?"

"Well, s'matter o' fact 'e sort of found me."

"What do you mean?"

---

10. smartly (smärt′ lē) *adv.*: Sharply.

11. menage (mə näzh′) *n.*: Household.

12. vicar's (vik′ ərz) *n.*: A vicar is a parish priest.

---

13. distemper (dis tem′ pər) *n.*: An infectious virus disease of young dogs.

Jack closed his eyes for a few moments before articulating carefully. "Thish is a big night, tha knows, Mr. Herriot. Darts championship. Lots of t'lads round at t'Dog and Gun—lotsh and lotsh of 'em. Big gatherin'."

"And our cat was there?"

"Aye, he were there, all right. Sitting among t'lads. Shpent t'whole evenin' with us."

"Just sat there, eh?"

"That 'e did." Jack giggled reminiscently. "By gaw 'e enjoyed 'isself. Ah gave 'em a drop out of me own glass and once or twice ah thought 'e was going to have a go at chuckin' a dart. He's some cat." He laughed again.

As I bore Oscar upstairs I was deep in thought. What was going on here? These sudden desertions were upsetting Helen and I felt they could get on my nerves in time.

I didn't have long to wait till the next one. Three nights later he was missing again. This time Helen and I didn't bother to search—we just waited.

He was back earlier than usual. I heard the door bell at nine o'clock. It was the elderly Miss Simpson peering through the glass. And she wasn't holding Oscar—he was prowling on the mat waiting to come in.

Miss Simpson watched with interest as the cat stalked inside and made for the stairs. "Ah, good, I'm so glad he's come home safely. I knew he was your cat and I've been intrigued by his behavior all evening."

"Where . . . may I ask?"

"Oh, at the Women's Institute. He came in shortly after we started and stayed there till the end."

"Really? What exactly was your program, Miss Simpson?"

"Well, there was a bit of committee stuff, then a short talk with lantern slides by Mr. Walters from the water company and we finished with a cake-making competition."

"Yes . . . yes . . . and what did Oscar do?"

She laughed. "Mixed with the company, apparently enjoyed the slides and showed great interest in the cakes."

"I see. And you didn't bring him home?"

"No, he made his own way here. As you know, I have to pass your house and I merely rang your bell to make sure you knew he had arrived."

"I'm obliged to you, Miss Simpson. We were a little worried."

I mounted the stairs in record time. Helen was sitting with the cat on her knee and she looked up as I burst in.

"I know about Oscar now," I said.

"Know what?"

"Why he goes on these nightly outings. He's not running away—he's visiting."

"Visiting?"

"Yes," I said. "Don't you see? He likes getting around, he loves people, especially in groups, and he's interested in what they do. He's a natural mixer."

Helen looked down at the attractive mound of fur curled on her lap. "Of course . . . that's it . . . he's a socialite!"

"Exactly, a high stepper!"

"A cat-about-town!"

It all afforded us some innocent laughter and Oscar sat up and looked at us with evident pleasure, adding his own throbbing purr to the merriment. But for Helen and me there was a lot of relief behind it; ever since our cat had started his excursions there had been the gnawing fear that we would lose him, and now we felt secure.

From that night our delight in him increased. There was endless joy in watching this facet of his character unfolding. He did the social round meticulously, taking in most of the activities of the town. He became a familiar figure at whist drives,[14] jumble

_____

14. whist (hwist) **drives:** Attempts to raise money for charities and other purposes by playing the card game whist.

sales,[15] school concerts and scout bazaars. Most of the time he was made welcome, but was twice ejected from meetings of the Rural District Council who did not seem to relish the idea of a cat sitting in on their deliberations.

At first I was apprehensive about his making his way through the streets but I watched him once or twice and saw that he looked both ways before tripping daintily across. Clearly he had excellent traffic sense and this made me feel that his original injury had not been caused by a car.

Taking it all in all, Helen and I felt that it was a kind stroke of fortune which had brought Oscar to us. He was a warm and cherished part of our home life. He added to our happiness.

When the blow fell it was totally unexpected.

I was finishing the evening surgery.[16] I looked round the door and saw only a man and two little boys.

"Next, please," I said.

The man stood up. He had no animal with him. He was middle-aged, with the rough weathered face of a farm worker. He twirled a cloth cap nervously in his hands.

"Mr. Herriot?" he said.

---

15. jumble sales: A British term for sales of contributed articles to raise money for charity.

16. surgery (sur′ jər ē) *n.*: A British term for "office hours."

"Yes, what can I do for you?"

He swallowed and looked me straight in the eyes. "Ah think you've got ma cat."

"What?"

"Ah lost ma cat a bit since." He cleared his throat. "We used to live at Missdon but ah got a job as plowman to Mr. Horne of Wederly. It was after we moved to Wederly that t'cat went missin'. Ah reckon he was tryin to find 'is way back to his old home."

"Wederly? That's on the other side of Brawton—over thirty miles away."

"Aye, ah knaw, but cats is funny things."

"But what makes you think I've got him?"

He twisted the cap around a bit more. "There's a cousin o' mine lives in Darrowby and ah heard tell from 'im about this cat that goes around to meetin's. I 'ad to come. We've been huntin' everywhere."

"Tell me," I said. "This cat you lost. What did he look like?"

"Gray and black and sort o' gingery. Right bonny[17] 'e was. And 'e was allus goin' out to gatherin's."

A cold hand clutched at my heart. "You'd better come upstairs. Bring the boys with you."

Helen was putting some coal on the fire of the bed-sitter.

"Helen," I said. "This is Mr.—er—I'm sorry, I don't know your name."

"Gibbons, Sep Gibbons. They called me Septimus because ah was the seventh in family and it looks like ah'm goin' t'same way 'cause we've got six already. These are our two youngest." The two boys, obvious twins of about eight, looked up at us solemnly.

I wished my heart would stop hammering. "Mr. Gibbons thinks Oscar is his. He lost his cat some time ago."

My wife put down her little shovel. "Oh . . . oh . . . I see." She stood very still for a

moment then smiled faintly. "Do sit down. Oscar's in the kitchen, I'll bring him through."

She went out and reappeared with the cat in her arms. She hadn't got through the door before the little boys gave tongue.

"Tiger!" they cried. "Oh, Tiger, Tiger!"

The man's face seemed lit from within. He walked quickly across the floor and ran his big work-roughened hand along the fur.

"Hullo, awd lad," he said, and turned to me with a radiant smile. "It's 'im, Mr. Herriot. It's 'im awright, and don't 'e look well!"

"You call him Tiger, eh?" I said.

"Aye," he replied happily. "It's them gingery stripes. The kids called 'im that. They were brokenhearted when we lost 'im."

As the two little boys rolled on the floor our Oscar rolled with them, pawing playfully, purring with delight.

Sep Gibbons sat down again. "That's the way 'e allus went on wi' the family. They used to play with 'im for hours. By gaw we did miss 'im. He were a right favorite."

I looked at the broken nails on the edge of the cap, at the decent, honest, uncomplicated Yorkshire[18] face so like the many I had grown to like and respect. Farm men like him got thirty shillings a week in those days and it was reflected in the threadbare jacket, the cracked, shiny boots and the obvious hand-me-downs of the boys.

But all three were scrubbed and tidy, the man's face like a red beacon, the children's knees gleaming and their hair carefully slicked across their foreheads. They looked like nice people to me. I didn't know what to say.

Helen said it for me. "Well, Mr. Gibbons." Her tone had an unnatural brightness. "You'd better take him."

---

17. bonny (bän' ē) *adj.*: Pretty.

18. Yorkshire: A former county of northern England.

The man hesitated. "Now then, are ye sure, Missis Herriot?"

"Yes . . . yes, I'm sure. He was your cat first."

"Aye, but some folks 'ud say finders keepers or summat like that. Ah didn't come 'ere to demand 'im back or owt of t'sort."

"I know you didn't, Mr. Gibbons, but you've had him all those years and you've searched for him so hard. We couldn't possibly keep him from you."

He nodded quickly. "Well, that's right good of ye." He paused for a moment, his face serious, then he stooped and picked Oscar up. "We'll have to be off if we're goin' to catch the eight o'clock bus."

Helen reached forward, cupped the cat's head in her hands and looked at him steadily for a few seconds. Then she patted the boys' heads. "You'll take good care of him, won't you?"

"Aye, missis, thank ye, we will that." The two small faces looked up at her and smiled.

"I'll see you down the stairs, Mr. Gibbons," I said.

On the descent I tickled the furry cheek resting on the man's shoulder and heard for the last time the rich purring. On the front door step we shook hands and they set off down the street. As they rounded the corner of Trengate they stopped and waved, and I waved back at the man, the two children and the cat's head looking back at me over the shoulder.

It was my habit at that time in my life to mount the stairs two or three at a time but on this occasion I trailed upwards like an old man, slightly breathless, throat tight, eyes prickling.

I cursed myself for a sentimental fool but as I reached our door I found a flash of consolation. Helen had taken it remarkably well. She had nursed that cat and grown deeply attached to him, and I'd have thought an unforeseen calamity like this would have up-

set her terribly. But no, she had behaved calmly and rationally.

It was up to me to do as well. I adjusted my features into the semblance of a cheerful smile and marched into the room.

Helen had pulled a chair close to the table and was slumped face down against the wood. One arm cradled her head while the other was stretched in front of her as her body shook with an utterly abandoned weeping.

I had never seen her like this and I was appalled. I tried to say something comforting but nothing stemmed the flow of racking sobs.

Feeling helpless and inadequate I could only sit close to her and stroke the back of her head. Maybe I could have said something if I hadn't felt just about as bad myself.

You get over these things in time. After all, we told ourselves, it wasn't as though Oscar had died or got lost again—he had gone to a good family who would look after him. In fact he had really gone home.

And of course, we still had our much-loved Sam, although he didn't help in the early stages by sniffing disconsolately where Oscar's bed used to lie then collapsing on the rug with a long lugubrious sigh.

There was one other thing, too. I had a little notion forming in my mind, an idea which I would spring on Helen when the time was right. It was about a month after that shattering night and we were coming out of the cinema at Brawton at the end of our half day. I looked at my watch.

"Only eight o'clock," I said. "How about going to see Oscar?"

Helen looked at me in surprise. "You mean—drive on to Wederly?"

"Yes, it's only about five miles."

A smile crept slowly across her face. "That would be lovely. But do you think they would mind?"

"The Gibbons? No, I'm sure they wouldn't. Let's go."

Wederly was a big village and the plowman's cottage was at the far end a few yards beyond the Methodist chapel. I pushed open the garden gate and we walked down the path.

A busy-looking little woman answered my knock. She was drying her hands on a striped towel.

"Mrs. Gibbons?" I said.

"Aye, that's me."

"I'm James Herriot—and this is my wife."

Her eyes widened uncomprehendingly. Clearly the name meant nothing to her.

"We had your cat for a while," I added.

Suddenly she grinned and waved her towel at us. "Oh aye, ah remember now. Sep told me about you. Come in, come in!"

The big kitchen-living room was a tableau[19] of life with six children and thirty shillings a week. Battered furniture, rows of much-mended washing on a pulley, black cooking range and a general air of chaos.

Sep got up from his place by the fire, put down his newspaper, took off a pair of steel-rimmed spectacles and shook hands. He waved Helen to a sagging armchair. "Well, it's right nice to see you. Ah've often spoke of ye to t'missis."

His wife hung up her towel. "Yes, and I'm glad to meet ye both. I'll get some tea in a minnit."

She laughed and dragged a bucket of muddy water into a corner. "I've been washin' football jerseys. Them lads just handed them to me tonight—as if I haven't enough to do."

As she ran the water into the kettle I peeped surreptitiously around me and I no-ticed Helen doing the same. But we searched in vain. There was no sign of a cat. Surely he couldn't have run away again? With a growing feeling of dismay I realized that my little scheme could backfire devastatingly.

It wasn't until the tea had been made and poured that I dared to raise the subject.

"How—" I asked diffidently. "How is—er—Tiger?"

"Oh, he's grand," the little woman replied briskly. She glanced up at the clock on the mantelpiece. "He should be back any time now, then you'll be able to see 'im."

As she spoke, Sep raised a finger. "Ah think ah can hear 'im now."

He walked over and opened the door and our Oscar strode in with all his old grace and majesty. He took one look at Helen and leaped onto her lap. With a cry of delight she put down her cup and stroked the beautiful fur as the cat arched himself against her hand and the familiar purr echoed round the room.

"He knows me," she murmured. "He knows me."

Sep nodded and smiled. "He does that. You were good to 'im. He'll never forget ye, and we won't either, will we mother?"

"No, we won't, Mrs. Herriot," his wife said as she applied butter to a slice of gingerbread. "That was a kind thing ye did for us and I 'ope you'll come and see us all whenever you're near."

"Well, thank you," I said. "We'd love to—we're often in Brawton."

I went over and tickled Oscar's chin, then I turned again to Mrs. Gibbons. "By the way, it's after nine o'clock. Where has he been till now?"

She poised her butter knife and looked into space.

"Let's see, now," she said. "It's Thursday, isn't it? Ah yes, it's 'is night for the Yoga class."

---

19. tableau (tab′ lō) *n.:* A dramatic scene or picture.

1. How have you felt when, like the Herriots, you've had to give up something that meant a lot to you?

Recalling

2. Explain how Herriot and his wife help the cat.
3. Where does the cat go each time it wanders off from the Herriots' apartment?
4. What do Herriot and his wife discover about the cat that makes them laugh?
5. Explain how the cat is reunited with his first owners.

Interpreting

6. What effect does the injured cat's purring have on Herriot and Tristan?
7. Why does Helen decide to give the cat up rather than claim "finders keepers"?
8. What qualities make this cat special?

Applying

9. Why do you think that many people enjoy having pets?

ANALYZING LITERATURE

Understanding the Narrative Essay

An **essay** is a brief and personal discussion of any topic that a writer wants to consider. A **narrative essay** considers the topic by telling a true story. In "Cat on the Go," Herriot gives a strong personal flavor to his narrative by telling you his thoughts and feelings. He writes about the healing cat, for example, ". . . it was sheer joy to watch the furry scarecrow fill out. . . ."

1. What is the topic of this narrative essay? What is Herriot's attitude toward the topic?
2. Identify three passages where Herriot tells you his thoughts or feelings about the topic.
3. How does Herriot's enjoyment of the cat increase your interest in the essay?
4. Compare and contrast reading a narrative essay and hearing a friend tell a story.

CRITICAL THINKING AND READING

Considering Another Perspective

This story is told from the point of view of James Herriot. That is why the sequence of events begins when Herriot first hears about the injured cat from Tristan. If the story had been told by Septimus Gibbons, however, it would have had a different shape.

1. How might the story have begun if Mr. Gibbons were telling it?
2. Which events in Herriot's story might *not* have been included in Gibbons's story?
3. Would Gibbons's story have ended in the same way? Why?

THINKING AND WRITING

Creating a Television Program

This essay has actually been made into a television program. Pretend that you were the writer hired to create this show. The producer has told you, however, that there is not enough time to include every episode. List the episodes that you think *must* appear in the program. Then write a memo to the producer defending your list. When you revise the memo, make sure it is convincing.

LEARNING OPTIONS

1. **Writing.** Write a short monologue from Oscar's point of view. Describe how you were injured and your feelings about the Herriots. Then explain why you like to attend the social gatherings around town. Finally discuss your feelings about leaving the Herriots and returning to your original owners. Write your monologue in the first person, using "I." Share your work with classmates to compare the feelings you imagine the cat had.
2. **Community Connections.** Find out what sort of services and agencies there are in your area for the protection and health care of animals. Compile your findings in a booklet.

GUIDE FOR READING

The Night the Bed Fell

Humorous Essay

A **humorous essay** is a brief work of nonfiction that is meant to amuse you. Many of James Thurber's humorous essays, like "The Night the Bed Fell," are about his lovable but silly relatives. During the night that Thurber tells about in this essay, each family member, including Thurber himself, has a different and mistaken idea of what is going on. The result is total confusion for the characters and a great deal of fun for the reader.

Focus

People love to tell funny stories about things that have actually happened to them. What makes such a story funny? How does the way it is told increase its comic effect? Recall a funny story about something that happened to you or one that someone told you. Make a list of the main events in the story, starting with what happened first and putting down each event in order. Is each item in the list funny in itself, or must we know the entire sequence before we will laugh at the story? As you read, pay attention to the way Thurber strings together the events in his essay.

Vocabulary

Knowing the following words will help you as you read "The Night the Bed Fell."

ominous (äm′ ə nəs) *adj.*: Threatening (p. 363)

allay (ə lā′) *v.*: Put to rest; calm (p. 363)

fortitude (fôr′ tə tood′) *n.*: Firm courage (p. 364)

perilous (per′ əl əs) *adj.*: Dangerous (p. 364)

deluge (del′ yooj) *n.*: A great flood or rush of anything (p. 365)

pungent (pun′ jənt) *adj.*: Sharp-smelling (p. 365)

extricate (eks′ trə kāt′) *v.*: Set free; disentangle (p. 365)

culprit (kul′ prit) *n.*: Guilty person (p. 366)

James Thurber

(1894–1961) lost the vision in one eye due to a childhood accident; however, he did not allow this disability to slow him down. He worked as a newspaper reporter and later wrote humorous pieces for *The New Yorker,* a famous magazine. In addition to being a talented writer, Thurber was a cartoonist. His amusing line drawings often accompany his writing. "The Night the Bed Fell," like many of his essays, describes the funny goings-on in his family.

The Night the Bed Fell

James Thurber

I suppose that the high-water mark of my youth in Columbus, Ohio, was the night the bed fell on my father. It makes a better recitation (unless, as some friends of mine have said, one has heard it five or six times) than it does a piece of writing, for it is almost necessary to throw furniture around, shake doors, and bark like a dog, to lend the proper atmosphere and verisimilitude[1] to what is admittedly a somewhat incredible tale. Still, it did take place.

It happened, then, that my father had decided to sleep in the attic one night, to be away where he could think. My mother opposed the notion strongly because, she said, the old wooden bed up there was unsafe: it was wobbly and the heavy headboard would crash down on father's head in case the bed fell, and kill him. There was no dissuading him, however, and at a quarter past ten he closed the attic door behind him and went up the narrow twisting stairs. We later heard ominous creakings as he crawled into bed. Grandfather, who usually slept in the attic bed when he was with us, had disappeared some days before. On these occasions he was usually gone six or eight days and returned growling and out of temper, with the news that the Federal Union[2] was run by a passel of blockheads and that the Army of the Potomac[3] didn't have a chance.

We had visiting us at this time a nervous first cousin of mine named Briggs Beall, who believed that he was likely to cease breathing when he was asleep. It was his feeling that if he were not awakened every hour during the night, he might die of suffocation. He had been accustomed to setting an alarm clock to ring at intervals until morning, but I persuaded him to abandon this. He slept in my room and I told him that I was such a light sleeper that if anybody quit breathing in the same room with me, I would wake instantly. He tested me the first night—which I had suspected he would—by holding his breath after my regular breathing had convinced him I was asleep. I was not asleep, however, and called to him. This seemed to allay his fears a little, but he took the precaution of putting a glass of spirits of camphor[4] on a little table at the head of his bed. In case I didn't arouse him until he was almost gone, he said, he would sniff the camphor, a powerful reviver. Briggs was not the only member of his family who had his crotchets.[5] Old Aunt Melissa Beall (who could whistle like a man, with two fingers in her mouth) suffered under the premonition that she was destined to die on South High Street, because she had been born on South High Street and married on South High Street. Then there was Aunt Sarah Shoaf, who never went to bed at night without the

---

1. verisimilitude (ver′ ə si mil′ə tōōd′) *n.*: The appearance of being true or real.
2. Federal Union: The Northern side during the Civil War. He is under the illusion that the Civil War has not yet ended.
3. Army of the Potomac: One of the Northern armies during the Civil War.

---

4. spirits of camphor: A liquid with a powerful odor.
5. crotchets (kräch′ its) *n.*: Peculiar or stubborn ideas.

fear that a burglar was going to get in and blow chloroform[6] under her door through a tube. To avert this calamity—for she was in greater dread of anesthetics than of losing her household goods—she always piled her money, silverware, and other valuables in a neat stack just outside her bedroom, with a note reading: "This is all I have. Please take it and do not use your chloroform, as this is all I have." Aunt Gracie Shoaf also had a burglar phobia, but she met it with more fortitude. She was confident that burglars had been getting into her house every night for forty years. The fact that she never missed

any thing was to her no proof to the contrary. She always claimed that she scared them off before they could take anything, by throwing shoes down the hallway. When she went to bed she piled, where she could get at them handily, all the shoes there were about her house. Five minutes after she had turned off the light, she would sit up in bed and say "Hark!" Her husband, who had learned to ignore the whole situation as long ago as 1903, would either be sound asleep or pretend to be sound asleep. In either case he would not respond to her tugging and pulling, so that presently she would arise, tiptoe to the door, open it slightly and heave a shoe down the hall in one direction, and its mate down the hall in the other direction. Some nights she threw them all, some nights only a couple of pair.

But I am straying from the remarkable incidents that took place during the night that the bed fell on father. By midnight we were all in bed. The layout of the rooms and the disposition[7] of their occupants is important to an understanding of what later occurred. In the front room upstairs (just under father's attic bedroom) were my mother and my brother Herman, who sometimes sang in his sleep, usually "Marching Through Georgia" or "Onward, Christian Soldiers." Briggs Beall and myself were in a room adjoining this one. My brother Roy was in a room across the hall from ours. Our bull terrier, Rex, slept in the hall.

My bed was an army cot, one of those affairs which are made wide enough to sleep on comfortably only by putting up, flat with the middle section, the two sides which ordinarily hang down like the sideboards of a drop-leaf table. When these sides are up, it is perilous to roll too far toward the edge, for

---

6. chloroform (klôr′ə fôrm′) *n.*: A substance used at one time as an anesthetic, or pain-killer, during operations because it can cause a person to pass out.

---

7. disposition (dis′ pə zish′ ən) *n.*: Arrangement.

then the cot is likely to tip completely over, bringing the whole bed down on top of one, with a tremendous banging crash. This, in fact, is precisely what happened about two o'clock in the morning. (It was my mother who, in recalling the scene later, first referred to it as "the night the bed fell on your father.")

Always a deep sleeper, slow to arouse (I had lied to Briggs), I was at first unconscious of what had happened when the iron cot rolled me onto the floor and toppled over on me. It left me still warmly bundled up and unhurt, for the bed rested above me like a canopy. Hence I did not wake up, only reached the edge of consciousness and went back. The racket, however, instantly awakened my mother, in the next room, who came to the immediate conclusion that her worst dread was realized: the big wooden bed upstairs had fallen on father. She therefore screamed, "Let's go to your poor father!" It was this shout, rather than the noise of my cot falling, that awakened Herman, in the same room with her. He thought that mother had become, for no apparent reason, hysterical. "You're all right, Mamma!" he shouted, trying to calm her. They exchanged shout for shout for perhaps ten seconds:

"Let's go to your poor father!" and "You're all right!" That woke up Briggs. By this time I was conscious of what was going on, in a vague way, but did not yet realize that I was under my bed instead of on it. Briggs, awakening in the midst of loud shouts of fear and apprehension, came to the quick conclusion that he was suffocating and that we were all trying to "bring him out." With a low moan, he grasped the glass of camphor at the head of his bed and instead of sniffing it poured it over himself. The room reeked of camphor. "Ugf, ahfg," choked Briggs, like a drowning man, for he had almost succeeded in stopping his breath under the deluge of pungent spirits. He leaped out of bed and groped toward the open window, but he came up against one that was closed. With his hand, he beat out the glass, and I could hear it crash and tinkle on the alleyway below. It was at this juncture that I, in trying to get up, had the uncanny sensation of feeling my bed above me! Foggy with sleep, I now suspected, in my turn, that the whole uproar was being made in a frantic endeavor to extricate me from what must be an unheard-of and perilous situation. "Get me out of this!"

The Night the Bed Fell 365

I bawled. "Get me out!" I think I had the nightmarish belief that I was entombed in a mine. "Gugh," gasped Briggs, floundering in his camphor.

By this time my mother, still shouting, pursued by Herman, still shouting, was trying to open the door to the attic, in order to go up and get my father's body out of the wreckage. The door was stuck, however, and wouldn't yield. Her frantic pulls on it only added to the general banging and confusion. Roy and the dog were now up, the one shouting questions, the other barking.

Father, farthest away and soundest sleeper of all, had by this time been awakened by the battering on the attic door. He decided that the house was on fire. "I'm coming, I'm coming!" he wailed in a slow, sleepy voice—it took him many minutes to regain full consciousness. My mother, still believing he was caught under the bed, detected in his "I'm coming!" the mournful, resigned note of one who is preparing to meet his Maker. "He's dying!" she shouted.

"I'm all right!" Briggs yelled to reassure her. "I'm all right!" He still believed that it was his own closeness to death that was worrying mother. I found at last the light switch in my room, unlocked the door, and Briggs and I joined the others at the attic door. The dog, who never did like Briggs, jumped for him—assuming that he was the culprit in whatever was going on—and Roy had to throw Rex and hold him. We could hear father crawling out of bed upstairs. Roy pulled the attic door open, with a mighty jerk, and father came down the stairs, sleepy and irritable but safe and sound. My mother began to weep when she saw him. Rex began to howl. "What in the name of heaven is going on here?" asked father.

The situation was finally put together like a gigantic jigsaw puzzle. Father caught a cold from prowling around in his bare feet but there were no other bad results. "I'm glad," said mother, who always looked on the bright side of things, "that your grandfather wasn't here."

RESPONDING TO THE SELECTION

Your Response

1. Do the events that Thurber describes seem as though they really happened? Why or why not?

Recalling

2. What is Briggs's crotchet, or peculiar idea?
3. Describe the layout of the rooms and their placement or grouping. Why is their placement important to the plot of the story?
4. In chronological, or time, order, list the actions that occur after Thurber's cot collapses.

Interpreting

5. Why does Thurber introduce the essay with a description of some of his relatives?
6. Identify the moment at which the events reach their climax.
7. What evidence is there that Thurber felt affection for his family?

Applying

8. Would you like to have known the Thurber family? Why or why not?

ANALYZING LITERATURE

Understanding the Humorous Essay

A **humorous essay** is a brief work of nonfiction that is meant to amuse you. In "The Night the Bed Fell" much of the humor comes from the contrast between what is really happening and what the characters think is happening. For example, Thurber's mother believes that her husband lies crushed in the wreckage of his bed when he is really safely asleep.

1. Contrast what actually happens when the bed falls and what each character thinks is happening.
2. Would the essay be as funny if you were as confused about what happened as the characters are? Why?
3. At the beginning of the essay, Thurber writes, "It makes a better recitation . . . than it does a piece of writing, for it is almost necessary to throw furniture around, shake doors, and bark like a dog, to lend the proper atmosphere and verisimilitude to what is admittedly a somewhat incredible tale." Do you think such theatrics would make this funny tale even funnier? Why or why not?

CRITICAL THINKING AND READING

Identifying Exaggeration

Writers of humorous essays often **exaggerate,** or enlarge, their descriptions to make them funnier. In "The Night the Bed Fell," for example, Thurber says that Briggs poured a "deluge of pungent spirits" on himself. Of course, we know that Briggs did not really *flood* himself with camphor. The contrast between what is really happening and the exaggerated description is humorous.

In each of the following passages, point out what is exaggerated and explain the contrast between the exaggeration and the reality.

1. "'Get me out of this!' I bawled. 'Get me out!' I think I had the nightmarish belief that I was entombed in a mine."
2. ". . . Herman, still shouting, was trying to open the door to the attic, in order to go up and get my father's body out of the wreckage."

THINKING AND WRITING

Creating a Humorous Essay

Recall the amusing events that you listed before reading the essay. Use this list to tell the story aloud to different friends. Each time you tell it, try to make it funnier by exaggerating one of the events. When you have perfected your narrative, write a humorous essay based on it. In revising the essay, make sure you have included the exaggerations that worked best when you told the story aloud. You may include humorous drawings, as Thurber did. When you are finished, share your essay with your classmates.

GUIDE FOR READING

Marjorie Kinnan Rawlings

(1896–1953) was born in Washington, D.C., but later moved to rural Florida, where "Rattlesnake Hunt" is set. There at Cross Creek she wrote about the world around her, and eventually, she became famous for her novels describing life in that part of the country. *The Yearling* (1938), for example, an American classic, was made into a successful film. Animals often play a major part in her work. As you will see, she was even fascinated by such creatures as rattlesnakes.

Rattlesnake Hunt

Description in an Essay

When writers describe people or scenes, they use language that appeals to your senses so that their descriptions come alive for you. For example, a writer describing a beach might tell about the surf that roars like an express train and the sand that feels powdery and warm. Good descriptions are just as important in essays as in other types of writing. You will be less likely to pay attention to what an essay writer says if you cannot see in your mind the people and places being discussed. In "Rattlesnake Hunt," Marjorie Kinnan Rawlings gives a vivid description of a desolate area in Florida where rattlesnakes live.

Focus

Do you know what you and a rattlesnake have in common? It's the rattle. No, *you* don't have a rattle, but the one that grows at the end of a rattlesnake's tail is made of the same substance as your toenails! Make some notes about other facts you may know about rattlers. Have you ever seen one in a zoo? As you read the following essay, notice how Rawlings's fear of the snakes begins to go away the more she learns about them.

Vocabulary

Knowing the following words will help you as you read "Rattlesnake Hunt."

data (dāt′ ə) *n.*: Information (p. 369)

desolate (des′ ə lit) *adj.*: Lonely; solitary (p. 369)

conventional (kən ven′ shə nəl) *adj.*: Ordinary; usual (p. 370)

translucent (trans lōō′ s'nt) *adj.*: Clear (p. 370)

arid (ar′ id) *adj.*: Dry and barren (p. 370)

mortality (môr tal′ ə tē) *n.*: Having to die someday (p. 371)

preferable (pref′ ər ə b'l) *adj.*: More desirable (p. 371)

camouflaged (kam′ ə fläzhd′) *v.*: Disguised (p. 371)

Rattlesnake Hunt

Marjorie Kinnan Rawlings

Ross Allen, a young Florida herpetologist,[1] invited me to join him on a hunt in the upper Everglades[2]—for rattlesnakes. Ross and I drove to Arcadia in his coupé[3] on a warm January day.

I said, "How will you bring back the rattlesnakes?"

"In the back of my car."

My courage was not adequate to inquire whether they were thrown in loose and might be expected to appear between our feet. Actually, a large portable box of heavy close-meshed wire made a safe cage. Ross wanted me to write an article about his work and on our way to the unhappy hunting grounds I took notes on a mass of data that he had accumulated in years of herpetological research. The scientific and dispassionate detachment of the material and the man made a desirable approach to rattlesnake territory. As I had discovered with the insects and varmints,[4] it is difficult to be afraid of anything about which enough is known, and Ross' facts were fresh from the laboratory.

The hunting ground was Big Prairie, south of Arcadia and west of the northern tip of Lake Okeechobee. Big Prairie is a deso-

late cattle country, half marsh, half pasture, with islands of palm trees and cypress and oaks. At that time of year the cattlemen and Indians were burning the country, on the theory that the young fresh wire grass that springs up from the roots after a fire is the best cattle forage. Ross planned to hunt his rattlers in the forefront of the fires. They lived in winter, he said, in gopher holes, coming out in the midday warmth to forage, and would move ahead of the flames and be easily taken. We joined forces with a big man named Will, his snake-hunting companion of the territory, and set out in early morning, after a long rough drive over deep-rutted roads into the open wilds.

I hope never in my life to be so frightened as I was in those first few hours. I kept on Ross' footsteps, I moved when he moved,

---

1. herpetologist (hur′ pə täl′ ə jist) *n.*: Someone who studies reptiles and amphibians.
2. Everglades: A large region of swampland in southern Florida, about 100 miles long and 50–75 miles wide.
3. coupé (ko͞o pā′) *n.*: A small, two-door automobile.
4. varmints (vär′ mənts) *n.*: Animals regarded as troublesome.

Rattlesnake Hunt 369

sometimes jolting into him when I thought he might leave me behind. He does not use the forked stick of conventional snake hunting, but a steel prong, shaped like an L, at the end of a long stout stick. He hunted casually, calling my attention to the varying vegetation, to hawks overhead, to a pair of the rare whooping cranes that flapped over us. In mid-morning he stopped short, dropped his stick, and brought up a five-foot rattlesnake draped limply over the steel L. It seemed to me that I should drop in my tracks.

"They're not active at this season," he said quietly. "A snake takes on the temperature of its surroundings. They can't stand too much heat for that reason, and when the weather is cool, as now, they're sluggish."

The sun was bright overhead, the sky a translucent blue, and it seemed to me that it was warm enough for any snake to do as it willed. The sweat poured down my back. Ross dropped the rattler in a crocus sack[5] and Will carried it. By noon, he had caught four. I felt faint and ill. We stopped by a pond and went swimming. The region was flat, the horizon limitless, and as I came out of the cool blue water I expected to find myself surrounded by a ring of rattlers. There were only Ross and Will, opening the lunch basket. I could not eat. Will went back and drove his truck closer, for Ross expected the hunting to be better in the afternoon. The hunting was much better. When we went back to the truck to deposit two more rattlers in the wire cage, there was a rattlesnake lying under the truck.

Ross said, "Whenever I leave my car or truck with snakes already in it, other rattlers always appear. I don't know whether this is because they scent or sense the presence of other snakes, or whether in this arid area

they come to the car for shade in the heat of the day."

The problem was scientific, but I had no interest.

That night Ross and Will and I camped out in the vast spaces of the Everglades prairies. We got water from an abandoned well and cooked supper under buttonwood bushes by a flowing stream. The camp fire blazed cheerfully under the stars and a new moon lifted in the sky. Will told tall tales of the cattlemen and the Indians and we were at peace.

Ross said, "We couldn't have a better night for catching water snakes."

After the rattlers, water snakes seemed innocuous enough. We worked along the edge of the stream and here Ross did not use his L-shaped steel. He reached under rocks and along the edge of the water and brought out harmless reptiles with his hands. I had said nothing to him of my fears, but he un-

---

5. crocus sack: A term used in the southern United States for a burlap bag.

one had come out or was still in the hole. Sometimes the two men dug the snake out. At times it was down so long and winding a tunnel that the digging was hopeless. Then they blocked the entrance and went on to other holes. In an hour or so they made the original rounds, unblocking the holes. The rattler in every case came out hurriedly, as though anything were preferable to being shut in. All the time Ross talked to me, telling me the scientific facts he had discovered about the habits of the rattlers.

"They pay no attention to a man standing perfectly still," he said, and proved it by letting Will unblock a hole while he stood at the entrance as the snake came out. It was exciting to watch the snake crawl slowly beside and past the man's legs. When it was at a safe distance he walked within its range of vision, which he had proved to be no higher than a man's knee, and the snake whirled and drew back in an attitude[7] of fighting defense. The rattler strikes only for paralyzing and killing its food, and for defense.

"It is a slow and heavy snake," Ross said. "It lies in wait on a small game trail and strikes the rat or rabbit passing by. It waits a few minutes, then follows along the trail, coming to the small animal, now dead or dying. It noses it from all sides, making sure that it is its own kill, and that it is dead and ready for swallowing."

A rattler will lie quietly without revealing itself if a man passes by and it thinks it is not seen. It slips away without fighting if given the chance. Only Ross' sharp eyes sometimes picked out the gray and yellow diamond pattern, camouflaged among the grasses. In the cool of the morning, chilled by the January air, the snakes showed no fight. They could be looped up limply over the steel L and dropped in a sack or up into

derstood them. He brought a small dark snake from under a willow root.

"Wouldn't you like to hold it?" he asked. "People think snakes are cold and clammy, but they aren't. Take it in your hands. You'll see that it is warm."

Again, because I was ashamed, I took the snake in my hands. It was not cold, it was not clammy, and it lay trustingly in my hands, a thing that lived and breathed and had mortality[6] like the rest of us. I felt an upsurgence of spirit.

The next day was magnificent. The air was crystal, the sky was aquamarine, and the far horizon of palms and oaks lay against the sky. I felt a new boldness and followed Ross bravely. He was making the rounds of the gopher holes. The rattlers came out in the mid-morning warmth and were never far away. He could tell by their trails whether

---

6. had mortality: Would die.

---

7. attitude: (at′ ə tood′) n.: In this case, a position or posture of the body.

the wire cage on the back of Will's truck. As the sun mounted in the sky and warmed the moist Everglades earth, the snakes were warmed too, and Ross warned that it was time to go more cautiously. Yet having learned that it was we who were the aggressors; that immobility meant complete safety; that the snakes, for all their lightning flash in striking, were inaccurate in their aim, with limited vision; having watched again and again the liquid grace of movement, the beauty of pattern, suddenly I understood that I was drinking in freely the magnificent sweep of the horizon, with no fear of what might be at the moment under my feet. I went off hunting by myself, and though I found no snakes, I should have known what to do.

The sun was dropping low in the west. Masses of white cloud hung above the flat marshy plain and seemed to be tangled in the tops of distant palms and cypresses. The sky turned orange, then saffron.[8] I walked leisurely back toward the truck. In the distance I could see Ross and Will making their way in too. The season was more advanced than at the Creek, two hundred miles to the north, and I noticed that spring flowers were blooming among the lumpy hummocks.[9] I leaned over to pick a white violet. There was a rattlesnake under the violet.

If this had happened the week before, if it had happened the day before, I think I should have lain down and died on top of the rattlesnake, with no need of being struck and poisoned. The snake did not coil, but lifted its head and whirred its rattles lightly. I stepped back slowly and put the violet in a buttonhole. I reached forward and laid the steel L across the snake's neck, just back of the blunt head. I called to Ross:

"I've got one."

He strolled toward me.

"Well, pick it up," he said.

I released it and slipped the L under the middle of the thick body.

"Go put it in the box."

He went ahead of me and lifted the top of the wire cage. I made the truck with the rattler, but when I reached up the six feet to drop it in the cage, it slipped off the stick and dropped on Ross' feet. It made no effort to strike.

"Pick it up again," he said. "If you'll pin it down lightly and reach just back of its head with your hand, as you've seen me do, you can drop it in more easily."

I pinned it and leaned over.

"I'm awfully sorry," I said, "but you're pushing me a little too fast."

He grinned. I lifted it on the stick and again as I had it at head height, it slipped off, down Ross' boots and on top of his feet. He stood as still as a stump. I dropped the snake on his feet for the third time. It seemed to me that the most patient of rattlers might in time resent being hauled up and down, and for all the man's quiet certainty that in standing motionless there was no danger, would strike at whatever was nearest, and that would be Ross.

I said, "I'm just not man enough to keep this up any longer," and he laughed and reached down with his smooth quickness and lifted the snake back of the head and dropped it in the cage. It slid in among its mates and settled in a corner. The hunt was over and we drove back over the uneven trail to Will's village and left him and went on to Arcadia and home. Our catch for the two days was thirty-two rattlers.

I said to Ross, "I believe that tomorrow I could have picked up that snake."

Back at the Creek, I felt a new lightness. I had done battle with a great fear, and the victory was mine.

---

8. saffron (saf' rən) adj.: Orange-yellow.
9. hummocks (hum' əks) n.: Areas of fertile, wooded land, higher than the surrounding swamp.

Your Response

1. Would you have been less or more brave than Rawlings on the rattlesnake hunt? Explain.

Recalling

2. Why does Rawlings go on the rattlesnake hunt?
3. Describe the area to which she, Will, and Ross travel.
4. Tell two facts she learns about rattlers.
5. How does she show that she has partly overcome her fear?

Interpreting

6. Why do Rawlings's feelings about snakes change when she holds one?
7. How do experience and knowledge influence her feelings about rattlers?
8. What reason can you suggest for rattlers having a "gray and yellow diamond pattern"?
9. At the end of the selection, why does Rawlings feel "a new lightness"? Is the victory truly hers?

Applying

10. Why does knowledge often drive away fear?

ANALYZING LITERATURE

Understanding Description in Essays

Descriptive passages include lively language and details that appeal to your senses. In this essay, for example, Rawlings writes: "Masses of white cloud . . . seemed to be tangled in the tops of distant palms and cypresses. The sky turned orange, then saffron." She helps you to see this scene by using many colors in her description: white, orange, and saffron. By using the verb "tangled," she gives you a vivid picture of the way the clouds look in the trees.

1. Find two other passages where Rawlings tells you the color of what she describes.

2. At the start of the essay, she writes: "In mid-morning he . . . brought up a five-foot rattlesnake draped limply over the steel L." Would this description have been better or worse if she had written "hanging" instead of "draped limply"? Why?

CRITICAL THINKING AND READING

Separating Fact From Opinion

A **fact** is something that can be proven, while an **opinion** is a person's belief or impression. Rawlings's statement that "The sweat poured down my back" is a fact. However, when she says, "'I believe that tomorrow I could have picked up that snake,'" she is stating an opinion.

As you read essays, you should be able to separate fact from opinion. Indicate which of the following passages from this essay are facts and which are opinions.

1. "Our catch for the two days was thirty-two rattlers."
2. "It seemed to me that the most patient of rattlers might in time resent being hauled up and down. . . ."
3. "We stopped by a pond and went swimming."
4. "If this had happened the week before, . . . I think I should have lain down and died on top of the rattlesnake. . . ."

THINKING AND WRITING

Writing a Description

The year is 2020. A distant planet has just entered into radio communication with Earth. The people of this planet are eager to discover what kind of animals exist here. Choose a type of animal that you have often observed and list its important qualities. Then use your list to write a description of it that will satisfy the curiosity of these extraterrestrial creatures. In revising your work, make sure your description gives them a clear picture of the animal you have chosen.

GUIDE FOR READING

James Dickey

(1923–   ) was born in Atlanta, Georgia, and attended Vanderbilt University. As a young man, he was a football player and a motorcycle enthusiast. Although these are not interests that are usually associated with poetry, Dickey is one of America's best-known poets. He is also famous for his novel *Deliverance* (1970), which was made into a film. In this selection, he demonstrates that poetry was not "invented as a school subject" and explains how to enjoy poetry as only a writer can.

How to Enjoy Poetry

Expository Essay

The purpose of an **expository essay** is to explain a subject or give information about it. You may have seen magazine articles with titles such as "How to Build Your Vocabulary" or "How to Operate a Computer." These articles explaining a process are expository essays. However, unlike many "How-to" articles, "How to Enjoy Poetry" does not give you rules that you *must* follow to achieve a goal. Instead, its purpose is to explain the value of poetry and offer suggestions for appreciating it.

Focus

The English language contains some words that people cannot define exactly. *Beauty* and *happiness* are two such words. *Poetry* is another. Sure, you probably know a poem when you see one in a book, but what would you say if someone asked you, "What is poetry?" To explore what your answer might be, try writing a definition of poetry. Just keep this in mind: Practically no two people agree upon what poetry is. Check your definition against James Dickey's as you read the essay.

Vocabulary

Knowing the following words will help you as you read "How to Enjoy Poetry."

emblems (em′ bləmz) *n.*: Signs; symbols (p. 376)

encounter (ən koun′ tər) *n.*: Meeting (p. 376)

compelling (kəm pel′ iŋ) *adj.*: Having a powerful effect (p. 377)

prose (prōz) *n.*: Nonpoetic language (p. 377)

definitive (di fin′ ə tiv) *adj.*: Final; the last word (p. 377)

inevitability (in ev′ ə tə bil′ i tē) *n.*: Certainty (p. 377)

interacts (in′ tər akts′) *v.*: Affects and is affected by (p. 378)

vital (vīt′ ′l) *adj.*: Essential to life; living (p. 378)

How to Enjoy Poetry

James Dickey

What is poetry? And why has it been around so long? Many have suspected that it was invented as a school subject, because you have to take exams on it. But that is not what poetry is or why it is still around. That's not what it feels like, either. When you really feel it, a new part of you happens, or an old part is renewed, with surprise and delight at being what it is.

Where Poetry Is Coming From

From the beginning, people have known that words and things, words and actions, words and feelings, go together, and that they can go together in thousands of different ways, according to who is using them. Some ways go shallow, and some go deep.

Your Connection
with Other Imaginations

The first thing to understand about poetry is that it comes to you from outside you, in books or in words, but that for it to live, something from within you must come to it and meet it and complete it. Your response with your own mind and body and memory and emotions gives the poem its ability to work its magic; if you give to it, it will give to you, and give plenty.

When you read, don't let the poet write down to you; read up to him. Reach for him from your gut out, and the heart and muscles will come into it, too.

Which Sun? Whose Stars?

The sun is new every day, the ancient philosopher Heraclitus[1] said. The sun of poetry is new every day, too, because it is seen in different ways by different people who have lived under it, lived with it, responded to it. Their lives are different from yours, but by means of the special spell that poetry brings to the *fact* of the sun—everybody's sun; yours, too—you can come into possession of many suns: as many as men and women have ever been able to imagine. Poetry makes possible the deepest kind of personal possession of the world.

The most beautiful constellation in the winter sky is Orion,[2] which ancient poets thought looked like a hunter, up there, moving across heaven with his dog Sirius.[3] What is this hunter made out of stars hunting for? What does he mean? Who owns him, if

---

1. Heraclitus (her′ ə klīt′ əs): A Greek philosopher who lived about 500 B.C.
2. Orion (ō rī′ ən)
3. Sirius (sir′ ē əs)

THE STARRY NIGHT, 1889
Vincent van Gogh
The Museum of Modern Art

anybody? The poet Aldous Huxley[4] felt that he did, and so, in Aldous Huxley's universe of personal emotion, he did.

> *Up from among the emblems of the*
>   *wind into its heart of power,*
> *The Huntsman climbs, and all his*
>   *living stars*
> *Are bright, and all are mine.*

------

4. Aldous Huxley: An English poet, essayist, and novelist (1894–1963).

Where to Start

The beginning of your true encounter with poetry should be simple. It should by-pass all classrooms, all textbooks, courses, examinations, and libraries and go straight to the things that make your own existence exist: to your body and nerves and blood and muscles. Find your own way—a secret way that just maybe you don't know yet—to open yourself as wide as you can and as deep as you can to the moment, the *now* of your own existence and the endless mystery of it, and perhaps at the same time to one other thing that is not you, but is out there: a handful of gravel is a good place to start. So is an ice cube—what more mysterious and beautiful *interior* of something has there ever been?

As for me, I like the sun, the source of all living things, and on certain days very good-feeling, too. "Start with the sun," D. H. Lawrence[5] said, "and everything will slowly, slowly happen." Good advice. And a lot *will* happen.

What is more fascinating than a rock, if you really feel it and *look* at it, or more interesting than a leaf?

> *Horses, I mean; butterflies, whales;*
> *Mosses, and stars; and gravelly*
> *Rivers, and fruit.*
>
> *Oceans, I mean; black valleys; corn;*
> *Brambles, and cliffs; rock, dirt, dust,*
> *ice . . .*

Go back and read this list—it is quite a list, Mark Van Doren's[6] list!—item by item. Slowly. Let each of these things call up an image out of your own life.

Think and feel. What moss do you see? Which horse? What field of corn? What brambles are *your* brambles? Which river is most yours?

The Poem's Way of Going

Part of the spell of poetry is in the rhythm of language, used by poets who understand how powerful a factor rhythm can be, how compelling and unforgettable. Almost anything put into rhythm and rhyme is more memorable than the same thing said in prose. Why this is, no one knows completely, though the answer is surely rooted far down in the biology by means of which we exist; in the circulation of the blood that goes forth from the heart and comes back, and in the repetition of breathing. Croesus[7] was a rich Greek king, back in the sixth century before Christ, but this tombstone was not his:

> *No Croesus lies in the grave you see;*
> *I was a poor laborer, and this suits*
> *me.*

That is plain-spoken and definitive. You believe it, and the rhyme helps you believe it and keep it.

Some Things You'll Find Out

Writing poetry is a lot like a contest with yourself, and if you like sports and games and competitions of all kinds, you might like to try writing some. Why not?

The possibilities of rhyme are great. Some of the best fun is in making up your own limericks.[8] There's no reason you can't invent limericks about anything that comes to your mind. No reason. Try it.

The problem is to find three words that rhyme and fit into a meaning. "There was a young man from . . ." *Where* was he from? What situation was he in? How can these things fit into the limerick form—a form everybody knows—so that the rhymes "pay off," and give that sense of completion and inevitability that is so deliciously memorable that nothing else is like it?

---

5. D. H. Lawrence: An English poet and novelist (1885–1930).
6. Mark Van Doren: An American poet, teacher, and critic (1894–1972).

7. Croesus (krē′ səs)
8. limericks (lim′ ər iks) *n.*: Nonsense poems of five lines.

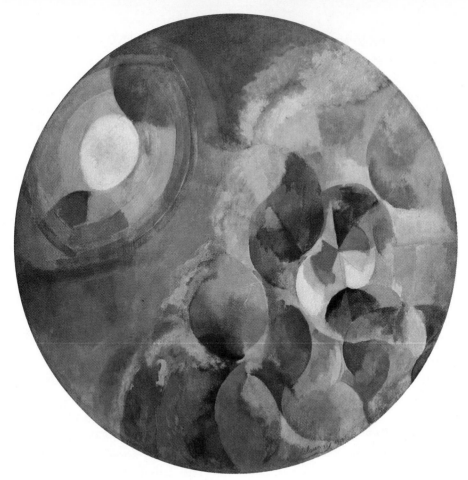

SIMULTANEOUS CONTRASTS: SUN AND MOON, 1913
Robert Delaunay
The Museum of Modern Art

How It Goes with You

The more your encounter with poetry deepens, the more your experience of your own life will deepen, and you will begin to see things by means of words, and words by means of things.

You will come to understand the world as it interacts with words, as it can be re-created by words, by rhythms and by images.

You'll understand that this condition is one charged with vital possibilities. You will pick up meaning more quickly—and you will *create* meaning, too, for yourself and for others.

Connections between things will exist for you in ways that they never did before. They will shine with unexpectedness, wide-openness, and you will go toward them, on your own path. "Then . . ." as Dante[9] says, ". . . Then will your feet be filled with good desire." You will know this is happening the first time you say, of something you never would have noticed before, "Well, would you look at *that*! Who'd 'a thunk it?" (Pause, full of new light)

"*I* thunk it!"

---

9. Dante (dän' tā): An Italian poet (1265–1321) whose most famous work is *The Divine Comedy.*

Your Response

1. How do you know when you like a poem? What reasons do you generally give?

Recalling

2. According to James Dickey, how can you get the most from a poem?
3. Why are rhythm and rhyme important to poetry?
4. How is poetry "like a contest with yourself"?

Interpreting

5. What does Dickey mean when he writes, "when you read, don't let the poet write down to you; read up to him"? Why would reading this way increase your enjoyment?
6. Why do you think Dickey relates rhythm in poetry to biology?
7. What does he mean by asking you "to open yourself as wide as you can and as deep as you can to the moment. . . ."?

Applying

8. Dickey says you can enjoy poetry more by focusing on yourself and also on "one other thing that is not you." Which "other thing" would you choose? Why?

ANALYZING LITERATURE

Understanding the Expository Essay

The purpose of an **expository essay** is to explain a subject rather than present a story. In "How to Enjoy Poetry," James Dickey explains why poetry is valuable not as a school subject but as a response to life. He also offers suggestions for getting the most from poems.

1. What key idea does Dickey offer under the heading "Your connection with other imaginations"? What key idea does he offer under the heading "Which sun? Whose stars?"
2. Identify three suggestions that he offers for increasing your enjoyment of poetry.
3. Which suggestion do you find most helpful? Why?

CRITICAL THINKING AND READING

Experimenting With a Suggestion

In the section of this essay entitled "Where to Start," Dickey suggests reading a list of things in a poem and responding to each item.

1. Choose three items from the list in the poem.
2. Freewrite about the picture that each of these items calls up in you.
3. Has writing about these items given you a better appreciation of the lines from the poem? Why or why not?

THINKING AND WRITING

Writing an Expository Essay

Imagine that a friend has moved to another city and you have told him or her about a new hobby you have taken up. This hobby can be anything you really like doing. Your friend wants to know about your hobby and to understand why you enjoy it so much. List the key aspects of your hobby and the reasons why it is fun. Then use this list to write a letter to your friend explaining what you do and why you enjoy it. In revising your letter, put yourself in your friend's place. Make sure that he or she will understand the value of what you do.

LEARNING OPTIONS

1. **Writing.** Poetry probably means very different things to you than it does to James Dickey. After all, he was born in 1923! Your world is very different from the one he grew up in. Write a poem in which you express what it is like to be you, living how and where you live. Collect the poems you and your classmates write. Copy them and publish an anthology called *Our World*.
2. **Speaking and Listening.** One way to share your enjoyment of a poem is to read it aloud to others. Pick a poem, and read it to the class. Be prepared to explain why you chose it.

GUIDE FOR READING

Chief Dan George

(1899–1981), a member of the Squamish Band, was born and raised on the Burrard Reserve in Canada's British Columbia. For many years he worked as a longshoreman on Vancouver's waterfront. Later he became an entertainer and a musician and also served as chief of his reserve for twelve years. At the age of sixty, he began appearing on Canadian television. He received an Academy Award nomination for his supporting role in the movie *Little Big Man* (1970).

I Am a Native of North America

Persuasive Essay

In a **persuasive essay** the author tries to convince readers to accept a certain point of view or to take a certain action. A good persuasive essay makes a strong argument for the author's point of view. Convincing arguments may include logical appeals to the reader's thinking or stirring appeals to the reader's emotions or both. In the following essay, Chief Dan George tries to persuade readers to accept his ideas by contrasting one way of life with another.

Focus

In this essay Chief Dan George describes how he grew up as a member of the Squamish Band of the Salish Indians. Among these people the greatest prestige is gained by giving away wealth. The ceremony at which this is done is called a *potlatch.* Often the people of one village invite those of another village for several days of feasting. During the festivities elaborate gifts are given to the guests. Imagine what such an occasion must be like, and write about your reactions to this idea. What does the potlatch suggest about the values of the Salish people? What traditions in your culture are similar to the potlatch? How are they different? Would you like to attend a potlatch? As you read, notice how other Salish beliefs and traditions relate to the potlatch.

Vocabulary

Knowing the following words will help you as you read "I Am a Native of North America."

distinct (di stinkt′) *adj.*: Separate and different (p. 381)

communal (kə myo͞o′ nəl) *adj.*: Shared by all (p. 381)

inlet (in′ let) *n.*: A narrow strip of water jutting into a body of land from a river, a lake, or an ocean (p. 381)

integration (in tə grā′ shən) *n.*: The mingling of different ethnic or racial groups (p. 382)

scorn (skôrn) *n.*: Complete lack of respect (p. 382)

I Am a Native of North America

Chief Dan George

In the course of my lifetime I have lived in two distinct cultures. I was born into a culture that lived in communal houses. My grandfather's house was eighty feet long. It was called a smoke house, and it stood down by the beach along the inlet. All my grandfather's sons and their families lived in this large dwelling. Their sleeping apartments were separated by blankets made of bull rush reeds, but one open fire in the middle served the cooking needs of all. In houses like these, throughout the tribe, people learned to live with one another; learned to serve one another; learned to respect the rights of one another. And children shared the thoughts of the adult world and found themselves surrounded by aunts and uncles and cousins who loved them and did not threaten them. My father was born in such a house and learned from infancy how to love people and be at home with them.

And beyond this acceptance of one another there was a deep respect for everything in nature that surrounded them. My father loved the earth and all its creatures. The earth was his second mother. The earth and everything it contained was a gift from See-see-am[1] . . . and the way to thank this great spirit was to use his gifts with respect.

I remember, as a little boy, fishing with him up Indian River and I can still see him as the sun rose above the mountain top in the early morning . . . I can see him standing by the water's edge with his arms raised above his head while he softly moaned . . . "Thank you, thank you." It left a deep impression on my young mind.

And I shall never forget his disappointment when once he caught me gaffing for fish[2] "just for the fun of it." "My Son," he said, "the Great Spirit gave you those fish to be your brothers, to feed you when you are hungry. You must respect them. You must not kill them just for the fun of it."

This then was the culture I was born into and for some years the only one I really knew or tasted. This is why I find it hard to accept many of the things I see around me.

I see people living in smoke houses hundreds of times bigger than the one I knew. But the people in one apartment do not even know the people in the next and care less about them.

It is also difficult for me to understand the deep hate that exists among people. It is hard to understand a culture that justifies the killing of millions in past wars, and is at this very moment preparing bombs to kill even greater numbers. It is hard for me to

---

1. See-see-am: The name of the Great Spirit, or "The Chief Above," in the Salishan language of Chief George's people.

2. gaffing for fish: Using a barbed spear to catch river fish.

understand a culture that spends more on wars and weapons to kill, than it does on education and welfare to help and develop.

It is hard for me to understand a culture that not only hates and fights its brothers but even attacks nature and abuses her. I see my white brother going about blotting out nature from his cities. I see him strip the hills bare, leaving ugly wounds on the face of mountains. I see him tearing things from the bosom of mother earth as though she were a monster, who refused to share her treasures with him. I see him throw poison in the waters, indifferent to the life he kills there; and he chokes the air with deadly fumes.

My white brother does many things well for he is more clever than my people but I wonder if he knows how to love well. I wonder if he has ever really learned to love at all. Perhaps he only loves the things that are his own but never learned to love the things that are outside and beyond him. And this is, of course, not love at all, for man must love all creation or he will love none of it. Man must love fully or he will become the lowest of the animals. It is the power to love that makes him the greatest of them all . . . for he alone of all animals is capable of love.

Love is something you and I must have. We must have it because our spirit feeds upon it. We must have it because without it we become weak and faint. Without love our self-esteem weakens. Without it our courage fails. Without love we can no longer look out confidently at the world. Instead we turn inwardly and begin to feed upon our own personalities and little by little we destroy ourselves.

You and I need the strength and joy that comes from knowing that we are loved. With it we are creative. With it we march tirelessly. With it, and with it alone, we are able to sacrifice for others.

There have been times when we all wanted so desperately to feel a reassuring hand upon us . . . there have been lonely times when we so wanted a strong arm around us . . . I cannot tell you how deeply I miss my wife's presence when I return from a trip. Her love was my greatest joy, my strength, my greatest blessing.

I am afraid my culture has little to offer yours. But my culture did prize friendship and companionship. It did not look on privacy as a thing to be clung to, for privacy builds up walls and walls promote distrust. My culture lived in big family communities, and from infancy people learned to live with others.

My culture did not prize the hoarding of private possessions; in fact, to hoard was a shameful thing to do among my people. The Indian looked on all things in nature as belonging to him and he expected to share them with others and to take only what he needed.

Everyone likes to give as well as receive. No one wishes only to receive all the time. We have taken much from your culture . . . I wish you had taken something from our culture . . . for there were some beautiful and good things in it.

Soon it will be too late to know my culture, for integration is upon us and soon we will have no values but yours. Already many of our young people have forgotten the old ways. And many have been shamed of their Indian ways by scorn and ridicule. My culture is like a wounded deer that has crawled away into the forest to bleed and die alone.

The only thing that can truly help us is genuine love. You must truly love us, be patient with us and share with us. And we must love you—with a genuine love that forgives and forgets . . . a love that forgives the terrible sufferings your culture brought ours when it swept over us like a wave crashing

WALKING IN BEAUTY (detail)
Clifford Brycelea
Courtesy of the Artist

along a beach . . . with a love that forgets and lifts up its head and sees in your eyes an answering love of trust and acceptance.

This is brotherhood . . . anything less is not worthy of the name.

I have spoken.

RESPONDING TO THE SELECTION

Your Response

1. What about Chief Dan George's childhood appeals to you? What doesn't?

Recalling

2. Name one thing people learned by living in the communal smoke houses.
3. According to the author, what makes humans the greatest of all creatures?

Interpreting

4. In your own words, summarize the differences between the "two distinct cultures" that the author lived in.
5. Chief Dan George says that his "white brother" is more clever than his people. What does he mean by the word *clever*?
6. What effect does the author create by using the term "white brother" to refer to the culture that sometimes harms his own?

Applying

7. Describe three specific ways in which life would change if people took Chief Dan George's words completely to heart.

ANALYZING LITERATURE

Understanding a Persuasive Essay

The purpose of a **persuasive essay** is to convince readers to accept a certain point of view or to take a certain action. In "I Am a Native of North America," Chief Dan George tries to persuade you that Native Americans have important values to offer European American culture. He supports his ideas with specific examples from his own life.

1. What example does he use to show that Native Americans have respect for nature?

2. Do his arguments appeal to your logical thinking, your feelings, or both? Give examples to support your answer.

CRITICAL THINKING AND READING

Appreciating Contrast Between Cultures

Contrast means showing the differences between two things. In his essay Chief Dan George makes important points by contrasting Native American culture with the culture of his "white brothers." Find contrasting statements about the following two topics:

1. people's attitudes toward other people
2. people's attitudes toward nature

THINKING AND WRITING

Writing a Persuasive Essay

Think of some aspect of Native American culture that you admire; for example, respect for the environment or the sharing of material wealth. Write a letter to the editor of your local or school newspaper urging readers to adopt that attitude. First make a list of specific ways in which your readers would benefit from the new attitude. Use the list as the basis for your essay. When you revise, make sure that your arguments are clearly stated so that readers will understand what they will gain by changing.

LEARNING OPTION

Multicultural Activity. Chief Dan George appeared only in films and television shows that portrayed Native Americans in respectful ways. Talk to two or three adults who remember the 1950's and 1960's. Ask them to recall how Native Americans were portrayed on television and in movies during those years. Take notes and bring your findings to class.

Essays in the Content Areas

THE LIBRARY
Jacob Lawrence
National Museum of American Art
The Smithsonian Institution

Isaac Asimov

(1920–1992) was born in Russia and grew up in Brooklyn. He earned a Ph.D. in biochemistry, a subject he taught at Boston University from 1949 to 1958, when he turned to full-time writing. It is said that since 1969 he wrote a book a month. His nonfiction works, such as the essay you are about to read, are admirable for making scientific and technological subjects understandable to the general reader. In this essay he explores the subject of endlessness. What does it mean for something to be without end?

Endlessness

Outlining

Outlining means organizing the content of a piece of writing to show the main ideas and supporting details. An outline might look as follows:

    I. First main topic
      A. First subtopic
        1. First supporting idea or detail
        2. Second supporting idea or detail
      B. Second subtopic
    II. Second main topic {The outline continues in the same way.}

By dividing an essay into its main ideas and supporting details, you will understand and remember more of what you read.

Focus

How do you use numbers outside school? Do you use them when shopping? Are they important in sports? List as many everyday uses for numbers as you can. Then take a look around where you are right now to see where numbers pop up, starting with the pages in a book or the face of a clock. We take these numbers for granted, but they have mysterious traits, one of which you will discover in the essay "Endlessness."

Vocabulary

Knowing the following words will help you as you read "Endlessness."

succession (sək sesh′ ən) *n.*: The act of coming after another in order (p. 388)

clamoring (klam′ ər iŋ) *v.*: Loudly demanding (p. 388)

expectantly (ek spek′ tənt lē) *adv.*: In a way that shows eager waiting (p. 389)

conceivable (kən sē′ və b'l) *adj.*: Imaginable (p. 389)

denumerable (di noō′ mər ə b'l) *adj.*: Countable—said of a set whose elements can be put in one-to-one correspondence with the natural integers (p. 389)

Endlessness

Isaac Asimov

The "Not-a-Number"

Anyone thinking about numbers must come to the conclusion that there are a great many of them, and feel at a loss to express just how many. In poetry, one could make use of some simile: "as many as the sands of the sea"; "as numerous as the stars that shine and twinkle in the Milky Way."

To the mathematician, however, similes are of no use. To him, it merely seems that the integers are formed by beginning with one, adding one to that for the next number, and one to that for the next number, and so on. Since the mathematical rules do not set any limits to addition (*any* two numbers may be added) there can be no end to this process. After all, however large a number is named—*however* large—though it stretch in a line of small figures from here to the farthest star, it is always possible to say "that number plus one" and have a still higher number.

The series of integers, if written in order, 1, 2, 3 . . . is "infinite," a word coming from Latin words meaning "no end." Consequently, when we can write the series of numbers thus: 1, 2, 3 . . . , we mean "1, 2, 3, and so on endlessly."

In the same way if we consider the negative numbers, −1, −2, −3, and so on, we can see that they too go on forever and can be written: −1, −2, −3 . . . Similarly, the series of positive imaginaries may be written as +1i, +2i, +3i . . . , and the negative imaginaries as −1i, −2i, −3i . . .

Now let's consider another kind of series of integers. Let's think of the even numbers: 2, 4, 6, 8, and so on. How many even numbers are there?

One way of arguing this question would be to say: Well, the integers can be divided into odd numbers and even numbers alternately, so that in the first ten numbers there are five odds and five evens, in the first hundred numbers there are fifty odds and fifty evens, and so on. This sort of thing would go on no matter how many integers are taken. Therefore, the total number of even integers is half the total number of all integers.

But this is not so. The number of integers is infinite, and one cannot talk of "a half of infinity."

Instead, consider the even integers this way. The series 2, 4, 6, 8 . . . can continue endlessly. There is no "largest even number" any more than there is a "largest number." For though you name an even number written in small numerals from here to the farthest star, it is always possible to say "that number plus two." Hence the series of even numbers should be written: 2, 4, 6 . . .

In the same way, odd numbers are 1, 3, 5 . . . ; the series of numbers, counting by fives , are 5, 10, 15. . . ; and the series of numbers counting by millions are 1000000, 2000000, 3000000 . . . All these series of integers are endless and that is all that infinity (or an infinite number) means.

Counting Without Counting

But this may not satisfy you. Surely, you may be thinking, even though the series of even numbers is endless and the series of all

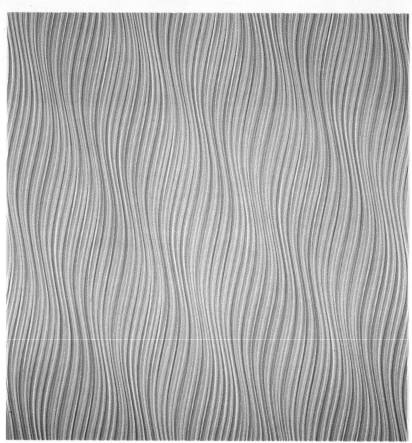

ORPHEAN ELEGY 1, 1978
Bridget Riley
Rowan Gallery

integers is endless, the fact still remains that there are only half as many even numbers as there are all integers, and that there are only a millionth as many even-million numbers. It stands to reason!

(Never trust an argument *only* because it stands to reason. It stands to reason that if a man is facing north, his back is toward the south. However, if he's standing at the South Pole and is facing north, his back is also toward the north.)

Well, then, let's settle the matter by finding out how many even numbers there are compared with all the integers. How, if the quantity is endless? Why, we'll count.

Let's first see what we mean by counting. In the ordinary meaning of the word, we count objects by assigning each one a num-

ber in succession. This object is number one, that is number two, the other is number three, and so on. When we finish, if the last object was assigned number ten, then there are ten objects.

But can we count without numbers? So used are we to numbers for the purpose, that this sounds as though I were asking, Can we count without counting?—and yet we can.

Suppose you have a number of lollipops (you don't know how many) and a crowd of clamoring children (you don't know how many). You distribute the lollipops, one to a child, and when you are finished, all the children have lollipops and you still have additional lollipops in your hand. Obviously, then, even without counting in the ordinary fashion, you know there were more lollipops than children. If, on the other hand, you ran out of lollipops while some children still stood expectantly waiting, you would know there were more children than lollipops.

But if, at the conclusion of the distribution, each child had a lollipop, and there were no children left unsatisfied and no lollipops left in your hand, then you would know beyond the shadow of a doubt, and without ever having counted in the usual fashion, that the number of children was equal to the number of lollipops.

This way of counting, then, which consists of lining up two series (one of children and one of lollipops; or one of all integers and one of even numbers) will tell you whether the two series are equal or unequal; and, if unequal, which is the larger.

Suppose we line up the series of all integers and all even numbers, then, as follows:

$$1 \; 2 \; 3 \; 4 \; 5 \; 6 \; 7 \; 8 \; 9 \; 10 \; . \; . \; .$$
$$\updownarrow \; \updownarrow \; \updownarrow \; \updownarrow \; \updownarrow \; \updownarrow \; \updownarrow \; \updownarrow \; \updownarrow \; \updownarrow$$
$$2 \; 4 \; 6 \; 8 \; 10 \; 12 \; 14 \; 16 \; 18 \; 20 \; . \; . \; .$$

As you see there is an even number for every conceivable integer, and you can obtain the even number by simply doubling the integer. No matter how far you go, no integer need be omitted and no even number is missing. (Every child, in other words, is being satisfied with a lollipop.) At no point, no matter how far you go, will you find an integer for which you can't write an even number, and each integer (no matter how many you've gone through) has a different even number attached to it.

Does this mean that there are exactly as many even numbers as there are integers all together? Well, the phrase "as many" doesn't really have the usual everyday meaning when we're talking about things that are endless. Instead it is more proper to say that the series of even numbers is "in one-to-one corre-

spondence" with the series of all integers; meaning that the even numbers can be lined up systematically with the integers so that there is one of the first series for every one of the second and vice versa.

You can also set up a series of numbers counting by millions and compare it with the series of all integers in the same way. For every integer there's an even-million number obtained by multiplying the integer by a million. For 1 there's 1000000, for 6 there's 6000000, for 2873 there's 2873000000 and so on. So there are "as many" numbers counting by a million as there are integers altogether. Or, at least, the two series are in one-to-one correspondence. Any series of numbers that is in one-to-one correspondence with the series of integers is said to be "denumerable." And the set of integers is also called "denumerable."

The Infinite in a Nutshell

Of course, the "infinite" gives one a notion of vastness and foreverness. It may even seem to you to have no usefulness.

However, even if we concerned ourselves only with small numbers, notions of "infinity" would crop up. For instance, suppose we were to divide 1 by $\frac{1}{10}$. Remembering the reciprocal rule, this is the same as 1×10 and therefore $1 \div \frac{1}{10} = 10$. Similarly, $1 \div \frac{1}{100} = 100$, and $1 \div \frac{1}{1000} = 1000$.

In fact, the smaller you make your divisor, the larger your quotient becomes.

Indeed, when you divide 1 (or any number) by a series of numbers that grow smaller and smaller, then the quotient grows larger and larger, and as the divisor grows endlessly small, the answer grows endlessly large.

However, what, you may wonder, is meant by "endlessly small"? Surely smallness has an end at zero. Ah, but smallness may be expressed in the form of a fraction. Thus $\frac{1}{10}$ is a small number, $\frac{1}{100}$ is smaller, $\frac{1}{1000}$ is smaller still. There is no limit to the smallness as you increase the number of zeros to $\frac{1}{10000000000000000}$ ... for no matter how far you increase it you never quite reach zero.

We may therefore also say: When you divide 1 (or any number) by a series of numbers that grows larger and larger, then the quotient grows smaller and smaller, and as the divisor grows endlessly large, the answer grows endlessly small.

Note, however, that we can never divide any number by 0. This operation is excluded from mathematics. And for a very good reason. What number, for instance, would be the quotient if we tried to divide 6, say, by 0? We would have $\frac{6}{0} = ?$ In other words, what number *times* zero comes out 6? There is no such number, since every number times 0 is 0. So we can never divide any number by 0.

The interval between any two numbers, say between 1 and 2, can be divided into any number of fractions by breaking it up into millionths, or trillionths, and each trillionth into trillionths and so on. This can be done for any smaller interval, such as that between $\frac{1}{4}$ and $\frac{1}{2}$ or between 0.0000000 and 0.0000001.

And yet mathematicians have managed to show that all conceivable fractions (that is, all rational numbers) can be arranged in such a way that a one-to-one correspondence can be set up with the series of integers. For every integer there will be a fraction, and vice versa, with no integers left out and no fractions left out. The series of all possible fractions is therefore denumerable.

Closer and Closer and Closer . . .

Consider a series of fractions like this: $\frac{1}{2}, \frac{1}{4}, \frac{1}{8}, \frac{1}{16}, \frac{1}{32}, \frac{1}{64}, \frac{1}{128}, \frac{1}{256}, \frac{1}{512}$, and so on endlessly.

Notice that each fraction is one-half the size of the preceding fraction, since the denominator doubles each time. (After all, if you take any of the fractions in the series, say $\frac{1}{128}$, and divide it by 2, that is the same as multiplying it by $\frac{1}{2}$, and $\frac{1}{128} \times \frac{1}{2} = \frac{1}{256}$, the denominator doubling.)

Although the fractions get continually smaller, the series can be considered endless because no matter how small the fractions get, it is always possible to multiply the denominator by 2 and get a still smaller fraction and the next in the series. Furthermore, the fractions never quite reach zero because the denominator can get larger endlessly and it is only if an end could be reached (which it can't) that the fraction could reach zero.

The question is, What is the sum of all those fractions? It might seem that the sum of an endless series of numbers must be endlessly large ("it stands to reason") but let's start adding, anyway.

First $\frac{1}{2}$ plus $\frac{1}{4}$ is $\frac{3}{4}$. Add $\frac{1}{8}$ and the sum is $\frac{7}{8}$; add $\frac{1}{16}$ and the sum is $\frac{15}{16}$; and $\frac{1}{32}$ and the sum is $\frac{31}{32}$, and so on.

Notice that after the first two terms of the series are added, the sum is $\frac{3}{4}$ which is only $\frac{1}{4}$ short of 1. Addition of the third term

REYTEY, 1968
Victor Vasarely
Solomon R. Guggenheim Museum

gives a sum that is only $\frac{1}{8}$ short of 1. The next term gives a sum that is only $\frac{1}{16}$ short of 1, then $\frac{1}{32}$, $\frac{1}{64}$, and so on.

In other words, as you sum up more and more terms of that series of fractions, you get closer and closer to 1, as close as you want, to within a millionth of one, a trillionth of one, a trillionth of a trillionth of one. You get closer and closer and closer and closer to 1, but you *never quite reach 1.*

Mathematicians express this by saying that the sum of the endless series of fractions $\frac{1}{2}$, $\frac{1}{4}$, $\frac{1}{8}$ . . . "approaches 1 as a limit."

This is an example of a "converging series," that is, a series with an endless number of members but with a total sum that approaches an ordinary number (a "finite" number) as a limit.

The Greeks discovered such converging series but were so impressed with the endlessness of the terms of the series that they did not realize that the sum might not be endless. Consequently, a Greek named Zeno[1] set up a number of problems called "paradoxes"[2] which seemed to disprove things that were obviously true. He "disproved," for instance, that motion was possible. These paradoxes were famous for thousands of

---

1. Zeno (zē′ no)
2. paradoxes (par′ ə däks′ iz) *n.:* Statements that seem to contain opposite meanings or to be unbelievable.

years, but all vanished as soon as the truth about converging series was realized.

Zeno's most famous paradox is called "Achilles[3] and the Tortoise." Achilles was a Homeric[4] hero renowned for his swiftness, and a tortoise is an animal renowned for its slowness. Nevertheless, Zeno set out to demonstrate that in a race in which the tortoise is given a head start, Achilles could never overtake the tortoise.

Suppose, for instance, that Achilles can run ten times as fast as the tortoise and that the tortoise is given a hundred-yard head start. In a few racing strides, Achilles wipes out that hundred-yard handicap, but in that time, the tortoise, traveling at one-tenth Achilles's speed (pretty darned fast for a tortoise), has moved on ten yards. Achilles next makes up that ten yards, but in that time the tortoise has moved one yard further. Achilles covers that one yard, and the tortoise has traveled an additional tenth of a yard. Achilles—

But you see how it is. Achilles keeps advancing, but so does the tortoise, and Achilles never catches up. Furthermore, since you could argue the same way, however small the tortoise's head start—one foot or one inch—Achilles could never make up any head start, however small. And this means that motion is impossible.

Of course, you know that Achilles *could* overtake the tortoise and motion *is* possible. Zeno's "proof" is therefore a paradox.

Now, then, what's wrong with Zeno's proof? Let's see. Suppose Achilles could run ten yards per second and the tortoise one yard per second. Achilles makes up the original hundred-yard head start in 10 seconds during which time the tortoise travels ten yards. Achilles makes up the ten yards in 1 second, during which time the tortoise travels one yard. Achilles makes up the one yard in 0.1 second during which time the tortoise travels a tenth of a yard.

In other words, the time taken for Achilles to cover each of the successive head starts of the turtle forms a series that looks like this: 10, 1, 0.1, 0.01, 0.001, 0.0001, 0.00001, and so on.

How much time does it take for Achilles to make up all the head starts? Since there are an endless number of terms in this Zeno series, Zeno assumed the total sum was infinite. He did not realize that some series of endless numbers of terms "converge" and have a finite sum.

For instance, the sum of the first two terms in the Zeno series above is 11; the sum of the first three is 11.1; of the first four, 11.11; of the first five, 11.111 and so on. As you see, if you add up all the endless series of terms, you get an endless decimal as the sum; 11.11111111111111111 . . . and so on forever.

But if you work out the decimal equivalent of the number $11\frac{1}{9}$, you find that it also is the endlessly repeating decimal 11.111111111111111111111111 . . . and so on forever.

The sum of the Zeno series is therefore $11\frac{1}{9}$ seconds and that is the time in which Achilles will overtake and pass the tortoise even though he has to work his way through an endless series of continually smaller head starts that the tortoise maintains. He *will* overtake the tortoise after all; motion *is* possible, and we can all relax.

---

3. Achilles (ə kil′ ēz): A legendary Greek hero who fought in the Trojan War, which the Greeks waged against the city of Troy in Asia Minor about 3,000 years ago.

4. Homeric (hō mer′ ik) *adj*.: The Greek poet Homer is said to have lived during the 8th century B.C. He wrote two epic poems, the *Iliad* and the *Odyssey*, about the Trojan War and the events that occurred afterward.

RESPONDING TO THE SELECTION

Your Response

1. Which ideas in the essay do you find most interesting? Explain.

Recalling

2. In mathematics what does infinity mean?
3. What is a converging series?
4. How does Asimov disprove Zeno's paradox?

Interpreting

5. What does Asimov mean by "counting without counting"?
6. How does Asimov use fractions to demonstrate the concept of the "endlessly small"?

Applying

7. What new ideas about infinity do you now have as a result of reading "Endlessness"?

READING IN THE CONTENT AREAS

Outlining

Outlining means organizing the content of a piece of writing to show the main ideas and supporting details. For example, the following is an outline of the first part of "Endlessness."

    I. Infinity
       A. Poet—can use simile to show it
       B. Mathematician—cannot use simile
          1. No limits to addition
          2. Any series of integers is infinite—can always be added to

Make an outline of the next part of the essay, headed "Counting Without Counting."

CRITICAL THINKING AND READING

Explaining Mathematics Inductively

Inductive reasoning means drawing a general conclusion from particular facts or cases. In "Endlessness" Asimov uses inductive reasoning to explain the general concepts with which his essay is concerned. For example, in the first part

he wishes to explain the general concept that the total number of even integers is infinite, like the total number of all integers. He does so by reasoning from a particular case.

> The series 2, 4, 6, 8 . . . can continue endlessly . . . [because] it is always possible to say "that [even] number plus two."

1. How does Asimov use inductive reasoning to show that the series of fractions 1/2, 1/4, 1/8 . . . will never reach zero?
2. How does he use inductive reasoning to show that the sum total of all fractions in this series will never quite reach one?

THINKING AND WRITING

Writing About Mathematics

Imagine that you are visiting a planet that has not discovered counting. Write an essay explaining the concept of counting to the people living on the planet. Revise your essay to make sure your explanation is clear.

LEARNING OPTION

Cross-curricular Connection. Find out about the work of Leonardo Fibonacci, a mathematician who lived in the thirteenth century. In particular, find out about his discovery of a special series of numbers that now bears his name: the Fibonacci Series. The first three numbers in the series are 1, 1, and 2. What operation must you perform on the first two numbers to get the third? Use the same method to get the fourth number in the series (3). Do you see the pattern? What is the fifth number in the series? How long could the series continue on?

Figure out the first eight numbers in the series, and choose any four numbers in a row. Multiply the two outside numbers, and then multiply the two inside numbers. What is the difference of the two products? Try this again with a different sequence of four. What do you notice about the difference of the products?

GUIDE FOR READING

H. N. Levitt

(1920–   ) was born and raised in New York City. During World War II he was a naval officer. After the war he pursued a career as a playwright and college professor of drama. However, he has always loved the visual arts too. He learned how to paint with watercolors at a well-known art school, and he has written many magazine articles about painters. In this article he tells why he considers Winslow Homer "America's Greatest Painter."

Winslow Homer: America's Greatest Painter

Setting a Purpose for Reading

A **purpose** is a reason for doing something. You can learn more from any work of nonfiction if you set a purpose for your reading before you start. One strategy for setting a goal is to imagine that you are a newspaper reporter gathering information for a story. Reading "Winslow Homer: America's Greatest Painter" as a reporter, for instance, you would use the journalistic formula *who? what? when? where? why?* and *how?* You might wonder *who* Winslow Homer was, *what* he did, *when* and *where* he lived, *how* he worked, and *why* he is considered a great painter.

Your information about Homer will not be complete, however, unless you look at his paintings (pages 396 and 398). Glancing at them before you begin will give you a general sense of his art.

Focus

Look at the paintings on pages 396 and 398. Which one do you like better? Look at it carefully, and take notice of the thoughts and feelings you have. Then imagine that you are one of the soldiers or the man on the boat. Write a description of what you are thinking and feeling at the moment. Compare your reactions with those of your classmates. Keep your response in mind as you read about Winslow Homer, the man who made the paintings.

Vocabulary

Knowing the following words will help you as you read "Winslow Homer: America's Greatest Painter."

cantankerous (kan taŋ′ kər əs) *adj.*: Bad-tempered (p. 395)

subtle (sut′ 'l) *adj.*: Delicately skillful or clever (p. 395)

brutality (broo tal′ ə tē) *n.*: Violence; harshness (p. 396)

vanquished (vaŋ′ kwisht) *n.*: The person defeated (usually a verb) (p. 397)

serenity (sə ren′ ə tē) *n.*: Calmness (p. 397)

subservient (səb sur′ vē ənt) *adj.*: Inferior (p. 398)

Winslow Homer:
America's Greatest Painter

H. N. Levitt

His oil paintings and watercolors are in all major American museums and collections today. But even when Winslow Homer was alive, they called him America's greatest painter.

That wasn't all they said about him. They also called him crusty, bad-tempered, cantankerous, grouchy, sour as a crab, and surly as a bear. He was all those things, and more.

His brother's wife—and Winslow's only female friend—thought Homer the most courteous gentleman she ever knew. She said he knew what he wanted in life, and he went about getting it without any fuss or feathers.

When it came to painting, he took five lessons, decided that was enough, then went on to become a self-taught genius.

Homer was born into a middle-class family on Feb. 24, 1836. The family lived near the harbor in Boston, so Homer's earliest memories were of ships, sailors, fishermen and the sea.

When he was six, the family moved to Cambridge, directly across the street from Harvard College. Sometimes Winslow's dad would suggest that the boy consider attending Harvard someday. But it was no use. All young Winslow wanted to do was fish and draw.

After a while, the family realized there was something special about Winslow, because that's all he would do—fish and draw, day in and day out, all year long.

But even if Homer had wanted to go to college, there would have been no money for it. When Homer was 13, his dad sold all and left to make his fortune in the California gold rush. He came back a few years later empty-handed.

But the family remained close. And once they realized how important art was to Homer, they encouraged it. In fact, his brothers secretly bought up his paintings at early exhibitions so he wouldn't get discouraged if no one else bought them. Those two brothers remained his best friends all his life.

When the Civil War broke out in 1861, Homer was a young artist already on his way to fame. As a freelance illustrator for *Harper's Weekly*, America's most important news magazine, he was considered one of the country's finest wood-block engravers.

In those days, an artist would cut illustrations into a wood block, which was then inked in black and printed on sheets of paper. Techniques like subtle shadowing and distant perspective were hard to achieve, but Homer's illustrations were unusually lively and strong.

Harper's Weekly offered Homer a good

PRISONERS FROM THE FRONT, 1866
Winslow Homer
The Metropolitan Museum of Art

job, and he could have remained a weekly illustrator all his life. But he wanted to work for no one but himself, so he turned the offer down.

Homer left New York to paint the war. He joined Gen. George McClellan's Army of the Potomac[1] as a freelance artist-correspondent. He painted scenes at the siege of Yorktown[2] and did many drawings of Abraham Lincoln, the tall, gaunt, serious president who was desperately trying to keep the Union together.

In a few short years, Homer's Civil War paintings brought him fame at home and abroad. He painted war as no other artist ever had. He emphasized not brutality but rather scenes of loneliness, camp life, endless waiting, and even horseplay on the battlefield.

Homer was a Yankee,[3] but he showed equal concern for soldiers from both the North and South. His paintings did not glorify war; they seemed to cry out for it to end.

His *Prisoners from the Front* made a rep-

---

1. Gen. George McClellan's Army of the Potomac: McClellan served for a time as the general in chief of the Union Army during the Civil War. The Union Army in the East was known as the Army of the Potomac.

2. Yorktown: Yorktown, Virginia, which Gen. McClellan occupied on May 4, 1862.

3. Yankee: Here, a native or inhabitant of a Northern state.

utation overnight. This one painting, done in Homer's honest, realistic style, showed the common humanity that linked North and South, victor and vanquished, Americans all. Homer's war paintings give us the best record we have of how the Civil War soldier actually looked and acted.

After the war, railroads and new industries changed America from a rural to an industrial society almost overnight. But Homer paid no attention. He went back to painting the things he liked: country scenes, farmers, beautiful women in fashionable clothes, and kids at play.

He never painted kids with the gushy sentimentalism of other American painters. And he didn't look down on young people. His paintings showed what was then a typical American upbeat attitude marked by humor and innocence. The public loved it.

And then something strange happened. Homer stopped painting. For three years, his brushes sat idle. He left his studio for Europe, but avoided the art world in Paris. Instead, he went to Tynemouth, England, a small fishing port on the North Sea.

It was there, at Tynemouth, that Winslow Homer witnessed the fierce, day-to-day struggle of men and women against the sea. Their hard, bitter, dangerous lives made him think critically about his own life and work.

After that, women, children and country life appeared less often in his paintings. What replaced them was the harsh existence of men of the sea. These heroic people became, in his mind, the best examples of mankind. That's apparent in his famous painting *The Life Line.* To Homer, the sea had lost its serenity and had become a powerful force of nature.

Homer began painting larger pictures too, and his style became more bold and powerful. Some complained that his paintings now looked unfinished. But he didn't

care. Nice finishing touches were no longer important.

Besides the sea and its people, Homer started painting scenes of the American wilderness. He did big, masculine pictures of hunting and fishing, canoeing the rapids, sitting around the campfire and trekking over rugged trails.

He painted large oils, but he also painted many watercolors. By the time he had hit his stride, he had become America's first great watercolor painter. It was he who developed the technique of using the white, unpainted paper as sparkling highlight.

Then, at 48, when he was selling just about everything he painted, he did another about-face.

He surprised his family, friends and fellow artists by turning his back on the city and the world of art. He packed up and left to spend the rest of his life—27 years—as a hermit on a rocky cliff overlooking the sea in Prouts Neck, Maine.

In typical, cantankerous, Yankee fashion, when asked how he could leave New York, the scene of his success, he said, "I left New York to escape jury duty."

In a more serious mood, he told his brother that his new, lonely life was the only setting in which he could do his work in peace, free from visitors and publicity seekers.

Winslow Homer finally came to love his life. It was at Prouts Neck that he finished one of his great masterpieces, *The Gulf Stream,* in 1899.

This painting showed a black man marooned in a broken-masted boat circled by sharks in the Gulf Stream.[4] It was an immediate sensation, but only one of a long series

---

4. Gulf Stream: The warm ocean current flowing from the Gulf of Mexico along the East Coast of the United States.

THE GULF STREAM, 1899
Winslow Homer
The Metropolitan Museum of Art

of oils and watercolors that Homer painted of American blacks. This was at a time when blacks were usually depicted as minstrel singers and servants, or in other subservient poses.

In his last years, Homer made another big change. Instead of painting scenes of men struggling against the sea and wilderness, he started painting the sea and wilderness alone.

Like a stubborn tree growing out of a rock, he stood on his lonely cliff and painted the sea, forever untamed and uncontrolled by man.

In 1910, just before he died, he wrote in a letter, "All is lovely outside my house and inside my house and myself." Winslow Homer was a simple, modest, unsentimental man—the kind of American we Americans like.

RESPONDING TO THE SELECTION

Your Response

1. Would you like to have known Winslow Homer? Why or why not?

Recalling

2. How did Homer's family know there was "something special" about him?
3. In what way did the Civil War change Homer's life? What other turning points did he have in his life?
4. Why are Homer's Civil War paintings unusual? How did *Prisoners From the Front* affect his reputation?
5. How did his work change after he lived in Tynemouth, England?

Interpreting

6. What do you think might have caused Homer to stop painting for three years?
7. How did Homer show his self-reliance and independent spirit throughout his life?
8. What does the author's last statement indicate about American values? Do you agree that these are values most Americans share? Support your answer.

Applying

9. Why do you think artists must have the ability to surprise the public?

READING IN THE CONTENT AREAS

Setting a Purpose for Reading

One way to set a purpose for reading is to pretend to be a reporter gathering information about a subject. After using this method with the essay about Winslow Homer, you should have the answers to the usual reporter's questions: *who, what, when, where, why,* and *how.*

1. Who was Winslow Homer?
2. What did he do?
3. When and where did he work?
4. Why is he considered a great painter?
5. How did he work?

CRITICAL THINKING AND READING

Evaluating the Writer's Opinions

The writer H. N. Levitt comments specifically on the Homer paintings that accompany this essay. He says, for example, that *Prisoners From the Front* (page 396) is "honest" and "realistic," showing the "common humanity" of soldiers from both sides. You can evaluate the writer's opinions by looking carefully at the picture yourself.

1. Describe what is happening in the scene, identifying the soldiers from each side.
2. Consider whether the scene is "realistic." What leads you to think that Homer either changed it or painted it realistically?

THINKING AND WRITING

Writing About a Painting

Imagine that you are an editor putting together a book of Winslow Homer's paintings for junior high school students. You have been assigned to write several paragraphs to accompany *The Gulf Stream.* Before starting, review what H. N. Levitt said about Homer's career in general and this work in particular. Then look at the picture closely. List its important qualities. For instance, you might want to mention the drama of the scene, the portrayal of a black man, and the way Homer has painted the ocean. Consider whether the painting has a theme—an idea that it communicates. When revising, check your writing for clarity.

LEARNING OPTION

Art. Have a class art exhibition for which each member of the class chooses a work of art. You can choose from art and photography books or magazines, posters, album covers, or drawings and paintings of your own. Write a brief paragraph describing why you like the work and find it meaningful. You might invite other classes to come and see the exhibit.

The Case for Short Words

Varying Rates of Reading

Not everything you read requires the same rate, or speed, of reading. You can choose to read at one of three basic rates. **Reading intensively** means reading carefully and slowly. You may stop after each paragraph or short section to summarize mentally what you have just read. **Scanning** means running your eyes over a page rapidly until you find specific information you are looking for. **Skimming** means reading quickly to get a general idea of what a book or selection is about.

Focus

The title of this selection gives you a clue to the author's opinion about short words. Working with a partner, take five minutes to create a list of one-syllable words in the following categories: animals, foods, and action words (verbs). How many words could you think of in each category? Compare your list with those of your classmates. How many words did you all find in each category?

Vocabulary

Knowing the following words will help you as you read "The Case for Short Words."

scald (skôld) *v.*: Burn with hot liquid (p. 401)

flit (flit) *v.*: Fly lightly and swiftly (p. 401)

terse (tʉrs) *adj.*: To the point (p. 401)

wrought (rôt) *adj.*: Formed; made out of (p. 401)

orators (ôr′ ət ərz) *n.*: Public speakers (p. 401)

pithy (pitʰ′ ē) *adj.*: Brief but full of meaning (p. 401)

laments (lə ments′) *v.*: Expresses deep sorrow; mourns (p. 401)

eloquence (el′ ə kwens) *n.*: Persuasive power (p. 403)

obligatory (əb lig′ ə tôr ē) *adj.*: Required (p. 403)

luminous (lōō′ mə nəs) *adj.*: Clear; easily understood (p. 403)

Richard Lederer

(1938–   ) has written several books about the English language, including *Anguished English* and *Get Thee to a Punnery.* In addition to teaching at St. Paul's School in Concord, New Hampshire, for over thirty years, Lederer has been vice president of SPELL (Society for the Preservation of English Language and Literature), is a regular contributor to magazines about language, and is a language commentator on National Public Radio. This selection is from his book *The Miracle of Language.*

The Case for Short Words

Richard Lederer

When you speak and write, there is no law that says you have to use big words. Short words are as good as long ones, and short, old words—like *sun* and *grass* and *home*—are best of all. A lot of small words, more than you might think, can meet your needs with a strength, grace, and charm that large words do not have.

Big words can make the way dark for those who read what you write and hear what you say. Small words cast their clear light on big things—night and day, love and hate, war and peace, and life and death. Big words at times seem strange to the eye and the ear and the mind and the heart. Small words are the ones we seem to have known from the time we were born, like the hearth fire that warms the home.

Short words are bright like sparks that glow in the night, prompt like the dawn that greets the day, sharp like the blade of a knife, hot like salt tears that scald the cheek, quick like moths that flit from flame to flame, and terse like the dart and sting of a bee.

Here is a sound rule: Use small, old words where you can. If a long word says just what you want to say, do not fear to use it. But know that our tongue is rich in crisp, brisk, swift, short words. Make them the spine and the heart of what you speak and write. Short words are like fast friends. They will not let you down.

The title of this chapter and the four paragraphs that you have just read are wrought entirely of words of one syllable. In setting myself this task, I did not feel especially cabined, cribbed, or confined. In fact, the structure helped me to focus on the power of the message I was trying to put across.

One study shows that twenty words account for twenty-five percent of all spoken English words, and all twenty are monosyllabic. In order of frequency they are: *I, you, the, a, to, is, it, that, of, and, in, what, he, this, have, do, she, not, on,* and *they.* Other studies indicate that the fifty most common words in written English are each made of a single syllable.

For centuries our finest poets and orators have recognized and employed the power of small words to make a straight point between two minds. A great many of our proverbs punch home their points with pithy monosyllables: "Where there's a will, there's a way," "A stitch in time saves nine," "Spare the rod and spoil the child," "A bird in the hand is worth two in the bush."

Nobody used the short word more skillfully than William Shakespeare, whose dying King Lear laments:

> *And my poor fool is hang'd! No,*
> *   no, no life!*
> *Why should a dog, a horse, a rat*
> *   have life,*
> *And thou no breath at all? . . .*
> *Do you see this? Look on her,*
> *   look, her lips.*
> *Look there, look there!*

OWH! IN SAN PAO, 1951
Stuart Davis
The Whitney Museum of American Art

Shakespeare's contemporaries made the King James Bible a centerpiece of short words—"And God said, Let there be light: and there was light. And God saw the light, that it was good." The descendants of such mighty lines live on in the twentieth century. When asked to explain his policy to Parliament, Winston Churchill responded with these ringing monosyllables: "I will say: it is to wage war, by sea, land, and air, with all our might and with all the strength that God can give us." In his "Death of the Hired Man" Robert Frost observes that "Home is the place where, when you go there,/They have to take you in." And William H. Johnson uses ten two-letter words to explain his secret of success: "If it is to be,/It is up to me."

You don't have to be a great author, statesman, or philosopher to tap the energy and eloquence of small words. Each winter I ask my students at St. Paul's School to write a composition composed entirely of one-syllable words. My students greet my request with obligatory moans and groans, but, when they return to class with their essays, most feel that, with the pressure to produce high-sounding polysyllables relieved, they have created some of their most powerful and luminous prose. Here are submissions from two of my students:

> What can you say to a boy who has left home? You can say that he has done wrong, but he does not care. He has left home so that he will not have to deal with what you say. He wants to go as far as he can. He will do what he wants to do.
>
> This boy does not want to be forced to go to church, to comb his hair, or to be on time. A good time for this boy does not lie in your reach, for what you have he does not want. He dreams of ripped jeans, shorts with no starch, and old socks.
>
> So now this boy is on a bus to a place he dreams of, a place with no rules. This boy now walks a strange street, his long hair blown back by the wind. He wears no coat or tie, just jeans and an old shirt. He hates your world, and he has left it.
>
> —Charles Shaffer

For a long time we cruised by the coast and at last came to a wide bay past the curve of a hill, at the end of which lay a small town. Our long boat ride at an end, we all stretched and stood up to watch as the boat nosed its way in.

> The town climbed up the hill that rose from the shore, a space in front of it left bare for the port. Each house was a clean white with sky blue or gray trim; in front of each one was a small yard, edged by a white stone wall strewn with green vines.
>
> As the town basked in the heat of noon, not a thing stirred in the streets or by the shore. The sun beat down on the sea, the land, and the back of our necks, so that, in spite of the breeze that made the vines sway, we all wished we could hide from the glare in a cool, white house. But, as there was no one to help dock the boat, we had to stand and wait.
>
> At last the head of the crew leaped from the side and strode to a large house on the right. He shoved the door wide, poked his head through the gloom, and roared with a fierce voice. Five or six men came out, and soon the port was loud with the clank of chains and creak of planks as the men caught ropes thrown by the crew, pulled them taut, and tied them to posts. Then they set up a rough plank so we could cross from the deck to the shore. We all made for the large house while the crew watched, glad to be rid of us. —Celia Wren

You too can tap into the vitality and vigor of compact expression. Take a suggestion from the highway department. At the boundaries of your speech and prose place a sign that reads "Caution: Small Words at Work."

RESPONDING TO THE SELECTION

Your Response

1. Did this essay convince you to use short words in your writing? Why or why not?
2. Which of the two student essays did you like better? What did you like about it?

Recalling

3. What do all the words in the first four paragraphs of the essay have in common?
4. What well-known authors does Lederer quote to make his case for short words?

Interpreting

5. When Lederer compares short words to specific objects—like sparks, the dawn, or a blade—he is creating powerful images. How does this help make his point?
6. In the last paragraph, the suggestion to set up a sign is not meant literally. Why do you think the author makes the suggestion?

Applying

7. Do you think the effectiveness of your writing would increase if you used more short words? Why or why not?

READING IN THE CONTENT AREAS

Varying Rates of Reading

Slow, intensive reading; rapid scanning; and rapid skimming are three useful ways of reading, depending on what you are reading and why you are reading it.

1. Did you use any of these methods to read "The Case for Short Words"? Explain. Which method did you use to answer the Recalling questions after the selection? Which method would you use when trying to decide whether to read another essay or book?
2. Scan "The Case for Short Words" to answer this question: Who wrote a sentence of ten two-letter words?

3. Skim the first student's essay to answer this question: Who is the "you" to whom the essay is addressed?

CRITICAL THINKING AND READING

Identifying Supporting Arguments

In making his case for short words, Richard Lederer relies on three different kinds of sources: his own writing, quotations of well-known writers and literary works, and students' writing. Identify the source of the argument in each passage below.

1. "Home is the place where, when you go there,/They have to take you in."
2. "What can you say to a boy who has left home?"
3. "Short words are like fast friends. They will not let you down."

THINKING AND WRITING

Writing Descriptively With Short Words

Imagine that you are entering a writing contest. You must describe a person, place, or object that you like. The only rule is that you may use only words of one syllable. After you have chosen your topic, make a list of words that describe your topic. They may be nouns, verbs, adjectives, or adverbs. Write your first draft quickly. Work with a partner to revise your essay. Help each other eliminate words that have more than one syllable. Publish your essays in a class scrapbook of writings with short words.

LEARNING OPTION

Writing. Rewrite one of the first four paragraphs of Richard Lederer's essay. Change as many one-syllable words to multisyllable words as you can without changing the meaning of the paragraph. Then compare the two paragraphs. Which seems the clearest and most powerful? Explain.

ONE WRITER'S PROCESS

Richard Lederer and "Short Words"

PREWRITING

Inspired by His Students A best-selling author and a teacher, Richard Lederer explains that the idea for his essay "was inspired by real-life examples of the power of short words." These examples came from "the many fine essays" submitted to him by his students "in response to an assignment on the topic of long and short words."

Planning the Text Lederer planned this essay carefully, just as he plans all his writing. "Good writing is not only rewriting; it's prewriting," he asserts.

DRAFTING

Write, Wash, Rinse, Write The greatest challenge for him in writing this essay was to make his words sound right. He says that "even though essays are made out of something we call prose, a caring writer tries always to write music." He therefore urges his students to read their writing aloud to themselves or to friends: "I want my students to wash the words around in their mouths and rinse them in their ears."

REVISING

It Took Ten Years Lederer has revised "The Case for Short Words" many times over the past ten years. To see the kinds of changes he has made, look at the box below. It shows two first-draft paragraphs of the essay. Look carefully at the revisions.

To get the full effect of his changes, first read the paragraphs without his changes. Then read the revision. Notice how the sounds of the words "crisp, brisk, swift" add to the "music" of the prose.

PUBLISHING

The Miracle of Language "The Case for Short Words" was first published in Lederer's weekly newspaper column about ten years ago. After revising the essay, he included it in his book *The Miracle of Language* (1991).

Seeing his work used, Lederer says, is both satisfying and deeply fulfilling. "The act of writing," he states, "extends my humanity and my mission as a teacher."

THINKING ABOUT THE PROCESS

1. What are some advantages of publishing an essay as a newspaper column, revising it, and then publishing it again in a book?
2. **Cooperative Activity** Together with several classmates, read aloud passages from essays you have read before and find examples of language that is especially musical. Share your findings with the class.

Here is a sound rule: ~~y~~ use small, old words where you can, if a long word says just what you want it to say, ~~don't~~ *do not* fear to use it.

No ¶ But know that our tongue is rich in *crisp, brisk, swift,* short words. Make them the spine and the heart of what you speak and write.

GUIDE FOR READING

Edwin Way Teale

(1899–1980) was born and raised in Joliet, Illinois. Up to the age of sixteen, he spent his summers at his grandparents' farm in Indiana, close to Lake Michigan. Here he developed a fascination with plants and animals that lasted all his life. He became a naturalist and a Pulitzer Prize-winning author of nature books. The journal entries that follow are remarkable for their perceptiveness and thoughtfulness. They will show you how much nature can teach a sensitive observer.

from Circle of the Seasons

Journal Writing

Journal writing is a way of recording events as they happen. Because a journal is personal, it usually includes a writer's thoughts, feelings, and insights as well as objective details. Many scientists keep journals as a record of observations and experiments. They can thereby keep track of their work. They can also use a journal to record information for future projects. Others, like Teale, treat journals as a place to do their best writing. Ultimately, such journals are published as books for the public.

Focus

People don't usually pay close attention to the natural things around them. For example, have you ever spent five minutes watching a fly zooming around the room? Have you ever watched an ant carrying a crumb twice its size across a sidewalk? Have you ever picked up an earthworm that had crawled above ground after a rainstorm? Choose some everyday natural occurrence to describe in detail. For example, you might write about a bird busily making its way around a lawn, pecking at seeds. What little things do you notice that you would normally overlook? You will see in this excerpt from *Circle of the Seasons* how a writer spent a lot of time paying very close attention to the little things in nature.

Vocabulary

Knowing the following words will help you as you read the excerpts from *Circle of the Seasons*.

susceptible (sə sep′ tə b'l) *adj.*: Easily affected by (p. 407)

apt (apt) *adj.*: Inclined; likely (p. 407)

invariable (in ver′ ē ə b'l) *adj.*: Not changing; uniform (p. 407)

opalescent (ō′ pə les′ 'nt) *adj.*: Showing a play of colors (p. 408)

from Circle of the Seasons

Edwin Way Teale

The following are excerpts from a journal that Edwin Way Teale kept for every day of a year. Scientists often use journals with dated entries as an ongoing record of their observations or experiments.

January 11

POISON IVY BERRIES. To the cedar woods at sunset. An overwintering catbird is feeding on the purple berries of the cat-briars and the gray berries of the poison ivy. Cows eat poison ivy leaves with immunity; birds eat the berries without ill effects. Only human beings, and only some human beings at that, are susceptible, through an allergy, to the torments of ivy poisoning. Yet those of us who fall victims, through this peculiarity in our own systems, are apt to bewail the presence of poison ivy in the world and to consider it an enemy lying in wait for our approach. Why was poison ivy put in the world?

The catbird, feeding in the quiet of this winter sunset, finding nourishment in the berries, supplies at least one of the answers. On the shifting sand of Fire Island,[1] there is another answer. There, the remarkably adaptive ivy, able to grow on barren sand as well as in swamps, anchors down the wind-blown earth. Each form of life, plant as well as animal, has its part to play. Whether the results delight or outrage man is no concern of nature's. Man plays, to be sure, a leading role in the drama of life. But he still is only a part of a cast that includes many, many actors.

January 24

THE WHITENESS OF THE SNOW. Looking across the white fields today, I am reminded that an invariable rule of nature is that nothing is invariable. "As like as two peas in a pod" is an exact statement of nature's way. For no two peas in a pod are ever exactly alike. Nature does not plagiarize herself, repeat herself. Her powers of innovation are boundless. No two hills or ants or oranges or sheep or snowflakes are identical. Ten thousand seem alike because we do not see them clearly enough, because our senses are too dull or inadequate or inaccurate to detect the differences.

And so it is with one of the oldest similes in the world: "As white as the snow." The whiteness of the snow is infinitely varied. In fact, its whiteness is produced by elements that are not white at all. The individual crystals that go into the make-up of a snowflake are transparent and colorless when they are created far up in the sky. They are like clear glass. It is when they are grouped together in flakes, when they lie in untold millions in a drift, that they appear white.

What is the explanation of this paradox? It is the same answer that explains how a transparent window pane when it is broken and powdered appears white while the intact pane is colorless. Both the infinite number of crystals that make up the snowdrift and

---

1. Fire Island: A long, narrow, sandy island off the south shore of Long Island, New York.

the vast number of particles that comprise the powdered glass have so many facets that they reflect all the rays of light in all directions. Put all the rays of the spectrum together and you have white just as when you take all the rays of the spectrum away you have black. It is the numberless crystals in the piled-up snow that turn it into a mound of the purest white.

Yet even this "purest white" has many subtle variations. The famous New York advertising photographer, H. I. Williams, once told me of his surprise in noting the differences in the whites recorded by his color camera. They all looked alike to his eyes. But the sensitive color film showed that some were tinged with blues or yellows or reds and some were pearly and opalescent. The white of a billiard ball, of a sheet of writing paper, of a dress shirt, of a tablecloth all were different. Probably no two tablecloths are exactly the same in whiteness, although our eyes are unable to detect the difference.

Similarly, it is likely that no two snowbanks are identical in the whiteness of their exterior. Their surroundings, the time of day, the conditions of the sky all contribute to their tinting. Even our eyes can note the blue in the shadows of trees stretching across the drifts and the pink glow of sunset spreading over an expanse of snow. But under the noonday sun, except when soot or mud has stained them or when old drifts have been discolored by deposits from the air, the whiteness of the snow remains all the same to our eyes—the purest white we know.

April 4

WORLD'S MOST VALUABLE ANIMAL. A long soaking rain before daybreak. And all along the way, when I walk for the morning papers, I find earthworms here and there stranded on the inhospitable cement of the sidewalk. Appearing naked and bewildered, they are in imminent danger of the early bird or of drying out in the sun-warmed air. This is the time of year when my morning walk is slowed by stops to put earthworms back on the ground where they belong. People probably wonder what treasure I am finding when they see me stoop so often!

And, in a way, I am dealing in treasure.

The pelt of a silver fox may sell for hundreds of dollars. The legs of a racehorse may be insured for a quarter of a million. Yet neither the silver fox nor the racehorse is the world's most valuable animal. This is the earthworm—a creature without fur and without legs; a creature that has neither paws nor eyes nor ears; a humble burrower, nature's plowman.

As frost has left the topsoil, earthworms have worked upward. They have begun once more their invaluable activity of plowing, pulverizing, aerating, fertilizing, leveling and thinning the soil. As many as 5,000 earthworms may plow through the earth of a single acre. During spring and summer and fall, they may bring as much as eighteen tons of new earth to the surface.

This labor is achieved with curious but effective equipment. Instead of legs, the earthworm employs hundreds of stiff bristles. Each body segment, except the first and last, is equipped with eight of these bristle-hooks. They are used to grip the soil on all sides and they explain the tugging of the robin when it seeks to drag an earthworm from the ground.

Underground, the earthworm pushes or literally eats its way through the soil. Its mouth, functioning like a suction pump, draws earth into its body. There it is pulverized and organic particles are digested. The rest is deposited as castings[2] at the mouth of the burrow. In its surface feeding, during

---

2. castings: (kas' tiŋz) *n.*: Waste material.

the hours of darkness, the creature usually anchors its tail in its burrow and then, elongating its body, moves in a circle like a tethered calf in its search for bits of decayed leaves.

At such times, it is warned of danger by curious senses, amazingly keen. Although it has no eyes, its skin is so sensitive to light that it warns the worm when dawn is breaking. Although it has no ears, it is so sensitive to earth vibrations that it is alarmed by the footfall of even an approaching shrew.[3]

This is the earthworm, that humble and invaluable creature I see so frequently along my way this morning.

---

3. shrew: (shrōō) *n.*: A small, slender, mouselike animal with soft, brown fur and a long pointed snout.

RESPONDING TO THE SELECTION

Your Response

1. What things would you like to set aside time to look at more closely? Why?

Recalling

2. What are Teale's answers to the question "Why was poison ivy put in the world?"
3. Explain the different tintings of color in snow.

Interpreting

4. Why is the earthworm "nature's plowman"?
5. What is the meaning of Teale's remark that humans are only part of the drama of life?
6. How strong is his argument for the idea that the earthworm is the most valuable animal?

Applying

7. In the first entry, Teale points out the value of poison ivy. What are some other aspects of nature he might have written about in a similar way?

READING IN THE CONTENT AREAS

Journal Writing

Journal writing can be a way of learning. It can stimulate a writer's thinking so that he or she sees meaning in the events recorded.

1. What is the specific observation that begins the January 24th entry?

2. What rule of nature does this observation lead Teale to recall?

CRITICAL THINKING AND READING

Observing and Inferring

Observing is the act of noting and recording facts and events. For example, when Teale notes and records that poison ivy anchors down the windblown earth on Fire Island, he is making an observation. **Inferring** means drawing a conclusion—often from observations. For example, after observing that the catbird is nourished by poison-ivy berries and earth is anchored down by the ivy, Teale makes the inference that "Each form of life . . . has its part to play."

Tell why you think that the following statement is an observation or an inference: "Yet neither the silver fox nor the racehorse is the world's most valuable animal."

THINKING AND WRITING

Writing a Journal Entry

Using your freewriting as a starting point, write an entry modeled on any one of the three by Teale. Include any inferences or other thoughts that come to you. When you revise your entry, make sure your observation is presented in a way that will be clear to any reader. Compare your entry with those written by others in your class.

Mari Sandoz

(1901–1966) was born in Nebraska but learned English only when she entered school; her Swiss parents spoke German at home. Sandoz worked as a teacher and a proofreader in a newspaper office before she became a successful writer. Influenced by her childhood on a frontier farm, she wrote many books about the American West. She was especially fascinated by the history and customs of Native Americans. In this excerpt from *These Were the Sioux,* she describes the upbringing of Sioux children.

from These Were the Sioux

Taking Notes

Taking notes is an excellent technique for remembering the most important information from your reading. Before you even start to take notes, however, you will find it helpful to skim through the selection to gain a general idea of it. Then you can read the piece more slowly, listing the main points. It is not necessary to use complete sentences in your list. Also, you can make note-taking easier by eliminating articles (*a, an, the*) and using abbreviations. As you read, pay special attention to words that indicate main ideas—*in conclusion, most important, the causes of,* and similar phrases. Finally, you may want to review your notes after writing them so they stay in your memory.

Focus

When did you learn to tie your shoes and to swim? When will you learn to drive? We learn things at different ages to succeed in our own time and culture. Imagine that you had been born in your hometown a hundred years ago. Make a list of things you might have had to learn when growing up at that time. What skills would you have needed? In this essay by Mari Sandoz, you will read about growing up in the traditional culture of the Sioux.

Vocabulary

Knowing the following words will help you as you read this excerpt from *These Were the Sioux.*

favoritism (fā′ vər ə tiz′ əm) *n.*: The showing of special kindness (p. 412)

rites (rīts) *n.*: Religious observances (p. 412)

usurped (yōō surpt′) *v.*: Took without right (p. 413)

tepid (tep′ id) *adj.*: Not warm or cold; lukewarm (p. 413)

enticing (en tīs′ iŋ) *adj.*: Tempting (p. 413)

regalia (ri gāl′ yə) *n.*: Splendid clothes and decorations (p. 414)

judicious (jōō dish′ əs) *adj.*: Wise (p. 414)

latent (lāt′ ′nt) *adj.*: Hidden and not fully developed (p. 414)

from These Were the Sioux

Mari Sandoz

By the time I was seven or eight I had begun to sense a special kind of individual responsibility among the Sioux, not only for oneself but for the family, the band, the whole tribe. Then one morning I saw something of the start of this. A small girl from the camp across the road came tapping shyly at our door, motioning to me.

"Ahh, I have a brother too now," she whispered, her dark eyes on the baby astride my hip. "He is just born."

I pushed the oatmeal back on the stove, glanced toward the stable where Mother was milking our cow and hurried across the road as fast as I could, my brother bobbing on my side. I slowed up at the smoky old canvas tipi, shy, too, now, but I did peer into the dusky interior where an Indian woman bent over the new baby on her lap. At the noise of our excitement, the tiny red-brown face began to pucker up tighter, but the mother caught the little nose gently between her thumb and forefinger and with her palm over the mouth, stopped the crying. When the baby began to twist for breath, she let go a little, but only a little, and at the first sign of another cry, she shut off the air again, crooning a soft little song as she did this, a growing song of the Plains Indians, to make the boy straight-limbed and strong of body and heart as the grandson of Bad Arm must be.

I watched the mother enviously. Our babies always cried, and so I had to ride them on my hip, but I knew that none of our small Indian friends made more than a whimper at the greatest hurt, even falling from the high limb of a tree. Now I saw what an old woman had tried to explain to me. During the newborn minutes, that newborn hour, Indian children, boy and girl, were taught the first and greatest lesson of their lives: that no one could be permitted to endanger the people by even one cry to guide a roving enemy to the village or to spoil a hunt that could mean the loss of the winter meat for a whole band or even a small tribe. In return the child would soon discover that all the community felt an equal responsibility toward him. Every fire became like that of his parents, welcoming the exploring, the sleepy or injured toddler. Every pot would have a little extra for a hungry boy, and every ear was open to young sorrow, young joys and aspirations. I also knew that never, in the natural events of this small boy's life, would he be touched by a punishing adult hand. If he grew up like the Sioux of the old hunting days he would be made equal to the demands of his expanding world without any physical restriction beyond the confines of the cradleboard.[1] I still remember the closed, distant faces of the Sioux when I was whipped for staying out to watch the *heyoka*[2] in the thunderstorm, and at other whippings as well.

---

1. cradleboard (krā′ d'l bôrd) *n.*: A board for carrying a baby.
2. heyoka (hā ō′ kə) *n.*: An Indian who made others laugh by doing things backward, for example, wearing warm clothes in summer and hardly any clothes in winter; dreaming of thunder was one qualification for becoming a *heyoka*.

CHEE-A-KA-TCHEE, WIFE OF NOT-TO-WAY, 1830–39
George Catlin
National Museum of American Art
The Smithsonian Institution

In the old days our Sioux neighbors still had their traditional set of precautions against immaturities and resentments among their young people. They avoided overprotecting the young and saved the eldest son from the mother's favoritism that could destroy the parents as well as the boy. By custom every son and daughter, too, was provided with a second father and mother at birth—usually friends of the blood parents, or some relatives outside of the immediate family. The second father of a boy was often selected partly for excellence as hunter, warrior, horse catcher, band historian, holy man who listened and advised, or medicine man—either healer or one learned in rites and ceremonials. Still earlier the man might have been a maker of arrows, spears or shields, an outstanding runner or gifted in decoying and snaring animals. His wife, the second mother, was preferably known as warmhearted, and fond of boys around the tipi, the lodge. Sometimes the youth showed a special and unexpected talent as he grew and then a third father might be selected, one gifted in this new bent. Or if the puberty dream was of thunder, a *heyoka* might be added as a sort of uncle.

The second mother took over much of the small boy's care so he would never shame his blood mother by trailing at her moccasin heel, never bring the scornful whisper, "Little husband! Little husband!" as he usurped another's place in her attention and affection. The Indians understood the anger and resentment that could grow up in the most tolerant, fortitudinous man if his wife preferred the son over the husband, used the boy against him, brought him humiliation in the village circle.

In the second mother's lodge the boy could tease and laugh in a way improper in his own home. He could talk freely, so long as it was respectful. And when a boy like Young One across the road went to war, whether in the old days against the Pawnees or the Crows, or later, to the Pacific or Korea,[3] the women of his second home could show emotion and cry out, "Be careful, our brother!" and "Be careful, our son!"

By the time Young One was six weeks old he was little trouble to anyone, either in the cradleboard propped against a tipi pole or riding a mother's back while she went about her work. He would be up there some of the time until he was a year old or more, out of harm's way, seeing all the world from the high place and unpossessed by the mother's eyes. Before Young One was two months old it was decided he must swim, "before he forget it," the older mother told us, by signs. I took my baby brother down to see this. The woman carried Young One into a quieter spot along the riverbank and with her hands under the chest and belly, she eased the boy into the shallow, tepid water until it came up

around him. Then, suddenly, his sturdy legs began to kick and his arms to flail out. The next time he lasted a little longer, and by the third or fourth time the woman could take her hands away for a bit while he held his head up and dog paddled for himself.

Winter babies, boys or girls, who couldn't be taught to swim early, were thrown into ponds or river holes in the spring by the father, the impact calculated to revive the fading urge to swim. Every Indian child had to keep himself afloat awhile if he slipped off into deep water, was caught in a cloudburst or in a river accident while the people were fleeing from enemies or a buffalo stampede.

The young Indian learned to make his own decisions, take the responsibility for his actions at an incredibly early age. When the baby began to crawl no one cried, "No, no!" and dragged him back from the enticing red of the tipi fire coals. Instead, his mother or anyone near watched only that he did not burn up. "One must learn from the bite of the fire to let it alone," he was told when he jerked his hand back, whimpering a little, and with tear-wet face brought his burnt finger to whoever was near for the soothing. The boy's eyes would not turn in anger toward the mother or other grownup who might have pulled him back, frustrated his natural desire to test, to explore. His anger was against the pretty coals, plainly the source of his pain. He would creep back another time but more warily, and soon he would discover where warmth became burning.

From birth the young Sioux was in the midst of the adult world. There was only one room in the lodge, and only one out-of-doors. Back when he was small his cradleboard often hung on a tipi pole or a meat rack, the wind swaying him drowsily, while the children played and raced and sang around him and one of his mothers or frequently several

---

3. the Pacific or Korea: World War II (1939–1945), fought on the Pacific Ocean and elsewhere, or the Korean War (1950–1953).

women worked nearby, busy with the meat or the hides or perhaps beading the regalia of the men.

But the little Sioux had to learn some use of his legs this summer. He spent more and more time on the ground, perhaps on a robe or soft grass but often alone, free to discover his body now and begin to get his discipline in the natural way, as he must be free to take his ideals and aspirations from the precepts and examples of those around him.

When the thrust of the boy's growing legs took on insistence, one of the fathers or perhaps an uncle lay on his back and held the baby erect for a short walk up his stomach and chest, laughing hard at the sturdy push of the legs, shouting that this was a warrior son, this was a great and powerful hunter. Perhaps the man was a young war chief, or, if older, just out of the evening council circle where any toddler could approach the headmen unhindered. He could see them smoking quietly, deliberating the common problems of today and tomorrow or planning ceremonials and hunts, perhaps selecting the warrior society to police the village for the next moon, and protect it from disturbances inside and out. The boy could hear the crier, always some old and very judicious and respected man, hurry through the camp with any news or with warnings of danger, or of a hunt coming up, perhaps carrying invitation sticks to a feast or a celebration, or proclaiming the council's decisions. And they were decisions, not orders, for no Sioux could tell anyone what to do. The only position a Sioux inherited was his membership in the tribe. He became a leader, a chief because some were willing to follow him and retained his position only as long as the following remained.

The young Sioux rode early. Sometimes before he could walk he was carried behind his father, clinging to the rawhide string of the man's breechclout.[4] He learned to climb up the foreleg of an old mare like a tree, mounting on the right side as the grown Indians all did, the man with the bow in his left hand when he leaped on, out of the way, and leaving the right hand free to draw the bowstring fast.

From back before he understood the words or the wisdom, the young Sioux heard the hero tales of his people told around the evening fires, but in his early years he learned most from the other children. They took joy in showing him all their knowledge, and in practicing the latent parent lying deep in everyone, eager to care for any small creature or being around. But he learned much, perhaps most, from the scorn and laughter of these peers, and from another boy's fist in his face. Eventually he discovered how to avoid some of the laughing, and the blows, or to fend them off.

When Bad Arm, the man who had once carried me home from the plum thicket, was asked if there wasn't injustice in this discipline by children he drew on his old pipe awhile. All life was injustice, he thought. Lightning found the good man and the bad; sickness carried no respect for virtue, and luck flitted around like the spring butterfly. "It is good to learn this in the days of the mother's milk. Discipline from the young comes as from the earth and is accepted like hunger and weariness and the bite of winter cold. Coming so, it hatches no anger against the grown-up ones, no anger and hatred to sit in the heart like an arrow pointed to shoot both ways."

So the young Sioux learned from his peers, learned from their companionship, their goodness and the power of their ridicule, the same ridicule he saw used against

---

4. breechclout (brĕch′ klout′) *n.*: A piece of cloth worn about the body at the hips.

SIOUX ENCAMPMENT, 1874–1884
Jules Tavernier
Laurie Platt Winfrey, Inc.

those in highest position sometimes, for even great war leaders bowed in humiliation before concentrated laughter. And he saw men and women of his people walk in dignity through the village circle, the peaceful, orderly village where normally one heard no quarreling in tipi or outside.

"It is better to use ridicule early—to keep the young on the good road," Bad Arm and the *heyoka* agreed, telling me that in this, had I been a Sioux, I should have had a real place, for ridicule from the girls and the women stings like the yellow-striped hornet.

In the old buffalo days the very young Sioux learned to snare and track small animals, even the rabbit, with his trick of doubling back on his trail, teaching the hunter to use his eyes while other creatures taught him to sharpen his nose and his ears. As the boy grew he was drawn into the hunting games as he was those of the village: prairie ball, running and jumping contests, tag, snow snake in the winter, and always wrestling and horse racing, the boys riding sometimes so small they seemed like some four-footed creature clinging to the mane and back. Young One would have seen the men pile their wagers in goods at the betting stake before the horses were whipped home with dust and whooping. He would have learned to ride in a dead run while hanging to the far side of his pony with a moccasin toe over the back, a hand twisted into the mane, ready for war. He would have been along on raids against enemy horse herds as

from *These Were the Sioux* 415

a young white man might study his father's methods of raiding a competitor's customers.

As the boy grew he ran with his village kind as young antelope run together. He teased the girls, grabbed bits of meat from the drying racks when he was hungry. He went to watch the older youths and young men stand in their courting blankets at this tipi or that one for a few words with the young daughter and could hardly wait until he, too, was a man. He imitated the warriors and ran their errands, hoping to be asked out on a raid, as was done for promising boys, particularly by the war society of a father or an uncle, much as a white youth would be eased toward his father's fraternity, and often with little more bloodshed. Except in a few tribal struggles for hunting grounds, Plains Indian fights were scarcely more dangerous than a hard-fought football game. The first-class coup—striking an enemy with the hand, the bow or the coup stick without harming him—was the highest war achievement, more important than any scalp.

Occasionally the boy was taken out on night guard of the village and the horse herds, or to scout the region for unauthorized war parties trying to slip away, endangering themselves and perhaps the village with avenging attacks. An Indian who gave up the right to cry at birth because it would bring enemies upon the people must not do the same thing by rash and foolish acts later.

Understanding of the regular ceremonials and rituals came gradually to the young Sioux. Eventually he realized what old Contrary told us through the interpretation of his teenage granddaughter, who cheerfully turned all the *heyoka* said around to its rightful meaning. The Sioux camp of any size was always set in a circle because all sacred things were round—the sun, the moon, the earth horizon, as one could plainly see. Even the tipis were round, and their openings as well as that of the whole camp always faced the east, to welcome and honor the light that brought the day and the springtime. But the simplest and perhaps the most profound ritual that the young Sioux saw was the most common. The first puff of the pipe at a smoking and the first morsel of food at a meal were always offered to the Great Powers—the earth, the sky and the four directions, which included everything that lay within their arms. All things were a part of these Powers, brothers in them, and anyone could understand what a brother was.

After his seventh birthday the Sioux boy never addressed his blood mother or sister directly again, speaking to them only through a third person. When he showed signs of coming manhood he was prepared for his puberty fasting by men close to the family, including some wise and holy one. There were also holy women among the Sioux, advising and officiating in many of the rites with both men and women but not for the puberty fasting, which was the youth's orientation into maleness. When he was ready the boy was escorted to some far barren hill and left there in breechclout and moccasins against the sun of day, the cold of night, without food or water. The ordeal was to strip away every superficiality, all the things of the flesh, to prepare for a dreaming, a vision from the Powers. Usually by the third or fourth day the youth had dreamed and was brought down, gaunt and weak. He was given a few drops of water at a time and some food, but slowly, and after he was restored a little, and bathed and feasted, his advisors and the holy man tried to interpret the vision that was to guide him in this manhood he was now entering.

RESPONDING TO THE SELECTION

Your Response

1. What about the way Sioux children were raised reminds you of how you were raised? What is different?

Recalling

2. What was "the first and greatest lesson" for the Sioux?
3. How did the Sioux feel about punishing children?
4. How did the young learn from their peers?
5. How were boys trained to be warriors?

Interpreting

6. Why would a young Sioux learn to feel responsible for the whole tribe?
7. What can you infer from this essay about the qualities that the Sioux valued?

Applying

8. Explain whether or not the Sioux methods of child-rearing would work today, outside of the Sioux tribe.

READING IN THE CONTENT AREA

Taking Notes

Taking notes will help you to remember the important ideas in your reading. First you should skim through the piece. Then you should read it slowly, listing the main ideas and using words or phrases rather than complete sentences. The following notes, for example, cover the first four paragraphs.

At early age—senses Sioux have special feeling for family and tribe
Sioux mother stops baby's breathing to prevent crying—noise could bring enemies, chase away game
Benefits: children cared for by whole tribe, not physically punished

1. Skim through the rest of the essay and then take notes on it.
2. Compare your notes with the essay, making sure you have recorded the main ideas.

CRITICAL THINKING AND READING

Understanding Cause and Effect

A **cause** is what brings about a result, or an **effect.** The writer of this essay tells you, for example, that a Sioux mother gently stops her baby's breathing when it cries. This action (cause) results in the baby's learning not to cry (effect).

On a separate piece of paper, write the missing cause.

1. *Cause:* ? *Effect*: The eldest son is protected from his mother's favoritism.
2. *Cause*: ? *Effect*: The Sioux are expert riders.

THINKING AND WRITING

Writing an Article About a Sioux Visitor

Imagine that a Sioux boy or girl from many years ago suddenly appears in your house. List some of the ways in which he or she would react to modern life. Then use the list to write a magazine article describing this miraculous visit. When revising your article, refer to Sandoz's essay to check that your portrait of a young Indian is accurate.

LEARNING OPTIONS

1. **Multicultural Activity.** Reservations for tribes of Native Americans exist all over the United States. Find out where the Native American reservation closest to your home is. Which nation or people live on the reservation? Did they always live in this region? You might work with a partner, each exploring a different aspect of life on the reservation today as well as the history of the people. Present your findings to the class.
2. **Writing.** Write an essay about the way you were raised. Describe your growing up experience so that someone from a different culture would understand it. What did you learn and when? What customs did you observe?

READING AND RESPONDING

Nonfiction

Nonfiction is concerned with people, places, things, and events. The nonfiction writer usually keeps several things in mind while writing: an idea to present (the topic), a purpose for presenting the idea, and an audience. To appreciate nonfiction fully, you should respond to the elements of nonfiction and to the writer's techniques.

RESPONDING TO PURPOSE The purpose is the reason for writing. A writer usually has both a general purpose and a specific purpose. The general purpose may be to explain or inform, to describe, to persuade, or to entertain. The specific purpose may be to change the reader's thinking about the topic in some way. It may be to explain the effect of an incident on the writer's life, or it may be to help the reader understand and marvel at an event in nature. Your response to the writer's purpose will affect your understanding of the work.

RESPONDING TO IDEAS AND SUPPORT The main ideas are the most important points the writer wants to make. Main ideas can be facts or opinions. Support is the information the writer uses to develop or illustrate the main ideas. Support includes facts to back up opinions, reasons to explain events, examples to illustrate ideas, and descriptive details to help you form a mental picture of the topic. What do you think of these ideas? How does this information relate to your experience and your life?

RESPONDING TO ORGANIZATION The writer organizes the ideas and support to accomplish the purpose and move the reader's thinking in the intended direction. The information may be arranged in chronological order, spatial order, order of importance, or any other order that best makes the ideas clear to the reader. How does the order help you grasp the writer's ideas?

RESPONDING TO TECHNIQUES Writers may use a variety of techniques to accomplish their purpose. They may use description, argumentation, or comparison and contrast. They may use emotional language to arouse your feelings. They may include anecdotes or quotations, or they may use unexpected grammar or sentence structure to create an effect. How do the author's techniques affect your response?

On pages 419–422 you can see an example of active reading and responding by Giang Kieu of Fitz Intermediate School in Santa Ana, California. The notes in the side column show Giang's thoughts and comments while reading the essay from *An American Childhood.* Your thoughts may be different, because each reader responds differently to an essay.

MODEL

from An American Childhood

Annie Dillard

Purpose: *Will this be about a typical American childhood? Or will it be about something unusual?*

Some boys taught me to play football. This was fine sport. You thought up a new strategy for every play and whispered it to the others. You went out for a pass, fooling everyone. Best, you got to throw yourself mightily at someone's running legs. Either you brought him down or you hit the ground flat out on your chin, with your arms empty before you. It was all or nothing. If you hesitated in fear, you would miss and get hurt: you would take a hard fall while the kid got away, or you would get kicked in the face while the kid got away. But if you flung yourself wholeheartedly at the back of his knees—if you gathered and joined body and soul and pointed them diving fearlessly— then you likely wouldn't get hurt, and you'd stop the ball. Your fate, and your team's score, depended on your concentration and courage. Nothing girls did could compare with it.

Technique: *She uses some terrific action words, but it could use some strong adjectives.*

Boys welcomed me at baseball, too, for I had, through enthusiastic practice, what was weirdly known as a boy's arm. In winter, in the snow, there was neither baseball nor football, so the boys and I threw snowballs at passing cars. I got in trouble throwing snowballs, and have seldom been happier since.

Purpose: *I like the way a girl is placed in a boy's world, as a friend and not as an enemy. Girls enjoy sports, too.*

On one weekday morning after Christmas, six inches of new snow had just fallen. We were standing up to our boot tops in snow on a front yard on trafficked Reynolds Street, waiting for cars. The cars traveled Reynolds Street slowly and evenly; they were targets all but wrapped in red ribbons, cream puffs. We couldn't miss.

I was seven; the boys were eight, nine, and ten. The oldest two Fahey boys were there—Mikey and Peter—polite blond boys who lived near me on Lloyd Street, and who already had four brothers and sisters. My parents approved Mikey and Peter Fahey. Chickie McBride was there, a tough kid, and Billy Paul

Ideas and Support: *I'm not sure how this passage helps support the purpose.*

and Mackie Kean too, from across Reynolds, where the boys grew up dark and furious, grew up skinny, knowing, and skilled. We had all drifted from our houses that morning looking for action, and had found it here on Reynolds Street.

It was cloudy but cold. The cars' tires laid behind them on the snowy street a complex trail of beige chunks like crenellated castle walls.[1] I had stepped on some earlier; they squeaked. We could have wished for more traffic. When a car came, we all popped it one. In the intervals between cars we reverted to the natural solitude of children.

I started making an iceball—a perfect iceball, from perfectly white snow, perfectly spherical, and squeezed perfectly translucent so no snow remained all the way through. (The Fahey boys and I considered it unfair actually to throw an iceball at somebody, but it had been known to happen.)

Purpose: *I like the way she expresses the childish side of the kids. They are just having fun.*

I had just embarked on the iceball project when we heard tire chains come clanking from afar. A black Buick was moving toward us down the street. We all spread out, banged together some regular snowballs, took aim, and, when the Buick drew nigh, fired.

A soft snowball hit the driver's windshield right before the driver's face. It made a smashed star with a hump in the middle.

Often, of course, we hit our target, but this time, the only time in all of life, the car pulled over and stopped. Its wide black door opened; a man got out of it, running. He didn't even close the car door.

Ideas and Support: *It would be good to hear him say something. I don't know much about him from this description.*

He ran after us, and we ran away from him, up the snowy Reynolds sidewalk. At the corner, I looked back; incredibly, he was still after us. He was in city clothes: a suit and tie, street shoes. Any normal adult would have quit, having sprung us into flight and made his point. This man was gaining on us. He was a thin man, all action. All of a sudden, we were running for our lives.

Wordless, we split up. We were on our turf; we could lose ourselves in the neighborhood backyards, everyone for himself. I paused and considered. Everyone had vanished except Mikey Fahey, who was just rounding the corner of a yellow brick house. Poor Mikey, I trailed him. The driver of the Buick sensi-

---

1. chunks like crenellated (kren' əl āt'əd) **castle walls:** The snow was in rows of square clumps like the notches along the top of castle walls.

bly picked the two of us to follow. The man apparently had all day.

He chased Mikey and me around the yellow house and up a backyard path we knew by heart: under a low tree, up a bank, through a hedge, down some snowy steps, and across the grocery store's delivery driveway. We smashed through a gap in another hedge, entered a scruffy backyard and ran around its back porch and tight between houses to Edgerton Avenue; we ran across Edgerton to an alley and up our own sliding woodpile to the Halls' front yard; he kept coming. We ran up Lloyd Street and wound through mazy backyards toward the steep hilltop at Willard and Lang.

He chased us silently, block after block. He chased us silently over picket fences, through thorny hedges, between houses, around garbage cans, and across streets. Every time I glanced back, choking for breath, I expected he would have quit. He must have been as breathless as we were. His jacket strained over his body. It was an immense discovery, pounding into my hot head with every sliding, joyous step, that this ordinary adult evidently knew what I thought only children who trained at football knew: that you have to fling yourself at what you're doing, you have to point yourself, forget yourself, aim, dive.

Mikey and I had nowhere to go, in our own neighborhood or out of it, but away from this man who was chasing us. He impelled us forward; we compelled him to follow our route. The air was cold; every breath tore my throat. We kept running, block after block; we kept improvising, backyard after backyard, running a frantic course and choosing it simultaneously, failing always to find small places or hard places to slow him down, and discovering always, exhilarated, dismayed, that only bare speed could save us—for he would never give up, this man— and we were losing speed.

He chased us through the backyard labyrinths[2] of ten blocks before he caught us by our jackets. He caught us and we all stopped.

We three stood staggering, half blinded, coughing, in an obscure hilltop backyard: a man in his twenties, a boy, a girl. He had released our jackets, our pursuer, our captor, our hero:

---

2. backyard labyrinths (lab′ ə rinths): The areas behind and between the houses were like a kind of maze.

he knew we weren't going anywhere. We all played by the rules. Mikey and I unzipped our jackets. I pulled off my sopping mittens. Our tracks multiplied in the backyard's new snow. We had been breaking new snow all morning. We didn't look at each other. I was cherishing my excitement. The man's lower pants legs were wet; his cuffs were full of snow, and there was a prow of snow[3] beneath them on his shoes and socks. Some trees bordered the little flat backyard, some messy winter trees. There was no one around: a clearing in a grove, and we the only players.

It was a long time before he could speak. I had some difficulty at first recalling why we were there. My lips felt swollen; I couldn't see out of the sides of my eyes; I kept coughing.

"You stupid kids," he began perfunctorily.

We listened perfunctorily indeed, if we listened at all, for the chewing out was redundant, a mere formality, and beside the point. The point was that he had chased us passionately without giving up, and so he had caught us. Now he came down to earth. I wanted the glory to last forever.

But how could the glory have lasted forever? We could have run through every backyard in North America until we got to Panama. But when he trapped us at the lip of the Panama Canal, what precisely could he have done to prolong the drama of the chase and cap its glory? I brooded about this for the next few years. He could only have fried Mikey Fahey and me in boiling oil, say, or dismembered us piecemeal, or staked us to anthills. None of which I really wanted, and none of which any adult was likely to do, even in the spirit of fun. He could only chew us out there in the Panamanian jungle, after months or years of exalting pursuit. He could only begin, "You stupid kids," and continue in his ordinary Pittsburgh accent with his normal righteous anger and the usual common sense.

If in that snowy backyard the driver of the black Buick had cut off our heads, Mikey's and mine, I would have died happy, for nothing has required so much of me since as being chased all over Pittsburgh in the middle of winter—running terrified, exhausted—by this sainted, skinny, furious red-headed man who wished to have a word with us. I don't know how he found his way back to his car.

---

3. prow of snow: The snow formed a V-shape, like the front of a ship.

Ideas and Support: *Did the chase take longer than it needed to?*

Technique: *She has some imagination. The things she describes are as strange as the man's behavior.*

Organization: *I'm still amazed that the man chased them, but why was there so much suspense?*

Respond: *I like the idea that boys and girls can get into the same kind of trouble, but I wonder why the man was so angry. I guess Annie and Mikey were pretty surprised, too.*

Annie Dillard (1945–) grew up in Pittsburgh, Pennsylvania. As a child, she loved reading, drawing, and observing the natural world. While attending college in Virginia, Dillard lived near a creek in a valley of the Blue Ridge Mountains. In 1974 she published *Pilgrim at Tinker Creek*, which describes her explorations of that environment. The book won the Pulitzer Prize for Nonfiction. This essay is an excerpt from *An American Childhood*, Dillard's memoirs of growing up in Pittsburgh.

RESPONDING TO THE SELECTION

Your Response

1. Would you want the young Annie Dillard as a friend? Why or why not?

Recalling

2. Why were the author and her friends throwing snowballs at passing cars?
3. What did the man who chased them look like?

Interpreting

4. What connection does the author make between playing football and being chased for throwing a snowball?
5. Why does the author call the man who chased her "our hero"?
6. How does the "hero" come down to earth?

Applying

7. The author says that nothing girls did could compare with playing football. Is there still a difference between girls' and boys' activities? Should there be?

ANALYZING LITERATURE

Understanding an Essay

A common topic for a personal essay is an incident that the writer experienced. Through vivid descriptive details, the author helps readers visualize what happened. Usually the author will also show why the event is significant.

1. How does the detail "He didn't even close the car door" help you visualize the event?
2. Find two other details that reveal something about the man.
3. Find three details that reveal how the author was feeling during or just after the chase.

THINKING AND WRITING

Describing a Suspenseful Event

Describe an event from your own life in which the outcome was in doubt for a while. For example, you might choose an athletic contest or a conflict with a friend. First make a list of descriptive details that will help readers see what happened. Then think about how you can build suspense. Have a classmate read your first draft. Together discuss the significance of the event and ways you might suggest this in your essay.

LEARNING OPTIONS

1. **Art.** Draw a picture of the chase scene as you envision it from the author's description. Think about how to show the suspense in your drawing. Your drawing may be realistic or abstract.
2. **Speaking and Listening.** You can hear the rhythm of the chase in Dillard's description of it. Prepare an oral reading of the section that starts with the man getting out of his car and that goes to the end.

YOUR WRITING PROCESS

"A sentence should contain no unnecessary words. . . . This requires not that the writer make all his sentences short . . . but that every word tell."

E. B. White

WRITING A SUMMARY

Have you ever summarized an important lesson for a classmate who missed it? If so, perhaps you found that reviewing and writing about the lesson was just as helpful for you as it was for your classmate.

Focus

Assignment: Summarize a series of ideas, a skill, or a procedure that you learned about in a class other than Language Arts.
Purpose: To inform a classmate who was not able to attend this class.
Audience: A friend from school or a classmate.

Prewriting

1. Brainstorm to list classes you enjoyed. Recall a lesson that you especially enjoyed. You might enjoy summarizing this lesson for a classmate.

2. Ask yourself questions. When you have selected a lesson to summarize, put yourself in your classmate's place. What questions would he or she ask about this lesson?

Student Model

Science class: Dissecting a Frog
Questions my classmate might ask:
• Which tools or instruments did you use?
• Which internal organs were you able to identify?
• What problems did you have? How did you solve them?
• What conclusions did you reach?

---

3. Freewrite. When you have listed some questions, freewrite your answers to them. Include as many details as you can, but do not stop to revise your writing. Then review your freewriting to see which details are the most important.

Drafting

1. Remember your audience. It will help to imagine a friend or classmate as you draft your summary. Remember that your aim is to make your friend feel as if he or she were *there.*

2. The sequence of events is important. To help your classmate understand the order in which events occurred, use words that clarify the time sequence.

> **Student Model**
>
> Ms. Johnson began by showing us a slide of herself standing at the Grand Canyon. _Then_ she described her hike down to Indian Gardens. The slides she showed _next_ told the story of her trip back up to the rim, and the _last_ slide we saw was a picture of Ms. Johnson after she had finished her hike.

Revising and Editing

1. Use a peer reviewer. Try showing your summary to a student who missed the lesson you are describing. Ask this person questions like the following:

- Does my summary make you feel as if you were there?
- Does my summary answer all your questions about the lesson?
- Have I included any unnecessary details?
- Would you rely on my summary in studying for a test on this lesson? Why or why not?

2. Vary your sentences. Read your summary aloud to see whether or not it sounds choppy or dull. If it does, vary the lengths and types of sentences you use so that your reader won't be bored.

> **Student Model**
>
> _after_
> First, Mr. Wallace explained the causes of the war. Then
> _conflict's major_
> he described some of the battles fought in the war. Finally, he pointed out the effects of the war.

3. Feel free to use informal language. Because your audience is a friend or classmate, you may use contractions and colloquial expressions. Make sure, however, that your sentences are clear and complete. Run-ons and sentence fragments may confuse your reader and distract him or her from the information you are trying to convey.

Grammar Tip

In deciding whether or not to use a contraction, read the sentence aloud. If it sounds too stiff and formal, then use the contraction. Remember to replace the missing letter or letters with an apostrophe.

Options for Publishing

- Find out from your teacher if anyone was absent for the lesson you summarized. If so, give that student a copy of your summary.
- Share your summary with the teacher of the class. Let him or her know that you learned something that day.
- Contribute to a class book of lesson summaries that students can use in studying for tests.

Reviewing Your Writing Process

1. Which details about the class did you remember most easily? Which took more time to recall? Explain.

2. Were you able to imagine your audience as you drafted your summary? Why or why not?

YOUR WRITING PROCESS

WRITING A "HOW-TO" ESSAY

The world of nonfiction includes "how-to" writing about a wide variety of activities. Helpful books and articles tell readers how to do anything, from fixing a leaky faucet to growing a more lovely rose. Like the essays in this unit, such pieces require just the right combination of clear information and an engaging style.

> **Focus**
>
> **Assignment:** Write a "how-to" essay for an activity you enjoy.
> **Purpose:** To convince someone to try this activity.
> **Audience:** People your age.

Prewriting

1. Study some models. Look in newspapers, magazines, library books—you'll find many sources of "how-to" articles that you can study. Read models, and with other students, discuss them and make observations.

2. Brainstorm a list of possibilities. Think about sports, music, arts and crafts, cooking, and games. Don't be afraid to choose an activity unfamiliar to many people. Sometimes the most unusual topics can serve as the basis for lively "how-to" essays.

3. Get specific. The more specific your topic, the better your writing can be. For example, "How to Throw a Curveball" will make a better essay than "How to Play Baseball."

4. Timelines. Most "how-to" essays guide readers through the steps they will have to follow. A timeline can help you organize the steps before you begin to write your draft. As you plan, fill in details in the correct sequence.

> **Student Model**
>
> Timeline for making a pizza
>
>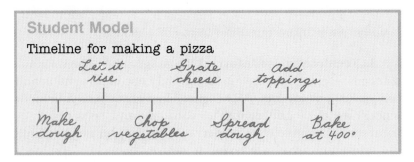

Drafting

1. Grab your reader's attention. Your introduction should make your topic clear and set the tone of your essay. Use your opening remarks to hook your reader with a joke, a story, or a fascinating description.

2. Use the present tense and include transitions. Consistently use the present tense when describing a process or procedure. Also, make the order and timing of the various steps clear by including words that show chronological order.

> **Student Model**
>
> <u>First</u>, lay out everything on the counter, including ingredients, a mixing bowl, and measuring spoons. <u>Next</u>, heat water and empty a package of yeast into the bowl.

3. Decide whom you are addressing. Many "how-to" essays directly address the reader by referring to him or her as "you." In many directions—for example, "Heat water"—the "you" is implied but not stated.

Revising and Editing

1. Don't settle for vague words. Eliminate adjectives and adverbs whenever you can by using precise nouns and verbs. Don't use a general noun when you can find a specific one; don't settle for an ordinary verb.

> **Student Model**
>
> *build camp*   *collect*   *twigs,*
> To ~~make~~ a fire, ~~get~~ some ~~little sticks,~~ some bigger ~~ones,~~ *sticks,*
>   *hefty logs. arrange*
> and some ~~real big ones,~~ ~~Put~~ them into piles.

2. Make sure you have defined your terms. Many activities have a vocabulary that won't be familiar to someone who has never tried these activities.

3. Ask a novice; ask a pro. Two kinds of peer reviewers will be valuable to you: someone who shares your enthusiasm for the activity and someone who has never tried it. For example, a fellow bowler can point out a detail you have forgotten, but someone who has never bowled can point out that you have used the term *gutter* without defining it clearly.

Grammar Tip

Rather than devoting a separate sentence to defining terms, try using **appositives** to get the job done. An appositive is a noun or noun phrase that immediately follows a noun or noun phrase and provides another way of saying the same thing.

Options for Publishing

• Have a classmate follow your directions to determine whether or not they are clearly written.
• Combine your essay with those of your classmates into an anthology entitled *How To.* Display the collection in your school library.

Reviewing Your Writing Process

1. Was it hard to break down the activity into a series of steps? Why or why not?
2. Did writing this essay give you a new appreciation for the activity you described? Explain.

SPRINGTIME FANTASY
Adolphe Faugeron

POETRY

Poetry is language that says more than ordinary language and says it with fewer words and in less space. Poets use language in a special way. Like other writers, poets choose words for their sense, but they also choose words for what they hint at or suggest, for the way they sound, and for the word pictures they create. Ordinary language makes sense. Poetry makes sense—and sound, and rhythm and music, and vision.

Short stories, essays, newspaper articles, your schoolbooks, and so on, are written in prose. Poetry is usually written in verse. Verse is language with a definite rhythm, or beat. It is usually arranged in columns down the page. Sometimes these columns of lines are divided into units called stanzas. Lines of verse often (but not always) rhyme. Although you could say that poetry is what is written in verse, it is always more than rhythm and rhyme. Poetry, as a great poet said, is the most memorable kind of language.

Poetry

Poetry differs from other forms of writing in the way it looks, the way it uses language, and the way it incorporates certain qualities of music. The poet Walt Whitman wrote, "To have great poetry, there must be great audiences, too." How does a member of an audience participate? You approach each poem actively. The following strategies will help you be an active reader of poetry:

QUESTION What is the poem saying? What questions come to mind as you read? Why does the poet include certain words and details? Search for answers to your questions as you read.

USE YOUR SENSES What images is the poet creating? How are these images developed? Let your imagination see pictures in your mind, and let your senses enjoy the poet's language.

LISTEN Much poetry is musical. Read the poem aloud to hear its sound and feel its rhythm. Often the words and rhythm suggest a mood or feeling. Let the poem's sound wash over you. How does the sound affect you?

CONNECT Bring your own experience and knowledge to the poem. What images and sounds are familiar? Which are new to you?

PARAPHRASE Put the poem in your own words. When you can express a poem in your own words, you can understand its meaning better.

RESPOND How does the poem make you feel as you read? Go beyond the poet's meaning and add your own. What does the poem say to *you*?

Try to use these strategies as you read the poems in this unit. They will help you increase your enjoyment and understanding of poetry.

On pages 431 and 433, you can see an example of active reading by Joanell Bookman of Eisenhower Middle School in Oklahoma City, Oklahoma. The notes in the side column include Joanell's thoughts and comments while reading "The Village Blacksmith." Your own thoughts may be different, because each reader responds differently to a poem.

The Village Blacksmith

Henry Wadsworth Longfellow

Question: *Who is the blacksmith?*

Under a spreading chestnut tree
    The village smithy[1] stands;
The smith, a mighty man is he,
    With large and sinewy[2] hands;
5 And the muscles of his brawny arms
    Are strong as iron bands.

Paraphrase: *The blacksmith is a large, strong man.*

His hair is crisp,[3] and black, and long,
    His face is like the tan;
His brow is wet with honest sweat,
10   He earns whate'er he can,
And looks the whole world in the face,
    For he owes not any man.

Listen: *Here is an interesting rhythm.*

Paraphrase: *He is a very good and honest man.*

Week in, week out, from morn till night,
    You can hear his bellows[4] blow;
15 You can hear him swing his heavy sledge,[5]
    With measured beat and slow,
Like a sexton[6] ringing the village bell,
    When the evening sun is low.

Use Your Senses: *He makes a lot of noise while he's working.*

And children coming home from school
20   Look in at the open door;
They love to see the flaming forge,
    And hear the bellows roar,
And catch the burning sparks that fly
    Like chaff from a threshing floor.

Connect: *I can understand why the kids like watching him do this unusual work.*

---

1. smithy (smith′ ē) *n.*: The workshop of a blacksmith.
2. sinewy (sin′ yo͞o wē) *adj.*: Tough and strong.
3. crisp (krisp) *adj.*: In this case, it means closely curled and wiry.
4. bellows (bel′ ōz) *n.*: A device for quickening the fire by blowing air on it.
5. sledge (slej) *n.*: Sledgehammer, a long, heavy hammer, usually held with both hands.
6. sexton (seks′ tən) *n.*: A church official in charge of ringing the bells.

25 He goes on Sunday to the church,
      And sits among his boys;
He hears the parson pray and preach,
      He hears his daughter's voice,
Singing in the village choir,
30   And it makes his heart rejoice.

It sounds to him like her mother's voice,
      Singing in Paradise!
He needs must think of her once more,
      How in the grave she lies;
35 And with his hard, rough hand he wipes
      A tear out of his eyes.

Toiling—rejoicing—sorrowing,
      Onward through life he goes;
Each morning sees some task begin,
40   Each evening sees it close;
Something attempted, something done,
      Has earned a night's repose.

Thanks, thanks to thee, my worthy friend,
      For the lesson thou hast taught!
45 Thus at the flaming forge of life
      Our fortunes must be wrought;
Thus on its sounding anvil shaped
      Each burning deed and thought.

Paraphrase: *He's a religious man.*

Question: *How did his wife die? How old was she?*

Use Your Senses: *This line looks very different from all the others.*

Connect: *It's best to forget the sad days and go on with life.*

Listen: *This line sort of stops, then starts again.*

Respond: *We can learn a lot from the blacksmith. I can see why Longfellow admires him. He lives simply, but he is kind and courageous.*

Henry Wadsworth Longfellow (1807–1882) was born in Maine. After graduating from Bowdoin College, he traveled in Europe, but returned to become a professor of languages at Bowdoin and later at Harvard. Longfellow is associated with a group of poets known as the Fireside Poets, since their work often attracted a family audience that would read the poems aloud while sitting around the fireplace. In many of his poems, Longfellow strove to portray the myths and values of the still-young nation. After the publication of his second book of poems, which included "The Village Blacksmith," he became recognized as one of the major poets in the United States.

RESPONDING TO THE SELECTION

Your Response

1. Do you admire the blacksmith? Explain.

Recalling

2. Why is the blacksmith able to look the whole world in the face?
3. Why does his daughter's voice make his heart rejoice?

Interpreting

4. Which details tell you that the blacksmith is an honest, hard-working man?
5. What does the tear in his eye indicate about him?

Applying

6. President Theodore Roosevelt once said in a Labor Day address: "Far and away the best prize that life offers is the chance to work hard at work worth doing." Do you think the village blacksmith would agree or disagree with this sentiment? Explain your answer.

ANALYZING LITERATURE

Understanding Theme in Poetry

Theme is the insight into life revealed by the poem. Sometimes the theme is stated directly. To fully understand it, paraphrase it, or express it in your own words.

1. Which lines reveal the blacksmith's philosophy of life?
2. Paraphrase these lines.
3. Which details indicate that the poet agrees with the blacksmith's philosophy of life?

CRITICAL THINKING AND READING

Understanding the Poet's Purpose

When Longfellow wrote in the mid-nineteenth century, the United States was still a rather young country. One of his purposes for writing was to present myths for the new land and to portray the values of our native American culture.

1. Which details in the poem show that the American culture during the nineteenth century valued independence?
2. Which details show that it valued sentiment, or tender feelings?
3. Which details show that it valued hard work?
4. Do you think views toward work in the later part of the twentieth century are different from those during Longfellow's time? Explain your answer.

THINKING AND WRITING

Writing About Work

Think of someone you know who enjoys his or her work. What does this person do? Why does this person take pleasure from the job? Write a short poem telling about a day in the work life of this person. Use similes to help you make your points. Revise your poem to make sure its meaning is clear. Prepare a final draft, and read it aloud to your classmates.

LEARNING OPTIONS

1. **Cross-curricular Connection.** When Longfellow wrote this poem, almost every village had a blacksmith. Nowadays, blacksmiths are rare. Discover what you can about working blacksmiths today. Also find out about modern jobs that involve working with metals. Your library's card catalog may have an entry for metal working, and you might interview an industrial arts teacher.
2. **Writing.** The poet makes it clear that the village children find it exciting to watch the blacksmith at work. Imagine that you are one of those children. Describe what you have seen to a friend or family member. What about him did you admire? Which of his specialized actions impressed you most?

Narrative Poetry

UNTITLED (CAT)
Noreen Anne Finn, Student
Erie, Pennsylvania
Courtesy of the Artist

GUIDE FOR READING

The Highwayman

Narrative Poetry

Narrative poetry is poetry that tells a story. Narrative poems have a special appeal. They present dramatic events in a vivid way, using some of the same elements as short stories: plot, characters, and dialogue, for example. Some narrative poems, like "The Highwayman," use words and phrases that are repeated throughout the work. These repetitions help to create a songlike rhythm and focus your attention on important details of the story.

Focus

In the days of travel in horse-drawn carriages, people feared encountering highwaymen—thieves who waited for their victims on lonely stretches of road. In the poem you are about to read, the highwayman is portrayed as a dashing, romantic figure. With a group of classmates, brainstorm to name legendary outlaws who have romantic reputations, such as Robin Hood. Make a chart like the one below, listing details about their lives that make them seem romantic.

Outlaw	Romantic Detail
Robin Hood	

Vocabulary

Knowing the following words will help you as you read "The Highwayman."

torrent (tôr′ ənt) *n.*: Flood (p. 437)

moor (moor) *n.*: Open, rolling land with swamps (p. 437)

breeches (brich′ iz) *n.*: Trousers that reach to or just below the knee (p. 437)

cascade (kas kād′) *n.*: Waterfall or anything tumbling like water (p. 439)

tawny (tô′ nē) *adj.*: Yellowish brown (p. 440)

strive (strīv) *v.*: Struggle (p. 441)

brandished (bran′ dish′d) *v.*: Waved in a threatening way (p. 442)

Alfred Noyes

(1880–1958) was both a poet and critic. He was born in Staffordshire, England, although he lived for many years in the United States and taught at Princeton University. Noyes often wrote about legendary figures from English history, such as Robin Hood and Sir Francis Drake. He wrote "The Highwayman," his best-known poem, about an outlaw and his love, while visiting Bagshot Heath. The poem may have been inspired by the fact that this region of England had once been terrorized by outlaws.

The Highwayman

Alfred Noyes

Part One

The wind was a torrent of darkness among the gusty trees.
The moon was a ghostly galleon[1] tossed upon cloudy seas.
The road was a ribbon of moonlight over the purple moor,
And the highwayman came riding—
5   Riding—riding—
The highwayman came riding, up to the old inn door.

He'd a French cocked-hat on his forehead, a bunch of lace at
      his chin,
A coat of the claret velvet, and breeches of brown doeskin.
They fitted with never a wrinkle. His boots were up to the
      thigh.
10   And he rode with a jeweled twinkle,
         His pistol butts a-twinkle,
His rapier hilt[2] a-twinkle, under the jeweled sky.

Over the cobbles he clattered and clashed in the dark innyard.
He tapped with his whip on the shutters, but all was locked
      and barred.
15   He whistled a tune to the window, and who should be waiting
      there
But the landlord's black-eyed daughter,
         Bess, the landlord's daughter,
Plaiting[3] a dark red love knot into her long black hair.

And dark in the dark old innyard a stable wicket[4] creaked
20   Where Tim the ostler[5] listened. His face was white and peaked.
His eyes were hollows of madness, his hair like moldy hay,
But he loved the landlord's daughter,
         The landlord's red-lipped daughter.
Dumb as a dog he listened, and he heard the robber say—

1. **galleon** (gal′ ē ən) *n.*: A large Spanish sailing ship.
2. **rapier** (rā′ pē ər) **hilt:** The large cup-shaped handle of a rapier,
which is a type of sword.
3. **plaiting** (plāt′ iŋ) *n.*: Braiding.
4. **stable wicket** (stā′ b′l wik′ it): A small door or gate to a stable.
5. **ostler** (äs′ lər) *n.*: Someone who takes care of horses at an inn
or stable.

25   "One kiss, my bonny[6] sweetheart, I'm after a prize to-night,
But I shall be back with the yellow gold before the morning
    light;
Yet, if they press me sharply, and harry[7] me through the day,
Then look for me by moonlight,
    Watch for me by moonlight,
30   I'll come to thee by moonlight, though hell should bar the
    way."

He rose upright in the stirrups. He scarce could reach her
    hand,
But she loosened her hair in the casement.[8] His face burnt
    like a brand[9]
As the black cascade of perfume came tumbling over his
    breast;
And he kissed its waves in the moonlight,
35   (O, sweet black waves in the moonlight!)
Then he tugged at his rein in the moonlight, and galloped
    away to the west.

---

6. bonny (bän′ ē) *adj.*: Scottish for pretty.
7. harry (har′ ē) *v.*: To disturb by constant attacks.
8. casement (kās′ mənt) *n.*: A window frame that opens on hinges.
9. brand (brand) *n.*: A piece of burning wood.

Part Two

He did not come in the dawning. He did not come at noon;
And out of the tawny sunset, before the rise of the moon,
When the road was a gypsy's ribbon, looping the purple moor,
40 A redcoat troop came marching—
            Marching—marching—
King George's men[10] came marching, up to the old inn door.

They said no word to the landlord. They drank his ale instead.
But they gagged his daughter, and bound her, to the foot of
        her narrow bed.
45 Two of them knelt at her casement, with muskets at their
        side!
There was death at every window;
            And hell at one dark window;
For Bess could see, through her casement, the road that *he*
        would ride.

They had tied her up to attention, with many a sniggering
        jest.[11]
50 They had bound a musket beside her, with the muzzle
        beneath her breast!
"Now, keep good watch!" and they kissed her. She heard the
        doomed man say—
Look for me by moonlight;
            Watch for me by moonlight;
I'll come to thee by moonlight, though hell should bar the
        way!

55 She twisted her hands behind her; but all the knots held
        good!
She writhed her hands till her fingers were wet with sweat or
        blood!
They stretched and strained in the darkness, and the hours
        crawled by like years,
Till, now, on the stroke of midnight,
            Cold, on the stroke of midnight,
60 The tip of one finger touched it! The trigger at least was hers!

The tip of one finger touched it. She strove no more for the
        rest.

---

10. King George's men: Soldiers serving King George of England.
11. sniggering (snig′ ər iŋ) **jest:** Sly joke.

Up, she stood up to attention, with the muzzle beneath her
    breast.
She would not risk their hearing; she would not strive again;
For the road lay bare in the moonlight;
65   Blank and bare in the moonlight;
And the blood of her veins, in the moonlight, throbbed to her
    love's refrain.

Tlot-tlot; tlot-tlot! Had they heard it? The horsehoofs ringing
    clear;
Tlot-tlot, tlot-tlot, in the distance? Were they deaf that they did
    not hear?
Down the ribbon of moonlight, over the brow of the hill,
70 The highwayman came riding—
      Riding—riding—
The redcoats looked to their priming![12] She stood up, straight
    and still.

Tlot-tlot, in the frosty silence! *Tlot-tlot,* in the echoing night!
Nearer he came and nearer. Her face was like a light.

---

12. priming (prī' miŋ) *n.*: The explosive used to set off the charge
in a gun.

75 Her eyes grew wide for a moment; she drew one last deep
        breath,
     Then her finger moved in the moonlight,
            Her musket shattered the moonlight,
     Shattered her breast in the moonlight and warned him—with
        her death.

     He turned. He spurred to the west; he did not know who stood
80 Bowed, with her head o'er the musket, drenched with her own
        blood!
     Not till the dawn he heard it, and his face grew gray to hear
     How Bess, the landlord's daughter,
            The landlord's black-eyed daughter,
     Had watched for her love in the moonlight, and died in the
        darkness there.

85 Back, he spurred like a madman, shouting a curse to the sky,
     With the white road smoking behind him and his rapier
        brandished high.
     Blood-red were his spurs in the golden noon; wine-red was his
        velvet coat;
     When they shot him down on the highway,
            Down like a dog on the highway,
90 And he lay in his blood on the highway, with a bunch of lace
        at his throat.

     .   .   .   .

     And still of a winter's night, they say, when the wind is in
        the trees,
     When the moon is a ghostly galleon tossed upon cloudy
        seas,
     When the road is a ribbon of moonlight over the purple moor,
     A highwayman comes riding—
95   *Riding—riding—*
     A highwayman comes riding, up to the old inn door.

     Over the cobbles he clatters and clangs in the dark innyard.
     He taps with his whip on the shutters, but all is locked and
        barred.
     He whistles a tune to the window, and who should be
        waiting there
100 *But the landlord's black-eyed daughter,*
            Bess, the landlord's daughter,
     Plaiting a dark red love knot into her long black hair.

Your Response

1. Who do you think was more brave, Bess or the highwayman? Why?

Recalling

2. Explain the highwayman's plans. (Lines 25–30)
3. How does Bess warn the highwayman of the soldiers' presence? (Lines 75–80)

Interpreting

4. How do the soldiers learn of the highwayman's plans to return to the inn?
5. Find three details that make the highwayman appear a romantic, or dashing, figure.
6. Find each mention of the color *red* in this poem. How does the repetition of this color add to the romantic quality of the poem?
7. How does the setting add to this quality?
8. Would this poem have been as effective if it had ended at line 90? Explain your answer.

Applying

9. What is it about outlaws that has made people romanticize them—or has made their lives seem romantic and glamorous?

ANALYZING LITERATURE

Understanding Narrative Poetry

Narrative poetry tells a story, using elements like plot, character, and setting. In "The Highwayman," for example, the two main characters are the outlaw and Bess. Using strong rhythm and repeated words, the poet tells how the love between Bess and the outlaw leads to their deaths.

1. Describe the two main characters.
2. How is the conflict resolved?
3. Where and when does most of the action take place?
4. How do the poem's rhythms and repetitions add to the drama of the story?

CRITICAL THINKING AND READING

Following the Sequence of Events

A storyteller creates an effect by the order in which he or she chooses to **sequence,** or arrange, the events. Noyes tells "The Highwayman" in **chronological sequence,** describing events in the order they occur.

1. List the important events of the poem in chronological sequence.
2. Would the poem be as effective if the sequence were changed and you knew right away what would happen? Why or why not?

THINKING AND WRITING

Summarizing a Narrative Poem

Summarizing a story means retelling it briefly in the correct order, giving only the essential details. Imagine that you are creating a movie based on this poem. In order to go ahead with your plans, you need a summary of the action. Look again at the list that you made of the poem's events. Turn this list into a summary of the story, adding only the most important details. In revising, make sure that your summary is brief but complete.

LEARNING OPTIONS

1. **Speaking and Listening.** Choose a passage of 10 to 20 lines from "The Highwayman" to read aloud to your classmates. Use your voice to bring out the meaning of the poem by changing the speed and volume with which you say words and phrases. Let the punctuation guide you in deciding when to pause at the end of a line or continue without interruption from one line to the next.
2. **Art.** Create a "Wanted" poster for the highwayman. Reread the poem to find the details you will need to include in your description of him. Then draw a sketch of the highwayman, briefly describe his crimes, and decide upon the amount of the reward for his capture.

GUIDE FOR READING

Robert Service

(1874–1958) was a Canadian poet who grew up in Glasgow, Scotland. He moved to Canada at the age of twenty and was hired by a bank in 1905. When the bank transferred him to a branch in the Yukon, Service began to write lively poems about the trappers and prospectors he met there. These poems were an immediate success. Soon he was able to leave the bank and concentrate on writing. In "The Cremation of Sam McGee," Service creates a memorable character with an intense hatred of the cold.

The Cremation of Sam McGee

Rhythm

Rhythm is the sound pattern created by combining stressed and unstressed syllables. In the following lines from "The Cremation of Sam McGee," for example, the stressed syllables (marked ´) receive more emphasis than the unstressed ones (marked ˘):

Aňd Ĭ looḱed ăt iť, aňd Ĭ thouǵht ă biť, aňd Ĭ looḱed ăt mў froźeň chuḿ;
Theň "Heŕe," saiď Ĭ, wĭth ă suddeň crý, "iš mў cre-́mă-toŕ-ĕuḿ."

The same general pattern of stressed and unstressed syllables continues throughout the poem. Other poems have different rhythms, and sometimes a poem's rhythm may change from line to line.

Focus

A character in this poem, Sam McGee, hates the cold, but he puts up with it because he is looking for gold in Alaska. Which do you find more uncomfortable: extreme cold or extreme heat? Write about the worst cold or the worst heat you have ever experienced. Describe the situation and how you felt. What did you do about getting warm or cooling off? As you read, notice the unusual way in which Sam conquers the cold.

Vocabulary

Knowing the following words will help you as you read "The Cremation of Sam McGee."

whimper (hwim′ pər) v.: Make low, crying sounds; complain (p. 445)

cremated (krē′ māt id) v.: Burned to ashes (p. 445)

ghastly (gast′ lē) adj.: Ghost-like; frightful (p. 446)

brawn (brôn) n.: Physical strength (p. 446)

stern (sturn) adj.: Strict; unyielding (p. 446)

loathed (lōthd) v.: Hated (p. 446)

scowled (skould) v.: Frowned (p. 447)

grisly (griz′ lē) adj.: Horrible (p. 447)

The Cremation of Sam McGee

Robert Service

There are strange things done in the midnight sun[1]
    By the men who moil[2] for gold;
The Arctic trails have their secret tales
    That would make your blood run cold;
5 *The Northern Lights have seen queer sights,*
    But the queerest they ever did see
Was that night on the marge[3] of Lake Lebarge
    I cremated Sam McGee.

Now Sam McGee was from Tennessee, where the cotton
    blooms and blows.
10 Why he left his home in the South to roam 'round the Pole,
    God only knows.
He was always cold, but the land of gold seemed to hold
    him like a spell;
Though he'd often say in his homely way that "he'd sooner
    live in hell."

On a Christmas Day we were mushing[4] our way over the
    Dawson trail.
Talk of your cold! through the parka's fold it stabbed like a
    driven nail.
15 If our eyes we'd close, then the lashes froze till sometimes
    we couldn't see;
It wasn't much fun, but the only one to whimper was Sam
    McGee.

And that very night, as we lay packed tight in our robes
    beneath the snow,
And the dogs were fed, and the stars o'erhead were dancing
    heel and toe,

---

1. the midnight sun: The sun visible at midnight in the arctic or
antarctic regions during the summer.
2. moil (moil) *v.:* To toil and slave.
3. marge (märj) *n.:* A poetic word for the shore of the lake.
4. mushing (mush' iŋ) *v.:* Traveling by foot over snow, usually with
a dog sled. "Mush" is a command to sled dogs to start or go faster.

He turned to me, and "Cap," says he, "I'll cash in[5] this trip,
    I guess;
20   And if I do, I'm asking that you won't refuse my last request."

Well, he seemed so low that I couldn't say no; then he says
    with a sort of moan:
"It's the cursèd cold, and it's got right hold till I'm chilled
    clean through to the bone.
Yet 'tain't being dead—it's my awful dread of the icy grave
    that pains;
So I want you to swear that, foul or fair, you'll cremate my
    last remains."
25   A pal's last need is a thing to heed, so I swore I would not
    fail;
And we started on at the streak of dawn; but God! he
    looked ghastly pale.
He crouched on the sleigh, and he raved all day of his home
    in Tennessee;
And before nightfall a corpse was all that was left of Sam
    McGee.

There wasn't a breath in that land of death, and I hurried,
    horror-driven,
30   With a corpse half hid that I couldn't get rid, because of a
    promise given;
It was lashed to the sleigh, and it seemed to say: "You may
    tax your brawn and brains,
But you promised true, and it's up to you to cremate those
    last remains."

Now a promise made is a debt unpaid, and the trail has its
    own stern code.
In the days to come, though my lips were dumb, in my
    heart how I cursed that load.
35   In the long, long night, by the lone firelight, while the
    huskies,[6] round in a ring,
Howled out their woes to the homeless snows—O God! how
    I loathed the thing.

And every day that quiet clay seemed to heavy and heavier
    grow;

---

5. cash in: A slang expression meaning "die."
6. huskies (hus' kēs) *n.*: Strong dogs used for pulling sleds over
the snow.

And on I went, though the dogs were spent and the grub
　　was getting low;
The trail was bad, and I felt half mad, but I swore I would
　　not give in;
40　And I'd often sing to the hateful thing, and it hearkened
　　with a grin.

Till I came to the marge of Lake Lebarge, and a derelict[7]
　　there lay;
It was jammed in the ice, but I saw in a trice it was called
　　the "Alice May."
And I looked at it, and I thought a bit, and I looked at my
　　frozen chum;
Then "Here," said I, with a sudden cry, "is my cre-ma-tor-
　　eum."

45　Some planks I tore from the cabin floor, and I lit the boiler
　　fire;
Some coal I found that was lying around, and I heaped the
　　fuel higher;
The flames just soared, and the furnace roared—such a
　　blaze you seldom see;
And I burrowed a hole in the glowing coal, and I stuffed in
　　Sam McGee.

Then I made a hike, for I didn't like to hear him sizzle so;
50　And the heavens scowled, and the huskies howled, and the
　　wind began to blow.
It was icy cold, but the hot sweat rolled down my cheeks,
　　and I don't know why;
And the greasy smoke in an inky cloak went streaking
　　down the sky.

I do not know how long in the snow I wrestled with grisly
　　fear;
But the stars came out and they danced about ere again I
　　ventured near;
55　I was sick with dread, but I bravely said: "I'll just take a
　　peep inside.
I guess he's cooked, and it's time I looked"; . . . then the
　　door I opened wide.

---

7. derelict (der′ ə likt′) *n*.: An abandoned ship.

And there sat Sam, looking cool and calm, in the heart of
    the furnace roar;
And he wore a smile you could see a mile, and he said:
    "Please close that door.
It's fine in here, but I greatly fear you'll let in the cold and
    storm—
60 Since I left Plumtree, down in Tennessee, it's the first time
    I've been warm."

There are strange things done in the midnight sun
    By the men who moil for gold;
The Arctic trails have their secret tales
    That would make your blood run cold;
65 *The Northern Lights have seen queer sights,*
    But the queerest they ever did see
Was that night on the marge of Lake Lebarge
    I cremated Sam McGee.

RESPONDING TO THE SELECTION

Your Response

1. Did you find this poem humorous? Why or why not?

Recalling

2. Where did Sam McGee come from? Why doesn't he go home? (Lines 8–11)
3. What does Sam ask the narrator to promise? (Lines 21–24)
4. How is the narrator to keep his promise? (Lines 41–48)
5. Describe what the narrator finds when he opens the furnace door? (Lines 53–61)

Interpreting

6. Compare and contrast Sam and the narrator.
7. In what way is the ending of this poem an elaborate practical joke? Explain the details that suggest Sam was playing a trick on his pal in order to get warm.

Applying

8. Do you agree with the narrator that "a promise made is a debt unpaid"? Why or why not?

ANALYZING LITERATURE

Understanding Rhythm

Rhythm is the pattern of stressed and unstressed syllables in the lines of a poem. Many poems have the same rhythmic pattern in each line.

1. Tap out the pattern of stressed and unstressed syllables in line 43. Find three other lines with this same rhythm.
2. How does the rhythm of line 44 differ from that of line 43? Find three other lines with the same rhythm as line 44.
3. What conclusion do you draw about the rhythmic pattern of this poem?

CRITICAL THINKING AND READING

Evaluating the Effects of Rhythm

Like a drumbeat, the pattern of stressed syllables in poetry can produce different moods: excitement, peace, sadness, for example. In evaluating the effects of rhythm, compare a passage from a poem with a similar passage written as a paragraph.

1. Use your own words to summarize lines 57–60 of the poem in a paragraph.
2. Read your own words and the lines of poetry aloud.
3. Compare and contrast the mood of the poetry with that of your paragraph.

THINKING AND WRITING

Patterning the Rhythm of a Poem

Imagine the narrator's reactions to Sam's trick. Freewrite about what you think the narrator said to Sam after he saw him looking cool and calm in the heart of the roaring furnace. Then use your freewriting as the basis for writing a new stanza for this poem. Using the same rhythmic pattern, write a stanza telling the narrator's reactions. Review your stanza, reading it aloud and tapping out the rhythm. Finally, prepare a proofread draft and read it to your classmates.

LEARNING OPTION

Speaking and Listening. With a group of classmates, prepare a choral reading of "The Cremation of Sam McGee." Choral reading refers to the reading aloud of a poem by a group of people. In a choral reading, some parts of the poem can be read by the whole group. Other parts, like the words of Sam McGee, can be read by one person. Decide which lines should be read by one person, and choose someone to read those lines. After you have practiced reading the poem as a group a few times, read it for the whole class.

GUIDE FOR READING

Sarah Cynthia Sylvia Stout
Would Not Take the Garbage Out

Rhyme

Rhyme is the repetition of a sound in two or more words or phrases. The common type of rhyme that occurs at the end of lines is called **end rhyme.** However, rhyme can occur within a line as well. Some rhymes are **exact rhymes,** like *peas* and *cheese.* The sounds of these words are exactly alike, except for the consonants at the beginning. Other rhymes are **half rhymes**—words whose sounds are similar but not identical, like *pans* and *hams.*

Rhyme is important for several reasons. You soon begin to listen for it, and the expectation of hearing sounds repeated keeps you interested in a poem. Also, a poet can vary the **rhyme scheme,** or pattern of rhymes, to focus your attention on a particular passage.

Focus

This poem is about a girl who refuses to do a certain chore. Write about a chore that you dislike. Say what you dislike about it, and describe the feelings you have as you are doing it. What would happen if no one ever did this chore? Would the consequences be negative or positive? As you read the poem, notice the results when Sarah stops doing her chore.

Vocabulary

Knowing the following words will help you as you read "Sarah Cynthia Sylvia Stout Would Not Take the Garbage Out."

scour (skour) *v.:* To clean by rubbing vigorously (p. 451)

candy (kan' dē) *v.:* To coat with sugar (p. 451)

rinds (rīndz) *n.:* Tough outer layers or skins (p. 451)

withered (with' ərd) *adj.:* Dried up (p. 451)

curdled (kʉr' d'ld) *adj.:* Thickened; clotted (p. 452)

rancid (ran' sid) *adj.:* Spoiled and bad-smelling (p. 452)

relate (ri lāt') *v.:* Tell (p. 452)

Shel Silverstein

(1932–   ) was born in Chicago, Illinois, and grew up hoping to be a dancer or a baseball player someday. Instead, his artistic talents led him to become one of America's most popular writers and cartoonists. Illustrated with his own drawings, his poetry books, such as *Where the Sidewalk Ends,* are enjoyed by young and old alike. In the poem you are about to read, he humorously tells the outrageous results of Sarah Cynthia Sylvia Stout's refusal to take the garbage out.

Sarah Cynthia Sylvia Stout Would Not Take the Garbage Out

Shel Silverstein

Sarah Cynthia Sylvia Stout
Would not take the garbage out!
She'd scour the pots and scrape the pans,
Candy the yams and spice the hams,
5 And though her daddy would scream and shout,
She simply would not take the garbage out.
And so it piled up to the ceilings:
Coffee grounds, potato peelings,
Brown bananas, rotten peas,
10 Chunks of sour cottage cheese.
It filled the can, it covered the floor,
It cracked the window and blocked the door
With bacon rinds and chicken bones,
Drippy ends of ice cream cones,
15 Prune pits, peach pits, orange peel,
Gloppy glumps of cold oatmeal,
Pizza crusts and withered greens,
Soggy beans and tangerines,
Crusts of black burned buttered toast,
20 Gristly bits of beefy roasts . . .
The garbage rolled on down the hall,
It raised the roof, it broke the wall . . .
Greasy napkins, cookie crumbs,
Globs of gooey bubblegum,
25 Cellophane from green baloney,
Rubbery blubbery macaroni,
Peanut butter, caked and dry,

From *Where the Sidewalk Ends: The Poems & Drawings of Shel Silverstein.*
Copyright © 1974 by Evil Eye Music, Inc. Reprinted by permission of HarperCollins
Publishers, Inc.

Curdled milk and crusts of pie,
Moldy melons, dried up mustard,
30 Eggshells mixed with lemon custard,
Cold french fries and rancid meat,
Yellow lumps of Cream of Wheat.
At last the garbage reached so high
That finally it touched the sky.
35 And all the neighbors moved away,
And none of her friends would come to play.
And finally Sarah Cynthia Stout said,
"OK, I'll take the garbage out!"
But then, of course, it was too late
40 The garbage reached across the state,
From New York to the Golden Gate
And there, in the garbage she did hate,
Poor Sarah met an awful fate,
That I cannot right now relate
45 Because the hour is much too late.
But children, remember Sarah Stout
And always take the garbage out!

 ## RESPONDING TO THE SELECTION

Your Response

1. Do you sympathize more with Sarah or with her father? Why?

Recalling

2. Name four chores that Sarah Cynthia Sylvia Stout does.
3. Find the lines that tell the reactions of her neighbors and friends. What do they do as a result of the situation?

Interpreting

4. At what point does the poem become unreal- istic? What is the effect of the poet's use of exaggeration?
5. What reason might the poet have—besides the fact that it is "late"—for not telling you what happened to Sarah?
6. What do you think was Sarah's "awful fate"?
7. The poet parodies, or humorously imitates, the type of story told to teach a lesson. How do you know the poet does not mean for you to take this lesson seriously?

Applying

8. Shel Silverstein's poems are recognized for their ability to make people laugh. Discuss with your classmates what makes something funny.

Understanding Rhyme

The repetition of sounds in two or more words, called **rhyme,** is a key element of poetry. In "Sarah Cynthia Sylvia Stout Would Not Take the Garbage Out," the poet uses rhymes that add humor, as they seem to pile up just as the garbage does.

1. Are the rhymes at the end of lines 25 and 26 exact rhymes or half rhymes?
2. Find one example of a rhyme in the middle, rather than at the end, of a line.
3. How might the poem be different if most of the rhyming words did not come right after one another?

CRITICAL THINKING AND READING

Evaluating the Effect of Rhyme

Rhyme sets up an expectation that keeps you alert. The list of discarded items in this poem, for example, might become boring without the delightful rhymes. Also, a change in the rhyme scheme can be very dramatic, marking a turning point in the poem. Most of the pairs of lines in this poem have end rhymes, but the pattern is broken at one point.

1. Identify the two lines in the poem that do *not* rhyme.
2. What important event in the story occurs at this point?
3. What is the effect of the sudden lack of rhyme?
4. Why do you think that the poet used the same rhyme seven times in a row after the break in rhyme?

THINKING AND WRITING

Writing a Rhymed Poem

Can you write a rhymed poem that will make your classmates laugh? Look again at your description of an unpleasant chore, and list the humorous aspects of the situation. Like Shel Silverstein, you may want to use exaggeration to increase the humor. Then turn your description and list into a funny, rhymed poem about the results of an undone job. After revising your poem, read it to some classmates to see whether they think it is amusing.

LEARNING OPTIONS

1. **Community Connections.** Find out more about waste disposal in your community. What happens to trash after it is picked up? What percentage of it is recycled? What happens to the trash that is not recycled? What is the cost to your community of trash removal? Then make a study of your family's trash. How much of it could be recycled? Find out about composting, the process by which some garbage is turned into fertilizer. When you have as many facts as you need, meet with a group of classmates to brainstorm a list of ideas for cutting down on the amount of trash that is created in your community.
2. **Art.** Make an illustration for the poem that shows some of the garbage that has piled up in Sarah Cynthia Sylvia Stout's house. Review the poem to get specific ideas about what to include in your illustration.

GUIDE FOR READING

Annabel Lee

Repetition in Poetry

Repetition is the use of a word or group of words more than once in a poem. Like rhyme, which is itself a form of repetition, this technique creates a variety of effects. In a quiet poem, for example, repetition creates a feeling of peacefulness, like the lapping waves of a calm sea. It can also create excitement and suspense in a poem with galloping rhythms, such as "The Highwayman." Still another use of repetition is to focus attention on important words and phrases. By employing several forms of repetition in "Annabel Lee," Poe creates a pattern of word-sounds very much like music.

Focus

In the poem you are about to read, the poet repeats certain words and phrases a number of times. You have probably heard songs that use repeated words or phrases. With two or three of your classmates, make a list of such songs. Think about different kinds of music: classical, folk, and popular. Say which of the songs mentioned you like best, and say what you like about it. As you read "Annabel Lee," look for the repeated words and phrases, and consider the effect they have on you. How do they help create a haunting melody like that of a sad song?

Vocabulary

Knowing the following words will help you as you read "Annabel Lee."

coveted (kuv′ it əd) *v.*: Envied (p. 456)

sepulcher (sep′ 'l kər) *n.*: Grave; tomb (p. 456)

demons (dē′ mənz) *n.*: Evil spirits (p. 456)

beams (bēmz) *v.*: Shines brightly (p. 456)

Edgar Allan Poe

(1809–1849) was born in Boston, the son of two actors who died before his third birthday. He was raised in the United States and England by John Allan, with whom he had a troubled relationship. Poe's adult life was difficult, too. He earned only a meager living from his writings. Still, during his short life he wrote poems and stories that have made him one of the best-known American authors. A critic has called his verse "easy but unforgettable," and "Annabel Lee," with its strange story and haunting melody, is both.

Annabel Lee

Edgar Allan Poe

It was many and many a year ago,
    In a kingdom by the sea.
That a maiden there lived whom you may know
    By the name of Annabel Lee;—
5 And this maiden she lived with no other thought
    Than to love and be loved by me.

She was a child and *I* was a child,
    In this kingdom by the sea.

But we loved with a love that was more than love—
10   I and my Annabel Lee—
With a love that the wingèd seraphs[1] of Heaven
        Coveted her and me.

And this was the reason that, long ago,
        In this kingdom by the sea,
15   A wind blew out of a cloud by night
        Chilling my Annabel Lee;
So that her highborn kinsmen[2] came
        And bore her away from me,
To shut her up in a sepulcher
20   In this kingdom by the sea.

The angels, not half so happy in Heaven,
        Went envying her and me:—
Yes! that was the reason (as all men know,
        In this kingdom by the sea)
25   That the wind came out of a cloud, chilling
        And killing my Annabel Lee.

But our love it was stronger by far than the love
        Of those who were older than we—
        Of many far wiser than we—
30   And neither the angels in Heaven above
        Nor the demons down under the sea,
Can ever dissever[3] my soul from the soul
        Of the beautiful Annabel Lee:—

For the moon never beams without bringing me dreams
35   Of the beautiful Annabel Lee;
And the stars never rise but I see the bright eyes
        Of the beautiful Annabel Lee;
And so, all the nighttide,[4] I lie down by the side
Of my darling, my darling, my life and my bride,
40   In her sepulcher there by the sea—
        In her tomb by the side of the sea.

---

1. seraphs (ser′ əfs) *n*.: Angels.
2. highborn kinsmen: Relatives of noble birth.
3. dissever (di sev′ ər) *v*.: Separate.
4. nighttide (nīt′ tīd′) *n*.: An old-fashioned way of saying nighttime.

RESPONDING TO THE SELECTION

Your Response

1. Would this poem make a good song? Explain.

Recalling

2. At what stage of life was the narrator of the poem when he fell in love?
3. What caused Annabel Lee's death?
4. Why can neither the angels nor the demons separate the narrator's soul from that of Annabel Lee? (Lines 27–33)
5. What does the narrator do "all the nighttide"? (Lines 34–41)

Interpreting

6. How can a love be "more than love"? (Lines 9–10)
7. How would you describe the love between the narrator and Annabel Lee?
8. Describe the narrator's mood.

Applying

9. The poet Countee Cullen once wrote, "Never love with all your heart,/It only ends in aching." Do you think the narrator of Annabel Lee would agree? Why or why not?

ANALYZING LITERATURE

Understanding Repetition in Poetry

Poets sometimes use certain words and phrases over and over in the same poem. This technique, called **repetition,** can make a poem seem almost like a piece of music. Poe's "Annabel Lee," in particular, seems to be woven together from repeated word-sounds.

1. Not including the title, how many times does the name "Annabel Lee" appear in the poem?
2. What line in the first stanza is repeated, almost exactly, in the next three stanzas?
3. Which adjective describing Annabel Lee is repeated three times in the poem?
4. How does the use of repetition help create a haunting melody?

CRITICAL THINKING AND READING

Evaluating the Effects of Repetition

A poet can use repetition for several reasons. It can help create a peaceful or disturbing rhythm in a poem. Also, by stressing certain words and phrases, it can show you that these are clues to the poem's meaning.

1. Is the rhythm created by the repetitions in this poem disturbing or restful? Give reasons for your answer.
2. Why do you think the writer repeats the name "Annabel Lee" so many times?
3. Why do you think he stresses the setting of the poem by repeating the word "sea"?

THINKING AND WRITING

Writing About a Narrative Poem

Write a letter to a friend explaining why you did or did not enjoy this poem. In your letter retell the story of the poem. Then explain the effect created by the use of repetition. As you revise your letter, make sure you have supported your opinion of the poem with details from it. Finally, proofread your letter and prepare a final draft.

LEARNING OPTIONS

1. **Art.** The poet describes Annabel Lee as beautiful, but he does not give any specific details about her appearance. How do you visualize the beauty of Annabel Lee? Draw a portrait of Annabel Lee as you imagine her. Make your drawing reflect the haunting mood of the poem by the colors you use and the style of the drawing.
2. **Writing.** Find out more about the life of Edgar Allan Poe and specifically about his marriage. Whom did he marry? How did she die? Are there any parallels between Annabel Lee and Poe's wife? Take notes on your findings and write a brief report.

GUIDE FOR READING

Gary Soto

(1952–   ) is a Mexican American, or Chicano, who grew up in the San Joaquin Valley in California. His first book of poetry, *The Elements of San Joaquin* (1977), describes the lives of migrant workers in that part of the country. Soto himself had worked in the fields as a migrant laborer, moving from farm to farm to harvest seasonal crops. One critic said that his poetry has "a lean, simple style." This description certainly is true of the poem "Oranges," a poem about the magic of an early love.

Oranges

The Speaker in a Narrative Poem

When a narrative poem is told by a character in the story, we call that character the **speaker.** This speaker refers to himself or herself as "I." It is important to remember, however, that the "I" telling the story is not the poet. The speaker is an imaginary person whom the poet has invented, just like a first-person narrator in a short story. In "Oranges," for example, the speaker is a character remembering "The first time" he "walked/With a girl."

Focus

In "Oranges" the speaker recalls a first date at the age of twelve. Write about the first occasion when you spent time alone with someone you liked very much. Recall what happened and how you felt during the experience. If you prefer, you may write about an imaginary meeting with someone you would like to know better. As you read the poem, compare your experience with the one described by the speaker.

Vocabulary

Knowing the following words will help you as you read "Oranges."

rouge (ro͞ozh) *n.:* A reddish cosmetic used to color the cheeks (p. 459)

tiered (tird) *v.:* Stacked in rows (p. 459)

bleachers (blēch′ ərz) *n.:* Benches stacked in rows for spectators at sporting events (p. 459)

hissing (his′ iŋ) *v.:* Making a sound like a prolonged *s* (p. 459)

Oranges

Gary Soto

The first time I walked
With a girl, I was twelve,
Cold, and weighted down
With two oranges in my jacket.
5 December. Frost cracking
Beneath my steps, my breath
Before me, then gone,
As I walked toward
Her house, the one whose
10 Porchlight burned yellow
Night and day, in any weather.
A dog barked at me, until
She came out pulling
At her gloves, face bright
15 With rouge. I smiled,
Touched her shoulder, and led
Her down the street, across
A used car lot and a line
Of newly planted trees,
20 Until we were breathing
Before a drug store. We
Entered, the tiny bell
Bringing a saleslady
Down a narrow aisle of goods.
25 I turned to the candies
Tiered like bleachers,
And asked what she wanted—
Light in her eyes, a smile
Starting at the corners

30 Of her mouth. I fingered
A nickel in my pocket,
And when she lifted a chocolate
That cost a dime,
I didn't say anything.
35 I took the nickel from
My pocket, then an orange,
And set them quietly on
The counter. When I looked up,
The lady's eyes met mine,
40 And held them, knowing
Very well what it was all
About.

     Outside,
A few cars hissing past,
45 Fog hanging like old
Coats between the trees.
I took my girl's hand
In mine for two blocks,
Then released it to let
50 Her unwrap the chocolate.
I peeled my orange
That was so bright against
The gray of December
That, from some distance,
55 Someone might have thought
I was making a fire in my hands.

Your Response

1. How do you feel about the speaker in the poem? Explain.

Recalling

2. Describe the girl when she first comes out of her house.
3. Why does the speaker try to pay for the candy with a nickel and an orange?
4. What is the last action of the speaker in the poem?

Interpreting

5. How does the speaker feel about the girl? Give evidence to support your answer.
6. What does the speaker mean when he says the saleslady knew "Very well what it was all/About"?
7. Why does the narrator still have the orange at the end of the poem?
8. What has the orange come to represent, or stand for, to the speaker?
9. What does the speaker mean when he describes his orange as "so bright against/The gray of December"?

Applying

10. Why is a first date such an important event in a person's life?

ANALYZING LITERATURE

Understanding the Speaker

A narrative poem can be told by a **speaker** who takes part in the story and refers to himself or herself as "I." The speaker is an invented character, not the poet talking to you directly.

You can perform an experiment to see the difference between a narrative poem told by a speaker and one told by the poet. Read "Oranges" again, and every time you see "I" change it in your mind to "he." Also, each time you see "we," change

it to "they." When you have made these changes, the poem will no longer have a speaker.

1. How is the poem different without a speaker?
2. Does the poem seem better to you with or without a speaker? Give reasons for your answer.

CRITICAL THINKING AND READING

Making Inferences About a Speaker

An **inference** is a reasonable conclusion you make based on stated information. In a poem like "Oranges," the poet does not tell you about the speaker directly. However, you can infer a great deal about the speaker from the way he talks, the details on which he focuses, and others' reactions to him. Your inferences will help you form an idea of his personality.

1. How does the saleslady act toward him?
2. How does his girlfriend act toward him?
3. The speaker seems to put special emphasis on the detail about the orange at the end of the poem. Why do you think this is so?
4. Does the speaker boast about this experience, or does he seem to be modest? Give reasons for your answer.
5. Based on all these clues, give a brief summary of the speaker's personality.

THINKING AND WRITING

Adding to a Narrative Poem

Every story involving two or more people has two or more different sides to it. Up to this point, we have heard only the boy's voice. How do you think the girl's side of the story would sound? Brainstorm to think of how her version might differ from the boy's. Which details of this story would she describe? Also, would she use short lines of poetry, as the boy does, or longer ones? Turn your ideas into another version of the story, using the girl as a speaker. When you revise your work, ask yourself whether the way you have written the poem is true to the girl's personality.

Figurative Language
and Imagery

WATERFALL NO. III, IAO VALLEY
Georgia O'Keeffe, 1939
Art Resource

The Magnificent Bull

The **Dinka** are an African people who live in southern Sudan to the west of the White Nile River. They are nomads, or wanderers. In the dry season, they live in riverside camps with their cattle. When the rains come, they move to permanent settlements, where they grow crops like millet, a cereal grass. Cattle are very important in the Dinka culture, and young men become deeply attached to their herds. "The Magnificent Bull" expresses the Dinka's strong feelings for their cattle.

Fog

Carl Sandburg (1878–1967), the son of Swedish immigrants, was born in Galesburg, Illinois. He was unique in winning the Pulitzer Prize for both poetry and history. Sandburg often wrote about the rough-and-tumble everyday world. By the time his first book appeared in 1916, Sandburg had been a farm worker, a stagehand, a railroad worker, a soldier, and a cook, among other things. He was working as a newspaper reporter when he wrote "Fog," a poem he jotted down one day while waiting to interview a Chicago judge.

Loo-Wit

Wendy Rose (1948–   ) was born in Oakland, California, to a Hopi father and a Scots-Irish-Miwok mother. She has said that she has "always felt misunderstood and isolated—whether with Indians or with non-Indians." Besides being a poet, Rose is also an anthropologist who has worked to protect Native American burial sites from developers and a painter who has illustrated some of her own books. Growing up in a city, she got to know Native American people from many different nations. In "Loo-Wit" she takes her subject from the Cowlitz people of Washington State.

Figurative Language

Figurative language is language that is not meant to be taken literally, or exactly according to the dictionary definitions of the words. One type of figurative language is **simile,** a comparison that uses the words *like* or *as* to point out a similar quality in two generally unlike things. For example: "In their brightly colored clothes, the children looked like a flower garden." The clothes and flower gardens are essentially unlike, but they are similar in being brightly colored.

A **metaphor** also points out a similar quality in two generally unlike things, but it does not use the words *like* or *as.* Sometimes a metaphor simply states that two things are the same. For example: "The children were a flower garden in their brightly colored clothes." You can also create a metaphor by writing about one thing as if it were another thing. For example: "The crowd *floods* into the open area, *swirls* around, and collects in *small pools* of people." In this metaphor the italicized words describe the crowd as if it were water.

An **extended metaphor** continues beyond a single phrase or sentence. You begin such a metaphor by saying, "Our country is a mighty ship, sailing the vast waters of history." Then you could extend the metaphor by describing the president as a captain, and so on.

Personification is a type of figurative language in which an animal, an object, or an abstract idea is given human qualities. For example: "As the storm came, the sea roared its anger." The sea cannot really be angry, but crashing waves may sound like an angry human.

Focus

The three poems in this section use figurative language to describe aspects of nature. Cattle, fog, and a volcano are depicted by poets who have observed them closely and thought about them. Think about some aspect of nature that you enjoy. It might be a kind of weather, an animal, or a plant. Write down your thoughts and feelings about the topic you have chosen.

Vocabulary

Knowing these words will help you as you read the poems.

shimmering (shim′ ər iŋ) *adj.*: Shining unsteadily (p. 464)

haunches (hônch′ iz) *n.*: An animal's legs (p. 466)

buttes (byo͞ots) *n.*: Steep hills standing in flat land (p. 468)

crouches (krou ch′ iz) *v.*: Stoops or bends low (p. 468)

unravel (un rav′ əl) *v.*: Become untangled or separated (p. 469)

dislodge (dis läj′) *v.*: Leave a resting place (p. 469)

The Magnificent Bull

Dinka Traditional

My bull is white like the silver fish in the river
white like the shimmering crane bird on the river bank
white like fresh milk!
His roar is like the thunder to the Turkish cannon[1] on the
   steep shore.
5 My bull is dark like the raincloud in the storm.
He is like summer and winter.
Half of him is dark like the storm cloud,
half of him is light like sunshine.
His back shines like the morning star.
10 His brow is red like the beak of the Hornbill.[2]
His forehead is like a flag, calling the people from a
   distance,
He resembles the rainbow.

I will water him at the river,
With my spear I shall drive my enemies.
15 Let them water their herds at the well;
the river belongs to me and my bull.
Drink, my bull, from the river; I am here
to guard you with my spear.

---

1. Turkish cannon: For more than two centuries, the Dinkas'
homeland, now called the Sudan, was ruled by Turkey.
2. Hornbill: A tropical bird with a huge, curved bill.

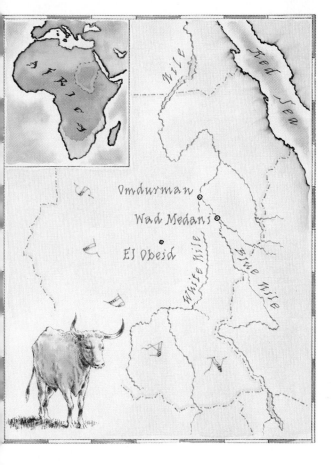

most? What difference does this reveal between our lives and the lives of the Dinka?

ANALYZING LITERATURE

Understanding Simile

A **simile** uses the words *like* or *as* to compare two essentially unlike things. Writers use similes to paint word pictures and to suggest positive or negative feelings about their subjects. For example, comparing a bull to a rainbow suggests positive feelings about the bull.

1. How does the speaker show positive feelings about the whiteness of the bull?
2. What positive quality is portrayed by comparing the bull's roar to the sound of a cannon?
3. How might a dark raincloud suggest positive feelings about the bull?
4. What other similes in the poem suggest positive feelings about the bull?

THINKING AND WRITING

Writing With Simile

Use similes to describe an animal you admire. It may be a pet or a wild animal. First list the physical traits and the actions of the animal. Then think of similes that capture its nature. Write a listing poem in the same style as "The Magnificent Bull." When you revise, make sure your similes show positive feelings about the animal.

LEARNING OPTIONS

1. **Speaking and Listening.** Animals play an important part in many African myths and folk tales. Find an African tale about an animal. Read it over several times until you are familiar with it. Then tell the story in your own words to your classmates.
2. **Multicultural Activity.** Find out more about the Dinka people and their cattle. Imagine you could spend a week living with a Dinka family. Write a letter about your experiences with them.

RESPONDING TO THE SELECTION

Your Response

1. Which description of the bull do you like best? Why?

Recalling

2. What color is the bull's brow?
3. Where does the speaker say his enemies should water their bulls?

Interpreting

4. What is one difference between summer and winter where the Dinka live?
5. Why might the river be a better watering place than the well?
6. How can you tell the speaker values the bull?

Applying

7. What animals do present-day Americans value

Fog
Carl Sandburg

The fog comes
on little cat feet.

It sits looking
over harbor and city
5 on silent haunches
and then moves on.

RESPONDING TO THE SELECTION

Your Response

1. Which words in the poem remind you most of fog that you have experienced or seen pictures of? Why?

Recalling

2. Being as specific as possible, describe the setting of this poem.
3. Describe the three things the fog does.

Interpreting

4. What impression of the fog does this poem create?
5. What is the effect of the writer's use of short lines?

Applying

6. Many poets have written poems about fog. What is it about this type of weather that makes it a good subject for a poem?

ANALYZING LITERATURE

Understanding Metaphor

A **metaphor** suggests that two essentially unlike things have something in common. A metaphor may state that one thing is another thing, or it may talk about one thing as if it were another thing.

1. How does the speaker suggest a comparison between fog and a cat without saying that fog is a cat?

2. What qualities of fog does the metaphor emphasize?

3. How would the meaning of the poem be different if the speaker had compared fog to a wolf?

CRITICAL THINKING AND READING

Evaluating the Effect of a Metaphor

Writers use figurative language to make descriptions more vivid and to add interest to their writing. Write a paragraph describing fog without using figurative language. Then compare your paragraph with the poem. Which captures the feeling of fog better? Why?

LEARNING OPTIONS

1. **Art.** Use crayons, watercolors, or some other medium to draw an illustration for the poem "Fog."

2. **Language.** Across the top of a piece of paper, list the following types of weather: foggy, cloudy, rainy, snowy, sunny, and windy. Under each type of weather, list as many words as you can think of that describe that kind of weather.

Loo-Wit[1]

Wendy Rose

The way they do
this old woman
no longer cares
what others think
5 but spits her black tobacco
any which way
stretching full length
from her bumpy bed.
Finally up
10 she sprinkles ashes
on the snow,
cold buttes
promise nothing
but the walk
15 of winter.
Centuries of cedar
have bound her
to earth,
huckleberry ropes
20 lay prickly
on her neck.
Around her
machinery growls,
snarls and plows
25 great patches
of her skin.
She crouches
in the north,
her trembling
30 the source
of dawn.
Light appears
with the shudder
of her slopes,

Eruption of Mount St. Helens

---

1. Loo-Wit: The name given by the Cowlitz People to
Mount St. Helens, an active volcano in Washington
State. It means "lady of fire."

35   the movement
of her arm.
Blackberries unravel,
stones dislodge;
it's not as if
40   they weren't warned.

She was sleeping
but she heard the boot scrape,
the creaking floor,
felt the pull of the blanket
45   from her thin shoulder.
With one free hand
she finds her weapons
and raises them high;
clearing the twigs from her throat
50   she sings, she sings,
shaking the sky
like a blanket about her
Loo-wit sings and sings and sings!

RESPONDING TO THE SELECTION

Your Response

1. Choose two phrases that you like from the poem. Explain what you like about them.

Recalling

2. How does Loo-Wit show that she doesn't care what others think of her?
3. What has bound Loo-Wit to the earth?

Interpreting

4. What kind of light appears when Loo-Wit shudders and trembles?
5. Who are "they" in line 40?
6. How are humans portrayed in the poem? What effect do they have on Loo-Wit?

Applying

7. Why do you suppose people tend to personify certain natural phenomena, like the wind (when it "kicks up") and storms (that show their "fury")?

ANALYZING LITERATURE

Understanding Extended Metaphor

"Loo-Wit" is an **extended metaphor** because the entire poem compares an erupting volcano to an old woman. The poem is also an example of **personification** because the volcano is seen as having human qualities. The extended metaphor creates two images at the same time, one of a woman and one of a volcano.

1. What human emotion does the poet give the volcano?
2. What parts of the volcano do the following words from the poem describe: "black tobacco," "her skin," "her throat"?
3. In what ways does the volcano act like a person?

THINKING AND WRITING

Writing an Extended Metaphor

Write a paragraph in which you use an extended metaphor to describe something. Choose what you want to describe, and think about what your subject reminds you of. Write down at least three points of comparison between the two things. When you have written a first draft, ask a classmate to read it and make suggestions. Then revise your work.

LEARNING OPTIONS

1. **Multicultural Activity.** In your library find a book of poetry by Native Americans. Choose a poem about nature and read it aloud to a group of your classmates. Tell them what you like about the poem, and point out any figurative language in the poem.
2. **Cross-curricular Connection.** Find out more about the eruption of Mount St. Helens in 1980. Were people warned ahead of time? Did they leave the mountain? Imagine that you are a television newscaster, and write a brief report about the eruption that you could read aloud on the air.

GUIDE FOR READING

The Bat

Theodore Roethke (1908–1963) was one of the best-known American poets writing after World War II. He won many awards for his work, including the Bollingen Prize, the Pulitzer Prize, and the National Book Award. In addition, he earned a reputation as a college teacher who challenged and inspired his students. Roethke was born and grew up in Saginaw, Michigan, where his father was a florist. As a boy, Roethke loved to play in and around the family greenhouse. These experiences gave him a feeling of kinship with nature that he never lost. In "The Bat" he writes with knowledge and humor about one of nature's more unusual creatures.

The Pasture

Robert Frost (1875–1963) is associated with New England, but he was born and spent his early years in San Francisco. When his father died, the family returned to its New England roots. Frost remained in that region for most of his life, making his living for a while as a farmer and part-time teacher. He was not well known as a writer until his first book of poetry, *A Boy's Will* (1913), appeared in Great Britain. Then, almost overnight, he became famous for his poems about New England people and landscapes. He won the Pulitzer Prize four times—more than any other poet. Frost used poetic forms that some writers thought old-fashioned. However, by combining these forms with the rhythms of everyday speech, he created highly original poems. "The Pasture" contains an invitation that makes you want to experience the joys of nature with the poet.

sugarfields

Barbara Mahone (1944–   ) was born in Chicago but spent most of her early years in Alabama. Her poems have appeared in many magazines and journals. A collection of her poems, *Sugarfields,* was published in 1970. About her work the poet has written, "I write poems for my children and their children. Because I want them to know who Mama was. . . . It's intimate stuff, of a very fragile nature. But it's history and legend that can be built upon." In "sugarfields" Mahone recalls part of her personal history.

470 Poetry

Images in Poetry

Images are the pictures that poets create with their words. As you read a poem, you can see these images in your mind's eye. Poets use lively and specific words so that you can see their images more clearly. In "The Pasture," for instance, Robert Frost says that a small calf is so young that "it totters" when its mother "licks it with her tongue." By using the specific verb *totters,* Frost paints a picture of the scene that is easy to visualize. In "sugarfields" Barbara Mahone creates an image for your ears by joining two words to make the new word *windsong.*

Focus

Below is a chart that lists the titles and the subjects of the three poems you are about to read. Copy the chart on a piece of paper. Then in the third column of the chart, list as many words as you can think of to describe each subject. If you are not at all familiar with the subject, let your imagination help you. As you read the three poems, fill in the fourth column of the chart with specific words that the poets use to create vivid word pictures of their subjects. Do any of the poets have the same impression of their subjects that you have? Fill in the third column with your own word pictures of these subjects.

Title	Subject	Your Words	Poet's Words
"The Bat"	bat		
"The Pasture"	calf in pasture		
"sugarfields"	sugarcane fields		

Vocabulary

Knowing the following words will help you as you read these poems.

amiss (ə mis´) *adv.*: In a wrong way; improper (p. 472)

totters (tät´ ərz) *v.*: Rocks or shakes as if about to fall; is unsteady (p. 473)

The Bat

Theodore Roethke

By day the bat is cousin to the mouse.
He likes the attic of an aging house.

His fingers make a hat about his head.
His pulse beat is so slow we think him dead.

5   He loops in crazy figures half the night
Among the trees that face the corner light.

But when he brushes up against a screen,
We are afraid of what our eyes have seen:

For something is amiss or out of place
10 When mice with wings can wear a human face.

RESPONDING TO THE SELECTION

Your Response

1. What effect did the poem have on your feelings about bats?

Recalling

2. What does the bat do at night?

Interpreting

3. Contrast the description of the bat in lines 3 and 4 with that in lines 5 and 6.
4. What details make the picture that the poet paints in line 10 so strange?

Applying

5. What is it about animals like bats and snakes that makes people both curious and afraid?

ANALYZING LITERATURE

Understanding Images

Images are pictures in words. By choosing lively and specific language, poets invite you to see the world in a fresh and original way. In "The Bat," for example, Roethke creates a vivid picture when he says that this creature's "fingers make a hat about his head."

1. Describe the picture that Roethke paints in lines 5 and 6.
2. Why do you think Roethke saved the image in line 10 for the end of the poem?

THINKING AND WRITING

Writing a Poem About an Animal

Write a brief poem about an animal that fascinates you. First, list the animal's interesting qualities. When you write, organize the lines in pairs, as Roethke does. When you revise, read your poem to a classmate and ask him or her whether your images are clear. Replace general words with lively and specific ones in your final draft.

The Pasture

Robert Frost

I'm going out to clean the pasture spring;
I'll only stop to rake the leaves away
(And wait to watch the water clear, I may):
I shan't be gone long.—You come too.

5   I'm going out to fetch the little calf
That's standing by the mother. It's so young
It totters when she licks it with her tongue.
I shan't be gone long.—You come too.

RESPONDING TO THE SELECTION

Your Response

1. Does the poem make you want to accept the poet's invitation? Why or why not?

Recalling

2. What two chores is the speaker going to do?

Interpreting

3. Although the speaker is going out to perform chores, he makes them sound attractive and inviting. What images make you feel like accompanying the speaker?
4. Why do you think the poet enclosed line 3 in parentheses?
5. Based on information in the poem, do you think the speaker is a grown man or a boy? Find evidence to support your answer.

Applying

6. An Indian holy book states: "What is work? and What is not work? are questions that perplex the wisest of men." Do you think the speaker in this poem considers the chores work? Find evidence to support your answer. How do you define work?

LEARNING OPTION

Speaking and Listening. Many of Robert Frost's poems are about nature. Find a collection of his poetry, and choose another of his nature poems to read to your classmates. Practice reading it aloud to yourself a few times. Then ask one other person to listen to you and to offer suggestions for improving your reading.

sugarfields

Barbara Mahone

treetalk and windsong are
the language of my mother
her music does not leave me.

let me taste again the cane
5   the syrup of the earth
sugarfields were once my home.

i would lie down in the fields
and never get up again
(treetalk and windsong
10   are the language of my mother
sugarfields are my home)

the leaves go on whispering secrets
as the wind blows a tune in the grass
my mother's voice is in the fields
15   this music cannot leave me.

 RESPONDING TO THE SELECTION

Your Response

1. What images do the words *treetalk* and *windsong* create in your mind?

Recalling

2. What phrase does the poet use to describe sugar cane?

3. Whose voice is in the sugar fields?

Interpreting

4. Lines 3 and 15 are slightly different. What effect does the difference create?

5. How do you know that the speaker has good memories of childhood?

6. Which words in the poem appeal to the sense of hearing?

7. There are no capital letters and almost no punctuation in the poem. What effect does that create?

Applying

8. Why do you suppose people often associate visual images with fond memories of their childhoods?

 **THINKING AND WRITING**

Writing About a Place

Think about a place where you like to be. It may be indoors or outdoors. Imagine that you are

SUGAR CANE HARVEST
Carlton Murrell
Courtesy of the Artist

going to create a travel brochure that tries to convince people to visit this place. List the things you like about it. Then list specific words that will create positive images in your readers' minds. Write a paragraph describing the place. When you revise, see if you have chosen just the right words to show how special the place is.

LEARNING OPTIONS

1. **Cross-curricular Connection.** Find out how and where sugar cane grows and how granu-lated table sugar is made from it. Then make a chart to illustrate the steps in the cultivation and processing of sugar cane.

2. **Speaking and Listening.** What musical instruments would you use to create the sounds of "treetalk" and "windsong"? Exchange ideas with a classmate. Find a recording of these instruments to play for the class, and say why you think the sounds these instruments create are like "treetalk" and "windsong."

GUIDE FOR READING

William Jay Smith

(1918–   ) was born in Winnfield, Louisiana. He has led a busy life—teaching college, writing poetry and essays, translating Russian and French poetry, and even serving in the Vermont state legislature for three years. His most successful writing has been his poetry for young people. When you read "Seal," you will see why. Lively and amusing, it shows that poetry can be pure and simple fun.

Seal

Concrete Poetry

Concrete poetry is poetry that is meant to be seen on the page, as well as heard like an ordinary poem. In a concrete poem, the words are arranged into a shape, often one that looks like the subject. The term *concrete* refers to the shape's being a specific, or concrete, representation of something.

Focus

The poem you are about to read describes vividly the antics of a lively seal. Make a list of four or five physical activities that you enjoy, like running, swimming, skating, dancing, or riding a bike. Then choose the one activity that makes you feel most alive. Write about this activity, describing it in a way that suggests the fun you get out of it. For example, if you choose to write about playing basketball, you might write about how you feel when you get your hands on the ball, when you break away from someone who is guarding you, when you see a clear path to the basket, when you sink a difficult shot, and so on.

Vocabulary

Knowing the following words will help you as you read "Seal."

feed (fēd) *n.:* The tiny particles that minnows feed on (p. 475)

swerve (swʉrv) *n.:* A curving motion (p. 475)

quicksilver (kwik′ sil′ vər) *n.:* The chemical element mercury, which is silver-white and flows easily (p. 475)

Seal

William Jay Smith

See how he dives
    From the rocks with a zoom!
  See how he darts
    Through his watery room
5 Past crabs and eels
    And green seaweed,
    Past fluffs of sandy
    Minnow feed!
  See how he swims
10 With a swerve and a twist,
  A flip of the flipper,
  A flick of the wrist!
  Quicksilver-quick,
  Softer than spray,
15 Down he plunges
  And sweeps away;
Before you can think,
Before you can utter
Words like "Dill pickle"
20 Or "Apple butter,"
  Back up he swims
  Past Sting Ray and Shark,
  Out with a zoom,
  A whoop, a bark;
25 Before you can say
    Whatever you wish,
    He plops at your side
    With a mouthful of fish!

RESPONDING TO THE SELECTION

Your Response

1. Do you think the poem makes the seal likeable? Why or why not?

Interpreting

2. Where do you think the poem is set? Give evidence to support your answer.
3. How would you describe the spirit, or mood, of the poem? Find at least three words that help create this mood.

Applying

4. If you saw seals in an aquarium, how might this poem affect your response to them?

ANALYZING LITERATURE

Understanding Concrete Poetry

Concrete poems are often lighthearted. When the words of a poem are arranged in a shape that imitates the subject or suggests something about it, the effect is usually playful.

1. How would the effect of "Seal" be changed if the poem did not have its unusual shape?
2. The lines of "Seal" are very short. What connection might there be between the shortness of the lines and the shape of the poem?
3. After reading the poem aloud, tell which of the following words or phrases best describes its rhythm: (a) slow and relaxed; (b) quick and lively; (c) powerful.

THINKING AND WRITING

Writing a Concrete Poem

Use the Focus writing you did to help you write a concrete poem. First, decide on a suitable shape. It should resemble, or suggest something about, your subject. You need not use rhyme, but try to write lines that have a definite rhythm. When you revise, think of the effect you are trying to achieve. Try to make everything about your poem contribute to that effect.

GUIDE FOR READING

Haiku

Taniguchi Buson (1715–1783) was a Japanese poet whose poems many Japanese of today know by heart. He was also a painter, and his sharp eye for detail no doubt helped him compose poems whose focus is on small things that express a great deal.

Otsuji (? –1772) wrote many essays about the art of writing haiku. He believed that a poet should view human life as part of the larger world of nature. He also felt that in the best haiku, emotions should be suggested, not expressed directly.

Kyorai (1651–1704) was the son of a physician to a royal family. He sought to write poems in which each word was necessary and none could be changed without destroying their meaning.

Matsuo Bashō (1644–1694) was born near Kyoto, Japan. In many of his haiku, he presents a scene in which a momentary feature stands out against an unchanging background. He evokes a whole landscape or an entire season by describing just a few key details.

Haiku

Haiku is a form of poetry that originated in Japan. A haiku has three lines; the first and third lines have five syllables each; the second line has seven. A haiku usually depicts a scene in nature and often implies a strong feeling. In a good haiku, a mere handful of words will make you see an entire scene and will convey a universal feeling, such as fear, surprise, regret, hope, or mystery.

Focus

Traditional haiku writers usually wrote about a moment experienced in nature, but a haiku can be about any moment that affects you deeply. Think of a simple scene that is vivid in your memory. It should be like a sharp, clear, unforgettable snapshot. Write two sentences about what this "mental photograph" shows. Try to make your sentences express as much about the scene as possible. As you read, notice what your sentences have in common with the haiku.

Vocabulary

In haiku simple words are used to create vivid images. Although you may think you know the meaning of each word, pause over each one and think about what it implies.

Three Haiku

translated from the Japanese by Harry Behn

Deep in a windless
wood, not one leaf dares to move. . . .
Something is afraid.
Buson

Into a forest
I called. . . . The voice in reply
was no voice I knew.
Otsuji

I called to the wind,
"Who's there?" . . . Whoever it was
still knocks at my gate.
Kyorai

RESPONDING TO THE SELECTION

Your Response

1. Which of the haiku created the strongest feeling in you? What was the feeling?

Recalling

2. Describe the real-life scene or situation that is the basis of each haiku.

Interpreting

3. In the haiku by Buson, what might be the "something" that is afraid?
4. Whose voice do you think replies to the poet in the haiku by Otsuji?
5. In the haiku by Kyorai, how might the continual knocking at the gate be explained?

Applying

6. Tell why you would, or would not, use the haiku form if you wanted to write a poem expressing strong personal feelings about something.

ANALYZING LITERATURE

Understanding Haiku

A haiku has three lines. The first and third lines have five syllables each; the second line has seven. One reason that readers enjoy haiku is that a single poem can be interpreted in different ways, and it is interesting to compare and discuss different interpretations.

1. Review your classmates' answers to question 3 under Responding to the Selection. Which seem to you good answers, though different from yours?
2. What was the basis for your answer to question 4 under Responding to the Selection?
3. Some readers think that the haiku by Kyorai is meant to be humorous. What reasons might be given for this interpretation?

RAVENS IN MOONLIGHT, 1882
Gengyo

Three Haiku

Bashō

translated by Daniel C. Buchanan

On sweet plum blossoms
The sun rises suddenly.
Look, a mountain path!

Has spring come indeed?
On that nameless mountain lie
Thin layers of mist.

Temple bells die out.
The fragrant blossoms remain.
A perfect evening!

RESPONDING TO THE SELECTION

Your Response

1. Which haiku creates the most pleasing picture in your mind? Why is it pleasing?

Recalling

2. In your own words, tell what the poet has noticed or observed in each haiku.

Interpreting

3. Why is the poet surprised in the first haiku?
4. In the second haiku, why is he uncertain that spring has come?
5. In the third haiku, why do you think he feels that the evening is perfect?

Applying

6. Reread the biography of Bashō. Then decide which one of these three haiku best illustrates what is said there about his poetry. Why did you pick the poem you did rather than either of the other two?

THINKING AND WRITING

Writing a Haiku

Write a haiku based on the description you wrote for the Focus activity. Remember the correct form: The first and third lines have five syllables each; the second has seven. As you revise your haiku, make every word count. Let the scene or moment you describe suggest your feelings about it. When you are satisfied that you have said all you can in seventeen syllables, share your haiku with your classmates.

Lyric Poetry

YOUNG GIRLS AT THE PIANO
Pierre Auguste Renoir
Joslyn Art Museum

GUIDE FOR READING

Washed in Silver

James Stephens (1880–1950) was a poet and storyteller who grew up in a poor neighborhood of Dublin, Ireland. As a young man, he worked for a lawyer, but in his free time he read all he could about Irish legends and fairy tales. His books include *The Crock of Gold* (1912), which is an imaginative novel, and *Songs From the Clay* (1915), a volume of poems. Stephens had a wonderful speaking voice and gave many readings of his poetry. "Washed in Silver" captures the magical quality of Irish legends.

Feelings About Words

Mary O'Neill (1908–　　) began writing to entertain her family as she grew up in a small town near Cleveland, Ohio. She kept her interest in writing even while making a career in advertising. When her own children grew up, she published many stories and poems for young people. One of her best-loved books is *Words, Words, Words* (1966). Her fascination with words is clearly seen in her poem "Feelings About Words."

The Flower-Fed Buffaloes

Vachel Lindsay (1879–1931) believed that poetry was most exciting when it was heard. He often traveled through the countryside reading his poems aloud and receiving shelter and food in return. One of his books, in fact, is called *Rhymes to Be Traded for Bread* (1912). Lindsay used strong rhythms in his poetry and often wrote about popular figures like baseball players and movie stars. In "The Flower-Fed Buffaloes," repeated words and phrases add to both the rhythm and the meaning.

Lyric Poetry

A **lyric poem** is the expression of a poet's personal thoughts and feelings in vivid and musical language. In ancient times lyric poetry was actually sung to the music of a stringed instrument known as a lyre. That is why such poetry was called *lyr*-ic and why we still refer to the words of songs as *lyrics*. While most lyric poems are no longer set to music, they still tend to be brief and melodic, like songs.

Any subject that calls up a poet's thoughts and feelings is suitable for a lyric poem. James Stephens, for example, describes the "silvery radiance" of moonlight; while Vachel Lindsay imagines the mighty buffaloes that "trundle around the hills no more."

Lyric poetry can take many forms, with different patterns of rhyme and rhythm. Most lyric poems, however, include vivid language that is filled with energy. Such lively words help you remember a poet's thoughts and feelings.

Focus

Make a list of songs whose lyrics you like. For each song pick out two or three vivid words or phrases that seem especially meaningful or clever to you. Then say what feeling those words and phrases create in you. Record your ideas in a chart like the sample one below. Afterward, brainstorm with your classmates to list the qualities of song lyrics that make them memorable.

Song	Memorable Words	Feelings Created

Vocabulary

Knowing the following words will help you as you read these poems.

squat (skwät) *adj.*: Short and heavy (p. 487)

glint (glint) *v.*: Gleam, flash, or glitter (p. 487)

saunter (sôn′ tər) *v.*: Walk about idly; stroll (p. 487)

preen (prēn) *v.*: Dress up; show pride in one's appearance (p. 487)

pomp (pämp) *n.*: An impressive show or display (p. 487)

trundle (trun′ d′l) *v.*: Move on wheels or as if on wheels (p. 488)

Washed in Silver

James Stephens

Gleaming in silver are the hills!
Blazing in silver is the sea!

And a silvery radiance spills
Where the moon drives royally!

5   Clad in silver tissue, I
March magnificently by!

RESPONDING TO THE SELECTION

Your Response

1. What mood does the poem create in you?

Interpreting

2. What does the poet mean by saying he is "Clad in silver tissue"?
3. Explain the poem's title.

Applying

4. Light is important in this lyric. How do different kinds of light affect people's moods?

ANALYZING LITERATURE

Understanding Lyric Poetry

A **lyric poem** expresses a poet's emotions and thoughts in lively and musical language. Most lyrics contain vivid words that communicate the poet's feelings in a memorable way. At the end of "Washed in Silver," Stephens declares: ". . . I/March magnificently by!" With this bold phrase he communicates feelings of triumph and delight.

1. In songs, words and phrases are often repeated. How many times does the word *silver* appear in this poem? What effect does the repetition of this word have on the poem?
2. What picture does the vivid phrase "the moon drives royally" bring to your mind? Why do you think Stephens uses this phrase rather than "the moon shines in the sky"?
3. What feelings does the poet communicate about the moonlit landscape?

LEARNING OPTION

Cross-curricular Connection. How many songs about the moon can you think of? Make a list of them. Look in songbooks. Ask people of your parents' and grandparents' generations if they can add any to your list. When you've found as many moon songs as you can, make a class list. Also, compare and contrast descriptions of the moon in recent songs with descriptions in older songs.

DOMINANT CURVE, APRIL 1936
Vasily Kandinsky
Solomon R. Guggenheim Museum

Feelings About Words

Mary O'Neill

Some words clink
As ice in drink.
Some move with grace
A dance, a lace.
5 Some sound thin:

Wail, scream and pin.
Some words are squat:
A mug, a pot,
And some are plump,
10 Fat, round and dump.
Some words are light:
Drift, lift and bright.
A few are small:
A, is and all.
15 And some are thick,
Glue, paste and brick.
Some words are sad:
"I never had . . ."
And others gay:
20 Joy, spin and play.
Some words are sick:
Stab, scratch and nick.
Some words are hot:
Fire, flame and shot.
25 Some words are sharp,
Sword, point and carp.
And some alert:
Glint, glance and flirt.
Some words are lazy:
30 Saunter, hazy.
And some words preen:
Pride, pomp and queen.
Some words are quick,
A jerk, a flick.
35 Some words are slow:
Lag, stop and grow,
While others poke
As ox with yoke.
Some words can fly—
40 There's wind, there's high;
And some words cry:
"Goodbye . . .
Goodbye . . ."

RESPONDING TO THE SELECTION

Your Response

1. Of all the words the poet mentions, which three are your favorites? Why? What feelings do you have about them?

Recalling

2. O'Neill calls some words "squat" and others "light." What examples does she give of each kind of word?

Interpreting

3. Why is *flick* a good example of a quick word?
4. Why is *goodbye* a word that cries?
5. Why does O'Neill call this poem "Feelings About Words"? What are her feelings about words?

Applying

6. Look at the painting by Wassily Kandinski on page 486. In what way is a poet's love of words similar to an artist's love of color and form?

CRITICAL THINKING AND READING

Understanding Connotation

Connotation refers to the feelings and associations words stir up in us. O'Neill explores the connotations of different words. For example, she says that *saunter* gives her a lazy feeling. When you read *saunter,* you, like her, may picture someone who moves in a lazy fashion.

When people use words to persuade you to buy or do things, they often rely on connotation. A company selling a new kind of soap, for instance, will choose a name that suggests cleanliness—like Rainwater or Springtime.

1. O'Neill lists words that suggest grace to her. List four words that suggest grace to you.
2. List four words that suggest sadness to you.
3. List four words that suggest gaiety to you.
4. A car manufacturer once hired the poet Marianne Moore to think of names for its latest models. Do you think it was a good idea to choose a poet for this job? Why or why not?

The Flower-Fed Buffaloes

Vachel Lindsay

The flower-fed buffaloes of the spring
In the days of long ago,
Ranged where the locomotives sing
And the prairie flowers lie low:—
5 The tossing, blooming, perfumed grass
Is swept away by the wheat,
Wheels and wheels and wheels spin by
In the spring that still is sweet.
But the flower-fed buffaloes of the spring
10 Left us, long ago.
They gore no more, they bellow no more,
They trundle around the hills no more:—
With the Blackfeet, lying low,
With the Pawnees,[1] lying low,
15 Lying low.

---

1. Blackfeet, Pawnees: The names of groups of Native Americans
who hunted buffalo.

RESPONDING TO THE SELECTION

Your Response

1. How does the poem make you feel about the passing of the buffaloes?

Recalling

2. According to the poem, in what ways has the prairie scene changed?
3. What has brought about this change?

Interpreting

4. Why does the poet describe the buffaloes as "flower-fed"? What is the effect of this image?
5. How does the repetition of the words "no more" in lines 11 and 12 emphasize the poem's meaning?

6. What is the implication of the words "lying low" in lines 13–15?
7. What does this poem suggest about progress?

Applying

8. The writer G. K. Chesterton defines progress as "leaving things behind us" and growth as "leaving things inside us." What do these definitions mean? What do you think is the difference between progress and growth?

CRITICAL THINKING AND READING

Appreciating Vivid Verbs

Poets and other writers use vivid, specific verbs to help you picture the actions they are de-

scribing. In "The Flower-Fed Buffaloes," Vachel Lindsay uses verbs like "bellow" and "trundle" to bring to life the vanished buffalo herds. Notice that the verb "trundle," for instance, is much more vivid and specific than the general verb *move*.

Replace the italicized word in each sentence with a more lively verb.

1. The lion *walked* through the jungle.
2. The airplane *traveled* down the runway.
3. The runner *went* around the track.

THINKING AND WRITING

Writing About a Lyric Poem

Imagine that a friend is going to give a public reading of "The Flower-Fed Buffaloes" and has asked for your help. List the important points that he or she should keep in mind while reading this poem aloud. Remember to consider when a reader's voice should be loud or soft. Also think about when a reader should pause or continue at the end of a line. Turn your list into a note to your friend that will help make the reading a success. Revise this note to make sure your friend will understand your instructions.

LEARNING OPTION

Multicultural Activity. Find out more about the Blackfeet, the Pawnees, and other Plains Indians who hunted buffaloes. How did they hunt? What parts of a buffalo did they use? Present your findings to the class.

The Courage That My Mother Had

Edna St. Vincent Millay (1892–1950) was born and raised in Rockland, Maine. Millay revealed her poetic talent very early, writing "Renascence," one of her most famous poems, when she was only nineteen years old. She published her first book of poetry while still only in her mid-twenties and quickly became a well-known poet. In 1923 she won a Pulitzer Prize for three of her works. Millay had a special fondness for the sonnet, a fourteen-line poem with a regular rhythm and pattern of rhymes. She published a collection of her sonnets in 1941. In "The Courage That My Mother Had," as in many of her lyric poems, she expresses strong emotions and intense feelings.

My Mother Pieced Quilts

Teresa Palomo Acosta (1949–   ) grew up in Texas. She became a journalist after studying at the University of Texas and Columbia University. As a girl, Acosta listened to her grandfather's stories about his childhood in Mexico and his life as a cowboy. These stories inspired her to begin reading literature. She wrote "My Mother Pieced Quilts" as an assignment for a university class. This poem was later read at the University of Southern California, during the first national festival of Chicano literature and art (1973). In "My Mother Pieced Quilts," Acosta follows in her grandfather's and mother's footsteps as a recorder of family history.

Figurative and Literal Language

Figurative language is language that has meaning beyond the usual dictionary definitions. It is the highly imaginative use of words. This type of language is often based on vivid comparisons that can help to change your usual way of seeing the world. By comparing a snowflake to a soldier, for instance, a writer can surprise you into looking at a snowstorm in a new way. Suddenly the bits of white may resemble an army retreating or attacking. This perception may lead you to see other aspects of a winter scene with fresh eyes.

Literal language refers to language that does not go beyond the dictionary definitions of the words. A literal description of a snowfall, for example, might include the ideas that each snowflake has six sides and that each falls at a certain rate of speed. Poets often weave literal and figurative language together in their work. This combination ensures that their poems will be both understandable and surprising.

Focus

The two poems you are about to read express strong, positive feelings about courageous women. Courage can be expressed in many different circumstances: sickness, poverty, war, oppression, to name a few. What does courage mean to you? Think about ordinary people you have known or heard about who seem courageous to you. What have they done that you see as courageous? Make a list of names for your own Hall of Fame for Courageous Individuals. Share your ideas with your classmates. As you read, see what traits the subjects of the poems have in common with the people on your list.

Vocabulary

Knowing the following words will help you as you read these two poems.

quarried (kwôr′ ēd) *v.*: Carved out of the ground (p. 492)

brooch (brōch) *n.*: A large ornamental pin worn on a dress (p. 492)

somber (säm′ bər) *adj.*: Dark and solemn (p. 495)

mosaic (mō zā′ ik) *adj.*: Made of different pieces combined to form a whole (p. 495)

testimonies (tes′ tə mō′ nēz) *n.*: Statements or declarations (p. 495)

muslin (muz′ lin) *n.*: A plain, strong kind of cotton (p. 496)

The Courage That My Mother Had

Edna St. Vincent Millay

The courage that my mother had
Went with her, and is with her still:
Rock from New England quarried;
Now granite in a granite hill.

5   The golden brooch my mother wore
She left behind for me to wear;
I have no thing I treasure more:
Yet, it is something I could spare.

Oh, if instead she'd left to me
10 The thing she took into the grave!—
That courage like a rock, which she
Has no more need of, and I have.

RESPONDING TO THE SELECTION

Your Response

1. What question or questions does the poem create in your mind?

Recalling

2. What quality does the speaker wish for?

Interpreting

3. Explain lines 3–4.
4. Why is a rock an effective metaphor for a courageous woman? How is courage also like granite?
5. What do lines 3–4 suggest about the importance of the mother's New England heritage?

6. In your own words, describe the feeling that the speaker expresses in this lyric poem.

Applying

7. The speaker implies that courage is a quality you either have or do not have. Do you think that a person could learn to be more courageous? Why or why not?

ANALYZING LITERATURE

Understanding Figurative Language

The poet uses both figurative language and literal language to express her strong feelings about her mother. For example, both literal and figurative language appear in the first stanza.

PORTRAIT OF HENRIETTE
Andrew Wyeth
Courtesy of the San Antonio Museum Association

1. Where in the stanza does the poet shift from a literal to a figurative description?
2. In which line of the third stanza does the poet start using figurative language again?
3. How would the poem be different if it were written entirely in literal language?

CRITICAL THINKING AND READING

Paraphrasing a Poem

Paraphrasing a poem means briefly restating it in your own words. Often you can clarify a difficult poem by paraphrasing it. However, you should realize that a paraphrase does not include many of the qualities that make a poem exciting. The following is a paraphrase of the first stanza of "The Courage That My Mother Had."

> When my mother died, she took her courage with her. In its strength, that courage reminded me of New England granite. Now the granite of her courage is buried with her in the hill, just as real granite is buried.

1. Paraphrase the other two stanzas.
2. Why is the poem more exciting than the paraphrase?

The Courage That My Mother Had 493

My Mother Pieced Quilts

Teresa Palomo Acosta

they were just meant as covers
in winter
as weapons
against pounding january winds

5   but it was just that every morning I awoke to these
october ripened canvases
passed my hand across their cloth faces
and began to wonder how you pieced
all these together
10 these strips of gentle communion cotton and flannel
      nightgowns
wedding organdies[1]
dime store velvets

how you shaped patterns square and oblong and round
positioned
15 balanced
then cemented them
with your thread
a steel needle
a thimble

20 how the thread darted in and out
galloping along the frayed edges, tucking them in
as you did us at night
oh how you stretched and turned and re-arranged
your michigan spring faded curtain pieces
25 my father's santa fe[2] work shirt
the summer denims, the tweeds of fall

in the evening you sat at your canvas
—our cracked linoleum floor the drawing board

---

1. **organdies** (or′ gən dēz) n.: Thin, crisp cotton fabrics used for items like dresses and curtains.
2. **Santa Fe** (san′ ta fā′): The capital of New Mexico.

me lounging on your arm
30 and you staking out the plan:
whether to put the lilac purple of easter against the red
    plaid of winter-going
into-spring
whether to mix a yellow with blue and white and paint the
corpus christi[3] noon when my father held your hand
35 whether to shape a five-point star from the
somber black silk you wore to grandmother's funeral

you were the river current
carrying the roaring notes
forming them into pictures of a little boy reclining
40 a swallow flying
you were the caravan master at the reins
driving your threaded needle artillery across the mosaic
    cloth bridges
delivering yourself in separate testimonies.

---

3. Corpus Christi (kor′ pəs kris′ tē): A city in southeast Texas.

oh mother you plunged me sobbing and laughing
45 into our past
into the river crossing at five
into the spinach fields
into the plainview[4] cotton rows
into tuberculosis wards
50 into braids and muslin dresses
sewn hard and taut to withstand the thrashings of twenty-
five years

stretched out they lay
armed/ready/shouting/celebrating

knotted with love
55 the quilts sing on

---

4. Plainview: A town in Texas.

RESPONDING TO THE SELECTION

Your Response

1. Is the mother someone you would like to know? Why or why not?

Recalling

2. What kinds of materials went into the quilts?

Interpreting

3. Like the quilts themselves, the poem is "pieced . . . together" from literal and figurative language. In what way were the quilts weapons? What battles has the mother fought?
4. To what is the speaker comparing her mother by using the word *canvases* in line 6?
5. How do the quilts reflect family history?
6. The speaker wonders how her mother was able to shape and cement the pieces of cloth to form a quilt. Find evidence that shows she also wonders how her mother was able to shape and cement the family.

Applying

7. Compare the mother in this poem with the mother in Millay's poem.

THINKING AND WRITING

Writing a Lyric Poem

Write a lyric poem about a courageous person. First brainstorm to list details that reveal this person's courage. Then shape these details into a poem expressing your feelings about this courageous person. Revise your poem to improve its musical quality. Prepare a final draft and share it with your classmates.

LEARNING OPTIONS

1. **Art.** With crayons, markers, or paints, draw a patchwork quilt. Draw pieces of fabric that have special meaning for you. They might be pieces of favorite clothing, clothing worn on a special occasion, or pieces of curtains or upholstery that remind you of your home.
2. **Language.** The poet refers to some fabrics not commonly used today: organdy and muslin, for example. Compile a list of these and of fabrics with which you are familiar. Write a few words to describe each fabric.

The Changing Seasons

BATCHEWANA WOOD, ALGOMA
J.E.H. MacDonald
Art Gallery of Ontario, Toronto

in Just-

E. E. Cummings (1894–1962) was born in Cambridge, Massachusetts. Cummings graduated from Harvard University in 1915. He served in World War I as an ambulance driver. After the war he worked as a painter and a poet. So successful a poet was he that, unlike many other poets, he was able to earn his living through his poetry. Individual liberty is a deeply rooted tradition in New England, and Cummings's life and writings are stamped with it. It is most clearly seen in the unusual way his poems are printed and in their strikingly original language. If you have not read any of Cummings's poems before, you will find "in Just-" a unique reading experience, and probably a delightful one.

Winter

Nikki Giovanni (1943–   ) was born in Knoxville, Tennessee, and grew up in Cincinnati, Ohio. She has received numerous awards and honors, among them a National Book Award nomination and election to the Ohio Women's Hall of Fame. Much of her poetry expresses the feelings and experiences of the African American community. She has also written about the joys and closeness of African American family life. In "Winter" Giovanni writes about a universal subject, the first signs of the coming of winter.

Stopping by Woods on a Snowy Evening

Robert Frost (1875–1963) lived in rural New England for most of his life. As a result, Frost's poetry presents a full picture of nature and of country life in New Hampshire, Vermont, and other parts of New England. Frost won the Pulitzer Prize four times. His poems that describe and comment on a rural scene or event are among his most popular, and among these "Stopping by Woods on a Snowy Evening" is one of his best. If the poem seems to draw you into the scene described, it is partly because the scene is one that Frost knew well from real life.

Sensory Language

Sensory language is language that appeals to your senses. Poets as well as other writers frequently include details that appeal to your sense of sight, hearing, touch, taste, or smell.

To convey her impression of the heat of summer, the poet Hilda Doolittle (known as H. D.) wrote these lines in her poem "Garden":

> Fruit cannot drop
> Through this thick air;
> Fruit cannot fall into heat
> That presses up and blunts
> The points of pears,
> And rounds the grapes.

The sensory language here helps you almost see and feel the heavy, almost visible heat.

Focus

The cycle of the seasons is one of the most fascinating aspects of the natural world. What kinds of seasonal changes are noticeable where you live? Make a chart like the one below, and list all the sensations that each season brings to mind.

Season	Sights	Sounds	Smells	Tastes	Physical Feelings
spring					
summer					
autumn					
winter					

Exchange charts with some classmates, and see how they compare.

People respond to the changing seasons in many different ways. As you read, notice how the poets have responded to the seasons.

Vocabulary

Knowing the following words will help you as you read these poems.

wee (wē) *adj.*: Very small; tiny (p. 500)

burrow (bur′ ō) *v.*: To dig a hole or tunnel, especially for shelter (p. 502)

downy (doun′ ē) *adj.*: Soft and fluffy; like soft, fine feathers (p. 504)

in Just-

E. E. Cummings

in Just-
spring   when the world is mud-
luscious the little
lame balloonman

5   whistles   far   and wee

and eddieandbill come
running from marbles and
piracies and it's
spring

10 when the world is puddle-wonderful

the queer
old balloonman whistles
far   and   wee
and bettyandisbel come dancing

15 from hop-scotch and jump-rope and

it's
spring
and
    the

20   goat-footed[1]

balloonMan   whistles
far
and
wee

---

1. goat-footed: Like the Greek god Pan, who
had the legs of a goat and was associated with
fields, forests, and wild animals.

Your Response

1. What feelings about spring does the poem create in you?

Recalling

2. What event does this poem describe?

Interpreting

3. From whose point of view—a child's or an adult's—is spring described? Which words seem especially appropriate for this group?
4. What is the effect of the poet's writing "eddie-andbill" and "bettyandisbel" instead of "Eddie and Bill" and "Betty and Isbel"?
5. How does the arrangement of lines on the page mimic the way the people in the poem move?
6. Look at the adjectives used to describe the balloon man. How does the description of him change as the poem progresses?
7. The Greek god Pan inspired people with his flute playing. What effect does the balloon-man's whistling have on the children?
8. Why does the poet call this poem "in Just-," instead of "In Spring"?

Applying

9. What is it about spring that often makes us want to abandon our chores to play?

Analyzing Literature

Understanding Sensory Language

Sensory language is language that appeals to your senses. Poets frequently use such language to give you a vivid impression of the physical world. Cummings creates words that boldly appeal to your senses.

1. To which of your senses do the words "mud-luscious" and "puddle-wonderful" appeal?
2. The poet created these words by joining a noun and an adjective. In what way do these words capture the spirit of the poem?
3. Using the poet's technique of joining a noun and an adjective, create three words you think would be appropriate for describing spring.

Learning Options

1. **Writing.** To conjure up the joys of spring, the poet joined together the words *mud* and *luscious* to create "mud-luscious" and *puddle* and *wonderful* to create "puddle-wonderful." Look at the list of words you wrote before reading the poem. Create some combinations of words that express your enjoyment of one of the seasons. For example, for summer you might write "plant-plentiful." Try to create at least three expressions. Then join with a classmate who chose the same season, and write a poem that uses each person's created words.
2. **Speaking and Listening.** Talk to two or three adults you know. Ask them what kinds of games they associated with spring when they were children. Ask each adult to explain the rules of one of the games to you. Then tell the rules to the class, and answer any questions about how the game is played.

Winter

Nikki Giovanni

Frogs burrow the mud
snails bury themselves
and I air my quilts
preparing for the cold

5   Dogs grow more hair
mothers make oatmeal
and little boys and girls
take Father John's Medicine[1]

Bears store fat
10 chipmunks gather nuts
and I collect books
For the coming winter

---

1. Father John's Medicine: An old-fashioned
cough syrup.

RESPONDING TO THE SELECTION

Your Response

1. Would you prepare for winter in the same way
   the poet does? Why or why not?

Recalling

2. What two things does the speaker do to prepare for winter?

Interpreting

3. In what way is the airing of quilts (line 3) a sign
   that winter is coming?

4. In what way does the collecting of books (line
   11) suggest the approach of winter?

5. In what way does this poem suggest that people and animals are alike?

Applying

6. If you were asked to write an additional stanza
   for "Winter," what details might you include that
   fit in with those of the four stanzas Giovanni
   wrote?

THINKING AND WRITING

Writing a Poem

Write a poem in which you describe the activities you think of in connection with any one of the seasons where you live. Before writing, think about and then list the details that express your idea of the coming of the season you chose.

Although the details of your poem will be different from Giovanni's, follow the pattern she used. Write three stanzas of four lines each. Keep the lines short. Let some of the details be about nature and other people, and let other details be about you.

Revise your poem and share it with your classmates.

Stopping by Woods on a Snowy Evening

Robert Frost

Whose woods these are I think I know.
His house is in the village, though;
He will not see me stopping here
To watch his woods fill up with snow.

5   My little horse must think it queer
To stop without a farmhouse near
Between the woods and frozen lake
The darkest evening of the year.

He gives his harness bells a shake
10 To ask if there is some mistake.
The only other sound's the sweep
Of easy wind and downy flake.

The woods are lovely, dark, and deep,
But I have promises to keep,
15 And miles to go before I sleep,
And miles to go before I sleep.

RESPONDING TO THE SELECTION

Your Response

1. If you were the speaker, would you stay longer in the woods or hurry to keep the promises? Explain your answer.

Recalling

2. Describe the setting—both the time and the place—of the poem.
3. Why has the speaker stopped by the woods?

Interpreting

4. What is the significance of the word *darkest* in line 8?

5. What does the speaker mean when he says that he has "promises to keep"?
6. What associations and feelings are stirred up by the word *sleep*? What might this word mean in this poem?

Applying

7. This is one of the most popular poems by one of America's best-loved poets. Why do you think it appeals to so many readers?

THINKING AND WRITING

Writing About a Poem

"Stopping by Woods on a Snowy Evening," like most poems, can be understood on many levels. Write an explanation for your classmates of what you think the poem might mean. Start by making notes on why the speaker feels he must move on, where you think he might be going, and what promises he must keep. You might think of the situation as a mystery to be solved. Draft your ideas into a paragraph. End your paragraph with a summary statement about the meaning of the poem. Revise your draft, checking that what you have said is clear and sensible. Proofread it and prepare a final draft. Then share your interpretation of the poem with your classmates.

LEARNING OPTION

Speaking and Listening. Practice reading the poem aloud several times, and then read it to a group of your classmates. When you read aloud a poem with rhythm and rhyme, be careful not to read it in a singsong voice. For example, do not overemphasize the beat of the lines, and do not pause for the same length of time whenever you reach the end of a line. Instead, imagine that you are simply telling something to someone in conversation. Read the words with natural pronunciation, and let the rhythm take care of itself. If there is no punctuation at the end of a line, read on, without pausing, to the first word of the next line.

Season at the Shore

Phyllis McGinley (1905–1978) was born in Ontario, Oregon. She is most famous for her lighthearted, humorous poetry, for which she won a Pulitzer Prize in 1961. McGinley, who wrote with humor and affection about ordinary life, once summed up the viewpoint of her work by saying. "Cheerfulness was always breaking in." In "Season at the Shore," she takes her cheerfulness and humor to the beach for a romp on the sand.

When the Frost Is on the Punkin

James Whitcomb Riley (1849–1916) was born in Indiana. He wrote so many poems in the dialect, or country speech, of his native state that he has come to be known as "the Hoosier poet." He knew the land and the people of Indiana very well, and he used his knowledge to write poems that are still a source of local pride. "When the Frost Is on the Punkin" is both a colorful picture of an Indiana farm such as Riley would have known and a lively tune in the dialect that was for him a kind of music. Reading it aloud will add to your enjoyment of the language.

Sound Devices

Sound devices are a poet's way of making language more expressive and musical. Two of the most frequently used of these devices are alliteration and onomatopoeia. **Alliteration** is the repetition of the same consonant sounds at the beginning of words. For example, in "Season at the Shore" McGinley writes, "sand in the sandwiches spread for luncheon." The consonant sound *s* is repeated.

Onomatopoeia is the use of a word that imitates or suggests the sound of what the word refers to. For example, in "When the Frost Is on the Punkin" Riley writes, "And you hear the kyouck and gobble of the struttin' turkey-cock." Here "kyouck" and "gobble" suggest the sounds a turkey makes.

Focus

In the two poems you are about to read, you will find examples of alliteration and onomatopoeia. Try using these two techniques yourself. Imagine that you are someplace where there are a lot of animals—a zoo, an animal preserve, or even a jungle. In a chart like the one below, list several animals you might find there. Then write down an onomatopoeic word to describe the sound the animal makes and an alliterative phrase to describe the animal. Two examples are given.

Animal	Sound	Descriptive Phrase
snake	hiss	slowly slithers
lion	grrr	roaring regally

As you read the poems, notice how the use of onomatopoeia in one and alliteration in the other add to their effectiveness.

Vocabulary

Knowing the following words will help you as you read "Season at the Shore" and "When the Frost Is on the Punkin."

adhesive (əd hē′ siv) *adj.*: Sticking (p. 508)

sibling (sib′ liŋ) *n.*: Brother or sister (p. 508)

odious (ō′ dē əs) *adj.*: Disgusting; offensive (p. 508)

gaiters (gāt′ ərz) *n.*: Coverings for the legs extending from the instep to the ankle or knee (p. 508)

stubble (stub′ ′l) *n.*: Short stumps of corn or grain (p. 513)

Season at the Shore

Phyllis McGinley

Oh, not by sun and not by cloud
And not by whippoorwill, crying loud,
And not by the pricking of my thumbs,
Do I know the way that the summer comes.
5 Yet here on this seagull-haunted strand,[1]
Here is an omen I understand—
Sand:

Sand on the beaches,
    Sand at the door,
10 Sand that screeches
    On the new-swept floor;
In the shower, sand for the foot to crunch on;
Sand in the sandwiches spread for luncheon;
Sand adhesive to son and sibling,
15 From wallet sifting, from pockets dribbling;
Sand by the beaker
    Nightly shed
From odious sneaker;
    Sand in bed;
20 Sahara[2] always in my seaside shanty
Like the sand in the voice
Of J. Durante.[3]

Winter is mittens, winter is gaiters
Steaming on various radiators.
25 Autumn is leaves that bog the broom.
Spring is mud in the living room
Or skates in places one scarcely planned.
But what is summer, her seal and hand?
Sand:

30 Sand in the closets,
    Sand on the stair,

---

1. strand (strand) *n.*: The ocean shore.
2. Sahara (sə har′ ə): A large desert in North Africa.
3. J. Durante (də ran′ tē): Jimmy Durante (1893–1980), an American comedian with a husky, scraping voice.

Desert deposits
   In the parlor chair;
Sand in the halls like the halls of ocean;
35   Sand in the soap and the sun-tan lotion;
Stirred in the porridge, tossed in the greens,
Poured from the bottoms of rolled-up jeans;
   In the elmy street,
      On the lawny acre;
40   Glued to the seat
      Of the Studebaker;[4]
Wrapped in the folds of the *Wall Street Journal;*[5]
Damp sand, dry sand,
Sand eternal.
45   When I shake my garments at the Lord's command,
What will I scatter in the Promised Land?
Sand.

---

4. Studebaker: A car that is no longer made.
5. *Wall Street Journal:* A well-known financial newspaper.

MULTICULTURAL CONNECTION

Celebrating Seasons in Different Cultures

For Phyllis McGinley, sand is a symbol of her summers spent at the seashore. People everywhere associate special signs and ceremonies with the seasons.

Around the world, the different seasons offer special occasions for rejoicing, whether it is time for planting, harvesting, or celebrating a religious or cultural event.

The harvest of the saguaro cactus. In the Sonoran Desert of southern Arizona, the Papago people celebrate the harvest of the fruit of the giant saguaro cactus, which symbolizes the end of spring and the arrival of summer. This traditional ceremony features saguaro wine and foods made from the cactus fruit as well as speeches, dances, and songs. All these activities are intended to bring on rains.

The rose festival. In Bulgaria, where rosebushes are cultivated by the millions for export, perfume, and medicine, the rose is the symbol of summer. A rose festival is held each year from May to June in the town of Kazanluk in the Valley of the Roses. It features ritual picking of roses and a parade of roses.

The rise of the Zambezi River. A folkloric event of the African country Zambia is the Ku Omboko ("Getting out of the water"). This event is held in February or March—depending on the rise of the Zambezi River—and is a signal of spring. The ceremony marks the occasion when the local residents move to higher grounds in order to avoid the floods. Much fanfare accompanies the event.

Exploring on Your Own

Find out more about how the seasons are celebrated around the world. Research cultural festivals for one of the seasons and share your report with the class.

Your Response

1. Did you find the poem humorous? Why or why not?

Recalling

2. What word is repeated more frequently than any other throughout the poem?
3. The poet thinks of sand as the "seal and hand" of summer. What things does she think of as standing for winter, autumn, and spring?

Interpreting

4. The poet includes a great number of images—word pictures—of sand in different places. What effect does the accumulation, or piling up, of details have on the poem? How is this effect reinforced by the repetition of the word *sand*?
5. To what senses does the poet appeal?
6. What is the poet's attitude toward sand?
7. Interpret, or explain the meaning of, the last three lines.
8. Why is "Season at the Shore" a better title for this poem than "Day at the Shore"?

Applying

9. What would you choose as the one thing that best represents summer? Why would this be your choice?

ANALYZING LITERATURE

Understanding Alliteration

   Alliteration is the repetition of the same consonant sound at the beginning of words. This sound device can reinforce meaning as well as contribute to the "music" of a poem. The line "Sand adhesive to son and sibling," in which the *s* sound is repeated, is a more effective line in McGinley's poem than a line such as "Sand adhesive to daughter and brother" would have been. Why?

1. Find three or four other examples of alliteration in which the *s* sound is repeated.
2. Why is this sound especially appropriate to the poem?
3. Find an example of alliteration in which some other consonant sound is repeated.

THINKING AND WRITING

Writing a Poem With Alliteration

   Write a four-line poem (it need not rhyme) in which you use alliteration. You may use one of the following subjects and the suggested consonant sound for alliteration, or you may choose another subject.

> The winter wind (*w*, as in *wail, whoosh, wild*)
> A snake (*s*, as in *slither, slimy, silent*)
> A guitar (*p*, as in *pluck, play, pick*)
> The rain (*d*, as in *downpour, damp, dreary*)

   When you revise, first check that your poem says what you want to say about the subject. Then see if you can replace any words to add alliteration to your poem.

   Read your poem to some of your classmates and listen to those they wrote.

LEARNING OPTION

Speaking and Listening. Find a collection of poems by Phyllis McGinley. Choose another light-hearted poem to read to the class. Practice reading it aloud several times. Then ask one other person to listen to you and make suggestions for improvements. After you read the poem to the class, point out some of the humorous devices.

When the Frost Is on the Punkin

James Whitcomb Riley

When the frost is on the punkin and the fodder's
    in the shock,[1]
And you hear the kyouck and gobble of the
    struttin' turkey-cock,
And the clackin' of the guineys,[2] and the cluckin' of
    the hens,
And the rooster's hallylooyer as he tiptoes on the
    fence;
5   O, it's then's the times a feller is a-feelin' at his
    best,
With the risin' sun to greet him from a night of
    peaceful rest,
As he leaves the house, bareheaded, and goes out
    to feed the stock,[3]
When the frost is on the punkin and the fodder's
    in the shock.

They's something kindo' harty-like about the
    atmusfere
10   When the heat of summer's over and the coolin' fall
    is here—
Of course we miss the flowers, and the blossums on
    the trees,
And the mumble of the hummin'-birds and buzzin'
    of the bees;
But the air's so appetizin'; and the landscape
    through the haze
Of a crisp and sunny morning of the airly[4] autumn
    days
15   Is a pictur' that no painter has the colorin' to mock[5]—

---

1. the fodder's in the shock: The corn or hay used to feed the
animals is stacked in piles, or shocks.
2. guineys (gin' ēs) guineas *n*.: Fowls with a featherless head,
rounded body, and dark feathers spotted with white.
3. stock (stäk) *n*.: Short for livestock, the domestic animals kept on
a farm.
4. airly (er' lē): Early.
5. mock (mäk) *v*.: Copy.

When the frost is on the punkin and the fodder's
in the shock.

The husky, rusty russel of the tossels[6] of the corn,
And the raspin' of the tangled leaves, as golden as
the morn;
The stubble in the furries[7]—kindo' lonesome-like,
but still
20 A-preachin' sermuns to us of the barns they growed
to fill;
The strawstack in the medder,[8] and the reaper in the
shed;
The hosses in theyr stalls below—the clover
overhead!—
O, it sets my hart a-clickin' like the tickin' of a
clock,
When the frost is on the punkin and the fodder's
in the shock!

25 Then your apples all is getherd, and the ones a
feller keeps
Is poured around the celler-floor in red and yeller
heaps;
And your cider-makin' 's over, and your wimmern-folks
is through
With ther mince[9] and apple-butter, and theyr souse[10] and
sausage, too! . . .
I don't know how to tell it—but ef sich a thing
could be
30 As the Angels wantin' boardin', and they'd call
around on *me*—
I'd want to 'commodate 'em[11]—all the whole-indurin'
flock—
When the frost is on the punkin and the fodder's
in the shock!

_____

6. tossels: Tassels, which are silky, threadlike tufts at the tip of
an ear of corn.
7. furries (fur' ēs) *n*.: Furrows, which are narrow grooves cut in
the ground by a plow.
8. medder (med' ar): Meadow.
9. mince (mins) *n*.: Mincemeat, a mixture of chopped apples,
spices, and sometimes meat, used as a pie filling.
10. souse (sous) *n*.: A pickled food.
11. 'commodate (käm' ə dāt') **'em:** Accommodate them, or give
them food and a place to stay.

Your Response

1. Which images of autumn in the poem appealed to you most? Why?

Recalling

2. In the first stanza, what details suggest "the times a feller is a-feelin' at his best"?
3. In the second stanza, what does the speaker especially like about the atmosphere and landscape of fall?
4. Summarize in your own words what sets the speaker's heart "a-clickin'" in stanza three.

Interpreting

5. What is the meaning or point of the last four lines of the poem?
6. Summarize the speaker's feelings about fall, "when the frost is on the punkin."
7. What can you conclude about the speaker and his way of life?
8. This poem is written in dialect rather than standard English. Why might the poet have decided to write it this way?

Applying

9. Although this poem is set in rural Indiana, it has long appealed to readers all over the country. Why do you think its appeal is so widespread?

■ A NALYZING LITERATURE

Understanding Onomatopoeia

Onomatopoeia is the use of a word that imitates or suggests the sound of what the word refers to. The word "cluckin'," for example, in the phrase "the cluckin' of the hens," suggests the sound hens make. This device adds vividness to a poet's descriptions of sound.

1. Besides "kyouck," "gobble," and "cluckin'," what other examples of onomatopoeia can you find in the first stanza?
2. Find two examples in each of the next two stanzas.
3. Of the examples you found, which seems to you most effective?
4. To which of your senses do these uses of onomatopoeia appeal?
5. Why is onomatopoeia so effective in poetry?

■ T HINKING AND WRITING

Writing a Travel Article

Write an article for your school newspaper or literary magazine about an imaginary trip you took to a zoo, an animal preserve, or a jungle. Using the phrases you wrote before reading these poems, describe the memorable sounds you heard. Use alliteration and onomatopoeia to make your descriptions vivid. When you revise your article, see if you can use more vivid words and phrases to make your description even more clear to someone who may never have heard the sounds you are writing about.

■ L EARNING OPTIONS

1. **Writing.** Even where the weather does not change a lot from summer to autumn, certain things mark the arrival of autumn—the start of the school year and fewer daylight hours, for example. Make a list of your own associations and feelings about autumn. Turn your list into a listing poem entitled "Autumn Is ____."
2. **Cross-curricular Connection.** What makes autumn different from the other seasons? Find out more about the seasons. What causes them, for example? What marks the beginning of each season? How do animals respond to the changes? Collect your findings in an illustrated report.

People in Their Variety

SNAPSHOT AT THE BEACH, 1891

Mother to Son

Langston Hughes (1902–1967) was born in Joplin, Missouri, and later lived in different parts of the country. He is most associated with Harlem, an area in New York City. Many of his poems, including "Mother to Son," use the rhythms of black music, especially jazz and blues. These poems present memorable, and sometimes powerful, portraits of black life. Often, as in "Mother to Son," they center on a character with a distinctive and forceful voice.

A Song of Greatness

The **Chippewa Indians** lived at one time on the shores of Lake Superior. Today, about 30,000 Chippewa live on reservations in the Midwest and West. "A Song of Greatness" recalls the Chippewa past when battles were fought and heroes were made.

    Mary Austin (1868–1934) lived most of her life in the Southwest, where she studied the ways of Native Americans.

I'm Nobody

Emily Dickinson (1830–1886) hardly ever traveled outside Amherst, Massachusetts, where she was born. When she died, she had written about 1,175 poems, but only seven had been published—anonymously. "I'm Nobody" reflects her life. She was a private person. But it does not reflect her destiny. Today, her fame is worldwide and her admirers are without number.

Life

Naomi Long Madgett (1923–   ) was born in Norfolk, Virginia, but has lived for much of her adult life in Detroit, Michigan. She retired from Eastern Michigan University in 1984 after sixteen years of teaching in the English Department. She has said, "I would rather be a good poet than anything else I can imagine." Her desire to write good poetry has led to seven collections of poetry and the appearance of poems in hundreds of anthologies. In "Life," Madgett uses a striking comparison to convey an idea about the way people live.

Martin Luther King

Raymond Richard Patterson (1929–   ) was born in New York City. Patterson has been a teacher for thirty years, both at the high school and at the college level. His poetry has appeared in poetry anthologies and in his own collection of poetry, *Twenty-six Ways of Looking at a Black Man and Other Poems.* "From Our Past" was the title of a weekly column on black history that Patterson wrote for several newspapers. "Martin Luther King" is also about history, paying tribute to a great man from America's past.

Tone

Tone in poetry is the poet's or speaker's attitude toward the subject, toward the reader, or toward himself or herself. It can often be described by such words as *serious, amused, sad, cheerful, proud,* or *mocking.* Tone comes from all the elements of a poem: the subject, what is said about it, the connotations of words, the rhythm, the figures of speech, and so on.

Focus

Role-playing with a group of four other classmates can help you gain a better understanding of how tone might change from poem to poem. Imagine that you are greeting people at a party. Speak to each of your classmates as if they were the following people: first, someone you have not seen in a very long time and are surprised and happy to see; second, someone you like who recently lost a much-loved pet; next, someone you dislike but wish to greet politely; and last, your best friend whom you see almost every day. When each of you has had a turn, discuss how your words, tone of voice, facial expressions, and gestures were used to convey the different attitudes. Which tone was the easiest to convey? Which was the most difficult? As you read the following poems, notice how the tone changes from speaker to speaker.

Vocabulary

Knowing these words will help you as you read the poems.

esteemed (ə stēmd′) *v.*: respected; held in high regard (p. 520)

banish (ban′ ish) *v.*: Send into exile (p. 521)

bog (bäg) *n.*: A small marsh or swamp (p. 521)

beset (bē set′) *v.*: Covered; set thickly with (p. 523)

profound (prō found′) *adj.*: Deeply or intensely felt (p. 523)

Mother to Son

Langston Hughes

Well, son, I'll tell you:
Life for me ain't been no crystal stair.
It's had tacks in it,
And splinters,
5   And boards torn up,
And places with no carpet on the floor—
Bare.
But all the time
I'se been a-climbin' on,
10   And reachin' landin's,
And turnin' corners,
And sometimes goin' in the dark
Where there ain't been no light.
So boy, don't you turn back.
15   Don't you set down on the steps
'Cause you finds it's kinder hard.
Don't you fall now—
For I'se still goin', honey,
I'se still climbin',
20   And life for me ain't been no crystal stair.

▌RESPONDING TO THE SELECTION

Your Response

1. Is the mother someone you would like to know? Is the son? Why or why not?

Recalling

2. What advice does the mother give the son?

Interpreting

3. The mother uses an extended metaphor to describe her life. What do the details in lines 3–7 suggest about this life?

4. What is the mother saying about her life in lines 8–13?

5. What is she telling her son in lines 14–17 about how to live?

Applying

6. Since our earliest days, Americans have valued stick-to-itiveness, or perseverance. What is it about our early history that would have made these traits desirable?

ORGANDY COLLAR, 1936
Edmund Archer
Whitney Museum of American Art

ANALYZING LITERATURE

Understanding Tone

Tone is the basic attitude expressed in a poem. It is like the emotional coloring you give your words in conversation by the way you use your voice. Just think, for example, of the different ways you can say the one word *Hello*!

1. How would you describe the tone of the first sentence (lines 1–7) of the poem?

2. How is the tone different in the next sentence (lines 8–13)?

3. Which of the following descriptions best fits the tone of the entire poem? Give reasons for your choice.
   a. Exhausted and hopeless
   b. Weary, yet strong and determined
   c. Lively and humorous
   d. Sorrowful and gloomy

A Song of Greatness

Chippewa Traditional

Mary Austin

When I hear the old men
Telling of heroes,
Telling of great deeds
Of ancient days—
5 When I hear that telling,
Then I think within me
I, too, am one of these.

When I hear the people
Praising great ones,
10 Then I know that I too—
Shall be esteemed:
I, too, when my time comes
Shall do mightily.

RESPONDING TO THE SELECTION

Your Response

1. What is your impression of the speaker?

Recalling

2. To whom is the speaker referring when he says in line 7, "I, too, am one of these"?

Interpreting

3. Who might the "great ones" (line 9) be?
4. What makes the speaker think that he shall "be esteemed" and "do mightily"?

Applying

5. How does the attitude of young people today toward heroes of the past compare with the attitude of the speaker in this poem?

CRITICAL THINKING AND READING

Comparing and Contrasting Tone

Tone is the speaker's attitude toward his or her subject. For example, the tone may be sorrowful or pleased, angry or accepting. You will find it easier to grasp the tone of a poem by comparing and contrasting it with the tone of another poem, especially one with a similar subject or point of view.

1. Describe the tone of "A Song of Greatness."
2. If you have not already done so, read the preceding poem, "Mother to Son." How are the subjects of "Mother to Son" and "A Song of Greatness" similar?
3. Finally, compare and contrast the tone of "A Song of Greatness" with the tone of "Mother to Son."

I'm Nobody

Emily Dickinson

I'm Nobody! Who are you?
Are you—Nobody—too?
Then there's a pair of us!
Don't tell! they'd banish us—you know!

5   How dreary—to be—Somebody!
How public—like a Frog—
To tell your name—the livelong June—
To an admiring Bog!

RESPONDING TO THE SELECTION

Your Response

1. Does the poem make you want to be "Nobody" too? Why or why not?

Recalling

2. What is it like to be a "Somebody"?

Interpreting

3. What does the word "Nobody" mean in this poem?
4. How does the speaker feel about discovering another nobody?
5. What does the word "public" suggest?
6. To what does the speaker compare being public?
7. What might the admiring bog stand for?

Applying

8. What is your opinion of the speaker's preference for being a nobody to being a somebody?

CRITICAL THINKING AND READING

Paraphrasing a Poem

Paraphrasing a poem means restating it in your own words. It is an excellent way of seeing through hard words, unusual sentence structures, and figurative language in order to come to a basic meaning of the poem.

The following lines are from a poem called "Solitude," by Alexander Pope. Notice how the paraphrase that follows them restates the meaning of the lines in simpler language.

Happy the man whose wish and care
A few paternal acres bound,
Content to breathe his native air
    In his own ground.

Paraphrase: A man is fortunate if everything he wants or worries about lies within the land he lives on. He is fortunate if he's happy at home and doesn't desire to travel.

Once you have paraphrased a poem, you can then reread it with greater understanding and enjoyment.

Write a paraphrase of "I'm Nobody." Be sure to restate the poem in your own words in a way that makes clear all that the poem is expressing.

Life

Naomi Long Madgett

Life is but a toy that swings on a bright gold chain
Ticking for a little while
To amuse a fascinated infant,
Until the keeper, a very old man,
5   Becomes tired of the game
And lets the watch run down.

RESPONDING TO THE SELECTION

Your Response

1. Do you agree with the poet's statement that life is a toy? Why or why not?

Recalling

2. What kind of "toy" does the poem describe?

Interpreting

3. Why is life amusing to the "fascinated infant"?
4. Why is "the keeper" a very old man?
5. What does the speaker mean by "the game" in line 5?
6. What happens when the keeper "lets the watch run down"?
7. In your own words, explain the meaning of this poem.

Applying

8. Like Naomi Long Madgett, many writers have used metaphors, or figurative comparisons, to describe life. For example, you probably know the expression, "Life is a bowl of cherries."

Working with your classmates, make a list of common metaphors describing life. Discuss the attitude toward life expressed in each.

LEARNING OPTIONS

1. **Cross-curricular Connection.** People rarely carry pocket watches anymore. Work with several classmates to find out more about the history of timepieces from the earliest sundials to the most modern digital watches. Create a timeline, indicating the period in which each type of timepiece was invented and used.

2. **Art.** In the poem "Life," the speaker compares life to a pocket watch. How do you describe life? Create a colorful collage that illustrates all the most important things in your life. Show it to the class and explain each part.

Martin Luther King

Raymond Richard Patterson

He came upon an age
Beset by grief, by rage—

His love so deep, so wide,
He could not turn aside.

5   His passion, so profound,
He would not turn around.

He taught this suffering Earth
The measure of Man's worth.

He showed what Man can be
10 Before death sets him free.

RESPONDING TO THE SELECTION

Your Response

1. Do you think the poem captures the spirit of Martin Luther King, Jr.? Why or why not?

Recalling

2. What does the speaker say that King taught us?

Interpreting

3. What tone does the speaker use in this poem?
4. What is meant by the "measure of Man's worth" in line 8?
5. To what might the speaker be referring when describing the "age" as "Beset by grief, by rage—" and the Earth as "suffering"?
6. What does the speaker mean by lines 9–10?

Applying

7. Martin Luther King was killed in 1968, working for what he believed in—equal rights for all people in the United States. What makes people who die for what they believe in especially admirable? Do you consider such people heroes? Why or why not?

THINKING AND WRITING

Writing to Express Tone

Write a paragraph, in the same tone as "Martin Luther King," about a person whom you admire. You might choose to write about a famous actor, athlete, or politician, or you might choose a friend, a relative, or a parent. First, freewrite about why you believe the person is worthy of admiration. As you write your first draft, you might include an example of your subject's actions or behavior that supports your reasons for admiring him or her. Let a classmate read your draft and offer suggestions. Then revise your paragraph and prepare a final draft.

GUIDE FOR READING

Father William

Lewis Carroll

(1832–1898) is the pen name of Charles Lutwidge Dodgson, who was born in Cheshire, England. Under his real name he wrote mathematical works, but as Lewis Carroll he wrote two of the most famous books for children of all time, *Alice's Adventures in Wonderland* and *Through the Looking Glass.* His outward life was very quiet and uneventful, but in works like "Father William" he found escape from his serious work into a delightfully zany, topsy-turvy world that still amuses children old and young.

Humor

Humor in poetry can arise from a number of sources, such as surprise, exaggeration, or the bringing together of unrelated things. The majority of funny poems, however, have two things in common: rhythm and rhyme. These devices often make language more lively and sharp. This more spirited language makes humorous situations even more humorous. For example, here is a little poem by Ogden Nash called "The Porcupine."

> Any hound a porcupine nudges
> Can't be blamed for harboring grudges.
> I know one hound that laughed all winter
> At a porcupine that sat on a splinter.

Take away the rhythm and rhyme and the humor vanishes.

Focus

In the poem you are about to read, a young man questions his father about some rather unusual behavior. There may have been times when you asked someone what they were doing and you received an explanation that made very little sense at all. Write about such a real situation, or invent an imaginary one. In the form of an interview, give your serious, logical questions and the zany replies of your interviewee. Then compare your interview with the one in the poem.

Vocabulary

Knowing the following words will help you as you read "Father William."

incessantly (in ses′ 'nt lē) *adv.*: Without stopping (p. 525)

sage (sāj) *n.*: A very wise man (p. 526)

supple (sup′ 'l) *adj.*: Flexible (p. 526)

shilling (shil′ iŋ) *n.*: A British coin. In Carroll's day, a shilling had much more monetary value than it has today. (p. 526)

Father William

Lewis Carroll

"You are old, Father William," the young man said,
    "And your hair has become very white;
And yet you incessantly stand on your head—
    Do you think, at your age, it is right?"

5 "In my youth," Father William replied to his son,
    "I feared it might injure the brain;
But, now that I'm perfectly sure I have none,
    Why, I do it again and again."

"You are old," said the youth, "as I mentioned before.
10   And have grown most uncommonly[1] fat;
Yet you turned a back-somersault in at the door—
    Pray, what is the reason of that?"

YOU ARE OLD FATHER WILLIAM, 1865
Sir John Tenniel
The Granger Collection

"In my youth," said the sage, as he shook his gray locks,
    "I kept all my limbs very supple
15 By the use of this ointment—one shilling the box—
    Allow me to sell you a couple?"

"You are old," said the youth, "and your jaws are too weak
    For anything tougher than suet;[2]
Yet you finished the goose, with the bones and the beak—
20 Pray, how did you manage to do it?"

"In my youth," said his father, "I took to the law,
    And argued each case with my wife;
And the muscular strength, which it gave to my jaw
    Has lasted the rest of my life."

---

1. **uncommonly** (un käm′ ən lē) *adv.*: Remarkably.
2. **suet** (so͞o′ it) *n.*: Fat used in cooking.

YOU ARE OLD FATHER WILLIAM, 1865
Sir John Tenniel
The Granger Collection

25   "You are old," said the youth, "one would hardly suppose
      That your eye was as steady as ever;
  Yet you balanced an eel on the end of your nose—
      What made you so awfully clever?"

  "I have answered three questions, and that is enough,"
30   Said his father. "Don't give yourself airs!
  Do you think I can listen all day to such stuff?
      Be off, or I'll kick you downstairs!"

R ESPONDING TO THE SELECTION

Your Response

1. Which of Father William's replies do you think is the most ridiculous? Why?

Recalling

2. What reason does Father William give for incessantly standing on his head?
3. What enables him to do back-somersaults?
4. How did he develop jaws strong enough to devour a goose, including the bones and beak?

Interpreting

5. What is it about Father William's physical condition that makes his behavior so absurd?
6. Why is it so comical that Father William refuses to answer any more questions?

Applying

7. Why do people like to laugh? Why do they enjoy telling utterly ridiculous stories?

A NALYZING LITERATURE

Understanding Humor in Poetry

Rhythm and rhyme are important aids to humorous poets, but they are not in themselves funny. The more common sources of humor include surprise, exaggeration, and bringing together unrelated things. For example, being elderly is not humorous, and neither (most of the time) is standing on one's head. However, an elderly person's standing on his or her head is funny because we usually associate standing on one's head with children. Such humor is based on bringing together unrelated things.

1. First rewrite any one of the pairs of stanzas in which a question is asked and then answered. Remove the rhythm and rhyme, but do not change the meaning. How is the humor affected by the changes you made?
2. Next find in "Father William" an example of humor based on surprise or the unexpected.
3. Find an example of humor that is based on exaggeration.

T HINKING AND WRITING

Writing a Humorous Poem

Using the questions and answers you wrote for your imaginary interview, write a humorous poem in dialogue with questions and replies. Your poem need not be as long as Carroll's, but it should be funny.

When you revise, read your poem to a friend to see if it is funny. Share your poem with your classmates.

GUIDE FOR READING

Oliver Herford

(1863–1935) was born in England but lived from childhood on in the United States. Once, passing a schoolhouse at night, he imagined the typical school day that lay ahead for the teacher and pupils. He entered the school and covered the chalkboard with drawings of animals. Next day, the teachers and pupils were as amused as they were surprised. This incident reveals two qualities of Herford's, his sense of humor and his fondness for animals as subjects. You will find both in his limericks.

Two Limericks

Limericks

A **limerick** is a poem of five lines. The first, second, and fifth lines have three rhythmic beats and rhyme with one another. The third and fourth lines have two beats, and they also rhyme. Using letters to represent the different rhyme sounds, you can describe the rhyme pattern of a limerick as *aabba*. Limericks are always lighthearted, humorous poems.

Focus

Humorous rhymes are an important part of successful limericks. To prepare for writing your own limerick, write the following line on a piece of paper:

There once was a girl (or boy) named ____ (supply a name).

Then list a number of words that rhyme with the name and that could be used in funny statements about the boy or girl named. Remember, some of the most humorous rhymes come from rhyming a word with a phrase. For example, you could rhyme the name *Susan* with the phrase *shoes on.* Since limericks have two sets of rhyming sounds, make a second list of rhyming words that could be used in your limerick. Then, as you read the limericks, pay attention to the rhyming pattern.

Vocabulary

Knowing the following words will help you as you read Herford's two limericks.

dote (dōt) *v.*: To be extremely fond (p. 529)

scale (skāl) *n.*: A series of musical tones (p. 529)

quail (kwāl) *v.*: Draw back in fear (p. 529)

Two Limericks

Oliver Herford

Said the Lion: "On music I dote,
But something is wrong with my throat.
    When I practice a scale,
    The listeners quail,
And flee at the very first note!"

A puppy whose hair was so flowing
There really was no means of knowing
    Which end was his head,
    Once stopped me and said,
"Please, sir, am I coming or going?"

RESPONDING TO THE SELECTION

Your Response

1. Which of the two limericks do you like better? Why?

Recalling

2. What activity does the lion say he performs?
3. Describe the puppy in the second limerick.

Interpreting

4. What is the lion really doing?
5. Why is the puppy's question funny?

Applying

6. Why do you think that the limerick form is never used for serious poetry?

ANALYZING LITERATURE

Understanding Limericks

A **limerick** has short lines; a swift, catchy rhythm; and heavily stressed rhymes. There are three beats in the first, second, and fifth lines, which rhyme, and two beats in the third and fourth lines, which also rhyme.

The following is a limerick about limericks. See if you can paraphrase it—restate it in your own words—to discover what it says about why limericks are amusing. (The word *conceits* in line 4 means "imaginative or clever ideas.")

Well, it's partly the shape of the thing
That gives the old limerick wing;
    These accordion pleats
    Full of airy conceits
Take it up like a kite on a string.

THINKING AND WRITING

Writing a Limerick

Using the opening line and the list of rhymes you have written, write a limerick of your own. When you revise, make sure that you do not damage the sense of your lines while getting them to rhyme. Also, check that your lines have the correct rhythm. Share your limerick with your classmates.

GUIDE FOR READING

Song of Orpheus

Myths in Poetry

Myths are traditional stories that have been passed on for generations. They reflect the most basic beliefs and ideals of the culture that created them. Many myths concern gods and goddesses and attempt to explain some aspect of nature or of human life. Over the years many poets have chosen myths as the basis for poems because myths are an important part of human history. In Greek mythology, Orpheus was the son of the god Apollo and the goddess Calliope, who was especially concerned with poetry. Orpheus was a poet whose music tamed wild animals and even charmed trees and rocks.

Focus

Literature is full of heroes who are able to do impossible things. Many of today's larger-than-life heroes are comic-book characters. List three comic-book superheroes along with the superpowers that they possess. What do the powers of today's comic-book heroes say about the beliefs and values of our culture? As you read the poem, compare the powers of the heroes you listed with those possessed by Orpheus.

Vocabulary

Knowing the following words will help you as you read "Song of Orpheus."

billows (bil′ ōz) *n.*: Large waves (p. 531)

grief (grēf) *n.*: Great sorrow (p. 531)

William Shakespeare

(1564–1616) is viewed by many as the greatest English writer of all times. Not much is known about his early life. He was born in Stratford-on-Avon and is believed to have attended grammar school there. Later, it is likely that he joined a group of actors who traveled around putting on plays. Shakespeare first received recognition as a playwright in London in 1592. In all, he wrote thirty-seven plays—about two per year. Some of his best-known works include *Romeo and Juliet, Hamlet,* and *Macbeth.* In addition to plays, Shakespeare wrote more than one hundred sonnets and other kinds of poems, including poems that appeared as songs in some of his plays. "Song of Orpheus" was written as part of his play *King Henry VIII.*

Song of Orpheus

from *King Henry VIII*

William Shakespeare

Orpheus with his lute made trees,
And the mountain tops that freeze,
   Bow themselves when he did sing:
To his music plants and flowers
5 Ever sprung; as sun and showers
   There had made a lasting spring.

Every thing that heard him play,
Even the billows of the sea,
   Hung their heads, and then lay by.
10 In sweet music is such art,
Killing care and grief of heart
   Fall asleep, or hearing, die.

ORPHEUS (detail)
Odilon Redon
The Cleveland Museum of Art

RESPONDING TO THE SELECTION

Your Response

1. Do you agree that music can take away our cares? Why or why not?

Recalling

2. What effect did Orpheus' music have on plants and flowers?

Interpreting

3. Why are mountains described as freezing?
4. Why do all things that hear Orpheus play hang their heads and then lie down?

Applying

5. Describe the skill of a musician you admire.

ANALYZING LITERATURE

Understanding Myths in Poetry

Some poets use **myths** in their poetry to remind their readers of the values of the ancient cultures from which the myths came.

1. What does the myth of Orpheus suggest about the ancient Greeks?
2. In the original myth, Orpheus could charm humans as well as rocks and trees. Why do you suppose the poet focuses on things that we don't think of as being able to respond?

READING AND RESPONDING

Poetry

Robert Frost has written, "A poem . . . begins in delight and ends in wisdom." Perhaps you experienced these feelings as you read and responded to the poems in this unit.

There is no precise definition for poetry, but it has special qualities that set it apart from other forms of literature. The language is imaginative, musical, and compact. The form may be unusual. Images and sound devices give you special insights into a poem.

Use the active reading strategies to respond to poetry.

RESPONDING TO LANGUAGE Poets use language to create new ways of seeing things. They often use figurative language, language that is not intended to be understood literally. Such figures of speech help you to see or think about something in a new and imaginative way. How does this language make you feel?

RESPONDING TO APPEARANCE Poetry can take a variety of forms. What does it look like on the page? Is its appearance related to the type of poetry it is, such as narrative or lyric? How does its appearance affect your expectations as you read it?

RESPONDING TO IMAGERY Poets appeal to the senses by creating images. Use your imagination and your senses to take in the images the poet might be developing. What senses are you using to respond to the images?

RESPONDING TO SOUND The music of poetry is created by sound devices. Read poems aloud and let the rhythm and the rhyme flow naturally. Listen for alliteration, onomatopoeia, and other musical devices. What is the effect of these sound devices? How do they contribute to the meaning of the poem?

RESPONDING TO THEME Many poems convey an important idea or insight about life. What do you think is the message of the poem? What special meaning does the poem have for you? How can you connect it to your life?

On pages 533 and 534, you can see an example of active reading and responding by Elizabeth Kerr of the Brookside School in Allendale, New Jersey. The notes in the side column include Elizabeth's thoughts and comments while reading "Miracles." Your own thoughts as you read may be different, because each reader responds differently to a poem.

LA BONNE AVENTURE (GOOD FORTUNE), 1939
René Magritte
Museum Boymans-van Beuningen, Rotterdam

Miracles

Walt Whitman

Why, who makes much of a miracle?
As to me I know of nothing else but miracles,
Whether I walk the streets of Manhattan,
Or dart my sight over the roofs of houses toward the sky,
5 Or wade with naked feet along the beach just in the edge of
the water,

Theme: *The title makes me think this poem will be about some impossible things that have happened in history.*

Sound: *The poet speaks in a regular way without using a specific rhyme or rhythm.*

Language: *This is unusual. I've heard of eyes darting, but not sight.*

Or stand under trees in the woods,
Or talk by day with any one I love . . .
Or sit at table at dinner with the rest,
Or look at strangers opposite me riding in the car,
10 Or watch honeybees busy around the hive of a summer
    forenoon[1]
Or animals feeding in the fields,
Or birds, or the wonderfulness of insects in the air,
Or the wonderfulness of the sundown, or of stars shining
    so quiet and bright,
Or the exquisite[2] delicate thin curve of the new moon in
    spring;
15 These with the rest, one and all, are to me miracles,
The whole referring, yet each distinct[3] and in its place.

To me every hour of the light and dark is a miracle,
Every cubic inch of space is a miracle,
Every square yard of the surface of the earth is spread with
    the same,
20 Every foot of the interior swarms[4] with the same.

To me the sea is a continual miracle,
The fishes that swim—the rocks—the motion of the waves—
    the ships with men in them,
What stranger miracles are there?

---

1. forenoon (fôr′ noon) *n*.: Morning.
2. exquisite (eks′ kwi zit) *adj*.: Very beautiful, especially in a delicate way.
3. distinct (dis tiŋkt′) *adj*.: Separate and different.
4. swarms (swôrmz) *v*.: Is filled or crowded.

Appearance: *The poet's use of "Or" so many times gives the poem a special look.*

Imagery: *I can picture all these things happening. They are normal, everyday things that make you feel good, light, and happy.*

Theme: *This means that if there were no miracles, nothing would exist. Life depends on miracles happening.*

Language: *This is a strange way of saying this. By "the same" he means "a miracle."*

Response: *I agree with what the poet says here and at the beginning. "As to me I know of nothing else but miracles." Nature is a miracle, and I can't picture the world without miracles.*

Walt Whitman (1819–1892) was born on Long Island but lived most of his life in Brooklyn, New York. He worked at many occupations—printer, carpenter, teacher, newspaper reporter—and praised the value of the common person in many of his poems. Called the father of modern poetry, most of his poems are highly original, using free verse to capture the various rhythms and moods of American life. They are collected in *Leaves of Grass*.

RESPONDING TO THE SELECTION

Your Response

1. Of all the "miracles" the poet mentions, which one do you find most full of wonder? Why?

Recalling

2. Find at least ten events the speaker considers miracles.
3. What are the first and second questions the speaker asks about miracles?

Interpreting

4. In what way is talking with a person you know a miracle?
5. In what way is the sea a continual miracle?
6. Think about the answer to the speaker's second question. How would you express the theme of the poem?

Applying

7. List at least five events you consider miracles

ANALYZING LITERATURE

Understanding Free Verse

Free verse is poetry that has no regular rhythmic pattern and no regular rhyme scheme. Usually, free verse uses the sounds and rhythms of natural speech to create its own unique musical quality. One way free verse creates rhythm is by using a similar word-order pattern from line to line.

1. What do you notice about word order in lines 4–14?
2. What do you notice about word order in lines 17–22?
3. What effect is created by the similar structure of the lines?

CRITICAL THINKING AND READING

Categorizing

A category is a group of related items. When you form categories, you put things that are sim-

ilar in the same group. For example, you might arrange the clothes in your closet into two groups: school clothes and play clothes. You might arrange the supplies you bring home into categories; for example, things that need to go directly into the refrigerator, canned goods, and cleaning supplies.

Arrange the events the speaker mentions in "Miracles" into groups.

1. Which events fit into the category "City Experiences"?
2. Which fit into the category "Wonders of the Natural World"?
3. Which fit into the category "Communicating With Others"?

THINKING AND WRITING

Writing a Poem About Miracles

Look over the list you created of things you consider miracles. Brainstorm with your classmates to add to this list. Then, using free verse, write a poem about miracles in everyday life. Revise your poem to be sure you have included enough details that appeal to the senses. Create a final draft, and share it with your classmates.

LEARNING OPTIONS

1. **Speaking and Listening.** Tell two or three people you know well about the theme of "Miracles." Interview them about what ordinary events they consider miracles. If they give you humorous replies, such as "Paying my bills" or "Getting an A in English," appreciate their humor and then ask them to take the question seriously. Share the responses you get with your classmates.
2. **Art.** Make a collage that illustrates the poem. You can cut pictures from discarded magazines and recycle such objects as old buttons, scraps of cloth, and pieces of yarn as part of your collage.

YOUR WRITING PROCESS

WRITING A LIMERICK

Write a limerick now. Say there was
An old man of some place, what he does
   Or perhaps what he doesn't.
   Or isn't or wasn't.
Want help with it? Give me a buzz.

"Poetry is all nouns and verbs."
Marianne Moore

There's no doubt about it—limericks are fun to read. As you may have discovered, however, they are even more fun to write. After all, who can resist the challenge of rhythmically setting up a joke and delivering its punch line in only five lines? See how inventive you can be when working together with several classmates on one of these rhyming jokes.

Focus

Assignment: Work with classmates to write a limerick.
Purpose: To entertain.
Audience: Your classmates and teacher.

Prewriting

1. Review the limerick form. Before you start to brainstorm with your partner or group, it's a good idea to review the patterns of rhythm and sound in a limerick. Read the definition of a limerick on pages 528 and 529.

2. Create a fill-in model. Create your own limerick model by writing a sentence or two with some of the words left out. Then save this model, or develop one of your own, to fill in during the drafting stage.

There once was a _____ from _____,
Who_____.
He (She) (It)_____
And _____,
And (But)_____.

3. Get in the mood. If you want to write a limerick, there's no better way to get into the swing of things than to read aloud a few that were written by others. With other members of your group, take turns reading aloud the three examples of limericks on page 529.

4. Brainstorm for humorous words. Which sounds funnier: "There once was a dog from the city" or "There once was a poodle from Perth"? Brainstorm to find specific and funny-sounding words that you can use. Also, try to come up with unpredictable or silly situations to include in your poem—the more outlandish, the better. List these words and situations.

Drafting

1. Write your first line. Refer to the model you created during the prewriting process. Fill it in with a few of the funny words you brainstormed to get.

2. Start to fill in your model. Work with your classmates to fill in each line of your model with appropriate words and descriptions. Don't be afraid to change your model if you have an inspiration.

Student Model

There once was a _cat_ from _Racine_,

Who_se eyes were a deep shade of green._

He (She) (It)_ blinked once or twice_

And _____,

And (But)_____.

---

3. Check your rhythms and rhymes by reading aloud. From time to time as you and your classmates fill in the blanks of your model, read your limerick aloud to one another. Look back at the prewriting chart to make sure that your poem is consistent with the limerick form.

Revising and Editing

1. Add punch to your poem. Is your limerick as catchy as it can be? Pay special attention to your verbs. In a limerick, the verbs drive the poem to its surprising conclusion.

2. Test your limerick on one or more peer editors. Exchange poems with another group. Consider the following questions as you review each other's work:

• Is the limerick humorous?
• Are the rhymes in the right places?
• Is the rhythm correct?

Writer's Hint

Be sure that the last word in the first line ends with a common enough sound so that you can easily find rhyming words for the second and fifth lines.

Tip for Using Verbs

Use lively **action verbs** that describe what someone or something is doing. Note, for example, the verbs "dote" and "quail" in the limerick at the top of page 529. These verbs are unusual—they aren't commonly used. That's what gives them an unpredictability and freshness. Keep these two qualities in mind as you choose strong action verbs for your own limerick.

Options for Publishing

• Have a person from your group read the limerick aloud to the class.
• Create a class book of limericks, complete with humorous illustrations.
• Hold a limerick contest in class. Select judges and determine a set of criteria to use for rating each poem.

Reviewing Your Writing

1. Did working with a group make it easier to write a limerick? Explain.
2. What part of writing a limerick were you best at?

YOUR WRITING PROCESS

WRITING A RESPONSE TO POETRY

> "If I feel physically as if the top of my head were taken off, I know that is poetry."
>
> **Emily Dickinson**

You probably have little trouble telling your friends and classmates how you responded to a movie, record, or television program. How would you tell them about your response to a poem? Suppose your class were assembling two anthologies of poetry, one titled *Hits* and the other *Misses*. Your job is to choose a poem you enjoyed for the first collection, or a poem you hated for the second, and write an explanation of your response.

Focus

Assignment: Choose a poem you especially liked or hated and explain your response.
Purpose: To tell why you responded the way you did.
Audience: Your classmates and teacher.

Prewriting

1. Recall your feelings. Did any of the poems in this unit make you want to slam the book shut and stop reading? Did any make you feel so enthusiastic that you wanted to discuss it with a friend or classmate? Write about a poem that caused you to react strongly, whether that reaction was positive or negative.

2. Respond to the poem without using words. Review the poem you have chosen; then make a drawing, painting, or collage that reflects how you feel when you read or hear the poem. You may depict a real scene, or you may just doodle or draw a pattern.

Student Model

"sugarfields" by Barbara Mahone

---

3. Freewrite about your response. After looking at your artwork, freewrite about your response to the poem. Don't worry about correct spelling, grammar, or punctuation. Jot down all your thoughts and feelings about the poem.

Drafting

1. Begin with a strong personal statement. Don't let your readers guess how you responded to the poem. Tell them immediately whether you responded positively or negatively.

> ### Student Model
>
> I know that Robert Frost's "Stopping by Woods on a Snowy Evening" is a famous poem, but I just don't see what the fuss is about.

2. Use quotations to back up your points. Readers will better understand your response if you illustrate your points with quotations from the poem. For instance, if you want to show how "The Highwayman" kept you in suspense, you might want to quote the following lines from the poem: "*Tlot-tlot; tlot-tlot*! Had they heard it? The horsehoofs ringing clear; / *Tlot-tlot, tlot-tlot*, in the distance? Were they deaf that they did not hear?"

Revising and Editing

1. Review your prewriting. In drafting your response, you may have lost sight of a feeling or thought you had about the poem. When you revise your rough draft, you might want to review your artwork and freewriting to see whether you left out anything important. If so, decide where in your essay you could include those feelings or ideas.

2. Replace vague words with precise terms. Your response will be more convincing if you are more specific.

> ### Student Model
>
> *onomatopoeia*
>
> In "The Highwayman" the use of ~~words that suggest sounds~~ really helped to keep me in suspense.

3. Get a response to your response. Have a classmate read your essay and answer the following questions:
- Are you clear about my reactions to the poem?
- Do I illustrate my points by quoting from the poem?
- Do I use precise terms whenever possible?

4. Proofread your response. Readers will more readily accept your response if it is free from errors in grammar and punctuation.

Grammar Tip

Indirect quotations are useful for summarizing what a poem's speaker or narrator said. Direct quotations, on the other hand, help to make a point in a stronger, more immediate way.

Options for Publishing

- Contribute the poem and your response to a class anthology titled *Hits* or for a class anthology titled *Misses*.
- Find a classmate who responded to the same poem and read one another's essays.

Reviewing Your Writing Process

1. Did you find it easier to write about a poem you liked or one you disliked? Explain.

2. Did drawing or painting help you to understand your response to the poem? Why or why not?

**AMANECER EN LA MONTAÑA
(DAWN ON THE MOUNTAIN), 1949**
Dr. Atl (Gerardo Murillo)
Patrimonio de Jalisco

MYTHS AND FOLK TALES AROUND THE WORLD

Gods and goddesses, talking animals, strange and wondrous events—these are some of the subjects of fables, myths, and folk tales. All such stories are very old. They come to us from the distant past. Although different writers retell these stories in print, most of them originated long before reading and writing began. They have survived by being handed down by word of mouth from generation to generation. Taken together, fables, myths, and folk tales make up what is known as the oral tradition of literature.

Why have these old tales survived through the centuries? One reason is that they are about subjects that people love to read or hear about. Superhuman characters and marvelous events always make for entertaining stories. Another reason is that these tales say so much about human nature and the world. In fact, they represent some of the earliest efforts of the human race to explain the world. Reading fables, myths, and folk tales should be both a pleasurable and rewarding experience.

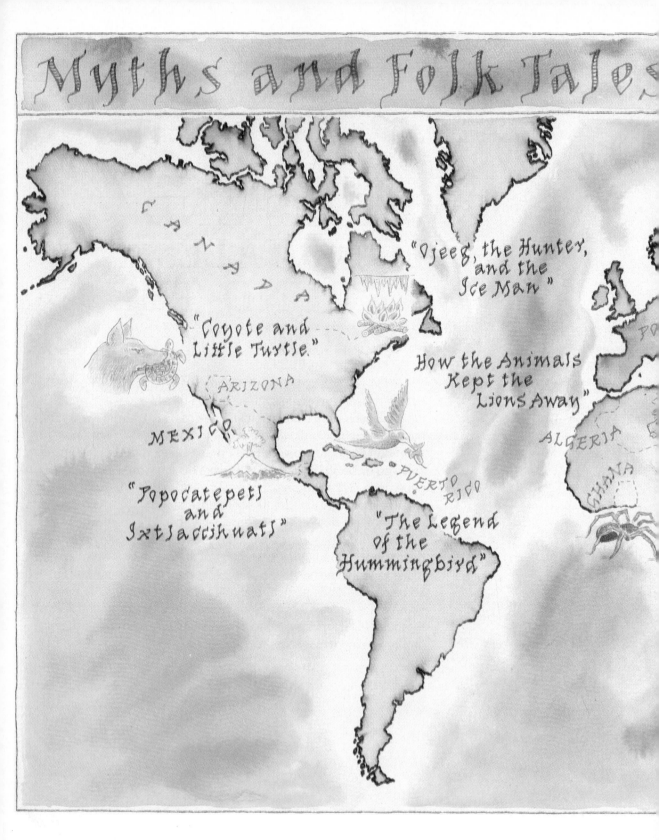

Myths and Folk Tales

"Ojeeg, the Hunter, and the Ice Man"

"Coyote and Little Turtle."

ARIZONA

CANADA

MEXICO

"How the Animals Kept the Lions Away"

ALGERIA

GHANA

PUERTO RICO

"Popocatepetl and Ixtlaccihuatl"

"The Legend of the Hummingbird"

Around the World.

"Let's Steal the Moon"

"The Fox and the Crow"

"The Pointing Finger"

GREECE

"Djuka Borrows a Pot"

SYRIA

CHINA

INDIA

THAILAND

VIETNAM

"The Little Lizard's Sorrow"

"The Mice that Set Elephants Free"

"The Wicked Weasel"

ZIMBABWE

0   1000   2000   3000   4000   5000   6000

Scale   in   Miles

Map   543

READING ACTIVELY

Myths and Folk Tales Around the World

BACKGROUND Myths and folk tales are among the oldest forms of literature. Myths are anonymous stories, often involving gods and goddesses, that either convey cultural ideals and beliefs or explain natural occurrences, such as the changing seasons or the path of the sun across the sky. Folk tales are similar to myths, but they are usually about ordinary people instead of gods. Fables are stories that teach moral lessons. The characters in fables are usually animals that speak and act like humans.

Every culture has developed its own tradition in regard to its myths and folk tales, and yet, when these traditions are compared and contrasted, many similarities become apparent. Most cultures have myths that explain natural events, fables that teach moral lessons, and folk tales that emphasize behaviors, attitudes, and ideals admired by the people who created them. As you read the stories in this unit, you will notice that different cultures, sometimes on opposite sides of the earth, have produced mythic and folk literature with common characters, themes, and purposes. You will also see how the literature of one culture can influence that of another.

READING STRATEGIES When reading the selections in this unit, you will encounter unique characteristics you may not have seen in the other forms of literature in this book. For example, the characters in fables are animals, but they speak and behave like people. The characters and places in the myths and folk tales have names that you may have trouble pronouncing. Many of the events in these tales fall into the category of fantasy, and the characters are often able to do strange or superhuman things.

Keep an open mind as you read these stories. Try to accept what they have to say and to learn as much as you can about the people in other cultures. You will find that although the tales were created long ago and sometimes far away, they convey feelings and ideas that people still have in today's world. Finally, as you read, interact with the literature by using the active reading strategies: question, visualize, predict, connect, evaluate, and respond.

Animal Fables

THE BLUE HORSE
Franz Marc

GUIDE FOR READING

Aesop

(about 620–560 B.C.) was an ancient Greek whose name was associated with a collection of wise tales about animals. Little is known about him, except that he was a slave who was later freed by his master. Actually many of Aesop's tales or fables were based on tales told long before his birth. Many of them were also rewritten by others after his death. They are fun to read and contain good advice.

The Town Mouse and the Country Mouse
The Fox and the Crow

Fables

A **fable** is a brief tale, in prose or verse, that teaches a lesson called a **moral.** Often this moral appears as a wise saying at the end of the tale. In Aesop's fables, the characters are animals who act like human beings and often illustrate human failings and weaknesses. However, other writers use human characters in their fables or even plants and objects that talk and behave like humans.

Focus

One of the fables you are about to read is about two mice who live in very different environments. One lives in a city, the other in the country. As the mice learn, each environment has both good qualities and bad.

Think about the place where you live. Is it a city, a small town, the suburbs, or a farm? Make a brief list of things you like about where you live. If you live in the country or in a small town, you might mention the clean air or the grass and trees. If you live in a city, you might enjoy the many things there are to do. Then list one or two things you do not especially like about where you live. When you finish reading the fable, see if your opinion of your hometown has changed at all.

Vocabulary

Knowing the following words will help you as you read these fables.

heartily (härt′ 'l ē) *adv.*: Warmly; completely (p. 547)

fare (fer) *n.*: Food (p. 547)

glossy (glôs′ ē) *adj.*: Smooth and shiny (p. 549)

surpass (sər pas′) *v.*: Be superior to (p. 549)

flatterers (flat′ ər ərz) *n.*: Those who praise a person insincerely in order to gain something for themselves (p. 549)

The Town Mouse and the Country Mouse

Aesop

Now you must know that a Town Mouse once upon a time went on a visit to his cousin in the country. He was rough and ready, this cousin, but he loved his town friend and made him heartily welcome. Beans and bacon, cheese and bread were all he had to offer, but he offered them freely. The Town Mouse rather turned up his long nose at this country fare, and said: "I cannot understand, Cousin, how you can put up with such poor food as this, but of course you cannot expect anything better in the country; come you with me and I will show you how to live. When you have been in town a week you will wonder how you could ever have stood a country life."

No sooner said than done: the two mice

set off for the town and arrived at the Town Mouse's residence late at night. "You will want some refreshment after our long journey," said the polite Town Mouse, and took his friend into the grand dining room. There they found the remains of a fine feast, and soon the two mice were eating up jellies and cakes and all that was nice. Suddenly they heard growling and barking.

"What is that?" said the Country Mouse.

"It is only the dogs of the house," answered the other.

"Only!" said the Country Mouse. "I do not like that music at my dinner."

Just at that moment the door flew open, in came two huge mastiffs,[1] and the two mice had to scamper down and run off.

"Good-by, Cousin," said the Country Mouse.

"What! going so soon?" said the other.

"Yes," he replied:

*"Better beans and bacon in peace
than cakes and ale in fear."*

---

1. mastiffs (mas' tifs) *n.*: Large, powerful, smooth-coated dogs with hanging lips and drooping ears. They were used for hunting and as watchdogs.

RESPONDING TO THE SELECTION

Your Response

1. Have you ever known someone from a place very different from your own? Did you feel or act differently around him or her? How did the person treat you?

Recalling

2. What disturbs the Town Mouse about his meal in the country?
3. What disturbs the Country Mouse about his meal in town?

Interpreting

4. Compare and contrast the two mice. Explain what traits each mouse represents.
5. Which mouse do you feel more sympathy for? Explain your answer.

Applying

6. Why do you think a fable with animal characters might teach a lesson better than a tale with human characters?

ANALYZING LITERATURE

Understanding Fables

A **fable** is a brief tale, in prose or verse, that teaches a lesson called a **moral**. In "The Town Mouse and the Country Mouse" each of the characters has a different approach to life. The moral suggests that the Country Mouse's point of view is better.

1. What is the moral of this fable?
2. Express the moral in your own words.
3. Explain why you agree or disagree with the moral.

THINKING AND WRITING

Writing a Fable

Write a fable with a moral that is the opposite of Aesop's lesson. The moral of your fable must be: *Better an interesting life with danger than a safe life that is dull.* Think of two contrasting animal characters for your fable. They can be animals of the same species, like the two mice, or different animals. Write a fable placing these characters in a modern setting. In revising your work, make sure that your tale really teaches the new moral. When you are finished, share your fable with your classmates.

The Fox and the Crow

Aesop

A Fox once saw a Crow fly off with a piece of cheese in its beak and settle on a branch of a tree. "That's for me, as I am a Fox," said Master Reynard,[1] and he walked up to the foot of the tree.

"Good day, Mistress Crow," he cried. "How well you are looking today: how glossy your feathers; how bright your eye. I feel sure your voice must surpass that of other birds, just as your figure does; let me hear but one song from you that I may greet you as the Queen of Birds."

The Crow lifted up her head and began to caw her best, but the moment she opened her mouth the piece of cheese fell to the ground, only to be snapped up by Master Fox. "That will do," said he. "That was all I wanted. In exchange for your cheese I will give you a piece of advice for the future—

"Do not trust flatterers."

---

1. Master Reynard (ren′ ərd): The fox in the medieval beast epic *Reynard the Fox;* therefore, a proper name for the fox in other stories.

RESPONDING TO THE SELECTION

Your Response

1. Do you think the Crow will ever be fooled again? Why or why not?

Recalling

2. How does the Crow lose the cheese?

Interpreting

3. What character traits do the Fox and the Crow represent?

4. How do the actions of these two animals support the moral?

5. The seventeenth-century Frenchman Jean de La Fontaine rewrote many of Aesop's fables and stamped them with his own style. He expressed the moral of "The Fox and the Crow" as follows: Learn that every flatterer/Lives at the flattered listener's cost. Compare this version of the moral with Aesop's. How would you rewrite the moral to stamp it with your own style?

Applying

6. What is it about human nature that allows flattery to do its work?

GUIDE FOR READING

India

This animal fable appears in the *Panchatantra,* a collection of stories from ancient India. Though scholars are unable to tell exactly when the stories were first created, they believe that these fables were first gathered together as a single work (the *Panchatantra,* which means the "Five Books") about 200 B.C.

Arthur W. Ryder completed his translation of the *Panchatantra* in 1925. When he called himself "the opposite of a scholar," he meant that his work could be enjoyed by book lovers everywhere.

The Mice That Set Elephants Free

Cultural Background

Like fables from other countries, those in the *Panchatantra* use as characters animals that can speak. The fables also illustrate valuable lessons about life. The mice and elephants in the story you are about to read exhibit traits that the writers believed an individual responsible for governing other people should have. These traits included intelligence, honor, and respect for the rights of others. Though the writers of the *Panchatantra* lived long ago in a very different culture, the lessons they taught about how people should treat one another still apply today.

Focus

Simply reading the title of this fable lets you know that it will concern mice and elephants. Make a list of everything you know about mice and another list of everything you know about elephants. Think about these animals' physical characteristics, their habitat, and the ways in which they behave. Compare your two lists. What differences are there between mice and elephants? What problems might arise when these two animals come in contact with each other?

Vocabulary

Knowing the following words will help you as you read "The Mice That Set Elephants Free."

diversions (də vur′ zhənz) *n.*: Things done for fun or relaxation (p. 551)

lumbering (lum′ bər iŋ) *adj.*: Awkward; clumsy (p. 551)

devise (di vīz′) *v.*: Think of; plan (p. 551)

prospered (präs′ pərd) *v.*: Grown; flourished (p. 551)

succession (sək sesh′ ən) *n.*: A number of persons or things

coming one after another (p. 551)

compassion (kəm pash′ ən) *n.*: A feeling of sorrow for others; a desire to help (p. 551)

reflected (ri flekt′ id) *v.*: Thought seriously (p. 552)

delivered (di liv′ ərd) *v.*: Set free; rescued (p. 552)

fettered (fet′ ərd) *adj.*: Tied up with ropes or chains (p. 552)

The Mice That Set Elephants Free

from **India: *The Panchatantra***

translated from the Sanskrit by Arthur W. Ryder

There was once a region where people, houses, and temples had fallen into decay. So the mice, who were old settlers there, occupied the chinks in the floors of stately dwellings with sons, grandsons (both in the male and female line), and further descendants as they were born, until their holes formed a dense tangle. They found uncommon happiness in a variety of festivals, dramatic performances (with plots of their own invention), wedding-feasts, eating-parties, drinking-bouts, and similar diversions. And so the time passed.

But into this scene burst an elephant-king, whose retinue numbered thousands. He, with his herd, had started for the lake upon information that there was water there. As he marched through the mouse community, he crushed faces, eyes, heads, and necks of such mice as he encountered.

Then the survivors held a convention. "We are being killed," they said, "by these lumbering elephants—curse them! If they come this way again, there will not be mice enough for seed.[1] Besides:

An elephant will kill you, if
He touch; a serpent if he sniff;
King's laughter has a deadly sting;
A rascal kills by honoring.[2]

Therefore let us devise a remedy effective in this crisis."

When they had done so, a certain number went to the lake, bowed before the elephant-king, and said respectfully: "O King, not far from here is our community, inherited from a long line of ancestors. There we have prospered through a long succession of sons and grandsons. Now you gentlemen, while coming here to water, have destroyed us by the thousand. Furthermore, if you travel that way again, there will not be enough of us for seed. If then you feel compassion toward us, pray travel another path. Consider the fact that even creatures of our size will some day prove of some service."

And the elephant-king turned over in his mind what he had heard, decided that the statement of the mice was entirely logical, and granted their request.

---

1. there will not be mice enough for seed: All the mice will die off.

2. An elephant . . . by honoring: This verse shows how the mice realize each kind of problem requires its own solution.

DARA SHIKOH RIDING AN ALBINO ELEPHANT, c. 1631
Mughal
Harvard University Art Museums

Now in the course of time a certain king commanded his elephant-trappers to trap elephants. And they constructed a so-called water-trap, caught the king with his herd, three days later dragged him out with a great tackle made of ropes and things,[3] and tied him to stout trees in that very bit of forest.

When the trappers had gone, the elephant-king reflected thus: "In what manner, or through whose assistance, shall I be delivered?" Then it occurred to him: "We have no means of deliverance except those mice."

So the king sent the mice an exact description of his disastrous position in the trap through one of his personal retinue, an elephant-cow[4] who had not ventured into the trap, and who had previous information of the mouse community.

When the mice learned the matter, they gathered by the thousand, eager to return the favor shown them, and visited the elephant herd. And seeing king and herd fettered, they gnawed the guy-ropes where they stood, then swarmed up the branches, and by cutting the ropes aloft, set their friends free.

"And that is why I say:

Make friends, make friends,
     however strong
  Or weak they be:
Recall the captive elephants
     That mice set free."

---

3. tackle made of ropes and things: The tackle was a huge piece of equipment made with pulleys, ropes, and poles.

---

4. elephant-cow: A female elephant.

Your Response

1. How do you feel when someone does you a favor? How do you feel when you return a favor?

Recalling

2. Why do the elephants march through the mouse community?
3. How do the mice convince the elephant-king to travel a different way in the future?
4. What happens to the elephants that causes them to call upon the mice for help?

Interpreting

5. What kinds of traits do the mice have? Which of their actions display these traits?
6. How would you describe the elephant-king's personality? Explain.

Applying

7. What problems must people sometimes overcome to live peacefully together?
8. What are the benefits of getting along with different kinds of people?

ANALYZING LITERATURE

Understanding Cultural Background

Fables usually teach lessons about life. They can also inform you about different times and cultures. Certain details in "The Mice That Set Elephants Free" can help you imagine what India looked like hundreds of years ago. For example, the mice lived in the ruins of stately houses and temples.

1. Identify another descriptive detail that helps to show what India was like long ago.
2. Identify an action of one of the characters in the fable that illustrates a custom of the people in India long ago.

CRITICAL THINKING AND READING

Understanding Poetry in Fables

"The Mice That Set Elephants Free" contains two short verses. The first, spoken by the mice, is a warning against various kinds of danger. In the second the author states the fable's moral.

1. Why are lessons in verse form easier to remember?
2. Do you think the second poem is an effective way to end the fable? Why or why not?

THINKING AND WRITING

Writing a Fable Episode

Write a scene that continues the fable you just read. Describe a second encounter between the mice and the elephants. What do you think the elephants and mice might say to one another the next time they meet? What danger might they both avoid by cooperating with one another? Make the animals behave as they do in the fable.

LEARNING OPTION

Cross-curricular Connection. The fable you just read shows how weak and strong animals were able to help each other. In reality, animals sometimes help people, too. For example, you may have learned in science class how snakes help farmers by killing pests that destroy crops or how birds eat insects, like mosquitoes, that bother us. People, in turn, can help animals by controlling hunting practices and creating wildlife preserves. Use your own knowledge and the information from books about ecology to present a report—either oral or written—about other ways that animals and people help one another today.

GUIDE FOR READING

Algeria

Though the Arab fable you are about to read comes from the deserts of Algeria in northwest Africa, it was probably inspired by a part of the *Panchatantra,* a collection of ancient tales from India. It is an example of how the literature of one culture can influence that of another. (See the Multicultural Connection, p. 557)

Inea Bushnaq was born in Jerusalem. Her other books include *The Arabs in Israel* and *Betrayal at the Vel d'Hiv.* She now lives in New York City.

How the Animals Kept the Lions Away

Humor in Fables

Before movie theaters and television, people of Arab countries often entertained one another and their children by telling tales. Whether in a cafe or at home by the fire, storytellers were sure to attract eager listeners. To keep their audiences involved, these storytellers told tales that were either a little scary or very funny. Many of the humorous tales involved animal characters who do ridiculous things or who outsmart one another.

Focus

Do you know what it means to "outsmart" someone? Have you ever been outsmarted? Perhaps you have outsmarted someone else. Write down a few examples of real experiences you have had or situations you have seen or read about that show how someone was outsmarted.

In the fable you are about to read, several animals—a rooster, a donkey, a ram, and a dog—work together to outsmart a dangerous foe.

Vocabulary

Knowing the following words will help you as you read "How the Animals Kept the Lions Away."

unfrequented (un frē′ kwənt əd) *adj.*: Not often visited (p. 555)

feigned (fānd) *v.*: Pretended (p. 555)

perseverance (pʉr sə vir′ əns) *n.*: Continued effort (p. 555)

discreet (dis krēt′) *adj.*: Careful about what one says (p. 555)

cantered (kan′ tərd) *v.*: Moved at an easy gallop (p. 555)

conceded (kən sēd′ əd) *v.*: Admitted as true (p. 555)

merit (mer′ it) *n.*: Worth; goodness (p. 555)

suppress (sə pres′) *v.*: Keep back (p. 556)

complied (kəm plīd′) *v.*: Did what was asked (p. 556)

chided (chīd′ əd) *v.*: Scolded (p. 556)

How the Animals Kept the Lions Away

from Algeria

Inea Bushnaq

Once when a tribe of Bedouins[1] moved their camp to a new site, they left behind them a lame rooster, a broken-backed donkey, a sick ram, and a desert greyhound suffering from mange. The animals swore brotherhood and determined to live together. They wandered until they came to an unfrequented oasis, where they decided to settle.

One day when the rooster was flying to the top of a tree, he noticed something important: the opening to a grain silo full of barley. The food was wholesome, and he began to visit the place daily. Soon his feathers became glossy as polished silk, and his comb began to glow like the fire inside a ruby. The donkey, observing the improvements, asked his friend, "How is it that your cap has grown so bright?" The rooster feigned surprise and tried to change the subject. But with the perseverance of his race, the donkey continued to pester the fowl until at last he said, "Very well, I shall show you the reason why my cap has grown so bright, but it must remain a secret between us." The donkey promised to be discreet and the rooster led him to the grain silo.

At the sight of the barley the donkey flung himself into the grain and fed until he could eat no more. Brimming with well-being, he danced back to the others and said, "I feel the urge to sing come upon me. With your permission I shall bray awhile!" The animals objected. "What if a lion should hear you?" they said. "He will surely come and devour us all!" But despite his friends, the donkey could not contain his high spirits. He cantered off by himself and began to bray long and noisily.

Now, a lion did hear the sound and came streaking across the wilderness on his silent feet until he was within one spring of the donkey. Almost too late the donkey became aware of the danger. "Sire," he said, "I see that my fate has been written, but I beg you to do me the favor not to devour me without my friends. It would be more honorable, considering that the animals of this oasis have sworn an oath of brotherhood to live together and die together, if you made an end of us all without exception." The lion conceded the merit of this plea and allowed the donkey to guide him to his friends.

When the other animals saw the donkey leading a lion toward them, they put their heads together and said, "How can we defend ourselves against a lion!" And they made their plans. When the lion came near they all

---

1. Bedouins (be′ do͞o inz′): Any of the Arab tribes that live a nomadic existence (moving from place to place in the desert).

KALİLA AND DIMNA: THE LION AND THE JACKAL, c. 1200 (detail)
Unknown Arabian Artist
Bibliothèque Nationale, Paris

said with one voice, "Greetings and welcome, uncle lion!" Then the ram butted him in his side and knocked the breath out of his lungs, the rooster flew up and pecked at his eyes, and the dog buried his teeth in the lion's throat. The lion died, of course. His flesh was given to the dog to eat, but the animals kept his skin and tanned it.

After that the four friends were able to live in peace for a time. However, soon the donkey was announcing, "I sense that I must bray again!" "Be still, O ill-omened animal!" said the others. But the donkey could not suppress his feelings, and his unmelodious call rang repeatedly in the air.

A second lion prowling that quarter of the desert was attracted to the braying. With water running in his mouth, he hurried to the oasis. Again the donkey invited the lion to kill all the animals of the oasis together, and the lion gladly complied. This time too the rooster, the ram, and the dog put their heads together when they saw the lion approaching and made a plan.

But what they said to the visitor was, "Welcome, may you be a thousand times wel-come!" Then the rooster hinted to the ram, "Our guest should be made comfortable and have a carpet to sit on!" The ram trotted into their dwelling and brought out the tanned lion skin. "Be ashamed, O ram!" chided the rooster when he saw him. "Our guest is of a noble tribe. His presence among us is an honor. Do you want to disgrace us by offering him that old, worn-out mat?" Meekly the ram carried the lion skin back into the house and brought it out a second time. This time the dog expressed impatience. "Surely we have a softer carpet than that, O ram! Besides, this one is quite faded." Obediently the ram took the lion skin inside and returned with it a third time. Now the donkey chimed in, "For one of such eminence as the lion, nothing but the finest can serve the occasion! Choose more carefully from among our store!" The ram withdrew into the house, but the lion did not linger further. He jumped to his feet and without bidding his hosts a formal farewell, ran away as fast as he was able.

Although the donkey continued to bray from time to time, no lion was seen near the animals' oasis again.

Your Response

1. Which of the animals do you think is the smartest? Why?

Recalling

2. How are the lions attracted to the oasis both times?

Interpreting

3. Why doesn't the rooster or the donkey tell the other animals about the grain?
4. Which of the animals seems to benefit the most from their pact of brotherhood? Which animal contributes the least?
5. Why does the second lion run away?

Applying

6. How do you and your friends benefit by cooperating with one another? How can people in general benefit from cooperation?

ANALYZING LITERATURE

Understanding Humor in Fables

Animal fables are often funny because of the personalities of the animals and because of what the animals do. For example, in this fable, the donkey cannot control himself and must bray even though he knows he might attract a lion.

1. How is the behavior of both lions humorous?
2. How is the way the animals speak funny?

THINKING AND WRITING

Comparing and Contrasting Characters

What a character does and says in a story reveals that character's personality. Write several paragraphs comparing and contrasting the personalities of two of the animals in "How the Animals Kept the Lions Away." Use the animals' actions and what they say to support your ideas.

MULTICULTURAL CONNECTION

The Panchatantra and Arabic Folk Tales

"How the Animals Kept the Lions Away" is a fable from Algeria. This and other Arabic folk tales were influenced by an ancient collection of fables from India, the *Panchatantra* (pun' chə tun' trə). "The Mice That Set Elephants Free," page 551, comes from this Indian collection.

A "how-to" book for rulers. The *Panchatantra*, which means "five books," was written by an Indian wise man named Vishnu Sharma. An ancient Hindu king asked Vishnu Sharma to teach his sons how to be good and clever kings. Vishnu Sharma then wrote the stories in the *Panchatantra* to guide the young princes.

From Indian to Arabic. The *Panchatantra* became well known outside of India as the stories were retold by travelers who had visited there. As early as the sixth century, the *Panchatantra* was translated into Pahlavi (Middle Persian) and then into Arabic. The *Panchatantra* had a great influence on Arabic folk tales and helped shape *The Arabian Nights*, a famous collection of Arabic stories.

From Arabic into many languages. The Arabic translation was later translated into several other languages, including Greek, Hebrew, and Spanish. From Greece, the stories traveled to the rest of Europe, where they came to be known as the *Tales of Bidpai*.

Exploring and Sharing

Find a fable that originated in another country. What moral lesson does it teach? Discuss the story in class.

GUIDE FOR READING

The Wicked Weasel

Motivation in Fables

Motivation refers to the reasons why characters in stories do certain things. Often in a fable, an animal acts in a certain way either to kill another animal for food or to avoid being killed and eaten. Understanding the different motivations of the animals in a fable can help you understand the lesson the fable teaches. In "The Wicked Weasel," the weasel, squirrels, and mice are motivated to act in certain ways for very different reasons.

Focus

Before reading "The Wicked Weasel," locate Thailand on the map that appears on pages 542 and 543. Then find the other countries that produced the animal fables collected in this unit. These countries include Greece, India, and Algeria. It is remarkable that the people in these countries, located far apart in Europe, Asia, and Africa, have told fables so similar to one another. Each contains talking animals, and in two of the fables, groups of animals must save themselves from being killed. Write a few sentences exploring possible reasons why these fables are so much alike.

As you read "The Wicked Weasel," ask yourself the following questions: How is this fable similar to other fables? Is an animal or a group of animals threatened by another? How do the animals get into trouble? Do the animals work together to save themselves?

Thailand

This animal fable comes from Thailand, a country in Southeast Asia. Once called Siam, Thailand is a land of mountains, deep valleys, and dense forests. In fact almost 60 percent of the country is forest. Along with Vietnam, Cambodia, and other countries, Thailand makes up what is known as Indochina.

Alan Feinstein (1931–   ) has traveled widely throughout the world and has collected stories from many of the countries he has visited. He is the author of a novel, *Triumph!*

The Wicked Weasel

from **Thailand**

Alan Feinstein

Years ago, when Pakchong was a forest, a weasel came traveling by one day. And he saw many mice and squirrels there.

"This looks like a good place for me to live," he said to himself. So he moved right into an empty cave and went to sleep.

Bright and early the next morning he awoke and went for a walk through the woods. When the mice and squirrels saw him they all fled behind bushes and trees. They had never seen a weasel before and he seemed so big to them that they thought it would be wise to keep away from this strange creature until they knew more about him. But the weasel paid no attention to them. He seemed quite harmless.

The weasel reached a hill in the middle of the forest.

"Ah, this looks like a perfect place for me to stay during the day," he said. And he climbed the hill. Then he sat down on a big stone right at the top.

"Would you please get off me?" said the stone.

"Why?" said the weasel. "You're not going anywhere."

"How long are you planning to sit on me?" asked the stone.

"Every day," answered the weasel. "For a hundred years if I want to."

So what could the poor stone do?

Sitting on the stone, the weasel lifted his front legs and looked toward the sky. And he held himself perfectly still.

When the mice and the squirrels saw the weasel sitting this way, looking toward the heavens, they were very curious. And the longer he sat there, the more curious they became. Finally, they decided to send a mouse and a squirrel to ask him what he was doing.

So the chosen mouse and squirrel scampered up the hill to him.

"What are you doing?" asked the mouse.

"Why are you sitting like that?" asked the squirrel.

"I'm praying," said the weasel, holding himself perfectly still.

The mouse and the squirrel watched him for a while. Then they came back down the hill to the other mice and squirrels and told them what the weasel had said.

They all watched the weasel for a long time. And the longer they watched him, the surer they became that he must be a great animal.

"We should pay him our respects," said the mice.

"Yes, we should indeed," agreed the squirrels.

When the sun went down, the weasel lowered his front legs and descended the hill.

The mice and the squirrels were waiting for him.

"We want to pay you our respects," they told him.

"Thank you," said the weasel.

Then all the mice and squirrels walked around him three times in a single line and then went home. But they didn't realize that the last mouse in line to walk past the weasel was not with them any more.

The following morning, the weasel climbed the hill again, sat down on the big stone, lifted his front legs and looked toward the heavens. And he sat perfectly still.

When the sun sank, the weasel came down from the hill and all the mice and squirrels walked around him again three times. Today a squirrel was the last one to pass the weasel. That was the end of the poor squirrel.

Every day the weasel would take the same position on the big stone and the mice and squirrels would wait for him to come down so they could walk around him three times to pay their respects. And every day there was one less of them.

Before long, some of the mice and squirrels noticed that there were many fewer of them than there used to be.

"Could the weasel be the cause of it?" they wondered.

So, the next morning, as soon as the weasel had taken his position on the hill, they went to his cave. And there they found the bones of the missing mice and squirrels.

"We must do something!" they cried.

"But what can we do?" they asked each other. "The weasel is so much bigger than we are."

They thought and thought. Then a squirrel had an idea. And he told it to the others.

So, they all went to the hill where the weasel was and waited for him to start down. And, as he did, several of the mice and squir-

SQUIRRELS, 1986
Cheng-Khee Chee
Courtesy of the Artist

rels who had crept around to the other side of the hill dashed up the back slope. When they reached the top of the hill, they pushed as hard as they could at the big stone.

The stone began to move.

They kept pushing.

The stone started falling. And it caught

up to the weasel and rolled right on top of him.

The weasel tried to get up. But he couldn't budge the stone. The mice and the squirrels danced with glee.

"Get off me, get off me!" the weasel cried to the stone.

"Why?" said the stone. "I'm not going anywhere."

"How long are you planning to sit on me?" whined the weasel.

"Oh, for about a hundred years," answered the stone.

Which is just what he did.

Your Response

1. Do you think the weasel got what he deserved? Explain.

Recalling

2. Why do the mice and squirrels stay away from the weasel at first?
3. When do the animals realize that the weasel is not so friendly?

Interpreting

4. What does the weasel do to win the other animals' trust?
5. In what way do the mice and squirrels change from the beginning to the end of the fable?

Applying

6. How else might the mice and squirrels have solved their problem?
7. What other stories can you think of in which someone gets hurt in the way he or she hurts others? Does this ever happen in real life? Explain.

ANALYZING LITERATURE

Understanding Motivation in Fables

Understanding why characters do things can add to your understanding of a story. For example, knowing that the weasel wants to eat the animals helps you understand his unusual behavior. Now think about the other characters.

1. Why must the mice and squirrels kill the weasel in the end?
2. Why does the rock say he is planning to sit on the weasel for a hundred years?

CRITICAL THINKING AND READING

Understanding Clues in Fables

The squirrel's idea for getting rid of the weasel is never directly stated. Certain clues in the fable, however, let you know that the animals are going to push the stone on the weasel, even before they do it.

1. As the weasel starts down the hill, some mice and squirrels run up the hill. What does this detail tell you about the animals' plan?
2. Identify two other clues that helped you know that the animals were going to push the stone down on the weasel.

THINKING AND WRITING

Extending Dialogue

At the end of the fable, the weasel pleads with the rock to get off him, and the rock refuses. What if the weasel had argued longer with the rock? Write a brief dialogue in which you extend the conversation between the rock and the weasel. What might the weasel say to convince the rock to move? How would the rock respond? Who would win the argument? Take care to punctuate direct quotations correctly.

LEARNING OPTION

Art. Imagine a newspaper cartoon called "The Wicked Weasel." Then draw your own cartoon illustrating the funnier scenes from the fable, such as the animals walking around the weasel or the weasel arguing with the stone on top of him. Color your cartoon and put the dialogue in balloons.

Tricksters, Rascals, and Fools

TEWA CLOWNS FOR A DONKEY RIDE
Neal David, Sr.
Private Collection

All Stories Are Anansi's

Folk Tales: The Trickster

Like fables, many folk tales contain animals that talk and behave like humans. One of the best-loved animal characters in folk tales is the **trickster,** who relies on brains rather than strength or speed. The trickster is usually able to outwit bigger and stronger animals. For many North American Indians, the coyote played the role of the shrewd trickster. In African folklore, however, the slyest creature is often Kwaku Anansi (kwä′ ko͞o ə nän′ sē), the spider.

Focus

On the map on pages 542 and 543, locate the country of Ghana on Africa's western coast. The Ashanti are one of the major groups of people who live in this West African country. Much of the land in Ghana is tropical forest, which is the setting of "All Stories Are Anansi's." Before you read, imagine the kinds of plants and animals you might actually find in a tropical forest and write a few sentences describing them.

Vocabulary

Knowing the following words will help you as you read "All Stories Are Anansi's."

yearned (yʉrnd) *v.*: Wanted very much (p. 565)

gourd (gôrd) *n.*: Fruit of a certain kind of plant; the dried, hollowed shell of this fruit is used as a drinking cup or dipper (p. 565)

acknowledge (ək näl′ ij) *v.*: To recognize and admit (p. 566)

Though English is the official language of Ghana, the traditional language of the Ashanti is Akan. In the tale several Akan words are used as names. Use the pronunciation key at the bottom of page 565 to help you pronounce these Akan words correctly.

The Ashanti

This folk tale comes from the **Ashanti** (ə shän′ tē), who ruled a large empire in West Africa during the 1700's and 1800's. Today, the Ashanti are an important people in the West African country of Ghana. They have made key contributions to farming, mining, and forestry. The Ashanti have also earned a reputation as skillful weavers.

Harold Courlander (1908–   ) received a Guggenheim fellowship for work on African culture and has written versions of folk tales from many nations.

All Stories Are Anansi's

from **the Ashanti (Ghana)**

Harold Courlander

In the beginning, all tales and stories belonged to Nyame,[1] the Sky God. But Kwaku Anansi, the spider, yearned to be the owner of all the stories known in the world, and he went to Nyame and offered to buy them.

The Sky God said: "I am willing to sell the stories, but the price is high. Many people have come to me offering to buy, but the price was too high for them. Rich and powerful families have not been able to pay. Do you think you can do it?"

Anansi replied to the Sky God: "I can do it. What is the price?"

"My price is three things," the Sky God said. "I must first have Mmoboro,[2] the hornets. I must then have Onini,[3] the great python. I must then have Osebo,[4] the leopard. For these things I will sell you the right to tell all stories."

Anansi said: "I will bring them."

He went home and made his plans. He first cut a gourd from a vine and made a small hole in it. He took a large calabash[5] and filled it with water. He went to the tree where the hornets lived. He poured some of the water over himself, so that he was dripping. He threw some water over the hornets, so that they too were dripping. Then he put the calabash on his head, as though to protect himself from a storm, and called out to the hornets: "Are you foolish people? Why do you stay in the rain that is falling?"

The hornets answered: "Where shall we go?"

"Go here, in this dry gourd," Anansi told them.

The hornets thanked him and flew into the gourd through the small hole. When the last of them had entered, Anansi plugged the hole with a ball of grass, saying: "Oh, yes, but you are really foolish people!"

He took the gourd full of hornets to Nyame, the Sky God. The Sky God accepted them. He said: "There are two more things."

Anansi returned to the forest and cut a long bamboo pole and some strong vines. Then he walked toward the house of Onini, the python, talking to himself. He said: "My wife is stupid. I say he is longer and stronger. My wife says he is shorter and weaker. I give him more respect. She gives him less respect. Is she right or am I right? I am right, he is longer. I am right, he is stronger."

When Onini, the python, heard Anansi talking to himself, he said: "Why are you arguing this way with yourself?"

---

1. **Nyame** (nē ä′ mē)
2. **Mmoboro** (mō bô′ rō)
3. **Onini** (ō nē′ nē)
4. **Osebo** (ō sä′ bō)
5. **calabash** (kal′ ə bash′) *n.*: A large fruit that is dried and made into a bowl or cup.

"All Stories Are Anansi's" in *The Hat-Shaking Dance And Other Ashanti Tales from Ghana,* by Harold Courlander with Albert Kofi Prempeh. Harcourt Brace Jovanovich. Reprinted by permission of Harold Courlander. © 1957, 1985 by Harold Courlander.

The spider replied: "Ah, I have had a dispute with my wife. She says you are shorter and weaker than this bamboo pole. I say you are longer and stronger."

Onini said: "It's useless and silly to argue when you can find out the truth. Bring the pole and we will measure."

So Anansi laid the pole on the ground, and the python came and stretched himself out beside it.

"You seem a little short," Anansi said.

The python stretched further.

"A little more," Anansi said.

"I can stretch no more," Onini said.

"When you stretch at one end, you get shorter at the other end," Anansi said. "Let me tie you at the front so you don't slip."

He tied Onini's head to the pole. Then he went to the other end and tied the tail to the pole. He wrapped the vine all around Onini, until the python couldn't move.

"Onini," Anansi said, "it turns out that my wife was right and I was wrong. You are shorter than the pole and weaker. My opinion wasn't as good as my wife's. But you were even more foolish than I, and you are now my prisoner."

Anansi carried the python to Nyame, the Sky God, who said: "There is one thing more."

Osebo, the leopard, was next. Anansi went into the forest and dug a deep pit where the leopard was accustomed to walk. He covered it with small branches and leaves and put dust on it, so that it was impossible to tell where the pit was. Anansi went away and hid. When Osebo came prowling in the black of night, he stepped into the trap Anansi had prepared and fell to the bottom. Anansi heard the sound of the leopard falling, and he said: "Ah, Osebo, you are half-foolish!"

When morning came, Anansi went to the pit and saw the leopard there.

"Osebo," he asked, "what are you doing in this hole?"

"I have fallen into a trap," Osebo said. "Help me out."

"I would gladly help you," Anansi said. "But I'm sure that if I bring you out, I will have no thanks for it. You will get hungry, and later on you will be wanting to eat me and my children."

"I swear it won't happen!" Osebo said.

"Very well. Since you swear it, I will take you out." Anansi said.

He bent a tall green tree toward the ground, so that its top was over the pit, and he tied it that way. Then he tied a rope to the top of the tree and dropped the other end of it into the pit.

"Tie this to your tail," he said.

Osebo tied the rope to his tail.

"Is it well tied?" Anansi asked.

"Yes, it is well tied," the leopard said.

"In that case," Anansi said, "you are not merely half-foolish, you are all-foolish."

And he took his knife and cut the other rope, the one that held the tree bowed to the ground. The tree straightened up with a snap, pulling Osebo out of the hole. He hung in the air head downward, twisting and turning. And while he hung this way, Anansi killed him with his weapons.

Then he took the body of the leopard and carried it to Nyame, the Sky God, saying: "Here is the third thing. Now I have paid the price."

Nyame said to him: "Kwaku Anansi, great warriors and chiefs have tried, but they have been unable to do it. You have done it. Therefore, I will give you the stories. From this day onward, all stories belong to you. Whenever a man tells a story, he must acknowledge that it is Anansi's tale."

In this way Anansi, the spider, became the owner of all stories that are told. To Anansi all these tales belong.

RESPONDING TO THE SELECTION

Your Response

1. What characteristics of spiders do you think prompted the Ashanti and other African peoples to cast one as the trickster figure in their folk tales?

Recalling

2. What does Anansi want from Nyame? What is Nyame's price?
3. How does Anansi capture the hornets, the python, and the leopard?

Interpreting

4. Why do you think Anansi values so highly what Nyame owns?
5. What is Anansi's attitude toward the other animals?
6. Why is Anansi able to do what great warriors and chiefs have tried to do but have been unable to do?

Applying

7. Why do you think people enjoy folk tales in which animals behave like humans?

ANALYZING LITERATURE

Understanding the Trickster in Folklore

The trickster is a character in folklore, usually an animal, who relies on brains rather than strength or speed to accomplish his or her goals. In "All Stories Are Anansi's," the spider fools animals that could easily defeat him in a contest of strength.

1. What qualities does Anansi display?
2. How does each of these qualities help him succeed?
3. Why do you think the trickster has been such a popular character in folklore?
4. Modern versions of the trickster appear in literature and movies. For example, Captain Kirk of *Star Trek* displays many of the trickster's characteristics. What other figures can be considered tricksters? Explain your choices.

CRITICAL THINKING AND READING

Making Inferences About Characters

An **inference** is a conclusion based on evidence. You can make inferences about animal characters in folk tales just as you would about a character in a short story or novel. In "All Stories Are Anansi's," the trickster helps you to make inferences about the other animals by pointing up their weaknesses.

1. What can you infer about the hornets based on their response to Anansi's warning?
2. What do you infer about the python when he keeps stretching to make himself as long as the pole?
3. Why must a trickster be able to make inferences about other animals?

THINKING AND WRITING

Writing a Folk Tale

Write your own folk tale about a trickster like Anansi. First give your character some goal to be achieved by trickery. Create three animal characters your trickster must deceive. When you revise your tale, try to increase the cleverness of the tricks. You might also try to make your tale convey an idea or teach a lesson. Share your folk tale with your classmates.

LEARNING OPTIONS

1. **Art.** What do you think the spider Anansi looks like? Is he large? Does he have long legs? What does his face look like? Using details from the tale you just read, make some imaginative drawings of Anansi as he captures the different animals. Display the drawings in your classroom.
2. **Cross-curricular Connection.** Use books from science class and from a library to find out more about spiders. In particular, learn about spiders that live in the tropical forests of West Africa. Prepare a brief presentation for class, outlining the spiders' appearances, surroundings, and feeding habits.

GUIDE FOR READING

The Hopi

The tale you are about to read comes from the Hopi, a Native American people. Set in the southwest United States, where the Hopi have lived for hundreds of years, the tale features one of the most humorous and popular characters in Native American literature, the Coyote.

Ekkehart Malotki was born in Germany but is now a naturalized American. He is a philologist and linguist who has extensively studied the Hopi language and oral tradition.

Coyote and Little Turtle

The Trickster's Victim

Folk tales often contain tricksters who use cleverness to get what they want, which is usually food. The trickster may want to steal food from another animal, or he may simply want to kill and eat the animal. The animal being tricked is the **trickster's victim.** Tricksters usually get what they want, but sometimes the trickster's victim turns out to be smarter than the trickster! In "Coyote and Little Turtle," you will discover how the well-known trickster Coyote is beaten at his own game.

Focus

Folk tales often contain characters who, although they may be small and weak, are able to outwit much larger and stronger foes. What stories do you know about small characters who use their brains to protect themselves from powerful enemies? Write a brief summary of one of these stories. How was the weaker character threatened? What method did he or she use to fend off the stronger one?

Vocabulary

Knowing the following words will help you as you read "Coyote and Little Turtle."

plodding (pläd′ iŋ) *adj.*: Walking or moving heavily (p. 569)
clambered (klam′ bərd) *v.*: Climbed with effort (p. 569)
resign (ri zīn′) *v.*: Accept without complaining (p. 569)
abruptly (ə brupt′ lē) *adv.*: Suddenly (p. 570)
persisted (pʉr sist′ id) *v.*: Refused to give up (p. 570)

consent (kən sent′) *v.*: Agree (p. 570)
intention (in ten′ shən) *n.*: Anything intended or planned (p. 572)
presently (prez′ ənt lē) *adv.*: Soon (p. 572)
gullible (gul′ ə b'l) *adj.*: Easily tricked (p. 572)

Coyote and Little Turtle

from **the Hopi**

Ekkehart Malotki

Aliksa'i.[1] They say people were living in Orayvi.[2] They had settled there long ago, I guess. And west of Leenangva the Turtles also had their home. At the spring there, marsh grass and rushes would grow. The same was true over at Mumurva, and it was this place that the Turtles usually headed to for food.

Now the rains had failed, and in pond after pond the water had dried up; neither rushes nor cattails[3] grew anymore. The poor Turtles were starving, so their mother said to them, "I suppose we have to leave for home. We can't find any food around here." They lived over at Sakwavayu, and they would have to return to that place.

Because it was the height of summertime, the ground was extremely hot. One of the children was still quite small and not very strong yet. He was the youngest of them all, and, because he suffered from the heat, the poor thing had crawled under a saltbush.[4] Under there the air was stirring a little, which helped him cool off somewhat, and finally he fell into a relaxing sleep.

All the Turtles were going to return home now, but the mother had so many offspring that I believe it completely escaped her that her baby was not with them. So when they started out, they forgot all about him and left him there. They made their way from Is-mo'wala south past Hovaqaptsomo. What a suffocating heat it was! The ground was burning hot, and the sand was dry and loose. Plodding along, they came to a ridge in the area of Songoopavi. They clambered up, and when they were on top, they turned around only to discover that the youngest was nowhere in sight. "Well," cried Mother Turtle, "some animal must have found him by now and has probably carried him off. We will never find him now. There is no point going back and looking for him. We have to go on."

So the Turtles marched on without waiting for the youngest one. They were sad but had to resign themselves to the situation.

They had already traveled far away when Little Turtle finally woke up. He arose and realized that the others had left him all by himself. The poor thing burst into tears and cried and cried. He crawled out from under the saltbush where he had slept. He glanced around and noticed that the others had headed south. Since they were turtles, they had ambled along scratching the ground

---

1. Aliksa'i (ə lēk' sī): Hopi for "Listen."

2. Orayvi (ô rä' vē): A Hopi place name. This and other place names in this folk tale are written with English letters so they can be sounded out.

3. rushes . . . cattails: Tall, grassy plants that grow in wet, marshy areas. Cattails have stalks topped with long, brown, fuzzy flowers that look like the tails of cats. The flexible leaves of both kinds of plants are used by the Hopis to weave mats and baskets.

4. saltbush: A hardy plant that is able to grow in salty marshes or in the desert.

with their bowlegged feet. The wretched baby began following their tracks into the area south of Ismo'wala, tears still streaming from his eyes. His crying sounded about like this:

Tingawsona, tingawsona.
Wa'oo, wa'oo.
Hi', hi', hi', hi'.[5]

This is how he was crying. The little creature was bathed in tears. He was suffering from the hot sand, for he was still a tiny baby.

It so happened that Coyote was hunting in that region, not far from Little Turtle, and Coyote's ears picked up the sound of an animal. He halted abruptly and said, "Who could be making that noise?" Standing there he strained his ears. Again he heard it.

Tingawsona, tingawsona.
Wa'oo, wa'oo.
Hi', hi', hi', hi'.

These were the sounds of this creature, whatever it was.

Coyote now headed straight toward the direction of the noise. Searching for whatever had caused the noise, he came upon the tiny Turtle. The moment Coyote reached him, the Turtle pulled in all his legs. Coyote, however, flipped him over and asked, "What were you singing?"

The Little Turtle replied, "I was not singing. I was crying."

"Come on, do it again. You were singing a really nice song," Coyote insisted.

"But I told you I wasn't singing; I was crying," Little Turtle protested. "My mother and family left for home without me, and that's why I was crying."

"Just sing once more, will you?" Coyote persisted. He was not going to give up. Little Turtle assured him again and again that he hadn't been singing. Coyote now resorted to threatening the tiny thing. "If you don't sing for me, I'll swallow you alive."

"All right, all right, that's fine with me. Being the creature that I am, I won't die if someone swallows me. If you do that I'll just live in the warmth of your stomach."

"You'd better sing for me. If you don't, I'll carry you to Nuvatukya'ovi and roll you down the snow all the way from the top of the peaks."

"All right, all right, that's fine with me. If you do that, I'll just have fun sliding down the snow."

Coyote gave it some thought and then he said again, "If you fail to sing for me, I'll tumble you in the hot sand."

"All right, all right, that's fine with me. For if you do that, I'll just enjoy myself rolling around in it," Little Turtle answered.

Again Coyote said, "If you don't sing for me I'll carry you to Qöma'wa and fling you down the bluff."[6]

"All right, all right, that's fine with me. You do that and I'll have a nice flight down to the ground."

Coyote was at a loss. He didn't know what else he could do to the little thing. Once again he racked his brain, and then he said, "Well, now, you sing for me. And if you don't consent, I'll carry you all the way to the Little Colorado and throw you in the water."

"Oh no, oh no! If that happens to me, I will die right away. Please don't do such a thing to me!" Little Turtle pleaded.

Coyote, however, lost no time and quickly grabbed him with his teeth. And with the Little Turtle in his mouth he rushed to Pa'utsvi so fast that his tail stuck out. From there the

---

5. Tingawsona . . . hi', hi': This is how the Little Turtle's crying sounds in the Hopi language.

6. bluff: A high, steep, wide cliff.

TURTLE SOUNDS
David Dawangyumptewa

river was not far. Coyote ran along without stopping. He was raising a trail of dust behind him. The parents of Little Turtle were still far away when Coyote reached the Little Colorado River. Surprisingly enough, it was flowing full. When Coyote came to its bank, he hurled the tiny turtle in. But he had barely thrown him in than Little Turtle stuck his head out of the water and shouted to Coyote, "How great! This is my home!"

Coyote grew furious now. Little Turtle had told him a lie. Evidently the water was his home, yet he had said that he would die if he was thrown in. Coyote was so angry that he yelled out his intention to eat the little thing. He leaped into the river after him. When Coyote jumped in, Little Turtle simply ducked under and was gone. And because the flow of the water was very strong there, Coyote was swept downstream, and the river pulled him under.

Presently Little Turtle surfaced again and shouted after Coyote, "All right, go on, you have no choice but to go along with the river! Nobody will pull you out. Why do you always have to believe everything right away? You brought this on yourself!"

Little Turtle now headed upstream, swimming along the edge of the river. When he reached Sakwavayu, his parents had not yet arrived so he waited for them. By evening a nice breeze set in, and just as the sun was going down, they became visible in the east. They came, and there, to their great surprise, was their child, the tiny one, the little baby. "Dear me, who brought you here?" his mother exclaimed.

"Well, Coyote found me and said he wanted to eat me. But I refused, so he told me one different thing after another. Finally, when I didn't sing for him, he threatened to throw me into the Little Colorado River. I replied that I would die right away, if he did that. So he grabbed me with his teeth and cast me into the river. That's why I got here so quickly."

"Thank heavens, Coyote is such a gullible creature! There is no way you could have drowned," his mother exclaimed. "Thanks indeed. Well, then, let's go; we are about home. It's quite close to here."

When they reached Sakwavayu, they all went in with great delight. Food was plentiful there. They just plunged into the water. "What a pleasure! From this day on we'll be living a pleasant life again," the mother said.

This is the way the Turtles came to their home. And here the story ends.

RESPONDING TO THE SELECTION

Your Response

1. Do you feel sorry for Coyote at the end? Why or why not?

Recalling

2. Why do the turtles have to leave their new home?
3. How does Little Turtle get left behind by the other turtles?
4. What happens to Coyote after Little Turtle escapes from him?

Interpreting

5. How would you describe Mother Turtle's reaction when she discovers that Little Turtle is missing?
6. Would Little Turtle have caught up with the others if Coyote had not carried him to the river? Why or why not?
7. Why do you think Coyote didn't realize that Little Turtle would not drown in the river?

Applying

8. When people are stranded in a wilderness as Little Turtle was, how do they use their brains to help them survive?

ANALYZING LITERATURE

Understanding the Trickster's Victim

Little Turtle's physical abilities as well as his brains help save him. For example, when he first sees Coyote, he retreats into his shell, a turtle's natural reflex in time of danger.

1. Identify two things that Little Turtle does that show he is smart.
2. Name one other physical ability that helps Little Turtle save himself.

CRITICAL THINKING AND READING

Making Inferences About Setting

"Coyote and Little Turtle" takes place in the southwest United States. Review the story, and make a list of details that are used to describe the landscape.

1. Name several of the different kinds of plants that were mentioned.
2. Based on the details in the tale, how does the presence of water affect the soil and plant life in the Southwest?

THINKING AND WRITING

Comparing and Contrasting Tricksters

Read another tale with a trickster character (you may choose a trickster tale in this section or find another). Compare the tale you have read with "Coyote and Little Turtle." How are the tricksters in these tales similar? How are they different? List your ideas. Then write several paragraphs comparing and contrasting the two. Begin your paragraphs with topic sentences.

LEARNING OPTION

Multicultural Activity. Today more than three thousand Hopi live on a reservation in northeastern Arizona. Imagine that you are going to visit a Hopi person your own age. In preparing for your trip, you will need to find out as much as you can about what it's like to be a Hopi. Ask your school or public librarian to help you identify sources that provide information about where a Hopi your age goes to school and how he or she spends free time.

MULTICULTURAL CONNECTION

The Hopi Trickster

By Joseph Bruchac

The story of "Coyote and Little Turtle" typifies the role played by the familiar figure of Coyote among the Hopi people of the Southwest. Like many Native American stories, it takes place in a landscape well known to its traditional audience.

A dry and ancient land. This region is a dry and ancient land dominated by mesas of red rock and wide expanses of desert with almost no trees except along the banks of the few rivers. The Hopi have occupied this area for many centuries, living on First Mesa, Second Mesa, and Third Mesa in well-organized towns made up of multiple-story dwellings, rather like apartment buildings, built of adobe bricks and logs.

Curious Coyote. The coyote, a smaller relative of the wolf, also does well in this difficult environment (the name "coyote" comes from the Aztec word *coyotl*). One of the most effective predators of the desert, it is known for its ability to eat almost anything and to thrive under the toughest conditions. Coyotes are also among the more wide-ranging and curious animals in nature, so it is not surprising that Coyote plays the role he does in this and other Hopi tales.

The Hopi Coyote. For the Hopi, Coyote tends to be what he is in this tale—a fool whose bad intentions are thwarted by his own gullibility. Stories of Coyote have long been enjoyed by Pueblo children and adults alike, who wait for the inevitable moment in every tale when Coyote will end up being too smart for his own good. However, like Wile E. Coyote in the popular cartoon, he is never totally defeated; the Hopi Coyote always comes back to life again. None the wiser, he goes on to yet another disastrous adventure.

The trickster. Trickster stories always serve a dual purpose: entertainment and instruction. There are many lessons in this story. Coyote's gullibility reminds us that it is not wise to believe everything we are told. Little Turtle's cleverness shows that even if you are small and weak, you can use your wits to overcome adversity. It is a great story for children. A story like this might be told by a Hopi grandmother or grandfather, sitting by the fire at night, the children gathered around to listen.

The Hopi people themselves are known as the people of peace, because of their long tradition of avoiding warfare. This story is a wonderful example of using an enemy's own weakness against him. In fact there are two tricksters in this story, the little turtle who tricks the coyote and the coyote who outsmarts himself.

Who is the trickster? Although Coyote is one of the favorite trickster animals among the many different Native American people, many different animals figure in the trickster tales heard throughout the continent. Raven is the most common trickster in the Northwest among such people as the Kwakiutl, the Nootka, and the Tlingit. Iktomi, the spider, is the trickster hero for the Lakotas on the Great Plains. Rabbit and Turtle are common tricksters in the region of the Great Lakes. Those animals are also sometimes seen in human form.

KOSHARE WITH WATERMELONS
Harry Fonseca
Private Collection

In some places the primary trickster is a more human figure. Gluskabe of the Abenaki in the extreme Northeast and Manabozho of the Ojibwa are two examples. Some of the same stories are found throughout the continent and credited to different tricksters.

Sometimes Coyote or some other trickster is a real hero, doing something that greatly benefits the people. There are many stories about how Coyote goes out and kills some monster that has been eating the people. In northern California a tale is told of a great sucking monster as big as a hill. Coyote allows it to swallow him and then cuts out its heart with his flint knife. Coyote then follows up his great deed, however, by doing something small, greedy, and foolish. Such trickster stories remind us that even heroes are capable of selfishness and failure and that no one is perfect.

The trickster is universal. In a sense when we ask who the trickster really is, there is only one answer. Trickster is you and Trickster is me. Trickster represents the basic potential for foolishness and bravery, greediness and great deeds, found in all human beings, whether young or old, women or men. When we hear trickster tales, we are listening to our own stories.

FURTHER READING

Bruchac, Joseph. *The Wind Eagle and Other Abenaki Folk Stories* (Bowman Books, 1985). In this collection you will find stories about the trickster Gluskabe.

Ramsey, Jarold, ed. *Coyote Was Going There* (Seattle, Washington: University of Washington Press, 1977). Included in this book is the Nez Percé version of the story of "Coyote and the Swallowing Monster."

Joseph Bruchac is a storyteller and writer of Abenaki, English, and Slovak descent. His poems, articles, and stories have appeared in hundreds of publications, from Cricket *to* National Geographic.

GUIDE FOR READING

The Pointing Finger

Folk Tale

A **folk tale** is a story made up by the common people of a country. It is handed down by word of mouth for many generations. Folk tales are especially interesting for what they imply about the values and beliefs of the people who create them.

Focus

In the folk tale you are about to read, several poor Chinese peasants are offered a gift. With a classmate act out a scene in which one of you, a magician, offers to grant a wish to the other. You might want to answer questions like these: Where has the magician come from? Why is he or she offering to grant this wish? Are there any conditions? What should you wish for? How might the granting of this wish change your life?

If several pairs act out their scenes, notice how each scene is different. How do the magicians make the offer? What different things are wished for? As you read, notice what the characters in this story wish for.

Vocabulary

Knowing the following words will help you as you read "The Pointing Finger."

tedious (tē′ dē əs) *adj.*: Long and boring (p. 577)

taint (tānt) *n.*: A trace (p. 577)

avarice (av′ ər is) *n.*: Greed for riches (p. 577)

proffered (präf′ ərd) *v.*: Offered (p. 577)

cupidity (kyo͞o pid′ ə tē) *n.*: Strong desire for wealth (p. 577)

China

Chinese literature is one of the great literatures of the world. Poems and tales have been produced in China for nearly 3,000 years. For most of China's history, literature, such as the folk tale you are about to read, has had an important place in people's lives.

Carol Kendall (1917–   ) has written two collections of Chinese tales. Translating Chinese is a special interest of hers.

Yao-wen Li (1924–   ) was born and raised in pre-Communist China and now lives in Kansas.

The Pointing Finger

from **China**

Carol Kendall and Yao-wen Li

Even P'eng-lai has its tedious days, and when time hung heavy over that fairy mountain isle in the Eastern Sea, the Eight Immortals who dwelt there remembered and talked of their previous existence as mortals on earth. Upon occasion they took disguises and transported themselves from P'eng-lai to their old world to nose about in human affairs in the hope of discovering improvements in human nature. On the whole, however, they found the mortals of today to have the same shortcomings and the same longcomings as those of yesterday.

It came about that one of the Immortals, on such a nosing-about expedition, was seeking an unselfish man. He vowed that when he found a man without the taint of greed in his heart, he would make of him an Immortal on the spot and transport him to P'eng-lai Mountain forthwith.[1]

His test for avarice was simple. Upon meeting a foot-traveler in lane or road, he would turn a pebble into gold by pointing his finger at it. He would then offer the golden pebble to the traveler.

The first person he met accepted the pebble eagerly, but then, turning it over and over between his fingers, his eyes beginning to gleam and glint, he said, "Can you do the same thing again? To those?" and he pointed at a small heap of stones at their feet.

The Immortal shook his head sadly and went on.

The second person looked at the proffered golden pebble long and thoughtfully. "Ah," he finally said, his eyes narrowed in calculation, "but this is a fine thing you would give me. It will feed my family for a year, and feed them well, but what then? Back to rice water and elm bark? That would be a cruelty. How could I face their tears and laments? Kind sir, as it is such an effortless task for you, perhaps you could turn your finger toward something a little larger, like, for example"—and he pointed at a boulder as big as himself beside the road—"that bit of stone?"

All along the way the story was the same, until the Immortal despaired of finding human beings whose cupidity did not outweigh their gratitude. After many a weary mile's walking, he came upon a man of middle years stumping along the lane and, greeting him, said, "I should like to make you a present." He pointed his finger at a stone, and it turned into gold before their eyes.

The man studied the gleaming chunk of stone, his head canted[2] to one side. "What sort of trick is that?" he asked with a frown.

---

1. forthwith (fôrth′ with′) *adv.*: At once.

2. canted (kant'd) *v.*: Tilted.

"No trick," said the Immortal. "Pick it up. Or would you prefer a larger stone?" He pointed his finger at a small rock, and it instantly blossomed gold. "Take it, brother. It is yours. I give it to you."

The man thought a while, then slowly shook his head. "No-o-o. Not that it's not a very clever trick, and a pretty sight to see."

With growing excitement the Immortal pointed at a larger rock and a larger, until their eyes were dazzled by the glint of gold all round them, but each time the man shook his head, and each time the shake became more decisive. Had he found his unselfish man at last? Should he transform him this instant into an Immortal and carry him back to P'eng-lai?

"But every human being desires *something*," the Immortal said, all but convinced that this was untrue. "Tell me what it is you want!"

"Your finger," said the man.

RESPONDING TO THE SELECTION

Your Response

1. If you could have either great riches or immortality, which would you choose? Why?

Recalling

2. What is the Immortal seeking on earth?
3. What does the test reveal?

Interpreting

4. In what way does the third man seem at first different from the first two?
5. Why does the Immortal grow more and more excited as he speaks with the third man?
6. What is suggested by the very last sentence?

Applying

7. What does this story imply about the values or beliefs of the people who told it?

ANALYZING LITERATURE

Understanding a Folk Tale

Folk tales are part of our oral tradition. They are created by ordinary people and preserved by word of mouth. The tale is passed down from one generation to the next for many years, even centuries. Usually, if a folk tale is at last written down, it is because someone felt it ought to be preserved so that people of other lands can enjoy it.

1. In what way does "The Pointing Finger" remind you of other folk tales?
2. This folk tale is several hundred years old. Why do you think it has lasted so long?

CRITICAL THINKING AND READING

Evaluating Generalizations

A **generalization** is an idea or statement that covers a great many specific cases. For example, near the end of "The Pointing Finger," the Im-

mortal says, "But every human being desires something." This is a generalization because the statement covers all human beings.

Generalizations need to be evaluated for their truth. To evaluate a generalization, look at the evidence. Does it indicate that the statement is solidly grounded in facts? Are there no exceptions—specific cases that do not fit the statement?

1. Evaluate the generalization that "every human being desires something."
2. Tell why it would or would not have been reasonable for the Immortal to make the generalization that all humans are greedy.

THINKING AND WRITING

Summarizing a Folk Tale

Summarizing a folk tale means retelling it in shortened form. Summarize "The Pointing Finger." Before you write, think about the several events that make up the story. Think about the characters' motives and purposes. When you write your summary, make clear not only what happens but also why it happens. When you revise, check your summary against the folk tale. Did you cover all the main incidents? Did you make clear why things happen as they do?

LEARNING OPTION

Performance. Think about what you would do or say to the Immortal if he tested you. Would you take the first pebble? Would you want more? Would you want the Immortal's power? Would you want to become an Immortal? Now write a brief skit showing an encounter with the Immortal that you and a friend can act out. Include stage directions and dialogue for both you and the Immortal. After practicing the skit, present it for the class.

The Little Lizard's Sorrow

Symbols in Folk Tales

A **symbol** is an object that stands for an idea but also has its own existence. A dove, for example, is a symbol of peace. Symbols are frequently used in folk tales to express an idea in a concrete and memorable way.

Focus

As in many other folk tales, a character in "The Little Lizard's Sorrow," a poor stranger, seeks to win a fortune for himself by making a wager, or bet. Every wager involves making a prediction; you can never be certain what the outcome will be. Think about times in your life when you have had to predict how an event would turn out. Then write a few sentences describing a time when you guessed correctly and a few describing how you lost a wager. What information had you used to make your prediction? What did you learn from your experience?

Many folk tales teach a valuable lesson about how to live, and sometimes more than one lesson is taught. As you read "The Little Lizard's Sorrow," think about what the tale is saying about greed and sharing with others.

Vocabulary

Knowing the following words will help you as you read "The Little Lizard's Sorrow."

emitting (ē mit′ iŋ) *v.*: Sending out or uttering (p. 581)

gaunt (gônt) *adj.*: Thin and bony (p. 581)

pauper (pô′ pər) *n.*: An extremely poor person (p. 581)

chortle (chor′ t'l) *v.*: Make an amused chuckling or snorting sound (p. 582)

domestic (də mes′ tik) *n.*: A servant for the home (p. 582)

harassed (hə rast′) *v.*: Troubled (p. 584)

Vietnam

Vietnam is a tropical country in Southeast Asia. The most popular form of literature in Vietnam is poetry, and poets are greatly respected there. This land also has a deeply rooted tradition of folk tales, of which "The Little Lizard's Sorrow" is an excellent example.

Mai Vo-Dinh (1933–   ), who translated the tale, was born in Vietnam. He came to live in the United States in 1960. He is not only a writer and translator of Vietnamese literature but also a painter and illustrator of books.

The Little Lizard's Sorrow

from **Vietnam**
Translated by Mai Vo-Dinh

There is in Vietnam a certain species of small lizard only three inches long with webbed feet and a short, round head. They are often seen indoors, running swiftly upside down on the ceiling or along the walls, emitting little snapping cries that sound like "Tssst . . . tssst!" Suppose that you drop an egg on the kitchen floor; the kind of sound you would make then, with the tip of your tongue between your teeth, is like the cry of these harmless, funny little lizards. Sounds of mild sorrow, of genuine shock but somehow humorous regret that seem to say, "Oh, if only I had been . . . If only I had known . . . Oh, what a pity, what a pity . . . Tssst! Tssst!"

There was once a very rich man whose house was immense and filled with treasures. His land was so extensive that, as the Vietnamese say, "Cranes fly over it with outstretched wings," for cranes only do so over very long distances. Wealth breeding vanity, one of the rich man's greatest pleasures was beating other rich men at a game he himself had invented. One player would announce one of his rare possessions, the other would counter the challenge by saying that he, too—if he really did—owned such a treasure.

"A stable of fifty buffalos," one man would say. The other would reply, "Yes, I also have fifty of them." It was then his turn to announce, "I sleep in an all-teak[1] bed encrusted with mother-of-pearl."[2] The first player would lose if he slept on cherry planks![3]

One day, a stranger came to the rich man's house. Judging from his appearance, the gatekeeper did not doubt that the visitor was a madman. He wanted, he said, to play the famous game with the mansion's master. Yet dressed in clothes that looked as if they had been mended hundreds of times, and wearing broken straw sandals, the stranger appeared to be anything but a wealthy man. Moreover, his face was gaunt and pale as if he had not had a good meal in days. But there was such proud, quiet dignity to the stranger that the servant did not dare shut the gates in his face. Instead, he meekly went to inform his master of the unlikely visitor's presence. Intrigued, the man ordered that the pauper be ushered in.

Trying to conceal his curiosity and sur-

---

1. teak (tēk) *n.*: Yellowish-brown wood used for furniture.
2. mother-of-pearl *n.*: The hard, pearly inside of certain seashells.
3. cherry planks *n.*: Wood from a cherry tree.

prise, the rich man offered his visitor the very best chair and served him hot, perfumed tea.

"Well, stranger, is it true that you have deigned[4] to come here to play a game of riches with me?" he began inquiringly.

The visitor was apparently unimpressed by the rich surroundings, giving them only a passing, casual look. Perfectly at ease, sipping his tea from the rare porcelain cup, he answered in a quiet though self-assured voice, "Yes, sir, that is if you, too, so wish."

"Naturally, naturally," the rich man raised his hand in a sweeping motion. "But, may I ask, with your permission, where you reside and what is your honorable occupation?"

The stranger gave a little chortle, visibly amused. "Sir, would you gain any to know about these? I came here simply to play your game; only, I have two conditions, if you are so generous as to allow them."

"By all means! Pray, tell me what they are," the rich man readily inquired.

The visitor sat farther back on the brocaded chair, his voice soft and confidential. "Well, here they are. A game is no fun if the winner does not win anything and the loser does not lose anything. Therefore I would suggest that if I win I would take everything in your possession—your lands, your stables, your servants, your house and everything contained in it. But if you win—" Here the stranger paused, his eyes narrowed ever so slightly, full of humorous malice, "If you win, you would become the owner of everything that belongs to me." The stranger paused again. "And what belongs to me, sir, you will have no idea of. I am one of the most fortunate men alive, sir. . . . And besides that," he added with a knowing look, "I

---

would remain in this house to serve you as a domestic the rest of my life."

For a long moment, the rich man sat back in silence. Another long moment went by, then the rich man spoke: "That's agreed. But, please tell me your other condition."

Eyes dreamy, the stranger looked out of the window. "My second condition, sir, is not so much a condition as a request. I hope you would not mind giving me, a visitor, an edge over you. May I be allowed to ask the first question?"

The rich man thought for a long second, then said, "That is also agreed. Let's begin."

"Do I really understand that you have agreed to both my conditions?" the stranger asked thoughtfully.

Something in the visitor's manner and voice hurt the rich man's pride. He was ready to stake his very life on this game that he himself had created. There was no way out. "Yes," he said. "Yes, indeed I have. Now tell me, please, what do you have that I have not got?" The stranger smiled. Reaching to his feet, he took up his traveling bag, a coarse cotton square tied together by the

four ends. Opening it slowly, ceremoniously, he took out an object and handed it to his host without a word. It was an empty half of a coconut shell, old and chipped, the kind poor people use as a container to drink water from.

"A coconut-shell cup!" the rich man exclaimed. One could not know whether he was merely amused or completely shattered.

"Yes, sir, a coconut-shell cup. A *chipped* shell cup. I use it to drink from on my wanderings. I am a wanderer," the visitor said quietly.

Holding the shell between his thumb and his forefinger and looking as if he had never seen such an object before, the rich man interrupted, "But, but you don't mean that I do not have a thing like this?"

"No, sir, you have not. How could you?" the stranger replied.

Turning the residence upside down, the man and his servants discovered odds and ends of one thousand and one kinds, but they were unable to produce a drinking cup made from a coconut shell. In the servants' quarters, however, they found a few such utensils, but they were all brand new, not chipped. One could imagine that the servants of such a wealthy man would not deign to drink from a chipped cup. Even a beggar would throw it away. . . .

"You see, sir," the stranger said to the rich man once they were again seated across the tea table, "you see, I am a wanderer, as I have said. I am a free man. This cup here is several years old and my only possession besides these poor clothes I have on. If you do not think me too immodest, I would venture that I treasure it more than you do all of your collections of fine china. But, from this day, I am the owner and lone master of all that belongs to you. . . ."

Having taken possession of the rich man's land, houses, herds and all

his other treasures, the stranger began to give them away to the poor and needy people. Then, one day, taking up his old cotton bag, he left the village and no one ever saw him again.

As for the dispossessed rich man, it is believed that he died of grief and regret and was transformed into this small lizard. Curiously, one sees him scurrying about only indoors. Running up and down the walls, crossing the ceiling, staring at people and furniture, he never stops his "Tssst, Tssst." Vietnamese children, in particular, are very fond of him for he looks so harassed, so funny.

But, oh, such sorrow, such regret, such self-pity.

Your Response

1. How do you feel about what the stranger did? Do you think the rich man deserved what happened to him? Explain.
2. Was it wise of the stranger to give all the riches to the poor? Why or why not?

Recalling

3. Describe the game the rich man plays with other rich men.
4. What two conditions for the game does the stranger request?
5. How does he defeat the rich man?
6. What does he do with his possessions?

Interpreting

7. Why does the stranger describe himself as one of the most fortunate men alive? Do you agree with this opinion? Why or why not?
8. Why does he treasure his coconut-shell cup more than the rich man treasures his china?
9. Why do you think the rich man is changed into a lizard rather than some other animal?
10. In what way does this folk tale teach a lesson in living?

Applying

11. J. Brotherton once wrote: "My riches consist not in the extent of my possessions but in the fewness of my wants." Would the stranger agree or disagree with him? Explain your answer.

ANALYZING LITERATURE

Understanding Symbols in Folk Tales

When some object—whether living or nonliving—seems to stand out as especially important in a folk tale, it is probably a **symbol.** In "The Little Lizard's Sorrow," the lizard and the coconut-shell cup are two such objects.

1. What human feelings are associated with the little lizard at the beginning and the end of the tale?
2. What, therefore, might the lizard symbolize?
3. What is said about the coconut-shell cup that suggests its importance to the stranger?
4. What might it symbolize?

THINKING AND WRITING

Writing a Folk Tale With a Symbol

Write a folk tale modeled on "The Little Lizard's Sorrow." Include an object that symbolizes some important idea you wish to express. When you revise your work, check that your symbol fits in well with the rest of the story and helps to reveal its meaning. Share your folk tale with your classmates.

LEARNING OPTION

Cross-curricular Connection. Lizards are fascinating animals and, together with snakes, make up 95 percent of all reptiles. Find out as much as you can about lizards. How are they different from and yet similar to their close relatives, the snakes? Where do they live? What do they eat? Try to find out what particular species of lizards live in Vietnam, the country from which "The Little Lizard's Sorrow" comes. Also try to discover what kinds of lizards, if any, live in your area. Then make a presentation for your class, sharing all that you have learned. You might include illustrations of lizards and their habitats.

GUIDE FOR READING

Djuha Borrows a Pot
Let's Steal the Moon

Fools in Folk Tales

Along with the trickster and the trickster's victim, another familiar character in folk tales is the **fool.** Folk tales feature different kinds of fools. In "Djuha Borrows a Pot," you will meet a **wise fool** named Djuha. The wise fool is like a trickster, because he only pretends to be foolish in order to get what he wants. In "Let's Steal the Moon," you will read about many **foolish fools.** As their name implies, these fools are the real thing. They have no common sense or judgment.

Focus

You probably have some ideas about the differences between a wise fool and a foolish fool. How might someone who is really wise pretend to be foolish? How might a real fool show just how foolish he or she is? Make a chart like the one below, marking one column Wise Fool and the other Foolish Fool. Then list as many characteristics and traits of each as you can.

Wise Fool	Foolish Fool

Vocabulary

Knowing the following words will help you as you read "Let's Steal the Moon."

patriarch (pā′ trē ärk) *n.:* An old, dignified man (p. 589)
luminary (lōō′ mə ner′ ē) *n.:* Something that gives off light (p. 589)
contemplation (kän tem plā′ shən) *n.:* Careful, serious thought or study (p. 589)

hoisting (hoist′ iŋ) *n.:* Raising with a pulley or rope (p. 591)
vied (vīd) *v.:* Competed (p. 591)
marauders (mə rôd′ ərs) *n.:* Roaming attackers or plunderers (p. 591)

Syria/Poland

Each of these stories is a sample from a popular series of tales. For centuries Djuha has been the most beloved of comic characters in Arab folklore, and the Yiddish-speaking citizens of Chelem in Poland have been delightfully misguided for years.

Inea Bushnaq ("Djuha Borrows a Pot") See biography on page 554.

Blanche Serwer-Bernstein ("Let's Steal the Moon"), psychologist and teacher of children's literature, has adapted eleven Jewish tales in her collection *Let's Steal the Moon.*

Djuha Borrows a Pot

from **Syria**

Inea Bushnaq

PREPARING MEDICINE FROM HONEY, 1224
Arab Painting
The Metropolitan Museum of Art

One day Djuha wanted to entertain his friends with a dinner of lamb stewed whole with rice stuffing, but he did not have a cooking pot large enough. So he went to his neighbor and borrowed a huge, heavy caldron of fine copper.

Promptly next morning, Djuha returned the borrowed pot. "What is this?" cried the neighbor, pulling a small brass pot from inside the caldron. "Oh yes," said Djuha, "congratulations and blessings upon your house! While your caldron was with me it gave birth to that tiny pot." The neighbor laughed delightedly. "May Allah[1] send blessings your way too," he told Djuha, and carried the two

---

1. Allah (al′ ə): The name for God in the Muslim religion.

cooking pots into his house.

A few weeks later Djuha knocked on his neighbor's door again to ask for the loan of the caldron. And the neighbor hurried to fetch it for him. The next day came and went, but Djuha did not return the pot. Several days passed and the neighbor did not hear from Djuha. At last he went to Djuha's house to ask for his property. "Have you not heard, brother?" said Djuha looking very grave. "The very evening I borrowed it from you, your unfortunate caldron—God grant you a long life—died!" "What do you mean, 'died'?" shouted the neighbor. "Can a copper cooking pot die?" "If it can give birth," said Djuha, "it can surely die."

RESPONDING TO THE SELECTION

Your Response

1. How do you feel about letting people borrow your things?

Recalling

2. When he borrowed his neighbor's pot the first time, how long did it take Djuha to return it?

3. What did Djuha claim happened to the pot the second time he borrowed it?

Interpreting

4. When do you think Djuha decided he wanted to keep his neighbor's pot?

5. Why do you think the neighbor hurried to fetch the pot the second time Djuha asked to borrow it?

Applying

6. How would you react to having a neighbor like Djuha?

ANALYZING LITERATURE

Understanding Wise Fools

To succeed at his plan, Djuha had to play the part of a fool convincingly. He may have known that he was succeeding when his neighbor laughed and carried the small pot along with the large one into his house.

1. Why do you think Djuha really gave his neighbor the small pot?

2. The second time Djuha asks for the caldron, the neighbor is eager to lend it. Why does Djuha want his neighbor to act this way?

LEARNING OPTIONS

1. **Performance.** With a partner, prepare a performance of "Djuha Borrows a Pot." Review the tale, and memorize the plot. As part of the oral tradition, this tale has probably been told in many slightly different versions, so you may want to improvise and embellish details of Djuha's prank. Use props and even costumes when you perform the tale for the class.

2. **Writing.** Write a brief tale in which Djuha uses a different scheme to trick somebody else. You may use the selection as a model. Remember that in order to succeed in his prank, Djuha must appear to be very foolish to the other person. Try not to reveal Djuha's plan until the very end of your tale.

Let's Steal the Moon
A Yiddish Tale
Blanche Serwer-Bernstein

The people of Chelem[1] loved their city and tried to improve it in every way. Whenever they heard of something new and different in another city, they wanted it for themselves. What is good for others is good for us, they reasoned.

Imagine how excited they became when they learned that in some towns the streets were lighted at night. What a brilliant idea! With street lamps there would be no need to stumble in the dark or to come right up to a person and peer closely into his face to recognize him, or guess when you came to a street corner, or lose your way because you made a wrong turn. A wonderful improvement, lamps in the streets! Why hadn't they thought of this before?

As was the custom, all the citizens of Chelem came together to discuss the appealing new notion of installing lights on their street corners.

As they sat in council, thinking the matter through, a white-bearded patriarch stood up and spoke, "Street lights, my friends, would cost us a great deal of money and where would the money come from? From our fund for the poor? That is forbidden!

"On the other hand, there is a luminary up in the sky that helps us for part of the month and leaves us in the dark for part of the month. There are nights when the moon shines and Chelem has enough light. There are other nights when there is no moon and Chelem is dark. Now, why can't the moon shine for us every night?"

"Why not?" wondered the people of Chelem, looking skyward and shaking their heads thoughtfully.

Then they drew closer to the old man, delighting in his great wisdom as he unfolded his plan. The wise patriarch persuaded the people of Chelem to wait for a night when the moon was large and full, shedding light into every nook and cranny of their dark streets. Then, to put it simply and directly, they would steal the moon and guard her safely until the dark nights of the month, when they would hang her in the skies to light up their streets.

"Steal the moon? Why not?" reasoned the people of Chelem, rubbing their chins in deepest contemplation.

Gimpel, who always had the most advanced ideas, suggested, "While we have it down, why not clean and polish it so that it will be brighter than ever?"

"Polish the moon? Why not?" agreed the people of Chelem, bewildered by the onrush of their own creative ideas.

They had no difficulty at all in capturing the moon. It was a simple matter. They filled a barrel with water and left it open, exposed

---

1. Chelem (k͟hel′ əm)

WATER CARRIER BY MOONLIGHT
Marc Chagall
The Metropolitan Museum of Art

to the moon's light. Then ten Chelemites stood ready with sackcloth.

The moon, unaware of the plot, moved into the barrel of water. When it was clearly trapped, the Chelemites covered the barrel with the heavy sackcloth and bound it down with thick strong rope. To make certain that everything was as it should be, they put the official seal of Chelem on the barrel and carried it carefully into the Synagogue[2] where it

would be safe from all harm. They checked every night to make sure the seal was not broken.

After two weeks, the nights became very dark and again they began to bump into each other on the streets, bruise their shins, and lose their way because of wrong turns in the darkness.

This was the time! They sent word through the town, and the people gathered to help take the moon out of the barrel and hang it in the sky. They were confident that, with all their minds working on the problem, there

---

2. Synagogue (sin' ə gäg): A place of worship in the Jewish religion.

would be a way of hoisting it up and securing it there. They knew it was possible, for hadn't they seen the moon up there month after month? Besides, they had collected all the ladders in Chelem and tied them together end to end in preparation for this moment.

Polishing cloths were also gathered in a gigantic heap in front of the Synagogue, where the important event would take place. The women of Chelem vied with each other for positions from which they could help in the polishing.

Then came the moment they had been planning for. They uncovered the barrel carefully, squinting their eyes so that they would not be blinded by the brilliance of the moon's light.

They opened their eyes wide. Their moon was gone! How could that be? They looked at each other in utter confusion.

Who could have released their moon, securely trapped in a water barrel and sealed by the official seal of the city of Chelem? Surely no Chelemite could have done it! Bandits? Marauders from a neighboring town? But the seal remained unbroken! They shook their heads and looked skyward, deeply disturbed by this mysterious happening.

One thing they were sure of. Had they set proper guards over their moon, it would have remained safe and they would have found a way to hang it in the sky. Far from being discouraged, they were confident that they would know how to do it next time.

RESPONDING TO THE SELECTION

Your Response

1. Did you find the behavior of the people of Chelem funny? Why or why not?

Recalling

2. What do the people of Chelem want for their city?
3. What was the patriarch's plan for lighting the city?
4. What do the people think has happened to the moon when they discover it is gone?

Interpreting

5. The patriarch is described as being very wise. Do you think the author really means this? Why or why not?
6. What really happened to the moon?

Applying

7. What does this tale suggest about the way people sometimes behave in groups?

ANALYZING LITERATURE

Understanding Foolish Fools

In "Djuha Borrows a Pot," you encountered the wise fool who only pretends to be foolish. The people in "Let's Steal the Moon," however, really are foolish.

1. Identify three things that the people of Chelem do that demonstrate their foolishness.
2. What lesson do you think a folk tale like this might intend to teach?

CRITICAL THINKING AND READING

Understanding Humorous Effects

The humor in "Let's Steal the Moon" is created not only by the people's foolish behavior but also by details the author uses. For example, whenever a ridiculous idea is suggested to the people of Chelem, they respond with an eager "Why not?"

1. What gesture do the Chelemites repeat to show they are thinking very hard? Why is this funny?
2. Identify details in the tale that show the suspense the Chelemites feel as they uncover the barrel. Why are these funny?

THINKING AND WRITING

Extending a Folk Tale

The citizens of Chelem remain foolish to the very end and are sure they will capture the moon the next time they try. Extend this folk tale by writing your version of the people's next attempt at stealing the moon. Try to balance narration with dialogue.

LEARNING OPTIONS

1. **Art.** Draw or paint a scene of your choice from "Let's Steal the Moon." Think about how to make your artwork express the humor in the folk tale. If you prefer, you might want to create a comic strip version of the tale, depicting each of its important scenes in a different frame. Also decide which pieces of dialogue to place in balloons that represent the characters' speech.

2. **Speaking and Listening.** There is really a town called Chelem (or Chelm) in Poland, but its more than 40,000 real inhabitants would probably not like to be called fools. Find out more about the Chelem that exists only in the tales. When were stories about the foolish people of Chelem first told? Who told them? Find more stories about the "wise men of Chelem." You might start with Blanche Serwer-Bernstein's book *Let's Steal the Moon: Jewish Tales, Ancient and Recent.* Then present the results of your research to the class, and read aloud another story about Chelem.

Transformations and Origins

THE SLEEPING GYPSY, 1897
Henri Rousseau
The Museum of Modern Art, New York

GUIDE FOR READING

Greece

The ancient Greeks often thought of **Demeter** (di mēt′ ər) and her daughter **Persephone** (pər sef′ ə nē) as a pair, calling them the Two Goddesses. Farmers honored and worshiped Demeter during the planting and harvesting of corn, as important a crop in the ancient world as it is today. The Greek poet Homer described Demeter as "blonde," giving her the color of ripened corn.

Anne Terry White (1896–   ), the reteller of this myth, was a teacher and has written many books for young people.

Demeter and Persephone

Myth

A **myth** is an ancient story about gods or heroes created to express beliefs or explain natural events. Among the matters that myths explain are how the world began, why the sun travels across the sky, and how humans gained fire. Since myths are stories, these mythical explanations of nature are both lively and imaginative. Therefore, they have lasted for generations.

Greek and Roman myths have had the greatest influence on our own culture. For hundreds of years, writers have retold these stories in the English language. "Demeter and Persephone" has been especially popular because it explains the rhythms of nature in terms of human emotions.

Focus

When myths were first created and told, people knew very few of the scientific reasons for natural occurrences. For example, when the ancient Greeks did not know why certain patterns in nature existed, they provided an explanation that involved the superhuman activities of their gods. If you didn't know about the Earth's orbit around the sun, how would you explain why the seasons change? Write a brief "myth" about the arrival of winter.

Vocabulary

Knowing the following words will help you as you read "Demeter and Persephone."

asunder (ə sun′ dər) *adv.*: Into parts or pieces (p. 595)

realm (relm) *n.*: Kingdom (p. 595)

defies (di fīz′) *v.*: Boldly opposes or resists (p. 595)

monarch (män′ ərk) *n.*: Ruler; king or queen (p. 595)

dominions (də min′ yənz) *n.*: Region over which someone rules (p. 596)

intervene (in′ tər vēn′) *v.*: Step into a situation (p. 596)

abode (ə bōd′) *n.*: Home (p. 598)

Demeter and Persephone

Anne Terry White

Deep under Mt. Aetna, the gods had buried alive a number of fearful, fire-breathing giants. The monsters heaved and struggled to get free. And so mightily did they shake the earth that Pluto, the king of the underworld, was alarmed.

"They may tear the rocks asunder and leave the realm of the dead open to the light of day," he thought. And mounting his golden chariot, he went up to see what damage had been done.

Now the goddess of love and beauty, fair Aphrodite,[1] was sitting on a mountainside playing with her son, Eros.[2] She saw Pluto as he drove around with his coal-black horses and she said:

"My son, there is one who defies your power and mine. Quick! Take up your darts! Send an arrow into the breast of that dark monarch. Let him, too, feel the pangs of love. Why should he alone escape them?"

At his mother's words, Eros leaped lightly to his feet. He chose from his quiver[3] his sharpest and truest arrow, fitted it to his bow, drew the string, and shot straight into Pluto's heart.

The grim King had seen fair maids enough in the gloomy underworld over which he ruled. But never had his heart been touched. Now an unaccustomed

warmth stole through his veins. His stern eyes softened. Before him was a blossoming valley, and along its edge a charming girl was gathering flowers. She was Persephone, daughter of Demeter, goddess of the harvest. She had strayed from her companions, and now that her basket overflowed with blossoms, she was filling her apron with lilies and violets. The god looked at Persephone

---

1. **Aphrodite** (af′ rə dīt′ ē)
2. **Eros** (er′ äs): In Greek mythology, the god of love, identified by the Romans with Cupid.
3. **quiver** (kwiv′ ər) n.: A case for arrows.

and loved her at once. With one sweep of his arm he caught her up and drove swiftly away.

"Mother!" she screamed, while the flowers fell from her apron and strewed the ground. "Mother!"

And she called on her companions by name. But already they were out of sight, so fast did Pluto urge the horses on. In a few moments they were at the River Cyane.[4] Persephone struggled, her loosened girdle[5] fell to the ground, but the god held her tight. He struck the bank with his trident.[6] The earth opened, and darkness swallowed them all— horses, chariot, Pluto, and weeping Persephone.

From end to end of the earth Demeter sought her daughter. But none could tell her where Persephone was. At last, worn out and despairing, the goddess returned to Sicily. She stood by the River Cyane, where Pluto had cleft[7] the earth and gone down into his own dominions.

Now a river nymph[8] had seen him carry off his prize. She wanted to tell Demeter where her daughter was, but fear of Pluto kept her dumb. Yet she had picked up the girdle Persephone had dropped, and this the nymph wafted[9] on the waves to the feet of Demeter.

The goddess knew then that her daughter was gone indeed, but she did not suspect Pluto of carrying her off. She laid the blame on the innocent land.

"Ungrateful soil!" she said. "I made you fertile. I clothed you in grass and nourishing grain, and this is how you reward me. No more shall you enjoy my favors!"

That year was the most cruel mankind had ever known. Nothing prospered, nothing grew. The cattle died, the seed would not come up, men and oxen toiled in vain. There was too much sun. There was too much rain. Thistles[10] and weeds were the only things that grew. It seemed that all mankind would die of hunger.

"This cannot go on," said mighty Zeus. "I see that I must intervene." And one by one he sent the gods and goddesses to plead with Demeter.

But she had the same answer for all: "Not till I see my daughter shall the earth bear fruit again."

Zeus, of course, knew well where Persephone was. He did not like to take from his brother the one joyful thing in his life, but he saw that he must if the race of man was to be preserved. So he called Hermes[11] to him and said:

"Descend to the underworld, my son. Bid Pluto release his bride. Provided she has not tasted food in the realm of the dead, she may return to her mother forever."

Down sped Hermes on his winged feet, and there in the dim palace of the king, he found Persephone by Pluto's side. She was pale and joyless. Not all the glittering treasures of the underworld could bring a smile to her lips.

"You have no flowers here," she would say to her husband when he pressed gems upon her. "Jewels have no fragrance. I do not want them."

When she saw Hermes and heard his message, her heart leaped within her. Her cheeks grew rosy and her eyes sparkled, for she knew that Pluto would not dare to disobey his brother's command. She sprang up,

---

4. River Cyane (sī′ an): A river in Sicily, an island just south of Italy.
5. girdle (gər′ d'l) *n.*: A belt or sash for the waist.
6. trident (trīd′ 'nt) *n.*: A spear with three points.
7. cleft (kleft) *v.*: Split or opened.
8. river nymph (nimf): A goddess living in a river.
9. wafted (wäft′ 'd) *v.*: Carried.

10. thistles (this′ 'lz) *n.*: Stubborn, weedy plants with sharp leaves and usually purplish flowers.
11. Hermes (hur′ mēz): A god who served as a messenger.

ready to go at once. Only one thing troubled her—that she could not leave the underworld forever. For she had accepted a pomegranate[12] from Pluto and sucked the sweet pulp from four of the seeds.

With a heavy heart Pluto made ready his golden car.[13] He helped Persephone in while Hermes took up the reins.

"Dear wife," said the King, and his voice trembled as he spoke, "think kindly of me, I pray you. For indeed I love you truly. It will be lonely here these eight months you are away. And if you think mine is a gloomy palace to return to, at least remember that your

---

12. pomegranate (päm' gran' it) *n.:* A round fruit with a red, leathery rind and many seeds.
13. car (kär) *n.:* chariot.

husband is great among the immortals. So fare you well—and get your fill of flowers!"

Straight to the temple of Demeter at Eleusis, Hermes drove the black horses. The goddess heard the chariot wheels and, as a deer bounds over the hills, she ran out swiftly to meet her daughter. Persephone flew to her mother's arms. And the sad tale of each turned into joy in the telling.

So it is to this day. One third of the year Persephone spends in the gloomy abode of Pluto—one month for each seed that she tasted. Then Nature dies, the leaves fall, the earth stops bringing forth. In spring Persephone returns, and with her come the flowers, followed by summer's fruitfulness and the rich harvest of fall.

RESPONDING TO THE SELECTION

Your Response

1. If you had been Zeus, how would you have solved the problem? Why?

Recalling

2. What motivates Pluto to take Persephone to his kingdom?
3. What does Demeter think has happened to Persephone? Why does she make the earth infertile?
4. How is the situation solved?
5. Why is Persephone unable to leave the underworld forever?
6. How does nature change as Persephone moves between the earth and the underworld?

Interpreting

7. Why is Persephone unhappy in the underworld?
8. Why is Pluto referred to as "the grim King"? How do you know that he truly loves Persephone?
9. Evaluate the judgment of the gods in regard to Persephone's fate. Do you think it just? Why or why not?

Applying

10. Why do you think the return of spring would be so important to ancient Greeks and Romans?
11. Create a celebration in honor of the returning spring. Briefly describe what you would have people wear, say, and do.

ANALYZING LITERATURE

Appreciating Myth

A myth is an ancient story about gods or heroes created to express beliefs or explain natural events. Often in myths the explanation of natural events has its roots in the powerful emotions of the gods and goddesses involved. The story of "Demeter and Persephone," for example, explains why "the earth stops bringing forth" in the fall and winter but blooms again in the spring.

1. Identify the feelings that Pluto experiences during the course of the story.
2. What emotions do Persephone and Demeter experience in this myth?
3. How do the powerful emotions of these three characters account for the change in seasons?
4. Why do you think that the emotions expressed in this myth have touched people for thousands of years?

CRITICAL THINKING AND READING

Contrasting Science and Myth

Science and myth explain natural events in different ways. While a scientific explanation contains facts and theories, a myth offers a highly imaginative story as an explanation. For example, a scientific account of lightning would mention the discharge of electricity. A myth, however, might tell a story about an angry god hurling a spear.

1. In what way can myths reveal truths about life?
2. Which do you think reveals truths about life more vividly—myths or science? Which reveals truths more accurately?

3. Which explanations do you think make a greater impact on our hearts and minds? Explain your answer.

THINKING AND WRITING

Writing a Myth

Imagine a society that uses myth rather than science to explain dramatic and destructive earthquakes. Briefly outline the lively story about gods or heroes that this society might have devised. For instance, the story might involve giants battling under the earth, a goddess stamping with her foot, or anything you can imagine. Then, using your outline, write the myth in greater detail. In revising your myth, make sure the characters, like those in "Demeter and Persephone," express strong emotions. When you are finished, share your myth with your classmates.

LEARNING OPTIONS

1. **Speaking and Listening.** Many myths that we know only in written form were originally sung or recited. Work with a small group of your classmates to give a dramatic reading of a portion of "Demeter and Persephone." Choose one or two passages to read. Then practice reading the passages aloud, paying attention to clues in the text that tell you what emotions are being expressed. Present your interpretation of the myth for the class.
2. **Art.** In "Demeter and Persephone," you read about the Greek underworld. What do you think this underworld looked like? Draw your version of the underworld, showing what you might find there. Include people or characters in your drawing.

GUIDE FOR READING

Phaëthon, Son of Apollo

Character in Myth: Hubris

Hubris is a Greek word meaning excessive pride or arrogance. The ancient Greeks believed very strongly in the separation between mortal humans and immortal gods. A human being who boasted of godlike powers was guilty of hubris and would almost certainly be punished. In "Phaëthon, Son of Apollo," you will see what happens to a young man who reaches too high.

Focus

Have you ever heard of someone "biting off more than he or she could chew?" This figure of speech means more than just having a huge mouthful of food. Have you ever decided to try something that turned out to require more energy, strength, or skill than you could muster? Write about such a time when you bit off more than you could chew. What did you want to accomplish? What hidden difficulties did you become aware of? What happened in the end?

Keep your answers to these questions in mind as you read about Phaëthon, who took on an overwhelming task.

Greece

Apollo (ə päl′ ō) was the son of Zeus and Leto. He is portrayed in Greek art as a handsome and athletic young man. He was known as the god of poetry and music, and he was often shown carrying the ancient stringed instrument called a lyre. He was also associated with the life-giving power of the sun, as you will see in this myth.

Olivia E. Coolidge (1908–   ), the modern teller of this myth, has written many books for young people about history and ancient legends.

Vocabulary

Knowing the following words will help you as you read "Phaëthon, Son of Apollo."

mortal (môr′ t'l) *n.*: A being who must eventually die (p. 601)

rash (rash) *adj.*: Reckless (p. 601)

deference (def′ ər əns) *n.*: Respect (p. 601)

implored (im plôrd′) *v.*: Begged (p. 601)

dissuade (di swād′) *v.*: Advise someone against an action (p. 602)

anointed (ə noint′ əd) *v.*: Rubbed oil or ointment on (p. 602)

precipitous (pri sip′ ə təs) *adj.*: Very steep (p. 603)

amber (am′ bər) *n.*: A yellowish or brownish substance that comes from certain trees (p. 604)

Phaëthon, Son of Apollo

Olivia E. Coolidge

Though Apollo always honored the memory of Daphne she was not his only love. Another was a mortal, Clymene,[1] by whom he had a son named Phaëthon. Phaëthon grew up with his mother, who, since she was mortal, could not dwell in the halls of Olympus[2] or in the palace of the sun. She lived not far from the East in the land of Ethiopia, and as her son grew up, she would point to the place where Eos,[3] goddess of the dawn, lighted up the sky and tell him that there his father dwelt. Phaëthon loved to boast of his divine father as he saw the golden chariot riding high through the air. He would remind his comrades of other sons of gods and mortal women who, by virture of their great deeds, had themselves become gods at last. He must always be first in everything, and in most things this was easy, since he was in truth stronger, swifter, and more daring than the others. Even if he were not victorious, Phaëthon always claimed to be first in honor. He could never bear to be beaten, even if he must risk his life in some rash way to win.

Most of the princes of Ethiopia willingly paid Phaëthon honor, since they admired him greatly for his fire and beauty. There was one boy, however, Epaphos,[4] who was rumored to be a child of Zeus himself. Since this was not certainly proved, Phaëthon chose to disbelieve it and to demand from Epaphos the deference that he obtained from all others. Epaphos was proud too, and one day he lost his temper with Phaëthon and turned on him, saying, "You are a fool to believe all that your mother tells you. You are all swelled up with false ideas about your father."

Crimson with rage, the lad rushed home to his mother and demanded that she prove to him the truth of the story that she had often told. "Give me some proof," he implored her, "with which I can answer this insult of Epaphos. It is a matter of life and death to me, for if I cannot, I shall die of shame."

"I swear to you," replied his mother solemnly, "by the bright orb of the sun itself that you are his son. If I swear falsely, may I never look on the sun again, but die before the next time he mounts the heavens. More than this I cannot do, but you, my child, can go to the eastern palace of Phoebus[5] Apollo— it lies not far away—and there speak with the god himself."

The son of Clymene leaped up with joy at his mother's words. The palace of Apollo was indeed not far. It stood just below the eastern horizon, its tall pillars glistening with bronze and gold. Above these it was white with gleaming ivory, and the great doors were flashing silver, embossed with pictures of earth, sky, and sea, and the gods that

1. **Clymene** (klim' ə nē)
2. **Olympus** (ō lim' pəs): A mountain in Northern Greece that was known as the home of the gods.
3. **Eos** (ē äs)
4. **Epaphos** (ep' ə fəs)

5. **Phoebus** (fē' bəs): Means "bright one" in Greek.

dwelt therein. Up the steep hill and the bright steps climbed Phaëthon, passing unafraid through the silver doors, and stood in the presence of the sun. Here at last he was forced to turn away his face, for Phoebus sat in state on his golden throne. It gleamed with emeralds and precious stones, while on the head of the god was a brilliant diamond crown upon which no eye could look undazzled.

Phaëthon hid his face, but the god had recognized his son, and he spoke kindly, asking him why he had come. Then Phaëthon plucked up courage and said, "I come to ask you if you are indeed my father. If you are so, I beg you to give me some proof of it so that all may recognize me as Phoebus' son."

The god smiled, being well pleased with his son's beauty and daring. He took off his crown so that Phaëthon could look at him, and coming down from his throne, he put his arms around the boy, and said, "You are indeed my son and Clymene's, and worthy to be called so. Ask of me whatever thing you wish to prove your origin to men, and you shall have it."

Phaëthon swayed for a moment and was dizzy with excitement at the touch of the god. His heart leaped; the blood rushed into his face. Now he felt that he was truly divine, unlike other men, and he did not wish to be counted with men any more. He looked up for a moment at his radiant father. "Let me drive the chariot of the sun across the heavens for one day," he said.

Apollo frowned and shook his head. "I cannot break my promise, but I will dissuade you if I can," he answered. "How can you drive my chariot, whose horses need a strong hand on the reins? The climb is too steep for you. The immense height will make you dizzy. The swift streams of air in the upper heaven will sweep you off your course.

Even the immortal gods could not drive my chariot. How then can you? Be wise and make some other choice."

The pride of Phaëthon was stubborn, for he thought the god was merely trying to frighten him. Besides, if he could guide the sun's chariot, would he not have proved his right to be divine rather than mortal? For that he would risk his life. Indeed, once he had seen Apollo's splendor, he did not wish to go back and live among men. Therefore, he insisted on his right until Apollo had to give way.

When the father saw that nothing else would satisfy the boy, he bade the Hours bring forth his chariot and yoke the horses. The chariot was of gold and had two gold-rimmed wheels with spokes of silver. In it there was room for one man to stand and hold the reins. Around the front and sides of it ran a rail, but the back was open. At the end of a long pole there were yokes for the four horses. The pole was of gold and shone with precious jewels: the golden topaz, the bright diamond, the green emerald, and the flashing ruby. While the Hours were yoking the swift, pawing horses, rosy-fingered Dawn hastened to the gates of heaven to draw them open. Meanwhile Apollo anointed his son's face with a magic ointment, that he might be able to bear the heat of the fire-breathing horses and the golden chariot. At last Phaëthon mounted the chariot and grasped the reins, the barriers were let down, and the horses shot up into the air.

At first the fiery horses sped forward up the accustomed trail, but behind them the chariot was too light without the weight of the immortal god. It bounded from side to side and was dashed up and down. Phaëthon was too frightened and too dizzy to pull the reins, nor would he have known anyway whether he was on the usual path. As soon as the horses felt that there was no hand controlling them, they soared up, up with fiery speed into the heavens till the earth grew pale and cold beneath them. Phaëthon shut his eyes, trembling at the dizzy, precipitous height. Then the horses dropped down, more swiftly than a falling stone, flinging themselves madly from side to side in panic because they were masterless. Phaëthon dropped the reins entirely and clung with all his might to the chariot rail. Meanwhile as they came near the earth, it dried up and cracked apart. Meadows were reduced to white ashes, cornfields smoked and

THE FALL OF PHAËTHON
Peter Paul Rubens

shriveled, cities perished in flame. Far and wide on the wooded mountains the forests were ablaze, and even the snowclad Alps were bare and dry. Rivers steamed and dried to dust. The great North African plain was scorched until it became the desert that it is today. Even the sea shrank back to pools and caves, until dried fishes were left baking upon the white-hot sands. At last the great earth mother called upon Zeus to save her from utter destruction, and Zeus hurled a mighty thunderbolt at the unhappy Phaëthon, who was still crouched in the chariot, clinging desperately to the rail. The dart cast him out, and he fell flaming in a long trail through the air. The chariot broke in pieces at the mighty blow, and the maddened horses rushed snorting back to the stable of their master, Apollo.

Unhappy Clymene and her daughters wandered over the whole earth seeking the body of the boy they loved so well. When they found him, they took him and buried him. Over his grave they wept and could not be comforted. At last the gods in pity for their grief changed them into poplar trees, which weep with tears of amber in memory of Phaëthon.

RESPONDING TO THE SELECTION

Your Response

1. Have you ever wished you had taken some good advice? Explain.

Recalling

2. Why does Phaëthon go to Apollo's palace?
3. Why does Apollo urge Phaëthon to make a wish different from his first one?
4. What is Phaëthon's secret reason for his request?
5. What natural features are explained in this myth?

Interpreting

6. Why do you think Phaëthon feels that he had to "always be first in everything"?

7. How does Phaëthon display his pride with his classmates? How does he display it with Apollo?
8. How might this story have been different if Phaëthon had resembled his father less?

9. Given Phaëthon's choice, tell what you would have requested from Apollo. Explain the reasons for your decision.

ANALYZING LITERATURE

Understanding Hubris

Hubris means excessive pride or arrogance. In this myth Phaëthon shows hubris by wanting to become an immortal. However, his attempt to assume his father's godlike powers threatens the earth and causes his own death.

1. Why do you think Phaëthon could not stand to be an ordinary human being?
2. Was Phaëthon's hubris his own fault or was it the result of the fact that he *was* the son of a god? Explain.
3. Was the punishment that Phaëthon received too harsh? Why or why not?
4. What lesson does this myth suggest?

CRITICAL THINKING AND READING

Recognizing Clues to the Outcome

Throughout this myth there are clues that Phaëthon's behavior may lead to disaster. You can find these hints by looking for remarks he makes or feelings he experiences that seem exaggerated or too intense. These indicate how desperate he is to prove that he is immortal.

1. Find two examples where Phaëthon feels that he would risk his life to get his way.
2. Why is his reaction to Apollo's embrace a clue to the coming disaster?

THINKING AND WRITING

Creating a Modern Myth

You and your literary agent have decided that the story of Phaëthon would make a wonderful best-selling novel. However, readers will not buy your book unless the story is up to date. Brainstorm to gather ideas for putting this myth into a modern setting. Phaëthon's father, for instance, cannot be a god, but he could be the president of a billion-dollar company. In this modern setting, perhaps Phaëthon wants to fly his father's corporate jet. Present your best ideas in a letter to your agent explaining the modern situation and setting for your novel. Then revise the letter to make sure your agent will be convinced that the book will sell.

LEARNING OPTIONS

1. **Cross-curricular Connection.** Locate Greece on a world map. In which hemispheres (northern, southern, eastern, western) is it located? Identify the lines of latitude that mark its northernmost and southernmost borders. Using this knowledge and the help of your science textbooks, determine approximately how many hours of sunlight Greece experiences in the months of December and June. Compare these estimates with the number of hours of sunlight your hometown experiences in the same months.
2. **Art.** Make a model of the chariot in which Phaëthon rides. You may use any medium you wish. Think about how to represent the horses and Phaëthon himself.
3. **Writing.** Write a newspaper story or television news report about Phaëthon's chariot ride. Make sure your account answers the reporter's basic questions: *who? what? when? where?* and *why?* Think about the kind of information your audience wants when deciding which details to include.

GUIDE FOR READING

Ojeeg, the Hunter, and the Ice Man

Conflict in Legend

A **conflict** is a struggle between opposing sides or forces. Conflict plays an important role in legend, just as it does in short stories and novels. One difference, however, is that a legend may present a struggle between a hero with special powers and a supernatural being. In this Indian legend, the hero Ojeeg battles with old man Peboan, the powerful spirit of winter. Their weapons are not bows or guns, but the forces of ice and fire.

Focus

The native peoples of North America built many different types of dwellings. The Sioux, for example, lived in tepees, cone-shaped tents made from the skins of animals that roamed the Great Plains. The Pueblo Indians of the Southwest, including the Hopi, lived in terraced dwellings made of stone or sun-dried clay called *adobe.* In the Maritime provinces of Canada, the Micmacs constructed two types of wigwam. One wigwam was oblong-shaped with open ends; the other was cone-shaped with a flap over the door. Which wigwam do you think they used in winter and which did they use in summer? Write a brief explanation for your choices. Which would be used in the story of Ojeeg?

Vocabulary

Knowing the following words will help you as you read "Ojeeg, the Hunter, and the Ice Man."

vanquish (van′ kwish) *v.:* Overcome (p. 607)

pummeled (pum′ ′ld) *v.:* Hit with repeated blows (p. 608)

extracted (ik strakt′ əd) *v.:* Obtained by drawing out (p. 608)

rendered (ren′ dərd) *v.:* Melted down (p. 608)

flaunted (flônt′ əd) *v.:* Displayed; showed off (p. 608)

shuddered (shud′ ərd) *v.:* Shook (p. 610)

grizzled (griz′ ′ld) *adj.:* Gray (p. 610)

flit (flit) *v.:* Fly lightly and rapidly (p. 610)

The Micmac

This tale comes from the **Micmac** (mik′ mak) Indians, who live in eastern Canada. Years ago, this tribe hunted, fished, and gathered clams for food. During the cold Canadian winter, they traveled by means of wooden toboggans and snowshoes. They kept themselves warm in wigwams covered with birchbark or animal skins.

Dorothy de Wit (1916–1980) retells this Micmac tale in her book *The Talking Stone: An Anthology of Native American Tales and Legends* (1979).

Ojeeg, the Hunter, and the Ice Man

from **the Micmac (Canada)**

Dorothy de Wit

On the shores of a large body of water, near the great evergreen forests of the north, there lived a hunter with his wife and young son. Their wigwam[1] stood by itself, far from the village, and they were very content, for Ojeeg was skilled with his arrows and brought as much game and furs to his wife as they had need of! The little boy would have been happy, indeed, if the snow had not been so deep or the winters so long. He did not miss companions to play with, for his father showed him the tracks of the grouse[2] and the squirrels. He pointed out the white coats of the rabbits and the weasel, and he trained him to use his bow carefully so that he would not waste his arrows.

But the cold grew more bitter as the long winter months dragged on. One day the boy saw a squirrel running around a stump, looking vainly for buried nuts, for the snow was too deep. Finally, the squirrel rested on his bushy tail, and as the boy came toward him, he said, "I am hungry, and there is no food to be found anywhere! Aren't you, too, tired of this ice and cold?"

"I am," said the hunter's son. "But what can we do against the power of the Ice Man? We are weak; he is cruel and strong!"

"You can cry! You can howl with hunger!" replied the squirrel. "Your father is a great hunter. He has strong power, and maybe he can vanquish the Ice Man if he sees your grief. Cry, cry, small brother! It may help!"

That night the young boy came into the wigwam, threw down his bow and arrows, and huddled beside the fire, sobbing. He would not answer his mother when she questioned him, and he would not stop crying. When his father came home, the boy's cries grew even louder, and nothing would make him stop, until at last the hunter asked, "Is it perhaps that you are lonely? That you do not like the snow and the cold?" At that the boy nodded his head. "Then," said the father, "I shall see if I have the power to change it."

He went out the next day on his snowshoes.[3] Long he traveled by the frozen water till he came to a narrow place that was

---

1. wigwam (wig′ wäm) *n.*: A shelter with a rounded top made by certain Native American groups.
2. grouse (grous) *n.*: A group of game birds.

3. snowshoes (snō′ shōoz′) *n.*: Racket-shaped pieces of wood crisscrossed with strips of leather, worn on the feet to prevent sinking in deep snow.

choked with huge blocks of ice. He took his sharp knife and a stone chisel, and he began to dig away at the chunks. Many hours he chipped and hacked and pummeled the ice, and in the end he heard the barricade crack! The ice began to move, and a part of it broke off and jostled and bumped around until more cracks appeared. The whole mass of ice began to float slowly away. The hunter rested and wiped the sweat from his face. Then he heard the voice of Peboan, the ice king, piercing the air: "You have won for now, my son! You are strong indeed, and your Manito power[4] is great! But I shall gain the final victory, for next year I will return, and I will bring even more snow! The North Wind will blow more fiercely, and the trees will break with the weight of the ice I will pile on their branches! The waters will freeze so that no matter how many warriors cross them, not a crack will appear. Then you will see, grandson, who is the master of winter!"

The hunter returned to his wigwam. The snows were melting, and green was returning to the earth. Sweet sap rose in the maple trees, and his little son shouted with joy! But the hunter remembered the threat which the ice king had made: "Next winter will be worse—much worse!"

So he set himself to cutting wood and piling it in great stacks; he gathered the resin[5] from the pine trees and formed it into great lumps. From the game which he brought home he extracted much fat, and this he rendered and stored in large oil pots. Baskets of evergreen cones and thick logs he stored up also. Then, when the maple and the oak flaunted their red and yellow banners at the dark hemlocks, he went somewhat apart from his own lodging and built a small, very tight new wigwam. He left his wife warm skins and food in quantity; then, with supplies for himself, he began stacking them, and the firewood, the resin lumps, the oil pots, and the baskets of cones, within his new lodging.

When the first snowfall whitened the ground, he bade his wife and son have courage and went to the new wigwam. He laced the skins tightly and closed the opening securely. With food and water at hand and warm furs to cover him, he built a very small

4. Manito (man′ ə tō′) **power:** Power that comes from nature spirits.
5. resin (rez′ ′n) *n.:* A sticky brownish or yellowish substance that comes from evergreen trees.

fire in the center of the fire hole and sat down to wait for Peboan.

At first the frost was light, and the snow melted quickly. At night the wind did not rise much, and the hunter thought, "Perhaps I have frightened old Peboan away! He will see that it is not so easy to win over me!" But as the winter deepened, the tent poles rattled more, the skins shuddered a bit, and it took more fire to warm the wigwam. Still, Peboan did not come. The hunter heard the great owl swoop through the trees at night. He heard weasels and rabbits move through the snow, and once the heavy footfall of a moose crashed through the drifts. The cold became intense.

Then, suddenly one night, the skins across the door opening were torn away and a gust of North Wind almost blew the fire apart! Peboan stood there, grizzled and bent. His face was lined and cruel, and his long beard hung with icicles. "I have come as I said I would," he shouted.

The hunter rose swiftly, tied up the door skins, and put more wood on the fire. A chill ran through him—the ice king's power was very great! "Grandfather, be seated at my fire. You are my guest here!" he said. The old one sat far from the fire and watched him.

"My power is great! I blow my breath—the streams stand still; the waters are stiff and hard like rock crystal!"

The hunter shivered and put another log on the fire. "The snow covers the land when I shake my head; trees are without any leaves, and their branches break with the weight of my ice!"

The hunter added some cones, and the flames leaped up. "No birds fly now, for they have gone far away. Only the hardy ones flit around, and they are hungry."

The hunter added more wood to the fire, for the air in the wigwam was becoming bitter cold, and frost hung on his eyebrows and nose. "The animals hide away and sleep through the long cold." Peboan laughed grimly as he saw the man draw his fur closer around him.

"Even the hunters do not leave their lodges. The children curl deep into their blankets for warmth and cry with hunger."

Then Ojeeg pulled out the resin lumps; first one, then another he tossed into the coals, and they burned hotly. Peboan shook his white head and moved as far away from the heat as he could. When the hunter saw that, he added yet another clutch of pitch and more logs. Sweat began to roll down the wrinkled face; the ice king huddled close to the wall of the wigwam; his icy garments began to melt.

Ojeeg took up the pots of oil and poured them onto the fire. The flames burned orange and red and blue! They licked at the old man's long robe, at his ice-covered feet, at his snowy mantle, and the Ice Man cried out in pain, "Enough, enough! I have seen your power, Ojeeg! Take back your fire and heat! Stifle your flames!" But the hunter only built up the fire higher, and the Ice Man became smaller and smaller, till at last he melted into a pool of water which ran over the ground and out, under the wigwam opening. When he saw that, Ojeeg, the hunter, untied the skins and looked out. The Ice Man was gone completely! Beyond his doorway the ground was brown and soft with pine needles, he could hear running water, and birds flew through the treetops. How long had he been in his wigwam? The spring was at hand!

Ojeeg put out his fire and ran toward his wife and son, who had come out and stood waiting to welcome him! The ice king would not make so long a visit next year! Only the white flowers of the snowdrop, fragile and small, remained to mark where Peboan had left his footprints!

Your Response

1. How do you feel about winter? If you have never experienced winter, do you think you would like it? Why or why not?

Recalling

2. Why does the hunter decide to make the snow and cold go away?
3. Describe Peboan when he appears at the wigwam. What powers does he have?
4. Why does the ice king vanish?

Interpreting

5. How do you know that the hunter is a hero, with more power than an ordinary person?
6. How does Ojeeg influence the way that seasons change?
7. Why do you think the Micmacs thought of ice as having godlike powers?

Applying

8. Explain what you learn about the Micmac tribe from reading this legend.

ANALYZING LITERATURE

Understanding Conflict in a Legend

A **conflict** is a struggle between opposing sides or forces. Sometimes tales and legends present conflicts by giving a supernatural twist to a real situation. For instance, the Micmac had to fight against the cold in the northern woods. Their legend of Ojeeg and the Ice Man dramatizes that struggle by telling about a battle between a hero and a magical ice king.

1. How does Ojeeg win the first fight?
2. What is his plan to win again?
3. When does it seem that Ojeeg might lose?
4. What does he do to make Peboan retreat?
5. Is Ojeeg's victory total? Explain.

CRITICAL THINKING AND READING

Evaluating a Personification

A **personification** is a figure of speech that gives human qualities to an idea, an object, or an aspect of nature. In this legend Peboan is a personification. Although he is magical, he represents the winter in human form. You can judge whether he is a suitable ice king by looking closely at his traits.

1. Is Peboan a suitable personification of winter? Why or why not?
2. Why is his face "lined and cruel"?
3. If you wanted to personify winter, what kind of person would you use?

THINKING AND WRITING

Creating a Personification

Imagine that an advertising agency is offering a prize for the best personification of winter. The agency will use the character created by the winner in a campaign to promote ski resorts. This character must therefore convey a positive image of the winter season. List the qualities that such a personification should have. Using your list, write a letter to the agency explaining your concept. As you revise your letter, make sure it will convince the agency, and you will win the prize.

LEARNING OPTION

Speaking and Listening. Form a small group to give a dramatic reading of "Ojeeg, the Hunter, and the Ice Man" for the class. Some group members can read the characters' dialogue, and others can read the narrative passages. As you practice, notice clues about how the characters might actually sound. For example, the ice king is a "grizzled and bent" old man. Those reading the narrative passages should try to convey a sense of the intense cold and the drama between Ojeeg and Peboan.

GUIDE FOR READING

The Aztecs

This folk legend comes to us from the **Aztec** Indians, who controlled a great empire in Mexico about 500 years ago. Some of their cities were even larger than European cities of that era. The Spanish destroyed this empire in 1521, but the influence of Aztec culture has continued in art, language, and food.

Juliet Piggott (1924–   ), whose version of this tale appears in her book *Mexican Folk Tales,* has also written about Japanese history and folklore.

Popocatepetl and Ixtlaccihuatl

Motivation in Legend

The term **motivation** refers to the reasons that people act as they do. Like characters in fiction, those in legends have reasons or motives for their behavior. In "The Wicked Weasel," for example, the weasel pretends to be praying in order to win the trust of the mice and squirrels. His motive for tricking them is his desire to eat them.

A storyteller may reveal the characters' motives or let you figure them out for yourself. In "Popocatepetl and Ixtlaccihuatl" the storyteller uses both of these methods.

Focus

Before you read "Popocatepetl and Ixtlaccihuatl," look at the painting on page 614. It is an artist's view of a volcano in the midst of erupting. What feelings does the painting evoke in you? What do you like about it? What don't you like? Write a few sentences about your reaction to the painting. Then write a few more exploring your thoughts about volcanoes. Have you ever seen one up close? Would you like to? To what human emotions could a volcano's eruption be compared? Have you ever "erupted"?

Vocabulary

Knowing the following words will help you as you read "Popocatepetl and Ixtlaccihuatl."

besieged (bi sēj'd') *v.:* Surrounded (p. 615)
decreed (di krēd') *v.:* Officially ordered (p. 615)
relished (rel' isht) *v.:* Especially enjoyed (p. 615)
brandishing (bran' dish iŋ) *v.:* Waving in a menacing way (p. 616)

unanimous (yōō nan' ə məs) *adj.:* Based on complete agreement (p. 616)
refute (ri fyōōt') *v.:* To prove someone wrong (p. 616)
routed (rout' əd) *v.:* Completely defeated (p. 618)
edifice (ed' ə fis) *n.:* Large structure (p. 618)

Popocatepetl and Ixtlaccihuatl

from Mexico

Juliet Piggott

Before the Spaniards came to Mexico and marched on the Aztec capital of Tenochtitlan[1] there were two volcanoes to the southeast of that city. The Spaniards destroyed much of Tenochtitlan and built another city in its place and called it Mexico City. It is known by that name still, and the pass through which the Spaniards came to the ancient Tenochtitlan is still there, as are the volcanoes on each side of that pass. Their names have not been changed. The one to the north is Ixtlaccihuatl[2] and the one on the south of the pass is Popocatepetl.[3] Both are snowcapped and beautiful, Popocatepetl being the taller of the two. That name means Smoking Mountain. In Aztec days it gushed forth smoke and, on occasion, it does so still. It erupted too in Aztec days and has done so again since the Spaniards came. Ixtlaccihuatl means The White Woman, for its peak was, and still is, white.

Perhaps Ixtlaccihuatl and Popocatepetl were there in the highest part of the Valley of Mexico in the days when the earth was very young, in the days when the new people were just learning to eat and grow corn. The Aztecs claimed the volcanoes as their own, for they possessed a legend about them and their creation, and they believed that legend to be true.

There was once an Aztec Emperor in Tenochtitlan. He was very powerful. Some thought he was wise as well, whilst others doubted his wisdom. He was both a ruler and a warrior and he kept at bay those tribes living in and beyond the mountains surrounding the Valley of Mexico, with its huge lake called Texcoco[4] in which Tenochtitlan was built. His power was absolute and the splendor in which he lived was very great.

It is not known for how many years the Emperor ruled in Tenochtitlan, but it is known that he lived to a great age. However, it was not until he was in his middle years that his wife gave him an heir, a girl. The Emperor and Empress loved the princess very much and she was their only child. She was a dutiful daughter and learned all she could from her father about the art of ruling, for she knew that when he died she would reign in his stead in Tenochtitlan.

Her name was Ixtlaccihuatl. Her parents

---

1. **Tenochtitlan** (te nôch′ tē tlän′): The Spanish conquered the Aztec capital in 1521.
2. **Ixtlaccihuatl** (ēs′ tä sē′ wät′l)
3. **Popocatepetl** (pŏ pō′ kä te′ pet′l)

4. **Texcoco** (tä skō′ kō)

ERUPTING VOLCANO, 1943
Dr. Atl (Gerardo Murillo)
Laurie Platt Winfrey, Inc.

and her friends called her Ixtla. She had a pleasant disposition and, as a result, she had many friends. The great palace where she lived with the Emperor and Empress rang with their laughter when they came to the parties her parents gave for her. As well as being a delightful companion Ixtla was also very pretty, even beautiful.

Her childhood was happy and she was content enough when she became a young woman. But by then she was fully aware of the great responsibilities which would be

hers when her father died and she became serious and studious and did not enjoy parties as much as she had done when younger.

Another reason for her being so serious was that she was in love. This in itself was a joyous thing, but the Emperor forbade her to marry. He wanted her to reign and rule alone when he died, for he trusted no one, not even his wife, to rule as he did except his much loved only child, Ixtla. This was why there were some who doubted the wisdom of the Emperor for, by not allowing his heiress to marry, he showed a selfishness and short-sightedness towards his daughter and his empire which many considered was not truly wise. An emperor, they felt, who was not truly wise could not also be truly great. Or even truly powerful.

The man with whom Ixtla was in love was also in love with her. Had they been allowed to marry their state could have been doubly joyous. His name was Popocatepetl and Ixtla and his friends all called him Popo. He was a warrior in the service of the Emperor, tall and strong, with a capacity for gentleness, and very brave. He and Ixtla loved each other very much and while they were content and even happy when they were together, true joy was not theirs because the Emperor continued to insist that Ixtla should not be married when the time came for her to take on her father's responsibilities.

This unfortunate but moderately happy relationship between Ixtla and Popo continued for several years, the couple pleading with the Emperor at regular intervals and the Emperor remaining constantly adamant. Popo loved Ixtla no less for her father's stubbornness and she loved him no less while she studied, as her father demanded she should do, the art of ruling in preparation for her reign.

When the Emperor became very old he also became ill. In his feebleness he channeled all his failing energies towards instructing Ixtla in statecraft, for he was no longer able to exercise that craft himself. So it was that his enemies, the tribes who lived in the mountains and beyond, realized that the great Emperor in Tenochtitlan was great no longer, for he was only teaching his daughter to rule and not ruling himself.

The tribesmen came nearer and nearer to Tenochtitlan until the city was besieged. At last the Emperor realized himself that he was great no longer, that his power was nearly gone and that his domain was in dire peril.

Warrior though he long had been, he was now too old and too ill to lead his fighting men into battle. At last he understood that, unless his enemies were frustrated in their efforts to enter and lay waste to Tenochtitlan, not only would he no longer be Emperor but his daughter would never be Empress.

Instead of appointing one of his warriors to lead the rest into battle on his behalf, he offered a bribe to all of them. Perhaps it was that his wisdom, if wisdom he had, had forsaken him, or perhaps he acted from fear. Or perhaps he simply changed his mind. But the bribe he offered to whichever warrior succeeded in lifting the siege of Tenochtitlan and defeating the enemies in and around the Valley of Mexico was both the hand of his daughter and the equal right to reign and rule, with her, in Tenochtitlan. Furthermore, he decreed that directly he learned that his enemies had been defeated he would instantly cease to be Emperor himself. Ixtla would not have to wait until her father died to become Empress and, if her father should die of his illness or old age before his enemies were vanquished, he further decreed that he who overcame the surrounding enemies should marry the princess whether he, the Emperor, lived or not.

Ixtla was fearful when she heard of her father's bribe to his warriors, for the only one whom she had any wish to marry was Popo and she wanted to marry him, and only him, very much indeed.

The warriors, however, were glad when they heard of the decree: there was not one of them who would not have been glad to have the princess as his wife and they all relished the chance of becoming Emperor.

And so the warriors went to war at their

ruler's behest, and each fought trebly[5] hard for each was fighting not only for the safety of Tenochtitlan and the surrounding valley, but for the delightful bride and for the right to be the Emperor himself.

Even though the warriors fought with great skill and even though each one exhibited a courage he did not know he possessed, the war was a long one. The Emperor's enemies were firmly entrenched around Lake Texcoco and Tenochtitlan by the time the warriors were sent to war, and as battle followed battle the final outcome was uncertain.

The warriors took a variety of weapons with them; wooden clubs edged with sharp blades of obsidian,[6] obsidian machetes,[7] javelins which they hurled at their enemies from troughed throwing boards, bows and arrows, slings and spears set with obsidian fragments, and lances, too. Many of them carried shields woven from wicker[8] and covered in tough hide and most wore armor made of thick quilted cotton soaked in brine.

The war was long and fierce. Most of the warriors fought together and in unison, but some fought alone. As time went on natural leaders emerged and, of these, undoubtedly Popo was the best. Finally it was he, brandishing his club and shield, who led the great charge of running warriors across the valley, with their enemies fleeing before them to the safety of the coastal plains and jungles beyond the mountains.

The warriors acclaimed Popo as the man most responsible for the victory and, weary though they all were, they set off for Tenoch-titlan to report to the Emperor and for Popo to claim Ixtla as his wife at last.

But a few of those warriors were jealous of Popo. Since they knew none of them could rightly claim the victory for himself (the decision among the Emperor's fighting men that Popo was responsible for the victory had been unanimous), they wanted to spoil for him and for Ixtla the delights which the Emperor had promised.

These few men slipped away from the rest at night and made their way to Tenoch-titlan ahead of all the others. They reached the capital two days later, having traveled without sleep all the way, and quickly let it be known that, although the Emperor's warriors had been successful against his enemies, the warrior Popo had been killed in battle.

It was a foolish and cruel lie which those warriors told their Emperor, and they told it for no reason other than that they were jealous of Popo.

When the Emperor heard this he demanded that Popo's body be brought to him so that he might arrange a fitting burial. He knew the man his daughter had loved would have died courageously. The jealous warriors looked at one another and said nothing. Then one of them told the Emperor that Popo had been killed on the edge of Lake Texcoco and that his body had fallen into the water and no man had been able to retrieve it. The Emperor was saddened to hear this.

After a little while he demanded to be told which of his warriors had been responsible for the victory but none of the fighting men before him dared claim the successful outcome of the war for himself, for each knew the others would refute him. So they were silent. This puzzled the Emperor and he decided to wait for the main body of his warriors to return and not to press the few

---

5. trebly (tre′ blē) *adv.*: Three times as much, triply.
6. obsidian (əb sid′ ē ən) *n.*: A hard, usually dark-colored or black, volcanic glass.
7. machetes (mə shet′ ēs) *n.*: Large, heavy-bladed knives.
8. wicker (wik′ ər) *n.*: A thin, flexible twig.

QUETZALCOATL
Laurie Platt Winfrey, Inc.

who had brought the news of the victory and of Popo's death.

Then the Emperor sent for his wife and his daughter and told them their enemies had been overcome. The Empress was thoroughly excited and relieved at the news. Ixtla was only apprehensive. The Emperor, seeing her anxious face, told her quickly that Popo was dead. He went on to say that the warrior's body had been lost in the waters of Lake Texcoco, and again it was as though his wisdom had left him, for he spoke at some length of his not being able to tell Ixtla who her husband would be and who would become Emperor when the main body of warriors returned to Tenochtitlan.

But Ixtla heard nothing of what he told her, only that her beloved Popo was dead. She went to her room and lay down. Her mother followed her and saw at once she was very ill. Witch doctors were sent for, but they could not help the princess, and neither could her parents. Her illness had no name, unless it was the illness of a broken heart. Princess Ixtlaccihuatl did not wish to live if Popocatepetl was dead, and so she died herself.

The day after her death Popo returned to Tenochtitlan with all the other surviving warriors. They went straight to the palace and, with much cheering, told the Emperor that his enemies had been routed and that Popo was the undoubted victor of the conflict.

The Emperor praised his warriors and pronounced Popo to be the new Emperor in his place. When the young man asked first to see Ixtla, begging that they should be married at once before being jointly proclaimed Emperor and Empress, the Emperor had to tell Popo of Ixtla's death, and how it had happened.

Popo spoke not a word.

He gestured the assembled warriors to follow him and together they sought out the few jealous men who had given the false news of his death to the Emperor. With the army of warriors watching, Popo killed each one of them in single combat with his obsidian studded club. No one tried to stop him.

That task accomplished Popo returned to the palace and, still without speaking and still wearing his stiff cotton armor, went to Ixtla's room. He gently lifted her body and carried it out of the palace and out of the city, and no one tried to stop him doing that either. All the warriors followed him in silence.

When he had walked some miles he gestured to them again and they built a huge pile of stones in the shape of a pyramid. They all worked together and they worked fast while Popo stood and watched, holding the body of the princess in his arms. By sunset the mighty edifice was finished. Popo climbed it alone, carrying Ixtla's corpse with him. There, at the very top, under a heap of stones, he buried the young woman he had loved so well and for so long, and who had died for the love of him.

That night Popo slept alone at the top of the pyramid by Ixtla's grave. In the morning he came down and spoke for the first time since the Emperor had told him the princess was dead. He told the warriors to build another pyramid, a little to the southeast of the one which held Ixtla's body and to build it higher than the other.

He told them too to tell the Emperor on his behalf that he, Popocatepetl, would never reign and rule in Tenochtitlan. He would keep watch over the grave of the Princess Ixtlaccihuatl for the rest of his life.

The messages to the Emperor were the last words Popo ever spoke. Well before the evening the second mighty pile of stones was built. Popo climbed it and stood at the top, taking a torch of resinous pine wood with him.

And when he reached to top he lit the torch and the warriors below saw the white smoke rise against the blue sky, and they watched as the sun began to set and the smoke turned pink and then a deep red, the color of blood.

So Popocatepetl stood there, holding the torch in memory of Ixtlaccihuatl, for the rest of his days.

The snows came and, as the years went by, the pyramids of stone became high white-capped mountains. Even now the one called Popocatepetl emits smoke in memory of the princess whose body lies in the mountain which bears her name.

RESPONDING TO THE SELECTION

Your Response

1. If you were either Ixtla or Popo, how would you have responded to the news of the other's death?

Recalling

2. Why are Ixtla and Popo unable to marry?
3. How does the emperor show his selfishness? What effect does his selfishness have on the safety of his kingdom?
4. What leads to Ixtla's death at the end of the war?
5. Why does Popo refuse to rule in Tenochtitlán?

Interpreting

6. Is the emperor a wise man? Why or why not?
7. On the basis of this legend, what traits do you think the Aztecs admired?

Applying

8. What traits do you think are necessary in a leader?

ANALYZING LITERATURE

Understanding Motivation in Legend

The term **motivation** refers to the reasons people act as they do. In "Popocatepetl and Ixtlaccihuatl" the storyteller often explains the characters' **motives,** or reasons for acting.

1. Which event is caused by selfishness?
2. Which is caused by jealousy?
3. Which are caused by love?
4. What do you think this legend indicates about the power of love?

CRITICAL THINKING AND READING

Identifying Imaginative Details

Legends are traditional tales passed down over the generations. Often they are based on the lives of people who actually once lived. However, legends are not history. The events they tell about have been filtered through a people's imagination and enlarged upon.

1. Which events in this legend might have been based on historical events?
2. Which events are highly imaginative and probably not based on historical events?

THINKING AND WRITING

Writing About a Legend

Imagine you are either Ixtla, Popo, or one of the jealous soldiers. Tell this story from this character's point of view. First list the details you would emphasize in your retelling of the myth. Arrange these details in chronological order. Then write your first draft. Revise your tale, making sure you have stayed in character. Prepare a final draft and share it with your classmates.

LEARNING OPTIONS

1. **Cross-curricular Connection.** The Aztecs settled in what is now Mexico in the twelfth century. Their empire flourished until the arrival of Spanish troops led by Hernán Cortés. Find pictures of what their cities, like Tenochtitlán, looked like. Then draw a map of an Aztec city, showing the arrangement of buildings. You may want to build a model of some Aztec pyramids.
2. **Cross-curricular Connection.** The volcanoes in this tale really exist, about thirty miles from Mexico City. Both are dormant, which means that they have not erupted in a long time. Ixtlaccihuatl last erupted in 1868, and though Popocatepetl last erupted in 1802, smoke still occasionally rises from its cone. Find out more about volcanoes. How are they formed? What is their structure like? Then build a model of one using whatever medium you like. Ask your science teacher to help find a way to make your volcano safely "erupt."

GUIDE FOR READING

The Legend of the Hummingbird

Legend: Universal Theme

A **universal theme** is an idea or a situation that has been common to many different groups throughout history. Such themes appear often in legends and folk tales. One repeated theme involves the problems that young people face when their love goes against the wishes of their families or society. In this legend the daughter of an Indian chief invites danger by falling in love with a young man from an enemy tribe.

Focus

Though it is located in the tropical zone, the rugged and hilly island of Puerto Rico rarely experiences temperatures exceeding 85 degrees Fahrenheit. Surprisingly, Puerto Rico does not have abundant wildlife. Fish are plentiful in the surrounding waters of the Caribbean Sea, but native land animals include mainly snakes, lizards, the mongoose, and birds—including hummingbirds. Plant life on the island includes many types of palm trees, bamboo, and a great variety of colorful and fragrant flowering plants.

In the tale you are about to read, two characters meet at a beautiful place "far up in the hills." To help you imagine what such a place would look like on a tropical island, make a sensory language chart like the one below. Use it to write descriptions of things on the island that would appeal to each of your senses.

Sights	Sounds	Smells	Tastes	Touch

Vocabulary

Knowing the following word will help you as you read "The Legend of the Hummingbird."

dreaded (dred′ əd) *adj.*: Feared (p. 621)

Puerto Rico

Puerto Rico (pwer′ tə rē′ kō) is a commonwealth of the United States located about 1,000 miles southeast of Florida. The earliest inhabitants of the island were the **Borinquen** Indians, from whom this legend comes. Some Puerto Ricans today can still trace their origins to this now-vanished tribe.

Pura Belpré (poo′ rä bel′ prā) (1899–1982), who retells this legend, was born in Puerto Rico and moved to New York City as a young woman. She wrote a number of books based on Puerto Rican folklore.

The Legend of the Hummingbird

from **Puerto Rico**

Pura Belpré

Between the towns of Cayey and Cidra, far up in the hills, there was once a small pool fed by a waterfall that tumbled down the side of the mountain. The pool was surrounded by pomarosa trees, and the Indians used to call it Pomarosa Pool. It was the favorite place of Alida, the daughter of an Indian chief, a man of power and wealth among the people of the hills.

One day, when Alida had come to the pool to rest after a long walk, a young Indian came there to pick some fruit from the trees. Alida was surprised, for he was not of her tribe. Yet he said he was no stranger to the pool. This was where he had first seen Alida, and he had often returned since then to pick fruit, hoping to see her again.

He told her about himself to make her feel at home. He confessed, with honesty and frankness, that he was a member of the dreaded Carib tribe[1] that had so often attacked the island of Borinquen.[2] As a young boy, he had been left behind after one of those raids, and he had stayed on the island ever since.

Alida listened closely to his story, and the two became friends. They met again in the days that followed, and their friendship grew stronger. Alida admired the young man's courage in living among his enemies. She learned to call him by his Carib name, Taroo, and he called her Alida, just as her own people did. Before long, their friendship had turned into love.

Their meetings by the pool were always brief. Alida was afraid their secret might be discovered, and careful though she was, there came a day when someone saw them and told her father. Alida was forbidden to visit the Pomarosa Pool, and to put an end to her romance with the stranger, her father decided to marry her to a man of his own choosing. Preparations for the wedding started at once.

Alida was torn with grief, and one evening she cried out to her god: "O Yukiyú, help me! Kill me or do what you will with me, but do not let me marry this man whom I do not love!"

And the great god Yukiyú took pity on her and changed her into a delicate red flower.

Meanwhile Taroo, knowing nothing of Alida's sorrow, still waited for her by the Pomarosa Pool. Day after day he waited. Sometimes he stayed there until a mantle of stars was spread across the sky.

---

1. Carib (kar′ ib) **tribe:** Native Americans who formerly inhabited the Southwest Indies and the northern coast of South America.
2. Borinquen (bō′ rēn ken′): Puerto Rico.

One night the moon took pity on him. "Taroo," she called from her place high above the stars. "O Taroo, wait no longer for Alida! Your secret was made known, and Alida was to be married to a man of her father's choosing. In her grief she called to her god, Yukiyú; he heard her plea for help and changed her into a red flower."

"Ahee, ahee!" cried Taroo. "O moon, what is the name of the red flower?"

"Only Yukiyú knows that," the moon replied.

Then Taroo called out: "O Yukiyú, god of my Alida, help me too! Help me to find her!"

And just as the great god had heard Alida's plea, he listened now to Taroo and decided to help him. There by the Pomarosa Pool, before the moon and the silent stars, the great god changed Taroo into a small many-colored bird.

"Fly, Colibrí, and find your love among the flowers," he said.

Off went the Colibrí, flying swiftly, and as he flew his wings made a sweet humming sound.

In the morning the Indians saw a new bird darting about among the flowers swift as an arrow and brilliant as a jewel. They heard the humming of its wings, and in amazement they saw it hover in the air over every blossom, kissing the petals of the flowers with its long slender bill. They liked the new bird with the music in its wings, and they called it Hummingbird.

Ever since then the little many-colored bird has hovered over every flower he finds, but returns most often to the flowers that are red. He is still looking, always looking, for the one red flower that will be his lost Alida. He has not found her yet.

Your Response

1. What advice would you have given to Alida and Taroo regarding their situation?

Recalling

2. How does Alida's father try to end her relationship with the stranger?
3. What happens to the two young lovers?

Interpreting

4. What does this legend tell you about the enduring quality of love?
5. Which facts of nature does this legend explain?

Applying

6. A proverb says: Love finds hidden paths. How does this legend prove the proverb?

ANALYZING LITERATURE

Understanding a Universal Theme

A **universal theme** is an idea or a situation common to many different groups throughout history. Such themes appear often in literature and folklore. In *Romeo and Juliet,* for instance, William Shakespeare writes about the problems that young people face when they fall in love. "The Legend of the Hummingbird" deals with the same universal theme. Like Romeo and Juliet, Taroo and Alida encounter serious difficulties.

1. What problems might they have faced even if Alida's family accepted Taroo?
2. Why do you think that Alida's father did not approve of her romance?
3. Would the lovers have been happier if Yukiyú did not change them? Why or why not?

CRITICAL THINKING AND READING

Recognizing Clues to Outcomes

As you read this legend, you can find clues in the story to what will happen. You can become better at finding such clues by not only understanding events but also thinking where they might lead. For instance, the fact that Alida and Taroo become friends so quickly suggests that they may fall in love as well.

1. Find two clues indicating that Alida's father may not accept her romance.
2. How is the title a clue to what will happen when Alida becomes a flower?

THINKING AND WRITING

Writing a Legend

Many legends tell about real people but exaggerate their achievements. Imagine that you have been arguing with a friend about who is the greatest baseball player, television actor, or any other performer. List some of the accomplishments of the person you have chosen, and then exaggerate the items you have listed. Using one of the items on your list, write a legend about this person. Remember that a legend is in the form of a story. As you revise your legend, make sure it will persuade your friend that you are right.

LEARNING OPTIONS

1. **Writing.** Imagine that you are either Taroo, who has been changed into a hummingbird, or Alida, who is now a red flower. Write a poem expressing your feelings about what has happened. You may or may not choose to use rhyme. You might also decide to make a drawing to illustrate your poem.
2. **Cross-curricular Connection.** The red flower mentioned in "The Legend of the Hummingbird" is never named. Investigate the plant life on Caribbean islands like Puerto Rico, and identify the names of several plants with red flowers that could indeed be the one in the folk tale.
3. **Art.** Draw a picture of the hummingbird searching through the flowers for Alida. Use any medium you wish.

GUIDE FOR READING

Greece

The name Daedalus (ded' 'l əs) means "artful craftsman" in Greek, and Daedalus deserved his name. According to legend, he learned his craft from the gods themselves. Not only did he design buildings, machines, and weapons for various Greek kings, but he also made wonderful toys for their children. His son, Icarus (ik' ə rəs), is remembered for the fateful flight recounted in this myth.

Josephine Preston Peabody (1874–1922), who wrote this version of the myth, was best known for her poetry and plays.

Icarus and Daedalus

Characters in Myth

Like people in real life or characters in fiction, the gods and heroes in myths have different ways of thinking and acting. Prometheus, for instance, is concerned about the results of his deeds, while Zeus is more stubborn and emotional. Hades is dark and forbidding, like his underworld kingdom, but Apollo loves the light.

You can understand the characters in myths by paying attention to what the storyteller says about them. You can also learn about them by observing what they say and do themselves. In "Icarus and Daedalus," you will meet a father and son who are quite different from each other.

Focus

Have you ever seen a movie or a television show about hang gliding or parachuting? Imagine what it must feel like to float hundreds of feet above the ground! Would you like it, or would it scare you? In the Greek myth you are about to read, a young boy named Icarus gets a chance to fly just like a bird. Write a few sentences describing in as much detail as possible the kind of flying experience you would most like to have. Where would you go? Would you make any stops? Explain the circumstances under which you became able to fly, and give your reasons for wanting to fly to the specific place or places you have chosen.

Vocabulary

Knowing the following words will help you as you read "Icarus and Daedalus."

cunning (kun' iŋ) *adj.*: Skillful; clever (p. 625)

veered (vird) *v.*: Changed directions (p. 625)

fledgling (flej' liŋ) *n.*: Young bird (p. 625)

rash (rash) *adj.*: Reckless (p. 625)

vacancy (va' kən sē) *n.*: Emptiness (p. 625)

sustained (sə stānd') *v.*: Supported (p. 626)

Icarus and Daedalus

Josephine Preston Peabody

Among all those mortals who grew so wise that they learned the secrets of the gods, none was more cunning than Daedalus.

He once built, for King Minos of Crete,[1] a wonderful Labyrinth[2] of winding ways so cunningly tangled up and twisted around that, once inside, you could never find your way out again without a magic clue. But the king's favor veered with the wind, and one day he had his master architect imprisoned in a tower. Daedalus managed to escape from his cell; but it seemed impossible to leave the island, since every ship that came or went was well guarded by order of the king.

At length, watching the sea-gulls in the air—the only creatures that were sure of liberty—he thought of a plan for himself and his young son Icarus, who was captive with him.

Little by little, he gathered a store of feathers great and small. He fastened these together with thread, moulded them in with wax, and so fashioned two great wings like those of a bird. When they were done, Daedalus fitted them to his own shoulders, and after one or two efforts, he found that by waving his arms he could winnow[3] the air

and cleave it, as a swimmer does the sea. He held himself aloft, wavered this way and that with the wind, and at last, like a great fledgling, he learned to fly.

Without delay, he fell to work on a pair of wings for the boy Icarus, and taught him carefully how to use them, bidding him beware of rash adventures among the stars. "Remember," said the father, "never to fly very low or very high, for the fogs about the earth would weigh you down, but the blaze of the sun will surely melt your feathers apart if you go too near."

For Icarus, these cautions went in at one ear and out by the other. Who could remember to be careful when he was to fly for the first time? Are birds careful? Not they! And not an idea remained in the boy's head but the one joy of escape.

The day came, and the fair wind that was to set them free. The father bird put on his wings, and, while the light urged them to be gone, he waited to see that all was well with Icarus, for the two could not fly hand in hand. Up they rose, the boy after his father. The hateful ground of Crete sank beneath them; and the country folk, who caught a glimpse of them when they were high above the treetops, took it for a vision of the gods— Apollo, perhaps, with Cupid after him.

At first there was a terror in the joy. The wide vacancy of the air dazed them—a glance downward made their brains reel. But when a great wind filled their wings, and Icarus

---

1. King Minos (mī′ nəs) **of Crete:** King Minos was a son of the god Zeus. Crete is a Greek island in the eastern Mediterranean sea, southeast of Greece.
2. Labyrinth (lab′ ə rinth′)
3. winnow (win′ ō) *v*.: Beat as with wings.

Icarus and Daedalus 625

DAEDALUS AND ICARUS
Albrecht Dürer

felt himself sustained, like a halcyon bird[4] in the hollow of a wave, like a child uplifted by his mother, he forgot everything in the world but joy. He forgot Crete and the other islands that he had passed over: he saw but vaguely that wingèd thing in the distance before him that was his father Daedalus. He longed for one draft of flight to quench the thirst of his captivity: he stretched out his arms to the sky and made towards the highest heavens.

Alas for him! Warmer and warmer grew the air. Those arms, that had seemed to uphold him, relaxed. His wings wavered,

drooped. He fluttered his young hands vainly—he was falling—and in that terror he remembered. The heat of the sun had melted the wax from his wings; the feathers were falling, one by one, like snowflakes; and there was none to help.

He fell like a leaf tossed down the wind, down, down, with one cry that overtook Daedalus far away. When he returned, and sought high and low for his poor boy, he saw nothing but the birdlike feathers afloat on the water, and he knew that Icarus was drowned.

The nearest island he named Icaria, in memory of the child; but he, in heavy grief, went to the temple of Apollo in Sicily, and there hung up his wings as an offering. Never again did he attempt to fly.

---

4. halcyon (hal′ sē ən) **bird** *n.*: A legendary bird, identified with the kingfisher, which could calm the sea by resting on it.

RESPONDING TO THE SELECTION

Your Response

1. In the same situation, would you have done what Icarus did? Why or why not?

Recalling

2. How does Daedalus plan to escape?
3. Paraphrase the warning he gives to Icarus.

Interpreting

4. Do you think that Daedalus was punished by the gods for daring an unusual deed? Explain.
5. Do you think Icarus was punished for disobeying his father? Explain.
6. What lesson does this myth teach?

Applying

7. Why do you think humans have always wanted to fly like birds?

ANALYZING LITERATURE

Understanding Characters in Myth

Like novels and short stories, myths present a variety of characters. In "Icarus and Daedalus," you learn about a famous father and son through what the storyteller says about them and what they do themselves.

1. Where does the storyteller inform you that Daedalus is "cunning"? In what ways does Daedalus display his cunning?
2. What does Daedalus reveal about himself in his words to his son?
3. At what point in the story does the storyteller hint that Icarus will disobey his father?
4. What does the boy's flying too close to the sun tell you about him?

CRITICAL THINKING AND READING

Comparing and Contrasting Characters

Comparing means finding similarities. **Contrasting** means showing differences. By comparing and contrasting Icarus and Daedalus, you can learn even more about them.

1. Find evidence to show that the father and son both are eager to escape the island.
2. How are the two similar in their first reaction to the experience of flying?
3. How are they different in the ways they adapt to this new experience?
4. Explain whether the contrast between them results more from the difference in their ages or from their differing personalities.

THINKING AND WRITING

Writing About Characters in Myth

Imagine that you are a reporter for an Athenian newspaper. You suddenly hear that an old man who just died on one of the Greek islands was Icarus. It turns out that he survived his fall into the sea and lived for many years, hiding his identity. Write a story for your newspaper with the following headline: The Secret Life of Icarus. In the story tell what happened to Icarus after his fall. Explain such matters as how he survived the accident, whether he felt sorry for what he did, why he never contacted his father, and whether he married. As you revise your account, make sure it will be interesting enough to sell newspapers.

LEARNING OPTION

Speaking and Listening. Imagine that you are Icarus. Write down your thoughts and feelings about your flight from Crete as if it were really happening. How does it feel at first? What about when the sun begins to melt the wax? Are you sorry you didn't follow your father's advice? When you have finished, revise your monologue to be read aloud, keeping in mind that the events should sound as though they are actually happening as you describe them. Read your monologue to the class, speaking as you think Icarus might have actually spoken.

GUIDE FOR READING

Zimbabwe

This tale comes from the south-central African country of Zimbabwe (zim bä′ bwā). Like other folk tales it teaches a lesson about life; however, its supernatural details and unusual ending give it a mysterious air all its own.

Alexander McCall Smith was born and raised in Zimbabwe. He has since traveled widely throughout that country gathering stories from both children and older people. "Children of Wax" is one such story.

Children of Wax

Metamorphosis

The word **metamorphosis** means a complete change in form. Some folk tales and myths use metamorphosis to explain how certain creatures came into being. In one Greek myth, a young girl named Arachne claims that she can weave more beautifully than the gods themselves. The gods punish the girl for her pride by changing her into a spider.

In the Arachne myth, metamorphosis is a form of punishment; in "Children of Wax," the change in form occurs for a different reason. As you read this tale, note the cause of the metamorphosis and the effect it has on the characters.

Focus

Have you ever wished you could do something that you knew was physically impossible? For example, wouldn't it be great if you could swim underwater for long periods of time without having to come up for air? Write about a wish that you have had and that you knew could never come true. Using words that appeal to the senses, describe in detail what the experience would be like.

In "Children of Wax," a young boy wants very badly to do something that he knows will cause him great harm. As you read this African folk tale, think about times when you have felt the same way as he does. How did you deal with the situation?

Vocabulary

Knowing the following words will help you as you read "Children of Wax."

penetrate (pen′ ə trāt) *v.*: To pass into or through (p. 629)
contented (kən tent′ əd) *v.*: Satisfied (p. 629)

peering (pēr′ iŋ) *v.*: Looking closely (p. 631)

Children of Wax

from Zimbabwe

Alexander McCall Smith

Not far from the hills of the Matopos[1] there lived a family whose children were made out of wax. The mother and the father in this family were exactly the same as everyone else, but for some reason their children had turned out to be made of wax. At first this caused them great sorrow, and they wondered who had put such a spell on them, but later they became quite accustomed to this state of affairs and grew to love their children dearly.

It was easy for the parents to love the wax children. While other children might fight among themselves or forget to do their duty, wax children were always dutiful and never fought with one another. They were also hard workers, one wax child being able to do the work of at least two ordinary children.

The only real problem which the wax children gave was that people had to avoid making fires too close to them, and of course they also had to work only at night. If they worked during the day, when the sun was hot, wax children would melt.

To keep them out of the sun, their father made the wax children a dark hut that had no windows. During the day no rays of the sun could penetrate into the gloom of this hut, and so the wax children were quite safe. Then, when the sun had gone down, the children would come out of their dark hut and begin their work. They tended the crops and watched over the cattle, just as ordinary children did during the daytime.

There was one wax child, Ngwabi,[2] who used to talk about what it was like during the day.

"We can never know what the world is like," he said to his brothers and sisters. "When we come out of our hut everything is quite dark and we see so little."

Ngwabi's brothers and sisters knew that what he said was right, but they accepted they would never know what the world looked like. There were other things that they had which the other children did not have, and they contented themselves with these. They knew, for instance, that other children felt pain: wax children never experienced pain, and for this they were grateful.

But poor Ngwabi still longed to see the world. In his dreams he saw the hills in the distance and watched the clouds that brought rain. He saw paths that led this way and that through the bush, and he longed to be able to follow them. But that was some-

---

1. the hills of the Matopos (mä to′ pōz): The blue granite mountains of Matabeleland (mat′ ə bē′ lē land), a part of Zimbabwe (zim bä′ bwā) in eastern Africa.

2. Ngwabi (əŋ gwä′ bē)

ON THE WAY TO THE VILLAGE (detail)
Gaylord Hassan
Courtesy of the Artist

thing that a wax child could never do, as it was far too dangerous to follow such paths in the night-time.

As he grew older, this desire of Ngwabi's to see what the world was really like when the sun was up grew stronger and stronger. At last he was unable to contain it any more and he ran out of the hut one day when the sun was riding high in the sky and all about there was light and more light. The other children screamed, and some of them tried to grab at him as he left the hut, but they failed to stop their brother and he was gone.

Of course he could not last long in such heat. The sun burned down on Ngwabi and before he had taken more than a few steps he felt all the strength drain from his limbs. Crying out to his brothers and sisters, he fell to the ground and was soon nothing more than a pool of wax in the dust. Inside the hut, afraid to leave its darkness, the other wax children wept for their melted brother.

When night came, the children left their hut and went to the spot where Ngwabi had fallen. Picking up the wax, they went to a special place they knew and there Ngwabi's eldest sister made the wax into a bird. It was a bird with great wings and for feathers they put a covering of leaves from the trees that grew there. These leaves would protect the wax from the sun so that it would not melt when it became day.

After they had finished their task, they told their parents what had happened. The man and woman wept, and each of them kissed the wax model of a bird. Then they set it upon a rock that stood before the wax children's hut.

The wax children did not work that night. At dawn they were all in their hut, peering through a small crack that there was in the wall. As the light came up over the hills, it made the wax bird seem pink with fire. Then, as the sun itself rose over the fields, the great bird which they had made suddenly moved its wings and launched itself into the air. Soon it was high above the ground, circling over the children's hut. A few minutes later it was gone, and the children knew that their brother was happy at last.

RESPONDING TO THE SELECTION

Your Response

1. Do you feel sorry about what happened to Ngwabi? Why or why not?

Recalling

2. How do the lives of the wax children differ from those of other children?
3. How is Ngwabi different from his siblings?

Interpreting

4. (a) What about the children could be true only in fantasy? (b) What is realistic about them?
5. Why do you think Ngwabi's eldest sister forms the melted wax into a bird and not another animal?
6. How do you think Ngwabi's brothers and sisters feel when they see the bird fly away? Why do they feel this way?

Applying

7. What other folk tales have you heard that describe how a character changes from one form into another?

ANALYZING LITERATURE

Understanding Metamorphosis

To understand Ngwabi's metamorphosis and its significance, you must understand how it occurs. It is Ngwabi's desire for freedom that causes him to run out into the sun's heat.

1. What do Ngwabi's brothers and sisters do after he melts into a pool of wax?
2. What is unusual about the way the bird comes to life?
3. What happens to the bird at the end?
4. How is the ending appropriate?

THINKING AND WRITING

Writing a Fantasy

In a fantasy anything can happen. Children can be made of wax and change into flying birds. People can fly or live underwater. Imagine your own fantastic characters. What do they look like? How do they act? Then imagine the world these fantasy people live in. Does it look like our world? How is it different? Write a brief fantasy, using the characters you imagined. Make sure you use realistic details in your fantasy, too.

LEARNING OPTION

Art. Choose a scene from the folk tale to depict in a diorama. Use a box at least as large as a shoe box and any other materials you like. Consider what should be seen in the background, such as a night sky with stars or the blazing midday sun. Also think about what things to show in three dimensions, such as the trees or the hut. Finally, how can you show the action of the story, such as the wax children working or Ngwabi as a bird flying away?

YOUR WRITING PROCESS

WRITING A COMPARISON AND CONTRAST

"The most beautiful thing we can experience is the mysterious. It is the source of all true art and science."

Albert Einstein

As you can see from several of the myths in this unit, many cultures try to explain natural phenomena with stories about gods and goddesses and remarkable humans. These stories answer questions like the following: Why are there seasons? Why day and night? Why rain? Why volcanoes? Myths give one answer, and scientific studies give another, but sometimes their answers have things in common.

Focus

Assignment: Write an essay that compares and contrasts explanations of a natural event provided by a myth and by science.
Purpose: To show how science and mythology are alike and how they are different.
Audience: Readers of a high-school science magazine.

Prewriting

1. Find a topic. Use a chart like the one following to do some preliminary thinking about possible topics. Work with a partner if possible.

Student Model

Natural Event	Scientific Explanation	Mythic Explanation
winter in the temperate zone	the changing relationship between Earth and the sun	the changing relationship between Pluto and Persephone

---

2. Do some research. You may think you understand why we experience winter, but are you really certain of all the facts and details? Use an encyclopedia or a science book to research the phenomenon you have chosen. Take careful notes.

3. Find likenesses *and* differences. You may find it easier to think of ways in which science and mythology are different. Keep in mind, however, that you want to think of similarities as well as differences. What basic ideas about the natural event do the mythic and scientific explanation share?

Drafting

1. Introduce your comparison/contrast. Have your first paragraph express your main idea. Don't settle for an obvious statement like "There are both similarities and differences."

> ### Student Model
>
> The more you know about hummingbirds, the more you begin to see that the Puerto Rican "Legend of the Hummingbird" is not far from fact.

2. Use your chart as a blueprint. The chart you completed to help you visualize the similarities and differences between mythic and scientific explanations will really come in handy now. Refer to it as a guide to help you include all those great ideas you had before you began to write.

3. Choose AAABBB or ABABAB. There are at least two ways to write comparisons and contrasts. In the first you make all your points about Topic 1 (the myth), then all your points about Topic 2 (science). In the other you move between points about Topic 1 and Topic 2, back and forth. Decide which method of organization you like best, but once you have settled on it, be consistent.

Revising and Editing

1. Check your logic. First reread your comparison and contrast to make sure that you followed the pattern you chose, either AAABBB or ABABAB. Then rethink each comparison and contrast. Is it accurate? Can it be written in a more logical way?

2. In a list treat similar items in a similar way. You may find that you have written a series of items or ideas. If so, make sure that each item is written in the same way.

> ### Student Model
>
> Hummingbirds are often brightly colored. They have patches of green, violet, red, and ~~some glow with~~ orange.

3. Use specific facts. When writing scientific explanations, use data (facts using numbers) and specific terms whenever possible. For example, the statement "The Earth rotates on its axis once every twenty-four hours" is much stronger than "The Earth turns around every day."

Writer's Hint

Spell out numbers or amounts of fewer than one hundred and any other numbers that can be written in one or two words. Also, use numerals for fractions, decimals, and percentages, as well as for addresses and dates.

Options for Publishing

• Submit your writing to your school magazine or newspaper or to a science magazine for high-school students.

• Have a science teacher read your comparison and contrast, and ask for his or her honest response.

• Read your comparison and contrast to a young child and to an adult. Ask each which explanation he or she prefers and why.

Reviewing Your Writing Process

1. Were the two explanations easier to compare or to contrast? Explain.

2. Based on your reading and writing, which way of explaining the world do you prefer—science or myth? Why?

YOUR WRITING PROCESS

WRITING A NEWS STORY

Have you ever wanted to be a newspaper reporter? Now is your chance to try your hand at journalism. Use the events of one of the folk tales in this unit as the basis of a news story. Imagine that your paper serves the community of people—or animals—that the story is about. Don't hesitate to make your descriptions colorful and entertaining. After all, lively and engaging writing helps to sell newspapers!

> **Focus**
>
> **Assignment:** Write a news story based on the events in a folk tale you have read.
> **Purpose:** To inform and entertain.
> **Audience:** The people (or animals) near the scene of the action.

Prewriting

1. Study news stories. With a partner or small group, read several newspaper stories. How do they begin? What kinds of information do they include? What makes them interesting to read?

2. Narrow your options. Review this unit. Then choose a folk tale that you especially enjoyed. Make sure that the one you choose contains enough information to make a good news story.

3. Ask the right questions. Reporters ask questions to get their information. Write down some questions based on the six key words (*who, what, when, where, why,* and *how*) of the newspaper trade.

Who? _____

What? _____

When? _____

Where? _____

Why? _____

How? _____

Then answer these questions before writing your story.

Drafting

1. Grab them with your lead. The opening paragraph of a news story, called the "lead," is very important. It should not only answer some of the six key questions, but it should also keep the reader guessing about what comes next.

This lead answers the questions *who* (eight immortals), *where* (from fairy mountain isle to our world), and *why* (to observe the behavior of mortals). It invites readers to continue, however, by not answering *when* the immortals came, *how* they will observe humans, and *what* will happen.

2. Stick to the facts. You probably have your own opinions about the events you are reporting, but leave these opinions out of your news story. Avoid words that make judgments instead of expressing facts. For instance, in writing about the town of Chelem, you would not want to judge the citizens as *foolish*.

3. Include a quotation. Direct quotations will add variety to your writing and believability to your story. Feel free to quote the characters in your story or to make up a suitable quotation.

Revising and Editing

1. No-frills language. Newspapers use language that is concise and direct. Work to simplify your language by eliminating all unnecessary words and by using specific nouns and active verbs.

3. "Hire" an editor. All good journalists have editors who help them revise and proofread their writing. You should, too. Have a classmate read your draft, make comments and suggestions, and later, help you proofread for errors. In turn you can act as his or her editor.

Grammar Tip

Make sure that pronouns agree with their nouns (antecedents) in both gender and number. You can check pronoun agreement by finding the antecedent of each pronoun you use.

Options for Publishing

• Use a word processor to format your story into columns. Put the headline across the top. If you wish, name your paper for the community where it is published, design or select a typeface for the name, and make your story front-page news.

• Combine your story with those of your classmates into a bulletin board newspaper that covers all places and times. Then choose a name for this journal of fables, myths, and legends.

Reviewing Your Writing Process

1. Did the tale you chose to retell make a good news story? Why or why not?

2. How did you decide what details to include?

3. How is your news story different from the folk tale?

SIERRA PEAK GLACIER (detail)
Edgar Payne
Courtesy of DeRu's Fine Arts

THE NOVEL

Like a short story, a novel is fiction. It is made up from an author's imagination, and it has the basic elements of fiction: plot, character, setting, and theme. The most obvious difference between a short story and a novel is length. A novel is longer—often much longer—than a short story. Because of its length, there are other differences, too. A novel often includes more characters than a short story. The plot may be more complicated. The setting may include a number of different places, and the time of the action may extend over months, years, and even decades. Most important, the total effect of a novel is different from that of a short story. A good short story makes a single, sharp impression on the reader. The effect of a novel, on the other hand, is like traveling to and getting to know a new part of the world. You get impression after impression, and you learn more and more about the people and their lives. At last, you feel that you have entered into that part of the world and that it has become part of you.

READING ACTIVELY

Bearstone

BACKGROUND This novel is set in a part of the country that the author, Will Hobbs, knows well: the stark peaks and lush valleys of southwestern Colorado. This region was once the home of a Native American people called the Utes. Their respect for the animals with which they shared this land is epitomized in their Bear Dance. Hobbs's tale of a Ute boy drawing upon his heritage as he struggles to build a future for himself is set against a rich backdrop of ranching, hunting, and mining, in a rugged and beautiful landscape.

READING STRATEGIES As you read the novel, you will discover that it offers advantages and presents problems that are different from those you encounter in shorter works of fiction. Some advantages of a novel include more in-depth and realistic development of the characters, a more complex plot, and the development of more than one theme. One of the problems is that, unlike a short story that can be read in one sitting, a novel is read at intervals over a longer period of time. Summarizing what you have learned after reading each section of the novel may help you remember what you have already read. Later, you can review your summaries about characters and events in previous sections. Also, interact with the novel by using the active reading strategies: question, visualize, predict, connect, and respond.

THEMES You will encounter the following themes as you read:

- The search for an identity
- The need to take responsibility for one's actions
- The struggles involved in growing up
- The rewards found in appreciating others

CHARACTERS Here is a brief introduction to the characters:

Cloyd—the Native American teenager who stays with an old rancher for the summer
Walter—the rancher who gives Cloyd a home
Susan—Cloyd's housemother at the group home
Rusty—Walter's outfitter friend, a professional hunter
Cloyd's grandmother—the woman who raised Cloyd

Bearstone

DREAMWALKER (detail)
Nancy Wood Taber
Courtesy of the Artist

GUIDE FOR READING

Will Hobbs

(1947–) was born in Pittsburgh, Pennsylvania. After graduating from Stanford University, he taught English and reading in southwestern Colorado for seventeen years. Now he writes full time. Besides *Bearstone,* he has written three other novels for young people: *Changes in Latitudes, Downriver,* and *The Big Wander.* Hobbs and his wife, Jean, enjoy backpacking with their nieces and nephews in the Weminuche wilderness area, where *Bearstone* takes place. He is familiar with all the places mentioned in the novel.

Bearstone, Chapters 1–6

Character

Characters are the people in a novel. As in a short story, characters have traits that make them seem like real people. Because a novel is longer than a short story, however, characters may be developed more fully—they can change and grow over time. In *Bearstone* you will get to know two major characters, a Ute boy named Cloyd Atcitty and an older man named Walter Landis.

Focus

In getting to know Cloyd, you will learn about some aspects of Ute culture. In the 1800's the Ute Indians signed a peace treaty with the United States government and were supposed to retain a large tract of land in Colorado for a reservation. When gold was discovered near Denver, however, the Utes were given less desirable land. Today some four thousand Utes live on three reservations in western Colorado and eastern Utah. Many still practice their traditional religion, the main ceremony of which is the Bear Dance, held in late spring. Why do you think the bear is important to the Utes? Make some notes about bears and what they represent to you. As you read *Bearstone,* notice the significance of the bear and other aspects of the Ute culture.

Vocabulary

Knowing the following words will help you as you read Chapters 1–6 of *Bearstone.*

summoned (sum′ ənd) *v.:* Called forth or gathered (p. 647)

precipice (pres′ i pis) *n.:* A vertical rock face or steep cliff (p. 649)

irrigation (ir ə gā′shən) *adj.:* Referring to an artificial means of supplying land with water (p. 650)

meager (mē′ gər) *adj.:* Of small amount; not full or rich (p. 652)

halter (hôl′ tər) *n.:* A rope, usually with a headpiece, for tying or leading an animal (p. 653)

skittish (skit′ ish) *adj.:* Nervous or jumpy (p. 653)

cinched (sincht) *v.:* Fastened a saddle on a horse (p. 653)

gorge (gôrj) *n.:* A deep, narrow pass between steep heights (p. 654)

Bearstone

Will Hobbs

Chapter 1

Cloyd stood a step from the door of the hospital room. His father was in that room. "Are you sure you have to see him in person to deliver those flowers?" the nurse asked.

"They won't pay me unless I deliver them in person."

Cloyd didn't think it would work if he told her who he was. He had run away from the Ute group home[1] in Colorado and hitched all the way to Window Rock, Arizona, to find his father. That's where the Navajos kept the records about everyone in the whole tribe, and there he found out that yes, there was a Leeno Atcitty, and his address was listed as the Indian Health Service Hospital in Window Rock. He was a patient there.

Cloyd wondered how he might get into his father's hospital room to see him. If he told them who he was, there would be trouble because he had run away. Then he had an idea. He used the last of his money to buy some flowers.

For years Cloyd had been asking every Navajo he happened to meet if they knew a man named Leeno Atcitty. "What does he look like?" they'd ask. Cloyd couldn't tell them; he'd never known his father. He'd grown up without him, with only his sister

---

1. **Ute** (yo͞ot or yo͞ot′ ē) **group home:** Cloyd has been living in a home for young members of his tribe. The Ute Indians live in western Colorado and eastern Utah.

and his grandmother. Cloyd knew just two things about his father—he was a Navajo, and he had disappeared after Cloyd was born. Nobody had seen him since.

When Cloyd was little, he used to talk to his sister about how badly he wanted to find his father, but she didn't seem to need to know him at all, so he had kept his dream inside. In the year since he'd been sent away, the more lonely he became, the stronger his desire grew to find his father. Now here he was with his heart pounding, following the nurse down the long hallway to his father's room.

The nurse stopped short of the door and said, "Why don't you let me take the flowers in."

Cloyd didn't know if this was going to work. He wasn't a good liar. He said, "I'm supposed to deliver them myself."

"I've never seen you here before. Who did you say you're working for?"

He knew he had to do something quick. Like a rabbit in the sagebrush, Cloyd was into the room.

What he saw terrified him. This wasn't even a human being. It was more like a shriveled-up mummy attached to a bunch of tubes. One went into his nose and one went into his arm. A third came out from under the sheet. How could this be his father? Was it even alive? "What's the matter with him?" he asked as evenly as he could.

"Have you ever heard of the expression

'brain dead'? It means his heart and his lungs still work, but his brain is . . . well, dead. I tried to tell you, it's not a pretty sight. He won't know about the flowers."

Cloyd had to keep talking, or the nurse would get onto him. He had to put away his terror, not show any emotion on his face. He was good at that. "How did this happen?"

"Car accident," she said. "I don't know any details."

"How long has he been like this?"

"Four years."

"Are you sure he's Leeno Atcitty?"

"Yes, of course."

"Where's he from?"

"I think I heard that once . . . Utah, I think. Monument Valley. I wonder if this could be the man you were looking for. Nobody ever sent him flowers before."

He knew it was his father. His father came from Monument Valley. Besides, the Navajos listed only one Leeno Atcitty.

Cloyd shrugged. "The people that ordered the flowers said he had a broken leg. Is there another Leeno Atcitty in the hospital?"

He sneaked one last look at his father. The terror returned full force. How could this . . . wrinkled, shrunken shell of a human being be his father? He forgot to wait for her reply. He turned and left without looking back.

"No," she said after him. "I'm sure there isn't. . . . There must have been some mistake."

He threw the flowers in the trash.

Chapter 2

Cloyd wanted to go home to Utah, back to White Mesa.[2] Every mile took him farther

---

2. White Mesa (mā′ sə): The town where Cloyd is from is named for a geological feature common to the Southwest: the mesa, a small, high, flat-topped area with steep sides.

THE ROCKING CHAIR RANCH
Ogden Pleissner
Shelburne Museum, Shelburne, Vermont

into Colorado, farther even than Durango, where he'd spent the lonely winter in the group home. He was looking out the window of the van at the beaver dams in the creek along the highway. There weren't any beaver dams where he came from.

His housemother didn't speak, and he was glad. She'd said it all before. How he couldn't go home for the summer, how she'd had this idea to put him on a ranch with an old man whose wife had died, and how much he was going to like it.

What was the old man going to be like? Cloyd wished he didn't have to meet this Walter Landis. Why wouldn't these people just leave him alone? All winter in the group home, through the miserable days in school, he had looked forward to going home for the summer. Now even that was being taken away from him. They were afraid his grandmother wouldn't make him mind, that she'd let him disappear into the canyons again. Cloyd thought about how good that would be, to disappear and be free. He wanted to run away again, hitchhike home to White Mesa. When he was trying to find his father, he'd hitched all over.

"Getting close," his housemother announced cheerfully. She pulled off the highway onto a bumpy dirt road. "Look, there's the river, Cloyd—the Piedra River—through the trees!"

Cloyd had already noticed the river and the big pines. It was so different from the high desert back home. He rolled the window down all the way. It smelled like . . . pine cones.

"Walter's is the only place north of the highway," Susan James said. "After his place, it's all wilderness for a hundred miles and more."

Cloyd noticed how she drove slowly and deliberately through the potholes, slower than she would have had to. There was only a short time left before she dropped him off.

Probably she was going to tell him to behave. This rancher was an old friend of hers. There, ahead, was the gate. Cloyd thought how much he didn't want to meet this stranger. He could hide and then hitch to Utah. He could visit his grandmother, at night when nobody would know. Then he would take off for the canyons. Nobody could find him in the canyons.

"Would you open the gate, Cloyd? Just look at that lovely orchard."

He got out of the van and opened the gate. Through the orchard he could see open fields, sheds, and a barn. Mostly hidden behind two blue spruce trees stood a gray two-story house. Somebody's home, not his. He could see a small figure stepping off the porch. Susan James was driving through the gate. Cloyd was supposed to close it behind her. He did, and then he bolted into the trees.

"Cloyd!" she called. "Cloyd, you come back here right now!"

He ran quickly and quietly. She was chasing him. Cloyd darted this way and that, then hid behind an enormous boulder. His heart was beating fast. He grinned; he knew she couldn't catch him. "For crying out loud," he heard her say.

Cloyd skittered twenty or more feet up the boulder's sloping backside, gained its nearly flat top, and lay on his belly. He heard her tramping around in the orchard and calling with her voice raised, thinking he was long gone. She was on her way back to the van when she and the old man met, not very far from the boulder. Cloyd could hear everything they said.

"So he's run off, has he, Susan?" the old man said. "And here I ain't even met him yet."

The voice sounded very old and very tired. Cloyd peeked over the edge and saw them talking. The old man's hands were in the pockets of his striped overalls, his shoulders were slumped, his bald head bowed. Purple veins stood out on his skull. The most surprising thing about him was his size. He was little. I'm taller and bigger than he is, Cloyd realized.

"Does he do that often—run away?" the old man asked.

"Only once before, and it sure got him in a whole lot of trouble. . . . I just thought being out here and working with you might be good for him. A chance with school out to get away from the group home where he's been getting into so much trouble. School has been a disaster for him."

"Oh? Well, I wasn't so good at school myself. . . ."

Cloyd saw his housemother frown. "I'll bet this is a lot worse than you ever did, Walter. He failed all seven of his classes. The school says he just won't do the work, but I'm not sure he even knows how. He's fourteen, but he missed four years of school back in Utah."

"Four years! Where was he?"

"Out in the canyons, herding his grandmother's goats. I think he's at least half-wild."

The old man grinned mischievously. "Now, ain't that somethin'."

Cloyd liked the old man's chuckle. The rancher didn't act like other grown-ups.

"So he was living with his grandmother?" Walter asked. "What about his parents—why isn't he with them?"

"His mother's dead—died when he was born. She was Ute. No one seems to know much about his father, just that he's a Navajo. He left when she died. Cloyd's always lived with his mother's people. So tell me about yourself, Walter. How've you been doing?"

"Not worth a darn. Since Maude passed away and I sold off the cows, I haven't even put up a hay crop."

"But look at these beautiful peaches," Susan James said brightly. "You can't tell me you're not taking care of this peach orchard."

"It's for her, Susan . . . for Maude. You know how she loved the peaches."

Cloyd peered into the thick green foliage. Until now, he hadn't noticed the trees around the boulder, he'd been so intent on listening. He was astonished. He never knew peach trees could grow so large, so full and lush, or set so much fruit. Peaches were treasured at White Mesa. He had always helped his grandmother harvest them, and it was a special time. But her trees couldn't begin to compare with these. He admired the rancher for owning these trees.

"Just look at all those baby peaches," Susan James said, pointing to branches loaded with fruit. "It amazes me that you can raise them here at all. I've never seen peaches at this altitude, much less in a canyon. Doesn't the cold air settle?"

The old man had that impish grin on his face again. "That's what makes it interesting."

"Do you still have that gold mine you always talked about? With the price of gold going up every day, you must be getting ideas."

The rancher sighed. "Oh, I've still got the Pride of the West, an' I still believe in her as much as ever, but I'm not so sure as I used to be that I'll ever get back there."

Cloyd turned onto his back and studied the cliffs high on the mountain above the river canyon. In reds and whites, the cliffs seemed like a huge chunk of the desert hovering over the forests. They reminded him of home. In a moment, he realized that the boulder underneath him made a perfect fit with a huge notch in the cliffs up above. It must have fallen long ago, leaving behind a shallow cave. He felt good about his insight. He wasn't stupid, like they thought. It was the first of June, a brilliant turquoise day, and he was out of school at last. He kind of liked the old rancher, too. I can hitchhike to Utah later, he thought. Anytime.

Sliding off the rock, Cloyd slipped through the orchard and vanished among the tall trees, then began to climb. He didn't know he was climbing toward a treasure and a turning point. He wanted only to reach that piece of desert in the sky.

Chapter 3

Under the cover of the big pines, Cloyd climbed the steep slope in leaps. As he climbed, the ranch buildings shrank until only their shiny metal roofs showed, and the peach orchard looked like a bright green circle with a sandy center. A herd of horses appeared in a pasture by the river. He was pleased to see that the old man had horses. He used to have a horse once.

Cloyd let his thoughts take him back to White Mesa, as they had all winter. Almost a year away from his grandmother and his sister, he'd had to live at White Mesa in his mind or wither away and become nobody. All winter in Durango as Cloyd sat in one classroom, then passed like a sleepwalker at the bell to the next, his spirit roamed the canyons with the flock. He put out of his mind now his other dream, the one he used to live for, the one that had turned into the man in the hospital bed in Window Rock. White Mesa was his whole world now.

Finally he stood atop the red-and-white sandstone cliffs. They had the same feel as the cliffs in the canyons where he used to take the goats. But he'd never seen a view like this one. This was a shining new world. To the north and east, peaks still covered with snow shone in the cloudless blue sky. He'd never seen mountains so sharp and rugged, so fierce and splendid. Below him, an eagle soared high above the old man's field. It was a good sign.

Then he remembered his grandmother's parting words as he left for Colorado. She told

him something he'd never heard before: their band of Weminuche Utes[3] hadn't always lived at White Mesa. Colorado, especially the mountains above Durango, had been their home until gold was discovered there and the white men wanted them out of the way. Summers the people used to hunt and fish in the high mountains, she'd said; they knew every stream, places so out of the way that white men still hadn't seen them. "So don't feel bad about going to Durango," she told him.

Cloyd regarded the distant peaks with new strength, a fierce kind of pride he'd never felt before. These were the mountains where his people used to live. Maybe he should stay at the ranch. Maybe he could follow the river all the way up to those peaks and stand atop the highest one. If he worked hard, there would be time off. Maybe the old man would let him take one of his horses.

Tucked under a high ridge, the outcrop suddenly lost the sun. He should be returning to the ranch. He wondered if his housemother had driven back to Durango with his duffel bag. Halfway down the side of the cliffs, he discovered a ledge that might lead across them. That's what he liked to do back in the canyon country: follow ledges across cliffs. You never knew what you might find. This one led to that shadowy cave, the notch he'd seen from the orchard. Its high, arching roof was indeed the perfect match to the backside of the boulder he'd climbed among the peach trees.

Cloyd sprang to the ledge. If he was careful, he could follow it, at least for a way. Below him the cliff fell more than a hundred feet. There was no good reason he had to get to the cave, yet he knew he would try it. The place itself was driving him on. The cliff houses in the canyons used to exert the same pull on him. He'd managed those climbs, nearly as

---

3. Weminuche (we mi noo′ chē) **Utes:** The people living in the northernmost sections of Ute territory.

difficult as this one, by using the natural cracks in the canyon walls and the handholds the Ancient Ones[4] had carved. And he'd stood many times in their ancient homes like nests, which were said to be unreachable without ladders. When he reached those places, he felt good, standing alone in a good place.

The ledge narrowed to a seam. Arms spread wide, fingers splayed on the sandstone, Cloyd started across it with his face to the cliff wall. Carefully he edged sideways on the tips of his toes with his right foot gingerly exploring, then choosing new footing, the left following after, until he was nearly there. With a swoon he realized he could no longer

---

4. the Ancient Ones: The ancestors of the Utes.

lean into the cliff. The shape of the rock had forced his body weight out over thin air, and he was in bad trouble. Stretched tight, the tendons above his heels began to quiver, then to tremble. His strength deserted him in a rush. He paused to rest, but his legs began to shake violently.

His fingers started to go numb. He fought the panic and tried to think. He knew he had to go forward, reach the cave, and rest. He'd never make it back unless he could rest.

Cloyd breathed deeply and summoned a little strength into his legs. He started out again, more quickly than before. Shuffling the last few steps, he fell gasping onto the chalky floor of the cave.

Once he caught his breath, Cloyd looked for what he might find. It would take his

ANASAZI—ANCIENT ONES
Paul Krapf
Courtesy of the Artist

mind off the return across the cliff. If this cave were back in the canyon country, he thought, it would have a ruin in it and maybe some picture writing. But it was bowl-smooth and empty, except for a large fin of sandstone broken loose from the wall and ceiling. He noticed something wedged between the wall and the fin—a shape that didn't look quite natural. He shimmied into the dark, narrow crack until his hands closed on some kind of a bundle, and then he backed out into the light to see what it was.

He knelt and examined it up close. He probed with his fingers. Turkey feathers and fur, probably rabbit: hundreds of tiny bits of feather and fur wrapped around cords of yucca fiber.[5] A blanket, a whole blanket in the style of the Ancient Ones.

Carefully he folded the blanket back and gasped to see a very small human face with empty eye sockets. The brown skin and black hair were still intact. At once he knew he was holding a burial in his hands, one of the Ancient Ones. His grandmother talked about such things, but he'd never seen one in all his time in the canyons. Her advice came to mind: behave carefully, treat the buried one with the utmost respect, and don't make any mistakes. The Ancient Ones are not people to be trifled with.

An infant, he realized. Buried in the position his grandmother had described, with the legs folded and tucked against the stomach. The best thing to do was think a good intention and return it to its resting place.

When Cloyd wriggled back with the bundle to the place where he'd found it, he saw the silhouette of a piece of pottery, a jar with handles and a short, slender neck. He brought it into the open where he could see

it, and took in its beauty and wholeness. Before this he'd found countless shards with similar black-lined designs, but never anything close to a whole pot. It was said they were worth a thousand dollars unbroken.

As he turned the pot on its side to admire it, something moved inside. He let the loose object fall gently into his hand. His heart leaped to see a small blue stone about two inches long, worn smooth by long handling. Turquoise. Two eyes, a snout, and a humped back. A bear. Surely, a bear to accompany the infant on the long journey.

His grandmother had told him about bears. The most important of all animals to the Utes, she'd said—friend and relative of man, bringer of strength and luck. If you could make a bear your personal guardian, you would be a strong man and lucky. In the old days, she said, when the people lived side by side with the bears, they would not kill them. That would bring on themselves the worst of bad luck.

Cloyd turned the smooth blue stone in his hand. He felt he was meant to cross the cliff and find this stone. He had earned this bearstone; his grandmother would understand. She was the only person he knew who remembered the old ways and believed in their power. He'd always wondered if there was anything to her tales. Now he was sure there was. With this token, he felt like a new and powerful person.

His grandmother had said that in the old days, people had a secret name that was known only to one other person—a name that described who they really were, not who the world thought they were. He had thought he would like to have such a name for himself, but this naming was no longer done. "I'll take a name for myself," he thought, eyeing the stone in his hand. "I don't need a father; I don't need anyone." Then he said aloud, "My name is Lone Bear."

___
5. yucca fiber: The stiff, cordlike fibers of the yucca plant, which has sword-shaped leaves and white flowers along a tall stem.

Cloyd returned the jar to the Ancient One. He tried to talk to the infant in his mind, told it that it must have reached its destination by now, and please, he'd like to have the stone on his own life's journey because he, Lone Bear, had great need of the strength and good luck it would bring.

Cloyd put the smooth stone in his pocket and started back across the precipice. This time his legs did not shake. His feet were sure, and his fingers exerted a powerful grip on the face of the cliff.

He raced down the mountain in the twilight, slowing his descent by clinging for moments to branches as he flew by them. With the bear in his pocket, he wasn't afraid of the oncoming darkness. In an odd sort of way, he was looking forward to seeing the curious old man at the ranch. Maybe the summer job wouldn't be so bad after all.

Maybe he could follow the river to the high peaks.

At any rate, he had the bearstone. He kept checking his pocket to make sure it was still there.

Chapter 4

It was dark. Walter tried to read his latest *Mining Gazette* in the parlor but couldn't concentrate for worrying about the teenager. He might've run off, but he might've slipped into the river. Swift and cold, the Piedra had drowned more than a few. He went outside, called the boy's name, and listened, but all he could hear was the river. Before too long he'd have to phone Susan James. He was supposed to call if Cloyd didn't show up.

Walter went inside and turned the heat down on the breaded pork chops he'd fixed. Since his wife died, he hadn't eaten regular meals. He'd eat a little of this and that, mostly from the canned goods in the basement. Old friends who dropped by would admonish him for not keeping up his strength, but as he told them, he was never hungry. With the boy coming, he'd had to get into town, do some shopping, plan some meals, and start thinking about how to cook them.

He thought he'd take his flashlight downstream and look along the riverbank. In the mudroom closet Walter collected his wool coat and sat down on the bench to pull on his rubber boots. Two soft knocks sounded on the door. "Come on in," he said.

The boy stepped inside, avoiding Walter's eyes. Walter noticed the jeans first, wet from the knees down, then the fresh mud on the sneakers. The boy had gotten wet only minutes before, and not in the river. Crossing the irrigation ditch, Walter realized. Then he saw the T-shirt, with a fishhook-shaped rip across the belly. The shirt was badly soiled, yet white enough to accent the darkness of Cloyd's face and arms, which were the deep-

est shade of brown. His limbs were rounded, undefined, and he was chunky overall in the way of Ute men. Shiny black hair hung straight to his shoulders. Cloyd's large, round face was devoid of expression, unless it was the mouth turning dourly down at the corners. A bloody scratch shone bright red against his dark brown cheek.

"Got some supper here," Walter said. "You like pork chops?"

Cloyd shrugged. "Okay, I guess."

Walter put away the coat and flashlight, thinking he'd best not embarrass the boy by mentioning his clothes or the scratches. But he wouldn't have the boy tracking through the house in muddy sneakers. "I like to leave my outside shoes here in this mudroom," he said over his shoulder as he left.

Cloyd joined him in the kitchen in wet socks. "I put your stuff up in your room," Walter said. "That's upstairs. The stairs are just off the parlor, and the bathroom is off the backside of the kitchen—that closed door over there. Would you like to shower and change clothes, or eat right away?"

"I'm hungry," Cloyd said softly.

Walter caught the black eyes darting toward him, then quickly away. "That'd be fine. Why, I'm hungry myself."

They ate quietly. Cloyd liked that. The old man wasn't all over him with questions. He looked around. The old man had an old-fashioned cookstove alongside the modern one. The cookstove was much like his grandmother's, only this one had bright blue enamel, where hers was all black and rusted in places. "You like that kind of stove?" he asked suddenly, pointing with a twist of the lips, as he finished up the food on his plate.

"Sure do. Still cook on it some, but mostly we used it for heating this side of the house in the winter. You can't beat them old stoves. Say, whyn't you have another go-round?" he said, indicating the pork chops and potatoes left on the platter. "Help yourself."

Cloyd shook his head. He felt freer refusing food.

"No? Make a good snack for tomorrow, then. But hang on. I've got something special to bring up from the basement for dessert."

On the old man's return, Cloyd sneaked a look at him. He sure was little. And he was really happy about his peaches—he had a big smile on his face and he carried the quart jar like it was a treasure.

"Like some?" Walter said with his grin.

Cloyd wasn't going to refuse this time; he nodded enthusiastically. These peaches were large as store-bought. He loved peaches. He allowed the old man to dish up two large scoops of vanilla ice cream with the fruit.

The old man dished himself up some peaches and joined him.

"We have peaches at home, too," Cloyd said. "Not as big as yours."

"Size don't matter. That's pretty country, Utah is. Any canyons where you come from?"

"All over," Cloyd said. "Lots of ruins . . . from the Ancient Ones."

"Cliff dwellers? Like at Mesa Verde? Now ain't that somethin'."

Cloyd was curious. He had to ask. "Any ruins around here?" he asked carefully.

"Well, up on Chimney Rock Mesa, down the river a few miles and up the other side."

"I mean real close."

"Well, they say they lived all along the river—I've found a few grinding stones and whatnot, a few arrowheads and some potsherds. . . ."

Cloyd felt the stone in his pocket. He almost wanted to tell, but he knew he shouldn't. It was his secret. It had to do with his secret name.

"So you had a look around today, did you . . . Cloyd?" the old man asked awkwardly.

Cloyd wanted to tell at least some of the truth. "I climbed up above the cliff," he said.

Walter perked up. "Why, that's one of my favorite places around the farm. I used to

climb up there myself. Haven't for a good while, though."

"How come you call it a *farm*? This place is a *ranch*."

"Well, my wife came from farm country in Missouri, and she always said a ranch was like a house, but a farm was a home."

Cloyd finished the last of the syrup from the jar. He wasn't hungry anymore.

As he went upstairs, Cloyd noticed the picture of the old man's wife. It was on top of the bookcase by the stairs. He tried to imagine the white-haired woman with the friendly smile saying to the old man, "A ranch is like a house, but a farm is a home." He thought about what it meant as he looked around his room, unpacked his things from his duffel bag, then lay down on the bed with the bearstone in the palm of his hand. This was a good place, Walter's farm.

Chapter 5

Walter knocked early on Cloyd's door. Cloyd woke to a warm house cheerful with the smell of sausage and eggs. Walter had fired up the cookstove and cooked breakfast on it. Cloyd ate with an eye on the fire showing through the draft slot. The old man opened the warmer door by the stovepipe and brought out sweet rolls.

"My grandmother keeps the frybread warm in there," Cloyd said.

"She raised you, didn't she?"

Cloyd nodded. He was beginning to feel uncomfortable. It sounded like Walter knew about his mother, how she died getting him born, how his father had run off. Walter wouldn't know what had happened to his father. He was the only one who knew that, and he wasn't going to tell anybody, not even his sister or grandmother.

"Where does your sister live?" Walter asked gently.

"Salt Lake.[6] She goes to a boarding school. I haven't seen her for a long time."

"That's too bad."

Cloyd felt more uncomfortable. He didn't want any pity. He wanted to talk about something else. "What are my jobs?" he asked.

The old man stroked the white stubble on his chin. "What needs doing worst around here is the foundation wall down in the basement. It has a bad crack in it. I don't know about you, but summer's no time to work indoors to my way of thinking, so I'm gonna put that one off. Irrigating the hayfields will keep me plenty busy, so I want to find you a project you can work on your own at. I've got something in mind, but I need to chew on it a little longer. Let's take a look around while I think about it—I'm just getting the hang of things myself after lettin' the farm set last year."

They went outside. Cloyd followed Walter up the stairway inside the big red barn. The loft upstairs was huge, and empty except for a dozen or so bales of hay off in one corner. Swallows were flying in and out by the hundreds. There were nests everywhere with baby birds.

"Sure feels empty, don't it?" Walter remarked. "I used to fill all this up with hay—fed a lot of cows. You see, Cloyd, I didn't hardly hit a lick last summer"

"How come?"

"On account of losing my wife. Hit me awful hard. Thought I didn't have anything to live for, to tell you the truth."

Cloyd didn't know what to say. He pointed with his lips to the meager haystack. "You don't have enough for your horses . . . for the winter."

"Oh, you saw the horses then. Yes, sir, it's time I baled some hay. Pretty soon the fields'll run to foxtails[7] if I don't, and then they won't be worth a darn to anybody."

"Did you ever have any kids?"

"No, never did," he said softly. "We'd of liked to, but it just never happened." There was a long silence, and Cloyd regretted the question.

"Say, I've got something I want to show you," Walter announced, and led Cloyd downstairs to the tack room.

Everywhere Cloyd looked were saddles and bridles and gear he didn't even know what to call. It was a wealth of leather, and he liked the smell of it. "I always used to ride bareback. . . ." he said cautiously. "I don't know anything about this stuff."

Walter beamed. "I could sure show you. If you'd like to ride, you could take your pick of the horses. Most are packhorses, but there's a few good saddle horses among 'em, and they need riding—I can't seem to find the time."

"What are packhorses?"

"Why, they're for carryin' loads—into the mountains, where there's no roads."

The mountains, Cloyd thought. He's all set up for the mountains. He's got the gear and the horses, and maybe he would take me. . . . "Do you go to the mountains?"

"That's a long story. . . . I've been keepin' horses for years, thinkin' I was going to get back up there and reopen a mine I've got up in the high country."

"You like mining?"

A big smile lit the old man's face. "You bet I do."

"What do you like about it?"

"Why, the gold, I suppose. Sounds crazy, but the price of gold yesterday was four hundred fifty-six dollars an *ounce*. When I was minin', gold was around thirty-two dollars. Makes a difference, don't it?"

---

6. Salt Lake: Salt Lake City, the capital of Utah.

7. the fields'll run to foxtails: When the hay goes to seed, its spiky tops will resemble foxes' tails.

"How come you quit if you liked it?"

"I got married, Cloyd. My wife made me promise to give it up."

The old man lowered his voice. "She was scared to death of mines, thinkin' they're cavin' in all the time. But what she never understood was that the Pride of the West won't cave in—never. I used to tell her it was safer than this house. There's not a stick of timberwork in that whole mine—it's a hard-rock gold mine if ever there was one. But now, back to the horses . . . how'd you like to look 'em over? We could take a feed bag and a halter up to the pasture and you could pick one out. I'm going to do some irrigating later, but you could—"

Cloyd shook his head. "What about my job?"

"We could line that out tomorrow. I want to see what you think of these horses."

They each had a feed bag and a halter. They found the horses in the shade of the big pines along the river upstream. There were ten of them. "They'll be pretty skittish," Walter said. "Haven't been rode."

Cloyd knew immediately which one he wanted: the blue roan, a big, well-muscled gelding. White hairs intermingled with gray underneath gave the roan a blue tinge all over. He wanted to call the horse to him, but he felt embarrassed having the old man see him. What if the horse wouldn't come? He had to try. "Hey-a, hey-a," Cloyd called softly. "Hey-a, hey-a." While the others shied away, the big roan came to him, slowly and alertly, its head held high to one side. Its nostrils flared as it caught the scent of the grain. Cloyd let the horse almost finish the grain before he slipped the halter over its head.

"Nice," Walter said. "Very nice. You made that look easy. I'm partial to that sorrel mare yonder—got a real easy gait."

They led the two horses back to the barn. Cloyd admired the roan's lines, the way it carried itself. At every moment it seemed about to bolt, yet never did. The horse wasn't giving up its freedom, he thought. We chose each other.

First they curried the horses,[8] then Walter showed him all about how to bridle and saddle his horse. The old man talked slow and made it easy to understand. "This blue roan's a smart'un. See how he puffs out his gut so you won't cinch him tight? And then the saddle falls off later and you with it."

Cloyd laughed. "Better not let him hear you. . . ."

"He thinks he's fooled us," Walter whispered. He turned away as if he was done, then winked and quickly cinched in a few more notches. "I wasn't born yesterday," he said.

Outside, Walter coached him on how to mount the big roan. "Confidence is the main thing. He's gonna be skittish—been too long since he had a man on his back. One quick move, and don't quit halfway. Let him feel your confidence."

As excited as he was, Cloyd calmed himself. He tried to talk to the big roan with his heart. You and me, blue horse, he thought. You're the most beautiful horse I've ever seen. I bet you can run fast. We'll be friends, you and me.

In one motion, much the way he used to when he rode bareback, he swung up into the saddle. The big roan lifted his head and took a step or two, then settled right down. Cloyd patted him on the neck.

"Well, I'll be," Walter chuckled. "He really took a shine to you. That horse never gave me the time of day."

"Does he have a name?"

"Never got around to it. None of 'em do."

---

8. they curried the horses: They used a circular comb with rows of teeth or ridges to clean the horses' coats.

They rode up the river trail through the big pines alongside the rapids. They followed the river for many miles, until the trail left it and climbed more than a thousand feet. The horse was surefooted and enjoyed the work. Cloyd was thrilled with the feel of the horse. He liked riding with the old man. He liked the wind in the trees and the gray jays and the way he felt. He hadn't felt this good in a long time. Finally he caught a glimpse of the river again, all white, in a gorge so deep and narrow it stirred his heart to beating loud. Like thousands of knives, the dark walls were flinty and jagged, so unlike the smooth sandstones of home. Cloyd remembered the snowy peaks he'd seen towering over the mountains. This gorge, he realized, was only the beginning of that higher country. He took the blue stone from his pocket and turned it slowly in his hand. Someday, he vowed, he'd see those peaks up close. He would see the home of the Utes.

The sun was dropping fast. They had to turn around and head back for the farm. He did a lot of thinking on the way. He would work hard for the old man, harder than the old man could ever have dreamed, and then he would ask the old man to take him to the mountains.

"Blueboy," he whispered, naming the horse. "You and me, Blue. We'll get to the mountains. Blueboy and Lone Bear."

It was dusk. They were back down on river level, not far from the farm. Blueboy reared, and then Cloyd saw a black form ahead lope across the trail with an unusual gait, followed by another, smaller black shape. "A bear!" he said, his voice filled with amazement. "A bear with a cub, isn't it?"

"Black bear," Walter said. "Sure enough."

"I've never seen one before. There aren't any bears back home."

"Somethin' else, ain't they? They live here, sure enough, but you don't see 'em that often. Born for the wild."

MY BEAR SPIRIT
Tom Uttech
Courtesy of the Artist

Chapter 6

Cloyd woke feeling good all over. As he yawned and stretched himself awake, he remembered his fleeting glimpse of the bear and the cub. What an amazing sight they were, he thought, and how lucky he'd been to see them. Or was it luck? He took the bearstone from under the pillow and turned it in his fingers. Lone Bear, he thought, that's the name I gave myself. These things were too wonderful to be accidents. His grandmother would understand. He recalled the feel of the powerful roan under him, and he heard the music in the old man's chuckle. He felt good, he felt strong. Now he wanted to prove himself.

"What's that job you were going to tell me about?" Cloyd asked at breakfast.

"Well, I'll need your help come haying time, bucking bales and putting up the hay, but of course that won't be until July. But I do have a project you could make a start on for me—I've been putting it off for a couple years now. Need to build a fence. I'm so busy irrigating the field, haying, fixing tractors and whatnot, I can't seem to get around to it."

"Show me about the fence. I can do that."

After breakfast, Cloyd followed Walter to a shed, where Walter picked out a posthole digger and a long steel bar. Cloyd grabbed the bar. It was six feet long and heavy, and he thought he could carry it better than the old man could. They walked through the lower field to the peach orchard and Walter's property line beyond it.

Walter set the tools down on the riverbank and led Cloyd along his line of short wooden survey stakes, one for each posthole that had to be dug, all the way across the end of the field from the river to the distant ditchbank at the base of the mountain. Then they walked back to the starting point. "What's this fence for?" Cloyd asked.

Walter's face went red suddenly as he looked away. Cloyd watched him closely.

"Well, Cloyd, I need to fence off a fellow that's been takin' advantage of me. This fellow—lives across the highway—he moves in from California a few years ago, buys himself a farm, and starts going broke, because he's no kind of farmer and won't listen if you try to help him, so he gets the idea he'll set himself up as a big-game guide—"

The old man ran short of breath, sputtered. Veins stood out on his forehead.

"He advertises in the big-city newspapers in Texas like he's an outfitter,[9] which he ain't licensed for, then he drives his hunters across my place in their four-wheel drives, tearin' up the field so bad you can't hay for the ruts. I only drive on the field myself when it's bone-dry. Then they park their trucks and horsetrailers right by the headgate where the trail takes out. He tells them I live on a county road with public access! The sheriff and the game warden, they've warned this fellow, but come fall he'll try it again. The sheriff says what I really need is a fence to go with my gate, and I guess he's right."

Walter's color returned, his breathing came easier. "You see, Cloyd, I've got the only access to a big piece of country up the Piedra here. There's no gov'ment trailhead anywhere near. So to get up the river to public land, folks have always had to come through my place. I don't mind when they ask beforehand and park downriver and walk or ride through, but this fellow doesn't know the meaning of courtesy. He's only out for himself."

---

9. outfitter: A person who provides equipment and serves as a guide for hunters.

Cloyd had watched with interest as Walter's anger rose. He could picture the neighbor from the other side of the highway driving up in the fall with his hunters and finding a new fence and a locked gate. The man would get out of his truck, walk along the fenceline, and see there was no way to get around it. Then he would have to turn around, and Walter would have won.

"Of course it's a two-year project, anyway," Walter said. "But we can make a start."

"I could finish this fence," Cloyd insisted.

"I don't think so. There's a lot of work in a fence like that. First off, since it's river bottom, you'll run into rocks sometimes, and to go deep enough to hold a post you'll have to break the rock with that bar and pull it out in pieces. Then there's all the posts to log out of the woods, wire to run—there's a lot of work in it. You'll be a help to me if you get some of the holes dug."

Walter dug the first hole to get Cloyd started. "No rocks in this'un," he said. "Lucked out."

Cloyd took the posthole digger from the old man, pulled out the next stake, and started to dig.

"Say," Walter said, "whyn't you hold off until I can fetch a pair of gloves for you and a jug of ice water. And a cap, too. I always wear one when I'm standin' out in the sun irrigatin'."

"I never wear a hat."

"There probably won't be much cloud cover until later in the month . . . usually doesn't start raining until the Fourth of July."

Cloyd shook his head. "I don't like hats."

"Suit yourself," Walter answered cheerfully. "Well, I better let the water into the field, or the grass is gonna burn up."

Cloyd let the old man disappear through the orchard, then started digging with all of his strength and determination. If he was going to get finished, he'd better get started. He could tell Walter had already forgotten he was going to bring back some gloves, but it didn't matter. He didn't like to use gloves.

The June days and Cloyd's line of completed postholes advanced steadily. His blisters healed, his hands grew callused. The white stubble on the old man's face lengthened into thick white whiskers. He said he was having a lark: he had never grown a beard in his whole life, and now he was going to. Cloyd liked the way it made him look. Like an old miner. He would look perfect, Cloyd thought, with a pick over his shoulder and leading a donkey.

Even though he didn't work with Walter during the day, Cloyd wasn't lonely. His mind was brimful of thinking as he worked the rhythm of the posthole digger. He thought about Blueboy and where they would ride that evening, and wondered if he would see another bear. The mountains he thought about, too, all the time. He'd made a promise to himself not to mention his plans to Walter until he had the fence finished, until he had proven himself, until he'd earned the mountains.

Every so often the blades of his posthole digger would strike a rock, and then Cloyd was in for a battle. First he'd try to dig another hole, but often he'd strike the same rock. Then there was no choice but to break it with the bar, and he would slam the bar down with all his might. He found a fierce satisfaction in breaking rock. And he knew the sound carried up to Walter in the field. The old man was surprised with how hard he could work and how many holes he had dug. Cloyd had never worked this hard before; he was surprising himself. In the early afternoon Walter would ring the porch bell, and they would eat a big meal. Then he'd go back to his postholes and work until Walter called him for supper.

In the evenings Cloyd would hurry out to saddle up the roan and take him for a ride. Blueboy could run like anything. The horse liked him, and he knew it. Cloyd felt good streaming along the river road with the wind in his hair. He talked to the horse all the time. The horse was the only one who knew his secret name and his secret plans.

Late in the evenings, Walter would read his mining journals. Cloyd liked to ask him what it was like in the high country. "Tell me about the mountains up real high," he'd say, "like where your mine is."

Walter would stroke his whiskers. "Oh, there's nothin' like it. Most beautiful country I've ever seen."

"Is there much water?"

"Oh, there's water everywhere. Little trickles runnin' off snowbanks, ponds, lakes, creeks, streams, baby rivers. . . . Some places the ground's so wet it's like walkin' on a sponge. It's as green as can be, and there's wildflowers everywhere you look."

"How high are the tops of the mountains?"

"Punch holes in the sky."

"Can you climb to the top?"

"If you got wings."

"What happens to the animals when winter comes?"

"Freeze solid," said the old man, with his tongue in his cheek. "Wouldn't you?"

It was a good time, talking about the mountains in the parlor. Walter would set his mining journal aside, the tiredness would leave his eyes, and a faraway look would come over him as he spoke. Cloyd liked to see him scratch his whiskers. He liked this old man, Walter Landis.

RESPONDING TO THE SELECTION

Your Response

1. Do you admire Cloyd? Why or why not?

Recalling

2. Why does Walter take such good care of his peach trees?
3. What does Cloyd find in the cave up on the cliff?

Interpreting

4. What effect does finding the bearstone have on Cloyd?
5. How does Cloyd show his respect for the Ancient Ones?
6. How is the secret name Cloyd chooses for himself a fitting name for him?
7. Why does Cloyd work so hard on the fence?

Applying

8. Walter's wife used to say that a ranch is a house, but a farm is a home. How would you describe the difference between a house and a home?

ANALYZING LITERATURE

Understanding Character

Characters are the people in a work of fiction. Authors reveal information about characters either by stating directly what they want you to know about a character, or by showing you what the character is like through the character's words, thoughts, and actions.

1. What do you learn about Cloyd from his attempt to find his father?
2. What does Cloyd's work on the fence tell you about him?
3. What do you learn about Walter from his decision not to question Cloyd about his wet clothes on the first night?
4. What does Walter reveal about his character by not making Cloyd work on his first day at the ranch?

CRITICAL THINKING AND READING

Understanding Cultural Differences

In *Bearstone* you get a glimpse of the Ute culture, which may be very different from your own. The Ute culture has influenced Cloyd's behavior and values in various ways.

1. What is Cloyd's attitude toward nature?
2. What are his feelings about his ancestors?

THINKING AND WRITING

Writing About Character

Sometimes, in order to know a character well, a writer may imagine that character's entire history without including it in the book. Knowing "where the character is coming from" helps the author see what the character would do in a given situation. Imagine that you are the author of *Bearstone*. Write a summary of either Cloyd's or Walter's life up to the time when the novel begins. Before drafting your summary, make a list of traits the character has. Then note events in the character's past that shaped his personality. When you revise your summary, check that it is written in chronological order.

LEARNING OPTIONS

1. **Multicultural Activity.** Find out more about either the Utes or the Navajos. Explore the group's history, religion, arts, relations with the United States government, its social customs, and its present-day way of life. Present your findings to the class.
2. **Art.** Make a sketch either of the landscape around Walter's farm as it is described in the novel or of Cloyd in the cave where he finds the bearstone.

MULTICULTURAL CONNECTION

Totem Animals in Different Cultures

For Cloyd and his fellow Utes, the bear is a totem animal, which means an animal regarded as a distant ancestor of the group. In some cultures animals viewed in this way appear on totem poles. Most of us have seen these poles with their colorful carvings of animal faces, but few of us probably know their deep significance for the Native Americans who made them. Totem poles are more than decorative art; they are symbols of the spirit that binds a group of people together.

More than a symbol. The animals, birds, and fish carved on each pole are emblems, or totems, representing a particular clan, group, or tribe. The totem is more than a symbol, however. It is believed to represent the group's distant ancestor in some strange, mystical way. The animal or thing (totems can also be plants and natural objects) is often thought to have actually entered the body of the group's oldest ancestor.

A visual family history. Many totem poles of the Native Americans of the Northwest are now in museums, but originally they were erected in front of people's homes. The figures of the family totems were carved from top to bottom by members of the group and then put in place by the entire community during a special feast called a *potlatch*. The totem poles told everyone who the family or group was and where they came from. They were a sort of visual family history, with no two totem poles exactly alike.

A widespread practice. Totems are not only carved on poles. Their images are engraved on weapons, painted on masks, and even tattooed on the bodies of clan members. Also, they are not unique to Native Americans. Totems exist among African peoples, the Australian Aborigines, and the inhabitants of Oceania, among others. Each culture has its own kinds of totems and its own set of beliefs about them.

For example, the Australian Aborigines have special ceremonies to honor their totems. During these ceremonies people paint totem animals like kangaroos, snakes, crows, and lizards on their bodies to announce membership in a particular clan.

The Zande people of the Sudan region in Africa choose their hundreds of totems from the many animals, birds, and insects native to their region. These include the lion, monkey, squirrel, hawk, crocodile, ant, and butterfly. Totems among the Zande are passed down from one generation to the next, either through the father's or the mother's side of the family. Zande girls, for instance, trace their totem to their mothers; and the boys, to their fathers.

Some groups, like the Kpelles of West Africa, believe that sorcerers and medicine men have totems of their own, in addition to a group totem. These individuals are believed to receive special healing powers from their totem. Among the Kpelles, people with the same individual totem must live in the same community.

Sacred animals. Totems are sacred to the peoples who believe in them. There are rules against killing and eating totem animals and against marriage between members of the same totem group.

When you look at a picture of a totem pole, think about what those mysterious figures meant to the people who carved them.

Exploring and Sharing

Look up the word *totem* in a dictionary. From which language does it come? Why do you think it had to be borrowed from another language?

Find photographs of totem poles in books about the beliefs of native peoples. If possible, show the photographs to the class and explain what you have learned about these totem poles.

UNTITLED
Jay Van Everen
The Montclair Art Museum

GUIDE FOR READING

Bearstone, Chapters 7–11

Plot

Plot is the series of related events in a story or novel. The events develop around one or more conflicts, or struggles between opposing sides. The early stages of the plot are usually devoted to giving readers background information and establishing the major conflict. Eventually the plot reaches a climax, or point of highest interest in the conflict. At the climax there is much dramatic tension between the opposing sides. After the climax the conflict is resolved.

In a novel the plot develops over a longer period of time, often through episodes. An **episode** is an incident complete in itself, including its own conflict, climax, and resolution. For example, the incident in which Cloyd climbs the cliff and discovers the burial of the Ancient One is an episode. The different episodes in a plot are unified by common characters and a common theme. In other words, the episodes in a novel all develop one major idea.

Focus

The mountains are important to Cloyd because his ancestors lived there. Where did your ancestors live? What do you know about that area (or those areas, if your parents came from different backgrounds)? Write about your ancestral homeland—what you know about it and what feelings you have about it.

Vocabulary

Knowing the following words will help you as you read Chapters 7–11 of *Bearstone*.

relentlessly (ri lent′ lis lē) *adv.*: Persistently or without stopping (p. 664)

raspy (ras′ pē) *adj.*: Rough and grating (p. 668)

erratically (er rat′ ik lē) *adv.*: Irregularly or inconsistently (p. 672)

livid (liv′ id) *adj.*: Grayish-blue with rage (p. 673)

grimaced (grim′ ist) *v.*: Twisted up the face as in pain (p. 675)

voluminous (və lōōm′ ə nəs) *adj.*: Large or full (p. 678)

adamant (ad′ ə mənt) *adj.*: Not giving in; unyielding (p. 680)

Chapter 7

The days were scorching. Weeks passed with no cloud cover at all. Cloyd kept working. The shade of the nearby timber beckoned, but he resisted. He was getting closer all the time to digging that last posthole. In the evenings he'd sneak looks at the calendar; he kept trying to guess how long it would take him to build the fence. Day by day he was realizing it was a much bigger project than he'd thought at first, just as the old man had said.

Sundays were something to look forward to, the only break in the routine. Walter would go into Durango for groceries and supplies, and Cloyd would spend the day with Blueboy.

At breakfast, Walter was all dressed up for town and working on a shopping list. It was another Sunday, but Cloyd wasn't feeling very good about it. He woke up feeling bad, and he didn't know why. He only knew he wasn't very happy.

They hardly spoke over breakfast. The talk between them was dying out little by little. There was only the work.

He knew Walter could tell he was feeling bad. The old man was a long time buttering his toast. At last he said, trying to sound cheerful, "Gonna take Blueboy out today, Cloyd?"

Cloyd shrugged.

"I sure hope so. Say, I've been wondering if you might like to give that fenceline a rest. Maybe do a little of this and a little of that, take some more time with the horse."

"I don't want to," Cloyd said stubbornly.

Walter left for Durango. Cloyd knew he didn't want to ride Blueboy. He didn't feel good enough. There was a little flame of anger in him that was starting to grow. The old man was saying he should give up. Walter didn't really expect anything from him. Walter had heard all about school, how he'd failed everything. Now Walter expected him to fail here too. Well, they were all wrong about him, wrong to say he was lazy. He wanted to show the old man.

Cloyd shouldered the posthole digger and dragged the bar along behind. He didn't have that many holes to go. He wanted to get the posts in the ground before Walter needed his help with the hay. Then that would leave only stringing the wire.

Concentrating on his welding, Walter was startled to notice Cloyd standing beside him. Removing his mask, Walter switched off the arc welder. "How's it going, Cloyd?" he asked cheerfully.

"I finished those holes."

Walter beamed. "Well, Cloyd, that's downright amazin', is what it is. I never seen the like."

"We should finish the fence. So you'll have it before hunting season."

"I'd sure like to see it finished, too, Cloyd, but there's a lot of work left in it, fallin' junipers[1] for posts and whatnot."

"I can start cutting the posts tomorrow."

The old man cast his eyes to the ground, removed his cap, ran his hand slowly over the top of his head and back. "Cloyd," he said finally, "I wish you'd let me cut the posts. After we get the hay in and it gets to rainin', I won't have to irrigate so much. I'll take out some junipers on the hill, clean 'em up so you can set 'em, then we'll string the wire together."

"You don't think I can do this job?"

"It's the chain saw I'm worried about. They're dangerous, Cloyd. I've used one for years, and I'm still scared of it. You see, sometimes a tree has a mind of its own, and there's plenty of ways you can make a mistake. Have you ever handled one?"

---

1. junipers: Evergreen trees with strong, straight trunks.

"You can show me," Cloyd insisted.

Walter saw how much it meant. At last he had to say, "Cloyd, I believe you can do just about anything you set your mind to."

Cloyd felt good as he walked up the field through the glowing late light to the barn. He took the bearstone out and turned it in his fingers, held it against his cheek. There was just enough evening left for him to visit the roan. "Hey-a, hey-a," he called, and the horse nickered back.

The roan was waiting by the pasture gate. Cloyd fed him a little grain and then curried him, thinking aloud all the while. "You and me, Blue, we're gonna go to the mountains. I'm gonna finish it, finish everything; then we can go to the mountains, you and me."

In the morning Walter poked around the machine shed and collected the saw, an axe, a plastic bottle of bar-and-chain oil, a pint can of engine oil, an empty gas can, and a leather bag of tools. He told Cloyd all about the saw, and it seemed to Cloyd to take forever. Two or three times Walter cautioned Cloyd to mix the engine oil in with gas. "Straight gas'll ruin her," he said. Cloyd didn't ask questions, and Walter didn't ask if he understood.

Walter knew the Utes weren't big talkers. He'd lived his whole life near the Colorado Utes, and his occasional contacts with them had taught him how to take things. The way Cloyd pointed with his lips—only the old Utes did that anymore, something about it being rude to point with the hand or finger. And like the old-time Utes, Cloyd looked away when he talked or was spoken to.

Yet for all the time they'd spent together, Walter wished he understood Cloyd better. In the evenings Cloyd no longer asked about the mountains; he was bone-weary from working too hard. The boy would fall asleep watching the television. He himself was tiring, too, even questioning the need to set the farm back to rights. He was back to the old routines again, standing in the hot sun all day long and tediously moving dirt and routing water. And Cloyd was working relentlessly, harder every day, for reasons of his own. To whatever end, their course was set. Cloyd couldn't be turned now. The only time he'd take for himself was a short visit mornings and evenings with the big roan. He'd work the currycomb and talk, talk, talk with the horse. If I could interview that horse, Walter mused, I'd know the boy a whole lot better.

Cloyd thought it would take only a few days to log out the posts he needed. He soon found out it wasn't going to be that easy. The junipers grew only here and there on the mountain. He wished he could use the jack pines or the straight young firs. But he knew why the old man wanted junipers—they'd never rot.

He had to range the hillside the length of the farm, hundreds of feet up the slope, to find his trees. If anything, the work was harder than digging the postholes. The saw was heavy and noisy; his ears were always ringing. He burned his thumb on the exhaust and cut the heel of his hand sharpening the chain. After he felled a juniper, he had to top it to a seven-foot length, trim it, then drag it down the hillside to the ditch. The heavy posts often snagged in the oakbrush and brought him tumbling down. Even though he had only fifty-seven posts cut, he knew he had to get off the hillside for a while. He decided to set the posts he had.

Placing a rock at the bottom of each hole the way the old man had suggested, Cloyd set the posts. He kept his eye on the tractor up the field as the old man drove around cutting the hay. Walter would need his help in a few days to buck the bales onto the trailer and stack them in the barn.

Cloyd set the fifty-seventh post as the sun

WATCHING THE FLOCK (detail)
Ray Swanson
Courtesy of the Artist

was setting on the next-to-last day of June. The posts reached less than halfway to the ditchbank. He wanted to go back up the hillside the next day and cut more posts, until he had all he needed, but he knew he'd lost. He could go back to the fenceline after haying, but it wouldn't be the same. He had wanted to get through with it before haying, and he'd lost. Now there would be too much work on the fence after haying. The work would be hot and endless, and there wouldn't be time left for him and Blueboy to go to the mountains. He'd been fooling himself about the mountains all along. The old man would never have let him go anyway.

The sun was down, the air was cooling fast. Exhausted, Cloyd leaned on the last post. He felt chilled one minute, burning up the next. He feared he might have fever from the ticks[2] in the oakbrush. When he looked down the line of fenceposts, it seemed senseless, what he'd done. The day before, he'd received a letter from his sister, and he didn't even know what it said. He could read a few words, but that was all. He was too embarrassed to ask the old man to read it to him. He longed for White Mesa. All he wanted was to go home. Looking across the field to the gray farmhouse in the trees, he wondered what had made him think he could belong here.

Walter was in the house, fixing a special supper for Cloyd. He'd been planning it all week: a Thanksgiving-style dinner with turkey and all the extras. He'd taken the day off to prepare the meal, but he hadn't been able to talk Cloyd out of working on the fenceline. When Cloyd finally came in, later than usual, he hadn't even a nod for the old man. Walter

could see how gloomy he was. Cloyd shoved his plate away after picking at the turkey. Walter, who never ate much, began to put away the mountain of leftovers.

In the parlor, Walter sought out his recliner. Cloyd collapsed with a sigh on the sofa. Walter glanced at his new *Mining Gazette* but set it aside. Something was terribly wrong, and he'd have to get the boy to tell him what it was. What could he say? Maybe he should try a new tack. "Tell me about that letter you got yesterday," he suggested awkwardly. "What do you hear from home?"

Cloyd battled the confusion washing over him. He felt angry at the old man, and he didn't know why. He thought about the letter in his pocket. What should he say?

"It's my letter," he said finally. "It's none of your business."

Walter felt sorry he had chosen the letter to try to talk about. "I didn't mean to pry, Cloyd," he apologized.

"I don't know what's in the letter!" Cloyd shouted, standing up. "I can't read it. I don't know how. There, are you satisfied?"

He felt the weight of the old man's eyes on him.

Leaning forward, the old man reached out and touched Cloyd's hand. The dark veins stood out on his forehead. "I'm sorry, Cloyd," he whispered. "I had no idea. Let me read it for you. Where's the letter?"

Cloyd wanted to hear the letter, but he hated his weakness being suddenly out in the open. Now the old man would think that he was stupid.

"Why, I could maybe help you in the evenings," Walter was saying. "And I could sure read you these mining papers. . . ."

"I don't want your help," Cloyd said. He had to get away.

In his confusion he bumped into the table and spilled the old man's coffee all over the mining newspapers. He had to get to his room and be by himself.

---

2. He feared . . . ticks: Ticks are wingless insects that can transmit diseases as they suck blood from a person or an animal.

"Leave me alone," he shouted at Walter as he ran for the stairs. "Leave me alone!"

Chapter 8

In the morning Cloyd was surprised to find Walter acting as if nothing had happened. "Time to buck them bales out of the field and up into the barn," the old man said cheerfully. Cloyd didn't respond. How could things ever be the same between them again? He kept his eyes on his plate and said nothing.

After breakfast, three pickups pulling horsetrailers drove into the farm. Two of the trucks were loaded heavily with saddles and camping equipment. The third carried at least a dozen barking hound dogs. Six men in blaze-orange vests got out of the trucks as the old man waved and walked down the drive to meet them. Had the old man been expecting them? Cloyd wondered. He hadn't talked about anyone coming.

The leader, very tall and sure of himself, stood in front of the rest and made small talk with the old man. Cloyd watched from behind a tractor in the shop. The tall man took off his cowboy hat, revealing a headful of wavy red hair. The wind, blowing in Cloyd's direction, carried their words to him. The two talked easily about Walter's new beard and his peaches. Apparently they were good friends.

The others standing around began to fidget, Cloyd saw. They were strangers. One of them asked in a Texas accent, "Does the wind always blow like this in Colorado?"

Cloyd saw the tall, red-haired man turn his shoulder and wink to Walter. "A question like that you oughta ask Walter here. Heck, I was just a kid when he invented this whole country. What about this wind, Walter—think it'll let up?"

The old man tugged at his cap. "It's been known to blow, that's for certain. Just workin' up to it this morning. Myself, I like to keep track of the wind by hangin' a chain on a post. If it stands out straight, that's a breeze, but when it gets to whippin' around and links snap off, why look out—it's likely to get windy by sundown."

Walter told it straight-faced, but when he finished he held his breath, and his ears turned red. Everyone was laughing. The old man's cheeks were all puffed out. Finally he blew the air out his nose, his head bobbing, and he stroked the white whiskers on his chin. "Yes sir," he concluded, "it can blow—not that it does very often."

Cloyd was amazed at how easily the old man got on with these people, laughing with them and having a good time. He hadn't even met some of them before. Who were these people?

Still laughing, the men turned to their preparations. Cloyd came out of the shed and watched them unload the horses. After they parked their trucks and trailers out of the way, they packed the horses, shouting instructions back and forth. Walter came over to Cloyd and said the tall man was his old friend. Walter was all excited, like the man was really important. "Rusty's the best outfitter in the San Juans," he said. "Best outdoorsman I ever saw. More'n likely he'll scare up a bear."

The red-haired man beckoned to Walter from beside the coal pile, where he was rigging the horses. The old man went to him and then into the house, returning with the salt and pepper shakers from the kitchen table. Suddenly Cloyd realized that these men had to have the old man's permission to hunt on his land, and that he had already given it to them. To hunt for bears?

With no warning, the old man was bringing the red-haired man over. "Got someone I'd like you to meet, Rusty," he said to his friend. "This here's Cloyd."

For an instant, before he looked away, Cloyd saw the bear hunter's eyes. The man thought that meeting Cloyd was a joke. The tall man stuck out his giant hand, and said in his raspy voice, "Glad to meet 'ya. 'Cloyd,' is it? Never heard a name like that before."

Walter had never tried to shake hands with Cloyd. Cloyd hated shaking hands. But he had no choice but to offer his now.

The red-haired man didn't just shake his hand, he crushed it. He didn't have to do that, Cloyd thought. It hurt really bad. Cloyd tried not to let his face show the pain. He glimpsed the man's mocking eyes. The eyes said Cloyd was nothing, nothing at all, only an Indian.

The old man was trying to get them to talk. "Cloyd here's real good with horses," Walter said, beaming. "That blue roan of mine has really taken a shine to him."

"Is that so?" the outfitter said with a short laugh. "Well, a horse ain't a dog, Cloyd. It could care less about you. All it cares about is getting fed. A horse is a work animal, not a pet."

Cloyd turned away. His hand was still throbbing. The bear hunter turned to his own business and mounted his horse. Cloyd imagined what he could do to the red-haired man's hand if he were twice the man's size. Break every bone in it.

Cloyd watched the riders and their dogs disappear upriver. He was furious, and the old man didn't even know it. Cloyd was sure now that he meant nothing to the old man. These men were his real friends. And they were bear hunters.

It was time to bring in the hay. The old man was going to drive the tractor, and he was supposed to buck the bales onto the trailer and afterward stack them up in the barn. The old man, he recalled, liked to brag about how heavy his bales were—eighty pounds. "People get their money's worth," he'd said. Eighty pounds was fine for Walter— the old man wasn't planning on bucking the bales himself. That would be Cloyd's job.

The old man was standing by the tractor, waiting, but Cloyd walked off down to the riverbank instead. A few minutes later he heard the tractor's motor fire. The old man was going to go ahead without him. Let him try, Cloyd thought. It's his hay, not mine.

Along the riverbank he saw several magpies and then a raven.[3] They reminded him of the canyons back home, and his sister, and he grew powerfully homesick. He brought the bearstone out of his pocket and tried to make a wish on it that he could go home. But the stone only reminded him of where he was and what the red-haired man was going to do. In a sudden burst of awareness he felt like he was the bear the man was after, and he could feel what it would be like to be chased by barking dogs and men on horses. He knew with awful certainty that the bear would be run down, cornered, and killed. Maybe it would be the mother bear, the one he'd seen with the cub. It was the old man's fault, he decided bitterly—he'd given his permission. If they killed a bear, the old man would have to pay. The old man never cared about me, he thought, these are his real friends.

Walter decided to bring in the hay all by himself. Something was wrong with Cloyd, he knew, but he shouldn't have walked off on him when he was needed most. Well, he would show this boy what Walter Landis was made of. He'd bucked a few bales in his life. Jumping off and back on the tractor, he pitched bale after bale onto the trailer like he was a young man again. His face was flushed bright red, his breathing came louder and

---

3. several magpies . . . raven: Birds that are known for their noisy calls. Magpies are black-and-white with long, tapering tails, and ravens are large all-black crows with straight, sharp beaks.

louder, but he wouldn't quit. He brought load after load to the barn, heaving and grunting and dragging the bales into place. He'd work until all the hay was in or his heart burst, whichever came first. He didn't care which.

He worked all morning and never came in for a meal. He worked all through the long afternoon, through the dusk, and into the darkness, until the last bale was up in the barn. Then he walked silently into the house, neglecting to take off his boots or his cap. Tracking dirt on the white parlor rug, he disappeared into his room, trailing bits of hay.

Walter was exhausted. He lay on his bed in his soiled overalls and boots and talked to his wife. "Maude," he said, "I'm an old fool, but I just don't know what to do with this boy. I sure wish you were here to help me. Something's got into him—I don't know what. He was doing so good. I guess we'll just hang on and see what happens. . . ."

The house fell silent. Cloyd was in his room, packing his duffel bag. The old man would get rid of him now. Tomorrow, he'd be back at Eaglewing. That would be all right. He didn't care anymore.

Chapter 9

At first light, Walter was usually up and cooking sausage and eggs. Cloyd waited awhile for him in the kitchen, then took a loaf of bread and a jar of peanut butter outside. It was easy to put off seeing the old man.

Several hours later Walter limped out of the house. Cloyd was surprised to see he had shaved his beard off. "Hay's in the barn, Cloyd," he announced cheerfully. "Lucky it didn't get rained on. Once you're into July—and today's the first—you're pressin' your luck."

Cloyd didn't know what to say. The old man was acting like nothing had happened.

"Wouldn't mind a bit if it rained anytime now," Walter continued. "Wouldn't have to irrigate so much. I'd better start the water back in today—the field's drying out bad. How 'bout you? Got anything in mind? Maybe you'd like to take that roan—"

"Make some more posts, I guess," Cloyd mumbled.

Walter hesitated. "Fine," he said uncertainly. "That's just fine."

Cloyd trudged across the field with the saw and the gas can. He'd left behind the pint of oil Walter wanted mixed with the gas.

It was another cloudless day. The last of the night's lingering cool air was burning off as he angled through the haystubble toward the hillside.

Before he climbed, he took a good look at his fenceposts, marching stout and straight all the way to the peach orchard. It was a strange feeling; they looked different. They didn't make him feel proud or good. They weren't his anymore.

He'd forgotten to bring along any drinking water. Already he was thirsty, and the sun was blazing. His head was pounding. Why was he still here? He'd expected to be sent on his way back to Durango, and instead he was being sent back to work as if nothing had happened.

He had to get out of the sun. He veered away from the hillside and followed the posts down to the orchard. He dropped the saw, lay in the grass at the base of the big boulder, and looked up at the trees. He could lie there all day, he thought. Ever since he'd come to the old man, there'd never been time to look at the world this way that he liked.

Suddenly the bear was back in his thoughts, and he could see it all happening. Men riding hard to keep up with their yapping dogs, the bear exhausted and desperate with no place to hide. He hated the outfitter, that red-haired man, with all his heart.

His thirst brought him back to the orchard. He swallowed hard and bitterly. The whole orchard was exploding with growth. The countless rock-hard peaches grew larger by the day—he'd been checking on them since the first day he came to the farm. He'd admired them, but now he hated them. These thriving trees of Walter's with their long, green leaves were so superior to his grandmother's it made him sick. Hers were pitiful.

He spat, but nothing came out. He had a bitter taste in his mouth, like poison. His grandmother's peaches were rare and beautiful only in the way he used to see them, not as they really were. But the old man's trees could have all the water they wanted, while his grandmother's, with their misshapen trunks and stunted, yellowed leaves, stood here and there against the sun and depended on the rain. Sometimes the rains didn't come at all and the peaches shriveled on the trees and there was no moisture to suck out of them.

All at once he heard dogs barking and men calling—the outfitter and his bear hunters had returned. Cloyd ran up the road toward the house, where the men had dismounted and were showing off their kill to Walter. Everyone talked at once, except for the red-haired man, who was acting like it was all in a day's work. A bear was heaped atop a nervous horse. It wasn't as big as Cloyd would have thought. It looked about like a big black dog. The old man was going to let his friend butcher it right there and hang it up in one of his sheds.

As if he were invisible, he walked among the preoccupied hunters with them taking no notice of him. He approached the bear and stared at it. The bear had nearly bitten its tongue in two. Its mouth was choked with clotted blood. A fly walked on one of its eyes.

Recounting the hunt, the men poked fun at each other. One man, the one who'd asked the old man about the wind, was especially happy—he was the one who shot it. "Bearskin for the den," he said proudly.

"Plenty of good sausage, too, and some for Walter here," the red-haired man said in his raspy voice. "What don't make sausage I'll feed to my dogs."

Suddenly Cloyd remembered all the sausage he'd eaten at the old man's table. It almost made him retch to think it might have been—probably was—*bear* meat he'd eaten all those mornings. He backed out of the clearing in front of the house, turned and ran back toward the peach orchard. A terrible revenge was taking shape in his mind.

Cloyd snatched up the saw from the tall grass at the base of the boulder. He filled it with gas, pink instead of its usual purple, the way it looked with the oil added in. Right now he didn't care how Walter wanted it. The old man was just fussy—he wouldn't even drive his truck without checking the oil first. Everything Walter did had to be in neat lines, like his windrows[4] and his fences. Everything had to be so clean, like the white rug in his parlor and his tractors, and everything had to be in its place in the house, the sheds, and the barn.

He grabbed up the saw and yanked the pull-cord with the saw in midair, as Walter had advised him never to do. The engine fired immediately and he gunned it until it screamed.

Cloyd wondered why he'd liked Walter in the first place, this fussy old white man who had a thousand times more than he needed and still had to have someone else do his work for him so he could get more. Maybe he'd worked for the old man because of finding the bearstone the first day. It was easy enough to see now—there was no connection between the good-luck token and the old man. Cloyd remembered how Walter laughed with the red-haired man and the other bear hunters when they first arrived. Laughs with Bear Hunters should be the old man's secret name, he thought bitterly.

He cut through the skin of the nearest tree and winced as he withdrew the saw. Beads of moisture were forming along the edges of the fresh wound. From one to the next he ran with the saw roaring at full throttle, and he cut each of the twenty-two peach trees most of the way through. Each time, as

---

4. windrows: Rows of cut hay raked together to dry before being made into heaps or stacks.

the saw's teeth bit into the thin bark, he hollered with hurt as if he felt the saw himself. He didn't want to cut them down, he wanted them to die slowly. Before they died, their leaves would yellow and the peaches shrivel, and they would look just like his grandmother's peaches.

Now he knew he was in big trouble, but that made it easier. He was only getting started. This time there wouldn't be any doubt he was going back to Eaglewing.

His mind racing and his throat so dry it seemed jammed with a wad of wool, Cloyd stumbled out of the orchard with the heavy saw. When his fifty-seven posts came into view all standing straight and lined up so perfectly, he pulled up for breath and caught himself admiring them. But what was the fence really for? To keep a man from crossing a field. It was a stupid reason to have worked so hard. At White Mesa he went with the goats wherever he wanted. None of the Utes put up fences or claimed a part of the mesa for their own. The animals went where there was feed, and there were no fences at all until some white men chained the trees out by their roots, dragged them into the arroyos,[5] and fenced the northern end of the mesa for beans.

Cloyd tried his shoulder against the first post. It wouldn't budge. He had set them deep, wedging rocks around the posts and packing them with clay soil. They'd set up like concrete. Why should Walter be so concerned about some people hunting deer and elk on his ranch while he thought it was fine for others to hunt bears? He was a fool to have worked for the old man.

The juniper posts wouldn't rot in two hundred years, but he didn't want them there at all. The field looked better without them.

The saw didn't want to start. After dozens

_____

5. arroyos (ə rȯi′ ōz): Rivulets or stream beds.

of attempts Cloyd made it idle erratically, but it cut out as soon as he tried the throttle. Eventually it caught at full throttle, and he discovered it would run if he didn't let up even a little bit. He walked along the line, sawing down the posts and thinking about people he didn't like. One post for the reading teacher who tried to make him read aloud, one for the speech teacher who always tried to make him get up in front of the class, and one for the nervous principal who was always saying, "Well, I guess I'll just have to use the board on you." One for each of the bear hunters. Two, three, four, five, six, sixteen for Walter and his friend, the red-haired man.

Half the posts remained when the saw began to kill as soon as it bit into the wood. Then it wouldn't fire at all. Cloyd checked the gas, which hissed as he loosened the cap. Boiling hot, most of it escaped. Maybe the saw did need oil mixed in with the gas, but who cared?

The saw was too hot; it wasn't going to start. Probably he'd ruined it by leaving out the oil. He felt like he was going to faint. He had to get out of the sun. He threw the saw down and walked off, waded the irrigation ditch at the edge of the field. Even though the water ran cool and clear, he didn't think to drink any. He started up the mountainside toward the sandstone outcrop where he'd found the blue stone.

On his way up, Cloyd saw the trucks and horsetrailers leave, and then he saw the old man walk down to the peach orchard. He turned and fled higher. When he reached the top of the cliffs and looked out, he was not soothed, as he had expected to be. The sight of the distant peaks did nothing to lift him out of the despair drowning him inside. Usually after he did something he knew was going to bring trouble, he felt better in a way—revenged. But with the old man it was different. He'd never felt this awful in his life; he'd never liked anybody this much, as much as he'd liked Walter. Suddenly he felt more alone than ever before, even more than in the first days in Durango after the tribe had sent him to Eaglewing.

This wasn't the same as getting into trouble with the teachers or the principal, or with his housemother. Those people were making him do things he didn't want to do. It was different with the old man. Once, he had really wanted to work for Walter, and it was good then. Now everything was spoiled. He had spoiled it.

His thirst grew so bad he couldn't swallow. But he was good at enduring pain. No one could ever take that away from him. Maybe he would run away. But first he would stand up to the old man for punishment the way he did with the principal, then go home and hide in the canyons. Walter would take him back to Eaglewing, but he wouldn't stay for long. No one could find him in the canyons.

Chapter 10

It was dark, and Cloyd was off the mountain. As he reached for the latch on the front door, the old man stepped out of the shadows, trembling with rage. He caught the boy by the shoulders with unnatural strength and shook him back and forth against the door. "What's the matter with you, anyway?" he roared.

Cloyd said nothing and let himself be shaken. He'd spent his own anger and had none left to counter the enormity of the old man's wrath.

Walter put his livid face against Cloyd's where the boy's eyes couldn't avoid his. "Who are you to come in here and ruin our peaches? You knew what those trees meant to me. Well? Speak to me!"

Cloyd turned his head aside and looked at the ground.

"Give me that little blue rock you keep in your pocket," Walter commanded.

Cloyd's mouth turned sharply down at the corners. "What rock?" he grunted.

Walter extended his hand, palm up. "Give it to me, Cloyd. I wasn't born yesterday. I've seen you more'n once sneakin' it in and out of your hand. C'mon, give it!"

There was nothing else to be done. He could see he owed it to the old man. He heaved a sigh and fetched it out of his pocket.

Walter took the stone and closed his fist on it. "You care about this little rock, eh? You won't say? I think you do. C'mon, I want to teach you something."

Walter stalked over to his machine shop with the boy in tow, flicked on the bare bulb suspended from the rafters, and set the blue stone on his anvil. Then he reached for the sledgehammer.

"A dose of your own medicine," the old man raged, holding the sledgehammer high over his head.

Cloyd's heart turned to lead. He waited passively for his punishment.

As Walter focused on his target, he paused with the hammer in midair and craned his neck in the bad light. "What is that thing?" he demanded.

"A bear," the boy answered quietly.

"A bear?" The old man took it in his hand and examined it up close. Cloyd edged forward.

"You care about this thing quite a bit, don't you?"

Cloyd wouldn't say. He backed off and looked at the ground.

"Oh, the heck with it," Walter stormed. "Here, keep it."

When Cloyd didn't respond, Walter reached over and shoved it into his pocket. "Go get your stuff. I just want to get rid of you."

It was late at night. As the pickup wound slowly through the foothills on its way to Durango, each of them kept silent, preoccupied with his own regrets. Just after they passed

SUMMER SOLITUDE, 1992
Lanny Grant
Courtesy of the Artist

through the little town of Bayfield, the head-lights illuminated a rabbit darting across the highway. Walter and Cloyd both winced at the thump under the wheels. In their broodings, that thump resounded like a judgment, and each was plunged deeper in remorse.

Fifteen more slow and silent miles, and they reached Durango. Walter stopped at a red light and stared down Main at the blinking yellows. At this hour Durango was a ghost town, and it seemed there were only the two of them in the world. "I couldn't miss him," Walter said with a sigh.

"Miss who?" Cloyd asked quickly. Somehow he was eager to talk with the old man.

"Oh, that darned rabbit back there. He seemed bound and determined."

"It wasn't your fault."

"I suppose not," Walter said slowly. "Just one of them things. Well, show me the way to your . . . Eaglewing."

Cloyd gave directions, and then the old man geared the truck down, and it crept toward the group home. They both knew they had only a few minutes' left. "I wonder if you'd mind if I looked over that turquoise piece of yours once more," Walter said.

The old man turned it over in his fingers, eyed it, and rubbed it thoughtfully, but he said nothing as he drove down the empty streets.

"Turn here," Cloyd said.

Walter sighed. "It's a sure-enough bear," he said. "Could even be a grizzly, from the shape of it. I went to the Bear Dance[6] once down at the reservation. . . ." he began, then stopped talking. A revelation was forging itself in his mind. At last he said, "You cut those peaches right after those fellows came in from their bear hunt. Isn't that right?"

Cloyd grimaced.

Walter scratched and scratched behind

---

6. Bear Dance: The Utes' principal religious and social ceremony held every year in the late spring.

his ear, and then he handed the stone back. "Well, that helps some, it sure does."

"Here it is," Cloyd said, and pointed to the house with his lips.

Walter slowed to a stop and eyed the group home. It wasn't what he expected; you couldn't tell it apart from all the other tract homes in the neighborhood. He drove on another block before he stopped. For a long time he said nothing. He took off his cap and raked his bald head with his fingers. Then he said, shaking his head a little, "Pigs might fly, but they're unlikely birds."

"What's that mean?"

"Just an old saying," he replied with a faint smile. "I never did know exactly, but I always liked the sound of it. Cloyd, Susan told me once you'd rather more'n anything just go home. Is that right?"

Cloyd shrugged guardedly.

"Well?"

"They won't let me."

"I suppose not," Walter agreed, as he slipped the truck into gear and drove off.

"What're you doing?" Cloyd mumbled.

"Takin' you home."

"How come?"

"You ain't gonna do any good here at this 'Eaglewing,' are you?"

"They won't let you."

"I don't see nobody," Walter said gruffly.

"They'll come and get me."

"I'll wait a week before I tell Susan. You'll have some time at home, whatever happens."

They left Durango behind and headed west up a steep grade. Cloyd barely thought about going home, he was so astonished and puzzled. He didn't know what to make of this old man. He'd liked him, and then he'd hated him, and now he didn't know what to think. Walter was taking him home. After a few more miles had passed and they were on their way down the western side of the mountains, he asked again, "How come you're doing this?"

"Maybe it'll help you get the bee out of your bonnet," the old man said coldly.

Cloyd didn't want to have to ask him what that meant. The old man was in a strange mood—better to keep quiet. He thought about the horse. He wished there'd been a chance to see Blueboy before he left.

The sun was rising over the high desert as they neared White Mesa. In the clear, thin air Cloyd took in the landmarks he'd grown up with. He almost wished he could share them with Walter, but they hadn't really made a peace. To the north, Blue Mountain, the sacred one, still wearing a patch of snow. To the east, the massive form of the Sleeping Ute lying on his back with arms folded across his chest, not yet ready to awake and vanquish his enemies. To the south, the glowing white cliffs of the San Juan as it flowed through Bluff, and beyond them the bare redlands of the Navajos with the towers of Monument Valley beginning to appear in the early light. To the west, the wooded slope of Cedar Mesa falling from the Bear's Ears to the river, gouged by the bottomless red-walled canyons. In those remote canyons was where he would hide, he decided. There, in the slickrock country, he could live wild and free.

As they drove south out of Blanding onto the windy mesa, Cloyd searched for something to say to thank the old man. There was something welling up inside him that he'd never felt before and that had to be expressed. Too soon he was pointing out the nondescript government house that was his grandmother's, the one with the summer ramada[7] of cottonwood branches on one side and the scraggly peach trees on the other. And then he was standing by the truck with

---

7. ramada (rə mä′ də): A garden structure made of crisscrossed branches on which flowering vines can grow. When attached to a house, a ramada is like an open porch.

60 YEARS A HERDER, 1986
Ray Swanson
Courtesy of the Artist

his duffel bag in his hand, and the old man was saying, "Good luck, Cloyd. Let's don't say good-bye with no hard feelin's. . . ."

Cloyd nodded, but it was all happening too fast, his feelings were too deep to be reached. He found no words at all, only waved slightly as the old man turned the truck around and drove away.

The pickup was small in the distance by the time he realized he'd lost something of priceless value. He waved forlornly, then furiously, as the truck vanished. With the suddenness of a cloudburst in the desert, tears ran down his face.

He stumbled around behind the house to the little shed and corral, to check in on the goats. They were all gone. There was no fresh dung there, either.

After smoke started to come from the chimney pipe, he went in. His grandmother looked up from the frybread dough she was kneading and gave a sharp cry.

A Ute woman in the old style, she was dark, earthy, and large, the mainstay of her diet being frybread. In her green velveteen blouse and voluminous red skirt, and in the way she knotted her long hair and wrapped it in bright yarn, she reflected the influence of the nearby Navajos. Not one to ask a flurry of questions, she made a joke about his ribs showing through his T-shirt and opened up a can of fruit cocktail. It was something for him to start on while she cooked the frybread in the oil she had boiling on the cookstove. She fed the people in her life, lavished affection on them, rarely asked anything, and never tried to control whether they came or went.

They squeezed honey on their frybread. Cloyd wanted to talk. He'd spoken no Ute in the last year, as the boys from the Colorado reservation no longer knew the language. Right away he found himself telling her about Walter, how they'd worked together, how there was a river flowing right through his farm.

"Good," she said. "I knew you would like it in Colorado."

He told her about the high mountains, how someday he'd like to go there and climb the highest peak he could find.

"Wouldn't that be something," she said, her eyes reflecting the vision. "This man you work for, he lives in a good way?"

"He's the best man I ever knew," Cloyd heard himself saying. "He's old—older than you. His wife died. He's all alone."

Suddenly he knew he had no desire to hide out in the canyons. But what was he to do?

They talked about his sister who was at the boarding school in Salt Lake City. She had visited, his grandmother said, and had reported that everything was fine.

"I'll go to Blanding on Saturday and get lots of groceries so we can put some fat on your ribs."

Though sometimes someone she knew stopped and picked her up, often enough she walked all the way. Cloyd saw how he could save her the ten miles into Blanding, ten miles back. He realized he'd made a decision. "Oh, I can't stay long," he said. "I have to leave tomorrow."

His grandmother's eyebrows rose. "Oh?"

"Walter needs me. We have a lot of work to do."

"Well, that's good. I'm glad you came to see me. How are you traveling?"

Cloyd gave the hitchhiking sign with his thumb.

"I have to go now," she said. "I have a job. There is a day-care center here now. I cook for them. I had to sell the goats when there was nobody to take care of them. Maybe someday we'll get them back." She paused at the door. "Live in a good way," she said in parting, as she always did.

Cloyd decided to leave right away. His grandmother would understand. But would the old man take him back?

Chapter 11

When Walter got home from Utah, he went directly to his bed and collapsed in his dirty overalls. He was exhausted. Unshaven, no sleep, nothing to eat, at his age driving to Utah and back: he'd been letting himself go to the dogs. And he didn't care. Right now he should be irrigating the field. The grass would burn up in the heat before long if he didn't. But he didn't care. He let himself sink into sleep like a heavy stone plunging into a well.

When he woke up he was hungry. Intent on drowning himself in sentiment, he went downstairs to the basement to fetch a jar of peaches. He sat on a crate a long time as the sunken window admitted less and less light. He brooded on the two dozen or so jars of peaches left on the shelf, her special Missouri peaches from those seedlings she'd brought along to Colorado. He'd told her that peaches wouldn't make it here, but she insisted. And there'd never been a time he'd gone downstairs for peaches that he hadn't remembered how it all happened.

Walter studied the crack that had appeared the length of the concrete basement wall just after his wife died. He got up and looked at it from across the room and then from the corner, where he eyeballed the length of the wall. He saw, or feared he saw, the foundation bulging in more than ever. As he had many times before, he outlined the work that had to be done to plumb the wall. Digging, pouring, timbering . . . He had the materials, the tools, the know-how—everything but the desire.

He didn't care anymore. About much of anything. He had for a while, when the boy was with him and they were working together to put the farm back in order. To what purpose? he wondered. He'd tried to make it like it was before, when his wife was alive, when the two of them and the farm were all one. On the surface, he and Cloyd had succeeded. But a farm isn't land and fenceposts and hay in the barn. As his wife always said, "A farm is a home." He'd failed the boy. When he'd had the chance to give him a home, he'd given him only work. But work for work's sake can't keep a soul going, Walter told himself. That's like pounding rocks in a prison yard. It's not the work that's awful, it's the lack of purpose.

She was gone. He could quit working the farm now. He himself had never been a farmer. He was a miner. He'd taken up farming for her, and gladly. They'd had all those good years making their living on the farm. Now he could quit, and lie down to rest. . . .

The next morning, Walter got up late and wandered outside to check on the horses. They had plenty of pasture and were able to drink from the river, but there was no telling when one might turn a leg in a varmint hole or get itself torn up in barbed wire. He felt bad when he saw the blue roan. He was never going to look at that horse again without thinking of the boy.

On the way back, he walked the irrigation ditch to see if a beaver hadn't moved in and started to dam it up. He sat down on the ditchbank with all the hayfields sloping away in front of him and tried to think of how to get his fields taken care of properly. Only one choice remained, really; he'd just been putting it off. He'd pick the best man he could and lease the second cutting to him. There were always industrious fellows around trying to raise more cows than they had the land to support. They had families to feed and mortgages[8] to pay off. He'd turned down plenty of requests as they'd seen him getting older.

He didn't really have to work anymore. The farm had been paid for years ago, and he didn't need much income to live the way he

---

8. mortgages (mör′ gij iz): Bank loans used to purchase property and paid off in monthly installments.

did. They'd always put some savings by, and he got a steady, if small, income from the mining claim his wife had finally convinced him to sell, the one near Monarch Pass. She'd wanted him to sell the Pride of the West, too, but he was so adamant about keeping it, she finally gave up. She even quit badgering him about his packhorses and mining equipment, and his occasional announcements that in a year or two he might reopen his mine. So many years had gone by, she knew he was just hanging on to a dream he'd had when he was young, and there wasn't any harm to it.

It was pleasant to sit on the ditchbank in the morning sun and imagine he was up at the mine, sitting on the ore dump with Snowslide Creek rushing by and the peaks all around, the grass green and the wildflowers all in bloom. And inside the mine, not far at all from where he'd left off tunneling, waited the heart of the mountain, a secret place, a marvelous fluke made millions of years before in the bowels of the earth: a room having no doors, its furniture and draperies the fantastic shapes of glistening, crystalline gold.

Walter looked up to see a figure stumbling toward him out of the dying peach trees and through the sawed-off fenceposts lying at sixes and sevens down at the low end of the farm. The figure was struggling with an awkward burden. The old man squinted for a better look. In a few moments, to his everlasting amazement, he made out the white T-shirt and jeans, the duffel bag, the shaggy black hair and the brown face of the boy. He stood up meekly, lifted his cap, and ran his trembling hand over and over his skull. "He's come back, Maude," he said quietly. "He's come back." Then he walked down to meet the boy.

They stood face-to-face in the middle of the field.

"I want to try again," Cloyd said, looking away.

Walter shook his head in wonder.

"Please, I'll do better," the boy pleaded, thinking he'd been turned down.

"My goodness, Cloyd, of course you can. Maybe I can do better, too."

The boy pointed toward the orchard with his lips. "I'm sorry about the trees."

"I see you are. Both of us was hurt bad. I like to think, though, that the hurt you get over makes you stronger. Now let's get you taken care of. You look like something the cat spit out."

Cloyd smiled wearily, and they walked down to the house. He showered, ate some sandwiches, and went upstairs to bed. When he woke up, Walter had his clothes cleaned and dried for him. Cloyd asked what work he should do next. Walter explained that he was leasing out the farm and wouldn't be working it anymore. "I've been thinking up a storm today, Cloyd. I don't have that much time left in my life—I'm old enough, I oughta be able to do what I really want. Farmin' was good to me, but now it's time to quit. I ain't a mule turnin' grist.[9] What I'm tryin' to say is, do you remember how I've got a mine up in the back country?"

"The Pride of the West?"

"That's right. Remember how I said I'm gonna reopen it someday? I've been sayin' that for years. Well . . . *now*, I figure, now's the time. I'd need your help gettin' up there, of course, but if I remember right, you were always askin' about the mountains. I think it might do us both a world of good to get up into that high country. How would that suit you, Cloyd?"

"Will we take the horses?"

"Of course. No roads in there. We'll have to pack in everything."

Cloyd beamed. "Can I ride Blueboy?"

---

9. a mule turnin' grist: Where water power was not available, harnessed mules turned the mechanism that caused the huge stones in gristmills to grind grain.

ILLUSTRATION FOR THE COVER
OF *BEARSTONE* (detail)
Patricia Mulvihill
Courtesy of the Artist

"You bet. I'll ride that sorrel mare."

"When can we go?"

"It might take a couple-three weeks to lease out the farm, get everything ready, and tie up all the loose ends. Tomorrow's the Fourth of July, so that still leaves us a good while up there before you have to be back in school. But before we get too serious about anything, let's take a day off. They got a rodeo up in Pagosa on the Fourth every year. I'm thinkin' you'd really enjoy it. You're about due for a payday—maybe you could spend some of your earnin's. And I'd get a chance to take those hot mineral baths they got there. Always does wonders for my bones."

Cloyd spent the afternoon riding Blueboy up the river and telling him the news about the mountains, over and over and over.

RESPONDING TO THE SELECTION

Your Response

1. Do you think Cloyd has a right to feel angry that Walter lets people hunt bears on his property?
2. What do you think of Walter's decision to return to mining?

Recalling

3. Why doesn't Cloyd cut the peach trees all the way down?
4. What does Cloyd's grandmother ask him about Walter?

Interpreting

5. Why does Cloyd become more isolated and withdrawn as he works on the fence?
6. What do Walter and Cloyd not understand about each other?
7. What difference between Walter and Cloyd is illustrated when Walter decides not to smash the bearstone?

Applying

8. Cloyd and the hunters have different feelings about bears. What can be done to resolve conflicts caused by differences between cultures?

ANALYZING LITERATURE

Understanding Plot Development

In a novel, the *plot,* or series of related events, develops through different *episodes.* Each episode, like the misunderstanding between Cloyd and Walter, has its own conflict, climax, and resolution.

1. For each episode listed below, describe the conflict, name the climax, and describe the resolution.

   a. Cloyd gets a letter from his sister.

   b. Rusty and the hunters arrive at the ranch.

   c. Rusty and his group return with a bear they have shot.

2. What aspect of Cloyd's personality causes all three of the conflicts?

CRITICAL THINKING AND READING

Making Predictions About Plot

You have read about half of the novel, and you have seen what conflicts have been established and how some of them have been resolved. You may already have some ideas about what is going to happen later in the plot. Answer these questions to make some predictions about the last half of *Bearstone*.

1. What does Cloyd's return to Walter suggest about the future of their relationship?
2. Do any clues suggest what might happen at the mine and in the mountains?
3. Do you think Cloyd has seen the last of Rusty? Why or why not?

THINKING AND WRITING

Writing About Plot

Use one of the predictions you made for Critical Thinking and Reading to write a summary of one possible outcome of the novel. Write a paragraph summarizing the ending you think is most likely and giving your reasons. When you revise, make sure you've clearly stated the reasons for your predictions.

LEARNING OPTIONS

1. **Multicultural Activity.** Find out more about the role of specific animals in Native American cultures. Choose two Native American nations to explore. Write a brief report of your findings.
2. **Speaking and Listening.** With four classmates role-play a meeting held at the end of August to decide where Cloyd will live for the next year. Each person should portray one of the following characters at the meeting: Cloyd, Walter, Susan James, Cloyd's grandmother, and the principal of the school that Cloyd attended in Durango.

MULTICULTURAL CONNECTION

Cultural Values and Conflicts

In this story Cloyd and the hunters come from different cultures and therefore have different ideas about killing bears. Frequently, the differences in the way people think and act are the result of their cultural background. What is considered appropriate behavior in one culture is often inappropriate in another. This can lead to misunderstandings.

Hunting in different cultures. Hunting is an activity that is viewed very differently by different cultures. Native American, African, and European hunters have traditionally killed animals for food and in self-defense. The Hindu people of India, on the other hand, consider their cattle sacred; they would never kill a cow.

Misunderstandings. Nonverbal communication is another area that differs from culture to culture and may cause misunderstandings. In the United States, avoiding eye contact may tell the other person that you are embarrassed or shy or are not interested in what is being said. In Japan and parts of Latin America, however, looking someone directly in the eye is considered impolite.

Signs of respect. In some countries there are other ways of showing respect when meeting a new acquaintance. Argentines customarily address people by a title (Señor, Señora, Doctor) when they are introduced. In sharp contrast, Australians greet everyone with a hearty "Good Day" (pronounced gə dī′) and are immediately on a first-name basis.

Ideas about pets. You might think that the subject of pets would be one area of cultural agreement; but one person's pet is another's pest. Dogs, for example, are man's best friend in the United States and much of Europe, but not in Arab countries. Arabs consider dogs unclean, and if they accidentally touch one, they must immediately wash their hands. Cats, however, are considered to bring good luck and are welcome even in Muslim temples or mosques.

Some people in Africa don't keep pets at all. The animals they come in contact with are usually wild and dangerous. To see Americans playing with cats or walking their dogs is a foreign experience for them.

Views of time. The concept of time itself varies from one culture to another. In the United States and northern Europe, people tend to work and play according to strict schedules. They define time in small units. In Mediterranean countries time is more fluid and less precise. If you told a Greek friend, for instance, to meet you somewhere at three o'clock, he might well arrive at three-thirty or four o'clock. He wouldn't understand why you were mad at him for being half an hour late. He might even accuse you of being early!

Avoiding conflicts. We can avoid such conflicts by finding out more about the cultures of our neighbors and by respecting their cultural values.

Cooperative Activity

Get together with a small group of students and list some things that a foreign student visiting your school should know. You may even want to compile your tips and suggestions in a book that can be given to visiting students.

GUIDE FOR READING

Bearstone, Chapters 12–16

Setting

The **setting** of a novel is the place and the time of the events. Setting is often closely related to other elements in the story. You have already seen some of the connections between the setting of *Bearstone* and the novel's characters and plot. In fact the plot of this novel would not be possible without the setting. Because Walter's ranch is near the Ute ancestral homeland, Cloyd finds the bearstone and decides to try to climb one of the mountains his ancestors lived on. In this section of the novel, you will see a new setting—Walter's mine and the mountains near it—and you will see how this setting affects the characters.

Focus

Will Hobbs, the author of *Bearstone*, lives in Colorado and knows the setting he describes quite well. You may not be familiar with this landscape. To help you imagine it, look carefully at the paintings that appear throughout the novel. Look particularly at the painting on pages 704 and 705, which is a rendering of the Rio Grande Pyramid and a rock formation called "The Window," actual places that Cloyd visits in the next section. Write down your reaction to it. What about it appeals to you? What wouldn't you like about it? As you read, notice Cloyd's reactions to the scene.

Vocabulary

Knowing the following words will help you as you read Chapters 12–16 of *Bearstone*.

claustrophobic (klôs′ trə fō′ bik) *adj.*: Related to an abnormal fear of being in an enclosed place (p. 686)

conjectured (kən jek′ chərd) *v.*: Guessed (p. 686)

reverentially (rev ə ren′ shə lē) *adv.*: Showing great respect and admiration (p. 695)

reverie (rev′ ə rē) *n.*: Daydream (p. 695)

begrudged (bē grujd′) *v.*: Resented (p. 700)

dormant (dor′ mənt) *adj.*: As if asleep; inactive (p. 700)

virulent (vir′ yo͞o lənt) *adj.*: Extremely poisonous or harmful (p. 700)

stratagem (strat′ ə jəm) *n.*: Trick or scheme (p. 700)

mired (mīrd) *v.*: Stuck in deep mud (p. 703)

Chapter 12

Today was the big day. Cloyd and Walter had been up since four in the morning shuttling the packhorses, mining equipment, food, and camping gear to the trailhead at the end of the road up the Pine River. It was mid-afternoon, and thunderclouds were gathering over the mountains. On their third and last trip to the trailhead, they stopped in Bayfield to buy a few last-minute supplies. Walter bought a fishing rod for Cloyd, and hooks and salmon eggs. "Used to be good fishing on the Pine—bet it still is. If the trout don't like the salmon eggs, you can dig worms with the camp shovel or catch grasshoppers. Maybe you can catch us some fresh dinner now and again."

They drove up the river road. Cloyd could hardly believe he was finally going to the mountains. A few miles north, Walter pulled off by the Pine River Cemetery. He told Cloyd he could wait a few minutes or come along. Cloyd looked in on the saddle horses in the gooseneck trailer, Blueboy, and the old man's sorrel mare, while Walter walked into the little cemetery. Then he caught up with the old man in front of a pair of graves.

At the far end of the plot was centered a single stone. Cloyd recognized the name *Landis.* Underneath there were two names, and one of them was Walter's.

"Why is your name on this?" Cloyd asked in undisguised confusion.

Walter scratched the thick white bristles of his beard. It was almost grown out again. "All they have to do is put the date on. Makes it easy."

Cloyd picked dandelions and piled the flowers on the grass. He thought about Walter in a box under the grass. "Do you have any relatives?"

"There's a few still around. My brother's on the Animas River down in New Mexico, and my wife's kin are back in Missouri."

Suddenly the wind began to blow. Cloyd looked up from the gravestones and saw the black clouds racing toward them from the mountains, where lightning flashed and rain hung in dark layers. He was chilled in his T-shirt, but he wanted to hear Walter talk. "Are people still alive after they die—like they say?"

"I don't know, really. Lots of folks believe there's life after death, but nobody knows for sure. Maybe your life is all there is. But that's plenty, ain't it? Make it good while you have it, is what I think, in case there ain't nothin' extra."

"Live in a good way. That's what my grandmother says."

"That's a fine way to put it."

The clouds overtook them and darkened the Pine River Valley. Thunder rumbled more frequently. A long bolt of lightning struck a few miles upriver, the concussion and unraveling thunder following behind. "Comin' our direction," Walter remarked with some anxiety.

Cloyd didn't want to cut off this talk with the old man. It was important. They could always run for the truck. "How come you stopped here—to talk to your wife?"

"Well, in a way. To tell her I'm goin' back to the mine, I guess."

"But she can't hear you."

"Prob'ly not, but it's more a matter of respect."

"How do you mean?"

"Showin' honor for her. I wouldn't do something this important without consulting her if she was alive. Matter of fact," he chuckled, "I wouldn't be doing it at all. But seeing the circumstances, she won't mind. She'd say, 'You go up there with Cloyd to that mine of yours and find your gold.'"

"But she isn't alive."

"No, that ain't right. Somehow, as long as I'm alive, she is too."

"Like she's a part of you?"

"People get like that, Cloyd. That's what's special about people."

The wind stopped abruptly, and Walter had that claustrophobic feeling he got when the air pressure was dropping fast around him. "Say, we better shake a leg," he said, and turned from the grave.

The old man wasn't much for running, but he shuffled along as briskly as he could. They were barely inside the truck when the wind and the rain struck. "Let's wait her out," Walter said. "No sense driving in this."

Cloyd reached into his jeans pocket and pulled out the bearstone, set it on the dashboard. "I want to tell you a secret about this," he said.

Walter appraised the stone up close, the turquoise bear he'd nearly destroyed in anger. "It's some piece," he said. "Forehead's dished out like a grizzly's, and this bulge here on the back, it's almost like it's a hump."

"I found it with one of the Ancient Ones—a baby—in those rocks up there, above your farm."

"In the cliffs? A burial? Why, if that ain't somethin'."

"Bears are special for Ute people—they bring strength and good luck."

"All the more reason you've got yourself something special here," Walter said. "Think how old this stone must be. This blue bear's a real treasure, Cloyd."

"When I found this, I gave myself a secret name. The Utes used to do that—they kept it secret except for one other person. You're the only one I'll ever tell my secret name to. It's Lone Bear. That's what it is—Lone Bear."

Walter conjectured what it might mean, the name Cloyd had taken for himself. It seemed like an awfully lonesome name. He wondered if the turquoise piece would bring the good luck the boy was hoping for.

"You know, Cloyd, some of that good luck just might rub off on the Pride of the West."

Chapter 13

Walter roused Cloyd when it was still dark in their camp at the trailhead. By the light of the gas lantern they set to work sorting their gear into eight loads for the eight packhorses. After sunrise Cloyd brought the horses into camp from the meadow by the river where they'd been hobbled overnight.

The packhorses stamped their feet and shied from the wooden frames lifted toward them. The packing dragged on all morning. Cloyd could hardly believe all the gear they were taking with them. Two groups of backpackers left up the trail while they were working. Finally the last knot was tied, the riding horses saddled. Cloyd and Walter led their animals to the wooden gate between the parking lot and the beginning of the trail.

"What's this sign say?" Cloyd asked.

"Weminuche Wilderness Area. No motorized vehicles beyond this point."

Cloyd looked up the trail and saw it climb through a dense stand of pines. The trunks weren't far enough apart to allow even a jeep through. "Why do they have to say that?" he asked.

"Why, that means motorbikes, I suppose, and snowmobiles in the winter. Good thing, too. Our horses are spooky enough without having to contend with motors. That 'Weminuche' there, that's the name of the Utes who used to live up here."

"I know. My grandmother said that's us. We're the Weminuche."

"Well, now ain't that somethin'."

And then they were under way, each leading a string of four packhorses. Walter rode in front on his sorrel mare; Cloyd followed on the big blue roan.

The canyon soon narrowed, and the trail climbed well above the river. Cloyd found himself looking down hundreds of feet into pools so clear he could see the stones on the bottom. Above them, rockslide paths fell through the spruce and aspen forests from the peaks. As high as they were, these peaks weren't the towering, jagged ones he'd seen from the cliffs that first day at the farm. Before long, he would stand on top of one of the very highest and look out over the world.

The farther they worked their way up the Pine, the more Cloyd marveled at the steady gait and sure-footedness of the roan. And when the horse had a chance, he'd swivel his eye back around and catch sight of the boy.

There was something Cloyd had been turning over and over in his mind and now, he decided, was the time to ask the old man about it. "Is it true, like he said, that horses don't care anything about you?"

The old man hitched himself up in the saddle and halfway turned around. "You mean like Rusty said? Don't pay no mind to his talk. He just hates to agree with anybody. It's just the way he is."

"But is it true?"

"I've always puzzled on that, same as you. Horses appreciate good treatment and a steady hand, but it's a fact they don't go out of their way to fetch your slippers. Maybe some really do care. I've had one or two that made me think so, but it seems like you never know for sure. What do you think?"

"Oh, I was just wondering."

Cloyd was mostly disappointed with the old man's answer. As they rode, he continued to turn it over in his mind. He leaned forward and patted the roan. "Blueboy," he thought, "you're not just any horse. You and me, Blue, you and me."

The roan rolled an eye back and snorted loudly.

The next day the horses labored up ever-steeper grades as the river fell in leaps from the high country. Cloyd watched his string carefully as they crossed the tricky scree slides[1] of fine rock that ran below them all the way to the river. Several times during the day they forded swift creeks that fed the Pine; with little urging, the roan crossed them easily. The others behind accepted his leadership.

Late in the afternoon they climbed out the canyon onto a large meadow, astonishingly green with knee-high grass and ringed by mountains that stabbed far above the line

---

1. scree slides: Small rock fragments that blanket a slope, making it extremely slippery.

where the trees stopped growing. A small stream here close to the Continental Divide,[2] the Pine River wound quietly in delicate meanders through the meadow. Walter said they'd lay over a day or two before they went up Snowslide Canyon to the mine. Cloyd was happy to make camp. As he'd been riding, he'd seen the trout darting through the riffles[3] between the pools. They set up the sheepherder tent in the trees at the meadow's edge.

At first light Cloyd was up digging worms in the black soil underneath the trees. On the meadow, he sneaked up on a pool and let his bait drift into a likely spot. In a moment the rod came alive in his hands, and he launched the flashing trout into the air and over his head. A large cutthroat trout in its orange-red colors lay gasping in the grass. It was the first fish he'd ever caught and the beginnings of a meal for him and the old man. He remembered his grandmother saying that when the Weminuche lived in the mountains, some of the men were so skilled that they could catch fish with their bare hands. That didn't seem possible. But now he knew how they must have felt when they caught the lightning-fast trout, however they did it.

Midway up the meadow Cloyd caught his second trout, and then his third at the upper end where the stream came rushing out of the trees. He'd discovered the fishing was better if he kept trying new water than if he stayed with one hole, even if he could see plenty of trout there. It seemed they would strike pretty quick, or not at all. He decided to look upstream in the trees for another good place to fish. After walking around the rapids through a thick spruce forest, he found an even bigger, more promising meadow above.

---

2. Continental Divide: A ridge along the Rocky Mountains that separates rivers flowing in an easterly direction from those flowing in a westerly direction.
3. riffles: A shallow part of a stream where the water is rippled and choppy.

BADLANDS, NM
William Berra
Fenn Galleries Ltd.

As Cloyd began to fish the upper meadow, white clouds boiled up out of the blue sky and quickly turned dark. The wind started to blow, but he was too excited to notice the wind or the clouds—he was landing trout. Several miles from camp, at the far end of the upper meadow, he caught his seventh. As he slid the new-caught fish onto the stringer he'd fashioned from a willow branch, he shook with cold and realized the temperature had been dropping for some time. He'd been out fishing longer than he thought. Without the sun it was hard to judge the time, but it could be past noon already. He saw the clouds spill down the mountainsides toward him, dark and loaded with moisture. A few more pools, maybe one more fish, and he would collect his trout and head for camp.

Lightning broke loose and thunder rumbled, not too far off. A cold wind rushed down the meadow. He wished he'd worn more than a T-shirt, but he hadn't thought he would be out long. He knew he'd better run for it; the storm was about to break. As he picked up his stringer and started out, lightning cracked barely upstream. The shock wave and his surprise threw him to the ground. Glancing back, he saw the big spruces bending under the weight of the wind, and hail angling down with terrific speed.

Cloyd thought he could race the hail into the trees between the meadows and nestle in under a good roof of branches. He ran for the trees with the rod held high in his right hand and the stringer of trout in his left. He ran with a laughing heart because the hail was already pounding the meadow behind him, and yet at full speed he would outrun it just in time.

With no warning his right leg sank to the hip, his chest and face struck the ground, the rod and stringer of fish flew. In the tall grass, he'd failed to see the narrow trench connecting the stream with the pond where beavers had built one of their domed lodges.

Pain coursed through and through his leg. He was sure he'd hurt it badly. With his weight on his left knee, Cloyd dragged the right leg out of the beaver run and lay on his left side, watching the wall of hail advance down the meadow. He had to wait for the pain to clear. Lightning ripped the meadow simultaneously with its deafening thunder. A heartbeat later the hail struck, stinging him and bouncing all around in the grass. Within seconds he was drenched and started to shake with cold. His T-shirt and jeans clung to him; they offered no protection. The feeling went out of his fingers. He lay motionless, unable to think.

In minutes the meadow was carpeted with a layer of hail. All of a sudden, it was winter. Cloyd had seen hailstorms in the high desert, but not like this one. Here the air itself had turned freezing cold. Shaking now from fear as well as cold, he forced himself to think. Managing another hundred yards to the trees meant nothing now. He had to reach camp, the old man, and a fire—or freeze to death. He tried the leg. It could take some of his weight. Nothing was broken.

Cloyd knew he had to start out immediately, but somehow it seemed important not to leave the rod and the fish behind. They couldn't be far. As he raked through the hail-flattened grass with his sneakers, he realized he couldn't feel his feet. There was the rod. He scooped it up and clamped his fingers around it. Lucky for him it wasn't broken. And here were the trout, stiff and staring.

Then he ran as best he could, shaking, tripping, falling. The hail turned to cold and steady rain. Something told him that he had no chance in the woods, the way he came up from the lower meadow. He had to find a trail. Was there a trail? He hadn't seen one all day. Maybe there would be one on the far side of the meadow, across the stream.

Cloyd couldn't feel the icy water as he plunged across the Pine River holding up his rod and reel and his fish. In fact, he'd stopped shaking and couldn't feel anything at all. His body was getting too cold, much too cold.

Across the meadow he found a trail and hastened wildly down it. After a while he was in the trees. The trail fell sharply, muddy and slick, turning this way and that. He veered through dark shapes as if in a dream. No sign of the lower meadow and the old man, and the cold was squeezing the life out of him. Through the dark trees, off the trail and down by the stream, a small patch of orange caught his eye. His mind dismissed the image, but as he stumbled forward, the idea of the orange color slowly worked its way to the surface. It was a tent. Cloyd stopped and stared through the trees at a trace of blue smoke hanging in the dark branches above the tent.

He could barely move. It took him a long time to reach the orange tent. Now he stood dumbly by the remains of a fire. There was no fire here, only a bit of blue smoke curling around the soggy stub of a log.

Cloyd faced the tent. "I need help," he said thickly.

Someone lifted the tent flap—a young man with glasses and a dark beard—and cursed in surprise. The man came out of the tent, took away the rod and the fish, and forced him to the ground and inside the small orange tent. Cursing softly, the man said not to worry. He rummaged through a sack, muttering something about long johns.

The man with the beard pulled Cloyd's wet clothes off. The boy looked curiously at his own body. It didn't seem to belong to him. He noticed he wasn't shaking anymore. He didn't even feel cold. Then the man was dressing him in different clothes. It took a long time. His elbows kept poking the tent. Everything was orange, orange all around.

The bearded man stuffed Cloyd into a sleeping bag and asked if he felt warmer. He couldn't even answer. Then he was alone.

The man had left. The cold and the quiet crept into one another comfortably. The world went dark; he felt himself falling asleep. He drifted deeper and deeper into the dark, like a leaf settling into the bottom of a deep pool. It was almost perfectly peaceful. He was so close to that perfect sleep when something intruded, one faraway nagging detail. He couldn't even tell what it was. After a while it was some kind of noise, very far away. A magpie or a raven squawking, or possibly even his sister come looking for him in the canyons and calling again and again. Yes, it was a human voice after all, nagging, calling, insisting, shouting, but it wasn't his sister. Gradually, light seeped into his eyes, and he saw a man with glasses and a black beard. Who was he?

The world was moving. No, he was moving, being dragged outside the orange tent into the dark trees, sleeping bag and all.

The man's glasses were fogged up. The man lay alongside him on his elbows blowing on the wet wood, making smoke. Some coals were glowing. The man kept wheezing on them. Finally they burst into a flame and the man placed a little stick across the flame and left again.

Branches were breaking somewhere. The tiny flame was gone. The man was back with his arms full of wood, and then he was on his elbows again, blowing until his face turned purple. The flame came back. The wood started to catch. The man left; branches were breaking. After a time he was back piling branches over the fire and blowing it into stronger and stronger flames. The flames grew brighter, bigger, stronger than the rain dripping from the trees.

The bearded man with fogged-up glasses was pulling him from the sleeping bag, standing him up close to the fire, arms locked around his chest. He could begin to feel the fire spreading warmth into his body. "You're going to be all right," the man was saying.

Cloyd struggled to get free of the sleeping bag. The man unzipped it, let it fall, and gained a new hold on him. Cloyd struggled again. "Hang on there," the man cautioned, "you're still medium rare. I'm gonna cook you until you're charbroiled."

Finally Cloyd's eyes cleared, and the man turned him loose. He could stand by the fire on his own. The man went for more wood. After many trips he'd built a bonfire. At its edge he boiled water in an aluminum pan and made coffee. When Cloyd drank it, he warmed from the inside out and at last became as warm as he could want to be.

"Think I'll clean your fish, if you don't mind," the man said. "They'd make a great hot meal for you, better than my freeze-dried stuff. You just stay by the fire there and make some more coffee if you like."

Cloyd nodded. The man went away through the trees to clean the fish at the stream. After he'd been gone some time, Walter rode into camp in his yellow rainslicker, leading the roan.

"Thank goodness you're okay, Cloyd," he said softly.

Walter's eyes took in the oversized clothes that weren't the boy's, a bruise below the right eye, a long scratch on his neck, the jeans and T-shirt drying by the fire. "I've been everywhere. I was afraid I wouldn't find you."

"I caught seven fish," Cloyd said.

The stranger came back with the fish cleaned and neatly arranged on the willow-branch stringer. Walter drank coffee with him and pieced together what had happened. Cloyd tended the frying trout.

The young man gave Cloyd a poke. "You must crave the taste of trout, the way you hung onto 'em."

A shy smile brightened the boy's face. "I guess so," he said.

Nothing ever tasted so warm or so good, Cloyd thought, as the three of them shared the fish. Except maybe new-made frybread.

Cloyd saw the worry finally leaving the old man's face. It seemed like the time to explain how he could have been so stupid. "I could have found a dry place in the trees, but I was running and fell into a hole."

The old man winked at the stranger and chuckled. "From the looks of it, the ground flew up and hit you in the face."

They all laughed. Cloyd pulled on his T-shirt and jeans. Not only dry, they were almost too hot for comfort. Walter went to his mare and pulled Cloyd's denim jacket from his saddlebags. Cloyd dismantled the fishing rod, then stood by the fire, turning his hands over even though they were warm already. He wanted to say something to the young man. He wouldn't have a chance to show it like with Walter. "Thank you," he said. Their eyes met for a moment. "You didn't have to . . . you didn't even know me, and you—"

"No big deal," the stranger said quickly. "You'd have done the same for me."

Chapter 14

For two days they rested in their campsite by the meadow. When Cloyd recovered his strength, they set out for the mine. Past the upper meadow where Cloyd had been caught by the cloudburst, Walter reined in his mare and motioned the boy and his string of pack-horses alongside. "That canyon there," he pointed, indicating a steep-sided cleft in the mountains across the river, "that's Snowslide. The Pride of the West is on up it a ways. Won't be long now."

They forded the river and angled away from it up Snowslide Creek. Cloyd took a last look up the Pine River and knew at once he'd found what he'd been looking for. A single peak rising alone and high above the others had just come into view, a sharp peak riding alone in the turquoise sky. "What's that?" he

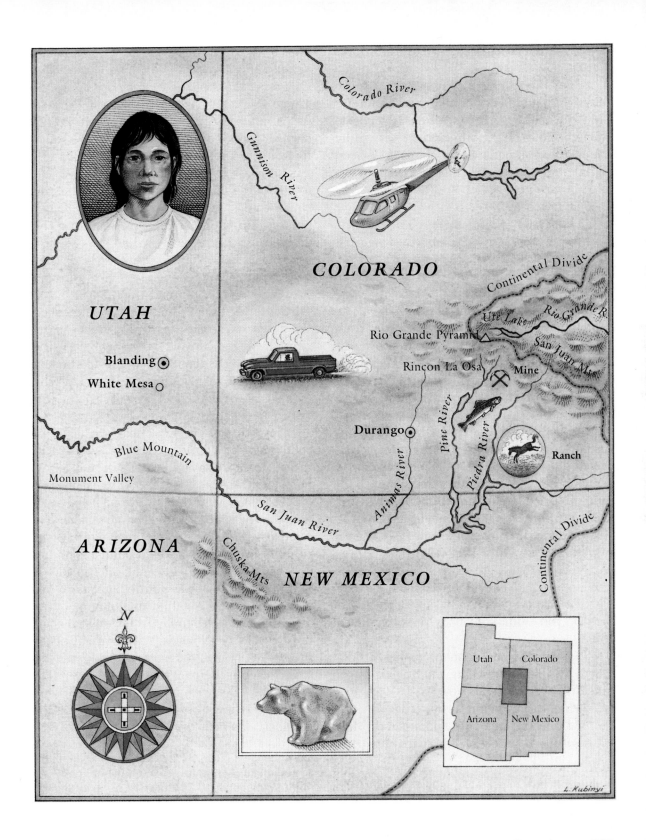

UTAH

Blanding

White Mesa

Colorado River

Gunnison River

COLORADO

Continental Divide

Ute Lake

Rio Grande Pyramid

Rio Grande R.

San Juan Mts

Rincon La Osa

Mine

Durango

Pine River

Piedra River

Ranch

Blue Mountain

Monument Valley

San Juan River

Animas River

ARIZONA

Chuska Mts

NEW MEXICO

Continental Divide

N

Utah | Colorado

Arizona | New Mexico

L. Rubinyi

called to the old man. "That mountain over there."

"That one yonder? Why, that's the Rio Grande Pyramid. Looks like one, don't it? That's where the Rio Grande River gets started—flows off the other side. That's quite a mountain, all right. Supposed to have been a grizzly and two cubs sighted on it about ten years ago."

"Grizzly bears?"

"That's right. Used to be plenty in this country, but that was some years ago. Of course we still have black bears."

"But this man saw three grizzly bears?"

"Says they was huntin' marmots[4] just above the tree line. Most folks think he saw a big cinnamon, which is a black bear when he's brown. The last grizzly bear proven in the state of Colorado—or south of Wyoming, for that matter—was killed near here in 1954. It's on display in a museum up in Denver."

Cloyd fingered the smooth bearstone in his pocket. He wondered if it might really represent a grizzly, as Walter had suggested. He remembered that the old Utes especially honored grizzlies. "Do *you* think there's any more grizzly bears?" he asked.

"Don't know—most likely not. It's been a bunch of years since that fellow saw 'em, if that's what they were. But if he was right, and nobody's killed 'em since, the cubs'd be in their prime now."

"Do you think somebody probably killed them?"

"Not that anybody's heard about. But if a fellow was to kill one, he might not let on since they're protected now."

"What's that mean, 'protected'?"

"On account of being endangered. That means there's so few of 'em that if anybody

kills one, there might be none left, so it's against the law."

For several hours they rode up Snowslide Canyon, crossing many of the wide, grassy paths among the sun-whitened hulks of spruces ripped from the edges of the slides high above. At the bottom of one of the avalanche chutes,[5] the old man and the boy found a big log and set out biscuits and canned pork for their midday meal. Walter pointed out the knee-high trees dotting the grassy route of the slide. "When they get just a bit bigger, the slide'll knock 'em down. They never quit trying, though. It's like building your house on a railroad track."

Scanning the skyline, the old man looked upstream. A smile crossed his face as he pointed up the canyon. "That peak with the ledge around the top like a crown sits directly above the mine. My tunnel's aimin' for the contact in the solid-gold heart of the mountain. The Pride of the West."

Cloyd thought about a heart made out of solid gold. It sounded like an awful cold heart. He didn't say so. "What's the contact?" he asked.

"A fissure vein of ore is what it is. Ore's the rock the gold is in. You see, gold is usually mixed with other minerals in veins that run through the mountain. If you find a good fissure vein, it'll never give out on you like a fault will. A fault leaves little pockets of ore called stringers. You find one of 'em, dig it out, and that's the end of it. But with a good fissure vein, you always have something to follow. Sometimes it'll narrow on you, maybe to inches, but then it'll widen out to eight feet or more."

Cloyd realized he would actually be mining soon, inside a mountain in the dark. Up

---

4. marmots (mär′ məts): Thick-bodied, burrowing rodents with coarse fur and short, bushy tails.

5. avalanche chutes (av′ ə lanch sho͞ots): Vertical hollowed-out paths cut in the side of a mountain by large rock slides.

to now he'd thought about it hardly at all. At White Mesa most people thought of mining as a bad thing, though many of the men worked off and on in the mines or at the ore-shipping depot. The uranium made you get sick and die early, his grandmother said. She never said if gold made you sick. But then he remembered what she had said about gold. It made people crazy and dishonest. First the white men promised the Utes they could keep the mountains forever, but that was before gold was discovered and the miners came pouring in. The white men forgot all about their promise. The Utes were told to stay out of the mountains. They couldn't roam around anymore and live in the old way. They were given tiny reservations in the low country and told to stay there and grow corn.

"You really think there's gold in your mine?" he asked skeptically.

"Why, I know there is! I crossed a vein of silver already, but I didn't even bother to follow it, 'cause in those days silver wasn't worth much unless it was real high-grade ore. I got a three-hundred-foot tunnel in already, an' I figure from the geology there can't be more'n a few more to the contact. I ain't really gambling, Cloyd. Why, I already found the contact, you see, where the vein breaks the surface way up the mountain. It's tilted at a pretty good angle, and the idea of the tunnel is to reach it inside the mountain and then stope up to the surface."[6]

"How come you didn't dig where you found it?"

"Sure wish I could have. But it's better mining sense to work upwards and let gravity move your rock for you—down ore chutes. It's too hard to move any quantity of rock uphill unless you've got heavy machinery."

The dubious cast to Cloyd's face told Walter he'd given the boy no feel for the joy of working in hard rock, the thrill of blasting and then returning to the drift always expecting to see a vein of high-grade ore laid open. "There's fabulous wealth in these mountains, Cloyd," he whispered reverentially. "And most of it hasn't been discovered yet. Let me tell you about the Cresson Mine up in the Cripple Creek District right here in Colorado. They were blastin' the face of the tunnel, following a fissure vein, and broke into a natural room forty feet long by twenty feet wide and fifteen feet high. A vug is what it was, like a geode—ever see a rock that's hollow in the middle with crystals all around? Well, this big room they found was a giant geode with the crystals sticking out the floor, the walls, the ceiling—everything was solid gold!"

It seemed from Walter's eyes that he was even now peering into the gold cave he'd described. Cloyd could see how much it meant to the old man. He would do his best for Walter, even though it sounded dark and cold and dangerous, and then he would climb the Rio Grande Pyramid for himself. "How much gold did they get from in there?" he asked politely, as the old man came out of his reverie.

"I recollect it was two and one-half million. At today's price—four hundred fifty dollars an ounce—that'd be . . . thirty-some million dollars from that one room!"

They continued up the canyon until Walter stopped at a bend in the trail and stared across the creek where a great pile of tailings[7] jutted from the mountainside. "The Pride of the West," Walter whispered. "It took me nearly forty years to get back, but I finally made it. And my goodness, it doesn't look a bit different. Mountains don't get old very fast, Cloyd. This mountain, it's like it blinked

---

6. stope up to the surface: Remove the ore from around a vertical mineshaft in such a way that "steps" are formed.

7. tailings: Ore discarded at the mouth of a mine.

while I went off a young man, looks again and sees me ridin' back plumb aged."

Walter and Cloyd set up the big sheepherder tent by the stream under a tall cluster of spruce. Once they had unpacked all the horses, they hobbled them in the grass across the creek where only a few rotted logs remained of the old man's corral. Then they climbed up the side of the ore dump and gained the landing on top, only to discover raw earth where the mine entrance should have been.

"Well, she's caved in, and not so long ago," Walter said, disappointed yet calm. "Just the portal, Cloyd. The topsoil slipped, is all. Inside it'll be fine, once we move this dirt out of the way. It's all hard rock once you're inside—we'll be in there drillin' in a few days."

"Drilling?" Cloyd asked vacantly. For a moment he'd hoped Walter would give it all up.

"Makin' holes in the rock—pretty deep— so we can slip the dynamite in and blast. We're going to have to do our drillin' the old way, with one of us holding the bit and the other pounding the sledgehammer. Slow going, but it works. They quit drilling by hand in the 1870s, way before my time. After that, double-jackin'—that's two men working like I said—was only for drilling contests or for fellows like me that didn't know any better mining back in the hills where you couldn't use machine drills. Drillin's hard work—can be dangerous, too."

"Dangerous?"

"One story I remember, there was these two men working high up on a scaffold in a big room inside a mine, and they were double-jackin' into the face up there. Must've been twenty-five feet up they was standing. Of a sudden their scaffolding busts, and the one doing the sledgework, he crashes down with it. Now his partner turning the bit, he grabs hold of his steel as he's falling, and it's stuck good and stout in the hole, so there he

is hanging from it pretty as you please. He starts hollerin' for help of course, only his buddy's got nothing to help him with, and there's nobody else around. So after about five minutes, the fellow up above can't hold on no longer, and he crashes down, too. His buddy says, 'Dang—I knew you was slow, but I had no idea it'd take you five minutes to fall twenty-five feet!' "

"Is that a true story?"

"Yes sir, that's a true story," the old man said as he stroked the bristles on his chin. But quickly his ears turned red and his cheeks puffed in and out as he tried to hold his breath and keep from laughing.

"True?" Cloyd repeated gravely.

Walter's cheeks collapsed and his breath exploded. "True . . . and then some," he said, slapping his knees.

Cloyd had to laugh, too. It was good to be laughing with the old man.

Chapter 15

It took three days of tedious handwork for them to clear the entrance. At last Cloyd's shovel broke through into empty space. He knelt and looked through the small opening. He saw only blackness but felt a steady flow of cool air escaping the mine through the hole he'd made. "Where's the air coming from?" he asked Walter.

"Oh, that's one of the lucky things about this mine—fresh air's always moving through it. Comes down from the surface through cracks in the formations."

Once they'd completely cleared the portal, Walter showed Cloyd how to rig his headlamp and how to ignite the gas that came from the water dripping on the carbide.[8] Then they started inside.

As they ventured down the center of the narrow railway, the air felt pleasantly cool.

---

8. how to ignite . . . carbide: Water and a substance called calcium carbide react chemically to produce the gas that burns in the headlamp.

Cloyd glanced constantly over his shoulder to the blinding white light of the portal; he banged his hard hat against a tooth of rock in the low ceiling. The cold surprised him, suddenly finding his bones. Next time he'd wear his sweatshirt and jacket. At the end of the tunnel, he was surprised by the ore car, big enough that both of them could have climbed in. "How'd you get this thing up here?" he asked.

"Oh, I had to take it apart with the torch and whatnot, machine new parts for bolting it back together, bring it in pieces up here on horseback, then reassemble it. The rails were somethin' else again."

In the morning they entered the mine ready for work. Cloyd held tight to the heavy drill bits and the long copper spoons. The one thing he liked was the feel of the hard hat and the hiss of burning gas in his headlamp. Before long, he told himself, he'd be accustomed to the strangeness inside the mountain. Working with the old man he wouldn't be so afraid of being trapped in the dark under the earth. At the end of the tunnel, Walter pointed out the vein of silver ore he'd been following many years before on his way to the gold contact. Cloyd was surprised to find it wasn't silver-colored at all, but black, peppered here and there in the quartz.[9]

"Now set those spoons and drills down," Walter said. "I'll tell you how we're going to start. We'll drill seven lucky holes in a circle around this vein, then three in the center about two feet apart in a triangle, anglin' 'em so they meet inside like the top of a pyramid."

"Then the dynamite?"

"Not yet. We drill a reliever at the top of the face, edgers on both sides, and a lifter at the bottom. If we do it right, we time the charges so the center comes out first, making space so's everything around it has somewhere to go when it's blasted a hair later. The lifter going last kicks it all out where we can muck it into the ore car."

"What do I do?"

"You're my partner when we're double-jackin'. That's one man working the drill bit, the other the sledgehammer. We'll stop every so often and fish out the dust with the spoons."

"How fast can we go?" Cloyd asked with little hope.

"Not fast at all. But what's time to a hog? I'll tell you what a good pace would be, though, so you know what those old-timers could do. A good pair of double-jackers could drill two inches a minute if they were going all out. Over a longer run, like an hour, they'd go maybe thirty inches."

"Why can't we?"

"We've got to play it safe. We're two days from help. Those drill heads make a mighty small target for a sledgehammer. Once I saw a Fourth of July drillin' contest up in Silverton that really made an impression on me—now this is a true story. The object of the competition was to see how deep you could drill in fifteen minutes. These two bull-strong Cornishmen[10] took their turn havin' at a six-foot-thick slab of Gunnison granite. The man on the sledge, early on in the contest, he's working at a good fifty-blow-per-minute pace. Of a sudden we see his hammer stopped up in the air. We realize he's just hit his partner's hand, and the crowd groans, but the hurt man yells, 'Bring it down! Bring it down!'"

"What did that mean?"

"He didn't want to quit even though he'd been hurt bad. So the sledgeman resumes hammering. We see the hand go red, the man's face showin' it's all he can do to keep the bit turning. His blood is mixing with the water flushin' out the dust. Every time the

---

9. quartz (kwôrts): An often colorless, very hard mineral that is a major part of many types of rock.

10. Cornishmen: Men from the region in southwest England called Cornwall, where mining is an important industry.

hammer comes down, the crowd is splashed with bloody water. Then it's time for the hurt man to take his turn with the sledge, and still he won't quit. When the hammer's up in the air, the blood runs down his arm until it's red all the way to the shoulder. That man never gave up until the timer gave the signal. Then he fainted dead away."

"He died?"

"No—blacked out."

"Did they win?"

"No," Walter said thoughtfully, "they didn't come close. But they finished. Couldn't pay men to do that no more. Then again, there's fools like us doing it for free!"

To Cloyd it all seemed impossibly strange and dangerous. But he would work. If he worked as hard as he had making the fence-line, he wouldn't feel the strangeness or the danger. And this time he'd trust in the old man and not blow up like before.

After seven days of bone-rattling drilling they were ready to blast. As Walter wished, Cloyd waited outside while he placed the dynamite in the drill holes and set the timing on the fuses.

Cloyd was exhausted. The cold had sapped all his strength. The work had been repetitive, painful, endless. In a pretty place he could enjoy working; in the mine he'd endured it only for the sake of the old man. At first they'd taken long breaks outside, down by the creek where they could lie in the grass, eat, and rest. But as the days went by, Walter stretched the working hours and made the breaks shorter. Close to the blasting, Cloyd could tell the old man didn't want to break at all or even sleep. He was so excited, he wanted to work through to the end to see what he would find.

At last all was ready. Walter came out of the mine to make sure Cloyd was standing well clear of the portal, then went back inside

to set off the charges. After awhile he came running out of the tunnel with a wild look in his eye, and yelled, "Fire in the hole! Fire in the hole!"

Cloyd smiled. The expression on the old man's face made it all worthwhile. Then came the waves of concussion as the charges rumbled inside the mine and dark clouds of smoke and dust poured out the entrance.

It was some time before the air cleared enough for them to reenter the mine. Cloyd was surprised to see how little progress the blast had made. No more than four feet. Walter knelt and examined piece after piece of the rock freed by the explosion. He'd hoped there might be at least some good silver ore for them to take home, but he was disappointed. "Poor makin's," he said. "Weak silver. Not even worth packing out for assay."[11]

They had nothing to show for their long days, Cloyd thought. But then, he'd never really believed they'd find anything. Now they'd have to shovel all the broken rock into the car and drop it over the edge of the dump outside. It would take many loads to clear out the tunnel for work on the next round. Yet Walter turned to the hand-mucking with new enthusiasm. "Next time we'll turn up something better," he said. "We're after gold anyway. You talk to that lucky bear of yours. This is still a promising vein, and silver can lead to gold."

Cloyd was convinced they were wasting their time, but he said nothing. He'd been trying to hide his feelings from the old man. Somehow there hadn't been any time for him to go fishing. Somehow, after the first few nights, there was no time set aside to sit around the campfire in the evenings. There'd only been time to work, eat, and sleep.

Shovelful by weary shovelful, he helped

---

11. packing out for assay (as' ā): Sending the ore to be analyzed for the purity of the metal it contains.

DEAD HORSE PASS
George Beard
Courtesy of Russell Beard

Walter muck out the tunnel. The bigger rocks he had to grapple with and lift by hand. Once the ore car was finally filled, they had to wedge its wheels to a stop every few feet, or it would speed out of control and hurtle over the dump down to the creek.

Each night, he'd noticed, the cold seemed to bite a little deeper. The fragile high-country summer was beginning to lose out to winter. He fretted that he was losing his chance at the peaks. It took them a whole day to clear the mine. The prospect of starting all over again on the next round of drilling was worse than the work itself. Six or seven more days of spine-wracking torment to endure before they'd be ready to blast again. Before long, he knew too well, they'd have to leave the mountains, and then school would start. His precious time in the mountains was being used to take the inside of one apart and move it outside. He was trying hard, but he wasn't sure he'd be able to hold up.

Three, four, five days of the second go-round passed. Cloyd worked in a trance, trying to concentrate on turning the bit between blows. There was only the penetrating cold and the hiss of burning acetylene in his headlamp, the numbing feel of cold steel in his hands, the stinging shock of the blow, and the harsh reports of the hammer rattling up and down the confines of the mine. It was enough to drive him crazy.

More and more, Walter begrudged himself the time it took to eat and sleep. He had to see what the next blast would turn up. He'd come up with fresh calculations and convinced himself he was closer than he'd thought to the contact, that artery of high-grade gold ore which would lead him directly to the heart of the mountain. His old obsession had taken over and he'd forgotten about the boy, about Cloyd's great desire to see the high country. He'd forgotten what he told Susan James,

that the trip wasn't so much for the mining as the chance to introduce the boy to the mountains.

Though it had lain dormant for almost forty years, the great illness of his youth—gold fever—had blossomed in its most virulent strain and invaded all his faculties. He'd slipped into the assumption that their enterprise was as exciting for Cloyd as it was for himself. Until, that is, they neared the second round of blasting. In a moment of clarity during their midday break he happened to read the boy's face. He realized he'd made the boy a prisoner of sorts again and must set him free at once. But he had to do it in such a way that Cloyd wouldn't feel compelled to stay and help out. He himself had no intention of quitting with the contact so near.

A stratagem came to mind. Not one his wife would have approved of, or he either under ordinary circumstances. It deviated by a substantial margin from the truth. A white lie, he told himself, for the boy's benefit. "Well, Cloyd, I've had it," he said disgustedly.

Surprised, Cloyd looked up and saw the disappointment all across the old man's face. "How do you mean?" he asked.

"Like they say in the oil business, it's a dry hole. We're wasting our time."

"But you won't know until you blow it up again and see."

A logical objection, Walter thought. He'd have to counter with bogus expertise. "Oh, I've been looking at the powder we've been fishing out of the drill holes with those spoons. Indications are bad, mighty poor. I figure we ought to give it up before we shoot what's left of the summer. Didn't you want to climb one of these mountains, maybe that Rio Grande Pyramid?"

"Maybe the gold's just a little farther," Cloyd insisted.

"Maybe. But chances are slim to none. If we quit now we'll have a little time—maybe a week—before we have to head back. Now what about that Pyramid? Let's get you some food packed, go over some maps—why, you could be ready to take out in the morning."

"Aren't you coming with me?"

For a moment, Walter was so touched that Cloyd would want him along, he almost abandoned his plan. Though he lacked the wind for climbing at high altitude, they could ride together and set up a base camp before the boy set out alone. But even more he was relishing the next blast and the treasure it might break loose. "My lungs couldn't take the thin air," he said. "That's close to fourteen thousand feet. I might have a fit or somethin'."

"We wouldn't have to go so high up."

"No, Cloyd, I'd rather stick close to camp here and just enjoy myself pokin' around, lookin' at the scenery, brewin' coffee and whatnot. You take Blueboy—you're better off on horseback as far as you can go. Take a packhorse too. Park your horses in the trees before you climb up above timberline."

Suddenly Walter was spooked. He shouldn't be letting the boy go off alone in the mountains. It was never a good idea, no matter how experienced you were. Yet he'd done it often enough when he was young. "Stay off of those peaks when the weather's comin' on. You know what that's about."

"I'll be careful," Cloyd promised.

Chapter 16

Mile by mile Cloyd rode up the gentle meadows of the Pine. As he saw the Rio Grande Pyramid gradually nearing, his confidence grew. He rode with beauty all around him. He rode on a powerful horse who was his friend. "Hey-a, Blueboy, hey-a!"

Cloyd's spirit was free and had all the running room in the world. There was no limit to where it might go or what was possible. "Hey-a," he sang. "Hey-a, hey-a, Blueboy."

The roan tried to break into a trot, even into a run, but the packhorse held him back. Cloyd could tell that Blueboy was taken with the morning's wild spirit; this day was made for the two of them. He dismounted and tied the packhorse to a tree, a little ways off the trail, and then he walked back to the roan and said, "Let's run, Blue, I mean really run."

And then they ran streaming through the meadows of the Pine. Cloyd and the horse were one, and they were flying through the wind and the light, while all around him shone the mountains and the trees and the river. Cloyd grinned as they ran, and then he broke into a smile. His teeth caught the wind. He couldn't stop smiling all the way up the meadow. This day was different. It was as if he was coming into a new world all bright and shining, and it was made for him.

They rested at the end of the meadow, and they drank from the stream. The roan was delighted with the meadow grass and tore at it as if he hadn't eaten for weeks. Cloyd lay on his back in the grass and watched the trees on the hillside sway in the wind. He wondered if trees could feel. He decided that they could. They liked to wrap themselves in the air, sway with the breeze, and let the air soothe their branches and every little needle.

Back on the horse, he leaned forward to speak. The roan swiveled an ear back. "Want to?" Cloyd whispered. "Want to, Blue?"

The roan exploded into a gallop, and they ran all the way back down the meadow. Then he collected the packhorse and continued on his way to the Pyramid. After several miles he had to leave the trail and strike upward through the dark spruce forest. There were no trails where he was going. Blueboy and the packhorse labored in the rapidly thinning air as Cloyd guided them through the deadfall.[12] Up, up they climbed. After a few miles Cloyd rested them on a bench where waterfalls spilled into a string of beaver ponds. The horses grazed while Cloyd ate his lunch. Contentment seeped through and through him. This place was almost enough, he felt so good. The peak, if he made it, would be surplus to store against the future. He resolved to see as much of the mountains as he could. Besides the Pyramid, he was taken with two other names: Ute Lake and the Rincon La Osa, "the corner of the bear."

As he climbed again, the spruces huddled in clusters, squatter than they grew below, and grassy slopes led to a world of wildflowers. He left the last of the trees behind and rode through windblown waves of reds, yellows, and blues. He could almost reach out and touch the Continental Divide. That's where, as Walter had explained, rivers bound for different oceans started out within spitting distance of each other.

He rested the horses while he took it all in. Here he was in the high, treeless world patched with snowbanks as far as he could see, the spongy, delicate, windlashed birthplace of rivers. A lone giant, the Pyramid loomed above and only a few miles away. He wondered if it could really be climbed. Close at hand, a spectacular formation in the Divide caught his fancy. It was called the Window, and it was so close he could see birds flying in the wide gap between its sheer walls. They were small birds, and they seemed to be flying loops for the sheer joy of it. They come to play, he realized. The air must pour through there like anything.

He noticed a bit of an elk trail leading to the Window across the steep scree slides of fine rock. On the spur of the moment he said to the roan, "You want to stand in that

Window, Blueboy? I sure do." He tied the packhorse and rode the roan toward the Window. He wanted to stand between those towering walls and feel the air currents, see the birds up close, and look over the other side.

They started across the elk trail. Once out on the scree slope, Cloyd thought the elk that cross it must be very sure-footed, or very brave. The fine rock slid under the roan's hoofs, and the steepness of the slope underneath them began to worry him. Maybe it's a mountain goat trail, he thought. Yet there was no place to turn around, no choice but to keep going forward.

They inched across the dizzying slope until they reached the Window, and then the roan balked about going up. "We're almost there," Cloyd encouraged him. Then he chuckled, and said, "Don't you want to stand on that windowsill?" With a jump, the roan gained the rock ledge and they were standing right where Cloyd wanted to be, in between those sheer walls like towers. He watched the swallows put on a show. He could even see the rainbow in their wing patches. To the north, across the Rio Grande country, a whole new world had opened up. It seemed like the wilderness had no end.

If only the old man could see us standing here, he thought—me and Blueboy in the Window. I wish my sister could, my grandmother, and Susan James. But especially the old man. What a wonderful day, he thought. And there's not a cloud in the sky.

Cloyd thought about the Pyramid. There was still time to climb it today. Tomorrow the weather could turn bad.

He realized it would be harder for the roan to step off the windowsill than it had been to scramble up. He could fall. Besides, he liked the idea of riding *through* the Window, and so he did. He rode through, and then he looped one of the towers until he

---

12. deadfall: A tangled mass of fallen trees and brush.

gained the ridgetop and picked up a thread of a trail. The slope was awful steep, but it wasn't all scree like the one he crossed before; there was quite a bit of grass on it. Halfway down, the roan pulled up and held his ground. In front of them, a spring popped out of the mountain and made a little bog on the slope. Cloyd didn't know why the roan wouldn't go across. The horse was looking around, but there was no passage above or below the muddy spot. "We don't mind the mud," Cloyd said. He smacked his lips and kicked the horse forward. "C'mon, Blueboy, you can do it. You can do it, Blueboy."

The roan tried the mud and eased into it. Afterward, Cloyd remembered how the horse glanced back at him, as if for reassurance.

The roan took another step and was into the mud all the way up to one of his front shoulders. His other three legs were scrambling, scrambling desperately for footing, but the one leg was trapped, and Blueboy was falling.

In the moment the horse went down, it was all a blur. Cloyd knew only that he was about to be crushed. He barely managed to free his feet from the stirrups and to lunge uphill as the roan fell on its side.

Cloyd was pinned in the mud, and all around his head were the four hoofs of the roan. He saw the horseshoes and even the nails in the horseshoes.

Cloyd saw Blueboy tense and prepare to kick. The roan had to kick for balance, to resist the pull of the slope underneath him, and when he did, he'd crush the boy's skull. Cloyd thrashed with all his might to free himself, but he was completely mired.

Their eyes met, in a moment Cloyd would never forget. Blueboy was poised to kick, and then he saw Cloyd's head there, and then he didn't kick, not at all, but slowly, slowly, rolled over on his back. All four legs arced

away from the boy, and then Blueboy tucked his legs in and tumbled down the mountain, slowly at first, then faster and faster like a trundling boulder.

The roan lay at the foot of the scree slope several hundred feet below. Full of dread, Cloyd freed himself from the mud and worked his way down to the horse. Blueboy was alive, but how badly hurt? His breathing came in spurts; he wasn't getting up. "Maybe you're okay," he told the horse, without believing it might be so. "Maybe you're okay. You gotta get up! Are your legs broken? Are you all busted up inside?"

Cloyd made the roan stand up. He was amazed to see Blueboy get up and then walk. He kept talking to the horse; he was so relieved and thankful. After a little while, he led Blueboy down to the tundra grass. Somehow, there were no broken bones, nothing to show but a few scratches. Somehow, they'd both lived through it. He led the horse down and around the base of the slope and back up to the packhorse.

Cloyd found a camp barely into the trees, by a trickle of a stream running off the snowbanks. There was no way he was going to try to climb the Pyramid this day. Brushing the dried mud off his clothes, he marveled at the sacrifice his horse had made. He shouldn't have taken Blueboy where he did. He wondered if he would climb the Pyramid at all; he wondered if he should even try. Maybe he should just get back to the old man while he was safe. He didn't really know what he was doing anyway. He'd almost killed the horse, could've got killed himself. What did he need to stand on the top of a mountain for anyway? Cloyd brooded through the long evening, finally crawled into his sleeping bag, and fell asleep by the fading fire. In his dreams, the horse kept falling over and over all night. He woke up, freezing in the cold night air. He should

PYRAMID AND WINDOW
Tom Lockhart
Courtesy of the Artist

have pitched his tent. He wished the day would come.

At first light he woke, and he knew he couldn't ride away and give up, leave his dream behind. Maybe he would fail, but at least he had to try. Maybe what happened with the roan was all a part of earning the peak, not a reason to give up. Hadn't the old man said that the hurt you get over makes you stronger?

He ate quickly and set out on foot. "Good-bye, Blueboy," he called over his shoulder. "I'm going for the top of the world."

Within a few hours he'd angled up the mountain far enough to emerge from the trees and find the Pyramid towering right in front of him. As yet not a cloud had formed over the mountains. Already he could see the mesas down in New Mexico. How much greater would be the view from the peak, where he would be able to see in all directions. With spirits rising he bounded from rock to rock on the talus slopes[13] tumbling from the ridge high above. The small rock-rabbits called pikas squeaked and scurried among the boulders on all sides. A marmot the size of a small dog stood on its hind legs and whistled shrilly at him. He grinned to think about how the old man called them whistle pigs. "Are you a whistle pig?" he asked playfully. The marmot whistled once more. "I guess you are. I wish I could whistle like that."

Clouds were forming quickly up and down the range as he reached the mountain. He could imagine what a lightning storm on the peak would be like; he wasted no time picking a route. There was only one by which

---

13. talus (tăl′ əs) **slopes:** Slopes with scattered piles of fallen rock.

he had a chance of reaching the summit, and that was the knife-edge in front of him where two planes of the Pyramid met. He left the pikas and the marmots behind and started picking his way up the knife-edge. Now it was all rock. Some of the rocks were loose and could take him with them. A fall down either face would be deadly, but the north side would be the worst. He'd slide a thousand feet on the snow before being pitched onto the boulders below.

Cloyd kept climbing and tried to keep his mind on each step, each handhold. The air was thin and seared his lungs. Every time he reached a spot that might have stopped him, he found a way around or located cracks and footholds that enabled him to continue. The clouds were building and starting to darken, but they were still in the distance. Cloyd felt strong. He remembered that first day at the old man's farm when he climbed to the out-crop, found the bearstone, and fastened his longing on these peaks. He fell into the rhythm of climbing and proceeded up the knife-edge at a steady, careful pace.

A calm joy lifted Cloyd up the final piece of the climb. He was as sure he'd make the top as he'd ever been of anything. He seemed to float up the last little bit and stepped to the very tip of the Pyramid.

Peaks on all sides were riding in the blue sky. Peaks everywhere, dancing, jutting up, all in motion. He had to sit down and grip the rock. Peaks, as far as he could see, peaks, rock and green tundra, snowbanks, spruce forests, river canyons.

As he caught his breath, Cloyd saw a big bird soaring far below. Probably it was an eagle. He enjoyed its mastery of the winds, then watched it disappear. A storm was gathering in the Needles, and shadows were overtaking the mountainsides. Out in the low country, the sun was still shining. He was amazed to recognize the Chuska Mountains[14] in the hazy distance. They were the same mountains he always saw from White Mesa. Home wasn't really so far away. Someday he'd go home, he knew, but it didn't have to be soon. Whenever it happened would be all right. Cloyd pulled the blue stone from his pocket and set the little bear on a flat rock at the very top of the mountain. "Lone Bear," he said aloud, "we're not so alone anymore."

Cloyd thought about how Walter liked to be deep in the cold darkness of his gold mine. He wished the old man could have stood here with him. He wanted to tell him *this* is the heart of the mountains, up here in the light where you can see forever. Where you feel like you're a part of it all, like the beating heart of the mountains is your own heart. He'd never felt this way before, free and peaceful at the same time. If only there was a way to show the old man how thankful he was, for this, for Blueboy, for everything. He could show he cared for Walter like a son for a father.

The wind began to blow hard, and the temperature was dropping. He'd have to start down soon. He wished he could stay longer and try to take it all in, but it didn't matter. He had fulfilled his dream. It would be something he could always keep with him.

Then he remembered what his grandmother had told him, how the Utes knew all these mountains. Other Utes like himself must have stood on this same peak years ago. They had probably done something special, said or sung something. Then Cloyd recalled a ceremony his grandmother had taught him, but which he'd never done. Taking the bearstone in his hand, he held it out and offered it in turn to the Four Directions, then to the Earth and the Sky.

---

14. Chuska Mountains: A group of mountains many miles to the southwest on the Arizona-New Mexico border.

RESPONDING TO THE SELECTION

Your Response

1. Do you like the setting? Would you enjoy back-packing there? Alone? With others?
2. Do you think Walter made the right decision to send Cloyd to the Rio Grande Pyramid alone? Why or why not?

Recalling

3. What makes Walter forget about giving Cloyd a rest and an outing?
4. How does Blueboy save Cloyd's life?

Interpreting

5. What signs are there that Cloyd's attitude toward Walter has changed since Cloyd returned from White Mesa?
6. In what way is the incident when Cloyd is lost in the hailstorm important to the novel? What does Cloyd learn from it?
7. What event at the beginning of the novel is similar to Cloyd's climbing of the Rio Grande Pyramid? How has Cloyd changed between then and now?

Applying

8. The mountains have a special meaning for Cloyd because his ancestors used to live there. What other kinds of places can have a special meaning for people? Explain what can make a place special.

ANALYZING LITERATURE

Understanding Setting

Setting is the place and the time of the events in a novel or story. It is often closely related to the plot and characters. Look at the map on page 693. Trace Cloyd's journey through the landscape. Then explain how each of the following locations is important to the novel:

1. Arizona (Navajo Reservation)
2. Durango, Colorado
3. Walter's ranch on the Piedra River
4. White Mesa, Utah (Ute Reservation)
5. the mine on the Pine River
6. the Rio Grande Pyramid

CRITICAL THINKING AND READING

Appreciating Details of Setting

To help readers "see" the setting of the novel, Will Hobbs uses words with specific meanings, like *talus* (a pile of fallen rocks) and *riffles* (choppy water in the shallow part of a stream). He also describes in detail the plants and animals found in the setting. Find at least five specific details that help you visualize the following scenes in the novel:

1. the hailstorm
2. the ride to the Rio Grande Pyramid

THINKING AND WRITING

Writing About Setting

Write a description of an outdoor setting that you know well. It can be a city or country spot. First make a list of details you want to include. Then, next to each item on your list, write specific words that will make your description come alive. Have a classmate read your first draft and point out what doesn't create a specific image in his or her mind. Revise your description to make it more vivid.

LEARNING OPTIONS

1. **Cross-curricular Connection.** Look at the map on page 693 and find the Continental Divide. Notice that it is not a straight line. Find out more about the Continental Divide. Outline your information and give a brief oral presentation about it.
2. **Language.** Compile an illustrated dictionary of geology (earth science) and mining terms from the novel. You may illustrate it with your own drawings or with photographs cut from old magazines.

ONE WRITER'S PROCESS

Will Hobbs and Bearstone

PREWRITING

Where to Begin? For Will Hobbs, "a novel begins with character and has to do with human relationships." When he began to think about writing *Bearstone,* he had two characters he was interested in, a young Ute boy and an old man. As Hobbs puts it, "I began to try to imagine what might happen if their paths were to cross. I began to explore a lot of 'what ifs' with these two central characters."

Fact Into Fiction The characters of Cloyd Atcitty and Walter Landis both evolved from people whom Hobbs knew about from his own experience. "Cloyd is based on a boy my wife was helping learn to read. . . . My wife liked him and would tell me about him almost every night. Walter is based on an old friend of ours who's a rancher in southwestern Colorado."

Setting plays an important role in *Bearstone,* and Will Hobbs knew exactly where he wanted the novel to take place. "The places in *Bearstone,* like The Window and the Rio Grande Pyramid, are all real places. The writing of the novel fulfilled my dream of setting a story for others to enjoy in the upper Pine River country of the Weminuche Wilderness, a very special place in the geography of my heart."

Hobbs tampered with the facts of his friend's life in order to get the setting he wanted. "I wanted my friend's ranch to be on the edge of the wilderness, so I 'moved' it about thirty miles. His gold mine really was called the Pride of the West, but I moved it about two hundred miles, to the heart of the Weminuche Wilderness."

DRAFTING

A Journey of Discovery Though some novelists map out their plots before they write a word, others have no idea where a story is going until they start writing it. For Will Hobbs, writing is "a journey of discovery. What I have at the beginning is one strong feeling, or a central image, and I begin to wrap the story around that. For *Bearstone* it was Cloyd's feelings. I find the story gradually by developing the characters and having them interact. Trial and error is definitely my method. I go off on tangents, but I usually learn something out there that will contribute."

Evolving Actions Sometimes the characters or even the setting takes over a story and tells the author what's coming. Hobbs says, "When the old man was about to smash the bearstone with his sledgehammer, I was just as surprised as Cloyd. I only knew how red-hot his anger was. I was also surprised when the bearstone first showed up, at the bottom of the pottery jar in the burial. I was looking into an empty pot, same as Cloyd, and the bearstone appeared on its own."

REVISING

Making Time Will Hobbs wrote the first draft of *Bearstone* in six weeks. Then he spent another eight years writing five more drafts until he was satisfied. For Hobbs, "The hardest part is always sitting down to work. It's easier to do anything else. After teaching all day, I was exhausted. But I'd make myself go to my study, and try to learn how to write better."

Being Patient It was only in the fifth or sixth version that the horse Blueboy became a fully developed character. "Before that, the horse was a prop, merely transportation. I got to thinking about all the wonderful animal stories I'd read over the years, and I wondered if Cloyd wouldn't appreciate an animal friend."

The Little Words In addition to looking at the big picture, a novelist has to consider each word to make sure it says exactly what he or she wants to express. Will Hobbs knew it was important to show, not tell, but for a long time he didn't know how to do that. Then he figured out that "showing means using the five senses as you write." Following is an example of revisions that he made:

Early Draft

He made a cut in the dozen or so peach trees, about a third of the way through. He didn't want them to die. He just wanted the leaves to wither and yellow, and the peaches to shrivel.

Revised

He cut through the skin of the nearest tree and winced as he withdrew the saw. Beads of moisture were forming along the edges of the fresh wound. From one to the next he ran with the saw roaring at full-throttle, and he cut each of the twenty-two peach trees most of the way through. Each time, as the saw's teeth bit into the thin bark, he hollered with hurt as if he felt the saw himself. He didn't want to cut them down, he wanted them to die slowly. Before they died, their leaves would yellow and the peaches shrivel, and they would look just like his grandmother's peaches.

In what specific ways does the revised passage appeal to your senses?

Getting Help As long as there are facts in fiction, those facts have to be accurate. To verify some of his information, Will Hobbs asked a girl in his reading class whose family kept horses to read the scene where Blue-boy falls down the mountainside and is unharmed. She confirmed not only that it could happen but that it *had* happened with one of her family's horses. She even gave Hobbs "the graphic detail of the horse tucking its legs as it began to tumble."

Will Hobbs also works with an editor at his book publisher. "My editor points out what is not working and leaves it to me to fix it. . . . In this story she encouraged me to show Cloyd's feelings and motivation more clearly than I had in earlier drafts."

PUBLISHING

Finding an Outlet Hobbs showed initiative and perseverance in seeking a publisher. At his local library, he found a copy of *Writer's Market* and started sending his manuscript to publishers. He says, "I got a letter that said the story had promise. A little encouragement went a long way."

Reader Response Hobbs was also gratified after the novel was published to get positive feedback from readers. "My favorite 'book report' on this novel was a phone call from a Navajo student. . . . He called to tell me how strongly he identified with the main character." Another young reader wrote Hobbs to tell him "the way you write, I can make my own movie in my head."

THINKING ABOUT THE PROCESS

1. How might Will Hobbs's teaching job have helped in his writing of *Bearstone*?
2. **Writing.** Write a sketch for a fictional character based on someone you know. Choose a specific setting and situation to frame your sketch. Then make a list of sensory details that will help readers understand the character. When you have written a draft, ask someone to read it and suggest places where more specific details would help. Take the suggestions into account when you revise.

GUIDE FOR READING

Bearstone, Chapters 17–22

Theme

A **theme** is a general idea about life presented in a novel or a short story. A theme may be stated directly by the narrator. More often a theme is suggested by what the characters do and what happens to them. In your reading of *Bearstone*, you have seen how Cloyd has grown and changed as a result of the friendship Walter has offered him. The changes in Cloyd brought about by his relationship with Walter point out a theme of the novel.

Focus

Novels often depict the changes in a central character that come about as a result of what happens to that character in the novel. Have you ever had an experience that changed the way you thought or acted? Write about an experience that changed your life or the life of someone you know. How was the experience significant? As you read the end of *Bearstone*, pay attention to the changes that Cloyd has undergone since you first met him.

Vocabulary

Knowing the following words will help you as you read Chapters 17–22 of *Bearstone*.

loping (lōp′ iŋ) *v.*: Moving along easily, with a long, swinging stride (p. 713)

squelched (skwelcht) *v.*: Crushed or overpowered (p. 713)

condescendingly (kän di send′ iŋ lē) *adv.*: In a superior or haughty way (p. 714)

savored (sā′ vərd) *v.*: Enjoyed with appreciation (p. 715)

confluence (kän′ flōō əns) *n.*: Place where two or more streams come together (p. 716)

waning (wān′ iŋ) *v.*: Approaching the end (p. 718)

brandished (bran′ disht) *v.*: Waved in a threatening way (p. 720)

uncanny (un kan′ ē) *adj.*: Strange in a frightening way (p. 722)

strenuous (stren′ yōō əs) *adj.*: Requiring great effort or energy (p. 730)

Chapter 17

Cloyd was eager now to be on his way back to the old man. But he wouldn't take the shortest way; there was more he wanted to see. Dropping through the deep timber, he picked up the Divide trail and followed it until he sighted Ute Lake, a deep green crater tucked under the north slope at timberline.

On the way down he saw three bull elk grazing in the lush grass along a rivulet that fed the lake. When they heard the horse coming down the switchbacks,[1] the elk hurried up the far side of the basin and into the brushy mountain willows beyond.

At lakeside, Cloyd made his camp and hobbled his horses in the good grass. Before long he had his rod and reel assembled and was searching for bait. He found a tiny grasshopper and dropped it on the surface of the deep and rocky lake, but the fish weren't interested. They could see its legs kicking, but they weren't interested. He tried the salmon eggs. No luck. The trout started hitting the surface for flies even tinier than gnats. He wondered if the old Utes had fished at this lake named after them, and how. He laughed out loud. He doubted they were fly fishermen.

As the sun was dropping behind the Needles, he sat by his fire and ate a chili supper. It tasted good, and the packhorse would have one less can to carry. Warmth and contentment spread through his body.

Cloyd's fourth morning found him riding out of Ute Lake up to the Divide and descending into the long alpine basin called the Rincon La Osa, which would lead him back to the valley of the Pine. This night he'd be at the mine with Walter, he thought happily. He thought about how he was going to tell the old man about that moment when his eyes

and Blueboy's met, that he'd found out the answer to the question of whether horses could care about you. The red-haired man was wrong about horses, at least about this one. He had a lot he wanted to talk about with Walter. He wondered if Walter would recognize how much he'd grown in four days' time.

He stopped to rest and eat berries on the bank of the Rincon stream as it wound its way slowly across a small meadow below the long basin. Kneeling by the stream to drink, he marveled at the clarity of the water, which seemed to magnify every pebble on the bottom. He became aware that he was looking as well at the dark backs of three large trout, motionless except for the fanning of their fins.

One of them, perhaps becoming aware of him, darted up a tiny inlet on his side of the creek. Cloyd followed and kept his eye on the fish moving slowly up the narrow passage. He'd like to catch this fish, he thought, catch it somehow without a fishing pole. Was it true what his grandmother had said, that in the old days some of the Utes could catch fish in their bare hands?

He would try. The fish would have to come back to the stream sometime. He could pick a spot and wait for it to come through.

With one knee on each bank, Cloyd straddled the inlet. Slowly he lowered his hands and then his arms into the icy water as deep as his arms were long. And then he waited.

Five minutes, ten minutes, he couldn't tell anymore. His arms went numb, his back ached, but he didn't move a muscle. He could see the trout slowly swimming toward him, pausing here and there for long minutes.

The trout was close now. Cloyd could see its mouth working, its bright orange markings. It was looking through the tunnel his hands and arms made. Would it retreat or dart between his hands before he could close on it? He held them as still as he could. It

---

1. switchbacks: Trails that follow a zigzag course, making it easier to climb up or down a steep slope.

GRIZZLY COUNTRY (detail)
Paul Krapf
Courtesy of the Artist

swam still closer. He began to narrow the gap between his freezing hands, slowly, slowly, slowly. Unsuspecting, the cutthroat swam between them. Cloyd closed in as calmly as he could. He dug with his nails, grasped the fish, and lifted it in one motion out of the water and onto the bank.

He stood up to ease the striking pain in his back. The horses whinnied. A dark shape was moving at the edge of the meadow. An animal loping with an unusual gait. A bear! A huge brown bear, and it was aware of him. It stood on its hind legs to have a look at him, and its head swayed back and forth. Cloyd was astonished at how tall it was. Its claws were enormous. The bear dropped quickly to all fours and suddenly disappeared into the trees.

The big fish flip-flopped against Cloyd's leg. He nudged it back into the water with his foot, then leaped across the Rincon stream and took off running in hopes of a second glimpse of the huge bear. Once in the trees Cloyd walked softly, looking all around, and tried to listen for the bear's passage. All he could hear was the furious pounding of his own heart.

In the quiet darkness of the trees, the bear was nowhere and everywhere. Suddenly Cloyd felt foolish and reckless for having tried to follow. He ran back to the sunlit meadow, to the horses. He wanted to hurry back to the camp on Snowslide Creek. He wanted to tell the old man about the bear.

It was late afternoon when he rode into camp. He was anxious to see Walter. The old man was drinking coffee and visiting by the campfire with his friend Rusty, the red-haired man.

Walter's face lit up when he saw Cloyd. "I didn't expect you until tomorrow or so," he said. "How'd everything go?"

"Fine," Cloyd mumbled. All his enthusiasm was squelched. The tall man was looking him over, like he did before. No handshake this time, but all the feelings were the same as before.

"Cloyd here's been out exploring the mountains. Did you climb that Rio Grande Pyramid?"

Cloyd nodded halfheartedly. He felt so disappointed that someone else was there, and worse, that it was the red-haired man. This wasn't how it was supposed to be.

"My goodness, that must've been something. I'll bet you could see hundreds of miles from up there."

"See any wildlife?" the outfitter asked abruptly.

Cloyd's heart began to pound. This wasn't as he'd pictured it, telling Walter how he'd caught the fish and seen the bear. But the outfitter had brought the subject up, and the man was making him feel bad again, sick even, as if he was suddenly burning up with fever. He cast wildly about thinking for what to say or do, but he couldn't think; he could only feel the resentment burning inside, and he wanted to prove himself, show that he wasn't a nothing, show that he knew something, something that would impress the big hunter. He'd seen a bear without having had to track it down with dogs. "Some elk . . ." he said, teetering on the brink, and then he added, ". . . and a bear."

"When'd you see the bear?" the man asked quickly.

"Today."

"What kind?"

Cloyd hesitated. "He was brown. I guess he was a brown bear."

"No such varmint. Black bear in a cinnamon phase. How big?"

"Taller than you, standing up."

The red-haired man smiled condescendingly. "Me standing up, you say, or the bear?"

"Both."

The man grunted. "You saw this bear standing on its hind legs? How far away was he?"

Now Cloyd regretted he'd said anything at all. Suddenly he didn't feel good about seeing the bear. The man was making him feel bad, making it seem in front of Walter like he was exaggerating. Maybe he was, a little, but he really didn't think so. What could he do now? He saw what he saw, and he wouldn't let the tall man shame him. "Just across the meadow," he said.

The man lifted his red eyebrows. "Oh, whereabouts?"

Again he hesitated. "Rincon," he said finally.

"Oh? La Vaca or La Osa?"

"La Osa."

"Rincon of the Bear, eh?" he said skeptically, with a wide grin. "Walter, you think he might've let his imagination get away from him up in that high altitude?"

Agitated, Walter got up. The conversation had gone badly. Cloyd had been embarrassed. His friend had no feel for the boy at all. "Why no, Rusty," he declared, "that ain't possible. Cloyd's got an eye for detail better'n mine by far."

The tall man rose, hung his coffee cup in the branch of a tree, and crossed the fire circle to Cloyd. He clapped Cloyd's shoulder. "No hard feelings, kid. I believed every word you said. I'm just part lawyer, I guess, and curious to boot. Say, I've got to be going, Walter—my brothers are expecting me for supper."

Walter put together a meal for the boy. They ate quietly. Walter didn't pester him; he could see Cloyd didn't want to talk just now. Walter let his mind drift, mulling things over. Like about how he'd been single-jacking all this time the boy was gone, day and night practically, when he'd told the boy he wouldn't. He was nearly ready to fire and should be getting some sleep, lest he make a mistake during the crucial preparation of the charges.

Cloyd's grown, Walter reflected. He's stronger, more like a young man than a boy. Because of how it went with Rusty, he'd have to wait awhile before asking Cloyd about the ride. They should've shared the ride in the first place. On the other hand, sometimes it was better to be out there on your own. That's when you really see things and learn something. Cloyd got to have the whole country to himself.

Tomorrow he'd fire the hole. Funny, it didn't really matter if he found anything. How could he expect to with only two blasts? That wasn't a significant amount of progress. But it was the trying again that made it worthwhile. This round might be his last ever. All his steels were dull, and it wouldn't do any good to try to sharpen them anymore— they needed retempering. The summer was run out anyway. His life, for that matter, was about run. But he'd come back to the Pride of the West the way he'd always wanted to, come full circle.

There was something weighing in the air tonight, Walter thought, something weighing on this time that should be savored. As he watched the boy in the firelight, he saw it building. Maybe Cloyd, too, was realizing that the summer was about over. It wouldn't do any good to talk about it. There'd be time yet for ending on the upside.

It was Cloyd who broke the long silence. "Why did he keep asking me about that bear I saw?"

"How do you mean?"

"He didn't believe me."

"Oh, he was trying to pick your memory."

Cloyd shook his head decisively. "He wanted to catch me saying something that wasn't right so he could prove I was making it up."

"Oh, no. I know Rusty awful well. He was so interested he could hardly hold himself still. Didn't you see how fast he took off? He was bustin' to get back to camp and get started after that bear. Sounded like a trophy."

Cloyd struggled against the panic that ripped him. His breath caught short, and his heart pounded in his ears. "It's not hunting season," he said, as calmly as he could. "Bear season was in June, wasn't it?"

"Open season on bears, Cloyd, or there's hunts off and on all year, I forget which."

Cloyd's mind raced. He'd given away the bear, and the outfitter was going to try to kill it. "Does he have those dogs with him?"

"They don't use any on this hunt. Too easy, they say. You see, Rusty and his brothers get together every summer for a pleasure-hunt. It's kind of a contest. The first brother to get himself a bear wins a prize of some kind."

"They can find a bear without dogs?"

"They're awful good. Rusty's the best trapper, tracker, and hunter in the San Juans. As a matter of fact, they're bowhunting."

"What do you mean?"

"Why, with bows and arrows. That's the way Rusty favors. He even writes articles for a magazine about bowhunting."

"There was a rifle in the case on his horse."

"Well, he'd have it along with him. But he prefers to bowhunt because it takes quite a bit more skill. It's like the Indians used to, only the arrows are made out of fiberglass or some-such and the head's like three razor blades in one. You wouldn't want to touch the thing—it'd take your thumb off. Even so, the odds against the hunter getting close enough are pretty long. Sometimes these guys come up empty-handed. Take this hunt for instance. They'll be heading back sometime soon and still have nothing to show. They probably won't come within miles of that bear of yours. Bears cover a lot of ground, you know. The chances of finding any one bear with that kind of head start are slim at best."

Cloyd wasn't reassured. The old man said the outfitter was the best trapper, tracker, and hunter in the mountains. This man might very well kill the bear, and he'd told him where to find it. Now he'd done it, spoiled everything. In the old days, his grandmother said, the Utes wouldn't kill bears. That would bring on the worst of bad luck, she said. Cloyd considered his secret name and fingered the bearstone in his pocket. He had to undo his mistake.

Chapter 18

Cloyd hoped to slip out of camp as soon as the moon rose to light his way. He struggled to stay awake after Walter fell asleep, but soon failed, worn out by his long ride off the Divide. The moon was high in the sky when he awoke. He feared that the red-haired man had already gone up the Rincon after the bear. The old man's breathing whistled its usual song; Cloyd was able to collect his jacket and slide through the tent flap without waking him.

He climbed in the moonlight to a vantage point above the confluence of the Rincon creek and the Pine River, and waited, his confidence collapsing all around him. He was alarmed by every sound the night made.

To his relief, he finally spotted the outfitter riding up the Pine trail. It was still all but dark, yet Cloyd recognized the profile of the tall man. He wondered why the man was alone, then recalled the contest among the brothers. The outfitter wanted the bear all for himself.

In the first light the outfitter trotted his horse along the flats at the bottom of the Rincon creek. From the point the man disappeared into the trees, the trail climbed so abruptly that his horse would be slowed to a walk. Cloyd ran to keep up. He wished he had Blueboy, but a horse would give him away turning over stones and breaking sticks. He had to follow so carefully that the best tracker in the mountains wouldn't know he was being followed.

Maybe the bear's gone over the mountains, Cloyd hoped, across the rockslides where even the red-haired man couldn't track him. But what if he had just killed a deer and would stay in the Rincon to feed a few days? What if he's eating berries along the stream in the meadow?

Cloyd hurried up the mountain, cutting the switchbacks and watching to make sure he didn't come too close to the man on horseback. Finally he could see through the trees to the meadow, the one where he'd seen the bear. He stopped to take off his jacket. He'd soaked himself with sweat. The outfitter, he guessed, was even now on the meadow looking for signs. Cloyd crawled to the edge of the trees and peeked around the trunk of a large spruce.

He saw the horse first, then the man kneeling in the grass where the bear had loped toward the trees and stood up. It hadn't taken the tall man much time to find the track of the bear. He was as skillful as Walter said, and after all, Cloyd thought bitterly, he'd been told right where to go.

As eager as he might be, the red-haired man took his time examining the signs, especially around the place where the bear stood up. Then he climbed the tongue of a talus slide to a spot well above the meadow where he crouched awhile and scanned in all directions with his large binoculars.

In a bowl like this any sound would carry,

Cloyd knew, yet the outfitter descended the slope as quietly as a cat. He's hunting, Cloyd realized—he's deadly serious. Cloyd remembered how the red-haired man had almost laughed at him. If the man knew, he would simply sneer at the suggestion that an unarmed boy on foot hoped to stop him.

How could it be done? Maybe make enough noise to warn the bear? That's what he'd been thinking as he rushed up the trail. But if he yelled and scared the bear away, wouldn't the man catch up again? How could the bear escape the best tracker in the country?

Cloyd watched the man return to the signs on the meadow. Most likely he hadn't caught sight of the bear through the binoculars.

The outfitter packed a daypack with his binoculars and what must have been food and water. Cloyd watched him string his bow and check his arrows one by one. How close would you have to get, Cloyd wondered, to hunt with a bow and arrow? The man hobbled his horse, entered the trees where the bear had, and disappeared.

The man's rifle must be in the saddle scabbard[2] on the horse, Cloyd reasoned. With the rifle he could make plenty of noise. The mountains would echo the shots all the way to the bear, wherever it was.

The rifle was there in the scabbard, as he'd hoped. But when Cloyd pulled the bolt back and exposed the chamber, there was no ammunition in it. He searched the saddlebags—no shells! The outfitter must have them in his daypack. The man was gone now, the chance to keep him in sight lost.

Cloyd knew he lacked the skill to track the man or the bear in the woods. His only chance now was to get back to the trees on the other side of the meadow, on the slope opposite the one the man was on. That way he could climb without being seen and find a high place where he might spot the outfitter again—if he was lucky.

Cloyd worked for most of an hour until he found a lookout close to timberline, high above the dogleg between the lower and upper meadows. Great ups and downs rippled the upper basin, where even now the outfitter or the bear or both might be hidden from view. Big patches of stunted spruce dotted the flanks of the basin, and thickets of brush grew everywhere, looking from this distance like tall grass. A thousand places he couldn't see. I'm an unlucky person, he thought.

Cloyd can't be too far off, Walter thought. He didn't take the horse. He'll be back. Walter's mind drifted back to his work, as he readied the charges for the second blast. Once you blast, he reflected, you forget about all the backbreaking work. Another three or four feet of the mountain is broken loose, and you just never know what you're going to find. Most times nothing but rock. A bonanza,[3] he mused, is a hole in the ground owned by a champion liar. But sometimes a man found good ore, and once in a million lifetimes, a fabulous strike like the Cresson Vug. It's really gambling, is what it is, he thought. They ought to make it illegal.

Walter came running out of the tunnel hollering, "Fire in the hole! Fire in the hole!" even though there was no one to hear it but himself. Muffled somewhat, the blast sent fewer clouds of fumes and dust than usual out of the mouth of the mine. He was concerned that the explosion lacked punch. When the air cleared enough for him to see,

---

2. saddle scabbard (skab′ ərd): A long sheath or case to hold a rifle.

3. bonanza: A very rich vein or pocket of ore (from the Spanish for "prosperity").

he entered the mine. So what if the air's still bad, he thought. No sense in an old man babying his lungs.

He groaned when he saw the blasted face at the end of the tunnel, recognizing at once what was wrong. The old face had been only partially blown out; two mounds of rock held the bulk of it fast. Two missed shots—worse than rotten luck. Two mounds of rock clinging there with crucial charges inside, unshot but possibly hair-triggered to blow when a man tried to pick at the surrounding rock to get at them.

Outside, he sat and thought about the missed shots. He could wait until next summer to try to pick them out, but then they'd be hanging over his head all winter and he'd still have to face them. He could give up on the Pride of the West, he supposed. But one thing he couldn't do—wait until somebody was blown up fooling around inside the mine. If he was going to remove them, he'd better try while he had the nerve and while the boy was safely away blowing off steam. "Maude, you were right—it's a risky business," he said aloud.

He lit the headlamp, shouldered the pick, and entered the tunnel. More than anything, he had to know if the missed shots hid some decent ore.

Chapter 19

The hours of careful waiting and watching ended as the tall white clouds turned dark and the wind began to blow. Cloyd glimpsed a figure moving swiftly for a low spot several miles up the basin. If it was the man on the track of the bear, it meant the bear had moved up the Rincon in the direction of the Divide.

Cloyd took off running. He avoided the meadows and tried to make time in the stands of timber and in the brush. He glimpsed the figure again clearing the top of the Divide, vanishing just as lightning struck up there. Apparently the outfitter had dropped his tracking and hurried up the ridge while Cloyd was in the brush. The man was taking a risk climbing into the weather, Cloyd thought. He must be closing in on the bear.

Cloyd broke into the open and made for the place where the man went over the top. As he climbed, it began to sprinkle; he had no rain gear. He ran stumbling up the ridge and into the wind with no thought but that he had to reach the bear in time.

As he topped out on the Divide, he found the outfitter's straw cowboy hat weighted and left in plain sight—as a sign for his brothers? Cloyd thought the man must be a little farther east on the Divide and a little below it. He had to be, it was the only hidden place. If he'd gone on down the steep slope to the west, he'd be visible.

The thundershower had passed by and was attacking the Pyramid. The day was waning now; he knew he had to guess right.

Yes, the outfitter had to be tucked out of sight on one of the small terraces angling to the north and dropping like stairs down to Ute Lake. The man—and the bear—must be about where he'd passed the day before on his way up from the lake.

Just in case the outfitter had somehow doubled back, Cloyd checked behind. His eye caught a flash of bright yellow. Riders in rainslickers, three of them coming up the Rincon and leading a fourth horse. The brothers. He left the ridgeline quickly.

Cloyd found the highest terrace, but the man wasn't there. He ran its length, then crawled to the far edge to avoid being seen as he gained a vantage point. Below him lay another little meadow surrounded by rockslides and brush. He made his way down to it among the rocks and ran for the far end. The

WIND RIVERS
Stephen Elliott
Claggett/Rey Gallery

wind blowing hard against him slowed him down.

When he dropped at the far end of the meadow to look below, he saw them on the next shelf. It *was* the bear he'd seen, a huge brown bear turning over rocks above the mountain willows at the edge of the meadow, looking maybe for pikas or marmots. The outfitter was stalking in a crouch. He sneaked along the line of brush until he drew close to the bear on the other side. The man carried his bow with an arrow in place. The bear wasn't aware of him.

Cloyd yelled with all his might. Strangely, neither the bear nor the man paid any attention. The red-haired man drew close to a gap in the brushline. Cloyd screamed again and again, desperately, with no result. As close as they were, the bear and the man were deaf and unreachable, like phantoms in a dream. Then he realized that he was yelling from above and into a sturdy wind, and his voice was being blown away, up and behind him.

Suddenly the tall man stood out in the open in front of the bear with the bow pulled all the way back and the arrow aimed. Sensing something, the bear stood up as if to have a better look and took the arrow in its neck.

The bear didn't fall. It roared in pain and charged the man through the opening in the brush with uncanny speed. But the outfitter hadn't wasted any time nocking a second arrow, and released it into the bear's chest.

Still the bear came on, all teeth and claws and blood, and knocked aside the bow the man lifted to shield himself. As the man spun away, the big bear hesitated, then stood up and tried to brush away the arrowshafts with its paws.

The man crouched and brandished a long-bladed knife. Returning to all fours, the bear took a few steps toward him, gave a strangled growl, and collapsed on its side.

The red-haired man circled the fallen bear several times. Then he knelt and ran his hand across its broad forehead. He inspected the teeth and the underside of one of the front paws, and sized the claws against his forefinger.

Cloyd fell to his belly in the cover of the rocks and let the bitterness roll over him in waves. He dreaded being seen by the outfitter now—that would make the man's victory complete. He'd gladly sink into the ground if he could. The uncaring wind shifted and carried the fragment of a shout from above and behind him. The others were coming, the brothers. He had to get out of there. He scuttled backward until he was well away from the lip of the shelf, then stood and ran off the downhill side into the rocks on the steep slope below. Above him, the riders crossed the spot he'd fled.

There was whooping and shouting as the three men met up with their brother and the dead bear, but Cloyd couldn't see them and he couldn't hear the outfitter's voice. He had to hear what the man would say. He worked his way through the talus until he was directly below them, then crept under the edge of the meadow where he could hear.

"Biggest bear I ever saw," said one. "You win again."

"You sure got the jump on us, Rusty, sneaking off in the night like that," said a second brother. "We came as soon as we saw your note. Heck of a bear. Did he charge you? How'd it go?"

"Look at the forehead," the outfitter said, not so loud as the others.

"What about it?"

"It's dished out."

"So?"

"Look at the hump on its back, the forehead, the teeth, the claws—that's a grizzly."

"Everybody knows there aren't any grizzlies left in Colorado," the third brother protested.

"Wasn't true. This here's a grizzly."

"If you say so—you're the expert. Well then, you've sure got yourself a trophy here, Rusty."

"What I've got myself here is a heck of a mess."

"Waddaya mean?"

"It's illegal to kill a grizzly. They're protected. Hundred thousand dollar fine and a year in jail."

"So . . . you didn't know it was a grizzly, did you?"

"It . . . crossed my mind—I couldn't tell for sure until I was up close. . . . It charged me—I had to defend myself."

That's a lie, Cloyd thought. That's not how it happened.

"Well, who's to know?" one of the brothers snapped. "Ain't nobody's business but yours."

"I got carried away."

There was a pause, then Cloyd heard the red-haired man's voice fill with what almost seemed like regret. "It's probably one of the two cubs that were reported around the Pyramid ten or twelve years ago."

"Look, Rusty," the same brother said, "Quit worrying. You made a terrific kill here, and it'll make a once-in-a-lifetime trophy."

"You guys think I can go ahead and display it in my home—show it to the game warden when he comes over to visit?"

"I see your point. You've got a problem here, don't you? How 'bout I just take it back to Texas with me. Let's skin it out right now."

"I don't know, Andy. I could lose my license over this—that's my livelihood we're talking about. Even if a grizzly's found dead, you're supposed to report it as soon as you can so the Department of Wildlife's scientific guys can study it."

"C'mon, we'll pack the skin out good and careful. No one'll ever see it. Tell you what. I'll give you a thousand dollars for it, make it worth your while. I'd really like to have that monster baring his teeth on the floor in front of the fireplace. Look at the size of those claws! From what you're saying, if you do report this thing, there's no way they aren't going to take it away from you. Then what if they don't like your story? You'll end up without the bear and in big trouble both!"

"We'd have to leave the carcass, Andy. Backpackers would come across it and report it. The bone structure would identify it as a grizzly. Sam Perkins—the game warden—he knows we're up here. I'd never get away with it. Besides, he's a good friend. The more I think about this, the more I'm convinced that the only way I'm going to come out at all on this deal is to get ahold of Sam right away. He's going to want to bring in the department helicopter and lift this grizzly out as soon as possible, before it starts to spoil. So let's get down to the guard station and radio this in."

"It's a shame."

"Sure is," the outfitter agreed. "But I'm not going to risk my business over it."

After the men were gone, Cloyd approached the bear. Kneeling close to its massive head, Cloyd asked the bear's forgiveness. He prayed that somehow this bear wasn't the last one. Hadn't there been two cubs? Maybe there are others that nobody knows about. Overcome with grief, he stayed into darkness. Cloyd vowed to the mighty grizzly that he would remember him forever, not lifeless like now, but standing tall and alert, sniffing the wind, still the most powerful animal in the mountains.

As he fled down the Rincon trail, the night was full of accusing voices. A large owl suddenly flapped out of the dark and almost struck him. He yelled sharply in terror. His grandmother had told him about owls. This one would be the dead bear's spirit freshly loosed from its body.

Chapter 20

It was no accident he'd seen the owl, Cloyd discovered. When, in the middle of the night, he stumbled into camp and lifted the flap of the canvas tent, his misgivings were verified. Instead of the musical comings and goings of the old man's breath, he was greeted by an uncanny silence. He had to fumble for a flashlight. Indeed, Walter was not there. His sleeping bag was rolled up as it always was during the day. The old man had not been to bed this night at all.

Cloyd ran up the ore dump and into the mine. His flashlight caught the trace of dust lingering in the air. There'd been a blast, he knew. And with that knowledge came the sickening realization that Walter had been working all along and had set off another round of blasting. He listened. All he could hear was the beating of his own heart. If Walter was working in there, he should be able to hear it: any sound carried in the mine. But there was no sound at all coming down the tunnel, only the uncanny silence. He called. No answer.

Cloyd found him face down at the end of the tunnel. Only the old man's head, shoulders, and right arm showed above the rubble. The explosion had made meat of one side of his face. Cloyd knelt close. Walter was still breathing, but he was unconscious. There was a nasty gash in his scalp on the back of his head, and it was all matted with blood. Cloyd went to work to free the old man from the rubble. He worked with the flashlight in his teeth, so he could use both hands. It took time. He fought the panic that was making his head swim. He had to be able to think. What was he going to do? How much time did the old man have? The legs were pinned badly, but at last he freed them, and then he saw the fracture. Surrounded by blood and dirt, the broken bone of the old man's lower leg was sticking out, and it had a sharp point on it.

Cloyd felt dizzy, he felt the panic rising again, and he fought it. He had to get Walter outside. He picked him up as gently as he could and started out of the mine. He didn't know if he'd be strong enough to make it, but he clenched his teeth, straightened his back, and kept moving. Cloyd let the flashlight drop from his fingers as he reached the portal; outside there was moonlight and even the first hint of dawn. Then it came to him, his only chance to get help fast. A helicopter. *A helicopter was coming to get the bear.* He stumbled and then recovered. It felt like he was carrying three hundred pounds. He told himself how light the old man was, and he kept going until he reached the tent.

Cloyd laid Walter down on a sleeping bag, then opened the other bag and spread it across him as a blanket. He knew he had to keep the old man warm. Then he ran down to the creek, drank from it, and splashed his face with the cold water. He had to think, and think right. Rusty said he was going to radio for a helicopter from the guard station. Where was that? He hadn't said—no clues at all. It could be any direction from where he killed the bear. How long would it have taken him to get there? There was no telling. How long before the helicopter came?

Dawn was coming on fast. Rusty probably reached the radio sometime in the evening. The helicopter could be coming anytime now; there was already enough daylight for them to fly. He could take Blueboy and head for the bear and hope to make it in time, but if he didn't—maybe he should ride all the way down the Pine to the trailhead and hitch to a phone and call for a helicopter. He had to choose, and it had to be the right decision. He went back to the old man. Walter was hurt so bad, and he was so fragile. There wasn't time enough to ride all the way down the Pine River, Cloyd decided. There just wasn't enough time.

He left drinking water by the old man's

shoulder, in case he came to, and then he saddled the roan. Cloyd walked him to the creek, where he took a long drink, and then a second. "Now we're gonna ride, Blueboy, we're gonna run. I want you to run like you've never run before."

He mounted the horse and took off flying. They galloped down Snowslide Creek and then up the Pine, until they were slowed by the steep Rincon trail. Was there time? Was he doing the right thing?

The roan was climbing, climbing. His gray coat was soaked with sweat, and in the morning light it shone a royal blue. He drank from the Rincon stream when they reached the meadow, and then he broke into a canter when the trail leveled out in the long upper basin. "Atta Blue," Cloyd encouraged him. "Atta Blueboy. Do it for me."

The climb out of the Rincon slowed them to a walk again, and it seemed to take forever. The sun was climbing fast. Noon wasn't that far off. When they were still in the thick mountain willows, he heard the chop-chop-chop of a helicopter and then looked up and saw it for a moment. He waved frantically, but he knew there was no way it could have seen him. At least the copter is heading toward the bear, he thought. It couldn't be on its way out.

The last pitch up the Divide was steep and slow, and the precious minutes were flying by. Finally they topped out. The roan's mouth was all covered with foam, and his sides were heaving. Cloyd urged his horse down the other side. "Run, Blue—it's going to take off! We're not going to make it!"

They came charging off the Divide. The helicopter came in sight, with its whirring blades and the awful noise and commotion they stirred. It was still on the ground. Cloyd couldn't see the bear—it was already loaded. Four men were walking back toward their horses and holding onto their hats. The roan pitched up to a stop and wouldn't budge, not

with the chopping and the scent of the bear all around. Cloyd leaped off and ran down the mountainside, and then the men saw him coming. He ran straight for the red-haired man and screamed in his ear. Rusty turned and sprinted, dived low under the whirling blades, and hollered for the pilot to shut the helicopter down.

Six men crowded around him. He told them about the old man, told them to hurry. One of the brothers said, "Hey, how'd you know about this helicopter? How'd you know to come up here?" The red-haired man was watching him closely, and so was the game warden. Cloyd didn't answer. He yelled at them, pleaded for them to hurry. They dragged the bear out of the helicopter. It was enormous.

"You get in with me," the man in uniform said. "You and me and the pilot. Rusty'll take care of your horse."

"Tell Walter," said the outfitter, "tell him I'll bring all of his horses and his stuff out. Tell him not to worry about a thing."

Cloyd looked up and saw the red-haired man's eyes. They were full of concern for his friend; they were even kind for once. The man leaned forward and said, "You done good, boy. However you done it, you done awful good."

Cloyd looked away. He saw the bear all in a heap, with its teeth showing and the tongue caught between them. Flies were buzzing all around, walking in its mouth and on its eyes.

"Let's get moving!" the game warden yelled. He gave Cloyd a push and a boost, then climbed in himself, using the bear for a step.

The copter started up, and then they lifted off. The men and the bear shrank below, and Cloyd caught sight of Blueboy on the mountain. Then they cleared the Divide and headed down the Rincon toward the old man. "So how did you know the helicopter

AMONG THE PINES
M. C. Poulsen
Courtesy of the Artist

would be coming?" the game warden asked him. "Do you know something about that bear?"

Cloyd knew what Rusty would have told the game warden. Something like what he told his brothers. That the bear charged, and he had to defend himself. He thought about how it really happened. How the bear stood up to sniff the wind, and took the arrow through its neck. He knew this was his chance to get back at the red-haired man, to really show him. His chance to get revenge.

And then Cloyd remembered the peach trees, and his awful revenge with the chain saw. He didn't want any more of that poison. He wouldn't say a thing. What was done was done. Rusty would figure out he'd been right there when it happened—that was enough.

The game warden was waiting for his answer. Cloyd shrugged and looked away, in so final a way that the man could tell he was going to have to wait forever. You might as well wait for a rock to speak.

Chapter 21

Cloyd wasn't allowed in to see the old man. He came to the hospital every day and waited, but they wouldn't let him in yet. He took the bearstone out of his pocket and asked the nurse to put it by Walter. She said she would put it right on his nightstand where he would see it. Walter's brother was there, from his ranch down at Aztec, and so was his sister-in-law from Missouri. They got to see him first. Finally Cloyd was allowed in. Half of Walter's face was bandaged, and his leg was in a cast that was held off the bed a little with a pulley. He smiled painfully when he saw Cloyd and beckoned him over. "I'm gonna make it, Cloyd," he said. "They can't kill this old hoss."

Cloyd didn't say anything. He didn't know what to say. He just stood by the old man. Walter rolled his eyes toward the nightstand.

"I sure appreciated seeing that blue bear of yours."

Cloyd looked at the bearstone in a new way. He'd been wishing, ever since he'd been to the top of the mountain, that he could find a way to show the old man how he felt about him. Now Cloyd knew what to do. He would give the old man his greatest treasure. "I want you to have it," Cloyd said, pointing to the bearstone with a twist of his lips.

The old man tried to hitch himself up in his bed. "Now wait a minute here, that's—"

Cloyd's eyes met Walter's. He wanted the old man to understand how grateful he was. "I want you to keep it," he said.

Walter saw into Cloyd's dark eyes and felt the strength and conviction of a man, not a boy. He was greatly humbled to receive such a token of affection. And at his age. This was a particular sort of joy he'd never felt in his whole life. He reached over to the nightstand and took the turquoise bear in his fingers. "I'll always treasure this piece, I surely will."

A tear escaped the old man's eye. "I'll think of you every time I see it." For a while Walter couldn't speak. "Now then," he said finally, "you and me have a lot of catchin' up to do. I heard about what you did, how you rode that blue horse up the Divide and got me that helicopter. Nobody else could've done as much, Cloyd."

With a quick smile, Cloyd said, "You would've done the same for me."

And then it was time to go. Walter could only have short visits. It was September, and school was starting. Cloyd came after school to see the old man and talk for a little while, and then the nurses let him come early in the morning as well. Walter was going to be in the hospital a long time. Cloyd could see he really needed company. He told Walter about how school was much better than before, how he was going to learn how to read. His house-mother got the school to give him a teacher all to himself for one period a day, since he was going to try.

A few weeks passed, and the old man seemed to be getting worse instead of better. Cloyd didn't know why. He was there when Walter's sister-in-law was saying good-bye, and then he found out something the old man had known for a while, but hadn't told him. "You won't mind it so bad, Walter," she said kindly. "You just can't manage on your own. If I could come and live at the farm, that would be another thing, but you know I have my own family back home. . . ."

"I wouldn't ask you to, Etta," Walter said.

"Well, I know you wouldn't have that. And Tom has his own ranch to keep up with. . . ."

The old man looked away through the window at the yellow leaves blowing from the trees, and he sighed.

His sister-in-law took his hand. "It's time to come in from the farm, Walter. Lots of folks have to face that. The nursing home's not going to be so bad, really, Walter. And I'll know you're getting good care."

The old man reached with his other hand and held fast. "I miss the farm awful bad, Etta. I could get my strength back on the farm."

"The doctor said it's going to be a long, slow process, Walter. You can't afford a live-in nurse. These bills have drawn you down too bad. Now, we already talked about all that, Walter."

And then she said good-bye. She had to catch a plane back to Missouri. Cloyd sat awhile with the old man. "What's going to happen to the farm?" he asked.

"Have to sell it to pay my board at the nursing home. But now, let's change the subject. Tell me what you did today. . . ."

The reading teacher was talking, and Cloyd wasn't even listening to her. He was thinking about Walter, about how he was getting worse instead of better. Pretty soon they would move him out of the hospital, and then he would wither away. It wouldn't take long. If he couldn't get back to his farm, he was going to wither away.

"Cloyd, I thought you wanted to work with me," the teacher said.

"I'm sorry. I was thinking."

It came to him in the group home, when all the kids were watching television, and he was looking at it but not seeing anything. The next day, in front of the school, Cloyd asked around among the bus drivers and found the one who came in from the east, a burly man in grease-stained overalls. "Does your bus come in from the Piedra?" he asked the driver.

The man shook his head. "Not nearly. Starts this side of Bayfield."

The boy's disappointment showed. "How come you're askin'?" the driver asked.

"I need to come in to school from there."

"Oh? Whereabouts?"

"A farm north of the highway."

"Ain't that the Landis place?"

"You know him?"

"I live out that way. You must be the kid helped out with him in the summer. Hey, I heard about you. Name's Wilson," he said, extending his grimy hand. "Wilson Webb. 'Scuse the grease—I work at a garage in between drivin' the bus. You see, I drive my pickup over to Bayfield and park it where the bus run starts. I'd be happy to bring you in from the Piedra if that's what you're askin'— wouldn't mind the company a bit."

Cloyd hurried back to the group home to tell his housemother. She wasn't there. He went to his room. A boy he'd never met before was unpacking a duffel bag and hanging up his clothes in Cloyd's closet. An army cot was set up between the beds. After a long moment of surprise, Cloyd asked him what was going on.

The boy shrugged. "Heard somebody was moving out. You, I guess."

"I didn't hear anything about it."

Cloyd fretted awhile in the living room, then saw Susan James driving up in the van and hurried out to see her. He stood quietly on the lawn and tried to read her face as she walked up. She knew something important.

"Have I got some news for you, Cloyd," she said excitedly.

Cloyd held his breath. He was always afraid of things dropped on him like this.

"The tribe says you can come home now, Cloyd."

"Home," he mumbled.

"White Mesa! They called this morning, Cloyd, and said everything looks a whole lot better at home, so—"

"How do you mean?" he asked guardedly.

"Well, the tribe heard about how hard you've been trying. They want to give you another chance at going to school right there in Blanding. Your grandmother's new job is working out, and your sister's on her way back from Salt Lake. Maybe your grandmother will get her goats back. Everybody's ready for you to come home, Cloyd."

He didn't know what to say. It was everything he'd hoped for all winter. "When?" he asked blankly.

"Right away! Well, tomorrow morning. Did you meet Charlie—in your room?"

Cloyd nodded.

"Sorry about that. When the people down at Towaoc heard about the vacancy, they sent Charlie up even though they were supposed to wait until tomorrow. But you know, there's a waiting list, and they've been desperately trying to find a place for him. . . . Why don't we go over to the hospital so you can say good-bye to Walter?"

Say good-bye to Walter? How could he do that, he asked himself, when the old man was slipping downhill? If he deserted Walter now . . . As much as he wanted to go back to

White Mesa, it wouldn't be right. It was his turn to pay back some of what he'd been given. "I can't go now," he told her. "Maybe after the winter . . ."

"Why not?"

"Walter needs me. He can't go back to the farm unless someone's there to do the chores and take care of—"

"But it's all arranged for him to go to the nursing home as soon as he—"

"He'll die there," Cloyd declared. "He's starting to die now."

She knew as much from visiting Walter herself. She'd been worrying terribly for him, knowing how badly he missed his farm. He'd been there so long he was like an old tree too deeply rooted for transplanting. "Tell me how it would all work, Cloyd. I guess you've got it all figured out."

Cloyd told her about the bus driver. He told her she'd have to get permission from the tribe for him to leave the group home and live with Walter.

"And permission from two school districts," she added. "You'd be out of boundaries. I don't know, Cloyd—it all sounds pretty tricky to me. I don't have any idea if the tribe would ever allow something like that. But then again, they might be able to see what kind of sacrifice you'd be making and why. Are you really sure about it yourself?"

Before he could answer, she told him, "Take a long walk and really think it over. Here's your chance to go home, Cloyd. Then come back and let me know what you've decided. If you want to stay with Walter until he's better, I'll do my best to make it happen."

Cloyd walked down to the river to think, crouched on the bank, and turned it all over in his mind. He saw himself standing at the door to a hospital room, discovering the shell of his father hooked up to a machine, and realizing finally that he didn't have a father. He saw himself finding the bearstone and killing the peach trees and following the old

COTTONWOOD RANCH (detail)
Roger P. Williams
Courtesy of the Artist

man up the Pine River to the mine. He saw himself standing alone atop the Rio Grande Pyramid and realizing a father had come into his life after all. He remembered the look in Blueboy's eye right before he tumbled down the mountain, and he recalled the bear. He'd never forget the bear. . . . *The hurt you get over makes you stronger.* It was all moving in a direction, he decided, making a pattern. And he had to know where it was all leading. If he went home now, he'd never know. It was all part of learning what it meant to live in a good way.

Chapter 22

It was the second Saturday in November, and they were repairing the foundation under the house. They'd started the weekend before. The project wasn't Walter's idea; Cloyd had remembered him worrying about it during the summer and reminded him of it. Walter had to admit it was a bad situation and getting worse. Walls, roof, and all would start to give before long.

Walter still had the cast on his leg, and he knew he couldn't negotiate the basement stairs. Wrapped up in a blanket, he sat in a chair at the top of the landing, where he could see the boy down below. He had to content himself with lending know-how and moral support.

Cloyd was mixing concrete. He'd carried the hundred-pound bags of cement downstairs himself, as well as countless buckets of sand and gravel, and now he was making concrete. It was chilly in the basement, but as long as he was working, he was warm enough in his denim jacket. He was happy taking care of the old man. He'd grown so used to wandering alone in the canyons, wandering alone in the school corridors, having his own private world. Now he wasn't alone anymore.

Cloyd felt strong. He could do whatever he set his mind to. He was never going to give up—he had a life to live. "Maybe it's all you've got," the old man had said. "Might as well make the most of it."

If he ever had any children, he was going to care about them, the way Walter cared. If he ever had a son, he was going to name him Walter. The old man would be dead and buried by then, he realized. It wouldn't matter. He would show them Walter's picture, and one day he would take them up to the meadows of the Pine River.

Cloyd checked the batch of concrete he was mixing. It was just about right. More water would weaken it. He hoped the weather would give them a few days. The snow from the October storm had thawed, leaving the ground unprotected. With the cold air moving in, he worried that the earth was freezing solid at this very moment. They needed the soil outside that broken wall to have some give in it, so there'd be room for the wall to move over. Cloyd had another reason, too, for hoping the ground would keep a few days and he could dig in it. Thinking about his secret reason made him feel good. He wished for a snowstorm that would blanket the ground and keep it warm. Maybe they'd get one—after breakfast he'd seen a thick layer of high clouds advance from the west and cover the sun. A good storm could be on its way. This time, Walter had said, the snow would stick, and winter would have come to stay.

Cloyd poured his concrete into the holes he had dug in the crawl space. Then he troweled the new footers smooth. The work went well, and he was pleased.

So was the old man. "Tomorrow we'll cut those railroad ties so's they fit between our concrete footers and that good wall. Then we'll build a framework between the two walls and jack it tight. With the railroad ties behind it, you know that good wall ain't gonna give. That other'n's gonna have to move over where it belongs."

Cloyd knew the plan by heart. He was pleased that he understood it so well, pleased that he was learning so many new things. When they jacked the framework tight between the two walls, the bulging one would start to give. Every day when he came home from school, he'd go down in the basement and crank the jack a little more. The crack in the wall would close up. When the wall was straight-up-and-down again, they'd simplify the supports that held it.

It was lunchtime, and it was warm in the kitchen with the cookstove fire going. The old man was fixing sandwiches. Walter made up the grocery lists, and Cloyd did the shopping in town. Every few days he'd go to the store during the lunch break at school. He had some friends this year, and sometimes they went with him. The teachers let him keep the groceries in their lounge; they even had a refrigerator for the fresh things. Walter insisted on doing the cooking. Cloyd thought that was fine. The doctor had said Walter needed to be doing things, only nothing strenuous.

On the kitchen table, with Walter's help, Cloyd struggled at writing a letter to his sister and his grandmother. He told them about Walter, how they'd gone into the mountains, that Walter had been hurt, that he was taking care of Walter until he got stronger. He knew Susan James had made sure they'd heard all those things, but he wanted to tell them himself. "I like the mountains, but I miss the desert," he wrote. "It's getting cold here now. Already it snowed once. I feed the horses in the morning, two bales of hay. Pretty soon I will shovel snow off the pond and chop a hole for them to drink. Blueboy is my favorite. He's strong and smart. When I come home, Walter is going to bring Blueboy, too. He's mine to keep."

For dessert they had doughnuts, the store-bought kind caked with powdered sugar. The old man broke one of his long-standing rules by suggesting they eat them in the parlor, where unavoidably the powdered sugar fell to the carpet. "Blends right in,"

ILLUSTRATION FOR THE COVER OF *BEARSTONE*
Patricia Mulvihill
Courtesy of the Artist

Bearstone 731

Walter chuckled. "Reminds me of a joke I'll bet you'd like."

The trace of a smile crossed Cloyd's face. "Oh?" he said, anticipating one of the old man's tall tales.

"This fellow was feeding doughnuts to his horse. Another fellow asks him what for. The first fellow says, 'To find out how many he'd eat before he asked for a cup of coffee.'"

Cloyd flashed a wide smile, and his round face shone like the sun. The old man was holding his breath, his head bobbing up and down, cheeks puffed out, lips drawn tight. Cloyd began to laugh, Walter's breath exploded, and then the old man was laughing too until his ears turned red.

They heard a vehicle pull up outside, and both went to the window to see. A young man was getting out of a white pickup with big red letters on the side.

"Durango Hardware and Nursery," Walter said. "Must be lost." The old man took his jacket from the peg in the mudroom and went outside to see if he could give directions.

The driver had taken off the glove on his right hand to turn the pages of his order book. "Here's your receipt," he said mechanically. He tore out a small yellow page and handed it to the old man. "The seedlings are in the back of the truck."

"Seedlings?" Walter protested.

"All paid for. Twenty-two peach trees. You are Cloyd Atcitty, aren't you?" the young man asked, reaching for his back pocket. "The manager gave me this map."

Cloyd stepped up. "I'm Cloyd Atcitty," he said. "I bought them. It was a surprise," he explained, motioning toward the old man with his lips.

For an instant, Walter's eyes found Cloyd's. The boy was glowing with pleasure.

"I never heard of anybody growing peaches around here," the driver offered skeptically. "Too cold, isn't it?"

"I suppose it is. . . ." Walter admitted, winking at Cloyd. "But we'll sure give it a try."

Your Response

1. Do you think that the novel's ending is realistic? Why or why not?

Recalling

2. How does Cloyd get the injured Walter to a hospital?
3. What choice does Cloyd have to make when the tribe says that he can return home?

Interpreting

4. What incidents near the end of the novel show that Cloyd has changed?
5. How does Cloyd's decision to stay and take care of Walter reflect back to the first chapter of the book?
6. In what ways has Walter become a father to Cloyd?
7. What does Cloyd do that makes him feel closer to his Ute heritage?

Applying

8. Walter says that the hurts you get over make you stronger. Why do you think this is so?

ANALYZING LITERATURE

Understanding Theme

A **theme** is the general idea about life presented through the characters and action in a novel. A theme may be suggested by what happens to the characters. Walter states one theme of the novel when he says that the hurts you get over make you stronger.

1. What evidence for the theme stated by Walter is given in the novel?
2. Below are topics dealt with in the novel. For each one write a complete sentence that expresses a theme of the novel.
   a. revenge
   b. people from different cultural backgrounds
   c. the beliefs of Native Americans
   d. a troubled young person
   e. making sacrifices for others

CRITICAL THINKING AND READING

Evaluating a Novel

Your opinion of a novel depends on the criteria, or standards, you use to evaluate it. For each category listed below, write a statement indicating what your criteria are. For example, for characters, you might say that they should be believable or realistic. After you have listed criteria, rank *Bearstone* on a scale of 1 to 4 in each category, with 1 being excellent; 2, good; 3, fair; and 4, poor.

a. characters   c. setting
b. plot   d. theme

THINKING AND WRITING

Writing About a Decision

Write an evaluation of Cloyd's decision to stay and take care of Walter. What pros and cons did he consider? Would you have made the same decision? Why or why not? Before writing, make a list of the pros and cons that you think are important. When you revise your writing, be sure you have stated and explained your opinion clearly.

LEARNING OPTIONS

1. **Writing.** Read one of Will Hobbs's other novels (listed on page 640). Notice the use of setting in it and find out more about the places described. As an alternative, read another novel about contemporary Native Americans and compare the central character with Cloyd Atcitty. Share your findings in a brief written report.
2. **Community Connections.** Find out more about the care of the elderly in your community. What services are available to help elderly people stay in their own homes? How much do the services cost? Who pays for them? What are local nursing homes like? How much do they cost?

YOUR WRITING PROCESS

WRITING A DESCRIPTIVE LETTER

It's a common dream among immigrants—to see the "old country," the place they or their parents or grandparents have left behind. In *Bearstone* Cloyd Atcitty feels that way about the mountains of Colorado, the home of his Ute ancestors. Imagine that you are Cloyd. You are thrilled at discovering the landscape of your ancestors, and you want to share your excitement with your sister.

> **Focus**
>
> **Assignment:** As Cloyd Atcitty, write a letter to your sister describing one of the landscapes you have seen.
> **Purpose:** To help your sister picture the landscape as you have seen it.
> **Audience:** Your sister.

Prewriting

1. Review the passages that describe the Colorado landscape. Do you want to describe Cloyd's first view of Walter's ranch and the mountains, the landscape on the ride up to the Pride of the West mine, or the vistas Cloyd sees on his solo trip to the Rio Grande Pyramid?

2. Take notes on the landscape. Once you have chosen a landscape to describe, review the section of the novel in which it is described and take notes. Organize your notes in a chart like the following. Leave the third column blank for later work.

> **Student Model**
>
> | Element | Details in Novel | My Own Words |
> |---------|-----------------|--------------|
> | Piedra River | swift, cold; all white in a gorge | |
> | orchard | thick green foliage; trees large, full, lush; branches loaded with fruit; huge boulder in middle | |

3. Find your own words. In the third column of the chart, describe the details in your own words.

Drafting

1. Start by making a personal connection with your reader. A letter is written to just one other person. In that sense, it's like having a conversation. Begin by asking a question or offering some information about yourself.

> **Student Model**
>
> Dear Sis,
> Are you surprised to get a letter from me? Well, I've learned how to read and write at the school here. So I thought it was time I started answering all the letters you've sent me over the years.

2. Add to the information in the chart. Use the chart you made as the basis for your description, but also describe what you did and how you felt in the landscape.

> **Student Model**
>
> The first thing I did when I got to Walter's ranch was run away. (That was the old Cloyd!) To my surprise, I found myself in a peach orchard. It reminded me of home—with one difference. This one got plenty of water and it was thriving. The leaves were thick and bright green, and huge peaches—some as big as your fist—weighed down the branches. It made me homesick, but it also made me angry that white people have all the luck while our grandmother has to work so hard to harvest the puny little peaches she gets.

3. End by inviting a response. You are more likely to get an answer to your letter if you ask a question or invite your reader to comment on something you've written.

Revising and Editing

1. Check the organization of your letter. Read over your letter to make sure that ideas are presented in a logical order and that there are transitions from one paragraph to the next.

2. Recruit a classmate to read your letter. Ask your reader questions like the following:
- Are any parts of the letter unclear?
- What questions do you have about the landscape?

3. Proofread for format. Reread your letter to make sure that it follows the correct format for a personal letter.

Writer's Hint

Events are best organized in chronological order, the order in which they happened. Descriptions of scenes can be organized spatially—from top to bottom, left to right, nearer to farther away—or in the order of importance—with the most important item first or last.

Options for Publishing

- With your classmates create a class mailbox. "Mail" your letter and wait for a reply. Also take a letter from the mailbox and write a reply.
- Help make a class bulletin-board display with all the letters.

Reviewing Your Writing Process

1. What was the most difficult thing about writing from Cloyd's point of view? The easiest?

2. Explain which stage of the writing process was most enjoyable for you: prewriting, drafting, or revising and editing.

YOUR WRITING PROCESS

WRITING A BOOK REVIEW

Thumbs up or thumbs down? That's the question every reviewer has to answer. Is a book worth reading or not—and why? Imagine that you are a book reviewer for a school radio station. Every week you have five minutes of air time to talk about a book and give it either thumbs up or thumbs down.

> **Focus**
>
> **Assignment:** Write a review of a novel for broadcast on a school radio station. Use passages from the novel to back up your opinion.
> **Purpose:** To evaluate the novel and convince listeners either to read it or not to read it.
> **Audience:** Your school community.

Prewriting

1. Establish your standards. In your opinion what makes a good novel? Work with a group of classmates to brainstorm standards for a good novel.

2. Zoom in on story elements. List these story elements: characters, plot, setting, theme, dialogue, and ending. With your group decide what makes each element successful.

3. Rank the novel according to your own standards. Use a scale like the one below to rank the book according to each of your standards.

Standard: Satisfying ending

1	2	3	4
Excellent	Good	Fair	Poor

Then give the novel an overall ranking.

4. Find passages to support your opinions. Unless you back up your general statements with examples from the novel, your audience will have no reason to trust your opinions.

Drafting

1. Grab your listeners' attention. To keep your listeners tuned in, you have to convince them that your review is going to be entertaining as well as informative. How do you do that? Ask a question they will want to answer. Make a provocative statement. Express your strongest opinion.

> **Student Model**
>
> If you like ordinary characters, common plots, and drab settings, stay away from *Bearstone*, by Will Hobbs. This well-written novel is only for those who appreciate a suspenseful plot, well-developed characters, and spectacular settings.

2. Summarize the plot—briefly. Your review won't make sense unless your listeners have some idea of what the novel is about. Don't tell them too much, however.

3. Be selective. Your listeners want to hear your most important raves or gripes about the novel. Pick three or four aspects of the novel to discuss. Mention your standards. Say how you rank the novel on each one and, where appropriate, cite passages to prove your point.

> **Student Model**
>
> If you have ever longed to see the Colorado wilderness, *Bearstone* will take you there. Whether he's describing a peach orchard, a snow-capped peak, or a lightning storm, Will Hobbs knows how to make a setting come alive for readers. Here is how he describes the main character caught in an unexpected storm:
>
> "Lightning broke loose and thunder rumbled, not too far off. A cold wind rushed down from the meadow. He wished he'd worn more than a T-shirt, but he hadn't thought he would be out long. He knew he'd better run for it; the storm was about to break."

Revising and Editing

1. Have someone read your review to you. Listen for places where you can use short, punchy words rather than long ones.

2. Get another opinion. Ask your reader questions like the following:
- Does the first sentence make you want to hear more?
- Are any of the sentences too long?
- Do the passages from the novel support my opinions?

3. Proofread your final copy. Make sure there are no spelling, punctuation, or grammar errors to trip you up as you read your review.

Grammar Tip

Make sure that you use verb tenses consistently. If you start out talking about the novel in the present tense, don't switch to the past tense in the middle of the review.

Options for Publishing

- Read your review aloud to friends or classmates who have not read the book.
- With some of your classmates, make an audio tape with several reviews on it. Lend the tape to classes that have not yet read the novels.
- Make a collection of written reviews into a class book called *Radio Reviews for Reading*.

Reviewing Your Writing Process

1. Was it helpful to work in a group when thinking about standards for judging a good novel? Why or why not?

2. Did you make more revisions after hearing your review read to you or after a peer editor commented on your work? Explain.

HANDBOOK OF THE WRITING PROCESS
Lesson 1: Prewriting

Writing is a process that involves several stages:

1. *Prewriting:* planning your writing
2. *Drafting:* creating a first version, or draft, of your writing
3. *Revising:* making improvements in your draft
4. *Proofreading:* checking for errors in grammar and usage, spelling, punctuation, capitalization, and manuscript form
5. *Publishing,* or *Sharing:* letting others read what you have written

This lesson will teach you the steps of prewriting.

STEP 1: ANALYZE THE SITUATION

To *analyze* something is to divide it into parts, or elements, and then to study these parts. Before writing, you should always analyze the elements of the writing situation in which you find yourself. To do so, ask yourself the following questions:

1. *Topic* (the subject you will be writing about): What exactly are you going to write about? Can you state your subject in a sentence? Is your subject too broad or too narrow?
2. *Purpose* (what you want your writing to accomplish): Do you want your writing to explain? To describe? To persuade? To tell a story? To entertain? What do you want your audience to learn or to understand?
3. *Audience* (the people who will read or listen to your writing): Who is your audience? What might they already know about your subject? What basic facts will you have to provide for them?
4. *Voice* (the way your writing will sound to your reader): What impression do you want to make? Do you want to sound formal or informal? Should you sound cool and reasoned or full of emotion?
5. *Content* (the subject and all the information you will provide about it): How much do you already know about this subject? What else do you need to find out? What libraries can you consult for newspapers, books, magazines, and other resources? Are there people you can ask for information?
6. *Form* (the shape that your writing will take, including its length and its organization): How do you picture your finished work? How long will it be? Will it be one paragraph or several? Will you use a special form like a verse or a drama? In what order will you present your information?

When you begin your prewriting, try to answer these questions. Doing so will help you to clarify your goals. If you are writing a paper for school, your teacher may give you a topic or may ask that the writing take a specific form. However, many decisions about the writing will still be up to you.

STEP 2: MAKE A PLAN

After thinking about the writing situation, you may find that you need more information. If so, you must decide how to gather this information. On the other hand, you may find that you already have too much information—that your topic is too broad. If this is the case, then you must decide how to narrow your topic. If you have the right amount of information but don't know how to present it clearly, you will have to choose a way to organize your information.

STEP 3: GATHER INFORMATION

There are many ways to gather information, to narrow a topic, and to organize ideas. You must find ways that work well for you. The following are some ways that you can try:

1. *Brainstorming:* Discuss the topic with a group of people. Follow these rules in your discussion: Try to generate as many ideas as possible. Do not pause to evaluate your ideas. This can be done later. Do not allow any member of the group to make negative comments about what another member says.

2. *Freewriting:* Write down everything that comes to your mind about the topic. Don't worry about spelling or about writing complete, grammatical sentences. Simply write nonstop for one to five minutes. Then read your freewriting and look for ideas you can use in your first draft.

3. *Clustering:* Write your topic in the middle of a piece of paper and circle it. Then write all the ideas you can think of that relate to your topic in circles around the main topic. Connect your circles with lines that show how your ideas, or subtopics, branch out from your main topic. You may even think of some ideas that branch off from your subtopics. If you need to narrow your topic, you might select one of your subtopics as a new main topic.

4. *Analyzing:* Divide your topic into parts that you can consider separately. Make notes about each part. Then study how the parts are related both to one another and to the main topic.

5. *Questioning:* Make a list of questions about the topic. Begin your questions with words like *who, what, where, when, why,* and *how.* Then answer the questions by doing research to find the information you need.

6. *Using Outside Sources:* Talk to other people about your topic. Conduct formal interviews. Read relevant books, pamphlets, newspapers, magazines, and reference works. Watch movies or television shows or listen to radio programs that deal with your topic.

7. *Making Charts* or *Lists:* Make a list or chart of relevant information. Possibilities include a time line, an ordered list of events, a pros-and-cons chart, a list of reasons, or a list of parts.

Any of these methods for finding information can also be used to identify a topic in the first place.

STEP 4: ORGANIZE YOUR NOTES

Once you have gathered enough information, you will have to organize it. Careful organization will make your writing easy to read and understand. The following methods of organization are common:

1. *Time Order,* or *Chronological Order:* organization in order of occurrence (from earliest to latest, for example)

2. *Spatial Order:* organization by position in space (from left to right, for example)

3. *Degree Order:* organization by size, amount, or intensity (from coldest to warmest, for example)

4. *Priority Order:* organization by importance, value, usefulness, or familiarity (from worst to best, for example)

CASE STUDY: PREWRITING

Pilar's English teacher asked the students in her class to write single paragraphs about their hobbies. Pilar chose to write about reading. Here are her preliminary notes for her paragraph:

- Topic: reading as a hobby

- Purpose: to inform

- Audience: my classmates and teacher
- Voice: informal and probably with some feelings
- Content: not sure. I have so many thoughts and feelings about reading, I don't know what to say.
- Form: single paragraph

Pilar reviewed her notes and decided that she needed to define her purpose more clearly. She decided to try freewriting:

I really enjoy reading—especially about kids my age and families. Some of my friends share my interests, but others prefer fantasy or adventure or travel reading—other friends don't read much. Too bad—they're missing something special. . . .

Pilar read her freewriting and realized that her purpose could be to persuade nonreading classmates that reading is fun. Pilar decided to gather more ideas and information by using the questioning technique:

What kinds of books do I enjoy? Where do I read? Why do I read? How do I read? When do I read? Whose books do I enjoy?

I love stories about kids like me. I usually read on the floor or all cozy in bed. I read for lots of reasons: to find out what other kids' lives are like (seeing how they manage things), for privacy, for company, because a friend has suggested the book, to get out of a grouchy mood, and also because I've liked other things by the writer. I read with or without a snack, with lots of noise or in silence. I usually read before bedtime to relax. I enjoy just about any books about kids.

Pilar looked over her notes and decided that in her paragraph she would first introduce the topic, "Why reading is a pleasurable hobby." Then she would give reasons why she enjoys reading, choosing three reasons and organizing them by degree, from least to most important.

ACTIVITIES AND ASSIGNMENTS

A. Answer the following questions about the case study:

1. Find the section of Pilar's notes in which she analyzed the writing situation. Which parts of her earliest notes needed to be expanded? Which were sufficient?
2. Why did Pilar freewrite? Why did she list questions and answer them?

B. Choose one of the following topics or one of your own: *sports, travel, pets,* or *outer space.* Prepare to write a paragraph about your topic. Follow these steps:

1. Make notes about the topic, purpose, audience, voice, content, and form of your paragraph.
2. Review your notes. Decide on a plan of action. To analyze the writing situation and to gather ideas, use prewriting techniques such as freewriting, clustering, analyzing, questioning, consulting outside sources, and making charts or lists.
3. Organize your notes; then make a rough outline for your paragraph. Your outline should include your main topic and two or three subtopics, or parts of the main topics. Under each subtopic, list specific details that you will include in your writing. Save your prewriting notes in a folder.

Lesson 2: Drafting and Revising

WRITING A DRAFT

Drafting follows prewriting and is the second stage in the writing process. When drafting, you simply write down ideas and information in sentence form. The following are important points to remember about drafting:

1. Write your rough draft slowly or quickly—whichever way works for you. Some writers like to work from detailed, thorough outlines and to write very slowly, correcting and polishing as they go. Other writers prefer to jot down brief outlines, write their rough drafts very quickly, and then go back to make corrections and revisions. Each of these methods is perfectly OK. Only you can decide which approach works best for you.
2. Do not try to make your rough draft a finished product. The main point of a draft is to get your ideas down on paper. Once this is done, you can go back and make improvements. Save concern over spelling, punctuation, and so on for the revision and proofreading stages of the writing process.
3. Refer to your prewriting notes as you draft. Do not ramble on about unrelated subjects—stick to your main topic.
4. Keep your audience and purpose in mind as you write. Try not to speak above or below the heads of your audience. Make sure that the ideas and information that you include are consistent with your purpose.
5. Be flexible. Don't be afraid to set aside earlier ideas if later ones work better. If you have already written part of a draft and a more interesting aspect of your topic comes to mind, use it! Remember, too, that you can always do more prewriting activities to gather more information or to focus your thinking.

6. Write as many rough drafts as you need. After you have written one draft, you might review it and realize that you need to add more information, to change your purpose, or to narrow your focus. If this happens, try some more prewriting activities and then write another draft. When you have a draft you are satisfied with, you are ready to go on to the next stage of the writing process—revising.

REVISING YOUR DRAFT

Revising is the process of reworking what you have written to make it as good as it can be. As you revise, use the Checklist for Revision on the next page. If you answer no to any of the questions on the checklist, then you will have to change, or revise, your draft accordingly.

EDITORIAL SYMBOLS

When you revise a rough draft, use the standard editorial symbols in the chart on the next page.

CASE STUDY: DRAFTING AND REVISING

Pilar used her prewriting notes from the last lesson to begin drafting her paragraph. Here is the beginning of her first rough draft.

> I love reading stories about kids like me for many reasons, and I think you should too. I like the privacy and also because a friend has suggested the book. I especially like to find out about other kids. How they handle their lives.

Pilar stopped writing and looked at her draft. She had given the three reasons she enjoyed reading and now had nothing more to say. She realized that her paragraph would never convince

CHECKLIST FOR REVISION

Topic and Purpose
- ☐ Is my topic clear?
- ☐ Does the writing have a specific purpose?
- ☐ Does the writing achieve its purpose?

Audience
- ☐ Will everything that I have written be clear to my audience?
- ☐ Will my audience find the writing interesting?
- ☐ Will my audience respond in the way I would like?

Voice, Word Choice
- ☐ Is the impression that my writing conveys the one that I intended it to convey?
- ☐ Is my language appropriately formal or informal?
- ☐ Have I avoided vague, undefined terms?
- ☐ Have I used vivid, specific nouns, verbs, and adjectives?
- ☐ Have I avoided jargon that my audience will not understand?
- ☐ Have I avoided clichés?
- ☐ Have I avoided slang, odd connotations, euphemisms, and gobbledygook (except for novelty or humor)?

Content/Development
- ☐ Have I avoided including unnecessary or unrelated ideas?
- ☐ Have I developed my topic completely?
- ☐ Have I supplied examples or details that support the statements that I have made?
- ☐ Are my sources of information unbiased, up-to-date, and authoritative?
- ☐ Are any quotations that I have used verbatim, or word-for-word?

Form
- ☐ Have I followed a logical method of organization?
- ☐ Have I used transitions, or connecting words, to make the organization clear?
- ☐ Does the writing have a clear introduction, body, and conclusion?

SYMBOL	MEANING	EXAMPLE
	move text	She wants / to go also
ℓ or —	delete	Meghan is quite / very happy.
∧	insert	of book / that
⌒	close up; no space	dish washer
⊙	insert period	was free
∧	insert comma	pencils, books / and pens
∨	add apostrophe	childrens books
∨ ∨	add quotation marks	The Raven
∼	transpose	to quickly run
¶	begin paragraph	book. If
/	make lower-case	the President
≡	capitalize	president / Adams

someone that reading was an interesting and fun hobby. Pilar set two goals for her next draft:

1. to keep her purpose more clearly in mind as she wrote, and
2. to give more reasons for her argument, with details to make the reasons persuasive.

Pilar wrote several more drafts of her paragraph. Here is her revised final draft:

Have you considered reading as a hobby?

When you have a free hour alone to relax ~~by yourself you might~~ try reading a good book.

Ask freinds ~~who know you~~ to reccommend

good books they think you'll like, or read

something ~~or other~~ by a Writer you enjoyed in

Find a comfortabel place to read and

school. ~~Get comfy,~~ see what happens.

Here's what happens for me ☉

Reading gives me both privacy and ~~I like the~~

company at the same time. When I'm involved

in a book I'm away from my every day world. I

can discover places, people, and information I

Most of all,

might never otherwise have known. I especially

like finding out about how other ~~kids~~ live their

situations I might find myself in

lifes. I actually learn about ~~real life.~~ And see

ways I might handle my own life. Maybe you'll

for

enjoy reading ~~because of~~ some of the same

reasons I do. Its a pleasure.

ACTIVITIES AND ASSIGNMENTS

A. Answer the following questions about the revised final draft in the case study:

1. Has Pilar corrected all the errors in her draft? Why isn't it necessary for all the errors to be corrected in the revision stage?
2. Why did Pilar delete material in the second and third sentences?
3. Why did Pilar add the sentence "Here's what happens for me"?
4. Why did Pilar delete the phrase "I like the" before the word "company"?
5. Why did Pilar take out the word "kids" in the third from the last sentence?
6. What transitional words did Pilar add to indicate that she was about to give the last reason why she enjoys reading?
7. Why did Pilar replace the words "real life" with other words?
8. What other revisions did Pilar make? Why did she make them?

B. Using your prewriting notes from the last lesson, write the rough draft of a paragraph on your topic. Then revise the draft until you are pleased with it.

Follow these steps for drafting and revising your paragraph:

1. Introduce your topic in a sentence or two.
2. Write the body of your paragraph, referring as necessary to your rough outline and to your prewriting notes. Do not spend time worrying about spelling and mechanics at this stage.
3. Write a conclusion of one or two sentences. In the conclusion, sum up the main idea of your paragraph.
4. Revise your draft, using the Checklist for Revision. Be sure that you can answer yes to every question. If not, use editorial symbols to make the necessary corrections.

Lesson 3: Proofreading and Publishing

PROOFREADING YOUR FINAL DRAFT

Once you have finished revising your rough draft, the next step is to make a clean copy and then proofread it. When you *proofread,* you check for errors in grammar and usage, spelling, punctuation, capitalization, and manuscript form. Use the checklist at right when proofreading.

If your answer to any of the questions in the checklist is no, use editorial symbols to make the necessary corrections on your final draft. Refer to a dictionary, writing textbook, or handbook of style as necessary.

PUBLISHING, OR SHARING YOUR WORK

After proofreading your final, revised draft, you are ready for the final step in the writing process—sharing your work with others. Much of the writing that you do for school will be handed in to your teachers. However, you can share your writing with other people as well. These are some of the many ways in which you can share your work:

1. Share your writing in a small group by reading it aloud or by passing it around for others to read.
2. Read your work aloud to the class.
3. Make copies of your writing for members of your family or for your friends.
4. Display your work on a classroom bulletin board.
5. Save your writing in a folder for later publication. At the end of the year, choose the best pieces from your folder and bind them together. Share the collection with your relatives and friends.
6. Submit your writing to the school literary magazine, or start a literary magazine for your school or for your class.
7. Submit your writing to your school or community newspaper.

CHECKLIST FOR PROOFREADING

Grammar and Usage
☐ Are all of my sentences complete? That is, have I avoided sentence fragments?
☐ Do all of my sentences express only one complete thought? That is, have I avoided run-on sentences?
☐ Do the verbs I have used agree with their subjects?
☐ Have all the words in my paper been used correctly? Am I sure about the meanings of all of these words?
☐ Is the thing being referred to by each pronoun (*I, me, this, each,* etc.) clear?
☐ Have I used adjectives and adverbs correctly?

Punctuation
☐ Does every sentence end with a punctuation mark?
☐ Have I used commas, semicolons, colons, hyphens, dashes, parentheses, quotation marks, and apostrophes correctly?

Spelling
☐ Am I absolutely sure that each word has been spelled correctly?

Capitalization
☐ Have I capitalized any words that should not be capitalized?
☐ Should I capitalize any words that I have not capitalized?

Manuscript Form
☐ Have I indented the first line(s) of my paragraph(s)?
☐ Have I written my name and the page number in the top, right-hand corner of each page?
☐ Have I double spaced the manuscript?
☐ Is my manuscript neat and legible?

---

8. Enter your writing in literary contests for student writers.
9. Submit your writing to a magazine that publishes work by young people.

CASE STUDY: PROOFREADING AND PUBLISHING

After revising her final draft, Pilar made a fresh, clean copy. Then she was ready for the proofreading stage. She read the Checklist for Proofreading on the previous page and applied each question to her revised draft. She found several errors. Pilar's paragraph with the proofreading corrections that she made is in the right column.

Pilar made a clean final copy of her paragraph. Then she shared her paragraph with other students in a small-group discussion.

ACTIVITIES AND ASSIGNMENTS

A. Answer the following questions about the case study:
1. What errors in spelling did Pilar correct during proofreading?
2. What capitalization error did Pilar correct?
3. What run-on sentence did she correct? How did she do this?
4. What punctuation errors did Pilar correct?
5. What error in manuscript form did she correct?
6. Are there any changes that you think should still be made in Pilar's paragraph?

Proofread to correct any errors in your draft. Share the final copy of your paragraph with your family, your teacher, and your classmates.

B. Make a clean copy of your revised draft from the last lesson. Then use the Checklist for Proofreading to check your revised draft. Using editorial symbols, make any necessary corrections on your final draft.

¶ Have you considered reading as a hobby? When you have a free hour alone to relax, try reading a good book. Ask friends to recommend good books they think you'll like, or read something by a writer you enjoyed in school. Find a comfortable place to read, and see what happens. Here's what happens for me: Reading gives me both privacy and company at the same time. When I'm involved in a book, I'm away from my everyday world. I can discover places, people, and information I might never otherwise have known. Most of all, I especially like finding out about how others live their lives. I actually learn about situations I might find myself in and see ways I might handle my own life. Maybe you'll enjoy reading for some of the same reasons I do. It's a pleasure.

HANDBOOK OF GRAMMAR AND REVISING STRATEGIES

STRATEGIES FOR REVISING PROBLEMS IN GRAMMAR AND USAGE
Problems of Sentence Structure

■ Run-on Sentences

GUIDE FOR REVISING: A run-on sentence results when no punctuation or coordinating conjunction separates two or more independent clauses. A run-on sentence also occurs when only a comma is used to join two or more independent clauses.

Strategy 1:	**Create two sentences by using a period to separate independent clauses.**
First Draft	Rikki-tikki-tavi is a curious and self-confident mongoose, he is also fearless in the face of danger.
Revision	Rikki-tikki-tavi is a curious and self-confident mongoose. He is also fearless in the face of danger.

Strategy 2:	**Use a comma and then a coordinating conjunction (*and, but, or, for, yet,* or *so*) to join the two sentences.**
First Draft	Pearl Buck was born in America , her family moved to China when she was very young.
Revision	Pearl Buck was born in America , but her family moved to China when she was very young.
Model From Literature	The other children screamed , and some of them tried to grab at him as he left the hut , but they failed to stop their brother and he was gone. —*Smith, p. 630*

■ Fragments

GUIDE FOR REVISING: A fragment is a group of words that does not express a complete thought. Although a fragment may begin with a capital letter and end with a period, it is only part of a sentence because it lacks a subject, a predicate, or both.

Strategy 1:	**Add a subject when necessary.**
First Draft	Leslie Marmon Silko was raised as a Pueblo Indian. Identifies strongly with this tradition.
Revision	Leslie Marmon Silko was raised as a Pueblo Indian. She identifies strongly with this tradition.
Model From Literature	Santo walked off by himself, clutching the story to his heart like a tangible thing. He went along the winding track to the main road where traffic passed to and from the city. —*Selvon, p. 49*

Strategy 2:	**Add a predicate when necessary.**
First Draft	In Pearl Buck's story "The Old Demon," the main character Mrs. Wang.
Revision	In Pearl Buck's story "The Old Demon," the main character Mrs. Wang values her family and her village.
Model From Literature	Every few steps, the girl, whose name was Sandra, would look at him out of the corner of her eye, . . . —*Soto, p. 71*

Strategy 3:	**Correct a phrase fragment by adding both a subject and a predicate.**
First Draft	After considering the plot, the setting, and the aliens in Asimov's "Hallucination."
Revision	After considering the plot, the setting, and the aliens in Asimov's "Hallucination," our reading group identified the story's theme as the value of courage.
Model From Literature	Through the dark trees, off the trail and down by the stream, a small patch of orange caught his eye. —*Hobbs, p. 691*

Problems of Clarity and Coherence

■ Effective Transitions

GUIDE FOR REVISING: You can help your readers by using transition words and phrases to signal connections and relationships between words, sentences, and paragraphs.

Strategy 1:	**Use transitions to indicate time relationships.**
First Draft	Mother frantically tried to open the attic door, and Mother and Herman shouted.
Revision	Mother frantically tried to open the attic door, and after a while both she and Herman shouted.
Model From Literature	When I stood up, I discovered my legs were shaking. —*Tan, p. 98*

Use transitions to indicate spatial relationships.

First Draft   You may see several paintings by Winslow Homer.

Revision   In the large gallery to the left, you may see several paintings by Winslow Homer.

Model From Literature   The sun was warm on their thawing bodies. Far above, it struck the cliffs and snowfields of the Citadel, so brightly that they had to squint against the glare.   —*Ullman, p. 40*

Strategy 3:   **Use transitions to indicate comparison or contrast.**

First Draft   The Town Mouse in Aesop's fable is willing to accept danger. The Country Mouse prefers safer surroundings.

Revision   The Town Mouse in Aesop's fable is willing to accept danger. The Country Mouse, in contrast, prefers safer surroundings.

Model From Literature   In poetry, one could make use of some simile. . . . To the mathematician, however, similes are of no use.   —*Asimov, p. 387*

■ **Vivid Modifiers**

GUIDE FOR REVISING: Modifiers such as adjectives, adverbs, and prepositional phrases describe subjects, verbs, objects, or other modifiers. Try to make your modifiers as vivid and specific as possible.

Strategy: **Replace vague or abstract modifiers with specific, concrete ones.**

First Draft   Since it was a nice day, I took my dog out.

Revision   Since it was a bright, cold day, I took my golden retriever for a brisk walk around the lake.

Model From Literature   Clad in silver tissue, I / March magnificently by!
                                          —*Stephens, p. 484*

GUIDE FOR REVISING: Personal pronouns must agree with their antecedents in number (singular or plural), person (first, second, or third), and gender (masculine, feminine, or neuter).

Strategy 1:	**Avoid shifts in person. Guard especially against careless use of the second-person pronoun *you* to refer to a third-person antecedent. Whenever you use the pronoun *you*, make sure it refers to the person you are speaking or writing to and not to any other person.**
First Draft	Ernesto Galarza spoke Spanish before he learned English. Miss Ryan was the kind of English teacher you needed in the barrio to learn English well.
Revision	Ernesto Galarza spoke Spanish before he learned English. Miss Ryan was the kind of English teacher he needed in the barrio to learn English well.
Model From Literature	The Moses sole is a flatfish, like the flounder you buy at the market, and it got its name from a traditional story told in Israel. —*Facklam, p. 319*

Strategy 2:	**Check to see that any personal pronoun you use agrees in number (singular or plural) with the noun that it replaces.**
First Draft	At first the local Chinese were not Jade Snow's patrons, since imported porcelain from China satisfied its tastes.
Revision	At first the local Chinese were not Jade Snow's patrons, since imported porcelain from China satisfied their tastes.
Model From Literature	The rattler strikes only for paralyzing and killing its food, and for defense. —*Rawlings, p. 371*

Strategy 3:	**Be sure to use a singular personal pronoun when its antecedent is a singular indefinite pronoun.**
First Draft	Theodore Roethke and William Jay Smith are noted American poets; each has chosen an animal as the subject of their poem.
Revision	Theodore Roethke and William Jay Smith are noted American poets; each has chosen an animal as the subject of his poem.
Model From Literature	Antonio and Felix were well liked and respected. Each had his own loyal following. —*Thomas, p. 86*

GUIDE FOR REVISING: A modifier placed too far away from the word it modifies is called a misplaced modifier. Misplaced modifiers may seem to modify the wrong word in a sentence. Always place a modifier as close as possible to the word it modifies.

Strategy:	**Move the modifying word, phrase, or clause closer to the word it should logically modify.**
First Draft	James Stephens was a poet in a poor neighborhood who grew up in Dublin.
Revision	James Stephens was a poet who grew up in a poor neighborhood of Dublin.
Model From Literature	As we emerged from the forest , we could see two small figures waiting impatiently on the other side of the road . —*Taylor, p. 120*

Problems of Consistency

GUIDE FOR REVISING: Subject and verb must agree in number. A singular subject needs a singular verb, and a plural subject needs a plural verb.

Strategy 1:	**When a word group, such as a subordinate clause or a prepositional phrase, comes between the subject and the verb, the verb must still agree with its subject and not with a noun in the word group.**
First Draft	The experiences of the narrator in Jack Finney's story "The Third Level" is mysterious.
Revision	The experiences of the narrator in Jack Finney's story "The Third Level" are mysterious.
Model From Literature	But the telling of these stories, which came from my mother's lips as naturally as breathing, was not the only way my mother showed herself as an artist. —*Walker, p. 312*

Strategy 2:	Use a singular verb with two or more singular subjects joined by *or* or *nor*. When singular and plural subjects are joined by *or* or *nor*, the verb must agree with the subject closest to it.
First Draft	Neither Margot nor the other children is happy in the sunless world that Ray Bradbury describes.
Revision	Neither Margot nor the other children are happy in the sunless world that Ray Bradbury describes.

Strategy 3:	A compound subject joined by *and* is usually plural and requires a plural verb.
First Draft	Demeter and Persephone was ancient Greek goddesses.
Revision	Demeter and Persephone were ancient Greek goddesses.
Model From Literature	Bennie and Oscar are behind him, followed by Carlos and Elias. —*Chávez, p. 227*

Strategy 4:	Many indefinite pronouns can agree with either a singular or plural verb. The choice depends on the meaning given to the pronoun.
First Draft	Some of the words in James Herriot's "Cat on the Go" is more common in Great Britain than in America.
Revision	Some of the words in James Herriot's "Cat on the Go" are more common in Great Britain than in America.
Model From Literature	All young Winslow wanted to do was fish and draw. —*Levitt, p. 395*

■ Confusion of Adjectives and Adverbs

GUIDE FOR REVISING: Adjectives modify nouns and pronouns. Adverbs modify verbs, adjectives, or other adverbs.

Strategy:	Be careful to make the correct use of troublesome adjective and adverb pairs such as *bad/badly, fewer/less,* and *good/well.*
First Draft	The other children behaved bad to Margot.
Revision	The other children behaved badly to Margot.
Models From Literature	She stroked the little animal for a moment. "Is he badly injured?" —*Herriot, p. 353*
	Look at him, Tudi . . . he looks bad . —*Chávez, p. 216*

First Draft	There are less characters in "Home" than in "Rip Van Winkle."
Revision	There are fewer characters in "Home" than in "Rip Van Winkle."
Models From Literature	Before long, some of the mice and squirrels noticed that there were many fewer of them than there used to be. —*Feinstein, p. 560*
	My three hundred dollars bought less than two hundred in old-style bills, but I didn't care. . . . —*Finney, p. 129*
First Draft	Israel Horovitz has dramatized Dickens's Christmas story good.
Revision	Israel Horovitz has dramatized Dickens's Christmas story well.
Model From Literature	The children were always good during the month of August, especially when it began to get near the twenty-third. —*Hoch, p. 53*

■ Inconsistencies in Verb Tense

GUIDE FOR REVISING: Check to see that you maintain consistent verb tenses from sentence to sentence. Verb tenses should not shift unnecessarily.

Strategy 1:	**Be sure that the main verbs in a single sentence or in a group of related sentences are in the same tense.**
First Draft	Cloyd asked all the Navajos he met if they know a man named Leeno Atcitty.
Revision	Cloyd asked all the Navajos he met if they knew a man named Leeno Atcitty.
Model From Literature	When the mice learned the matter, they gathered by the thousand, eager to return the favor shown them, and visited the elephant herd. —*Ryder, p. 552*

Strategy 2:	**When you want to describe the earlier of two actions that occurred at different times in the past, use a verb in the past perfect tense. This tense is formed with the helping verb _had_ and the past participle of the main verb.**
First Draft	When he took possession of the rich man's land, the stranger began to give it away to the poor.
Revision	When he had taken possession of the rich man's land, the stranger began to give it away to the poor.
Model From Literature	On one weekday morning after Christmas, six inches of new snow had just fallen. We were standing up to our boot tops in snow on a front yard on trafficked Reynolds Street, waiting for cars. —_Dillard, p. 419_

Problems With Incorrect Words or Phrases

■ Nonstandard Pronoun Cases

GUIDE FOR REVISING: Use the nominative case for a personal pronoun that is either the subject of a sentence or a predicate nominative. Use the objective case for a personal pronoun when it is a direct object, an indirect object, or an object of a preposition.

Strategy 1:	**Be sure to identify the case of a personal pronoun correctly when the pronoun is part of a compound subject or a compound object. It is often helpful to reword the sentence in your mind.**
First Draft	The students most interested in haiku were Tamara and me.
Revision	The students most interested in haiku were Tamara and I. [Could be reworded as follows: Tamara and I were the students most interested in haiku.]
Model From Literature	My father had died two years before, leaving us with a few pieces of Sears, Roebuck furniture and not much else, and my mother had taken Doris and me to live with one of her younger brothers. —_Baker, p. 332_

Strategy 2:	Personal pronouns in the possessive case show possession in two ways. Possessive pronouns show possession when they come before nouns. Certain personal pronouns also show possession when used by themselves. Note that these pronouns sometimes have different forms (*mine, yours, his, hers, its, ours, yours, theirs*).
First Draft	My theory is that Sarah Cynthia Sylvia Stout drowned in the garbage. What's your ?
Revision	My theory is that Sarah Cynthia Sylvia Stout drowned in the garbage. What's yours ?
Model From Literature	When I looked up, The lady's eyes met mine , . . . —*Soto, p. 459*

■ Wrong Words or Phrases

GUIDE FOR REVISING: Words or phrases that are suitable in one context may be inappropriate in another.

Strategy 1:	Check to see that you have not mistaken one word for another because they sound alike, are spelled similarly, or are easily confused.
First Draft	Isaac Asimov grew up in a family of Russian emigrants in Brooklyn, New York.
Revision	Isaac Asimov grew up in a family of Russian immigrants in Brooklyn, New York.
Strategy 2:	Be sure that the words and phrases you use express your exact meaning.
First Draft	As a child, Russell Baker hated dealing with magazines.
Revision	As a child, Russell Baker hated selling the *Saturday Evening Post.*

■ Double Negatives

GUIDE FOR REVISING: A double negative is the use of two or more negative words in one clause to express a negative meaning.

Strategy:	Use only one negative word to give a clause or sentence a negative meaning.
First Draft	The quilt in the Smithsonian Institution is not like no other in the world.
Revision	The quilt in the Smithsonian Institution is not like any other in the world.

Problems of Readability

■ **Sentence Variety**

GUIDE FOR REVISING: Varying the length and structure of your sentences will improve your writing and help you to hold your readers' attention.

Strategy 1: **Combine two or more short simple sentences to make a longer simple sentence, a compound sentence, or a complex sentence.**

First Draft Rudyard Kipling received a Nobel Prize in 1907. He was forty-two years old.

Revision Rudyard Kipling received a Nobel Prize in 1907, when he was forty-two years old.

Model From Literature Polishing cloths were also gathered in a gigantic heap in front of the Synagogue, where the important event would take place. —*Bernstein, p. 591*

Strategy 2: **Separate rambling compound or complex sentences into two or more shorter sentences.**

First Draft After participating in World War I, Ernest Hemingway lived in Paris during the 1920's, where he met noted writers such as Ezra Pound and Gertrude Stein, and it was also there that he wrote his first important novels.

Revision After participating in World War I, Ernest Hemingway lived in Paris during the 1920's. There he met noted writers such as Ezra Pound and Gertrude Stein. It was also there that he wrote his first important novels.

Model From Literature When the sun sank, the weasel came down from the hill and all the mice and squirrels walked around him three times. Today a squirrel was the last one to pass the weasel. That was the end of the poor squirrel. —*Feinstein, p. 560*

Strategy 3:	Begin your sentences with different openers: subjects, adjectives and adverbs, phrases, and clauses.
First Draft	Robert Herrick was born in London in 1591. He was a goldsmith's apprentice as a boy. He later became a minister.
Revision	Robert Herrick was born in London in 1591. As a boy, he was a goldsmith's apprentice. Later he became a minister.
Model From Literature	Bright and early the next morning he awoke and went for a walk through the woods. When the mice and squirrels saw him they all fled behind bushes and trees.
	—Feinstein, p. 559

Problems of Conciseness

■ Wordy Phrases

GUIDE FOR REVISING: Wordy phrases and clauses weaken your writing by diminishing the focus and impact of your ideas.

Strategy:	You may be able to eliminate a wordy clause by rewriting the sentence.
First Draft	Frost's "Stopping by Woods on a Snowy Evening," which is a famous poem, has a mysterious ending.
Revision	Frost's "Stopping by Woods on a Snowy Evening" is a famous poem with a mysterious ending.

■ Redundancy

GUIDE FOR REVISING: Redundancy is the unnecessary repetition of an idea. Redundancy makes writing heavy and dull.

Strategy:	Eliminate redundant modifiers in your sentences.
First Draft	A fable is a short, brief story that teaches a lesson.
Revision	A fable is a brief story that teaches a lesson.
First Draft	A legend is a widely told story about the past that people tell everywhere.
Revision	A legend is a widely told story about the past.

Problems of Appropriateness

■ Inappropriate Diction

GUIDE FOR REVISING: There are two levels of standard English usage: formal English and informal English. The problem of inappropriate diction results when words or phrases that are generally accepted in informal conversation or writing are included in formal writing or when overly formal language is used in informal writing.

Strategy:	**Choose the appropriate level of diction based on your subject, audience, and writing occasion.**
First Draft	Salutations, Rena! Did you conclude that "Hallucination" was compatible with your taste in short stories?
Revision	Hi, Rena! Did you like "Hallucination"?
Model From Literature	"That was the luckiest time of all, Tee Baby. It got me acquainted with Mr. Amos Pickens, and if that ain't luck, what could it be!" —*Clifton, p. 80*

■ Clichés and Slang

GUIDE FOR REVISING: Clichés are expressions that were once fresh and vivid but are now stale. People often use clichés in casual conversation, but in writing expressions like *busy as a bee* or *sharp as a tack* sound vague and tired. Like cliché, slang is often used in conversation. Slang words and expressions tend to be popular only for a short time among certain groups of people. In formal writing slang should be avoided.

Strategy 1:	**Replace clichés with clear, direct words or with a fresh expression of your own.**
First Draft	The fog was as thick as pea soup.
Revision	The fog was so thick that we could not continue our journey.
Model From Literature	Fog hanging like old Coats between the trees. . . . —*Soto, p. 459*

Strategy 2:	**Replace slang words and expressions with clear, direct words.**
First Draft	Dickinson thinks that being a public dude or a celeb is a bummer.
Revision	Dickinson thinks that being public or famous is a burden.

SUMMARY OF GRAMMAR

Nouns A **noun** is the name of a person, place, or thing.

A **common noun** names any one of a type of people, place, or thing. A **proper noun** names a specific person, place, or thing.

Common nouns	Proper nouns
writer	Mari Sandoz, O. Henry
city	Los Angeles, Atlantic City

Pronouns **Pronouns** are words that stand for nouns or for words that take the place of nouns.

Personal pronouns refer to (1) the person speaking, (2) the person spoken to, or (3) the person, place, or thing spoken about.

	Singular	Plural
First Person	I, me, my, mine	we, us, our, ours
Second Person	you, your, yours	you, your, yours
Third Person	he, him, his, she, her, hers, it, its	they, them, their, theirs

Drink, *my* bull, from the river; *I* am here/to guard *you* with *my* spear. —*Dinka traditional p. 464*
He arose and realized that the others had left *him* all by himself.
  —*from the Hopi, trans. by Malotki, p. 569*

Demonstrative pronouns direct attention to specific people, places, or things.
this lamp   *these* rugs   *that* chair   *those* tables

An **interrogative pronoun** is used to begin a question.
"*What* is this?" cried the neighbor, pulling a small brass pot from inside the caldron.
  —*from Syria, trans. by Bushnaq, p. 587*
Who is the author of "Circle of the Seasons"?

Indefinite pronouns refer to people, places, or things, often without specifying which ones.
Many of the players were tired.
Everyone bought *something.*

Verbs A **verb** is a word that expresses time while showing an action, a condition, or the fact that something exists.

An **action verb** is a verb that tells what action someone or something is performing.

Bears *store* fat
Chipmunks *gather* nuts. . . .
  —*Giovanni, "Winter," p. 502*

A **linking verb** is a verb that connects a word at or near the beginning of a sentence with a word at or near the end.

By day the bat *is* cousin to the mouse.
  —*Roethke, p. 472*
Her eyes *grew* wide for a moment. . . .
  —*Noyes, p. 442*

Helping verbs are verbs that can be added to another verb to make a single verb phrase.
All day yesterday they *had read* in class about the sun. —*Bradbury, p. 105*

Adjectives An **adjective** is a word used to describe a noun or pronoun or to give a noun or pronoun a more specific meaning. Adjectives answer these questions:

What kind?	*red* rose, *small* bowl
Which one?	*this* spoon, *those* pots
How many?	*four* hours, *many* tomatoes
How much?	*no* rain, *little* money

The articles *the, a,* and *an* are adjectives. *An* is used before a word beginning with a vowel sound.

A noun may sometimes be used as an adjective.
family home   *science* fiction

Adverbs An **adverb** is a word that modifies a verb, an adjective, or another adverb. Adverbs answer the questions *Where? When? In what manner? To what extent?*

He ran *outside.* (modifies verb *ran*)
She *never* wrote us. (modifies verb *wrote*)
Close the window *quickly.* (modifies verb *close*)
We were *very* sad. (modifies adjective *sad*)
They left *too* suddenly. (modifies adverb *suddenly*)

Prepositions A **preposition** is a word that relates the noun or pronoun following it to another word in the sentence.

across the road	*near* the corner
except me	*during* the show
at school	*with* them

Conjunctions A **conjunction** is a word used to connect other words or groups of words.

Coordinating conjunctions connect similar kinds or groups of words.
lions *and* tigers   small *but* strong

Correlative conjunctions are used in pairs to connect similar words or groups of words.

both Keith *and* Chuck   *neither* they *nor* I

Interjections   An **interjection** is a word that expresses feeling or emotion and functions independently of a sentence.

"Gugh," gasped Briggs, floundering in his camphor.   *—Thurber, p. 366*

"Oh, no. Spirit! *Oh,* no, no!"   *—Horovitz, p. 297*

Sentences   A **sentence** is a group of words with two main parts: a complete subject and a complete predicate. Together these parts express a complete thought.

The use of this poison as a shark repellent was an exciting idea.   *—Facklam, p. 320*

A fragment is a group of words that does not express a complete thought.

Into the room quietly.

Strolled until night came.

Subject-Verb Agreement   To make a subject and verb agree, make sure that both are *singular* or both are *plural.* Two or more singular subjects joined by *or* or *nor* must have a singular verb. When singular and plural subjects are joined by *or* or *nor*, the verb must agree with the closest subject.

He is at the door.

They drive home every day.

Jeff or *Sam is* absent.

Both *pets are* hungry.

Either the *chairs* or the *table is* on sale.

Neither the *tree* nor the *shrubs were* in bloom.

In winter, in the snow, there *was* neither *baseball* nor *football.*   *—Dillard, p. 419*

Phrases   A **phrase** is a group of words, without a subject and verb, that functions in a sentence as one part of speech.

A **prepositional phrase** is a group of words that includes a preposition and a noun or pronoun.

near the town   with them

inside our house   beneath the floor

An **adjective phrase** is a prepositional phrase that modifies a noun or pronoun by telling what kind or which one.

Friends *in the barrio* explained that the director was called a principal, . . .   *—Galarza, p. 337*

An **adverb phrase** is a prepositional phrase that modifies a verb, an adjective, or an adverb by pointing out where, when, in what manner, or to what extent.

I had not yet put the sheet *on him.* *—Téllez, p. 3*

An **appositive phrase** is a noun or pronoun with modifiers, placed next to a noun or pronoun to add information and details.

As a freelance illustrator for *Harper's Weekly, America's most important news magazine,* he was considered one of the country's finest woodblock engravers.   *—H. N. Levitt, p. 395*

A **participial phrase** is a participle modified by an adjective or adverb phrase or accompanied by a complement. The entire phrase acts as an adjective.

Taking the staff from him, the man pulled up the line of clothes, untied the knots and shook them out.   *—Ullman, p. 39*

An **infinitive phrase** is an infinitive with modifiers, complements, or a subject, all acting together as a single part of speech.

He came into the room *to shut the windows* while we were still in bed and I saw he looked ill.   *—Hemingway, p. 197*

Clauses   A **clause** is a group of words with its own subject and verb.

An **independent clause** can stand by itself as a complete sentence.

A **subordinate clause** cannot stand by itself as a complete sentence; it can only be part of a sentence.

An **adjective clause** is a subordinate clause that modifies a noun or pronoun by telling *what kind* or *which one.*

He was a descendant of the Van Winkles *who figured so gallantly in the chivalrous days of Peter Stuyvesant,* . . .   *—Irving, p. 134*

Subordinate **adverb clauses** modify verbs, adjectives, or adverbs by telling *where, when, in what manner, to what extent, under what condition,* or *why.*

"When they get married, I will be able to pay back the five gulden."   *—Singer, p. 150*

SUMMARY OF CAPITALIZATION AND PUNCTUATION

CAPITALIZATION

Capitalize the first word in sentences.

Bright and early the next morning he awoke and went for a walk through the woods.
—*Feinstein, p. 559*

Capitalize all proper nouns and adjectives.

Amy Tan	Amazon River	Thanksgiving Day
Florida	October	Italian

Capitalize a person's title when it is followed by the person's name or when it is used in direct address.

Doctor   Chief Dan George   Dame Van Winkle

Capitalize titles showing family relationships when they refer to a specific person, unless they are preceded by a possessive noun or pronoun.

Aunt Sarah Shoaf   Buddy's uncle

Capitalize the first word and all other key words in the titles of books, periodicals, poems, stories, plays, paintings, and other works of art.

Bearstone   *The Flying Tortilla Man*
"All Summer in a Day"   "Season at the Shore"

Capitalize the first word and all nouns in letter salutations and the first word in letter closings.

Dear Mr. Herriot,   Yours truly,

PUNCTUATION

End Marks   Use a **period** to end a declarative sentence, an imperative sentence, and most abbreviations.

They returned to the pueblo for the ceremonials and special days.   —*Silko, p. 167*
"Gentry, call a meeting."   —*Asimov, p. 193*
It takes years of study and research to complete a Ph.D.   —*Facklam, p. 322*

Use a **question mark** to end a direct question or an incomplete question in which the rest of the question is understood.

Has spring come indeed?   —*Bashō, p. 480*
"Go ahead, let her talk. What about it? Explain what?"   —*Serling, p. 253*

Use an **exclamation mark** after a statement showing strong emotion, an urgent imperative sentence, or an interjection expressing strong emotion.

"It's Oscar—he's gone!"   —*Herriot, p. 355*
"Get me out of this!"   —*Thurber, p. 365*
"Bah! Humbug!"   —*Horovitz, p. 266*

Commas   Use a **comma** before the conjunction to separate two independent clauses in a compound sentence.

Stories of his doings came to us from many sources, for he was still easily recognized by the dark patch on his shoulders.   —*Annixter, p. 64*

Use commas to separate three or more words, phrases, or clauses in a series.

There were two filling stations at the intersection with Union Avenue, as well as an A&P, a fruit stand, a bakery, a barber shop, Zuccarelli's drugstore, and a diner shaped like a railroad car.
—*Baker, p. 332*
The air was crystal, the sky was aquamarine, and the far horizon of palms and oaks lay against the sky.   —*Rawlings, p. 371*

Use commas to separate adjectives of equal rank. Do not use commas to separate adjectives that must stay in a specific order.

He did *big, masculine* pictures of hunting and fishing. . . .   —*Levitt, p. 397*
They were also hard workers, one wax child being able to do the work of at least two ordinary children.   —*Smith, p. 629*

Use a comma after an introductory word, phrase, or clause.

"Grandmother, you must go in," Little Pig's wife's soft voice said.   —*Buck, p. 157*
In his corner, Antonio was doing what all fighters do when they are hurt.   —*Thomas, p. 90*
By the time Stacey and I arrived at the house, Mr. Andersen's car was already parked in the dusty drive.   —*Taylor, p. 115*

Use commas to set off parenthetical and nonessential expressions.

For instance, the sum of the first two terms in the Zeno series above is 11. . . .   —*Asimov, p. 392*

Use commas with places and dates made up of two or more parts.

Ray Bradbury was born in *Waukegan, Illinois.*
On *July 20, 1969,* American astronauts first set foot on the moon.

Use commas after items in addresses, after the salutation in a personal letter, after the closing in all letters, and in numbers of more than three digits.

Linden Lane, Durham, N.C.   My dear Cal,
Sincerely yours,   1,372,597

Use a comma to set off a direct quotation.

"Wait, Commander," said Sam, in a strangled voice.   —*Asimov, p. 191*

Semicolons   Use a semicolon to join independent clauses that are not already joined by a conjunction.

When Santo heard the story he was amazed; he wanted to know if the children didn't have to pay for the toys.   —*Selvon, p. 45*

Use semicolons to avoid confusion when independent clauses or items in a series already contain commas.

Your response with your own mind and body and memory and emotions gives the poem its ability to work its magic; if you give to it, it will give to you, and give plenty.   —*Dickey, p. 375*

Colons   Use a colon before a list of items following an independent clause.

The following words are examples of onomatopoeia: *buzz, hiss, jingle,* and *cluck.*

Use a colon in numbers giving the time, in salutations in business letters, and in labels used to signal important ideas.

4:30 A.M.   Dear Ms. Landis:
Danger: Landslide Area Ahead

Quotation Marks   A **direct quotation** represents a person's exact speech or thoughts and is enclosed in quotation marks.

In 1910, just before he died, he wrote in a letter, "All is lovely outside my house and inside my house and myself."   —*Levitt, p. 398*

An **indirect quotation** reports only the general meaning of what a person said or thought and does not require quotation marks.

When Humaweepi asked him what they would eat, the old man had waved his hand at the sky and earth around them.   —*Silko, p. 168*

Always place a comma or a period inside the final quotation mark of a direct quotation.

"It's no good, Triss," I said gently. "It's got to be done."   —*Herriot, p. 352*

Place a question mark or exclamation mark inside the final quotation mark if the end mark is part of the quotation; if it is not part of the quotation, place it outside the final quotation mark.

As Rikki-tikki went up the path, he heard his "attention" notes like a tiny dinner gong; and then the steady "*Ding-dong-tock!* Nag is dead—dong! Nagaina is dead *Ding-dong-tock!*"
     —*Kipling, p. 22*

Does that poem by Robert Frost start with the line, "I'm going out to clean the pasture spring"?

Underline the titles of long written works, movies, television and radio shows, lengthy works of music, paintings, and sculptures.

<u>A Christmas Carol</u>   <u>Star Trek</u>   <u>The Mona Lisa</u>

Use quotation marks around the titles of short written works, episodes in a series, songs, and titles of works mentioned as parts of collections.

"The Old Demon"   "Cat on the Go"
"Let's Steal the Moon"   "Annabel Lee"

Hyphens   Use a hyphen with certain numbers, after certain prefixes, with two or more words used as one word, and with a compound modifier that comes before a noun.

fifty-four   self-employed
daughter-in-law   happy-go-lucky friend

Apostrophes   Add an apostrophe and *-s* to show the possessive case of most singular nouns.

Aesop's fables   the author's story
Dickens's novels

Add an apostrophe to show the possessive case of plural nouns ending in *-s* and *-es.*

the bats' squeaks   the Brookses' home

Add an apostrophe and *-s* to show the possessive case of plural nouns that do not end in *-s* or *-es.*

the women's hats   the mice's whiskers

Use an apostrophe in a contraction to indicate the position of the missing letter or letters.

They're never opened; you just put blank paper in the envelope.   —*Finney, p. 130*

GLOSSARY OF COMMON USAGE

accept, except
Accept is a verb that means "to receive" or "to agree to." *Except* is a preposition that means "other than" or "leaving out." Do not confuse these two words.
> The Amigo brothers *accepted* the challenge and prepared for the match.
> All the children *except* Margot played.

affect, effect
Affect is normally a verb meaning "to influence" or "to bring about a change in." *Effect* is usually a noun, meaning "result."
> The unexpected appearance of Bandit deeply *affects* Colin.
> In James Thurber's essay, the collapse of the bed has many humorous *effects*.

among, between
Among is usually used with three or more items. *Between* is generally used with only two items.
> "Zoo" was *among* the stories I liked best.
> There was a special relationship *between* Colin and Bandit in "Last Cover."

amount, number
Amount refers to a mass or a unit, whereas *number* refers to individual items that can be counted. Therefore, *amount* generally appears with singular nouns, and *number* appears with plural nouns.
> To start her career as an artist, Jade Snow Wong needed a huge *amount* of determination.
> In "The Night the Bed Fell," the family members draw a *number* of mistaken conclusions.

bad, badly
Use the predicate adjective *bad* after linking verbs such as *feel, look,* and *seem.* Use *badly* whenever an adverb is required.
> At the beginning of "Amigo Brothers," Felix and Antonio feel *bad* about the upcoming fight.
> When Charley finds he's stepped back in time to 1894, he is *badly* confused at first.

because of, due to
Use *due to* if it can logically replace the phrase *caused by.* In introductory phrases, however, *because of* is better usage than *due to.*
> Washington Irving's popularity was largely *due to* his use of setting to re-create early America.
> *Because of* Mrs. Wang's belief that people should

care for one another, she makes the ultimate sacrifice for her family and village.

beside, besides
Do not confuse these two prepositions, which have different meanings. *Beside* means "at the side of" or "close to." *Besides* means "in addition to."
> In Hemingway's "A Day's Wait," the father sits *beside* his son to comfort him.
> No one *besides* me had read Hemingway's *The Old Man and the Sea*.

can, may
The verb *can* generally refers to the ability to do something. The verb *may* generally refers to permission to do something.
> Anansi *may* tell all stories if he *can* deliver the hornets, the python, and the leopard to Nyame, the Sky God.

compare, contrast
The verb *compare* can involve both similarities and differences. The verb *contrast* always involves differences. Use *to* or *with* after *compare.* Use *with* after *contrast.*
> Stan *compared* Nikki Giovanni's "Winter" *with* Robert Frost's "Stopping by Woods on a Snowy Evening."
> Utzel's life at the end of Singer's story *contrasts with* his situation at the beginning.

different from, different than
Different from is generally preferred over *different than.*
> Similes are *different from* metaphors because similes use the words *like* or *as* to make comparisons.

farther, further
Use *farther* when you refer to distance. Use *further* when you mean "to a greater degree or extent" or "additional."
> The speaker in Robert Frost's poem is tempted to ride *farther* into the snowy woods.
> The reference to his age *further* irritates Father William.

fewer, less
Use *fewer* for things that can be counted. Use *less* for amounts or quantities that cannot be counted.
> Which animals have *fewer* fans: sharks or rattlesnakes?
> Ordinary people have *less* understanding of nature than the warrior priest Humaweepi has.

good, well

Use the predicate adjective *good* after linking verbs such as *feel, look, smell, taste,* and *seem.* Use *well* whenever you need an adverb.

> The speaker in "Oranges" *feels good* about his meeting with the girl.
> Rudyard Kipling *describes* Indian animals *well.*

hopefully

You should not loosely attach this adverb to a sentence, as in "Hopefully, the rain will stop by noon." Rewrite the sentence so *hopefully* modifies a specific verb. Other possible ways of revising such sentences include using the adjective *hopeful* or a phrase like *everyone hopes that.*

> James Dickey writes *hopefully* about everyone's ability to enjoy poetry.
> At the end of "Hallucination," Dr. Gentry seems *hopeful* about the future of the project.

its, it's

Do not confuse the possessive pronoun *its* with the contraction *it's,* standing for "it is" or "it has."

> If a rattler thinks *it's* not seen, it will lie quietly without revealing *its* location.

lay, lie

Do not confuse these verbs. *Lay* is a transitive verb meaning "to set or put something down." Its principal parts are *lay, laying, laid, laid. Lie* is an intransitive verb meaning "to recline." Its principal parts are *lie, lying, lay, lain.*

> The seal *lays* its flipper on a rock.
> Sam McGee *lies* down in his sleigh for the last time.

leave, let

Be careful not to confuse these verbs. *Leave* means "to go away" or "to allow to remain." *Let* means "to permit."

> After the fox had eaten the cheese, he *left* the crow sitting forlorn and hungry in the tree.
> The aliens *let* the people destroy themselves.

like

Like is a preposition that usually means "similar to" or "in the same way as." *Like* should always be followed by an object. Do not use *like* before a subject and a verb. Use *as* or *that* instead.

> A story *like* "A Boy and a Man" by James Ramsay Ullman uses suspense to hold the reader's interest.
> The journey of Icarus does not end *as* he expected.

loose, lose

Loose can be either an adjective (meaning "unattached") or a verb (meaning "to untie"). *Lose* is always a verb (meaning "to fail to keep, have, or win").

> There is often only a *loose* connection between the speaker of a poem and the poem's author; sometimes there is no link whatever between the two.
> When no one recognizes him, Rip Van Winkle feels that he is *losing* his mind.

many, much

Use *many* to refer to a specific quantity. Use *much* for an indefinite amount or for an abstract concept.

> Winslow Homer painted *many* Civil War scenes.
> Gwendolyn Brooks has won *much* praise for her poems and stories.

of, have

Do not use *of* in place of *have* after auxiliary verbs like *would, could, should, may, might,* or *must.*

> Russell Baker writes that his lack of gumption *must have* saddened his mother.

raise, rise

Raise is a transitive verb that usually takes a direct object. *Rise* is intransitive and never takes a direct object.

> Miss Hopley *raises* Ernesto's sense of self-esteem.
> Rip rubs his eyes, *rises* from the ground, and looks around for his gun.

set, sit

Do not confuse these verbs. *Set* is a transitive verb meaning "to put (something) in a certain place." Its principal parts are *set, setting, set, set. Sit* is an intransitive verb meaning "to be seated." Its principal parts are *sit, sitting, sat, sat.*

> The speaker *sets* the planks in the furnace.
> Mama, Maud Martha, and Helen *sit* on the porch in their rocking chairs.

than, then

The conjunction *than* is used to connect the two parts of a comparison. Do not confuse *than* with the adverb *then,* which usually refers to time.

> Rena liked "The Pointing Finger" more *than* "The Wicked Weasel."
> Robert Service grew up in Scotland and *then* moved to Canada at the age of twenty.

that, which, who

Use the relative pronoun *that* to refer to things or people. Use *which* only for things and *who* only for people.

> The season *that* E. E. Cummings describes is spring.
>
> Lyric poems, *which* express personal emotions, are often brief.
>
> One writer *who* has vividly described the experiences of African Americans is Alice Walker.

their, there, they're

Do not confuse the spelling of these three words. *Their* is a possessive adjective and always modifies a noun. *There* is usually used either at the beginning of a sentence or as an adverb. *They're* is a contraction for *they are.*

> The family members in Gwendolyn Brooks's short story are extremely anxious about *their* home.
>
> For most people, *there* are few creatures more terrifying than sharks.
>
> Ron and Nan are in the class production of *The Monsters Are Due on Maple Street; they're* rehearsing right now in the auditorium.

to, too, two

Do not confuse the spelling of these words. *To* is a preposition that begins a prepositional phrase or an infinitive. *Too,* with two o's, is an adverb and modifies adjectives and other adverbs. *Two* is a number.

> Jade Snow Wong paid constant attention *to* her kiln.
>
> Josh thought that his paper on *A Christmas Carol* was *too* short, so he added another paragraph.

> *Two* poems that Thelma especially liked were Theodore Roethke's "The Bat" and Nikki Giovanni's "Winter."

unique

Because *unique* means "one of a kind," you should not use it carelessly to mean "interesting" or "unusual." Avoid such illogical expressions as *most unique, very unique,* and *extremely unique.*

> Pearl Buck's forty years in China gave her a *unique* insight into Chinese customs and traditions.

when, where, why

Do not use *when, where,* or *why* directly after a linking verb such as *is.* Reword the sentence.

> Faulty: Suspense is *when* an author increases the reader's tension.
>
> Revised: An author uses suspense to increase the reader's tension.
>
> Faulty: Algeria is *where* the fable "How the Animals Kept the Lions Away" is told.
>
> Revised: The fable "How the Animals Kept the Lions Away" is told in Algeria.

who, whom

In formal writing remember to use *who* only as a subject in clauses and sentences and *whom* only as an object.

> Vachel Lindsay, *who* believed that poetry should be heard rather than read, used strong rhythms.
>
> Langston Hughes, *whom* we discussed yesterday, was a leader of an important cultural movement during the 1920's called the Harlem Renaissance.

HANDBOOK OF LITERARY TERMS AND TECHNIQUES

ALLITERATION   *Alliteration* is the repetition of initial consonant sounds. Writers use alliteration to create musical effects and to draw attention to certain words or ideas. Shel Silverstein uses alliteration for humorous effect in the title of his poem "*Sarah Cynthia Sylvia Stout,*" on page 451. In the following lines from "Who Has Seen the Wind," Christina Rossetti uses alliteration to imitate the sound of the wind:

> Who *h*as seen the wind
> Neither you nor I:
> But *wh*en the trees bow down their heads
> The *w*ind is passing by.

In "The Highwayman," on page 437, Alfred Noyes uses alliteration to imitate the sound of horseshoes on a stone pavement:

> Over the *c*obbles he *cl*attered and
>   *cl*ashed in the dark innyard.

ALLUSION   An *allusion* is a reference to a well-known person, place, event, literary work, or work of art. Understanding what a writer is saying often depends on recognizing allusions. E. E. Cummings's "goat-footed balloonman" in the poem "in Just-," on page 500, is an allusion to Greek myths about the god Pan. Pan was a goat-footed god associated with spring.

ANAPEST   See *Meter.*

ANECDOTE   An *anecdote* is a brief story about an interesting, amusing, or strange event. Writers tell anecdotes for specific reasons. For example, in "Cat on the Go," on page 351, James Herriot tells several anecdotes about the character named Oscar. Herriot tells these anecdotes to amuse the reader and to reveal Oscar's unusual personality.

ANTAGONIST   An *antagonist* is a character or force in conflict with a main character, or protagonist. In "Rikki-tikki-tavi," on page 13, there are two antagonists, the cobras Nag and Nagaina. The protagonist is the mongoose, Rikki.
See *Conflict* and *Protagonist.*

ATMOSPHERE   See *Mood.*

AUTOBIOGRAPHY   *Autobiography* is a form of nonfiction in which a person tells his or her own life story. This text contains several excerpts from autobiographies, including the selections from Ernesto Galarza's *Barrio Boy,* on page 337, and from Jade Snow Wong's *No Chinese Stranger,* "A Time of Beginnings," on page 343.

Because autobiographies are about real people and events, they are a form of nonfiction. The best autobiographies contain many elements of short stories, including plot, setting, and characters. Most autobiographies, including *Barrio Boy,* are written in the first person. However, a few autobiographies, like *Fifth Chinese Daughter,* are written in the third person.
See *Biography, Nonfiction,* and *Point of View.*

BALLAD   A *ballad* is a songlike poem that tells a story, often one dealing with adventure and romance. Most ballads are written in four- to six-line stanzas and have regular rhythms and rhyme schemes. A ballad often features a refrain—a regularly repeated line or group of lines.

The following stanza is from the traditional English ballad "Willie O'Winsbury":

> The king has called on his merry men all,
> By thirty and by three,
> Saying, "Fetch me this Willie O'Winsbury,
> For hanging he shall be."

Originally, ballads were not written down. They were composed orally and then sung. As these early *folk ballads* passed from singer to singer, they often changed dramatically. As a result, folk ballads usually exist in many different forms.

Many writers of the modern era have used the ballad form to create *literary ballads*—written imitations of folk ballads. The influence of the ballad tradition can be seen in Alfred Noyes's "The Highwayman," on page 437. While Noyes's poem is not written in typical ballad form, it does tell a story of adventure in rhyming stanzas.
See *Oral Tradition* and *Refrain.*

BIOGRAPHY   *Biography* is a form of nonfiction in which a writer tells the life story of another person. Examples from the text include "Eugenie Clark and the Sleeping Sharks," on page 319, and "Winslow Homer: America's Greatest Painter," on page 395. Because biographies deal with real people and real events, they are classified as nonfiction.
See *Autobiography* and *Nonfiction.*

BLANK VERSE   *Blank verse* is poetry written in unrhymed iambic pentameter lines. The following lines from Robert Frost's "Birches" are written in blank verse:

> When I see birches bend to left and right
> Across the lines of straighter darker trees,
> I like to think some boy's been swinging them.

See *Meter.*

CHARACTER   A *character* is a person or animal who takes part in the action of a literary work. The *main character* is the most important character in a story, poem, or play. A *minor character* is one who takes part in the action but who is not the focus of attention. In Pearl Buck's "The Old Demon," on page 155, the main character is Mrs. Wang. Her grandson and his wife are minor characters.

Characters are sometimes classified as flat or round. A *flat character* is one-sided and often stereotypical. A *round character,* on the other hand, is fully developed and exhibits many traits—often both faults and virtues. In O. Henry's "The Ransom of Red Chief," on page 25, Sam, Bill, and Red Chief are flat characters. In Washington Irving's "Rip Van Winkle," on page 133, the title character is round, or fully developed.

Characters can also be classified as dynamic or static. A *dynamic character* is one who changes in the course of the work. A *static character* is one who does not change. Rip Van Winkle is a dynamic character. Sam, Bill, and Red Chief are static characters.
See *Characterization, Hero/Heroine,* and *Motivation.*

CHARACTERIZATION   *Characterization* is the act of creating and developing a character. Writers use two major methods of characterization—direct and indirect.

When describing a character *directly,* a writer simply states the character's traits, or characteristics. In "Song of the Trees," on page 111, Mildred Taylor describes Stacey directly, saying, "Stacey thought of himself as the man of the house . . . "

When describing a character *indirectly,* a writer depends on the reader to draw conclusions about the character's traits. Sometimes the writer describes the character's appearance, actions, or speech. At other times the writer tells what other participants in the story say and think about the character. The reader then draws his or her own conclusions.

See *Character* and *Motivation*.

CINQUAIN See *Stanza.*

CLIMAX See *Plot.*

CONCRETE POEM A *concrete poem* is one with a shape that suggests its subject. The poet arranges the letters, punctuation, and lines to create an image, or picture, on the page. William Jay Smith's "Seal," on page 477, is a concrete poem. Its swirling shape suggests the form of a seal's body and the way the seal moves.

CONFLICT A *conflict* is a struggle between opposing forces. Conflict is one of the most important elements of stories, novels, and plays because it causes the action.

There are two kinds of conflict: external and internal. An *external conflict* is one in which a character struggles against some outside force. For example, in "A Boy and a Man," on page 37, the character Rudi struggles against nature to save the life of a man who has fallen into a crevasse.

An *internal conflict* is one that takes place within the mind of a character. The character struggles to make a decision, take an action, or overcome a feeling. For example, in "A Day's Wait," on page 197, the character Schatz struggles with his feelings of fear and despair because he believes he is dying.

See *Plot.*

COUPLET See *Stanza.*

DACTYL See *Meter.*

DENOUEMENT See *Plot.*

DESCRIPTION A *description* is a portrait, in words, of a person, place, or object. Descriptive writing uses images that appeal to the five senses—sight, hearing, touch, taste, and smell. See *Image.*

DEVELOPMENT See *Plot.*

DIALECT A *dialect* is the form of a language spoken by people in a particular region or group. The English language is divided into many dialects. British English differs from American English. The English spoken in Boston differs from that spoken in Charleston, Chicago, Houston, or San Francisco. This variety adds richness to the language. Dialects differ in pronunciation, grammar, and word choice.

Writers use dialects to make their characters seem realistic. In the following selection from Lucille Clifton's "The Luckiest Time of All," on page 79, the character speaking uses a dialect from the rural southern United States:

> It was just this time, spring of the year, and me and my best friend Ovella Wilson, who is now gone, was goin to join the Silas Greene. Usta be a kinda show went all through the South, called it the Silas Greene show. Somethin like the circus. Me and Ovella wanted to join that thing and see the world. Nothin wrong at home or nothin, we just wanted to travel and see new things and have high times. Didn't say nothin to nobody but one another. Just up and decided to do it.

DIALOGUE A *dialogue* is a conversation between characters. In poems, novels, and short stories, dialogue is usually set off by quotation marks:

> "Were they cute?" Alfonso asked.
> "I guess so."
> "Do you think you could recognize them?"
> —Gary Soto, "Broken Chain"

In a play, dialogue follows the names of the characters, and no quotation marks are used:

CARLOS. What do you want?

TORTILLA MAN. What makes you think I want anything?

— Denise Chávez, *The Flying Tortilla Man*

See *Drama.*

DIMETER See *Meter.*

DRAMA A *drama* is a story written to be performed by actors. Although a drama is meant to be performed, one can also read the *script,* or written version, and imagine the action. The script of a drama is made up of dialogue and stage directions. The *dialogue* is the words spoken by the actors. The *stage directions,* usually printed in italics, tell how the actors should look, move, and speak. They also describe the setting and effects of sound and lighting.

Dramas are often divided into parts called *acts.* The acts are often divided into smaller parts called *scenes. The Flying Tortilla Man,* on page 211, is a one-act drama. All of its action takes place in one act that has nine scenes.

DRAMATIC IRONY See *Irony.*

DYNAMIC CHARACTER See *Character.*

ESSAY An *essay* is a short nonfiction work about a particular subject. Most essays have a single major focus and a clear introduction, body, and conclusion.

There are many types of essays. A *narrative essay,* like "Rattlesnake Hunt," on page 369, tells a story about a real-life experience. An *expository essay,* like the excerpt from *These Were the Sioux,* on page 411, relates information or provides explanations. A *persuasive essay,* like "I Am a Native of North America," on page 381, presents and supports an opinion. Most essays contain passages that describe people, places,

or objects. However, there are very few purely descriptive essays.

See *Description, Exposition, Narration,* and *Persuasion.*

EXPOSITION *Exposition* is writing or speech that explains a process or presents information. This Handbook of Literary Terms is an example of exposition. So are the introductions to the selections in this text.

In the plot of a story or drama, the *exposition,* or introduction, is the part of the work that introduces the characters, setting, and basic situation. See *Plot.*

EXTENDED METAPHOR In an *extended metaphor,* as in a regular metaphor, a subject is spoken or written of as though it were something else. However, extended metaphor differs from regular metaphor in that several comparisons are made. Carl Sandburg uses extended metaphor in his poem "Fog," on page 466. The poem points out a number of similarities between fog and a cat. Like a cat, the fog is silent and moves stealthily.

See *Metaphor.*

FABLE A *fable* is a brief story or poem, usually with animal characters, that teaches a lesson, or moral. The moral is usually stated at the end of the fable.

The fable is an ancient literary form found in many cultures. The fables written by Aesop, a Greek slave who lived in the sixth century B.C., are still popular with children today. Many familiar expressions, such as "crying wolf," "sour grapes," and "crying over spilt milk," come from Aesop's fables. Other famous writers of fables include La Fontaine, the seventeenth-century French poet, and James Thurber, the twentieth-century American humorist. Thurber called his works fables for our time, and many of them have surprise endings. See the fables by Aesop and others on pages 547, 549, 551, 555, and 559. See *Irony* and *Moral.*

FANTASY   *Fantasy* is highly imaginative writing that contains elements not found in real life. In Jack Finney's "The Third Level," on page 127, traveling through time is a fantastic element. Science fiction stories, such as Isaac Asimov's "Hallucination," on page 179, contain elements of fantasy.
See *Science Fiction.*

FICTION   *Fiction* is prose writing that tells about imaginary characters and events. Short stories and novels are works of fiction. Some writers base their fiction on actual events and people, adding invented characters, dialogue, settings, and plots. Other writers of fiction rely on imagination alone to provide their materials.
See *Narration, Nonfiction,* and *Prose.*

FIGURATIVE LANGUAGE   *Figurative language* is writing or speech that is not meant to be taken literally. The many types of figurative language are known as *figures of speech.* Common figures of speech include hyperbole, metaphor, personification, and simile.

Writers use figurative language to state ideas in vivid and imaginative ways. For example, in "The River," by Javier Héraud, the speaker uses figurative language to express his own wildness:

I am a river,
I flow each moment more
   furiously,
more violently

The speaker does not mean, literally, that he is a river. However, by using figurative language to compare himself to a river, the speaker conveys the idea of his wildness vividly and imaginatively.
See *Metaphor, Personification, Simile,* and *Symbol.*

FIGURE OF SPEECH   See *Figurative Language.*

FLASHBACK   A *flashback* is a section of a literary work that interrupts the sequence of events to relate an event from an earlier time.

FLAT CHARACTER   See *Character.*

FOLK BALLAD   See *Ballad.*

FOLK TALE   A *folk tale* is a story composed orally and then passed from person to person by word of mouth. Folk tales originated among people who could neither read nor write. These people entertained one another by telling stories aloud, often ones dealing with heroes, adventure, magic, or romance. Eventually, modern scholars like Wilhelm and Jakob Grimm began collecting these stories and writing them down. In this way folk tales have survived into the present day. The Brothers Grimm collected many European folk tales and published these as *Grimm's Fairy Tales.* The Grimms' tales include such famous stories as "Cinderella," "Rapunzel," and "The Bremen Town Musicians." In the United States, scholars have also collected folk tales. These tales deal with such legendary heroes as Pecos Bill, Paul Bunyan, Mike Fink, and Davy Crockett. "The Little Lizard's Sorrow," on page 581, is a retelling of a Vietnamese folk tale.
See *Fable, Legend, Myth,* and *Oral Tradition.*

FOOT   See *Meter.*

FORESHADOWING   *Foreshadowing* is the use, in a literary work, of clues that suggest events that have yet to occur. Writers use foreshadowing to build their readers' expectations and to create suspense. For example, at the beginning of *The Monsters Are Due on Maple*

Street, on page 247, the narrator makes the following statement:

> NARRATOR'S VOICE. Maple Street. Six-forty-four P.M. on a late September evening. [*A pause*] Maple Street in the last calm and reflective moment . . . before the monsters came!

The narrator's comment foreshadows, or predicts, what will happen later in the play. It leads the reader or audience to feel suspense and to expect the arrival of monsters. Later the reader or audience is surprised to find out who the monsters really are.

FREE VERSE   *Free verse* is poetry not written in a regular rhythmical pattern, or meter. Walt Whitman's "Miracles," on page 533, is written in free verse. So are the traditional Chippewa Indian song, "A Song of Greatness," on page 520, and Langston Hughes's "Mother to Son," on page 518.

In a free verse poem the poet is free to write lines of any length or with any number of stresses, or beats. Free verse is therefore less constraining than *metrical verse,* in which every line must have a certain length and a certain number of stresses.
See *Meter.*

GENRE   A *genre* is a division or type of literature. Literature is commonly divided into three major genres: poetry, prose, and drama. Each major genre is in turn divided into lesser genres, as follows:
1. *Poetry:* lyric poetry, concrete poetry, dramatic poetry, narrative poetry, epic poetry
2. *Prose:* fiction (novels and short stories) and nonfiction (biography, autobiography, letters, essays, and reports)
3. *Drama:* serious drama and tragedy, comic drama, melodrama, and farce
See *Drama, Poetry,* and *Prose.*

HAIKU   The *haiku* is a three-line Japanese verse form. The first and third lines of a haiku have five syllables apiece. The second line has seven syllables. A writer of haiku uses images to create a single, vivid picture, generally of a scene from nature. See the examples of haiku on pages 479 and 480.

HEPTAMETER   See *Meter.*

HEPTASTICH   See *Stanza.*

HERO/HEROINE   A *hero* or *heroine* is a character whose actions are inspiring or noble. Often heroes and heroines struggle mightily to overcome foes or to escape difficulties. This is true, for example, of Demeter in "Demeter and Persephone," on page 595. The most obvious examples of heroes and heroines are the larger-than-life characters in myths and legends. However, characters who are more ordinary than Demeter can also act heroically. For example, in Alfred Noyes's poem on page 437, the landlord's daughter, Bess, sacrifices her own life to save that of the highwayman. This is a heroic deed, and Bess is therefore a heroine.

Note that the term *hero* was originally used only for male characters, while heroic female characters were always called *heroines.* However, it is now acceptable to use *hero* to refer to females as well as to males.

HEXAMETER   See *Meter.*

HUBRIS   *Hubris* is excessive pride. In "Phaëthon, Son of Apollo," on page 601, the central character is guilty of hubris.

IAMB   See *Meter.*

IMAGE   An *image* is a word or phrase that appeals to one or more of the five senses. Writers use images to describe how their subjects look, sound, feel, taste, and smell. In the following lines from the poem "Kansas Land," Gordon Parks uses images of sight, sound, and smell to re-create the natural wonders of life in Kansas:

Cloud tufts billowing across the round
  blue sky.
Butterflies to chase through grass high
  as the chin.
Junebugs, swallowtails, red robin and
  bobolink,
Nights filled with soft laughter, fire
  flies and restless stars,
The winding sound of crickets rubbing
  dampness from their wings.
Silver September rain, orange-red-brown
  Octobers and white Decembers with
  hungry
Smells of hams and pork butts curing in
  the smokehouse.

IMAGERY   See *Image.*

INCITING INCIDENT   See *Plot.*

IRONY   *Irony* is the general name given to literary techniques that involve surprising, interesting, or amusing contradictions. In *verbal irony,* words are used to suggest the opposite of their usual meanings. In *dramatic irony,* there is a contradiction between what a character thinks and what the reader or audience knows to be true. In *irony of situation,* an event occurs that directly contradicts the expectations of the characters, the reader, or the audience. O. Henry uses irony in his short story "The Ransom of Red Chief," on page 25. In this story, two men kidnap a young boy in a seemingly easy scheme to get ransom money. In an ironic twist, the boy proves to be so wild and mischievous that the two men end up paying his father to take him back.

IRONY OF SITUATION   See *Irony.*

LEGEND   A *legend* is a widely told story about the past, one that may or may not have a founda-

tion in fact. Every culture has its own legends—its familiar, traditional stories. Examples of legends in the text include "Ojeeg, the Hunter, and the Ice Man," on page 607, and "Popocatepetl and Ixtlaccihuatl," on page 613. The former is a legend from the Micmac Indians of Canada. The latter is a legend from the Aztec Indians of Mexico.
See *Oral Tradition.*

LIMERICK   A *limerick* is a humorous, rhyming, five-line poem with a specific meter and rhyme scheme. Most limericks have three strong stresses in lines 1, 2, and 5 and two strong stresses in lines 3 and 4. Most follow the rhyme scheme *aabba.* See the limericks by Oliver Herford, on page 529.

LYRIC POEM   A *lyric poem* is a highly musical verse that expresses the observations and feelings of a single speaker. Examples of lyric poems in the text include "My Mother Pieced Quilts," on page 494, and "I'm Nobody," on page 521.

MAIN CHARACTER   See *Character.*

METAMORPHOSIS   A *metamorphosis* is a change in shape, or form. Many ancient Greek and Roman myths involve characters who undergo dramatic changes. One famous collection of these myths, by the Roman poet Ovid, is called *Metamorphoses.*

In the tale "Children of Wax," on page 629, a curious boy is transformed into a beautiful bird when he disobeys a natural law.
See *Myth.*

METAPHOR   A *metaphor* is a figure of speech in which something is described as though it were something else. A metaphor, like a simile, works by pointing out a similarity between two unlike things. In "A Far Cry From Africa," the West Indian poet Derek Walcott uses the following metaphor:

A wind is ruffling the tawny pelt
  Of Africa.

A "tawny pelt" is a brownish-yellow animal hide. By comparing Africa to a tawny pelt, Walcott suggests two similarities. First, the African grasslands are like a tawny pelt because they are brownish-yellow in color. Second, Africa itself is like that proud, strong animal that wears a tawny pelt—the lion.
See *Extended Metaphor* and *Simile*.

METER The *meter* of a poem is its rhythmical pattern. This pattern is determined by the number of stresses, or beats, in each line. To describe the meter of a poem, you must *scan* its lines. *Scanning* involves marking the stressed and unstressed syllables, as follows:

The life | Ĭ leád | Ĭ wánt | tŏ bé

As you can see, each stress is marked with a slanted line (ˊ) and each unstressed syllable with a horseshoe symbol (˘). The stressed and unstressed syllables are then divided by vertical lines (|) into groups called *feet*.

The following types of feet are common in English poetry:

1. *Iamb:* a foot with one unstressed syllable followed by one stressed syllable, as in the word "begín"

2. *Trochee:* a foot with one stressed syllable followed by one unstressed syllable, as in the word "péople"

3. *Anapest:* a foot with two unstressed syllables followed by one stressed syllable, as in the phrase "on the séa"

4. *Dactyl:* a foot with one stressed syllable followed by two unstressed syllables, as in the word "happiness"

5. *Spondee:* a foot with two stressed syllables, as in the word "downtown"

6. *Pyrrhic:* a foot with two unstressed syllables, as in the last two syllables of the word "unév|enly"

7. *Amphibrach:* a foot with one unstressed syllable, one stressed syllable, and another unstressed syllable, as in "the shimmer"

8. *Amphimacer:* a foot with a stressed syllable, one unstressed syllable, and another stressed syllable, as in "Jáck and Jíll"

Depending on the type of foot that is most common in them, lines of poetry are described as *iambic, trochaic, anapestic,* or *dactylic.*

Lines are also described in terms of the number of feet that occur in them, as follows:

1. *Monometer:* verse written in one-foot lines

Thŭs Í
P̆ass bý
Ănd díe
    —Robert Herrick, "Upon His Departure"

2. *Dimeter:* verse written in two-foot lines

There was | a woman
Who lived | on a hill.
If she's | not gone,
She lives | there still.
    —Anonymous

3. *Trimeter:* verse written in three-foot lines

Where dips | the rock|y highland
Of Sleuth | Wood in | the lake,
There lies | a leaf|y island
Where flapp|ing her|ons wake
The drows|y wat|er rats;
    —W.B. Yeats, "The Stolen Child"

4. *Tetrameter:* verse written in four-foot lines

When wĕar|ў̆ wĭth | thĕ lŏng | dăy's cáre,
 And earth|lў̆ change | frŏm pain | tŏ pain,
And lóst, | ănd reád|ў̆ tŏ | dĕspair,
 Thў̆ kĭnd | vŏice cáls | mĕ báck | ăgáin
  —Emily Brontë, "To Imagination"

5. *Pentameter:* verse written in five-foot lines

Ămĭdst | thĕse scénes, | Ŏ Píl|grĭm, séek'st|
 thŏu Róme?
Vaín ĭs | thў̆ seárch|—thĕ pómp | ŏf Róme | ĭs
 fléd
  —Francisco de Quevedo, "Rome in Her
  Ruins"

A six-foot line is called a *hexameter.* A line with seven feet is a *heptameter.*

A complete description of the meter of a line tells the kinds of feet each line contains, as well as how many feet of each kind. Thus the lines from Quevedo's poem would be described as *iambic pentameter,* with one variation, a trochee, in the second line. *Blank verse* is poetry written in unrhymed iambic pentameter. Poetry that does not have a regular meter is called *free verse.* See *Blank Verse* and *Free Verse.*

MINOR CHARACTER   See *Character.*

MONOMETER   See *Meter.*

MOOD   *Mood,* or *atmosphere,* is the feeling created in the reader by a literary work or passage. Writers use many devices to create mood, including images, dialogue, setting, and plot. Often a writer creates a mood at the beginning of a work and then sustains this mood throughout. Sometimes, however, the mood of the work changes dramatically. For example, the mood of most of "A Boy and a Man," on page 37, is tense and suspenseful. This mood changes after the man is rescued from the crevasse.

MORAL   A *moral* is a lesson taught by a literary work. A fable usually ends with a moral that is directly stated. For example, Aesop's fable "The Fox and the Crow," on page 549, ends with the moral "Do not trust flatterers." A poem, novel, short story, or essay often suggests a moral that is not directly stated. The moral must be drawn by the reader, based on other elements in the work. See *Fable.*

MOTIVATION   A *motivation* is a reason that explains or partially explains a character's thoughts, feelings, actions, or speech. Writers try to make their characters' motivations, or motives, as clear as possible. If the motives of a main character are not clear, then the character will not be believable.

Characters are often motivated by needs such as food and shelter. They are also motivated by feelings such as fear, love, and pride. In "Last Cover," on page 59, Colin's fierce, protective love for his pet fox motivates him to go into the woods each day and to create a beautiful drawing. In turn, admiration for Colin's drawing motivates Father to support Colin's plan to become an artist.

MYTH   A *myth* is a fictional tale that explains the actions of gods or heroes or the origins of elements of nature. Myths are part of the oral tradition. They are composed orally and then passed from generation to generation by word of mouth. Every ancient culture has its own mythology, or collection of myths. The stories on pages 595, 601, and 625 of your text are retellings, in writing, of myths from ancient Greece and Rome. These Greek and Roman myths, known collectively as *classical mythology,* tell about such gods as Zeus, Demeter, and Apollo.
See *Oral Tradition.*

NARRATION   *Narration* is writing that tells a story. The act of telling a story is also called *nar-*

ration. Fictional works such as novels and short stories are examples of narration. So are poems that tell stories, such as "The Cremation of Sam McGee," on page 445. Narration can also be found in many kinds of nonfiction, including autobiographies, biographies, and newspaper reports. A story told in fiction, nonfiction, poetry, or even in drama is called a *narrative.*
See *Narrative Poem* and *Narrator.*

NARRATIVE   See *Narration.*

NARRATIVE POEM   A *narrative poem* is a story told in verse. Narrative poems often have all the elements of short stories, including characters, conflict, and plot. Examples of narrative poems include "The Highwayman," on page 437, and "Annabel Lee," on page 455.

NARRATOR   A *narrator* is a speaker or character who tells a story. A *third-person narrator* is one who stands outside the action and speaks about it. A *first-person narrator* is one who tells a story *and* participates in its action.

In some dramas, like *The Monsters Are Due on Maple Street,* on page 247, there is a separate character called "The Narrator" who introduces, comments on, and concludes the play. See *Point of View.*

NONFICTION   *Nonfiction* is prose writing that presents and explains ideas or that tells about real people, places, objects, or events. Autobiographies, biographies, essays, reports, letters, memos, and newspaper articles are all types of nonfiction.
See *Fiction.*

NOVEL   A *novel* is a long work of fiction. Novels contain all of the elements of short stories, including characters, plot, conflict, and setting. However, novels are much longer than short stories. The writer of novels, or novelist, can therefore develop these elements more fully than a writer of short stories can. In addition to its main plot, a novel may contain one or more subplots, or independent, related stories. A novel may also have several themes. This text contains one full-length novel, *Bearstone,* by Will Hobbs, on page 641. See *Fiction.*

OCTAVE   See *Stanza.*

ONOMATOPOEIA   *Onomatopoeia* is the use of words that imitate sounds. *Crash, buzz, screech, hiss, neigh, jingle,* and *cluck* are examples of onomatopoeia. *Chickadee, towhee,* and *whippoorwill* are onomatopoeic names of birds.

In her poem "Onomatopoeia," Eve Merriam uses words to re-create the sounds of water splashing from a faucet:

> The rusty spigot
> sputters,
> utters
> a splutter,
> spatters a smattering of drops,
> gashes wider;
> slash,
> splatters,
> scatters,
> spurts,
> finally stops sputtering
> and plash!
> gushes rushes splashes
> clear water dashes.

ORAL TRADITION   The *oral tradition* is the passing of songs, stories, and poems from generation to generation by word of mouth. Folk songs, folk tales, legends, and myths all come from the oral tradition. No one knows who first created these stories and poems. They are *anonymous.*

Here is an anonymous poem from the oral tradition:

> Monday's child is fair of face,
> Tuesday's child is full of grace,
> Wednesday's child is full of woe,

Thursday's child has far to go,
Friday's child is loving and giving,
Saturday's child works hard for its
  living,
And a child that is born on the Sabbath
  day
Is fair and wise and good and gay.

See *Folk Tale, Legend,* and *Myth.*

PARALLELISM   See *Repetition.*

PENTAMETER   See *Meter.*

PERSONIFICATION   *Personification* is a type of figurative language in which a nonhuman subject is given human characteristics. In "Feeling About Words," on page 486, Mary O'Neil personifies words, describing some as "lazy" and some as full of "pride" and "pomp." In the following lines from the poem "Minor Elegy," Henriqueta Lisboa personifies death:

How do you recognize death?
Maybe she looks gray.
Does she give out calling cards, with
  her name correctly embossed?
Will she waylay us in the hall?

PERSUASION   *Persuasion* is used in writing or speech that attempts to convince the reader or listener to adopt a particular opinion or course of action. Newspaper editorials and letters to the editor use persuasion. So do advertisements and campaign speeches given by political candidates. In "How to Enjoy Poetry," on page 375, James Dickey attempts to persuade the reader to start reading poetry.

PLOT   *Plot* is the sequence of events in a literary work. In most novels, dramas, short stories, and narrative poems, the plot involves both characters and a central conflict. The plot usually begins with an *exposition* that introduces the setting, the characters, and the basic situation. This is followed by the *inciting incident,* which introduces the central conflict. The conflict then increases during the *development* until it reaches a high point of interest or suspense, the *climax.* The climax is followed by the *falling action,* or end, of the central conflict. Any events that occur during the falling action make up the *resolution* or *denouement.*

Some plots do not have all of these parts. Some stories begin with the inciting incident and end with the resolution. In some the inciting incident has occurred before the opening of the story.
See *Conflict.*

POETRY   *Poetry* is one of the three major types of literature, the others being prose and drama. Defining poetry more precisely isn't easy, for there is no single, unique characteristic that all poems share. Poems are often divided into lines and stanzas and often employ regular rhythmical patterns, or meters. However, some poems are written out just like prose, and some are written in free verse. Most poems make use of highly concise, musical, and emotionally charged language. Many also make use of imagery, figurative language, and special devices of sound such as rhyme.

Major types of poetry include lyric poetry, narrative poetry, and concrete poetry. E.E. Cummings's "In Just—," on page 500, and Teresa Palomo Acosta's "My Mother Pieced Quilts," on page 494, are both lyric poems. Alfred Noyes's "The Highwayman," on page 437, is a narrative poem. William Jay Smith's "Seal," on page 477, is a concrete poem.

Other forms of poetry include *dramatic poetry,* in which characters speak in their own voices, and *epic poetry,* in which the poet tells a long, involved tale about gods or heroes.
See *Concrete Poem, Genre, Lyric Poem,* and *Narrative Poem.*

POINT OF VIEW   *Point of view* is the perspective, or vantage point, from which a story is told. Three commonly used points of view are first person, omniscient third person, and limited third person.

In stories told from the *first-person point of view,* the narrator is a character in the story and refers to himself or herself with the first-person pronoun *I.* The story "Two Kinds," on page 93, is told by a first-person narrator—the story's main character.

The two kinds of third-person point of view, limited and omniscient, are called "third person" because the narrator uses third-person pronouns such as *he* and *she* to refer to the characters. There is no *I* telling the story.

In stories told from the *omniscient third-person point of view,* the narrator knows and tells about what each character feels and thinks. "Rikki-tikki-tavi," on page 13, is written from the omniscient third-person point of view.

In stories told from the *limited third-person point of view,* the narrator relates the inner thoughts and feelings of only one character, and everything is viewed from this character's perspective. "A Boy and a Man," on page 37, is written from the limited third-person point of view. See *Narrator.*

PROSE   *Prose* is the ordinary form of written language. Most writing that is not poetry, drama, or song is considered prose. Prose is one of the major genres of literature and occurs in two forms, fiction and nonfiction.
See *Fiction, Genre,* and *Nonfiction.*

PROTAGONIST   The *protagonist* is the main character in a literary work. In "Rikki-tikki-tavi," on page 13, the protagonist, or main character, is Rikki, the mongoose.
See *Antagonist* and *Character.*

PYRRHIC   See *Meter.*

QUATRAIN   See *Stanza.*

REFRAIN   A *refrain* is a regularly repeated line or group of lines in a poem or song. In the following lines from a traditional Eskimo poem, the refrain has been italicized:

> I wonder what the dear south wind
>   has on its mind
>   *as it blows past?*
> Does it think about the small people
>   who live north of us?
> Does it think of them,
>   *as it blows past?*

REPETITION   *Repetition* is the use, more than once, of any element of language—a sound, word, phrase, clause, or sentence. Repetition is used in both prose and poetry. In prose a situation or character may be repeated with some variations. A subplot, for example, may repeat, with variations, the circumstances presented in the main plot. Poets make use of many varieties of repetition. *Rhyme, alliteration,* and *rhythm* are all repetitions of sounds or sound patterns. A *refrain* is a repeated line. Patterns of rhythm and rhyme may be repeated throughout a long poem, as in "The Cremation of Sam McGee," by Robert Service, on page 445.

The following poem makes use of a type of repetition called *parallelism.* In parallelism a grammatical pattern is repeated but the words are changed.

> Grandfather sings, I dance.
> Grandfather speaks, I listen.
> Now I sing, who will dance?
> I speak, who will listen?
>
> Grandfather hunts, I learn.
> Grandfather fishes, I clean.
> Now I hunt, who will learn?
> I fish, who will clean?

Grandfather dies, I weep.
Grandfather buried, I am left alone.
When I am dead, who will cry?
When I am buried, who will be alone?
    —Shirley Crawford, "Grandfather"

See *Alliteration, Meter, Plot, Rhyme,* and *Rhyme Scheme.*

RESOLUTION   See *Plot.*

RHYME   *Rhyme* is the repetition of sounds at the ends of words. Poets use rhyme to lend a songlike quality to their verses and to emphasize certain words and ideas. Many traditional poems contain *end rhymes,* or rhyming words at the ends of lines. See, for example, the end rhymes in Robert Frost's "The Pasture," on page 473. Another common device is the use of *internal rhymes,* or rhyming words within lines. Notice, for example, the internal rhymes in the following passage from Edgar Allan Poe's "Annabel Lee," on page 455:

    For the moon never *beams* without
        bringing me *dreams*
      Of the beautiful Annabel Lee;
    And the stars never *rise* but I see
        the bright *eyes*
      Of the beautiful Annabel Lee

See *Rhyme Scheme.*

RHYME SCHEME   A *rhyme scheme* is a regular pattern of rhyming words in a poem. To indicate the rhyme scheme of a poem, one uses lowercase letters. Each rhyme is assigned a different letter, as follows:

Under a spreading chestnut *tree*	a
The village smithy *stands;*	b
The smith, a mighty man is *he,*	a
With large and sinewy *hands;*	b
And the muscles of his brawny *arms*	c
Are strong as iron *bands.*	b
—Henry Wadsworth Longfellow, "The Village Blacksmith"	

The rhyme scheme of these lines is thus *ababcb.*

RHYTHM   *Rhythm* is the pattern of beats, or stresses, in spoken or written language.
See *Meter.*

ROUND CHARACTER   See *Character.*

SCAN/SCANNING   See *Meter.*

SCENE   See *Drama.*

SCIENCE FICTION   *Science fiction* is writing that tells about imaginary events that involve science or technology. Many science fiction stories are set in the future. "All Summer in a Day," on page 105, is a science fiction story. In this story Ray Bradbury describes events that take place in the future on the planet Venus. *The Monsters Are Due on Maple Street,* on page 247, is a science fiction drama.

SENSORY LANGUAGE   *Sensory language* is writing or speech that appeals to one or more of the five senses.
See *Image.*

SESTET   See *Stanza.*

SETTING   The *setting* of a literary work is the time and place of the action. The time includes not only the historical period—the past, present, or future—but also the year, the season, the time of day, and even the weather. The place may be a specific country, state, region, community, neighborhood, building, institution, or home. Details such as dialects, clothing, customs, and modes of transportation are often used to establish setting.

    In most stories the setting serves as a backdrop—a context in which the characters interact. In some stories the setting is crucial to the plot.

For example, the weather on the planet Venus is central to the plot of Ray Bradbury's story "All Summer in a Day," on page 105. Setting can also help to create a mood, or feeling. In "The Third Level," on page 127, the writer's description of a summer evening in a small Illinois town creates a mood of peace and innocence:

> It's a wonderful town still, with big old frame houses, huge lawns and tremendous trees whose branches meet overhead and roof the streets. And in 1894, summer evenings were twice as long, and people sat out on their lawns, the men smoking cigars and talking quietly, the women waving palm-leaf fans, with the fireflies all around, in a peaceful world. To be back there with the First World War still twenty years off, and World War II over forty years in the future . . . I wanted two tickets for that.

See *Mood*.

SHORT STORY A *short story* is a brief work of fiction. Like a novel, a short story presents a sequence of events, or plot. The plot usually deals with a central conflict faced by a main character, or protagonist. Like a lyric poem, a short story is concise and creates a single effect, or dominant impression, on its reader. The events in a short story usually communicate a message about life or human nature. This message, or central idea, is the story's *theme*.
See *Conflict, Plot,* and *Theme*.

SIMILE A *simile* is a figure of speech that uses *like* or *as* to make a direct comparison between two unlike ideas. Everyday speech often contains similes such as "pale as a ghost," "good as gold," "spread like wildfire," and "clever as a fox."

Writers use similes to describe people, places, and things vividly. Poets, especially, create similes to point out new and interesting ways of viewing the world. In the following poem, Maxine Kumin uses a simile that compares the wings of moths beating against a screen to the end of a piece of film hitting the spool of a movie projector:

> Once he puts out the light
> moth wings on the window screen slow
> and drop away *like film lapping the spool
> after the home movie runs out.*
> —Maxine Kumin, "The Hermit Has a
> Visitor"

SPEAKER The *speaker* is the imaginary voice assumed by the writer of a poem. In other words, the speaker is the character who tells the poem. This character, or voice, often is not identified by name. The speaker in the following lines by poet Sylvia Plath is a mirror:

> I am silver and exact. I have no
> preconceptions
> Whatever I see I swallow immediately
> Just as it is, unmisted by love or dislike.
> I am not cruel, only truthful—
> —Sylvia Plath, "Mirror"

See *Narrator*.

SPONDEE See *Meter*.

STAGE DIRECTIONS *Stage directions* are notes included in a drama to describe how the work is to be performed or staged. Stage directions are usually printed in italics and enclosed within parentheses or brackets. Some stage directions describe the movements, costumes, emotional states, and ways of speaking of the characters. For example, these stage directions from *The Flying Tortilla Man,* on page 211, tell how the characters should move:

> **TORTILLA MAN.** Boy, once you get over your wonder, you can start dealing with life. Sit up there . . . you're slouched over like you're afraid.
> **CARLOS.** [*Peering over the edge of the Flying Tortilla*] I am!
> **TORTILLA MAN.** You, my young explorer, afraid of this . . . [THE TORTILLA MAN *begins to jump up and down on the tortilla.*]

CARLOS. [*Begging* THE TORTILLA MAN *to stop*] Oh please, Mr. Juan, won't you stop doing that? I think I'll just sit here, if you don't mind.

See *Drama*.

STANZA   A *stanza* is a formal division of lines in a poem, considered as a unit. Many poems are divided into stanzas that are separated by spaces. Stanzas often function just like paragraphs in prose. Each stanza states and develops a single main idea.

Stanzas are commonly named according to the number of lines found in them, as follows:
1. *Couplet:* a two-line stanza
2. *Tercet:* a three-line stanza
3. *Quatrain:* a four-line stanza
4. *Cinquain:* a five-line stanza
5. *Sestet:* a six-line stanza
6. *Heptastich:* a seven-line stanza
7. *Octave:* an eight-line stanza

Theodore Roethke's "The Bat," on page 472, is written in couplets:

By day the bat is cousin to the mouse.
He likes the attic of an aging house.

His fingers make a hat about his head.
His pulse beat is so slow we think him dead.

Robert Frost's "Stopping by Woods on a Snowy Evening," on page 504, is written in quatrains:

Whose woods these are I think I know.
His house is in the village, though;
He will not see me stopping here
To watch his woods fill up with snow.

My little horse must think it queer
To stop without a farmhouse near
Between the woods and frozen lake
The darkest evening of the year.

Division into stanzas is common in traditional poetry and is often accompanied by rhyme. Notice, for example, that in each of the stanzas from the Frost poem, the first, second, and fourth lines rhyme. That is, each stanza follows the rhyme scheme *aaba*. However, some rhyming poems are not divided into stanzas, and some poems divided into stanzas do not contain rhyme. See, for example, Nikki Giovanni's "Winter," on page 502, which is divided into unrhymed quatrains.

STATIC CHARACTER   See *Character*.

SUBPLOT   See *Novel*.

SURPRISE ENDING   A *surprise ending* is a conclusion that is unexpected. Sometimes a surprise ending follows a false resolution. The reader thinks that the conflict has already been resolved but then is confronted with a new twist that changes the outcome of the plot. Often a surprise ending is *foreshadowed,* or subtly hinted at, in the course of the work. Writer O. Henry was a master of the surprise ending. See the surprise ending of his story "The Ransom of Red Chief," on page 25.
See *Foreshadowing* and *Plot*.

SUSPENSE   *Suspense* is a feeling of anxious uncertainty about the outcome of events in a literary work. Writers create suspense by raising questions in the minds of their readers. For example, in "A Day's Wait," on page 197, Ernest Hemingway raises questions about why the boy is acting so strangely and whether the boy will recover from his illness. In "A Boy and a Man," on page 37, James Ullman makes the reader wonder whether the character Rudi will succeed in saving the life of the explorer trapped in the crevasse.

SYMBOL   A *symbol* is anything that stands for or represents something else. Symbols are common in everyday life. A dove with an olive branch in its beak is a symbol of peace. A blindfolded woman holding a balanced scale is a symbol of justice. A crown is a symbol of a king's status and authority.

TERCET   See *Stanza.*

TETRAMETER   See *Meter.*

THEME   A *theme* is a central message, concern, or purpose in a literary work. A theme can usually be expressed as a generalization, or general statement, about human beings or about life. The theme of a work is not a summary of its plot. The theme is the central idea that the writer communicates.

A theme may be stated directly by the writer, although this is unusual. In "Utzel and His Daughter, Poverty," on page 149, Isaac Bashevis Singer states his theme directly: ". . . all a man possesses he gains through work, and not by lying in bed and being idle." This statement is a generalization that applies to all human beings. Singer illustrates this theme by telling the story of what happens to Utzel and his daughter.

Most themes are not directly stated but are implied. When the theme is implied, the reader must figure out what the theme is by looking carefully at what the work reveals about people or about life.

TRIMETER   See *Meter.*

TROCHEE   See *Meter.*

VERBAL IRONY   See *Irony.*

GLOSSARY

READING THE GLOSSARY ENTRIES

The words in this glossary are from selections appearing in your textbook. Each entry in the glossary contains the following parts:

1. Entry Word. This word appears at the beginning of the entry, in boldface type.

2. Pronunciation. The symbols in parentheses tell how the entry word is pronounced. If a word has more than one possible pronunciation, the most common of these pronunciations is given first.

3. Part of Speech. Appearing after the pronunciation, in italics, is an abbreviation that tells the part of speech of the entry word. The following abbreviations have been used:

n. noun   **p.** pronoun   **v.** verb

adj. adjective **adv.** adverb **conj.** conjunction

4. Definition. This part of the entry follows the part-of-speech abbreviation and gives the meaning of the entry word as used in the selection in which it appears.

KEY TO PRONUNCIATION SYMBOLS USED IN THE GLOSSARY

The following symbols are used in the pronunciations that follow the entry words:

Symbol	Key Words	Symbol	Key Words
a	asp, fat, parrot	b	bed, fable, dub
ā	ape, date, play	d	dip, beadle, had
ä	ah, car, father	f	fall, after, off
		g	get, haggle, dog
e	elf, ten, berry	h	he, ahead, hotel
ē	even, meet, money	j	joy, agile, badge
		k	kill, tackle, bake
i	is, hit, mirror	l	let, yellow, ball
ī	ice, bite, high	m	met, camel, trim
		n	not, flannel, ton
ō	open, tone, go	p	put, apple, tap
ô	all, horn, law	r	red, port, dear
o͞o	ooze, tool, crew	s	sell, castle, pass
oo	look, pull, moor	t	top, cattle, hat
yo͞o	use, cute, few	v	vat, hovel, have
yoo	united, cure, globule	w	will, always, swear
oi	oil, point, toy	y	yet, onion, yard
ou	out, crowd, plow	z	zebra, dazzle, haze
u	up, cut, color	ch	chin, catcher, arch
ʉr	urn, fur, deter	sh	she, cushion, dash
		th	thin, nothing, truth
ə	a in ago	t͟h	then, father, lathe
	e in agent	zh	azure, leisure
	i in sanity	ŋ	ring, anger, drink
	o in comply	′	[indicates that a
	u in focus		following **l** or **n** is a
ər	perhaps, murder		syllabic consonant, as in
			able (ā′ b'l)]

This pronunciation key is from *Webster's New World Dictionary*, Second College Edition. Copyright © 1986 by Simon & Schuster. Used by permission.

A

abet (ə bet′) *v.* To help or encourage

abode (ə bōd′) *n.* Home

abruptly (ə brupt′ lē) *adv.* Suddenly

accessible (ak ses′ ə b'l) *adj.* Easy to get

acknowledge (ak näl′ ij) *v.* To recognize and admit

adamant (ad′ ə mənt) *adj.* Unyielding; inflexible

addled (ad′ 'ld) *adj.* Muddled and confused

adhesive (əd hē′ siv) *adj.* Sticking

aeon (ē′ än) *n.* A very long period of time

aesthetic (es thet′ ik) *adj.* From an artistic point of view

akimbo (ə kim′ bō) *adv.* Hands on hips, with elbows pointing outward

algae (al′ jē) *n.* Plants like seaweed that live in water or damp places

allay (ə lā′) *v.* To put to rest; calm

amber (am′ bər) *n.* A brownish-yellow substance; *adj.* of a brownish-yellow color

ambulance (am′ byə ləns) *n.* A specially equipped vehicle for carrying the sick or wounded

amends (ə mendz′) *n.* Things given or done to make up for injury or loss

amiss (ə mis′) *adv.* In a wrong way; improper

Anglophile (aŋ′ glə fīl) *n.* A person who is strongly devoted to England, its people, customs, or influence

anoint (ə noint′) *v.* To rub oil or ointment on

anonymous (ə nän′ ə məs) *adj.* With no name known

apparition (ap′ ə rish′ ən) *n.* Ghost

appease (ə pēz′) *v.* To satisfy

appraisal (ə prā′ z'l) *n.* Judgment of something's or someone's quality

apprehensive (ap′ rə hen′ siv) *adj.* Anxious; fearful

apprentice (ə pren′ tis) *v.* To receive financial support and instruction in a trade in return for work

apt (apt) *adj.* Inclined; likely

aptitude (ap′ tə to͞od′) *n.* Talent; ability

arched (ärcht) *adj.* Curved

arid (ar′ id) *adj.* Dry and barren

Arkansas (är′ k'n sô′) [<Fr. < Siouan tribal name; ? "downstream people"] State of the south central United States

arrogant (ar′ ə gənt) *adj.* Proud; self-important

arroyo (ə roi′ ō) *n.* A dry gully or ravine

assent (ə sent′) *n.* Agreement

assortment (ə sôrt′ mənt) *n.* A group or collection of different kinds of things

astonish (ə stän′ ish) *v.* To amaze

astrophysics (as′ trō fiz′ iks) *n.* The science of the physical properties of the stars, planets, and other heavenly bodies

asunder (ə sun' dər)   *adv.* Into parts or pieces

audible (ô' də b'l)   *adj.* Loud enough to be heard

avarice (av' ər is)   *n.* Greed for riches

awe (ô)   *n.* A mixed feeling of fear and wonder

B

banish (ban' ish)   *v.* To send into exile

bantam (ban' təm)   *n.* A small chicken

bark (bärk)   *n.* Any boat, especially a small sailing boat

barometer (bə räm' ə tər)   *n.* An instrument for measuring atmospheric pressure

barrage (bə räzh')   *n.* A heavy attack

barrio (bär' ē ō)   *n.* Part of a town or city where most of the people are Hispanic

bay (bā)   *v.* To bark with deep, prolonged tones

beam (bēm)   *v.* To shine brightly

begrudge (bē gruj')   *v.* To resent

belligerent (bə lij' ər ənt)   *adj.* Showing a readiness to fight

bellow (bel' ō)   *v.* To roar with a powerful, reverberating sound

bellows (bel' ōz)   *n.* A device for quickening the fire by blowing air on it

berserk (bər sʉrk')   *adj.* Into a violent or destructive rage

beset (bi set')   *v.* Covered; set thickly with

besiege (bi sēj')   *v.* To surround

bias (bī' əs)   *n.* Preference; leaning; prejudice

bilious (bil' yəs)   *adj.* Bad-tempered; cross

billow (bil' ō)   *n.* A large wave; *v.* To surge or swell

bleachers (blēch' ərz)   *n.* Benches stacked in rows for spectators at sporting events

blemish (blem' ish)   *n.* A defect or scar

blissfully (blis' fool ē)   *adv.* Very happily

bog (bäg)   *n.* A small marsh or swamp

bonnet (bän' it)   *n.* [Brit.] An automobile hood

brandish (brand' dish)   *v.* To wave in a threatening way

bravado (brə vä' dō)   *n.* Pretended courage

brawn (brôn)   *n.* Physical strength

breeches (brich' iz)   *n.* Trousers that reach to or just below the knee

brooch (brōch)   *n.* A large ornamental pin worn on a dress

brooding (brōod' iŋ)   *n.* Thinking in a worried way

brutality (broo tal' ə tē)   *n.* Violence; harshness

buffet (bə fā')   *n.* A piece of furniture with drawers and cupboards for dishes, table linen, and so on

burly (bʉr' lē)   *adj.* Heavy and muscular

burrow (bʉr' ō)   *v.* To dig a hole or tunnel, especially for shelter

bustle (bus' 'l)   *v.* To hurry

butte (byoot)   *n.* A steep hill standing in flat land

C

calabash (kal' ə bash')   *n.* A large fruit that is dried and made into a bowl or cup

calico (kal' ə kō)   *n.* A coarse and cheap cloth

calligrapher (kə lig' rə fər)   *n.* Someone skilled in the art of beautiful handwriting

camouflage (kam' ə fläzh')   *v.* Disguise

candy (kan' dē)   *v.* To coat with sugar

canebrake (kān' brāk)   *n.* A dense growth of cane plants

cant (kant)   *v.* To tilt

cantankerous (kan taŋ' kər əs)   *adj.* Bad-tempered

canter (kan' tər)   *v.* To move at an easy gallop

cantonment (kan tän' mənt)   *n.* Temporary quarters assigned to troops

canvas (kan' vəs)   *n.* Closely woven cloth used for tents and sails

carp (kärp)   *n.* A fresh-water fish living in a pond or other quiet water

cascade (kas kād')   *n.* A waterfall or anything tumbling like water

casement (kās' mənt)   *n.* A window frame that opens on hinges

castings (kas' tiŋz)   *n.* Waste material

cataract (kat' ə rakt')   *n.* An eye disease in which the lens becomes clouded over, causing partial or total blindness

catastrophe (kə tas' trə fē)   *n.* A sudden disaster or misfortune

catgut (kat' gut')   *n.* A tough string or thread used in surgery

chemistry (kem' is trē)   *n.* The chemical makeup and reaction of substances

Cherokee (cher' ə kē)   *n.* [<tribal name *Tsárăgĭ*, prob. < Choctaw *chiluk-ki*, "cave people"] A member of a tribe of Iroquoian Native Americans most of whom were moved from the southeast United States to Oklahoma

chide (chīd)   *v.* To scold

chivalrous (shiv' 'l rəs)   *adj.* Courteous

chloroform (klôr' ə fôrm')   *n.* A substance used at one time as an anesthetic

chortle (chôr' t'l)   *v.* To make an amused chuckling or snorting sound

cinch (sinch)   *v.* To fasten a saddle on a horse

clamber (klam' bər)   *v.* To climb with effort

clamor (klam' ər)   *v.* To cry out; to demand loudly

clan (klan)   *n.* A group of people, often relatives

claret (klar' it)   *adj.* Purplish-red

claustrophobic (klôs' trə fō' bik)   *adj.* Pertaining to an abnormal fear of being in an enclosed place

cleft (kleft)   *v.* Split or opened

coarse (kôrs)   *adj.* Inferior; crude; common

comely (kum' lē)   *adj.* Attractive; pretty

collaborate (kə lab' ə rāt')   *v.* Work together

comforter (kum' fər tər)   *n.* A long, woolen scarf

commence (kə mens')   *v.* To begin

commit (kə mit′) *v.* To deliver for safekeeping; entrust; **commit to memory** to learn by heart

commotion (kə mō shən) *n.* Noisy reaction; confusion

communal (kə myoo′ nəl) *adj.* Shared by all

comparable (käm′ pər ə b′l) *adj.* Similar

compassion (kəm pash′ ən) *n.* A feeling of sorrow for others; a desire to help

compel (kəm pel′) *adj.* To have a powerful effect

competent (käm′ pə tənt) *adj.* Capable

complaint (kəm plānt′) *n.* An illness

comply (kəm plī′) *v.* To do what is asked

compulsion (kəm pul′ shən) *n.* A driving force

concave (kän kāv′) *adj.* Hollow and curved like the inside of an empty ball

concede (kən sēd′) *v.* To admit as true

conceivable (kən sē′ və b′l) *adj.* Imaginable

concussion (kən kush′ ən) *n.* Violent shaking

condescendingly (kän′ di send′ iŋ lē) *adv.* In a superior or haughty manner

confluence (kän′ floo əns) *n.* Place where two or more streams come together

confound (kən found′) *v.* To confuse

conjecture (kən jek′ chər) *v.* To guess

conniving (kə nīv′ iŋ) *adj.* Scheming in an underhanded way

consent (kən sent′) *v.* To agree

consolation (kän′ sə lā′ shən) *n.* Something that makes one feel better

conspire (kən spīr′) *v.* To combine; to work together

consternation (kän′ stər nā′ shən) *n.* Sudden confusion and frustration

consultation (kän′ s′l tā′ shən) *n.* Discussion

contemplation (kän tem plā′ shən) *n.* Careful, serious thought or study

content (kən tent′) *v.* To satisfy

conventional (kən ven′ shən ′l) *adj.* Ordinary; usual

convey (kən vā′) *v.* To make known

corroborate (kə räb′ ə rāt′) *v.* Confirm; support

councilor (koun′ sə lər) *n.* Adviser

countenance (koun′ tə nəns) *n.* Face

coupe (koo pā′) *n.* A small, two-door automobile

court (kôrt) *v.* To try to win someone's love

covet (kuv′ it) *v.* To envy

covey (kuv′ ē) *n.* A small flock of birds

crafty (kraf′ tē) *adj.* Sly, cunning

cremate (krē′ māt) *v.* To burn to ashes

crevasse (kri vas′) *n.* Deep crack

crotchet (kräch′ it) *n.* A peculiar or stubborn idea

crouch (krouch′) *v.* To stoop or bend low

crucial (kroo′ shəl) *adj.* Of great importance

cul-de-sac (kul′ də sak′) *n.* A blind alley; a deadend street

culprit (kul′ prit) *n.* Guilty person

cunning (kun′ iŋ) *adj.* Skillful; clever

cunningly (kun′ iŋ lē) *adv.* In a tricky or sly way

cupidity (kyoo pid′ ə tē) *n.* Strong desire for wealth

curdle (kur′ d′l) *v.* To thicken; clot

curfew (kur′ fyoo) *n.* A time in the evening beyond which certain people must not be out on the streets

currency (kur′ ən sē) *n.* Money

D

dabbling (dab′ liŋ) *n.* The act of dipping lightly in water

dark (därk) *adj.* Entirely or partly without light

data (dāt′ ə) *n.* Information

dawdle (dôd′ l) *v.* Waste time by being slow

debut (dā byoo′) *n.* First appearance before the public

decipher (di sī′ fər) *v.* To make out the meaning of

decreed (di crēd′) *v.* Officially ordered

deference (def′ ər əns) *n.* Respect

defiant (di fī′ ənt) *adj.* Boldly resisting

definitive (di fin′ ə tiv) *adj.* Final; the last word

deft (deft) *adj.* Skillful

defy (di fī′) *v.* To boldly oppose or resist

deign (dān) *v.* To graciously agree to do something beneath one

deliver (di liv′ ər) *v.* To set free; rescue

delude (di lood′) *v.* To fool; to mislead

deluge (del′ yooj) *n.* A great flood or rush of anything

demeanor (di mēn′ ər) *n.* Outward behavior; manner

democracy (di mäk′ rə sē) *n.* Government in which the people hold the ruling power

democrat (dem′ ə krat′) *n.* A person who believes in and upholds government by the people

demon (dē′ mən) *n.* Evil spirit

denumerable (di noo′ mər ə b′l) *adj.* Countable; said of a set whose elements can be put in a one-to-one correspondence with the natural integers

derelict (der′ ə likt′) *v.* An abandoned ship

derive (di rīv′) *n.* To receive from someone or something

desolate (des′ ə lit) *adj.* Lonely; solitary

despair (di sper′) *n.* Loss of hope

desperation (des pər ā′ shən) *n.* Recklessness that comes from despair

despise (di spīz′) *v.* Look down on with scorn

despondent (di spän′ dənt) *adj.* Lacking hope; depressed

destitute (des′ tə toot′) *adj.* Living in complete poverty

deteriorate (di tir′ ē ə rāt′) *v.* To become worse

devise (di vīz′) *v.* To think of; plan

dignitary (dig′ nə ter′ ē) *n.* Person holding a high position or office

diligent (dil′ ə jənt) *adj.* Careful and steady

dim (dim) *adj.* Not bright; somewhat dark; not clearly seen

disarray (dis ə rā′) *n.* Untidiness

discreet (dis krēt′) *adj.* Careful about what one says

disdain (dis dān′) *v.* To scorn; regard as unworthy

disembowel (dis′ im bou′ əl) *v.* To take out the inner organs

dislodge (dis laj′) *v.* To leave a lodging or resting place

dismayed   (dis mād′)   *adj.* Upset; worried

dispel   (dis pel′)   *v.* To scatter and drive away

disposition   (dis′ pə zish′ ən)   *n.* Arrangement

dissever   (di sev′ ər)   *v.* To separate

dissuade   (di swād′)   *v.* To advise someone against an action

distemper   (dis tem′ pər)   *v.* An infectious virus disease of young dogs

distinct   (dis tiŋkt′)   *adj.* Separate and different

distinction   (dis tiŋk′ shən)   *n.* Difference of meaning

distinguished   (dis tiŋ′ gwisht)   *adj.* Famous or outstanding

distracted   (dis trakt′ id)   *adj.* With the mind drawn away in another direction

distraught   (dis′ trôt′)   *adj.* Extremely upset

diversion   (də vʉr′ zhən)   *n.* Something done for fun or relaxation

divisor   (də vī′ zər)   *n.* The number or quantity by which the dividend is divided to produce the quotient

domestic   (də mes′ tik)   *adj.* Of the home and family

dominion   (də min′ yən)   *n.* Region over which one rules

dormant   (dôr′ mənt)   *adj.* As if asleep; inactive

dote   (dōt)   *v.* To be extremely fond

downy   (doun′ ē)   *adj.* Soft and fluffy, like soft, fine feathers

draggled   (drag′ 'ld)   *adj.* Wet and dirty

dreaded   (dred′ əd)   *adj.* Feared

E

ecstatic   (ik stat′ ik)   *adj.* Delighted

edifice   (ed′ ə fis)   *n.* Large structure

elaboration   (ē lab ə rā′ shən)   *n.* Gestures that make an action seem complicated

elevation   (el′ ə vā′ shən)   *n.* A high place

eloquence   (el′ ə kwens)   *n.* Persuasive power

elude   (i lōōd′)   *v.* To escape or keep away from

elusive   (i lōō′ siv)   *adj.* Hard to find

emaciated   (i mā′ shē āt′ ed)   *adj.* Extremely thin, starving

emblem   (em′ bləm)   *n.* Sign; symbol

emerge   (i mʉrj′)   *v.* To become visible

emit   (i mit′)   *v.* To send out or utter

emphatic   (im fat′ ik)   *adj.* Felt with emphasis; forceful; definite

enamel   (i nam′ 'l)   *n.* Glassy colored substance used as coating on metal, glass, or pottery

encounter   (in koun′ tər)   *n.* Meeting

endow   (en dou′)   *v.* Provide with some talent or quality

entice   (in tīs′)   *v.* To tempt

entrails   (en′ trālz)   *n.* The inner organs of animals

epidemic   (ep′ ə dem′ ik)   *n.* Outbreak of a contagious disease

equivalent   (i kwiv′ ə lənt)   *n.* A thing similiar to another thing

erratically   (er rat′ ik ə lē)   *adv.* Irregularly or inconsistently

esteem   (ə stēm′)   *v.* To respect; to hold in high regard

evident   (ev′ ə dent)   *adj.* Obvious

ewer   (yōō′ ər)   *n.* A large water pitcher with a wide mouth

exalting   (eg zôl′ tiŋ)   *adj.* Filled with honor, joy, and glory

exclaim   (iks klām′)   *v.* To cry out; speak or say suddenly and vehemently

exhilarated   (eg zil′ ə rāt id)   *adj.* Thrilled; excited

expectant   (ik spek′ tənt)   *adj.* Showing eager waiting

exquisite   (eks′ kwi zit)   *adj.* Very beautiful, especially in a delicate way

extract   (ik strakt′)   *v.* To draw out

extricate   (eks′ trə kāt)   *v.* To set free; disentangle

exuberance   (ig zōō′ bər əns)   *n.* High spirits

exultation   (eg′ zəl tā′ shən)   *n.* Rejoicing

F

falter   (fôl′ tər)   *v.* To show uncertainty; act hesitantly

fanciful   (fan′ si fəl)   *adj.* Playfully imaginative

fantasia   (fan tā′ zhə)   *n.* A musical composition of no fixed form, with a structure determined by the composer's fancy

fantasize   (fan′ tə sīz)   *v.* To have daydreams; indulge in fantasies

fare   (fer)   *n.* Food

favoritism   (fā′ vər it iz'm)   *n.* Showing special kindness

feed   (fēd)   *n.* The tiny particles that minnows feed on

feign   (fān)   *v.* To pretend

feint   (fānt)   *v.* To pretend to make an attack

fennel   (fen′ 'l)   *n.* A tall herb

fettered   (fet′ ərd)   *adj.* Tied up with ropes or chains

fiasco   (fē as′ kō)   *n.* A complete failure

file   (fīl)   *v.* To move in line

finicky   (fin′ i kē)   *adj.* Particular or fussy

firing   (fīr′ iŋ)   *n.* The application of heat to harden or glaze pottery

firmament   (fʉr′ mə mənt)   *v.* The sky, viewed poetically as a solid arch or vault

fitting   (fit′ iŋ)   *adj.* Suitable; proper

flagon   (flag′ ən)   *n.* A container for liquids with a handle, narrow neck, spout, and sometimes a lid

flat   (flat)   *n.* An apartment

flatterer   (flat′ ər ər)   *n.* One who praises a person insincerely in order to gain something for oneself

flaunt   (flônt)   *v.* To display; to show off

fledgling   (flej′ liŋ)   *n.* A young bird

flinch   (flinch)   *v.* To move back, as if away from a blow

flit   (flit)   *v.* To fly lightly and rapidly

flock   (fläk)   *n.* Group of sheep

flush   (flush)   *v.* To drive from hiding

fluster   (flus′ tər)   *v.* To make nervous

forbidding   (fər bid′ iŋ)   *adj.* Looking harmful or unpleasant

forlorn   (fər lôrn′)   *adj.* Hopeless; miserable

formidable   (fôr′ mə də b'l)   *adj.* Impressive

forthwith (fôrth′ with′) *adv.* At once

fortitude (fôr′ tə tood′) *n.* Firm courage

fragile (fraj′ 'l) *adj.* Delicate; easily broken

fraudulent (frô′ jə lənt) *adj.* Acting with fraud; deceit

free-lance (frē′ lans′) *adj.* Working independently by selling services to individual buyers

furtively (fur′ tiv lē) *adv.* In a sly or sneaky way

G

gabardine (gab′ ər dēn′) *n.* A cloth of wool, cotton, rayon, or other material, used for suits and dresses

gaiter (gāt′ ər) *n.* Covering for the leg extending from the instep to the ankle or knee

galleon (gal′ ē ən) *n.* A large Spanish ship of the 15th and 16th centuries, used as both a warship and a trader

gambol (gam′ b'l) *n.* Play, frolic

garment (gär′ mənt) *n.* An article of clothing; costume

gaunt (gônt) *adj.* Thin and bony

gaze (gāz) *v.* To look intently and steadily

geology (jē äl′ ə jē) *n.* The science dealing with the physical nature and history of the earth

ghastly (gast′ lē) *adj.* Ghostlike; frightful

girdle (gər′ d'l) *n.* A belt or sash for the waist

glacier (glā′ shər) *n.* Large mass of ice and snow

gleeful (glē′ fəl) *adj.* Merry

glint (glint) *v.* To gleam, flash, or glitter

glisten (glis′ 'n) *v.* To shine or sparkle

gloat (glōt) *v.* To gaze or grin in scornful triumph

gloomy (gloom′ ē) *adj.* Causing gloom; dismal; depressing

glossy (glôs′ ē) *adj.* Smooth and shiny

gnarled (närld) *adj.* Knotty and twisted

gnawing (nô′ iŋ) *adj.* Tormenting; bothering

gorge (gôrj) *n.* A deep, narrow pass between steep heights

gourd (gôrd) *n.* The fruit of a certain kind of plant; the dried, hollowed shell of this fruit used as a drinking cup or dipper

gout (gout) *n.* A disease characterized by swelling and pain in the hands and feet

grave (grāv) *adj.* Serious

grief (grēf) *n.* Great sorrow

grieve (grēv) *v.* To feel sorrow for a loss

grimace (grim′ is) *v.* A twisting of the face as in expressing pain

grisly (griz′ lē) *adj.* Horrible

grizzled (griz′ ld) *adj.* Gray

grotesque (grō tesk′) *n.* A strange or distorted character

grouse (grous) *n.* A group of game birds

gullible (gul′ ə b'l) *adj.* Easily tricked

gumption (gump′ shən) *n.* Courage and enterprise

H

haggard (hag′ ərd) *adj.* Looking worn from grief or illness

halter (hôl′ tər) *n.* A rope, usually with a headpiece, for tying or leading an animal

harass (hə ras′) *v.* To trouble or worry

haughty (hôt′ ē) *adj.* Showing pride in oneself and contempt for others

haunch (hônch) *n.* An animal's lower back; hip

hearth (härth) *n.* The stone or brick floor of a fireplace

heartily (härt′ 'l ē) *adv.* Warmly; completely

heed (hēd) *n.* Attention

henceforth (hens fôrth′) *adv.* From this time on

herpetologist (hur′ pə täl′ ə jist) *n.* Someone who studies reptiles and amphibians

hexagonal (hek sag′ ə n'l) *adj.* Six-sided

hissing (his′ iŋ) *v.* Making a sound like a prolonged *s*

hoisting (hoist′ iŋ) *n.* Raising with a pulley or rope

holocaust (häl′ ə kôst′) *n.* In ancient times an offering burned to the gods

hover (huv′ ər) *v.* To hang in the air

hummock (hum′ ək) *n.* Area of fertile, wooded land, higher than the surrounding swamp

hunch (hunch) *v.* To stand with one's back bent

hurl (hurl) *v.* To throw with force or violence

Husky (hus′ kē) *n.* A strong dog used for pulling a sled over the snow

hymn (him) *n.* A song of praise

I

idiograph (id′ ē ə graf′) *n.* A symbol that stands for a thing or idea without expressing the sounds that make up its name

immeasurable (i mezh′ ər ə b'l) *adj.* So great that it cannot be measured

immense (i mens′) *adj.* Vast

impartiality (im pär′ shē al′ i tē) *n.* Fairness; not taking sides

impetuous (im pech′ oo wəs) *adj.* Moving with great force or violence

implore (im plôr′) *v.* To beg

impressive (im pres′ iv) *adj.* Having a strong effect on the mind or emotions

improvise (im′ prə vīz′) *v.* To make with the tools and materials at hand, usually to fill an unforeseen and immediate need

impudence (im′ pyoo dəns) *n.* Lack of respect

incense (in′ sens) *n.* Any of various substances that produce a pleasant odor when burned

incessant (in ses′ 'nt) *adj.* Without stopping

incomprehensible (in′ käm pri hen′ seb'l) *adj.* Not able to be understood

incredulous (in krej′ oo ləs) *adj.* Unwilling or unable to believe

incredulously (in kre′ joo ləs lē) *adv.* In a disbelieving way

incubation (in′ kyoo bā′ shən) *n.* The phase in a disease between the infection and the first appearance of symptoms

indifferent (in dif′ ər ənt)   *adj.* Uninterested

industrious (in dus′ trē əs)   *adj.* Hard-working

inert (in ᵿrt′)   *adj.* Without power to move

inertia (in ᵿr′ shə)   *n.* The tendency of an object to remain at rest if it is at rest, or to remain moving if it is moving—unless it is disturbed by an outside force

inevitable (in ev′ ə tə b'l)   *adj.* Certain to happen

inflammatory (in flam′ ə tôr′ ē)   *adj.* Characterized by pain and swelling

ingenious (in jēn′ yəs)   *adj.* Clever and inventive

inlet (in′ let)   *n.* A narrow strip of water jutting into a body of land from a river or lake or ocean

insolent (in′ sə lənt)   *adj.* Disrespectful

integer (in′ tə jər)   *n.* Any positive or negative whole number

integration (in tə grā′ shən)   *n.* The mingling of different ethnic or racial groups

intention (in ten′ shən)   *n.* Anything intended or planned

interact (in′ tər akt′)   *v.* To affect and be affected by

interplanetary (in′ tər plan′ ə ter′ ē)   *adj.* Between planets

interpreter (in tᵿr′ prə tər)   *n.* Someone who translates from one language to another

interrogation (in ter′ ə gā′ shən)   *n.* Situation where people are formally questioned

intervene (in′ tər vēn′)   *v.* To step into a situation

interwoven (in′ tər wō′ vən)   *adj.* Mixed together

intricacy (in′ tri kə sē)   *n.* The quality of being hard to follow or understand

intrigue (in trēg′)   *v.* To fascinate

invariable (in ver′ ē ə b'l)   *adj.* Not changing; uniform

ironical (ī rän′ i k'l)   *adj.* In a different way from what is expected

irrevocable (i rev′ ə kə b'l)   *adj.* Unchangeable

irrigation (ir′ ə gā′ shən)   *adj.* Referring to an artificial means of supplying land with water

J

jubliant (jo͞o′ b'l ənt)   *adj.* Joyful and triumphant

judicious (jo͞o dish′ əs)   *adj.* Wise

K

keener (kēn′ ər)   *adj.* Sharper and quicker

Kentucky (kən tuk′ ē)   *n.* [<Iroquoian (Wyandot), level land, plain] Eastern central state of the United States

kiln (kiln)   *n.* An oven to bake pottery

kilometer (ki läm′ ə tər)   *n.* 1,000 meters or about ⅝ of a mile

kindling (kin′ dliŋ)   *n.* Bits of dry wood for starting a fire

knoll (nōl)   *n.* A small, rounded hill

L

lackadaisical (lak′ ə dā′ zi kəl)   *adj.* Showing a lack of interest

lackluster (lak′ lus′ tər)   *adj.* Lacking brightness; dull

laconic (lə kän′ ik)   *adj.* Using few words

lacy (lā′ sē)   *adj.* Haivng a delicate, open pattern, like lace

lament (lə ment′)   *v.* To express deep sorrow for; mourn

lariat (lar′ ē it)   *n.* A rope for tethering grazing horses; lasso

latent (lāt′ 'nt)   *adj.* Hidden and not fully developed

lattice (lat′ is)   *n.* An openwork structure of crossed strips or bars of wood, metal, and the like

leer (lir)   *v.* To look with harmful intent

leeward (lē′ wərd)   *adj.* Sheltered from the wind

legacy (leg′ ə sē)   *n.* Something handed down by a parent or an ancestor

lethal (lē′ thəl)   *adj.* Deadly

liability (lī ə bil′ ə tē)   *n.* A disadvantage

lichen (lī′ kən)   *n.* Any of a large group of small plants

limerick (lim′ ər ik)   *n.* A nonsense poem of five lines

lith (līth)   *adj.* Flexible and supple

livid (liv′ id)   *adj.* Grayish-blue; sometimes taken to mean pale, white, or red

loathe (lō*th*)   *v.* To hate

lollop (läl′ əp)   *v.* To move in a clumsy or relaxed way, bobbing up and down or from side to side

loping (lōp′ iŋ)   *adj.* Moving in a hesitant way

lorry (lôr′ ē)   *n.* [Brit.] A motor truck

lull (lul)   *v.* To calm by gentle sounds or motions

lumbering (lum′ bər iŋ)   *adj.* Awkward; clumsy

luminary (lo͞o′ mə ner′ ē)   *n.* Something that gives off light

luminous (lo͞o′ mə nəs)   *adj.* Clear; easily understood

lute (lo͞ot)   *n.* An old-fashioned stringed instrument like a guitar

M

machete (mə shet′ ē)   *n.* Large, heavy-bladed knife

madly (mad′ lē)   *adv.* Insanely; wildly or furiously; foolishly; extremely

majestic (mə jes′ tik)   *adj.* Grand; lofty

malice (mal′ is)   *n.* Ill will or spite

malleable (mal′ ē ə b'l)   *adj.* Able to be hammered, pounded, or pressed into various shapes without breaking

maneuver (mə no͞o′ vər)   *n.* A planned movement or procedure

mantle (man′ t'l)   *n.* A loose, sleeveless cloak or cape

marauder (mə rôd′ ər)   *n.* A roaming attacker or plunderer

marred (märd)   *v.* Disturbed

martial (mär′ shəl)   *adj.* Suitable for war

masterful (mas′ tər fəl)   *adj.* Able to force one's will on others

mastiff (mas′ tif)   *n.* A large, powerful, smooth-coated dog with hanging lip and drooping ears

maxim (mak′ sim)   *n.* Wise saying

meager (mē′ gər)   *adj.* Of poor quality; small in amount

meek (mēk) *adj.* Patient and mild

melancholy (mel' ən käl' ē) *adj.* Sad, gloomy

melodious (mə lō' dē əs) *adj.* Pleasing to hear

menace (men' is) *n.* Danger, threat

menacing (men' is iŋ) *adj.* Threatening

menage (mə näzh') *n.* Household

merit (mer' it) *n.* Worth; goodness

mesa (mā' sə) *n.* A flat tableland with steep sides

mesmerize (mez' mər īz') *v.* To hypnotize

mesmerizing (mez' mər īz' iŋ) *adj.* Hypnotizing

metamorphose (met' ə môr' fōz) *v.* To change

metamorphosis (met' ə môr' fə sis) *n.* A change of form

milling (mil' iŋ) *v.* Moving in a circular or random motion

mined (mīnd) *adj.* Filled with buried explosives that are set to go off when stepped on

miracle (mir' ə k'l) *n.* An event or action that apparently contradicts known scientific laws and is hence thought to be due to supernatural causes

mired (mīrd) *adj.* Stuck in deep mud

misanthrope (mis' ən thrōp') *n.* A person who hates or mistrusts everyone

Missouri (mi zoor' ē) *n.* [<Algonquian, literally, people of the big canoes] Middle Western state of the central United States

mobilize (mō' bə līz') *v.* To put into motion

mock (mäk) *v.* To copy

moil (moil) *v.* To toil and slave

momentum (mō men' təm) *n.* The increasing force of a moving object

monarch (män' ərk) *n.* A ruler; king or queen

monitoring (män' ə tər' iŋ) *v.* Watching or keeping track of

monogrammed (män' ə gramd') *adj.* Having a design made up of two or more letters

monotone (män' ə tōn) *v.* A single, unchanging tone

moor (moor) *n.* Rolling land with swamps

morbid (môr' bid) *adj.* Of, having, or caused by disease; unhealthy

morgue (môrg) *n.* A place where the bodies of dead persons are kept to be examined or identified before burial

morose (mə rōs') *adj.* Gloomy; ill-tempered

mortal (môr' t'l) *n.* A being who must eventually die

mortality (môr tal' ə tē) *n.* Having to die someday

mortician (môr tish' ən) *n.* An undertaker; funeral director

mortuary (mor' choo wer' ē) *n.* A place where dead bodies are kept before burial or cremation, such as a morgue or funeral home

mosaic (mō zā' ik) *adj.* Made of different pieces combined to form a whole

mourning (môr' niŋ) *v.* Feeling sorrow for the death of a loved one

murder (mur' dər) *v.* To kill unlawfully and with malice

murky (mur' kē) *adj.* Heavy and obscure with smoke or mist

mush (mush) *v.* To travel by foot over snow, usually with a dog sled

muslin (muz' lin) *n.* A plain, strong kind of cotton cloth

mustache (mus' tash) *n.* The hair on the upper lip of men

mutilated (myoot' 'l āt' əd) *adj.* Damaged or injured

mutton (mut' 'n) *n.* Sheep

muzzled (muz' 'ld) *adj.* Prevented from talking or expressing an opinion

N

narcissism (när' sə siz'm) *n.* Self-love; excessive interest in one's own appearance, comfort, importance, or abilities

neurophysiology (noor' ō fiz' ē äl' ə jē) *n.* The study of the brain and nervous system

nimble (nim' b'l) *adj.* Moving quickly and lightly

nonchalant (nän' shə länt') *adj.* Casual

O

obligatory (əb lig' ə tôr ē) *adj.* Required

obliging (ə blīj' iŋ) *adj.* Ready to do favors

obscure (äb skyoor') *adj.* Unknown; isolated

obsequious (əb sē' kwē əs) *adj.* Much too willing to serve or obey; overly submissive

obsidian (əb sid' ē ən) *n.* A hard, usually dark-colored or black, volcanic glass

obstinate (äb' stə nit) *adj.* Stubborn

odious (ō' dē əs) *adj.* Disgusting; offensive

oil painting (oil' pānt' iŋ) *n.* A picture painted in oil colors

ominous (äm' ə nəs) *adj.* Threatening

ontogeny (än täj' ə nē) *n.* The life cycle of a simple organism or individual

ooze (ooz) *v.* To flow or leak slowly

opalescent (ō' pə les' 'nt) *adj.* Showing a play of colors like an opal

opaque (ō pāk') *adj.* Not letting light pass through

orator (ôr' ət ər) *n.* A public speaker

organdy (or' gən dē) *n.* Thin, crisp cotton fabric used for items like dresses and curtains

ostler (äs' lər) *n.* Somone who takes care of horses at an inn or stable

outskirts (out' skurtz) *n.* Part of district remote from the center or midst

Ozark (ō' zärk) **Mountains** *n.* [<Fr. *aux Arcs,* to the (region of the) Arc (Arkansas) Indians] Highland region in NW Arkansas, SW Missouri, and NE Oklahoma

P

pamper (pam' pər) *v.* To treat carefully; coax

pandemic (pan dem' ik) *adj.* Prevalent over a whole area; universal

paradox (par' ə däks') *n.* A statement that seems contradictory, unbelievable, or absurd but that may actually be true in fact

parasite (par′ ə sīt) *n.* An animal that lives on another organism in order to get food, protection, or both

passive (pas′ iv) *adj.* Inactive

pathetic (pə thet′ ik) *adj.* Arousing pity, sorrow, and sympathy

pathological (path′ ə läj′ i k'l) *adj.* Due to or involving disease

patriarch (pa′ trē ärk) *n.* An old, dignified man

pauper (pô′ pər) *n.* An extremely poor person

peer (pēr) *v.* To look closely

peeved (pēvd) *adj.* Irritated

penetrate (pen′ ə trāt) *v.* To pass into or through

perfunctorily (pʉr funk tôr′ i lē) *adv.* As if routinely or as a matter of course

perilous (per′ əl əs) *adj.* Dangerous

perpetual (pər pech′ ळ wəl) *adj.* Never stopping

perseverance (pʉr sə vir′ əns) *n.* Continued effort

persist (pʉr sist′) *v.* To say or to do over and over again

persistent (pər sis′ tənt) *adj.* Constantly recurring

perspective (pər spek′ tiv) *n.* The appearance of objects or scenes as determined by their relative distance and positions; a specific point of view

pestilent (pes′ t'l ənt) *adj.* Deadly; annoying

petrol (pet′ rəl) *n.* [Brit.] Gasoline

phantasmagoria (fan taz′ mə gôr′ ē ə) *n.* An early type of magic-lantern show consisting of various optical illusions

phantom (fan′ təm) *n.* Something that seems to appear to the sight but has no physical existence

philanthropy (fi lan′ thrə pē) *n.* A desire to help mankind; benevolence

philharmonic (fil′ här män′ ik) *adj.* Loving or devoted to music

philosophy (fi läs′ ə fē) *n.* Originally, love of, or the search for, wisdom or knowledge

phylogeny (fī läj′ ə nē) *n.* The development of a species or group

pilgrimage (pil′ grəm ij) *n.* A long journey to a place of interest

pious (pī′ əs) *adj.* Good; virtuous

pithy (pith′ ē) *adj.* Brief but full of meaning

plaiting (plāt′ iŋ) *n.* Braiding

plankton (plaŋk′ tən) *n.* Very small animal and plant life that floats or drifts in the water

pliant (plī′ ənt) *adj.* Easily bent; adaptable

plodding (pläd′ iŋ) *adj.* Walking or moving heavily

poise (poiz) *v.* To balance

pomegranate (päm′ gran′ it) *n.* A round fruit with a red, leathery rind and many seeds

pomp (pämp) *n.* Impressive show or display

ponderous (pän′ dər əs) *adj.* Very heavy, bulky

posting (pōs′ tiŋ) *n.* Notice of the racing time of each swimmer

pound (pound) *n.* A unit of money used by the British

precipice (pres′ i pis) *n.* A vertical rock face or steep cliff

precipitation (pri sip′ ə tā′ shən) *n.* Great speed

precipitous (pri sip′ ə təs) *adj.* Very steep

predatory (pred′ ə tôr′ ē) *adj.* Living by capturing and feeding on other animals

predestined (prē des′ tind) *adj.* In this case, marked to die early

preen (prēn) *v.* To dress up; show pride in one's appearance

preening (prēn′ iŋ) *n.* The act of cleaning and trimming feathers with a beak

preferable (pref′ ər ə b'l) *adj.* More desirable

premium (prē′ mē əm) *n.* An additional charge

prescribed (pri skrib′'d) *adj.* Advised as a medicine by a doctor

presently (prez′ 'nt lē) *adv.* In a little while

presumptuous (pri zump′ choo wəs) *n.* Overstepping ordinary bounds of courtesy

prevalent (prev′ ə lənt) *adj.* Widely accepted

priming (prī′ miŋ) *n.* The explosive used to set off the charge in a gun

prodigy (präd′ ə jē) *n.* A child of unusually high talent

proffer (präf′ ər) *v.* To offer

profound (prə found′) *adj.* Deeply or intensely felt

prolapse (pro′ laps) *n.* An internal organ that has fallen out of place

Promethean (prə mē′ thē ən) *adj.* Life-bringing, creative, or courageously original

prominent (präm′ ə nənt) *adj.* Widely and favorably known

promissory (präm′ i sôr′ ē) **notes** *n.* Written promises to pay someone a certain sum of money

prone (prōn) *adj.* Lying face downward

prose (prōz) *n.* Nonpoetic language

prosper (präs′ pər) *v.* To grow; flourish

providence (präv′ ə dəns) *n.* A godsend; a valuable gift

provisional (prə vizh′ ən 'l) *adj.* Temporary; depending on future events

provision (prō vizh′ ən *n.* A stock of food and supplies

psychology (sī käl′ ə jē) *n.* The science dealing with the mind

pummel (pum′ 'l) *v.* To hit with repeated blows

pungent (pun′ jənt) *adj.* Sharp-smelling

Q

quaff (kwäf) *v.* To drink in a thirsty way

quail (kwāl) *v.* To draw back in fear

quarry (kwôr′ ē) *v.* To carve out of the ground

quaver (kwā′ vər) *v.* To shake or tremble

quicksilver (kwik′ sil′ vər) *adj.* Quick; changeable; unpredictable; like the chemical element mercury, which is silver-white and flows easily

quip (kwip) *v.* To make a witty remark

quiver (kwiv′ ər) *n.* A case for arrows

R

radiant (rā′ dē ənt) *adj.* Shining brightly

rancid (ran′ sid) *adj.* Spoiled and bad smelling

rapt (rapt) *adj.* Giving complete attention; totally carried away by something

rash (rash) *adj.* Reckless

raspy (ras′ pē) *adj.* Rough and grating

realm (relm) *n.* A kingdom

reconnoiter (rē kə noit′ ər) *v.* To look around

redundant (rē dun′ dənt) *adj.* No longer needed; in excess

reflect (ri flekt′) *v.* To think seriously

refuge (ref′ yōōj) *n.* A place of safety or shelter

refute (ri fyōōt′) *v.* To prove someone wrong

regalia (ri gāl′ yə) *n.* Splendid clothes and decorations

register (rej′ is tər) *n.* A record containing a list of names

relate (ri lāt′) *v.* To tell

relentlessly (ri lent′ lis lē) *adv.* Persistently or without stopping

relevant (rel′ ə vənt) *adj.* Relating to the matter at hand; to the point

relish (rel′ ish) *v.* To especially enjoy

remit (ri mit′) *v.* To forgive or pardon; put back

remonstrance (ri män′ strəns) *n.* The act of protesting or pleading

render (ren′ dər) *v.* To melt down

repellent (ri pel′ ənt) *n.* Something that pushes away

reproach (ri prōch′) *v.* To blame; scold

resign (ri zīn′) *v.* To accept without complaining

resigned (ri zīn′ ′d) *adj.* In a yielding and uncomplaining manner

resilient (ri zil′ yənt) *adj.* Springing back into shape

resin (rez′ ′n) *n.* A sticky brownish or yellowish substance that comes from evergreen trees

resolute (rez′ ə lōōt′) *adj.* Of firm purpose

resourceful (ri sôrs′ fəl) *adj.* Able to deal effectively with problems

retrieve (ri trēv) *v.* To find and bring back

retrospect (ret′ rə spekt′) *n.* A looking back on the past

reverentially (rev′ ə ren′ shə lē) *adv.* In a manner showing great respect and admiration

reverie (rev′ ər ē) *n.* Dreamy thinking or imagining

revoke (ri vōk′) *v.* To cancel, withdraw

rheumatism (rōō′ mə tiz′m) *n.* Pain and stiffness of the joints and muscles

riffle (rif′ ′l) *n.* A shallow area in a stream

rigorous (rig′ ər əs) *adj.* Strict; thorough

rind (rīnd) *n.* Tough outer layer or skin

rite (rīt) *n.* Religious observance

rodeo (rō′ dē ō′) *n.* A public exhibition or competition of the skills of cowboys

rouge (rōōzh) *n.* A reddish cosmetic used to color the cheeks

rout (rout) *v.* To completely defeat

rudder (rud′ ər) *n.* A flat piece of wood or metal attached to the rear of a boat and used for steering

ruff (ruf) *n.* A band of fur around the necks of animals or birds

runt (runt) *n.* The smallest animal of a litter

S

saffron (saf′ rən) *n.* An orange-yellow color

sage (sāj) *n.* A very wise man

saline (sā′ līn) *n.* A salt solution

sanction (saŋk′ shən) *n.* Support

sanctuary (saŋk′ choo wer′ ē) *n.* A place of protection

sarcastically (sär kas′ ti klē) *adv.* In a mocking or sneering manner

sauciness (sô′ sē nes) *n.* Liveliness; spirit

saunter (sôn′ tər) *v.* To walk about idly; stroll

savor (sā′ vər) *v.* To enjoy

scald (skôld) *v.* To burn with hot liquid

scale (skāl) *n.* A series of musical tones

scapegoat (skāp′ gōt) *n.* A person or group blamed for the mistakes or crimes of others

scorn (skôrn) *n.* A strong dislike for someone or something thought to be inferior

scour (skour) *v.* To clean by rubbing vigorously

scourge (skurj) *n.* The cause of serious trouble

scowl (skoul) *v.* To frown

scrim (skrim) *n.* A light, semi-transparent curtain

scrooge (skrōōj) *n.* A hard, miserly misanthrope

scurry (skur′ ē) *v.* To run hastily; scamper

scuttle (skut′ ′l) *v.* To run or move quickly; scurrcy

seismology (sīz mäl′ ə jē) *n.* A geophysical science dealing with earthquakes and related phenomena

sentimental (sen′ tə men′ t′l) *adj.* Acting from feeling rather than from practical motives

sepulcher (sep′ ′l kər) *n.* Grave; tomb

seraph (ser′ əf) *n.* Angel

serenity (sə ren′ ə tē) *n.* Calmness

severe (sə vir′) *adj.* Harsh

sexton (seks′ tən) *n.* A church official in charge of ringing the bells

shadowing (shad′ ō iŋ) *v.* Shading an area in a picture or painting

sheen (shēn) *n.* Brightness; shininess

shilling (shil′ iŋ) *n.* A British coin worth five pennies

shimmering (shim′ ər iŋ) *adj.* Shining with an unsteady light

shrew (shrōō) *n.* A small, slender, mouselike animal with soft, brown fur and a long, pointed snout

shrewdest (shrōōd′ əst) *adj.* Cleverest

shrouded (shroud′ əd) *adj.* Hidden from view

shudder (shud′ ər) *v.* To shake

sibling (sib′ liŋ) *n.* A brother or sister

sieve (siv) *n.* A utensil with many tiny openings; strainer

sinew (sin′ yōō) *n.* Tendon

sinewy (sin′ yōō wē) *adj.* Tough and strong

skids (skidz) *n.* Planks or logs on which a heavy object can be slid

skittish (skit′ ish) *adj.* Nervous or jumpy

slacken (slak′ ′n) *v.* To become less active

slither (slith′ ər) *v.* To slide

slough (slōō) *n.* A swamp, bog, or marsh that is part of an inlet or backwater

sluggish (slug′ ish) *adj.* Lacking energy

sluice (slo͞os) *n.* An artificial channel or passage for water, having a gate or valve at its head to regulate the flow

smartly (smärt′ lē) *adv.* Sharply

snorkel (snôr′ k'l) *v.* To swim underwater using snorkel, or breathing tube, that extends above the surface of the water

snowshoes (snō′ sho͞oz′) *n.* Racket-shaped pieces of wood crisscrossed with strips of leather, worn on the feet to prevent sinking in deep snow

snug (snug) *adj.* Cozy; comfortable

solemn (säl′ əm) *adj.* Serious; somber

solemnize (säl′ əm nīz) *v.* To honor

solitary (säl′ ə ter ē) *adj.* Single

somber (säm′ bər) *adj.* Dark and solemn

somnolent (säm′ nə lent) *adj.* Sleepy, drowsy

spectacle (spek′ tə k'l) *n.* Something to look at; unusual display

spectacles (spek′ tə k'lz) *n.* A pair of eyeglasses

spectator (spek′ tā tər) *n.* A person who sees or watches something without taking an active part

specter (spek′ tər) *n.* A ghost or ghostlike appearance

spectral (spek′ trəl) *adj.* Like a specter; phantom; ghostly

spectroscope (spek′ trə skōp′) *n.* An optical instrument used for forming spectra for study

spittoon (spi to͞on′) *n.* A jarlike container into which people spit

squat (skwät) *adj.* Short and heavy

squelched (skwelcht) *adj.* Crushed or overpowered

stable (stā′ b'l) *n.* A building in which horses or cattle are sheltered and fed

staccato (stə kät′ ō) *adj.* Made up of sharp, separate little elements

stalk (stôk) *v.* To walk slowly and stiffly

stealthy (stel′ thē) *adj.* Secretly; slyly

steed (stēd) *n.* A high-spirited riding horse

stern (sturn) *adj.* Strict; unyielding

still (stil) *n.* A photograph made from a single frame of a motion picture and used for advertising it

straggly (strag′ lē) *adj.* Spread out

straightforward (strāt′ fôr′ wərd) *adj.* Direct; frank; honest

strand (strand) *n.* The ocean shore

stratagem (strat′ ə jəm) *n.* Trick or scheme

strenuous (stren′ yo͞o əs) *adj.* Requiring great effort or energy

stride (strīd) *v.* To walk with long steps, especially in a vigorous manner

strive (strīv) *v.* To struggle

stubble (stub′ 'l) *n.* Short stumps of corn or grain

studio (sto͞o′ dē ō′) *n.* A room or rooms where an artist or photographer works

subscribe (səb skrīb′) *v.* To support

subservient (səb sur′ vē ənt) *adj.* Inferior

subtle (sut′ 'l) *adj.* Delicately skillful or clever

succession (sək sesh′ ən) *n.* The act of coming after another in order

succulent (suk′ yoo lent) *adj.* Juicy

sullen (sul′ ən) *adj.* Silent and keeping to oneself because angry or hurt

summon (sum′ ən) *v.* To call forth or gather

supercilious (so͞o′ pər sil′ ē əs) *adj.* Proud; scornful

supple (sup′ 'l) *adj.* Flexible

suppress (sə pres′) *v.* To keep back

surge (surj) *v.* To move in a violent swelling motion

surpass (sər pas′) *v.* To be superior to

surreptitious (sur′ əp tish′ əs) *adj.* Secret

susceptible (sə sep′ tə b'l) *adj.* Responsive

suspiciously (sə spish′ əs lē) *adv.* In a suspecting way

sustain (sə stān′) *v.* To support

swagger (swag′ ər) *v.* To walk in a showy, proud way

swarm (swôrm) *v.* To be filled or crowded

swerve (swurv) *n.* A curving motion

sylvan (sil′ vən) *adj.* Of or characteristic of woods and forests

T

tableau (tab′ lō) *n.* A dramatic scene or picture

taco (tä′ kō) *n.* A Mexican dish consisting of a fried, folded tortilla filled with chopped meat, shredded lettuce, and the like

taint (tānt) *n.* A trace

tangible (tan′ jə b'l) *adj.* Real or solid

taut (tôt) *adj.* Tightly stretched

tawny (tô′ nē) *adj.* Yellowish-brown

teak (tēk) *n.* Yellowish-brown wood

technology (tek näl′ ə jē) *n.* The ideas of science applied to practical problems

tedious (tē′ dē əs) *adj.* Long and boring

tempest (tem′ pist) *n.* A violent storm

tentative (ten′ tə tiv) *adj.* Hesitant; uncertain

tepid (tep′ id) *adj.* Not warm or cold; lukewarm

termagant (tur′ mə gənt) *adj.* Scolding

terse (turs) *adj.* To the point

testimony (tes′ ti mō′ nē) *n.* Statement or declaration

tether (teth′ ər) *v.* To fasten with a rope or chain

thistle (this′ 'l) *n.* A stubborn, weedy plant with sharp leaves and usually purplish flowers

threadbare (thred′ ber′) *adj.* Worn, shabby

tiered (tird) *adj.* Stacked in rows

titanic (tī tan′ ik) *adj.* Having great size, strength, or power

torrent (tôr′ ənt) *n.* A flood

totter (tät′ ər) *v.* To rock or shake as if about to fall; to be unsteady

tracheotomy (trā′ kē ät′ ə mē) *n.* An operation in which the trachea, or windpipe, is cut to make an artificial breathing hole

transformation (trans′ fər mā′ shən) *n.* A change in condition and outward appearance

translucent (trans lo͞o′ s'nt) *adj.* Clear

transmission (trans mish′ ən) *n.* The passage of radio waves through space between the transmitting station and the receiving station

trebly   (tre′ blē)   *adv.* Three times as much; triply

tribulation   (trib′ yə lā′ shən)   *n.* Great misery or distress

trident   (trīd′ 'nt)   *n.* A spear with three points

trifle   (trī′ f'l)   *n.* Something of little value or importance

triumphant   (trī um′ fənt)   *adj.* Rejoicing for victory; exulting in success

trundle   (trun′ d'l)   *v.* To move on wheels or as if on wheels

tumultuous   (tōō mul′ choo wəs)   *adj.* Noisy and violent

turmoil   (tur′ moil′)   *n.* Uproar; confusion

U

unanimous   (yōō nan′ ə məs)   *adj.* Based on complete agreement

unbiased   (un′ bī′ əst)   *adj.* Without prejudice; fair

uncanny   (un kan′ ē)   *adj.* Unfamiliar; strange in a frightening way

undeleterious   (un del′ ə tir′ ē əs)   *adj.* Healthy, full of well-being

unfrequented   (un frē kwənt′ əd)   *adj.* Not often visited

unique   (yōō nēk′)   *adj.* Highly unusual or rare

unison   (yōō′ nə sən)   *n.* Complete agreement; harmony

unravel   (un rav′ əl)   *v.* To become untangled or separated

unrequited   (un′ ri kwī′ t'd)   *adj.* Unreturned

urchin   (ur′ chin)   *n.* A mischievous boy

usurp   (yōō surp′)   *v.* To take without right

utilize   (yōōt′ 'l īz′)   *v.* To make useful

V

vacancy   (vā′ kən sē)   *n.* Emptiness

vandal   (van′ d'l)   *n.* A person who damages or destroys things on purpose

vanquish   (van′ kwish)   *v.* To overcome

varmint   (vär′ mənt)   *n.* An animal regarded as troublesome

veer   (vir)   *v.* To change direction

venomously   (ve′ nəm əs lē)   *adv.* Full of ill will

verdict   (vur′ dikt)   *n.* A decision or judgment

verge   (vurj)   *n.* The edge or brink

verisimilitude   (ver′ ə si mil′ ə tōōd′)   *n.* The appearance of being true or real

vertebrate   (vər′ tə brāt′)   *n.* An animal with a backbone

vibrant   (vī′ brənt)   *adj.* Throbbing with life and activity; lively; energetic

vicar   (vik′ ər)   *n.* A parish priest in the Anglican Church

vie   (vī)   *v.* To compete

virago   (vi rä′ gō)   *n.* A quarrelsome woman

virulent   (vir′ yōō lənt)   *adj.* Extremely poisonous or harmful

visage   (viz′ ij)   *n.* Face

vital   (vīt′ 'l)   *adj.* Essential to life; living

vitality   (vī tal′ ə tē)   *n.* The power to live or go on living

vitalize   (vīt′ 'l īz′)   *n.* To make vital; give life to

vital signs   (vīt′ 'l sīnz′)   *n.* Indicators of the efficient functioning of the body; especially pulse, temperature, and respiration

vitamin   (vīt′ ə min)   *n.* Any of a number of complex organic substances found in most foods

vixen   (vik′ s'n)   *n.* A female fox

void   (void)   *n.* Emptiness

voluminous   (və lōōm′ ə nəs)   *adj.* Large or full

W

waft   (wâft)   *v.* Carry

wages   (wāj′ əz)   *n.* Money paid to an employee for work done

wane   (wān)   *v.* To approach the end

warbler   (wôr′ blər)   *n.* Songbird

wary   (wâr′ ē)   *adj.* Cautious

wassail   (wäs′ 'l)   *n.* A spiced drink used in celebrating

watercolor   (wôt′ ər kul′ ər)   *n.* A pigment or coloring matter that is mixed with water for use as a paint; a painting done with such paints

wee   (wē)   *adj.* Very small, tiny

wheedle   (hwē′ d'l)   *v.* To persuade a person by flattery or coaxing

whimper   (hwim′ pər)   *v.* To make low, crying sounds; complain

wicker   (wik′ ər)   *n.* A thin, flexible twig

wigwam   (wig′ wäm)   *n.* A shelter with a rounded top made by certain Native American groups

willful   (wil′ fəl)   *adj.* Wanting one's own way; self-willed

wily   (wī′ lē)   *adj.* Sly

wince   (wins)   *v.* Draw back

winnow   (win′ ō)   *v.* To beat as with wings

wistfully   (wist′ fəl lē)   *adj.* Showing vague yearnings

wither   (with′ ər)   *v.* Dry up

wonderful   (wun′ dər fəl)   *adj.* That causes wonder; marvelous; amazing

wonderland   (wun′ dər land′)   *n.* An imaginary land full of wonders

wonderment   (wun′ dər mənt)   *n.* Astonishment

wonderworker   (wun′ dər wurk′ ər)   *n.* One who performs miracles or wonders

wondrous   (wun′ drəs)   *adj.* Wonderful; extraordinary

wrought   (rôt)   *adj.* Formed; made out of

Y

yearn   (yurn)   *v.* Want very much

yucca   (yuk′ ə)   *adj.* Plants with stiff sword-shaped leaves and white flowers

INDEX OF FINE ART

INDEX OF SKILLS

CRITICAL THINKING AND READING

LEARNING OPTIONS

READING IN THE CONTENT AREAS

THINKING AND WRITING

INDEX OF TITLES BY THEMES

GROWING AND CHANGING

OUR LIVING EARTH

RITES OF PASSAGE

THE SEARCH FOR SELF

INDEX OF AUTHORS AND TITLES

Page numbers in *italics* refer to biographical information

ACKNOWLEDGMENTS (continued)

Isaac Asimov
"Hallucination" by Isaac Asimov, published in *Boy's Life*. Copyright © 1985 by the Boy Scouts of America. Reprinted by permission of the author.

Atheneum Books for Young Readers, an imprint of Simon & Schuster Children's Publishing Division
Bearstone by Will Hobbs. Copyright © 1989 by Will Hobbs. "Construction" from *8 A.M. Shadows* by Patricia Hubbell. Copyright © 1965 by Patricia Hubbell. Reprinted with permission.

Elizabeth Barnett, Literary Executor for the Estate of Norma Millay Ellis
"The Courage That My Mother Had" by Edna St. Vincent Millay. From *Collected Poems,* HarperCollins. Copyright © 1954, 1982 by Norma Millay Ellis. Reprinted by permission of Elizabeth Barnett, Literary Executor.

Susan Bergholz Literary Services
The Flying Tortilla Man by Denise Chávez. Copyright © 1989 by Denise Chávez. Reprinted by permission of Susan Bergholz Literary Services, New York.

Gwendolyn Brooks
"Home" from *The World of Gwendolyn Brooks,* Harper & Row. Reprinted by permission of the author.

Canongate Press PLC
"Children of Wax" by Alexander McCall Smith, from *Children of Wax: African Folk Tales.* © Alexander McCall Smith 1989. Reprinted by permission of Canongate Press PLC.

Don Congdon Associates, Inc.
"All Summer in a Day" by Ray Bradbury. Copyright © 1954; renewed 1982 by Ray Bradbury. "The Third Level" by Jack Finney. Copyright © 1950; renewed 1977 by Jack Finney. Reprinted by permission of Don Congdon Associates, Inc.

Congdon & Weed, Inc.
"No Gumption" from *Growing Up* by Russell Baker. Copyright © 1982 by Russell Baker. Reprinted by permission of Congdon & Weed, Inc.

Harold Courlander
"All Stories Are Anansi's" from *The Hat-Shaking Dance and Other Ashanti Tales from Ghana* by Harold Courlander with Albert Kofi Prempeh. Copyright © 1957 by Harcourt Brace Jovanovich, Inc.; 1985 by Harold Courlander. Reprinted by permission of the author.

Current History, Inc.
"A puppy whose hair was so flowing" by Oliver Herford. From *The Century Magazine,* copyright 1912. Reprinted by permission of Current History, Inc.

Delacorte Press, a division of Bantam Doubleday Dell Publishing Group, Inc.
"The Luckiest Time of All" excerpted from the book *The Lucky Stone* by Lucille Clifton. Copyright © 1979 by Lucille Clifton. Reprinted by permission of Delacorte Press, a division of Bantam Doubleday Dell Publishing Group, Inc.

Adriaan de Wit for the Estate of Dorothy de Wit
"Ojeeg, the Hunter, and the Ice Man" retold by Dorothy de Wit in *The Talking Stone,* edited by Dorothy de Wit. Copyright © 1979 by Dorothy de Wit. Reprinted by permission.

Dial Books for Young Readers, a division of Penguin Books USA Inc.
From *Song of the Trees* by Mildred D. Taylor. Copyright © 1975 by Mildred Taylor. Reprinted by permission of Dial Books for Young Readers, a division of Penguin Books USA Inc.

Doubleday, a division of Bantam Doubleday Dell Publishing Group, Inc.
"The Ransom of Red Chief" from *The Tales of O. Henry* by O. Henry. "The Bat" copyright 1938 by Theodore Roethke from *The Collected Poems of Theodore Roethke* by Theodore Roethke. Reprinted by permission of Doubleday, a division of Bantam Doubleday Dell Publishing Group, Inc.

Dutton Children's Books, a division of Penguin Books USA Inc.
"The Flower-Fed Buffaloes" from *Going-to-the-Stars* by Vachel Lindsay. Copyright 1926 by D. Appleton & Co., renewed 1954 by Elizabeth C. Lindsay. A Hawthorn book. Reprinted by permission of Dutton Children's Books, a division of Penguin Books USA Inc.

Farrar, Straus & Giroux, Inc.
"Utzel and His Daughter, Poverty" from *Stories for Children* by Isaac Bashevis Singer. Copyright © 1962, 1967, 1968, 1970, 1972, 1973, 1974, 1975, 1976, 1979, 1980, 1984 by Isaac Bashevis Singer. Excerpt from "A Far Cry From Africa" from *Collected Poems* 1948–1984 by Derek Walcott. Copyright © 1962, 1963, 1964, 1986 by Derek Walcott. "Seal" from *Laughing Time: Nonsense Poems* by William Jay Smith. Copyright © 1953, 1955, 1956, 1957, 1959, 1968, 1974, 1977, 1980 by William Jay Smith. Reprinted by permission of Farrar, Straus & Giroux, Inc.

Feinstein, Alan S.
"The Wicked Weasel" from *Folk Tales from Siam* by Alan S. Feinstein. © 1969 by Alan S. Feinstein. Reprinted by permission of the author.

Harcourt Brace & Company
"Broken Chain" from *Baseball in April and Other Stories* by Gary Soto. Copyright © 1990 by Gary Soto. "Eugenie Clark and the Sleeping Sharks" from *Wild Animals, Gentle Women,*

Little, Brown and Company

From *Let's Steal the Moon* by Blanche Serwer-Bernstein. Text copyright © 1970, 1987 by Blanche L. Serwer-Bernstein. "The Porcupine" from *Verses from 1929 On* by Ogden Nash. Copyright 1944 by Ogden Nash. First appeared in *The Saturday Evening Post.* By permission of Little, Brown and Company.

Liveright Publishing Company

"In Just-" is reprinted from *Complete Poems: 1904–1962* by E. E. Cummings, edited by George James Firmage, by permission of Liveright Publishing Corporation. Copyright 1923, 1951, by E. E. Cummings. Copyright © 1976 by George James Firmage. Copyright © 1991 by the Trustees for the E. E. Cummings Trust.

Tom Lowenstein

Lines from "A Forgotten Man's Song about the Winds" (Talitgak traditional) reprinted from *Eskimo Poems from Canada and Greenland* translated by Tom Lowenstein. Copyright © 1973 by Tom Lowenstein. Reprinted by permission of the translator.

Macmillan Publishing Company and A.P. Watt Ltd.

Lines from "The Stolen Child" from *Collected Poems of W. B. Yeats* (New York: Macmillan, 1956).

Ekkehart Malotki

"Coyote and Little Turtle" collected, translated, and edited by Ekkehart Malotki, from *Gullible Coyote: A Bilingual Collection of Hopi Coyote Stories* by Ekkehart Malotki with the assistance of Michael Lomatuway'ma. Copyright © 1985, The Arizona Board of Regents. Reprinted by permission of the author.

McIntosh and Otis, Inc.

From *These Were the Sioux* by Mari Sandoz. Copyright © 1961 by Mari Sandoz. Copyright © renewed 1989 by Caroline Pifer. Reprinted by permission of McIntosh and Otis, Inc.

William Morrow & Company, Inc.

"Winter" from *Cotton Candy on a Rainy Day* by Nikki Giovanni. Copyright © 1978 by Nikki Giovanni. By permission of William Morrow & Company, Inc.

Naomi Long Madgett

"Life" from *One and Many* by Naomi Long Madgett. Copyright 1956. Reprinted by permission of the author.

John G. Neihardt Trustee

"The Magnificent Bull," Dinka Traditional, from *Black Elk Speaks* by John G. Neihardt (Flaming Rainbow). Copyright © 1985.

New American Library

"Miracles" from *Leaves of Grass* by Walt Whitman.

New Directions Publishing Corporation

Lines from "Garden" by H.D., *Collected Poems 1912–1944.* Copyright © 1982 by the Estate of Hilda Doolittle. Reprinted by permission of New Directions Publishing Corporation.

Harold Ober Associates Incorporated.

"The Old Demon" by Pearl S. Buck, originally published in *Cosmopolitan.* Copyright 1939 by Pearl S. Buck. Copyright © renewed 1966 by Pearl S. Buck. Reprinted by permission of Harold Ober Associates Incorporated.

Pantheon Books, a division of Random House, Inc.

"How the Animals Kept the Lions Away" and "Djuha Borrows a Pot" from *Arab Folktales* by Inea Bushnaq. Copyright © 1986 by Inea Bushnaq. Reprinted by permission of Pantheon Books, a division of Random House, Inc.

Raymond R. Patterson

"Martin Luther King" by Raymond R. Patterson. Copyright © 1971 by Raymond R. Patterson. Reprinted by permission of the author.

Pocket Books, a division of Simon & Schuster, Inc.

"The Case for Short Words" from *The Miracle of Language* by Richard Lederer. Copyright © 1991 by Richard Lederer. Reprinted by permission of Pocket Books, a division of Simon & Schuster, Inc.

The Putnam Publishing Group

"Rip Van Winkle" from *A Legend of the Kaatskill Mountains* by Washington Irving. G.P. Putnam & Sons, 1871. "Two Kinds" by Amy Tan from *The Joy Luck Club* by Amy Tan. Copyright © 1989 by Amy Tan. Reprinted by permission of the Putnam Publishing Group.

Random House, Inc.

"Father William" from *The Complete Works of Lewis Carroll* by Lewis Carroll. Lines from "Minor Elegy" by Henriqueta Lisboa, translated by Willis Barnstone and Nelson Cerqueira. Reprinted from *A Book of Women Poets from Antiquity to Now* edited by Aliki Barnstone and Willis Barnstone, Schocken Books. Reprinted by permission.

Marian Reiner

"Feelings About Words" from WORDS, WORDS, WORDS by Mary O'Neill. Copyright © 1966 Mary O'Neill. Copyright renewed 1994 Erin Baroni and Abigail Hagler. Haiku by Buson, Otsuji, and Kyorai from *More Cricket Songs: Japanese Haiku* translated by Harry Behn. Copyright © 1964 by Harry Behn. Copyright © renewed 1992 by Prescott Behn, Pamela Behn Adam and Peter Behn. All rights reserved. Reprinted by permission of Marian Reiner.

Marian Reiner for Eve Merriam

"Onomatopoeia" from *It Doesn't Always Have to Rhyme* by Eve Merriam. Copyright © 1964 by Eve Merriam. Copyright © renewed 1992 by Eve Merriam. All rights reserved. Reprinted by permission of Marian Reiner for the author.

Wendy Rose
"Loo-Wit" from *The Halfbreed Chronicles and Other Poems* by Wendy Rose. Copyright © 1985 by Wendy Rose. Reprinted by permission of the author.

St. Martin's Press, Inc., New York, NY, and Harold Ober Associates Incorporated.
"Cat on the Go" from *All Things Wise and Wonderful* by James Herriot. Copyright © 1976, 1977 by James Herriot. Reprinted by permission of St. Martin's Press, Inc., New York and Harold Ober Associates Incorporated.

William Saroyan Foundation
"The Hummingbird That Lived Through Winter" from *Dear Baby* by William Saroyan. Copyright 1935, 1936, 1939, 1941, 1942, 1943, 1944 by William Saroyan. Reprinted by permission of the William Saroyan Foundation.

Scribner, an imprint of Simon & Schuster, Inc.
"A Day's Wait" from *Winner Take Nothing* by Ernest Hemingway. Copyright 1933 by Charles Scribner's Sons; copyright renewed © 1961 Mary Hemingway. "Rattlesnake Hunt," from *Cross Creek* by Marjorie Kinnan Rawlings. Copyright 1942 Marjorie Kinnan Rawlings; copyright renewed © 1970 Norton Baskin. Reprinted by permission of Scribner, an imprint of Simon & Schuster, Inc.

Sam Selvon
"The Mouth-Organ" from *Foreday Morning: Selected Prose 1946–1986* by Sam Selvon, edited and introduced by Kenneth Ramchand and Susheila Nasta. Copyright © Sam Selvon 1989. Reprinted by permission of the author.

The Rod Serling Trust
The Monsters are Due on Maple Street by Rod Serling. Copyright © 1960 by Rod Serling, copyright renewed 1978 by Carolyn Serling, Jodi Serling, and Anne Serling Sutton. Reprinted by permission of The Rod Serling Trust.

Estate of Robert Service
"The Cremation of Sam McGee" by Robert Service. 1910 Dodd Mead & Co., by permission of the Estate of Robert Service.

Leslie Marmon Silko
From "Humaweepi, The Warrior Priest" by Leslie Marmon Silko. Reprinted by permission of the author.

Simon & Schuster, Inc.
Pronunciation key from *Webster's New World Dictionary,* Second College Edition. Copyright © 1984 by Simon & Schuster, Inc. Reprinted by permission.

Gary Soto and Poetry
"Oranges" by Gary Soto. First appeared in *Poetry,* copyright © 1983 by The Modern Poetry Association and is reprinted by permission of the author and the editor of *Poetry.*

Stoddart Publishing Co. Limited
"I Am a Native of North America" by Chief Dan George, from *My Heart Soars* copyright © 1974 by Clarke Irwin. Reprinted by permission of Stoddart Publishing Co., Limited.

Teale, Nellie D.
From *Circle of the Seasons* by Edwin Way Teale. Copyright 1953 by Edwin Way Teale. Copyright renewed 1981 by Nellie D. Teale. Reprinted by permission of Nellie D. Teale.

Rosemary A. Thurber
"The Night the Bed Fell" by James Thurber. Copyright © 1933, 1961 James Thurber. From *My Life and Hard Times,* published by Harper & Row. Reprinted by permission.

TriQuarterly
Lines from "The River" by Javier Héraud, translated by Paul Blackburn. From *TriQuarterly,* No. 13-14, Fall/Winter issue, 1969. Copyright © 1969 by *TriQuarterly,* Evanston, IL. Reprinted by permission of the publisher.

The University of Chicago Press
"The Mice That Set Elephants Free," from *The Panchatantra,* translated from the Sanskrit by Arthur W. Ryder. Copyright 1953 by Mary E. Ryder and Winifred Ryder. Reprinted by permission of the publisher, The University of Chicago Press.

University of Notre Dame Press
From *Barrio Boy* by Ernesto Galarza. Copyright © 1971 by University of Notre Dame Press. Reprinted by permission.

Viking Penguin, a division of Penguin Books USA Inc.
Lines from "The Hermit Has a Visitor" from *Our Ground Time Here Will be Brief* by Maxine Kumin. Copyright © 1972 by Maxine Kumin. "Season at the Shore" from *Times Three* by Phyllis McGinley. Copyright 1954 by Phyllis McGinley, renewed © 1982 by Phyllis Hayden Blake. Originally published in *The New Yorker.* Reprinted by permission of Viking Penguin, a division of Penguin Books USA Inc.

Mai Vo-Dinh
"The Little Lizard's Sorrow" from *The Toad is the Emperor's Uncle, Animal Folktales from Viet-Nam,* told and illustrated by Mai Vo-Dinh. Copyright © 1970 by Mai Vo-Dinh. Reprinted by permission of the author.

Frederick Warne Books, a division of Penguin Books USA, Inc.
"The Legend of the Hummingbird" from *Once in Puerto Rico* by Pura Belpré. Copyright © 1973 by Pura Belpré.

Western Publishing Company, Inc.
"The Bride of Pluto" (retitled "Demeter and Persephone") adapted from *Golden Treasury of Myths and Legends* by Anne Terry White. Copyright © 1959 Western Publishing Company, Inc. Reprinted by permission.

Jade Snow Wong and Curtis Brown, Ltd.
From "A Time of Beginnings" in *No Chinese Stranger* by Jade Snow Wong. Copyright © 1975 by Jade Snow Wong. Reprinted by permission of the author and Curtis Brown, Ltd.

Juliet Wood (née Piggott)
"Popocatepetl and Ixtlaccihuatl" from *Mexican Folk Tales* by

Juliet Piggott. Copyright © 1973 Juliet Piggott. Reprinted by permission of the author.

Writers & Artists Agency
A Christmas Carol: Scrooge and Marley adapted from Charles Dickens by Israel Horovitz. Reprinted by permission.

ART CREDITS
Boldface numbers refer to the page on which the art is found.

Cover and Title Page: *Heaven's Bounty,* Tom Darro, Overland Trail Fine Art Gallery; **v:** *Noon Wash,* 1991, Jonathan Green, From the collection of Mary and Michael James, Chicago, Illinois, Courtesy of the artist; **vi:** *Three Days and Three Nights* (detail), 1985, Paul Sierra, 44 × 60″, Oil on canvas, Courtesy of Gwenda Jay Gallery, Chicago, Illinois; **vii:** *Owh! In San Pao,* 1951, Stuart Davis, Oil on canvas, 52 1/4 x 41 3/4″, Collection of Whitney Museum of American Art, Purchase; **viii:** *Ravens in Moonlight,* 1882, Gengyo, Photo by John Lei/Omni-Photo Communications, Inc., © LEA; **ix:** *Turtle Sounds* (detail), David Dawangyumptewa, Jerry Jacka Photography; **x:** *Grizzly Country* (detail), Paul Krapf, Courtesy of the artist; **xii:** *Noon Wash,* 1991, Jonathan Green, From the collection of Mary and Michael James, Chicago, Illinois, Courtesy of the artist; **5:** *General With Sword,* Francisco Vidal, Courtesy of the artist; **8:** *General Looking at the Eclipse,* Francisco Vidal, Courtesy of the artist; **9:** *General Looking at the Eclipse* (detail), Francisco Vidal; **11:** *The Callers,* Executed c. 1926, Walter Ufer, Oil on canvas, 50 1/2 x 50 1/2″, National Museum of American Art, Smithsonian Institution, Gift of Mr. and Mrs. Crosby Kemper, Jr.; **12:** *Rudyard Kipling* (detail), 1899, P. Burne-Jones, By courtesy of the National Portrait Gallery, London; **24:** *O. Henry,* Artist Unknown, UPI/Bettmann Newsphotos; **46:** *Thinking,* Carlton Murrell, Courtesy of the artist, Photo by John Lei/Omni-Photo Communications, Inc.; **48:** *Sugar Cane,* Carlton Murrell, Courtesy of the artist; **57:** *Jovenes,* 1991, Tony Ortega, Mixed media, Courtesy of the artist; **60:** *Brer Fox,* Bob Kuhn, Sportsman's Edge/King Gallery; **63:** *Courtship,* Bonnie Marris, © 1988 The Greenwich Workshop, Inc., Trumbull, Connecticut 06611; **71:** *Alone,* Diana Zelvin, Courtesy of the artist; **74:** *La Esquina y La Bicicleta (The Corner and The Bicycle)* (detail), Tony Ortega, Monotype, Courtesy of the artist; **79:** *Mom and Dad* (or) *Portrait of a Lady With Kittens,* 1944, William H. Johnson, National Museum of Art, Smithsonian Institution, Gift of the Harmon Foundation; **96:** *Atelier,* Byron Birdsall, Courtesy of Artique, Ltd.; **103:** *Early Summer on the Farm,* Karl Rodko, Superstock; **106:** *Sunrise IV,* 1937, Arthur Dove, Hirshhorn Museum and Sculpture Garden, Smithsonian Institution; **113:** *Before Dawn,* 1985, Romare Bearden, Courtesy of the Public Library of Charlotte and Mecklenburg County; **116:** *Georgia Landscape,* Hale Aspacio Woodruff, National Museum of American Art, Washington, D.C., Art Resource, New York; **118:** *Spring Fever* (detail), 1978, Romare Bearden, Courtesy of the Estate of Romare Bearden; **122:** *Brothers,* 1934, Malvin Gray Johnson, Oil on fabric—canvas, National Museum of American Art, Washington, D.C., Art Resource, New York; **132:** *Washington Irving* (detail), Daniel Huntington, The National Portrait Gallery, Smithsonian Institution, Washington, D.C./Art Resource, New York; **133:** *Rip in the Mountains,* Albertus Del Orient Browere, Shelburne Museum, Shelburne, Vermont, Photograph by Ken Burris; **136:** *Rip at the Inn,* Albertus Del Orient Browere, Shelburne Museum, Shelburne, Vermont, Photograph by Ken Burris; **139:** *Rip Van Winkle Asleep,* Albertus Del Orient Browere, Shelburne Museum, Shelburne, Vermont, Photograph by Ken Burris; **142:** *Return of Rip Van Winkle,* 1829, John Quidor, National Gallery of Art, Washington, Laurie Platt Winfrey, Inc.; **147:** *The Four-Leaf Clover,* 1873, Winslow Homer, Oil on canvas, 36 x 52 cm., © The Detroit Institute of Arts, Bequest of Robert H. Tannahill; **154:** *Pearl S. Buck* (detail), Vita P. Solomon, The National Portrait Gallery, Smithsonian Institution, Washington, D.C./Art Resource, New York; **175:** *Her World,* 1948, Philip Evergood, The Metropolitan Museum of Art, Arthur H. Hearn Fund, 1950 (50.29), Copyright © 1986 by The Metropolitan Museum of Art; **206:** *Parade Curtain After Picasso,* 1980, Oil on canvas, 48 x 60″, © David Hockney, 1980; **213:** *Los Cholos,* 1985, Tony Ortega, Oil on canvas, Courtesy of the artist; **218:** *I Am Your Mexican Cowboy,* 1989, Jose Esteban Martinez, Oil on canvas, Courtesy of Vorpal Gallery, New York; **226:** *La Mesera (The Waitress),* 1923, Oil on board, 104 x 120 cm, Abraham Angel, Collection INBA–Museo de Arte Moderno, Mexico D.F., Reproduction authorized by the Instituto Nacional de Bellas Artes y Literatura, Photo by John Lei/Omni-Photo Communications, Inc.; **229:** *Flying Tiles,* 1965, Francisco Toledo, Photo courtesy of Mary-Anne Martin/Fine Art, New York; **232:** *I Am Singing at Your Window,* 1988, Jose Esteban Martinez, Oil on canvas, Courtesy of Vorpal Gallery, New York; **237:** *The New Rich,* 1941, Antonio Ruiz, Oil on canvas, 12 5/8 x 16 5/8″, Collection, The Museum of Modern Art, New York, Inter-American Fund; **243:** *Three Days and Three Nights,* 1985, 44 x 60″, Oil on canvas, Paul Sierra, Courtesy of Gwenda Jay Gallery, Chicago, Illinois; **262:** *Charles Dickens,* Artist Unknown, The Granger Collection, New York; **308:** *Reclining Woman,* 1952, John Robinson, Private Collection, Courtesy of the artist; **317:** *Self Portrait,* 1934, Malvin Gray Johnson, National Museum of American Art, Smithsonian Institution, Gift of the Harmon Foundation; **349:** *Iced Coffee,* Fairfield Porter, Courtesy Private Collection, Brookline, Massachusetts; **364, 365, 366:** Copyright ©1933, 1961 James Thurber, From *My Life and Hard Times,* Published by Harper & Row; **376:** *The Starry Night,* 1889, Vincent van Gogh, Oil on canvas, 29 x 36 1/4″, Collection, The Museum of Modern Art, New York, Acquired through the Lillie P. Bliss Bequest; **378:** *Simultaneous Contrasts: Sun and Moon,*

1913, Robert Delaunay, Oil on canvas, 53″ diameter, Collection, The Museum of Modern Art, New York, Mrs. Simon Guggenheim Fund; **383:** *Walking in Beauty* (detail), Clifford Brycelea, Courtesy of the artist; **385:** *The Library,* 1960, Jacob Lawrence, National Museum of American Art, Smithsonian Institution, Gift of S. D. Johnson and Son, Inc.; **388:** *Orphean Elegy 1,* 1978, Bridget Riley, Rowan Gallery; **391:** *Reytey,* 1968, Victor Vasarely, , Solomon R. Guggenheim Museum, New York, Photo by Carmelo Guadagno © The Solomon R. Guggenheim Foundation, New York; **396:** *Prisoners From the Front,* 1866, Winslow Homer, The Metropolitan Museum of Art, Gift of Mrs. Frank B. Porter, 1922 (22.207), Copyright © 1980 by The Metropolitan Museum of Art; **398:** *The Gulf Stream,* 1899, Winslow Homer, The Metropolitan Museum of Art, Wolfe Fund, 1906, Catherine Lorillard Wolfe Collection (06.1234), Copyright © 1980 by The Metropolitan Museum of Art; **402:** *Owh! In San Pao,* 1951, Stuart Davis, Oil on canvas, 52 1/4 x 41 3/4″, Collection of Whitney Museum of American Art, Purchase; **410:** *Mari Sandoz* (detail), Louise Austen, University Archives, Love Library, University of Nebraska; **412:** *Chee-A-Ka-Tchee, Wife of Not-to-Way,* 1835–1836, George Catlin, National Museum of American Art, Smithsonian Institution, Gift of Mrs. Joseph Harrison, Jr.; **415:** *Sioux Encampment,* c. 1874–1884, Jules Tavernier, Oil on canvas, 171.5 x 99 cm, The Oakland Museum, Oakland, California, The Kahn Collection, Laurie Platt Winfrey, Inc.; **428:** *Springtime Fantasy,* Adolphe Faugeron, Superstock; **433:** *Henry Wadsworth Longfellow* (detail), Thomas B. Read, The National Portrait Gallery, Smithsonian Institution, Washington, D.C./Art Resource, New York; **435:** *Untitled (cat),* Noreen Anne Finn, Student, Erie, Pennsylvania, Courtesy of the artist; **436:** *Alfred Noyes,* Artist Unknown, New York Public Library Picture Collection; **455:** *Belgium,* 1915, J. E. H. MacDonald, Oil on cardboard, 52.7 x 74.9 cm, Art Gallery of Ontario, Toronto, Purchase, 1963, Photo by Larry Ostrom; **461:** *Waterfall No. III, Iao Valley,* 1939, Georgia O'Keeffe, Art Resource; **462:** *Brass Buffalo Pendant From Cameroon,* Bamum, Staatliche Museum für Völkerkunde, Munich; *Carl Sandburg* (detail), 1951, Emerson C. Burkhart, The National Portrait Gallery, Smithsonian Institution, Washington, D.C./Art Resource, New York; **475:** *Sugar Cane Harvest,* Carlton Murrell, Courtesy of the artist, Photo by John Lei/Omni-Photo Communications, Inc.; **478:** *Ravens in Moonlight* (detail), 1882, Gengyo, Photo by John Lei/Omni-Photo Communications, Inc., © LEA; **480:** *Ravens in Moonlight,* 1882, Gengyo, Photo by John Lei/Omni-Photo Communications, Inc., © LEA; **481:** *Young Girls at the Piano,* Pierre Auguste Renior, Joslyn Art Museum, Omaha, Nebraska; **482:** *James Stephens* (detail), Sir William Rothenstein, The Tate Gallery, London/Art Resource, NY; **486:** *Dominant Curve,* April 1936, Vasily Kandinsky, Solomon R. Guggenheim Museum, New York, Photo by David Heald © The Solomon R. Guggenheim Foundation, New York; **489:** *The Buffalo Trail,* 1867–1868, Albert Bierstadt, M. and M. Karolik Collection, Courtesy, Museum of Fine Arts, Boston; **490:** *Edna St. Vincent Millay* (detail), 1934, Charles Ellis, The National Portrait Gallery, Smithsonian Institution, Washington, D.C./Art Resource, New York; **493:** *Portrait of Henriette,* An-

drew Wyeth, Courtesy of the San Antonio Museum Association, San Antonio, Texas; **495:** *Crazy Quilt,* Artist Unknown, Yakima Valley Museum and Historical Association, Photo by Rod Hansen; **497:** *Batchewana Wood, Algoma,* J.E.H. MacDonald, Oil on canvas, 21.6 × 26.7 cm, Art Gallery of Ontario, Toronto, Gift of Student's Club, Ontario College of Art, 1933; **498:** *E. E. Cummings* (detail), 1958, Self-Portrait, The National Portrait Gallery, Smithsonian Institution, Washington, D.C./Art Resource, New York; **506:** *James Whitcomb Riley* (detail), John Singer Sargent, © 1994 Indianapolis Museum of Art, Painted on commission from Art Association; **515:** *Snapshot at the Beach,* 1891, Superstock; **516:** *Langston Hughes* (detail), c. 1925, Winold Reiss, Gift of W. Tjark Reiss, in memory of his father, Winold Reiss, The National Portrait Gallery, Smithsonian Institution, Washington, D.C./Art Resource, New York; *Emily Dickinson,* Artist Unknown, The Granger Collection, New York; **519:** *Organdy Collar,* 1936, Edmund Archer, Oil on canvas, 19 x 16″, Collection of Whitney Museum of American Art, Purchase; **525, 526:** *You Are Old Father William,* 1865, Sir John Tenniel, The Granger Collection; **530:** *William Shakespeare* (detail), Artist Unknown, By courtesy of the National Portrait Gallery, London; **531:** *Orpheus,* Odilon Redon, The Cleveland Museum of Art, Gift of J. H. Wade, 26.25; **533:** *La Bonne Aventure (Good Fortune),* 1939, René Magritte, Gouache on paper, 33.5 x 40.7 cm., Museum Boymans-Van Beuningen, Rotterdam © 1993 C. Herscovici/ARS, New York; **540:** *Amanecer en la Montaña (Dawn on the Mountain),* 1949, Dr. Atl (Gerardo Murillo), Patrimonio de Jalisco, Reproduction authorized by the Instituto Nacional de Bellas Artes y Literatura, Photo by John Lei/Omni-Photo Communications, Inc.; **545:** *The Blue Horse,* Franz Marc, Superstock; **550:** *Dara Shikoh Riding an Albino Elephant* (detail), c. 1631, Mughal, Opaque watercolor on paper, 9 1/2 x 13 3/8″ (sight), Courtesy of the Arthur M. Sackler Museum, Harvard University Art Museums, Private Collection; **552:** *Dara Shikoh Riding an Albino Elephant,* c. 1631, Mughal, Opaque watercolor on paper, 9 1/2 x 13 3/8″ (sight), Courtesy of the Arthur M. Sackler Museum, Harvard University Art Museums, Private Collection; **554:** *Kalîla and Dimna: The Lion and the Jackal Dimna* (detail), c. 1200–1220, Arabian painting, Bibliothéque Nationale, Paris; **556:** *Kalîla and Dimna: The Lion and the Jackal Dimna* (detail), c. 1200–1220, Arabian painting, Bibliothéque Nationale, Paris; **558:** *Squirrels* (detail), 1986, Cheng-Khee Chee, Chinese ink and watercolor on rice paper, 25 x 37″, Courtesy of the artist; **560:** *Squirrels,* 1986, Cheng-Khee Chee, Chinese ink and watercolor on rice paper, 25 x 37″, Courtesy of the artist; **563:** *Tewa Clowns for a Donkey Ride,* Neal David, Sr., Private Collection, Photo by Native American Painting Reference Library; **568:** *Turtle Sounds* (detail), David Dawangyumptewa, Photo by Jerry Jacka Photography; **571:** *Turtle Sounds,* David Dawangyumptewa, Photo by Jerry Jacka Photography; **575:** *Koshare With Watermelons,* Harry Fonseca, Private Collection, Photo courtesy of Native American Painting Reference Library; **586:** *Preparing Medicine From Honey* (detail) from *De Materia Medica of Dioscorides: The Pharmacy,* 1224, Arab painting, Copyist: Abdallah ibn al-Fadl, The Metropolitan Museum of Art, Cora

Timken Burnett Collection of Persian Miniatures and Other Persian Art Objects, Bequest of Cora Timken Burnett, 1957 (57.51.21), Copyright © 1986 by The Metropolitan Museum of Art; **587:** *Preparing Medicine From Honey* from *De Materia Medica of Dioscorides: The Pharmacy,* 1224, Arab painting, Copyist: Abdallah ibn al-Fadl, The Metropolitan Museum of Art, Cora Timken Burnett Collection of Persian Miniatures and Other Persian Art Objects, Bequest of Cora Timken Burnett, 1957 (57.51.21), Copyright © 1986 by The Metropolitan Museum of Art; **590:** *Water Carrier by Moonlight,* Marc Chagall, The Metropolitan Museum of Art, Bequest of Scofield Thayer, 1982 (1984.433.56), Copyright © 1989 by The Metropolitan Museum of Art; **593:** *The Sleeping Gypsy,* 1897, Henri Rousseau, Oil on canvas, 51″ x 6′7″, Collection, The Museum of Modern Art, New York, Gift of Mrs. Simon Guggenheim; **600:** *The Fall of Phaëthon* (detail), Peter Paul Rubens, The Granger Collection, New York; **603:** *The Fall of Phaëthon,* Peter Paul Rubens, The Granger Collection, New York; **612:** *Erupting Volcano* (detail), 1943, Dr. Atl (Gerardo Murillo), Laurie Platt Winfrey, Inc.; **614:** *Erupting Volcano,* 1943, Dr. Atl (Gerardo Murillo), Laurie Platt Winfrey, Inc.; **617:** *Quetzalcoatl,* from *Codex Borbonicus* (copy), Mixtec, c. A.D. 1500, M.N.A.H., Biblioteca, Laurie Platt Winfrey, Inc.; **624:** *Daedalus and Icarus* (detail), Albrecht Dürer, The Granger Collection, New York; **626:** *Daedalus and Icarus,* Albrecht Dürer, The Granger Collection, New York; **628:** *On the Way to the Village* (detail), 1973, Gaylord Hassan, Oil, 36 x 36″, Courtesy of the artist; **630:** *On the Way to the Village* (detail), 1973,

Gaylord Hassan, Oil, 36 x 36″, Courtesy of the artist; **636:** *Sierra Peak Glacier* (detail), Edgar Payne, Courtesy of DeRu's Fine Arts; **639:** *Dreamwalker* (detail), Nancy Wood Taber, Courtesy of the artist; **642:** *The Rocking Chair Ranch,* Ogden M. Pleissner, Shelburne Museum, Shelburne, Vermont; **647:** *Anasazi—Ancient Ones,* Oil, 20 x 30″, Paul Krapf, Courtesy of the artist; **654:** *My Bear Spirit,* Tom Uttech, Courtesy of the artist; **661:** *Untitled,* Jay Van Everen, n.d., Oil and lacquer on board, 26 1/4 x 37 1/4″, Collection of The Montclair Art Museum, Gift of Mr. and Mrs. Rick Mielke; **665:** *Watching the Flock* (detail), Ray Swanson, Oil, 40 x 30″, Courtesy of the artist; **669:** Illustration for the cover of *Bearstone* (detail), Patricia Mulvihill, Courtesy of the artist; **674:** *Summer Solitude,* 1992, Lanny Grant, Oil, Courtesy of the artist; **677:** *60 Years a Herder,* 1986, Ray Swanson, Oil, 40 x 24″, Courtesy of the artist; **681:** Illustration for the cover of *Bearstone* (detail), Patricia Mulvihill, Courtesy of the artist; **688:** *Badlands, NM,* Bill Berra, Oil, 14 x 18″, Fenn Galleries Ltd.; **699:** *Dead Horse Pass,* George Beard, Courtesy of Russell Beard, Photo by John Lei/Omni-Photo Communications, Inc.; **704:** *Pyramid and Window,* Tom Lockhart, Courtesy of the artist; **712:** *Grizzly Country* (detail), Paul Krapf, Courtesy of the artist; **719:** *Wind Rivers,* Stephen Elliott, Courtesy of the Claggett/Rey Gallery; **724:** *Among the Pines,* M. C. Poulsen, Oil/linen, 36 x 30″, Courtesy of the artist; **728:** *Cottonwood Ranch* (detail), Roger P. Williams, Oil, 30 x 44″, Courtesy of the artist; **731:** Illustration for the cover of *Bearstone,* Patricia Mulvihill, Courtesy of the artist

PHOTOGRAPH CREDITS

2: Courtesy of Niki Grace; **36:** AP/Wide World Photos; **38:** Keith Gunnar/Bruce Coleman, Inc.; **44:** Calgary Herald; **52:** Patricia M. Hoch; **58:** New York Public Library; **68:** Dianne Trejo; **78:** © Rollie McKenna; **92:** G. P. Putnam's Sons; **99:** Courtesy of Amy Tan; **104:** Thomas Victor; **128:** Culver Pictures, Inc.; **148, 166:** Thomas Victor; **168:** Peter Menzel; **171:** Ralph Loony/Superstock; **172:** Gary Meszaros/Bruce Coleman, Inc.; **174:** Mark Leighton/UPI/Bettmann Newsphotos; **178:** Thomas Victor; **196:** Courtesy of Mario Sanchez; **200:** Larry Burrows/*Life* Magazine © Time Warner Inc.; **246:** International Creative Management; **248:** Frank Wing/Stock Boston, Inc.; **255:** Jean-Pierre Pieuchot/The Image Bank; **259:** Donald E. Carroll/The Image Bank; **265, 269, 275, 278, 284, 288, 298:** The Guthrie Theatre; **310:** Courtesy of Craig Browning; **313:** Harvey Lloyd/The Stock Market; **315:** Thomas Victor; **318:** Dave Gannon; **320:** Norman Owen Tomalin/Bruce Coleman, Inc.; **325:** Ron and Valerie Taylor/Bruce Coleman, Inc.; **328:** Thomas Victor; **330, 333:** Russell Baker; **336:** Mae Galarza; **339:** Rodney Jones; **342, 344, 346:** Jade Snow Wong; **350:** John Wyand; **352:** Mike Mazzaschi/Stock Boston, Inc.; **357:** Louis Panuse/DPI; **362:** UPI/Bettmann Newsphotos; **368:** AP/Wide World Photos; **369:** Dr. M. P. Kahl/Bruce Coleman, Inc.; **370:** Wendell D. Metzen/Bruce Coleman, Inc.; **374:** Thomas Victor; **380:** Alan Markfield/ Globe Photos, Inc.; **386:** Thomas Victor; **394:** John Kleinhans; **400:** Ken Williams; **406:** AP/Wide World Photos; **418:** Courtesy of Giang Kieu; **423:** Thomas Victor; **430:** Courtesy of Joanell Bookman; **444, 450:** AP/Wide World Photos; **454:** UPI/Bettmann Newsphotos; **458:** Dianne Trejo; **462:** (bottom) Pat Wolk, Courtesy of Wendy Rose; **466:** Andrei Lloyd/The Stock Market; **468:** Roger Werth/Woodfin Camp & Associates; **470:** (top) AP/Wide World Photos; (bottom) Dmitri Kessel/*Life* Magazine © Time Warner Inc.; **472:** Sdeuard C. Bisserot/Bruce Coleman, Inc.; **476:** Sonja H. Smith; **482:** (bottom) The Bettmann Archive; **484:** Harald Sund; **498:** (bottom) Dmitri Kessel/*Life* Magazine © Time Warner Inc.; **500:** David Herman/Superstock; **503:** Gordon R. Gainer/The Stock Market; **505:** Steward Henderson/The Image Bank; **506:** (top) AP/Wide World Photos; **509:** Jerry Simions/Superstock; **513:** David Barnes/The Stock Market; **516:** (center, top) Courtesy of The Huntington Library, San Marino, California; (bottom) Courtesy of Naomi Long Madgett; **517:** William E. Stafford; **523:** Declan Haun/Black Star; **524, 528:** New York Public Library; **532:** Courtesy of Elizabeth Kerr; **534:** UPI/Bettmann Newsphotos; **620:** Lois and George Cox/Bruce Coleman, Inc.; **622:** Bob and Clara Calhoun/Bruce Coleman, Inc.; **640:** Photo by Jean Hobbs, Courtesy of Will Hobbs; **649, 686:** John Lei/Omni-Photo Communications, Inc.

ILLUSTRATION CREDITS